An Introduction to Database Systems

Third Edition

An Introduction to Database Systems

Third Edition

C. J. DATE
IBM Corporation

 ADDISON-WESLEY PUBLISHING COMPANY
Reading, Massachusetts • Menlo Park, California
London • Amsterdam • Don Mills, Ontario • Sydney

Sponsoring Editor: William B. Gruener
Production Editor: Martha K. Morong
Designer: Herbert E. Caswell
Illustrator: Robert Gallison
Cover Design: Richard Hannus

This book is in the
Addison-Wesley Systems Programming Series
Consulting editors: IBM Editorial Board

Library of Congress Cataloging in Publication Data

Date, C. J.
 An introduction to database systems.

 (The systems programming series)
 Includes bibliographies and index.
 1. Data base management. I. Title.
QA76.9.D3D37   1981   001.64   80-17603
ISBN 0-201-14471-9

Reprinted with corrections, February 1982

ISBN 0-201-14471-9
GHIJ-HA-8987654

For Lindy

THE SYSTEMS PROGRAMMING SERIES

Foreword

The field of systems programming primarily grew out of the efforts of many programmers and managers whose creative energy went into producing practical, utilitarian systems programs needed by the rapidly growing computer industry. Programming was practiced as an art where each programmer invented his own solutions to problems with little guidance beyond that provided by his immediate associates. In 1968, the late Ascher Opler, then at IBM, recognized that it was necessary to bring programming knowledge together in a form that would be accessible to all systems programmers. Surveying the state of the art, he decided that enough useful material existed to justify a significant codification effort. On his recommendation, IBM decided to sponsor The Systems Programming Series as a long term project to collect, organize, and publish those principles and techniques that would have lasting value throughout the industry.

The Series consists of an open-ended collection of text-reference books. The contents of each book represent the individual author's view of the subject area and do not necessarily reflect the views of the IBM Corporation. Each is organized for course use but is detailed enough for reference. Further, the Series is organized in three levels: broad introductory material in the foundation volumes, more specialized material in the software volumes, and very specialized theory in the computer science volumes. As such, the Series meets the needs of the novice, the experienced programmer, and the computer scientist.

Taken together, the Series is a record of the state of the art in systems programming that can form the technological base for the systems programming discipline.

The Editorial Board

ABOUT THE AUTHOR

Mr. Date is an Advisory Programmer with IBM General Products Division, San Jose, California.

On graduating in mathematics from Cambridge University (England) in 1962, Mr. Date joined Leo Computers Ltd., London, as a programmer and programming instructor. He moved to IBM in 1967 as an instructor to help develop and teach a comprehensive training program in computer system fundamentals, System/360 assembler language, and PL/I. Subsequently he helped to establish the IBM European Laboratories Integrated Professional Training Program (ELIPT), a cooperative education scheme intended for computer professionals in the IBM development laboratories in Austria, England, France, Germany, the Netherlands, and Sweden. This involved developing and teaching several new courses, covering such topics as system programming techniques and Operating System/360 (both externals and internals).

In 1970, Mr. Date worked on a database language project in IBM (UK). Since that time he has been more or less continuously active in the database field, both inside and outside IBM. In particular he designed and taught a highly successful course on database concepts in the IBM ELIPT program mentioned previously. The present book has benefited greatly from the author's experience in teaching this course. Mr. Date is also responsible for the design of a proposed database programming language known as UDL (Unified Database Language). In addition Mr. Date has lectured widely on database topics—particularly on relational database—both in the United States and in many other countries. He is a member of ACM and the ACM Special Interest Group on Management of Data (SIGMOD). For some time he was actively involved in a British Computer Society working group on relational database. He is the author/coauthor of several technical papers.

Preface
to the
First Edition

Computers have already had a considerable impact on many aspects of our society. Medicine, law enforcement, government, banking, education, transportation, planning—these are only some of the fields in which computers are already playing a highly significant role. Over the next few years we can expect a vast increase in the range of computer applications and a corresponding increase in the effect computers will have on our daily lives. The two areas of computer technology that will make the new applications possible—indeed, in most cases they are absolutely fundamental—are telecommunications and the integrated database.

In the years ahead, then, database systems will become increasingly widespread and increasingly important. At present, however, they represent a new and relatively unexplored field, despite the fact that the number of systems installed or under development is growing at considerable speed. There is a real need for a good basic textbook that covers the fundamental concepts of such systems in a clear and concise manner. This book represents an attempt to meet the need.

The reader is assumed to be professionally interested in some aspect of data processing. He or she may, for example, be a systems analyst or designer, an application programmer, a systems programmer, a student following a university or similar course in computer science, or a teacher of such a course. (The book is in fact based on an intensive course in the subject that the author has been teaching to professional staff within IBM over a considerable period of time.) Generally speaking, the reader is expected to have a reasonable appreciation of the capabilities of a modern computer system, with particular reference to the file-handling features of such a system. He or she should also have some knowledge of at least one high-level programming language. Since these prerequisites are not particularly demanding, I am hopeful that the book will prove suitable as an introductory text for anyone concerned with using or implementing a database system, or for anyone who simply wishes to broaden a general knowledge of the computer science field.

The book is divided into six major parts:*

1. Database System Architecture
2. The Relational Approach
3. The Hierarchical Approach
4. The Network Approach
5. Security and Integrity
6. Review, Analysis, and Comparisons

Each part in turn is subdivided into a number of chapters. Part 1 provides a general introduction to the concepts of a database system, and in particular outlines three distinct approaches to the design of such a system, namely, the relational, hierarchical, and network approaches. Part 2 then examines the relational approach in considerable detail; Part 3 performs the same function for the hierarchical approach; and Part 4 does the same for the network approach. Part 5 presents a discussion of the problems of security and integrity in a database system. Part 6 draws together some of the more important themes introduced earlier in the book and considers them in somewhat more depth.

The structure just outlined requires some justification. As explained, Part 2 is concerned with the relational approach. In fact, it is largely devoted to an exposition of the ideas of Dr. E. F. Codd, the recognized authority in the relational database field. It is only fair to point out, however, that most commercial systems currently available (1974) are based on one of the other two approaches. Why, then, the emphasis on the relational approach? There are at least two answers to this question.

1. The relational approach may be viewed as the beginnings of a theory of data; as such, it provides an excellent basis for understanding and comparing the other two approaches, and a convenient measure or yardstick against which any existing system can be judged. The soundness and permanence of the theory would make it an ideal vehicle for tutorial purposes, even if it possessed no other advantages.

---

*In the third edition the material on security and integrity has been deferred to a supplemental volume.

2. The fact that most existing systems are not relational may be viewed as the natural outcome of the way in which computing technology itself has developed. The comparatively small capacity and high access times of early direct-access devices, the traditional emphasis on sequential media such as tape and cards, the limited amount of storage available in the computer itself—these and similar considerations had significant repercussions on the original design of most early systems. With modern hardware and techniques, however, it seems possible to design and build a system that does not have the shortcomings of earlier designs. To be more specific, many authorities now believe that the future will see the implementation of one or more large-scale systems based on the relational approach. (Since this was first written, in fact, a number of commercial systems incorporating relational concepts have begun to appear on the scene.)

From these remarks the reader will conclude, quite rightly, that the text is somewhat biased throughout in favor of the relational approach. Obviously the author believes that such a bias is justified; but it would be dishonest not to warn the reader that the bias is there.

Despite the views just expressed, however, the hierarchical and network approaches are obviously extremely important, and they possess the advantage of having several years' experience behind them. Parts 3 and 4 therefore deal with these approaches in some detail (and I hope fairly, in spite of my prejudices). Part 3 is based entirely on an existing system, IBM's Information Management System (IMS), which is already operating successfully in a number of computer installations. This system has been chosen as the basis for Part 3 both because it is a good example of the hierarchical approach and, of course, because it is an important system in its own right. For similar reasons, Part 4 is based on the proposals of the Data Base Task Group (DBTG) of the CODASYL COBOL Committee. I hope, therefore, that Parts 3 and 4 will serve not only as a general introduction to the hierarchical and network approaches, but also specifically as a tutorial on the IMS and DBTG systems. However, teaching specific systems is not the major aim of the book; rather, the object is to describe some general concepts, using specific systems primarily for purposes of illustration. (For this reason many otherwise important systems are little more than just mentioned.) Even so, the descriptions of IMS and DBTG, in particular, do go into a fair amount of rather specific detail.* The reader who is not too interested in the finer detail of these systems may omit certain portions of the text if he or she wishes—principally Chapters 19–22, and certain sections (appropriately indicated) of Chapter 24.

---

*The same is true of System R in the third edition.

A note on terminology. Like many other new subjects, the field of database systems possesses as yet no commonly agreed nomenclature. In particular, the terminology of IMS differs in many respects from that of DBTG. This book attempts to reconcile the differences by relating both IMS and DBTG terminology to a "neutral" terminology defined in Parts 1 and 2. (Once this has been done, however, the "correct" terminology for each system is generally employed in subsequent discussions.) The terminology of Parts 1 and 2, in turn, is an amalgam derived from many sources.

A few further points about the structure of the book:

1. I have tried to write a textbook, not a reference work. Of course, these two objectives are not wholly incompatible—indeed, I hope that to a large extent both are achieved—but whenever they clash, I have aimed at the first rather than the second. To this end I have not hesitated to omit minor points in the interests of clarity, nor to simplify others for the same reason, although as a general rule I have attempted to be as thorough as possible. (The reader is referred elsewhere for further details where appropriate.)

2. Since it is a textbook, most chapters are followed by a set of exercises, of which the reader is strongly urged to attempt at least a few. Answers, sometimes giving additional information about the subject of the question, will be found at the end of the book.

3. Each chapter is followed by a list of references, many of them annotated. References are identified in the text by numbers in square brackets. For example, [1.3] refers to the third item in the list of references at the end of Chapter 1, namely, a paper by the CODASYL Systems Committee published in the *BCS Computer Bulletin,* Vol. 15, No. 4, and also in *Communications of the ACM,* Vol. 14, No. 5.

There remains only the pleasant task of acknowledging the help I have received in writing this book. I am grateful, first, to Dr. Codd for a great deal of encouragement, for permission to make use of much of his published material, particularly in Part 2, and for his helpful comments on the initial draft. The following people also very kindly read that draft and produced many valuable criticisms and suggestions: Joel Aron, Jan Hazelzet, Roger Holliday, Paul Hopewell, Larry Lewis, Salah Mandil, Bill McGee, Herb Meltzer, John Nicholls, Terry Rogers, and Tom Work. I would also like to thank Professor Julius T. Tou, the organizer of the 4th International Symposium on Computers and Information Science (Miami Beach, Florida, 14–16 December 1972), and Plenum Publishing Corporation (publishers of the proceedings) for permission to use a paper I presented at that symposium as the basis for Chapter 3. Thanks should also be given to the many IBM students whose comments on the original course from which this book is derived have been most helpful. Finally, I am grateful to IBM for allowing much of the work of preparing the book to be done using company time and resources. I must emphasize, however, that I am entirely responsible for the contents of the book; the views expressed are my own and in no way represent an official statement on the part of IBM.

Palo Alto, California   C. J. D.
November 1974 (revised March 1981)

Preface
to the
Second Edition

Many changes have occurred in the field of database development since the first edition was written. The DBTG data manipulation language and subschema data description language have been accepted by the CODASYL COBOL Committee for incorporation into COBOL, and a number of DBTG-based systems are now commercially available. Secondary indexing and various other features have been added to IMS. Commercial systems based on relational concepts have started to become available. Various standardization activities are under way. Perhaps most significant of all, universities and similar institutions throughout the world are displaying an unprecedented level of interest in the subject. The present edition is an attempt to reflect some of this activity. It includes a great deal of new material, which is of course its primary raison d'être; however, the opportunity has also been taken to correct some errors from the first edition and to improve the presentation in many places. Many new references have also been included, most of them with annotation.

Some of the more significant differences between this edition and the previous one are summarized below.

Part 1: The overall systems architecture has been revised to incorporate ANSI/SPARC terminology. The comparative presentation of the three approaches has been unified and extended.

Part 2: The treatment of relational data structure has been expanded into a separate chapter; chapters on SEQUEL and Query By Example have been added; and the chapter on further normalization has been totally rewritten and includes an improved treatment of third normal form and the new fourth normal form. All other chapters have been considerably revised.

Part 3: A chapter on secondary indexing has been introduced. Other chapters have been revised in accordance with the latest version of IMS.

Part 4: All chapters have been revised to incorporate changes made by the Data Description Language and COBOL Committees of CODASYL.

*Part 5:** Both chapters have been revised to incorporate IMS and DBTG changes. Additional relational systems have been included. The treatment of integrity constraints and concurrency has been greatly expanded.

Part 6: This part is completely new.

Once again it is a great pleasure to acknowledge the assistance I have received in producing this book. I am particularly pleased to have the chance to thank the many people who commented favorably on the first edition and encouraged me to expand it into its present form. In this regard, I would especially like to mention Ted Codd, Frank King, Ben Shneiderman, and Mike Stonebraker. I am also deeply indebted to the following people for helping me over numerous technical questions and for reviewing and criticizing various portions of the draft of this edition: David Beech, Don Chamberlin, Rod Cuff, Bob Engles, Ron Fagin, Peter Hitchcock, Roger Holliday, Bill Kent, Bill Lockhart, Ron Obermarck, Vern Watts, and Moshe Zloof. As with the previous edition, I am extremely grateful to IBM for supporting me in this work. I would also like to thank Technical Publishing Company, publishers of *Datamation,* for permission to base the revisions in Chapter 3 on an article that appeared in that journal in April 1976; and ACM, for permission to base portions of Part 6 on material from three papers (references [26.1], [27.1], and [28.3]) for which ACM holds the copyright. Last but not least, I would like to express my appreciation to the staff of Addison-Wesley for the tremendous enthusiasm, encouragement, and patience they have shown throughout the production of both editions.

San Jose, California   C. J. D.
June 1977 (revised March 1981)

---

*In the third edition this material has been deferred to a supplemental volume.

Preface
to the
Third Edition

The field of database technology continues to evolve at an ever-increasing rate: so much so, in fact, that several more or less distinct subfields within it are beginning to emerge as disciplines in their own right. At the same time there are signs that some of the older-established areas are settling down to a state of comparative stability. Although the time is clearly ripe for a new edition of this book, it is regrettably no longer feasible to treat the subject adequately within a single volume and still keep that volume to a reasonable size. The material has therefore been divided into two parts, which can be categorized very roughly as "basic" and "advanced"; the present volume contains the "basic" material, and the "advanced" material is deferred to a projected supplemental volume. However, the present volume does form a complete and self-contained book in itself. In most respects, in fact, it provides a total replacement for the whole of the previous edition; the only exception is that the material on security and integrity (Part 5 in the second edition), which in a sense was less "basic" than the rest of that edition, has been deferred to the supplemental volume. This omission is counterbalanced in the present book by the introduction of much new material, in particular by a greatly expanded treatment of the relational approach.

The major differences between this edition and its predecessor are summarized below. It may be helpful to observe that, in the case of Parts 1, 2, 3, and 5, the changes are mostly either clarifications of, or additions—albeit very significant additions—to, the material found in the previous book. By contrast, the changes in Part 4 include numerous changes of *fact* (reflecting changes in the corresponding source documents). In other words, Part 4 of the second edition must now be considered obsolete; Parts 1, 2, 3, and 5 are still reasonably accurate so far as they go, but cannot be regarded as being totally up to date.

Part 1. Chapter 1 has been revised to provide a gentler overall introduction to the subject and a better description of the ANSI/SPARC architecture. Chapter 2 has been extended to include a discussion of *B*-trees and a brief introduction to extendible hashing.

Part 2. This has been almost totally rewritten. Chapter 4 has been expanded to provide a better explanation of relational structure, and in particular to incorporate two fundamental integrity rules. Chapters 5–10 (replacing Chapters 7 and 10 of the second edition) provide a comprehensive description of the relational system System R, using it as a vehicle to illustrate numerous relational system concepts.* Chapter 11 on Query By Example (Chapter 8 in the second edition) has been revised to bring it more into line with the released QBE product from IBM. Chapter 12 (Chapter 6 in the second edition) provides a much fuller treatment of the relational algebra than before. Chapter 13 (Chapter 5 in the second edition) presents the relational calculus, both tuple and domain versions, somewhat more formally than before, and uses QUEL (the language of the INGRES system) for its examples rather than DSL ALPHA, which was never implemented. Chapter 14 (Chapter 9 in the second edition) has been extended to include the concept of good and bad decompositions, the "final" fifth normal form, and a much better treatment of fourth normal form. Finally, Chapter 11 in the second edition ("Some Relational Systems") has been deleted, although most of its content still survives in the form of annotation within the bibliographies.

Part 3. This has been extended to include material on field level sensitivity (Chapter 17), the use of multiple PCBs (Chapter 18), and a new chapter on Fast Path databases (Chapter 22).

Part 4. This material has been totally revised in accordance with the most recent CODASYL specifications and the working documents of the ANS COBOL Committee (X3J4) and ANS Data Description Language Committee (X3H2). In addition, the answers to the exercises have been significantly improved.

Part 5 (Part 6 in the second edition). Chapter 27, a thorough treatment of the Unified Database Language UDL, is a greatly expanded version of the old Section 25.2. Chapter 28 is an extended version of the old Section 25.3.

---

*Just as this book was going to press (January 1981), a new database program product known as SQL/DS was announced by IBM. SQL/DS, which runs under the DOS/VSE operating system, incorporates almost all the features of System R.

One further change is that the term "data model," much used in the previous editions, has largely been dropped from the present book. This term has unfortunately been given a variety of meanings by different workers in the field and has consequently become the source of some confusion. Nor can I pretend to be blameless in this regard: The term does appear (in Chapter 12), with a meaning somewhat different from that ascribed to it in previous editions. The terminology of database systems is, regrettably, still in a state of flux.

I am grateful to the many friends and colleagues who have helped me by offering suggestions or by reviewing and commenting on portions of the draft of this edition—in particular, to David Beech, Don Chamberlin, Ted Codd, Bob Engles, Ron Fagin, Bill Kent, Pete Lazarus, Jim Panttaja, Franz Remmen, Reind van de Riet, Bob Smead, and, most especially, Phil Shaw, who performed the most thorough job of reviewing the manuscript that any writer could wish for. I would also like to thank Karen Takle Quinn and Per Groth for helping me to use the IBM Santa Teresa Library QBE system, and Paul Pittman, Russ Williams, and members of the System R development team for assisting me in experiments with System R. As with the previous editions, I am pleased to acknowledge the support I have received from IBM in writing this book. I would also like to thank ACM for permission to include some short quotations from three papers (references [1.14], [4.6], and [5.1]) for which ACM holds the copyright. And, finally, it is a real pleasure to express once again my appreciation of the friendliness, cooperation, and professionalism shown by everyone at Addison-Wesley throughout the production of this edition.

San Jose, California   C. J. D.
March 1981

Contents

CHAPTER 7
SYSTEM R DATA MANIPULATION

CHAPTER 8
EMBEDDED SQL

CHAPTER 9
THE EXTERNAL LEVEL OF SYSTEM R

CHAPTER 10
THE INTERNAL LEVEL OF SYSTEM R

PART 3
THE HIERARCHICAL APPROACH

CHAPTER 20
IMS LOGICAL DATABASES

CHAPTER 21
IMS SECONDARY INDEXING

CHAPTER 22
IMS FAST PATH DATABASES

PART 4
THE NETWORK APPROACH

CHAPTER 23
THE ARCHITECTURE OF A DBTG SYSTEM

CHAPTER 24
DBTG DATA STRUCTURE

CHAPTER 25
THE EXTERNAL LEVEL OF DBTG

CHAPTER 26
DBTG DATA MANIPULATION

Part 1
Database System Architecture

Part 1 consists of three introductory chapters. Chapter 1 sets the scene by explaining what a database is and defining an outline architecture for a database system. This architecture serves as a framework on which all later chapters of the book will build. Chapter 2 is a brief introduction to some techniques for physically arranging the data in the stored database. Chapter 3 is perhaps the most important chapter; it concerns a problem that is central to the design of any database system, namely, the problem of how the database is to be viewed by the users. (It is normal to shield users from details of how the data is physically stored and to allow them to view the database in a form more suited to their requirements.) Chapter 3 introduces the three major approaches to this problem, namely, the relational, hierarchical, and network approaches, and thus paves the way for the next three parts of the book.

1
Basic
Concepts

1.1 WHAT IS A DATABASE SYSTEM?

Database technology has been described as "one of the most rapidly growing areas of computer and information science" [1.14]. As a field, it is still comparatively young; manufacturers and vendors did not begin to offer database management system products until well into the 1960s (although it is true that certain earlier software packages did include some of the functions now associated with such systems [1.13, 1.15]). Despite its youth, however, the field has quickly become one of considerable importance, both practical and theoretical. The total amount of data now committed to databases can be measured, conservatively, in the billions of bytes; the financial investment involved is represented by a correspondingly enormous figure; and it is no exaggeration to say that many thousands of organizations have become critically dependent on the continued and successful operation of a database system.

So what exactly is a database system? Basically, it is nothing more than a computer-based recordkeeping system: that is, a system whose overall purpose is to record and maintain information.[1] The information concerned can be anything that is deemed to be of significance to the organization the

---

1. The terms "data" and "information" are treated as synonymous in this book. Some writers distinguish between the two, using "data" to refer to the values physically recorded in the database and "information" to refer to the *meaning* of those values as understood by some user. The distinction is clearly important—so important that it seems preferable to make it explicit, where relevant, instead of relying on a somewhat arbitrary differentiation between two essentially similar terms.

3

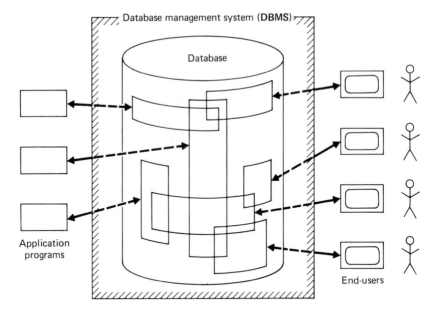

Fig. 1.1 Simplified picture of a database system.

system is serving—anything, in other words, that may be necessary to the decision-making processes involved in the management of that organization. Figure 1.1 shows a greatly simplified view of a database system.

Figure 1.1 is intended to show that a database system involves four major components: data, hardware, software, and users. We consider each of these briefly below. Later in the chapter we shall discuss each one in rather more detail.

Data

The data stored in the system is partitioned into one or more *databases*. For tutorial purposes it is usually convenient to assume that there is just one database, containing the totality of all stored data in the system, and we will generally make this simplifying assumption, since it does not substantially invalidate any of the subsequent discussion. There are good reasons why such a restriction should not be enforced in practice, however, as will be seen later.

A database, then, is a repository for stored data. In general, it is both *integrated* and *shared*.

By "integrated" we mean that the database may be thought of as a unification of several otherwise distinct data files, with any redundancy among those files partially or wholly eliminated. For example, a given database might contain both EMPLOYEE records, giving name, address, department, salary, etc., and ENROLLMENT records, representing the enrollment of employees in training courses. Suppose that in order to carry out the process of course administration, it is necessary to know the department for each enrolled student. There is clearly no need to include this information, redundantly, in ENROLLMENT records, because it can always be discovered by referring to the corresponding EMPLOYEE records.

By "shared" we mean that individual pieces of data in the database may be shared among several different users, in the sense that each of those users may have access to the same piece of data (and may use it for different purposes). Such sharing is really a consequence of the fact that the database is integrated; in the EMPLOYEE/ENROLLMENT example cited above, the department information in EMPLOYEE records is shared by users in the personnel department and users in the education department. Another consequence of the same fact (that the database is integrated) is that any given user will normally be concerned only with some subset of the total database; moreover, different users' subsets will overlap in many different ways. In other words, a given database will be perceived by different users in a variety of different ways. (Even when two users share the same subset of the database, their views of that subset may differ considerably at a detailed level. This topic is discussed more fully in Section 1.4.)

The term "shared" is frequently extended to cover, not only sharing as just described, but also *concurrent* sharing: that is, the ability for several different users to be actually accessing the database—possibly even the same piece of data—*at the same time.* (A database system supporting this form of sharing is sometimes referred to as a multiuser system.)

Hardware

The hardware consists of the secondary storage volumes—disks, drums, etc.—on which the database resides, together with the associated devices, control units, channels, and so forth. (We assume that the database is too large to be held in its entirety within the computer's primary storage.) This book does not concern itself very greatly with hardware aspects of the system, for the following reasons: First, these aspects form a major topic in their own right; second, the problems encountered in this area are not peculiar to database systems; and third, those problems have been very thoroughly investigated and documented elsewhere.

Software

Between the physical database itself (i.e., the data as actually stored) and the users of the system is a layer of software, usually called the database management system or DBMS. All requests from users for access to the database are handled by the DBMS. One general function provided by the DBMS is thus the shielding of database users from hardware-level detail (in much the same way that programming-language systems for languages such as COBOL shield programming users from hardware-level detail). In other words, the DBMS provides a view of the database that is elevated somewhat above the hardware level, and supports user operations (such as "get the EMPLOYEE record for employee Smith") that are expressed in terms of that higher-level view. We shall discuss this function, and other functions of the DBMS, in considerably more detail later.

Users

We consider three broad classes of user. First, there is the *application programmer,* responsible for writing application programs that use the database, typically in a language such as COBOL or PL/I. These application programs operate on the data in all the usual ways: retrieving information, creating new information, deleting or changing existing information. (All these functions are performed by issuing the appropriate request to the DBMS.) The programs themselves may be conventional batch applications, or they may be "on-line" programs that are designed to support an end-user (see below) interacting with the system from an on-line terminal.

The second class of user, then, is the *end-user,* accessing the database from a terminal. An end-user may employ a *query language* provided as an integral part of the system, or (as mentioned above) he or she may invoke a user-written application program that accepts commands from the terminal and in turn issues requests to the DBMS on the end-user's behalf. Either way the user may again, in general, perform all the functions of retrieval, creation, deletion, and modification, although it is probably true to say that retrieval is the most common function for this class of user.

The third class of user is the *database administrator,* or DBA (not shown in Fig. 1.1). Discussion of the DBA function is deferred to Section 1.5.

This completes our preliminary description of the major aspects of a database system. The rest of this chapter will consider these topics in somewhat more detail.

1.2 OPERATIONAL DATA

In one of the earliest tutorials on the subject [1.16], Engles refers to the data in a database as "operational data," distinguishing it from input data, output data, and other kinds of data. We give below a modified version of Engles's original definition of *database:*

- A database is a collection of stored operational data used by the application systems of some particular enterprise.

This definition requires some explanation. "Enterprise" is simply a convenient generic term for any reasonably self-contained commercial, scientific, technical, or other organization. Some examples are:

Manufacturing company,

Bank,

Hospital,

University,

Government department.

Any enterprise must necessarily maintain a lot of data about its operation. This is its "operational data." The operational data for the enterprises listed above would probably include the following:

Product data,

Account data,

Patient data,

Student data,

Planning data.

As already mentioned, operational data does *not* include input or output data, work queues, or indeed any purely transient information. "Input data" refers to information entering the system from the outside world (typically on cards or from a terminal); such information may cause a change to be made to the operational data but is not itself part of the database. Similarly, "output data" refers to messages and reports emanating from the system (printed or otherwise displayed at a terminal); again, such a report contains information derived from the operational data, but is not itself part of the database.

As an illustration of the concept of operational data, let us consider the case of a manufacturing company in a little more detail. Such an enterprise will wish to retain information about the *projects* it has on hand; the *parts* used in those projects; the *suppliers* who supply the parts; the *warehouses* in which the parts are stored; the *employees* who work on the projects; and so on. These are the basic entities about which data is recorded in the database. (The term "entity" is widely used in database systems to mean any distinguishable object that is to be represented in the database.) See Fig. 1.2.

It is important to note that in general there will be *associations* or *relationships* linking the basic entities together. These are represented by connecting arrows in Fig. 1.2. For example, there is an association between suppliers and parts: Each supplier supplies certain parts, and conversely, each part is supplied by certain suppliers. Similarly, parts are used in projects, and conversely, projects use parts; parts are stored in warehouses, and warehouses store parts; and so on. Note that these relationships are all bidirectional: that is, they may all be traversed in either direction. For example, the relationship between employees and departments may be used to answer both of the following questions: (a) Given an employee, find the corresponding department; (b) given a department, find all corresponding employees.

The significant point about relationships such as those illustrated in Fig. 1.2 is that they are *just as much a part of the operational data as are the associated entities.* They must therefore be represented in the database. Later we will consider the various ways in which this can be done.

Figure 1.2 also illustrates a number of other points.

1. Although most of the relationships in the diagram associate *two* types of entity, this is by no means always the case. In the example there is one arrow connecting three types of entity (suppliers–parts–projects). This could represent the fact that certain suppliers supply certain parts to certain projects. This is *not* the same as the combination of the suppliers–parts association and the parts–projects association (in general). For example, the

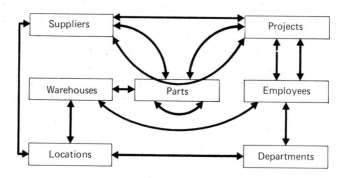

Fig. 1.2 An example of operational data.

information that "supplier S2 supplies part P4 to project J3" tells us *more* than the combination "supplier S2 supplies part P4" and "part P4 is used in project J3"—we cannot deduce the first of these three associations knowing only the second and third (but we *can* deduce the second and third knowing the first). More explicitly, if we know that S2 supplies P4 and that P4 is used in J3, then we can deduce that S2 supplies P4 to some project Jx, and that some supplier Sy supplies P4 to J3, but we cannot infer that Jx is J3 or that Sy is S2. False inferences such as these are examples of what is sometimes referred to as the *connection trap*.

2. The example also shows one arrow involving only *one* type of entity (parts). This represents an association between one part and another: for example, the fact that some parts are components of other parts (a screw is a component of a hinge assembly, which is also considered as a part).

3. In general, the same entities may be associated in any number of relationships. In the example, projects and employees are linked in two relationships. One might represent the relationship "works on" (the employee works on the project), the other the relationship "is the manager of" (the employee is the manager of the project).

Many database texts (and systems) consider entities and relationships as two fundamentally dissimilar types of object. However, an association between entities may itself be considered as an entity. If we take as our definition of entity "an object about which we wish to record information," then an association certainly fits the definition. For example, "part P4 is stored in warehouse W8" is an entity about which we may wish to record information, e.g., the appropriate quantity. Thus in this book we shall tend to view relationships merely as special types of entity.

1.3 WHY DATABASE?

Why should an enterprise choose to store its operational data in an integrated database? The broad answer to this question (elaborated below) is that a database system provides the enterprise with *centralized control* of its operational data—which, as the reader should realize by now, is one of its most valuable assets. This is in sharp contrast to the situation that prevails in many enterprises today, where typically each application has its own private files—quite often its own private tapes and disk packs, too—so that the operational data is widely dispersed, and is therefore probably difficult to control.

The foregoing implies that in an enterprise with a database system there will be some one identifiable person who has this central responsibility for the operational data. This person is the database administrator (DBA) mentioned in Section 1.1. We shall be discussing the role of the DBA in detail later; for the time being, it is sufficient to note that the job will involve both a high degree of technical expertise and the ability to understand and interpret management requirements at a senior level. (In practice the DBA may consist of a team of people rather than just one person.) It is important to realize that the position of the DBA within the enterprise is a very senior one.

Let us consider some of the advantages that accrue from having centralized control of the data, as discussed above.

- Redundancy can be reduced.

In nondatabase systems each application has its own private files. This can often lead to considerable redundancy in stored data, with resultant waste in storage space. For example, a personnel application and an education-records application may each own a file containing department information for employees. As we suggested in Section 1.1, these two files can be integrated, and the redundancy eliminated, *if* the DBA is aware of the data requirements for both applications—i.e., *if* the DBA has the necessary overall control.

We do not mean to suggest that *all* redundancy should necessarily be eliminated. Sometimes there are sound business or technical reasons for maintaining multiple copies of the same data. In a database system, however, redundancy should be *controlled*—that is, the system should be aware of the redundancy and should assume responsibility for propagating updates (see the next point below).

- Inconsistency can be avoided (to some extent).

This is really a corollary of the previous point. Suppose that a given fact about the real world—say, the fact that employee E3 works in department D8—is represented by two distinct entries in the database, and that the system is not aware of this duplication (in other words, the redundancy is not controlled). Then there will be some occasions on which the two entries will not agree (that is, when one and only one has been updated). At such times the database is said to be *inconsistent*. Obviously, a database that is in an inconsistent state is capable of supplying incorrect or conflicting information.

It is clear that if the given fact is represented by a single entry (i.e., if the redundancy is removed) such an inconsistency cannot occur. Alternatively, if the redundancy is not removed but is controlled (by making it known to the system), then the system could guarantee that the database is never inconsistent *as seen by the user,* by ensuring that any change made to either of the two entries is automatically made to the other. This process is known as *propagating updates*—where the term "update" is used to cover all the operations of creation, deletion, and modification. (Note, however, that few systems today are capable of automatically propagating updates; that is, most current systems do not support controlled redundancy at all.)

- The data can be shared.

We discussed this point in Section 1.1, but it is so important that we stress it again here. It means not only that existing applications can share the data in the database, but also that new applications can be developed to operate against that same stored data. In other words, the data requirements of new applications may be satisfied without having to create any new stored files.

- Standards can be enforced.

With central control of the database, the DBA can ensure that all applicable standards are followed in the representation of the data. The applicable standards may include any or all of the following: company, installation, departmental, industry, national, and international standards. Standardizing stored data formats is particularly desirable as an aid to *data interchange* or migration between systems.

- Security restrictions can be applied.

Having complete jurisdiction over the operational data, the DBA (a) can ensure that the only means of access to the database is through the proper channels, and hence (b) can define authorization checks to be carried out whenever access to sensitive data is attempted. Different checks can be established for each type of access (retrieve, modify, delete, etc.) to each piece of information in the database. [Note that without such checks the security of the data may actually be *more* at risk in a database system than in a traditional (dispersed) filing system.]

- Integrity can be maintained.

The problem of integrity is the problem of ensuring that the data in the database is accurate. Inconsistency between two entries representing the same "fact" is an example of lack of integrity (which of course can occur only if redundancy exists in the stored data). Even if redundancy is eliminated, however, the database may still contain incorrect data. For example, an employee may be shown as having worked 200 hours in the week, or a list of employee numbers for a given department may include the number of a nonexistent employee. Centralized control of the database helps in avoiding these situations, insofar as they can be avoided, by permitting the DBA to define validation procedures to be carried out whenever any update operation is attempted. (Again we are using the term "update" to cover all the operations of modification, creation, and deletion.) It is worth pointing out that data integrity is even more important in a database system than in a "private files" environment, precisely because the database is shared; for without appropriate validation procedures it is possible for a program with errors in it to generate bad data and thus to "infect" other innocent programs using that data.

■ Conflicting requirements can be balanced.

Knowing the overall requirements of the enterprise—as opposed to the requirements of any individual user—the DBA can structure the database system to provide an overall service that is "best for the enterprise." For example, a representation can be chosen for the data in storage that gives fast access for the most important applications at the cost of poor performance in some other applications.

Most of the advantages listed above are fairly obvious. However, one other point, which is not so obvious—although it is implied by several of the foregoing—must be added to the list, namely, *the provision of data independence*. (Strictly speaking, this is an *objective* rather than an advantage.) This concept is so important that we devote a separate section to it.

1.4 DATA INDEPENDENCE

Data independence may be most easily understood by first considering its opposite. Most present-day applications are data-dependent. This means that the way in which the data is organized in secondary storage and the way in which it is accessed are both dictated by the requirements of the application, *and, moreover, that knowledge of the data organization and access technique is built into the application logic.* For example, it may be decided (for performance reasons) that a particular file is to be stored in indexed sequential form. The application, then, must know that the index exists and must know the file sequence (as defined by the index), and the internal structure of the application will be built around this knowledge. In addition, the precise form of the various accessing and exception-checking procedures within the application will depend very heavily on details of the interface presented by the indexed sequential software.

We say that an application such as this one is *data-dependent* because it is impossible to change the storage structure (how the data is physically recorded) or access strategy (how it is accessed) without affecting the application, probably drastically. For example, it would not be possible to replace the indexed sequential file above by a hash-addressed file without making major modifications to the application. It is interesting to note, incidentally, that the portions of the application requiring alteration in such a case are the portions that communicate with the file-handling software, and that the difficulties involved are quite irrelevant to the problem the application was written to solve—they are difficulties *introduced* by the structure of the file-handling software interface.

In a database system, however, it would be extremely undesirable to allow applications to be data-dependent, for at least the following two reasons.

1. Different applications will need different views of the same data. For example, suppose that before the enterprise introduces its integrated database, we have two applications, A and B, each owning a file containing the field "customer balance." Suppose, however, that application A records this value in decimal, whereas application B records it in binary. It will still be possible to integrate the two files and to eliminate the redundancy, provided that the DBMS performs all necessary conversions between the stored representation chosen (which may be decimal or binary or something else again) and the form in which each application wishes to see it. For example, if the decision is to hold the value in decimal, then every access from B will require a conversion to or from binary.

This is a fairly trivial example of the sort of difference that may exist in a database system between an application's view of the data and what is physically stored. Many other possible differences are considered later.

2. The DBA must have the freedom to change the storage structure or access strategy (or both) in response to changing requirements without having to modify existing applications. For example, the enterprise may adopt new standards; application priorities may change; new types of storage device may become available; and so on. If applications are data-dependent such changes involve corresponding changes to programs, thus tying up programmer effort that would otherwise be available for the creation of new applications. For example, one large installation has approximately 25 percent of its programming effort devoted to this sort of maintenance activity [1.16]. Clearly this is a waste of an extremely valuable resource.

It follows that the provision of data independence is a major objective of database systems. We can define data independence as the *immunity of applications to change in storage structure and access strategy*—which implies, of course, that the applications concerned do not depend on any one particular storage structure and access strategy. In Section 1.5, we present an architecture for a database system that provides a basis for achieving this objective. Before then, however, let us consider in more detail the types of change that the DBA may wish to make (and that we may wish applications to be immune to).

We start with some definitions.

A *stored field* is the smallest named unit of data stored in the database. The database will, in general, contain many *occurrences* or *instances* of each of several *types* of stored field. For example, a database containing information about parts would probably include a stored field type called "part number," and there would be one occurrence of this stored field for each distinct part.[2]

A *stored record* is a named collection of associated stored fields. Again we distinguish between type and occurrence. A stored record *occurrence* or *instance* consists of a group of related stored field occurrences (and represents an association between them). For example, a stored record occurrence might consist of an occurrence of each of the following stored fields: part number, part name, part color, and part weight. The association between them is of course that they all represent properties of some particular part. We say that the database contains multiple occurrences of the "part" stored record *type* (again, one occurrence for each distinct part). In most systems, the stored record occurrence is the unit of access to the database—i.e., the unit that may be retrieved or stored in one access by the DBMS (see Chapter 2).

[As an aside, we note that it is common to drop the qualifiers "type" and "occurrence" and to rely on context to indicate which is meant. Although there is a slight risk of confusion the practice is convenient, and we will adopt it ourselves from time to time in what follows.]

A *stored file* is the (named) collection of all occurrences of one type of stored record.[3]

In most present-day systems an application's logical record is identical to a stored record. However, as we have already seen, this is not necessarily so in a database system, because the DBA may make changes to the storage structure—that is, to the stored fields and records—while the corresponding logical fields and records do *not* change. For example, the "part weight" field mentioned above could be stored in binary to economize on storage space, whereas a given COBOL application might see it as a PICTURE item (i.e., as a character string). A difference such as this—involving data type conversion on a particular field on each access—is comparatively minor,

---

2. "Part" here refers to a *kind* of part, say hinges (that is, not to a specific individual hinge).

3. For simplicity we ignore the possibility of a stored file containing more than one type of stored record. This simplifying assumption does not materially affect any of the subsequent discussion.

however; in general, the difference between what the application sees and
what is actually stored can be considerable. This fact is illustrated by the
following subsections describing aspects of the database storage structure
that may be subject to variation. (A more complete list will be found in
Engles [1.16].) The reader should consider in each case what the DBMS
would have to do to protect an application from such variation (and indeed
whether such protection can always be achieved).

Representation of numeric data

A numeric field may be stored in internal arithmetic form (e.g., in packed
decimal) or as a character string. In each case the DBA must choose an
appropriate base (e.g., binary or decimal), scale (fixed or floating point),
mode (real or complex), and precision (number of digits). Any of these aspects may be changed to improve performance or to conform to a new standard or for many other reasons.

Representation of character data

A character string field may be stored in any of several character codes
(e.g., EBCDIC, ASCII).

Units for numeric data

The units in a numeric field may change—from inches to centimeters, for
example, during the process of metrication.

Data coding

In some situations it may be desirable to represent data in storage by coded
values. For example, the "part color" field, which an application sees as a
character string ('RED' or 'BLUE' or 'GREEN' . . .), may be stored as a
single decimal digit, interpreted according to the table 1 = 'RED',
2 = 'BLUE', and so on.

Data materialization

Normally the logical field seen by an application corresponds to some
unique stored field (although, as we have already seen, there may be differences in data type, units, and so on). In such a case the process of materialization—that is, constructing an occurrence of the logical field from the
corresponding stored field occurrence and presenting it to the application—may be said to be direct. Occasionally, however, a logical field will
have no single stored counterpart; instead, its values will be materialized by
means of some computation performed on a set of several stored field
occurrences. For example, values of the logical field "total quantity" may
be materialized by summing a number of individual quantity values. "Total

quantity" here is an example of a *virtual* field, and the materialization process is said to be indirect. (Note, however, that the user may see a difference between real and virtual fields, inasmuch as it would probably not be possible to create or modify an occurrence of a virtual field, at least not directly.)

Structure of stored records

Two existing types of stored record may be combined into one. For example, the record types (part number, color) and (part number, weight) may be integrated to give (part number, color, weight). This commonly occurs as pre-database applications are brought into the database system. It implies that an application's logical record may consist of some subset of a stored record (that is, some of the stored fields may be invisible to that particular application).

Alternatively, a single type of stored record may be split into two. For example, (part number, color, weight) may be broken down into (part number, color) and (part number, weight). Such a split would allow less frequently used portions to be stored on slower devices, for example. The implication here is that an application's logical record may contain fields from several stored records.

Structure of stored files

A given stored file may be physically implemented in storage in a wide variety of ways. For example, it may be entirely contained within one storage volume (e.g., one disk pack), or it may be spread across several volumes of several different types. It may or may not be physically sequenced according to the values of some stored field. It may or may not be sequenced by some other means, e.g., by one or more associated indexes or by means of embedded pointers. It may or may not be accessible via hash-addressing. The stored records may or may not be blocked. But none of these considerations should affect applications in any way (other than in performance, of course).

The list above implies that the database is (or should be) able to *grow* without affecting existing applications. Indeed, enabling the database to grow without impairing existing applications is the single major reason for providing data independence. For example, it should be possible to extend an existing stored record type by the addition of new field types (representing, typically, further information concerning some existing type of entity or relationship; e.g., a "unit cost" field might be added to the "part" stored record). These new fields will simply be invisible to all previous applications. Similarly, it should be possible to add entirely new types of stored record to the database, again without requiring any change to existing applications; such records would typically represent completely new types of entity or relationship (e.g., a "supplier" record type could be added to the "parts" database).

1.5   AN ARCHITECTURE FOR A DATABASE SYSTEM

We are now in a position to outline an architecture for a database system (Figs. 1.3, 1.4, and 1.5). Our aim in presenting this architecture is to provide a framework on which we can build in subsequent chapters. Such a framework is extremely useful for describing general database concepts and for explaining the structure of individual systems; but we do not claim that every database system can be neatly matched to this particular framework, nor do we mean to suggest that this particular architecture provides the only possible framework. However, the architecture does seem to fit a large number of systems reasonably well; moreover, it is in broad agreement with that proposed by the ANSI/SPARC Study Group on Data Base Management Systems [1.17, 1.18]. (We choose not to follow the ANSI/SPARC terminology in every detail, however.)

The architecture is divided into three general levels: internal, conceptual and external (Fig. 1.3). Broadly speaking, the *internal* level is the one closest to physical storage, that is, the one concerned with the way in which the data is actually stored; the *external* level is the one closest to the users, that is, the one concerned with the way in which the data is viewed by individual users; and the *conceptual* level is a "level of indirection" between the other two. If the external level is concerned with *individual* user views, the

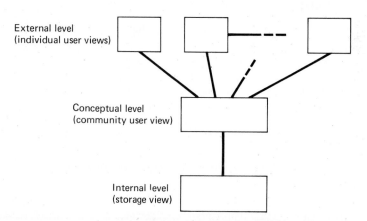

Fig. 1.3 The three levels of the architecture.

conceptual level may be thought of as defining a *community* user view. In other words, there will be many "external views," each consisting of a more or less abstract representation of some portion of the database, and there will be a single "conceptual view," consisting of a similarly abstract representation of the database in its entirety.[4] (Remember that most users will not be interested in the total database, but only in some restricted portion of it.) Likewise, there will be a single "internal view," representing the total database as actually stored.

An example will help to make these ideas clearer. Figure 1.4 shows the conceptual structure of a simple personnel database, the corresponding internal structure, and two corresponding external structures (one for a PL/I user, the other for a COBOL user). Of course, the example is completely hypothetical—it is not intended to resemble any actual system—and many irrelevant details have been deliberately omitted.

We interpret Fig. 1.4 as follows.

- At the conceptual level, the database contains information concerning an entity type called EMPLOYEE. Each EMPLOYEE has an EMPLOYEE_NUMBER (six characters), a DEPARTMENT_NUMBER (four characters), and a SALARY (five digits).

- At the internal level, employees are represented by a stored record type called STORED_EMP, eighteen bytes long. STORED_EMP contains four stored field types: a six-byte prefix (presumably containing control information such as flags or pointers) and three data fields corresponding to the three properties of EMPLOYEE. In addition, STORED_EMP records are indexed on the EMP# field by an index called EMPX.

- The PL/I user has an external view of the database in which each employee is represented by a PL/I record containing two fields (department numbers are of no interest to this user and are omitted from the view). The record type is defined by an ordinary PL/I structure declaration in accordance with the normal PL/I rules.

- Similarly, the COBOL user has an external view in which each employee is represented by a COBOL record containing, again, two fields (salaries are omitted). The record type is defined by an ordinary COBOL record description in accordance with the normal COBOL rules.

---

4. When we describe some representation as abstract we mean merely that it involves user-oriented constructs (such as logical records and fields) rather than machine-oriented constructs (such as bits and bytes).

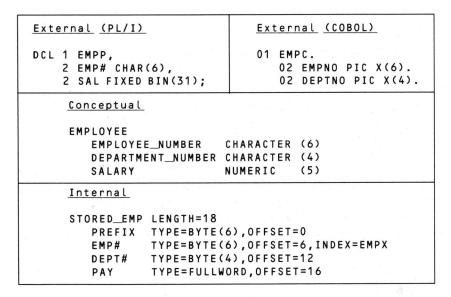

Fig. 1.4 An example of the three levels.

- Notice that corresponding objects at the three levels can have different names at each level. For example, the COBOL employee number field is called EMPNO, the corresponding stored field is called EMP#, and the corresponding conceptual object is called EMPLOYEE_NUM-BER. (The system must be aware of the correspondences. For example, it must be told that the COBOL field EMPNO is derived from the conceptual object EMPLOYEE_NUMBER, which in turn is represented by the stored field EMP#. Such correspondences, or *mappings,* have not been shown in Fig. 1.4.)

Now let us examine the components of the architecture in somewhat more detail (Fig. 1.5).

The *users* are either application programmers or on-line terminal users of any degree of sophistication. (The DBA is an important special case.) Each user has a *language* at his or her disposal. For the application programmer it will be a conventional programming language, such as COBOL or PL/I; for the terminal user it will be either a query language or a special-purpose language tailored to that user's requirements and supported by an on-line application program. For our purposes the important thing about the user's language is that it will include a *data sublanguage* (DSL), that is, a subset of the total language that is concerned with database objects and

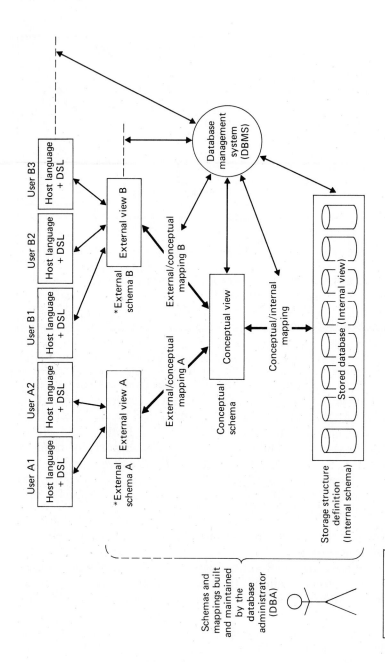

Fig. 1.5 Database system architecture.

* User interface

operations. We talk about the data sublanguage as being embedded in a *host language.* A given system may support multiple host languages and multiple data sublanguages.

In principle, any given data sublanguage is really a combination of two languages: a *data definition language* (DDL), which provides for the definition or description of database objects (as they are perceived by the user), and a *data manipulation language* (DML), which supports the manipulation or processing of such objects. Consider the PL/I user of Fig. 1.4. The data sublanguage for that user consists of those PL/I features that are used to communicate with the database. The DDL portion consists of those declarative constructs of PL/I that are needed to declare database objects: the DECLARE statement itself (DCL), certain PL/I data types, possibly special extensions to PL/I to support new objects that are not handled by existing PL/I. (Current PL/I [1.27] does not actually include any specific database features.) The DML portion consists of those executable statements of PL/I that transfer information to and from the database—again, possibly including special new statements.

The foregoing explanation assumes that the data sublanguage and the host (PL/I in the example) are fairly "tightly coupled"—that is, to the user the two are not really separable. In current practice this is usually not the case, at least so far as *programming* languages are concerned. Instead (a) the *definitions* are completely outside the application program, and are written in a DDL that does not even faintly resemble the user's host language, and (b) the *manipulation* is done by CALLing standard subroutines (provided as part of the DBMS), and is therefore again outside the host language framework. In other words, in most systems today the data sublanguage and the host are very *loosely* coupled. A tightly coupled system provides a more uniform set of facilities for the user, but obviously involves more effort on the part of the designers and developers of the system (which accounts for the status quo). It seems likely that there will be a gradual movement toward more tightly coupled systems over the next few years.

To return to the architecture: We have already indicated that an individual user will generally be interested only in some portion of the total database; moreover, the user's view of that portion will generally be somewhat abstract when compared with the way in which the data is physically stored. In ANSI/SPARC terms an individual user's view is called an *external view.*[5] An external view is thus the content of the database as it is seen by

---

5. External views were called data submodels in the first edition of this book, and external models (following [1.17]) in the second. There is a great deal of confusion over terminology in this area. Following [1.18], we now prefer "view" for a set of occurrences and "schema" for the definition of a view.

some particular user (that is, to that user the external view *is* the database). For example, a user from the personnel department may regard the database as a collection of department record occurrences plus a collection of employee record occurrences (and may be quite unaware of the supplier and part record occurrences seen by users in the purchasing department). In general, then, an external view consists of multiple occurrences of multiple types of *external record*.[6] An external record is *not* necessarily the same as a stored record. The user's data sublanguage is defined in terms of external records; for example, a DML "get" operation will retrieve an external record occurrence, rather than a stored record occurrence. (We can now see, incidentally, that the term "logical record" used in Section 1.4 actually refers to an external record. From this point on we will generally avoid the term "logical record.")

Each external view is defined by means of an *external schema,* which consists basically of definitions of each of the various types of external record in that external view. (The external schema is written using the DDL portion of the data sublanguage. That DDL is therefore sometimes called an *external DDL.*) For example, the employee external record type may be defined as a six-character employee-number field plus a fixed binary salary field, and so on. In addition there must be a definition of the *mapping* between the external schema and the underlying conceptual schema (described below). We shall discuss this mapping later.

We turn now to the conceptual level. The *conceptual view* is a representation of the entire information content of the database, again in a form that is somewhat abstract in comparison with the way in which the data is physically stored. (It may also be quite different from the way in which the data is viewed by any particular user. Broadly speaking, it is intended to be a view of the data "as it really is," rather than as users are forced to see it by the constraints of [for example] the particular language or hardware they are using.) The conceptual view consists of multiple occurrences of multiple types of *conceptual record;*[7] for example, it may consist of a collection of department record occurrences plus a collection of employee record occur-

---

6. For the time being we assume that all information is represented in the form of records. Later we will see that information may be represented in other ways as well, e.g., in the form of "links" (see Chapter 3). For a system using such alternative methods, the definitions and explanations given in this section will require suitable modification.

7. Footnote 6 applies to the conceptual level also. It should also be stressed that there may well be other, preferable ways of modeling the operational data of the enterprise at the conceptual level. For example, instead of dealing in terms of "conceptual records" it may be more desirable to consider "entities," and perhaps "relationships" too, in some more direct fashion. However, such questions are beyond the scope of this introductory chapter.

rences plus a collection of supplier record occurrences plus a collection of
part record occurrences. . . . A conceptual record is not necessarily the
same as either an external record, on the one hand, or a stored record, on
the other. The conceptual view is defined by means of the *conceptual
schema,* which includes definitions of each of the various types of conceptual record. (The conceptual schema is written using another data definition
language—the *conceptual DDL.*) If data independence is to be achieved,
these definitions must not involve any considerations of storage structure or
access strategy—they must be definitions of information content *only.* Thus
there must be no reference to stored field representations, physical
sequence, indexing, hash-addressing, or any other storage/access details. If
the conceptual schema is made truly data-independent in this way, the external schemas, which are defined in terms of the conceptual schema (see
below), will, a fortiori, be data-independent too.

   The conceptual view, then, is a view of the total database content, and
the conceptual schema is a definition of this view. However, it would be
misleading to suggest that the conceptual schema is nothing more than a set
of definitions much like the simple record definitions in a COBOL program
today. The definitions in the conceptual schema are intended to include a
great many additional features, such as the authorization checks and validation procedures mentioned in Section 1.3. Some authorities would go so far
as to suggest that the ultimate objective of the conceptual schema is to
describe the complete enterprise—not just its operational data, but also how
that data is used: how the data flows from point to point within the enterprise, what the data is used for at each point, what audit controls are to be
applied at each point, and so on. It must be emphasized, however, that few
systems today—if any—actually support a conceptual level of anything
approaching this degree of comprehensiveness; in most existing systems the
conceptual view is really little more than a simple union of all individual
users' views, possibly with the addition of some simple authorization and
validation procedures. But it seems clear that database systems of the future
will eventually be far more sophisticated in their support of the conceptual
level. We will discuss this topic in more depth toward the end of this book.

   The third level of the architecture is the internal level. The *internal view*
is a very low-level representation of the entire database; it consists of multiple occurrences of multiple types of *internal record.*[8] "Internal record" is
the ANSI/SPARC term for the construct that we have been calling a *stored*
record (and we shall generally continue to use this latter term); the internal
view is thus still at one remove from the physical level, since it does not deal
in terms of *physical* records or blocks, nor with any device-specific con-

---

8. Footnote 6 applies to the internal level also.

straints such as cylinder or track sizes. (Basically the internal view assumes an infinite linear address space. Details of how this address space is mapped to physical storage are highly implementation-specific and are not explicitly addressed in the architecture.) The internal view is described by means of the *internal schema,* which not only defines the various types of stored record but also specifies what indexes exist, how stored fields are represented, what physical sequence the stored records are in, and so on. (The internal schema is written using yet another data definition language—the *internal DDL.*) In this book we shall tend to use the term "stored database" in place of "internal view," and "storage structure definition" in place of "internal schema." Also, we shall generally (but not invariably!) use the unqualified term "database" as a synonym for "stored database," thus reserving it to mean what is actually stored; but the reader should be warned that this latter interpretation is by no means universal.[9]

Referring again to Fig. 1.5, the reader will observe two levels of *mapping,* one between the external and conceptual levels of the system and one between the conceptual and internal levels. The *conceptual/internal mapping* defines the correspondence between the conceptual view and the stored database; it specifies how conceptual records and fields map into their stored counterparts. If the structure of the stored database is changed—i.e., if a change is made to the storage structure definition—the conceptual/internal mapping must be changed accordingly, so that the conceptual schema may remain invariant. (It is the responsibility of the DBA to control such changes.) In other words, the effects of such changes must be contained below the conceptual level, so that data independence can be achieved.

An *external/conceptual mapping* defines the correspondence between a particular external view and the conceptual view. In general, the same sort of differences may exist between these two levels as may exist between the conceptual view and the stored database. For example, fields may have different data types, records may be differently sequenced, and so on. Any number of external views may exist at the same time; any number of users may share a given external view; different external views may overlap. Incidentally, some systems permit the definition of one external view to be expressed in terms of others, rather than always requiring an explicit defini-

---

9. In exceptional situations application programs may operate directly at the internal level rather than at the external level. Needless to say, this practice is not recommended; it represents a security risk (since the authorization checks are bypassed), and an integrity risk (since the validation procedures are bypassed), and the programs are data-dependent to boot; but sometimes it is the only way to obtain the required function or performance—just as a COBOL programmer might occasionally need to use assembler language to satisfy certain functional or performance objectives today.

tion of the mapping to the conceptual level (a very useful feature if several external views are closely related to one another).

Turning again to Fig. 1.5, we see that there still remain three topics for discussion: the database management system, the database administrator, and the user interface. The *database management system* (DBMS) is the software that handles all access to the database. Conceptually what happens is the following: (1) A user issues an access request, using some particular data manipulation language; (2) the DBMS intercepts the request and interprets it; (3) the DBMS inspects, in turn, the external schema, the external/conceptual mapping, the conceptual schema, the conceptual/internal mapping, and the storage structure definition; and (4) the DBMS performs the necessary operations on the stored database. For example, consider what is involved in the retrieval of a particular external record occurrence. In general, fields will be required from several conceptual record occurrences. Each conceptual record occurrence, in turn, may require fields from several stored record occurrences. Conceptually, at least, then, the DBMS must retrieve all required stored record occurrences, construct the required conceptual record occurrences, and then construct the required external record occurrence. At each stage data type or other conversions may be necessary.

(The foregoing description assumes that the entire process is interpretive, which usually implies rather poor performance. In practice, of course, it will sometimes be possible for access requests to be *compiled* in advance, thus avoiding the interpretive overheads.)

To return to Fig. 1.5: The *database administrator* (DBA), who has already been discussed to some extent, is the person (or group of persons) responsible for overall control of the database system. The DBA's responsibilities include the following.

Deciding the information content of the database

It is the DBA's job to decide exactly what information is to be held in the database—in other words, to identify the entities of interest to the enterprise and to identify the information to be recorded about those entities. Having done this, the DBA must then define the content of the database by writing the conceptual schema (using the conceptual data definition language). The object (compiled) form of this schema is used by the DBMS in responding to access requests. The source (uncompiled) form acts as a reference document for the users of the system.

Deciding the storage structure and access strategy

The DBA must also decide how the data is to be represented in the database, and must specify the representation by writing the storage structure definition (using the internal data definition language). In addition, the associated mapping between the storage structure definition and the conceptual schema must also be specified. In practice, either the internal DDL or the conceptual DDL will probably include the means for specifying this mapping, but the different definitions should be clearly separable. Like the conceptual schema, the internal schema and corresponding mapping will exist in both source and object form.

Liaising with users

It is the business of the DBA to liaise with users, to ensure that the data they require is available, and to write the necessary external schemas (using the appropriate external data definition language; as already suggested, there may be several distinct external DDLs). In addition, the mapping between any given external schema and the conceptual schema must also be specified. In practice the external DDL will probably include the means for specifying this mapping, but the schema and the mapping should be clearly distinguishable. Each external schema and corresponding mapping will exist in both source and object form.

Defining authorization checks and validation procedures

As already suggested, authorization checks and validation procedures may be considered as logical extensions of the conceptual schema. The conceptual DDL will include facilities for specifying such checks and procedures.

Defining a strategy for backup and recovery

Once an enterprise is committed to a database system, it becomes critically dependent on the successful operation of that system. In the event of damage to any portion of the database—caused by human error, say, or a failure in the hardware or supporting operating system—it is essential to be able to repair the data concerned with a minimum of delay and with as little effect as possible on the rest of the system. (For example, the availability of data that has *not* been damaged should not be affected in any way.) The DBA must define and implement an appropriate recovery strategy, involving, for example, periodic dumping of the database to a backup tape and procedures for reloading the relevant portions of the database from the latest tape.

Monitoring performance and responding to changes in requirements

The DBA is responsible for so organizing the system as to get the performance that is "best for the enterprise," and for making the appropriate adjustments as requirements change. As already mentioned, any change to details of storage and access must be accompanied by a corresponding change to the definition of the mapping to storage, so that the conceptual schema may remain constant.

It is clear that the DBA will require a number of utility programs to help with these tasks. Such utilities would be an essential part of a practical database system, although they have not been shown in Fig. 1.5. Below are some examples of the sort of utilities that would be necessary.

- Loading routines (to create the initial version of the database).

- Reorganization routines (to rearrange the database to reclaim space occupied by obsolete data, for example).

- Journaling routines (to note each operation against the database, together with identification of the user performing the operation and a record of the before and after states).

- Recovery routines (to restore the database to an earlier state after a hardware or program failure).

- Statistical analysis routines (to assist in monitoring performance).

Utility programs may be thought of as special system-supplied applications (except for the journaling routines, which must be part of the central DBMS itself). Some utilities will operate directly at the internal level (see Footnote 9).

One of the most important DBA tools is the *data dictionary* (not shown in Fig. 1.5). The data dictionary is effectively a database in its own right—a database that contains "data about data" (that is, *descriptions* of other objects in the system, rather than simply "raw data"). In particular, all the various schemas (external, conceptual, internal) are physically stored, in both source and object form, in the dictionary. A comprehensive dictionary will also include cross-reference information, showing, for instance, which programs use which pieces of data, which departments require which reports, and so on. In fact, the dictionary may even be integrated into the database it describes, and thus may include its own description. It should be possible to query the dictionary just like any other database, so that, for example, the DBA can easily discover which programs are likely to be affected by some proposed change to the system.

The last component in Fig. 1.5 is the *user interface*. This may be defined as a boundary in the system below which everything is invisible to the user. By definition, therefore, the user interface is at the *external* level. However, as we shall see later (in Chapter 9), there are some situations in which the external view cannot differ significantly from the relevant portion of the underlying conceptual view.

1.6   DISTRIBUTED DATABASES

We conclude this chapter with a brief mention of the subject of *distributed database*. Distributed database technology is a comparatively recent development within the overall database field [1.26]. A distributed database is, typically, a database that is not stored in its entirety at a single physical location, but rather is spread across a network of computers that are geographically dispersed and connected via communication links. As an (oversimplified) example, consider a banking system in which the customer accounts database is distributed across the bank branch offices, such that each individual customer account record is stored at that customer's local branch. In other words, the data is stored at the location at which it is most frequently used, but is still available, via the communications network, to users at other locations (for example, users at the bank's central office). The advantages of such a distribution are clear: It combines the efficiency of local processing (no communication overhead) for most operations, together with all the advantages discussed earlier (in particular, data sharing) provided by a centralized system. But of course there are disadvantages too: The communication overhead may be quite high, and also there are significant technical difficulties in implementing such a system.

A key objective for a distributed system is that *it should look like a centralized system to the user*. That is, the user should not normally need to know where any given piece of data is physically stored (so that applications are independent of the manner in which the data is distributed, making it possible to change the distribution without affecting those applications —another aspect of data independence). Thus the fact that the database is distributed should be relevant only at the internal level, not at the external or conceptual levels. Few systems today, if any, go very far toward meeting this objective.

EXERCISES

The material presented in this chapter is not difficult, but it does involve a somewhat bewildering array of terminology. To ensure that you have absorbed the most important ideas, you are urged to attempt the following questions.

1.1 Draw a diagram of the database system architecture presented in Section 1.5.

1.2 Define the following terms.

database: integrated, shared	external schema, view, DDL
database system	conceptual schema, view, DDL
DBMS	internal schema, view, DDL
DBA	external/conceptual mapping
user	conceptual/internal mapping

entity	data sublanguage
relationship	data dictionary
data independence	security
stored file, record, field	integrity
DML	

1.3 What are the advantages of using a database system?

1.4 What are the disadvantages of using a database system?

REFERENCES AND BIBLIOGRAPHY

1.1 CODASYL Systems Committee. "A Survey of Generalized Data Base Management Systems." Technical Report (May 1969). Available from ACM and IAG.

1.2 CODASYL Systems Committee. "Feature Analysis of Generalized Data Base Management Systems." Technical Report (May 1971). Available from ACM, BCS, and IAG.

These two lengthy documents (over 900 pages between them) complement each other in the following sense: [1.1] consists of independent descriptions of a number of systems (that is, a separate chapter is devoted to each system); [1.2] consists of feature-by-feature comparisons of a (slightly different) set of systems. The following systems are covered: ADAM ([1.1] only), COBOL ([1.2] only), DBTG ([1.2] only), GIS, IDS, ISL-1 ([1.1] only), IMS ([1.2] only), MARK IV, NIPS/FFS, SC-1, TDMS, UL/1.

1.3 CODASYL Systems Committee. "Introduction to 'Feature Analysis of Generalized Data Base Management Systems.' " *Comp. Bull.* **15,** No. 4 (April 1971); also *CACM* **14,** No. 5 (May 1971).

Adapted from the initial section of [1.2]. A useful introduction to some of the basic concepts of a database system.

1.4 GUIDE/SHARE Data Base Task Force. "Data Base Management System Requirements." (November 1971). Available from SHARE Inc., 111 E. Wacker Drive, Chicago, Illinois 60601.

A detailed statement by representatives of the IBM users' associations of the features required of an ideal database system.

1.5 R. G. Canning. "Trends in Data Management." Part 1, *EDP Analyzer* **9,** No. 5 (May 1971); Part 2, *EDP Analyzer* **9,** No. 6 (June 1971).

These two issues of *EDP Analyzer* contain outline descriptions of the following systems: TOTAL, DBOMP, MARS III, CZAR, Disk Forte, SERIES, IMS (Version 2), and dataBASIC. In each case notes are included on some actual users' experience of the system. A brief tutorial on database is also included.

1.6 G. C. Everest. *Data Base Management: Objectives, System Functions, and Administration.* New York: McGraw-Hill (1977).

1.7 D. C. Tsichritzis and F. H. Lochovsky. *Data Base Management Systems.* New York: Academic Press (1977).

Includes descriptions of IMS, System 2000, IDMS, TOTAL, and ADABAS.

1.8 D. Kroenke. *Database Processing: Fundamentals, Modeling, Applications.* Palo Alto, Calif.: Science Research Associates (1977).

Includes descriptions of ADABAS, System 2000, TOTAL, IDMS, IMS, and MAGNUM.

1.9 R. G. Ross. *Data Base Systems: Design, Implementation, and Management.* New York: Amacom (1978).

Includes very brief summaries of over 20 implemented systems.

1.10 A. F. Cardenas. *Data Base Management Systems.* Boston: Allyn and Bacon (1979).

Includes descriptions of TOTAL, IMS, and System 2000.

1.11 I. R. Palmer. "Data Base Systems: A Practical Reference." Q. E. D. Information Sciences Inc., 141 Linden Street, Wellesley, Mass. 02181 (June 1975).

Contains outlines of over 20 implemented systems, as well as a checklist including about 50 more, and some interesting case studies.

1.12 D. A. Jardine (ed.). *Data Base Management Systems: Proceedings of the SHARE Working Conference on Data Base Management Systems, Montreal, Canada, July 23–27, 1973.* North-Holland (1974).

This book includes papers on user requirements, future trends, user experience with a number of systems (IMS, TOTAL, IDS, DMS 1100, and EDMS), and statements of plans and intentions by a number of vendors (Burroughs, Cincom, CDC, Honeywell, IBM, UNIVAC, and XDS).

1.13 W. C. McGee. "Generalized File Processing." *Annual Review in Automatic Programming,* Vol. 5 (eds., Halpern and Shaw). Elmsford, N.Y.: Pergamon Press (1969).

The paper that first introduced the term "schema" (though not quite with the ANSI/SPARC meaning). A most readable survey with examples taken from a number of early systems.

1.14 E. H. Sibley. "The Development of Data Base Technology." Guest Editor's Introduction to *ACM Comp. Surv.* **8,** No. 1: Special Issue on Data Base Management Systems (March 1976).

1.15 J. P. Fry and E. H. Sibley. "Evolution of Data Base Management Systems." *ACM Comp. Surv.* **8,** No. 1 (March 1976).

1.16 R. W. Engles. " A Tutorial on Data Base Organization." *Annual Review in Automatic Programming,* Vol. 7 (eds., Halpern and McGee). Elmsford, N.Y.: Pergamon Press (1974).

A good introduction to database concepts. The major topics included are a theory of operational data, a survey of storage structures and accessing techniques, and a discussion of data independence.

1.17 ANSI/X3/SPARC Study Group on Data Base Management Systems. Interim Report. *FDT* (*ACM SIGMOD* bulletin) **7**, No. 2 (1975).

1.18 D. C. Tsichritzis and A. Klug (eds.). "The ANSI/X3/SPARC DBMS Framework: Report of the Study Group on Data Base Management Systems." *Information Systems* **3** (1978).

These two documents are the Interim and Final Reports of the so-called ANSI/SPARC Study Group. The ANSI/X3/SPARC Study Group on Data Base Management Systems (to give it its full title) was established in late 1972 by the Standards Planning and Requirements Committee (SPARC) of ANSI/X3. ANSI/X3 is the American National Standards Committee on Computers and Information Processing. The objectives of the Study Group were to determine the areas, if any, of database technology for which standardization activity was appropriate, and to produce a set of recommendations for action in each such area. In working to meet these objectives the Study Group took the view that *interfaces* were the only aspect of a database system that could possibly be suitable for standardization, and so defined a generalized architecture or framework for a database system and its interfaces. The Final Report provides a detailed description of this architecture and of some of the 42 identified interfaces. The Interim Report is an earlier working document but is still of interest; in some areas it provides additional detail.

1.19 D. A. Jardine (ed.). *The ANSI/SPARC DBMS Model: Proceedings of the Second SHARE Working Conference on Data Base Management Systems, Montreal, Canada, April 26–30, 1976.* North-Holland (1977).

The proceedings of a conference (papers and discussions) devoted to the ANSI/SPARC proposals as documented in the interim report [1.17].

1.20 B. Yormark. "The ANSI/X3/SPARC/SG DBMS Architecture." In [1.19].

An overview of the interim report [1.17].

1.21 B. Langefors. "Theoretical Analysis of Information Systems." Lund, Sweden (1966, 1973).

1.22 B. Sundgren. "Conceptual Foundation of the Infological Approach to Data Bases." *Proc. IFIP TC-2 Working Conference on Data Base Management Systems* (eds., Klimbie and Koffeman). North-Holland (1974).

The work of Langefors [1.21] and Sundgren has many points in common with the ANSI/SPARC proposals, which they anticipated by a number of years. Until recently, however, their ideas did not receive much general acceptance except in Scandinavia.

1.23 P. P. Uhrowczik. "Data Dictionary/Directories." *IBM Sys. J.* **12**, No. 4 (1973).

An introduction to the basic concepts of a data dictionary system. An implementation using IMS physical and logical databases is outlined (see Part 3 of this book).

1.24 Data Dictionary Systems Working Party of the British Computer Society. Report. Joint Issue: Data Base (ACM SIGBDP newsletter) **9,** No. 2; SIGMOD Record (ACM SIGMOD bulletin) **9,** No. 4 (December 1977).

> An excellent description of the role of the data dictionary; includes a brief but good discussion of the conceptual schema.

1.25 M. R. Stonebraker. "A Functional View of Data Independence." *Proc. 1974 ACM SIGMOD Workshop on Data Description, Access and Control.*

> This paper is an attempt to provide a precise framework for dealing with the problem of data independence. Seven classes of transformation of a stored database from one representation to another are identified and rigorously defined. The following examples give some idea of the types of transformation in each of the seven classes.
>
> 1. Physical relocation of stored files
>
> 2. Conversion of stored field values from one data type to another
>
> 3. Replacement of one hashing algorithm by another
>
> 4. Addition of indexes
>
> 5. Duplication of stored data
>
> 6. Splitting one stored record into two
>
> 7. Combining two stored records into one
>
> It is suggested that a measure of the degree of data independence provided by a particular system may be obtained by considering the transformations supported (in a data-independent fashion) in each of the seven classes. The paper concludes with a brief examination of three specific systems in the light of these ideas: RDMS, ISAM, and IMS.

1.26 CODASYL Systems Committee. "Distributed Data Base Technology—An Interim Report." *Proc. NCC* **47** (June 1978).

1.27 American National Standard Programming Language PL/I. ANSI Document X3.53-1976. American National Standards Institute, Inc., 1430 Broadway, New York, NY 10018.

2
Storage
Structures

2.1 INTRODUCTION

The purpose of this chapter is to provide an introduction to the way in which data may be organized in secondary storage. By "secondary storage" here we really mean present-day direct access media, such as disk packs, drums, and so on. In other words:

- We are not considering purely sequential media, such as tape, since such media in general impose far too many restrictions to be useful in a database system[1] (for example, it is not generally possible to perform "update in place" on tape).

- We make no attempt to predict what future media may be like. Note, however, that if a new device—say, a large-capacity associative memory—were to be produced, the enterprise could take immediate advantage of it, provided data independence had been achieved.

One other introductory remark: In this chapter we are not concerned with specific systems. The storage structures provided in individual systems are considered to some extent in later chapters.

This chapter, then, is concerned with the internal level of the system (and also, to some extent, with what lies below that level—remember that the internal level is still slightly above the level of physical storage). As explained in Chapter 1, user operations are expressed (via the DML) in terms

---

1. Tapes do have a use in database systems as a medium for journaling and dumping operations. However, tapes are not normally used for storing the operational database itself.

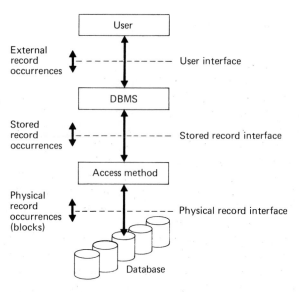

Fig. 2.1 The stored record interface.

of external records, and must be converted by the DBMS into corresponding operations on internal or stored records. These latter operations must be converted in turn to operations at the actual hardware level, that is, to operations on physical records or blocks. The component responsible for this internal/physical conversion is called an *access method* (Fig. 2.1). The access method consists of a set of routines whose function is to conceal all device-dependent details from the DBMS and to present the DBMS with a *stored record interface*.[2] The stored record interface thus corresponds to the internal level, just as the user interface corresponds to the external level. [The physical record interface (see Fig. 2.1) corresponds to the actual hardware level.]

[The ANSI/SPARC term for the access method is "storage subsystem." As an aside, we note that the access method may be thought of as a logical extension of the DBMS, and indeed in some systems the two are

---

2. Many existing access methods actually do rather more. Thus many of the functions attributed in what follows to the DBMS may in practice be performed by the access method; for example, the access method may provide secondary indexes of its own. However, we choose to assume a rather elementary access method as a more suitable basis for describing possible storage structures. The existence of more complex access methods does not invalidate any of the subsequent discussion.

packaged together. In other cases, the DBMS relies on the underlying operating system to provide the access method function. To fix our ideas we
assume this latter structure.]

The stored record interface permits the DBMS to view the storage
structure as a collection of stored files, each one consisting of all occurrences of one type of stored record (see Chapter 1). Specifically, the DBMS
knows (a) what stored files exist, and, for each one, (b) the structure of the
corresponding stored record, (c) the stored field(s), if any, on which it is
sequenced, and (d) the stored field(s), if any, that can be used as search
arguments for direct access. This information will all be specified as part of
the storage structure definition. Note that points (c) and (d) amount to saying that the DBMS knows what access statements it can issue against the
stored file. Note, too, that the unit that crosses the stored record interface is
one stored record occurrence.

The DBMS does *not* know (a) anything about physical records
(blocks); (b) how stored fields are associated to form stored records
(although in practice this will almost invariably be via physical adjacency);
(c) how sequencing is performed (e.g., it may be by means of physical contiguity, an index, or a pointer chain); or (d) how direct access is performed
(e.g., it may be via an index, a sequential scan, or hash-addressing). This information is specified to the access method, not to the DBMS.

As an illustration, let us suppose that the storage structure includes a
stored file of PARTs, where each stored record occurrence consists of a part
number (P#), a part name (PNAME), a color (COLOR), and a weight
(WEIGHT). Part of the storage structure definition might then go as follows:

```
STORED FILE PART_FILE
     PART   LENGTH = ...,   SEQUENCE = ASCENDING(P#)
         P#       TYPE = ..., INDEX = P#_INDEX
         PNAME    TYPE = ...
         COLOR    TYPE = ...
         WEIGHT   TYPE = ...
```

This definition is intended to convey the following information.

■ The stored file of PARTs exists.

■ The corresponding stored record has a particular structure.

■ The stored record occurrences are sequenced on ascending P# values
    (note that the sequencing mechanism is *not* specified).

■ The P# stored field is indexed, so that direct access may be performed
    by supplying a value for this field.

(Of course, many other details of the storage structure may have to be specified, too.)

We make one other assumption: When a new stored record occurrence is first created and entered into the database, the access method is responsible for assigning it a unique *stored record address* (SRA). This value distinguishes that stored record occurrence from all others in the database. It may, for example, be simply the physical address of the occurrence within the storage volume (together with a volume identification), or alternatively an identification for the appropriate stored file together with an offset within that file (considering the file as a byte string). The SRA for a particular occurrence is returned to the DBMS by the access method when the occurrence is first created, and may be used by the DBMS for subsequent direct access to the occurrence concerned. We assume here that the SRA for a given occurrence does not change until the occurrence is physically moved as part of a database reorganization (if then).

The SRA concept permits the DBMS to build its own access mechanisms (indexes, pointer chains, etc.), over and above those maintained by the access method. This is illustrated by many of the examples in Section 2.2.

2.2   POSSIBLE REPRESENTATIONS FOR SOME SAMPLE DATA

In this section we take a simple collection of sample data and consider some of the many ways it could be represented in storage (at the level of the stored record interface). The sample data is shown in Fig. 2.2. It consists of information about five suppliers; for each supplier we wish to record a supplier number (S#), a supplier name (SNAME), a status value (STATUS), and a location (CITY). We assume that each supplier has a unique supplier number, and also that each supplier has one name, one status value, and one location.

S#	SNAME	STATUS	CITY
S1	Smith	20	London
S2	Jones	10	Paris
S3	Blake	30	Paris
S4	Clark	20	London
S5	Adams	30	Athens

Fig. 2.2 Sample data.

In what follows, the assumption, unless we explicitly state otherwise, will be that each stored file is sequenced by the access method on its *primary key*. [This term will be defined rigorously in Chapter 4; for the present we assume that it is well understood. Basically it signifies a field (combination) whose values uniquely identify the records in the file.] The mechanism by which this sequencing is performed will not be shown.

The first (and simplest) representation consists of a single stored file containing five stored record occurrences, one for each supplier. Figure 2.2 may be considered an illustration of this. This representation has the advantage of simplicity but would probably be inadequate in practice. Suppose, for example, that we had 10,000 suppliers instead of just five, but that they were located in only ten different cities. If we assume that the amount of storage required for a *pointer* is less than that required for a city name, the representation illustrated in Fig. 2.3 will clearly save some storage space in such a situation.

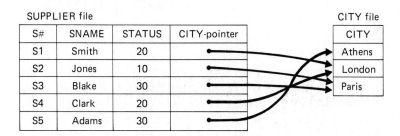

Fig. 2.3 Factoring out the CITY values.

Here we have two stored files, a supplier file and a city file, with pointers out of the former into the latter. These pointers are SRAs. The *only* advantage of this representation (compared with the previous one) is the saving in space. For example, a request to find all properties of a given supplier will require at least one more access than before; a request to find all suppliers in a given city will involve several more accesses. Note, incidentally, that it is the DBMS, not the access method, that maintains the pointers; the access method is not aware of the connection between the two files. (The connection must be stated in the definition of the mapping from the conceptual schema to storage.)

If the query "Find all suppliers in a given city" is an important one, the DBA may choose the alternative representation shown in Fig. 2.4. Here again we have two stored files, a supplier file and a city file, but this time there are pointers out of the latter into the former (each city stored record

CITY file

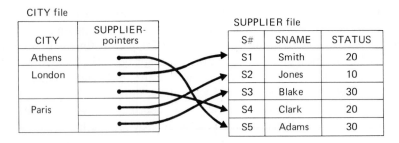

Fig. 2.4 Indexing on CITY.

occurrence contains pointers to all corresponding supplier stored record occurrences). It should be obvious that this is better than the previous representation for queries asking for all suppliers in a given city but worse for queries asking for all attributes of a given supplier. The storage requirement is basically the same.

The city file in Fig. 2.4 serves as an *index* to the supplier file (equivalently, the supplier file is *indexed by* the city file). The purpose of an index is to provide an *access path* to the file it is indexing—that is, a way of getting to the records in that indexed file. A given file may have many associated access paths. One path that is always available is the simple sequential path—it is always possible to perform an exhaustive search through the file, record by record, according to the basic sequence (usually the primary key sequence) supported by the underlying access method. Other types of access path are discussed later in this section.

Returning to the topic of indexing: An index, then, is a file in which each entry (record) consists of a data value together with one or more pointers. The data value is a value for some field of the indexed file (the *indexed field*), and the pointers identify records in the indexed file having that value for that field. An index can be used in two ways. First, it can be used for *sequential* access to the indexed file—sequential access, that is, according to values of the indexed field. (In other words, it imposes an ordering on that indexed file.) Second, it can also be used for *direct* access to individual records in the indexed file on the basis of a given value for that same field.

In general, then, the advantage of indexing is that (usually) it speeds up retrieval. The disadvantage is that it may slow down update. For example, suppose supplier S2 moves from Paris to London and consider what must be done to support this change in Fig. 2.4, compared with what must be done in Fig. 2.3.

Note, incidentally, that the city file shown in Fig. 2.4 is an index controlled by the DBMS, not by the access method. It is in fact a *dense, secondary* index. "Dense" means that it contains an entry for every stored record occurrence in the indexed file; this means that the indexed file need not contain the indexed field—in the example, the supplier file no longer includes a city field. (We shall consider *non*dense indexing in Section 2.3.) "Secondary" means that it is an index on a field other than the primary key.

Figure 2.5 shows a representation of the data that combines the two previous representations, and thus possesses the advantages of each. Of course it also has the update disadvantage mentioned earlier, and in addition it requires slightly more storage.

Another disadvantage of *secondary* indexes in general is that each stored record occurrence in the index must contain an unpredictable number of pointers (because the indexed field will not usually contain a distinct value for each stored record occurrence in the indexed file). This fact complicates the job of the DBMS in applying changes to the database. An alternative to the previous representation that avoids this problem is illustrated in Fig. 2.6.

In this representation each stored record occurrence (supplier or city) contains just one pointer. Each city points to the first supplier in that city. That supplier then points to the second supplier in the same city, who points to the third, and so on, up to the last, who points back to the city. Thus for each city we have a *chain* of all suppliers in that city (another example of an access path). The advantage of this representation is that it is easier to apply changes. The disadvantage is that, for a given city, the only way to access the nth supplier is to follow the chain and access the 1st, 2nd, . . . , $(n - 1)$th suppliers, too. If each access involves a seek operation, the time taken to access the nth supplier may be quite considerable.

As an extension of the foregoing representation, we could make the chains two-way (so that each stored record occurrence contains exactly *two* pointers). Such a representation might be chosen if deleting a supplier is a common operation, for example, since it simplifies the process of pointer adjustment necessitated by such an operation. Another extension would be to include a pointer in each supplier direct to the corresponding city (as we did in Fig. 2.3), to cut down on the amount of chain-traversing required for certain types of query.

The representation shown in Fig. 2.6 (using pointer chains) is a simple example of *multilist organization*. In Fig. 2.6 we chained together all suppliers in the same city; in other words, for each city we had a *list* of corresponding suppliers. In exactly the same way (by means of additional pointers) we could also have a list of suppliers for each distinct status value, for example. The reader should try sketching this representation for the

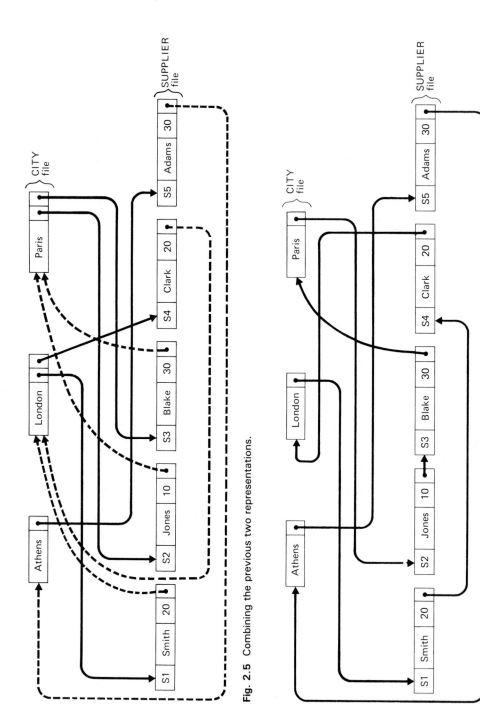

Fig. 2.5 Combining the previous two representations.

Fig. 2.6 Using pointer chains.

sample data. In general, a multilist organization can clearly contain any number of such lists.

To return to secondary indexing: Just as it is possible to provide any number of lists in the multilist organization, it is also possible to provide any number of secondary indexes in an indexing organization. In the extreme case we have the situation illustrated in Fig. 2.7: an index on every secondary field, or *inverted organization*. (The symbol ↑ is used to mean "pointer to.")

SNAME index			STATUS index			CITY index			SUPPLIER file
SNAME	Pointers		STATUS	Pointers		CITY	Pointers		S#
Smith	↑ S1		10	↑ S2		Athens	↑ S5		S1
Jones	↑ S2		20	↑ S1, ↑ S4		London	↑ S1, ↑ S4		S2
Blake	↑ S3		30	↑ S3, ↑ S5		Paris	↑ S2, ↑ S3		S3
Clark	↑ S4								S4
Adams	↑ S5								S5

Fig. 2.7 Inverted organization.

However, although inverted organization will perform well for a request for all suppliers with a given property (say, a status of 20), a request for all properties of a given supplier will take a long time to answer. In practice, therefore, we frequently compromise by providing a *regular* organization (as shown in Fig. 2.2) together with secondary indexes on certain selected fields. (Note that this involves redundant storage of the indexed field values.) This is one of the most common storage structures in current use.

Another representation that should be mentioned is the *hierarchical* organization, illustrated in Fig. 2.8. Here we have one stored file containing three (hierarchical) stored record occurrences, one for each city. Part of each stored record occurrence consists of a variable-length list of supplier

Fig. 2.8 Hierarchical organization.

entries, one for each supplier in that city, and each supplier entry contains supplier number, name, and status. (A variable-length list contained within a record like this is sometimes called a *repeating group.*) As in many previous examples, we have here factored out the CITY values, but we have chosen this time to represent the association between a city and its suppliers by making the city and suppliers all part of one stored record occurrence (instead of using pointers, as in Fig. 2.4, for example). Incidentally, a secondary index such as that in Fig. 2.4 is in fact a hierarchical file.

The last representation we shall consider is a *hash-addressing organization.* Hash-addressing, or simply *hashing,* is another example of an access path. The basic idea of hash-addressing is that each stored record occurrence is placed in the database at a location whose address (SRA) may be computed as some function (the *hash function*) of a value that appears in that occurrence—usually the primary key value. Thus, to store the occurrence initially, the DBMS computes the SRA and instructs the access method to place the occurrence at that position; and to retrieve the occurrence subsequently, the DBMS performs the same computation as before and then requests the access method to fetch the occurrence at the computed position. The advantage of this organization is that it provides very fast direct access on the basis of values of the hashed field.

As an example of hash-addressing, let us assume that the S# values are S100, S200, S300, S400, S500 (instead of S1, S2, S3, S4, S5), and let us consider the hash function:

SRA = remainder after dividing (numeric part of) S# value by 13

(a simple example of a fairly common class of hash function—"division/remainder").[3] The SRAs for the five suppliers are then 9, 5, 1, 10, 6, respectively, giving us the representation shown in Fig. 2.9 (where we have assumed that these SRA values simply represent record positions within the stored file).

In addition to showing how hashing works, the example also shows why the hash function is necessary. It would be theoretically possible to use an "identity" hash function, i.e., to use the (numeric) primary key value for any given occurrence directly as the SRA for that occurrence. However, this is usually inadequate in practice, because the range of primary key values is generally much wider than the range of available SRAs. For example, suppose that supplier numbers are in fact three digits wide, as specified above. This allows a theoretical maximum of 1000 different suppliers, whereas in practice there may be a maximum of only ten. To avoid a colossal waste of

---

3. For reasons that are beyond the scope of this text, the divisor is usually chosen to be prime.

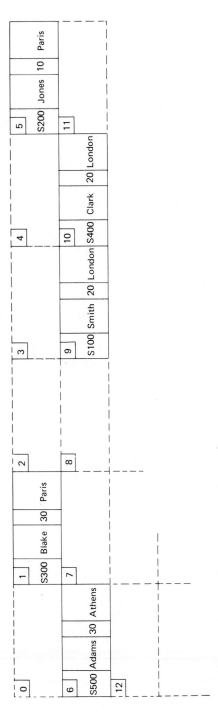

Fig. 2.9 A hash-addressing organization.

storage space, we ideally require a hash function that will reduce any value in the range 0–999 to one in the range 0–9. To allow a little room for future growth, it is usual to extend the target range by 20 percent or so; thus in the example, we actually choose a function that generates values in the range 0–12 rather than 0–9.

The example also illustrates one of the disadvantages of hash-addressing: The sequence of stored record occurrences within the stored file will almost certainly not be the primary key sequence (in addition, there may be gaps of arbitrary size between consecutive occurrences). In fact, a stored file in a hash-addressing organization is usually (not invariably) considered to have no particular sequence.

Another disadvantage of hash-addressing is the possibility of *collisions*—that is, two distinct stored record occurrences whose keys hash to the same SRA. For example, suppose that the sample data also included a supplier with an S# value of S1400. This supplier would collide (at SRA 9) with supplier S100, given the same hash function as before. The implication is that the hash function has to be made more complicated to handle this sort of situation. One possibility is to make the SRA (derived as above) the start point for a sequential scan. Thus to insert supplier S1400 (assuming that suppliers S100–S500 already exist), we go to SRA 9 and search forward from this position for the first free location. The new supplier will be stored at SRA 11. To retrieve supplier S1400 subsequently, we go through a similar process.

Our survey of some storage structures permitted by the stored record interface is now complete. In conclusion we should stress the fact that there is no such thing as a "best" storage structure. What is "best" depends on what is important to the enterprise. It is the responsibility of the DBA to balance a large number of conflicting requirements in choosing a storage structure. The considerations that must be taken into account include retrieval performance, the difficulty of applying changes, the amount of storage space available, the ease with which the database may be reorganized and the desired frequency of such reorganization, problems of recovery, and so on.

2.3   THE PHYSICAL RECORD INTERFACE: INDEXING TECHNIQUES

The physical record interface is the interface between the access method and the physical database. The unit that crosses this interface is one physical record occurrence (one block). The really significant difference between this interface and the stored record interface discussed in Section 2.2 is that here the concept of physical contiguity becomes significant. Physical contiguity provides an important means of representing the sequence of stored record occurrences within their stored file, making use of (a) the physical sequence of stored record occurrences within one block, and (b) the physical sequence of blocks on the medium. This has two implications in the area of index design.

First, it is possible to construct *nondense* indexes. The idea here is that the file being indexed is divided into groups, with several stored record occurrences in each group, such that the following conditions hold.

- For any two groups, all the stored record occurrences in one precede all those in the other (with respect to the sequencing being imposed on the file).

- Within any one group, the file sequence is represented by physical contiguity.

(In practice a group may be one block, one track, or any other convenient unit of storage space.) The index then contains one entry per group, giving (typically) the highest value of the indexed field occurring in the group and a pointer to the start of the group. The sequence of groups is represented by the sequence of entries in the index.

The term "nondense" refers to the fact that the index does *not* contain an entry for every stored record occurrence in the indexed file. Thus the stored record occurrences *must* contain the indexed field (contrast the situation with a dense index—Fig. 2.4). Figure 2.10 illustrates the situation in which the group is one track.

The second point arising from the availability of physical sequencing is the possibility of constructing *multilevel* (tree structure) indexes. The reason for providing an index in the first place is to remove the need for sequential scanning of the indexed file. However, sequential scanning is still necessary in the *index*. If the index gets very large, that fact in itself can cause a significant performance problem. The solution is to construct an index to the index. For one common example, see Fig. 2.11.

Here the indexed file is divided into groups of one track each. The *track index* contains an entry for each such track (as in Fig. 2.10). The track

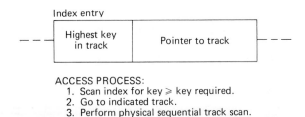

Index entry

| Highest key in track | Pointer to track |

ACCESS PROCESS:
1. Scan index for key ⩾ key required.
2. Go to indicated track.
3. Perform physical sequential track scan.

Fig. 2.10 An example of nondense indexing.

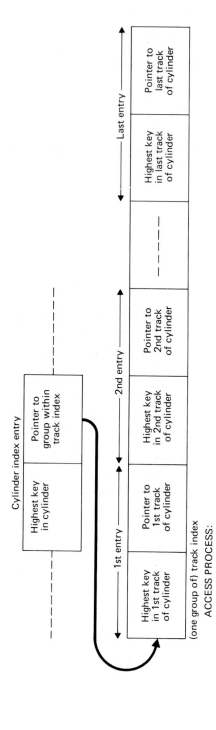

Fig. 2.11 An example of multilevel indexing.

index in turn is divided into groups, each of which consists of the entries for all tracks of one cylinder in the indexed file, and a *cylinder index* contains an entry for each such group in the track index. (Each group within the track index is normally recorded at the beginning of the appropriate cylinder of the indexed file, to cut down on seek activity.)

In general, a multilevel index can contain any number of levels, each of which acts as a nondense index to the level below. (It *must* be nondense; otherwise nothing is achieved.) If we were to take the technique to its logical conclusion, the top level would contain a single entry; in practice, however, a top level consisting of a single block (containing many entries) is the most that can be required.

B-trees

One particular form of multilevel or tree structure index that has become extremely popular in recent years is the *B-tree*. *B*-trees were described in a paper by Bayer and McCreight in 1972 [2.16]. Since that time numerous variations on the basic idea have been proposed by Bayer and other investigators. The variation discussed by Knuth [2.1] is one of the most common indexing techniques found in modern systems; in particular, the index structure of IBM's Virtual Storage Access Method, VSAM, is similar to Knuth's structure [2.17]. (However, the VSAM version was invented independently and includes additional features of its own, such as the use of compression techniques [see later]. In fact, a precursor of the VSAM structure was described as early as 1969 by H. K. Chang [2.21].)

In Knuth's variation the index consists of two parts: the sequence set and the index set (VSAM terminology). The *sequence set* consists of a single-level dense index to the actual data; the entries in the index are blocked, and the blocks are chained together, such that the data file ordering represented by the index is obtained by taking the entries (in physical order) in the first block on the chain, followed by the entries (in physical order) in the second block on the chain, and so on. Thus the sequence set provides fast sequential access to the data. The *index set,* in turn, provides fast *direct* access to the sequence set (and thus to the data too). The index set is actually a tree structure index to the sequence set; in fact, it is the index set that is the real *B*-tree, strictly speaking. (The combination of index set and sequence set is sometimes called a B^+-tree.) A simple example is shown in Fig. 2.12.

We explain Fig. 2.12 as follows. The values 6, 8, 12, . . . , 97, 99 are values of the indexed field, F say. Consider the top node, which consists of two value entries (50 and 82) and three pointers. Data records with F less than or equal to 50 can be found (eventually) by following the left pointer from this node; similarly, records with F greater than 50 and less than or

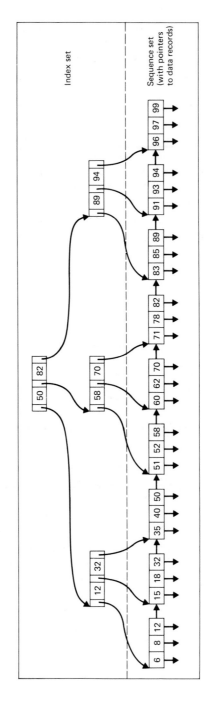

Fig. 2.12 Part of a simple *B*-tree (Knuth's variation).

equal to 82 can be found by following the middle pointer, and records with F greater than 82 can be found by following the right pointer. The other nodes of the index set are interpreted similarly; note in particular that (for example) following the right pointer from the first node at the second level takes us to all records with F greater than 32 *and less than or equal to 50* (by virtue of the fact that we have already followed the left pointer from the higher node).

The *B*-tree (index set) shown in Fig. 2.12 is somewhat unrealistic, however, for the following two reasons: First, the nodes of a *B*-tree do not normally all contain the same number of value entries; second, they normally do contain a certain amount of free space. In general, a *B-tree of order n* has at least n but not more than $2n$ value entries at any given node (and, if it has k value entries, then it also has $k + 1$ pointers). No data value appears in the tree more than once. We give the algorithm for searching for a particular value V in the structure of Fig. 2.12; the algorithm for the general *B*-tree is a simple generalization.

```
set N to the top node;
repeat until N is a sequence-set node;
    let X, Y be the data values in node N (X < Y);
    if V ≤ X
    then set N to the left lower node of N;
    if X < V ≤ Y
    then set N to middle lower node of N;
    if V > Y
    then set N to right lower node of N;
end;
if V occurs in node N then exit (found);
if V does not occur in node N then exit (not found);
```

A problem with tree structures in general is that insertions and deletions can cause the tree to become *unbalanced*. A tree is unbalanced if the terminal nodes are not all at the same level—i.e., if different terminal nodes are at different depths below the top node. Since searching the tree involves a secondary storage access for every node visited, search times can become very unpredictable in an unbalanced tree. The notable advantage of *B*-trees is that the *B*-tree insertion/deletion algorithm guarantees that the tree will remain balanced. We briefly consider insertion of a new value, V say, into a *B*-tree of order n. (The algorithm as described handles the index set only, since, as explained earlier, it is the index set that is the *B*-tree proper. A trivial extension is needed to deal with the sequence set also.)

First, the search algorithm is executed to locate, not the sequence set node, but that node (N say) at the lowest level of the index set in which V logically belongs. If N contains free space, V is inserted into N and the process terminates. Otherwise, node N (which must contain $2n$ values) is *split* into two nodes N_1 and N_2; the lowest n values of the set consisting of the original $2n$ values plus the value V are placed in the left node N_1, the highest n values of this set are placed in the right node N_2, and the middle value, W say, is promoted to the "parent" node of N, P say, to serve as a separator value for nodes N_1 and N_2. (Future searches for a value V', on reaching node P, will be directed to node N_1 if $V' \le W$ and to N_2 if $V' > W$.) An attempt is now made to insert W into P, and the process is repeated. In the worst case, splitting will occur all the way to the top of the tree and the tree will increase in height by one level (but even then will remain balanced).

The deletion algorithm is essentially the inverse of the procedure just described.

2.4 GENERAL INDEXING TECHNIQUES

In the previous section we presented two techniques, nondense indexing and multilevel indexing, that can be applied at the physical record interface. In theory these techniques *could* be applied at the stored record interface too, but such application would be unlikely in practice since the techniques depend so much on the concept of physical contiguity. By way of contrast, the following techniques may be used in indexes at either level:

> Indexing on field combinations,
>
> Selectivity in the index,
>
> Compression techniques,
>
> Symbolic pointer representation.

Indexing on field combinations

It is possible to construct an index on the basis of the values of two or more fields in combination. For example, Fig. 2.13 shows an index to the sample data of Fig. 2.2 on the field combination CITY and STATUS (in that order).

CITY/STATUS	Pointers
Athens/30	↑ S5
London/20	↑ S1, ↑ S4
Paris/10	↑ S2
Paris/30	↑ S3

Fig. 2.13 Indexing on CITY/STATUS.

With such an index we can respond to such queries as "Find all suppliers in Paris with status 10" in one scan of the index. If the combined index did not exist, this query would involve (a) finding all suppliers in Paris, (b) finding all suppliers with status 10, and (c) extracting the suppliers common to both lists. Since steps (a) and (b) could perfectly well be performed in the reverse order, moreover, we would have a strategy problem (that is, deciding which to do first).

Note that the combined index also acts as an index on the CITY field, inasmuch as all the entries for a given city are at least consecutive within the index. (A separate index will have to be provided if indexing on STATUS is required, however.) In general, an index on the combination of n fields F_1, $F_2, \ldots, F_n$ (in that order) will also serve as an index on F_1, as an index on the combination F_1F_2 (or F_2F_1), as an index on the combination $F_1F_2F_3$ (in any order), and so on. Thus the total number of indexes required to provide complete indexing in this way is not so large as might appear at first glance.

Selectivity in the index

The reader should realize that it is not necessary to provide access via the index to every record occurrence in the indexed file. In some situations it may be useful to have index entries for selected values only of the indexed field. For example, consider an employee file in which 95 percent of the employees have a status of exempt and 5 percent have a status of nonexempt. It would scarcely be worth providing a general index on the status field. On the other hand, it might be very useful to have an index pointing to all nonexempt employees—in other words, to select a subset of the set of possible values to be indexed.

Compression techniques

Compression techniques are ways of reducing the amount of storage required for a given set of stored data. One common technique is to replace each individual data value by some representation of the difference between it and the data value next to it. Such a technique can be used wherever the data will be accessed *sequentially*—for example, within an index or within one "group" of a file for which a nondense index exists (see Section 2.3).

To fix our ideas, let us take as an example a single block of an index to an employee file. (In practice, compression techniques are much more frequently used in indexes rather than in data files.) We suppose that the first four entries in this block are for the following employees.

```
ROBERTON
ROBERTSON
ROBERTSTONE
ROBINSON
```

Employee names are 12 characters long (so that each of these names may be considered—in its uncompressed form—to be padded at the right with the appropriate number of blanks).

The first compression technique we can apply is to replace those characters at the front of each entry that are the same as those in the previous entry by a corresponding count: *front compression*. This gives us

```
0-ROBERTONbbbb
6-SONbbb
7-TONEb
3-INSONbbbb
```

(The trailing blanks are now shown explicitly as b.)

The second compression technique is *rear compression*. One way to apply rear compression in the example would be to eliminate all trailing blanks (again, replacing them by an appropriate count). Further compression can be achieved by dropping all characters to the right of the one required to distinguish this entry from its two adjacent entries. This gives us

```
0-7-ROBERTO
6-2-SO
7-1-T
3-1-I
```

where the second number in each entry is a count of the number of characters recorded. (We have assumed that the next entry does not have ROBI as its first four characters when decompressed.) Note, however, that we have actually lost some information from this index. That is, when decompressed, it looks like this:

```
ROBERTO?????
ROBERTSO????
ROBERTST????
ROBI????????
```

(where ? represents an unknown character). This is permissible only on the assumption that the values are recorded in full *somewhere* (in this case, in the indexed file).

Symbolic pointer representation

So far we have assumed that all pointers are SRAs. As suggested in Section 2.1, however, SRA values may change when a stored file is reorganized. If this does happen when a given stored file is reorganized, then all files pointing into it—in particular, all indexes—will need to be updated to contain the revised SRA values. Reorganization can thus become a time-consuming and very costly process. The problem can be avoided, however, by using *sym-*

bolic pointers. That is, SRA-valued pointers can be replaced by the corresponding primary key values. An index entry for supplier S1, for example, will now contain, not the address (SRA) of the S1 record, but the actual data value 'S1'. This value can then be used to locate the corresponding record (we assume that it is always possible to access records directly on the basis of their primary key). An index using symbolic keys will clearly not need to be updated just because the indexed file has been reorganized (the symbolic value 'S1' still identifies the record for supplier S1, even if that record has been moved and its SRA has changed). Of course, access via that index will be slower than access via an index that uses direct pointers.

Figures 2.14 and 2.15 show the result of applying this technique to the representations of Figs. 2.4 (indexing on CITY) and 2.7 (inverted organization), respectively. In Fig. 2.15, note that the need for the supplier stored file has disappeared entirely.

CITY file

CITY	S#
Athens	S5
London	S1
	S4
Paris	S2
	S3

SUPPLIER file

S#	SNAME	STATUS
S1	Smith	20
S2	Jones	10
S3	Blake	30
S4	Clark	20
S5	Adams	30

Fig. 2.14 Indexing on CITY (symbolic pointers).

SNAME index

SNAME	S#
Smith	S1
Jones	S2
Blake	S3
Clark	S4
Adams	S5

STATUS index

STATUS	S#
10	S2
20	S1, S4
30	S3, S5

CITY index

CITY	S#
Athens	S5
London	S1, S4
Paris	S2, S3

Fig. 2.15 Inverted organization (symbolic pointers).

EXERCISES

Exercises 2.1–2.3 may prove suitable as a basis for group discussion; they are intended to lead to deeper consideration of various design problems. Exercises 2.5 and 2.6 have rather a mathematical flavor.

2.1 A company database is to contain information about the divisions, departments, and employees of the company. Each employee works in one department; each department is part of one division. Invent some sample data and sketch some possible storage structures for this data. Where possible, state the relative advantages of each structure—i.e., consider how typical retrieval and update operations would be handled in each case. *Hint:* The constraints "each employee works in one department" and "each department is in one division" are structurally similar to the constraint "each supplier has one city." (They are all examples of many-to-one relationships.) A difference between this exercise and the supplier–city example is that we would probably like to record more information in the database for departments and divisions than we did for cities.

2.2 Repeat Exercise 2.1 for a database that is to contain information about customers and items. Each customer may order any number of different items; each item may be ordered by any number of customers. *Hint:* There is a many-to-many relationship here between customers and items. One way to represent such a relationship is by means of a *double index*. A double index is an index that is used to index two data files simultaneously. A given entry corresponds to a *pair* of related data records, one from each of the two files, and contains two indexed values and two pointers. Can you think of other ways of representing many-to-many (-to-many- . . .) relationships?

2.3 Repeat Exercise 2.1 for a database that is to contain information about parts and components (a component is itself a part and may have further components). *Hint:* How does this problem differ from that in Exercise 2.2?

2.4 The first ten values of the indexed field in a particular indexed file are as follows.

```
ABRAHAMS,GK
ACKERMANN,LZ
ACKROYD,S
ADAMS,T
ADAMS,TR
ADAMSON,CR
ALLEN,S
AYRES,ST
BAILEY,TE
BAILEYMAN,D
```

(Each is padded with blanks at the right to a total length of 15 characters.) Show the values actually recorded in the *index* if the compression techniques described in Section 2.4 are applied. What is the percentage saving in space? Show the steps involved in retrieving (or attempting to retrieve) the stored record occurrence for ACKROYD,S and ADAMS,V. Show also the steps involved in inserting a stored record occurrence for ALLINGHAM,M.

2.5 Suppose that we have a multilevel index such that the lowest level contains an entry for each of N stored data record occurrences, and each level above the lowest contains an entry for every block in the level below. Suppose also that each block in the index contains n index entries, and that the index is extended up to a single block at the top level. Derive expressions for the number of *levels* in the index and the number of *blocks* in the index.

2.6 Let us define "complete indexing" to mean that an index exists for every distinct field combination in the indexed file. How many indexes will be necessary to provide complete indexing for a file defined on (a) 3 fields; (b) 4 fields; (c) N fields?

REFERENCES AND BIBLIOGRAPHY

These references are organized into groups, as follows: [2.1–2.5] are textbooks that either are devoted entirely to the topic of this chapter or at least include a detailed treatment of it. [2.6–2.8] are tutorials. [2.9] and [2.10] are very early papers that nevertheless are still relevant. [2.11] and [2.12] discuss hashing, [2.13–2.15] combined indexes, [2.16–2.18] other indexing techniques (including *B*-trees), and [2.19–2.21] compression techniques. [2.22–2.24] are attempts to develop a theoretical basis for the subject. Finally, [2.25–2.28] discuss some miscellaneous techniques.

See also [1.16].

2.1 D. E. Knuth. *The Art of Computer Programming. Vol. III: Sorting and Searching.* Reading, Mass.: Addison-Wesley (1973).

Includes a comprehensive analysis of search algorithms (Chapter 6). For *database* searching, where the data resides in secondary storage, the most directly applicable sections are 6.2.4 (Multiway Trees), 6.4 (Hashing), and 6.5 (Retrieval on Secondary Keys).

2.2 D. Lefkovitz. *File Structures for On-Line Systems.* Rochelle Park, N.J.: Spartan Books (1969).

2.3 J. Martin. *Computer Data-Base Organization.* Englewood Cliffs, N.J.: Prentice-Hall (1975).

This book is divided into two major parts: Logical Organization and Physical Organization. Part II consists of an extensive description (over 300 pages) of storage structures and associated access strategies.

2.4 G. Wiederhold. *Database Design.* New York: McGraw-Hill (1977).

This book (15 chapters) includes a good survey of secondary storage devices and their performance parameters (one chapter, about 40 pages) and a comprehensive analysis of corresponding storage structures (three chapters, over 200 pages).

2.5 S. P. Ghosh. *Data Base Organization for Data Management.* New York: Academic Press (1977).

A rather formal treatment.

2.6 G. G. Dodd. "Elements of Data Management Systems." *ACM Comp. Surv.* **1**, No. 2 (June 1969).

2.7 W. D. Maurer and T. G. Lewis. "Hash Table Methods." *ACM Comp. Surv.* **7,** No. 1 (March 1975).

2.8 D. Comer. "The Ubiquitous *B*-tree." *ACM Comp. Surv.* **11,** No. 2 (June 1979).

2.9 W. W. Peterson. "Addressing for Random-Access Storage." *IBM J. R & D* **1,** No. 2 (April 1957).

2.10 W. Buchholz. "File Organization and Addressing." *IBM Sys. J.* **2,** No. 2 (June 1963).

2.11 R. Morris. "Scatter Storage Techniques." *CACM* **11,** No. 1 (January 1968).

This paper is concerned primarily with hashing techniques as they apply to the symbol table of an assembler or compiler. However, it is a useful survey of the techniques available and should prove valuable to anyone concerned with the problems of storage structure design.

2.12 V. Y. Lum, P. S. T. Yuen, and M. Dodd. "Key-to-Address Transform Techniques: A Fundamental Performance Study on Large Existing Formatted Files." *CACM* **14,** No. 4 (April 1971).

An investigation into the performance of several different hashing algorithms. The conclusion is that the division/remainder method seems to be the best all-round performer.

2.13 V. Y. Lum. "Multi-attribute Retrieval with Combined Indexes." *CACM* **13,** No. 11 (November 1970).

The paper that introduced the technique of indexing on field combinations.

2.14 J. K. Mullin. "Retrieval-Update Speed Tradeoffs Using Combined Indices." *CACM* **14,** No. 12 (December 1971).

A sequel to [2.13] that gives performance statistics for the combined index scheme for various retrieval/storage ratios.

2.15 B. Shneiderman. "Reduced Combined Indexes for Efficient Multiple Attribute Retrieval." *Information Systems* **2,** No. 4 (1976).

Proposes a refinement of Lum's combined indexing technique [2.13] that considerably reduces the storage space and search time overheads. For example, the index combination ABCD, BCDA, CDAB, DABC, ACBD, BDAC—see the answer to Exercise 2.6(b)—could be replaced by the combination ABCD, BCD, CDA, DAB, AC, BD. If each of A, B, C, D can assume 10 distinct values, then in the worst case the original combination would involve 60,000 index entries, the reduced combination only 13,200 entries.

2.16 R. Bayer and C. McCreight. "Organization and Maintenance of Large Ordered Indexes." *Acta Informatica* **1,** No. 3 (1972).

2.17 R. E. Wagner. "Indexing Design Considerations." *IBM Sys. J.* **12,** No. 4 (1973).

A good description of indexing concepts, with details of the techniques—including compression algorithms—used in IBM's Virtual Storage Access Method, VSAM.

2.18 M. R. Vose and J. S. Richardson. "An Approach to Inverted Index Maintenance." *BCS Comp. Bull.* **16**, No. 5 (May 1972).

Describes a multilist approach to the construction and maintenance of secondary indexes. This method avoids some of the problems of variable-length index entries. Each data record occurrence is represented within the system by a "sequential index number" (SIN), assigned when the occurrence is first stored. SIN values are assigned in ascending sequence. The "basic index" contains an entry for every data record occurrence, giving its SIN and its physical address, and it is in this index that multilist organization is used. For each indexed field, each basic index entry gives the SIN of the next occurrence having the same value in that field. For each value of each indexed field, pointers are maintained to the start and the end of the chain within the basic index.

2.19 B. A. Marron and P. A. D. de Maine. "Automatic Data Compression." *CACM* **10**, No. 11 (November 1967).

Gives two compression/decompression algorithms: NUPAK, which operates on numeric data, and ANPAK, which operates on alphanumeric or "any" data (i.e., any string of bits).

2.20 D. A. Huffman. "A Method for the Construction of Minimum Redundancy Codes." *Proc. IRE* **40** (September 1952).

Huffman coding is a character coding technique that can result in significant data compression if all characters do not occur with equal frequency. The basic idea is that bit string encodings are assigned to represent characters in such a way that different characters are represented by strings of different lengths, and the most commonly occurring characters are represented by the shortest strings. Also, no character has an encoding (of n bits, say) such that those n bits are identical to the first n bits of some other character encoding. As a simple example, suppose the data to be represented involves only the characters A, B, C, D, E, and suppose that the relative frequency of occurrence of these characters is as given in the following table (second column).

Character	Frequency	Code
E	35%	1
A	30%	01
D	20%	001
C	10%	0001
B	5%	0000

Character E has the highest frequency and is therefore assigned the shortest code, a single bit, say a 1-bit. All other codes must then start with a 0-bit, and must be at least two bits long (a lone 0-bit would not be valid, since it would be indistinguishable from the leading bit of other codes). Character A is assigned the next shortest code, say 01; characters D, C, and B are assigned 001, 0001, 0000, respectively (see the table). With these assignments the expected average length of a coded character, in bits, is

$$0.35 * 1 + 0.30 * 2 + 0.20 * 3 + 0.10 * 4 + 0.05 * 4 = 2.15 \text{ bits,}$$

whereas if every character were assigned the same number of bits, as in a conventional character coding scheme, we should need three bits per character (to allow for five different characters).

2.21 H. K. Chang. "Compressed Indexing Method." *IBM Technical Disclosure Bulletin II,* No. 11 (April 1969).

2.22 D. Hsiao and F. Harary. "A Formal System for Information Retrieval from Files." *CACM* **13,** No. 2 (February 1970).

This paper is an attempt to unify the ideas of various storage structures—inverted organization, indexed sequential organization, multilist organization, and so on—into a "generalized file structure," and so to form a basis for a theory of storage structures. A "general retrieval algorithm" is presented for retrieving occurrences satisfying an arbitrary Boolean combination of "attribute = value" conditions from the generalized structure.

2.23 D. G. Severance. "Identifier Search Mechanisms: A Survey and Generalized Model." *ACM Comp. Surv.* **6,** No. 3 (September 1974).

2.24 M. E. Senko, E. B. Altman, M. M. Astrahan, and P. L. Fehder. "Data Structures and Accessing in Data-Base Systems." *IBM Sys J.* **12,** No. 1 (1973).

This paper is in three parts:
  I. Evolution of Information Systems,
  II. Information Organization,
  III. Data Representations and the Data Independent Accessing Model.
Part I consists of a short historical survey of the development of database systems. Part II describes the entity set model, which corresponds to the conceptual level in the ANSI/SPARC architecture. Part III forms an introduction to the Data Independent Accessing Model (DIAM), which is an attempt to describe a database in terms of four successive levels of abstraction: the entity set (highest), string, encoding, and physical device levels. These four levels may be thought of as a more detailed, but still abstract, definition of the lower portions of the architecture in Fig. 1.5. We may characterize the three lower levels of the four as follows.

- *String level.* Access paths to data are defined as ordered sets or "strings" of data objects. Three types of string are identified: atomic strings (example: a string connecting field values to form a PART stored record occurrence), entity strings (example: a string connecting PART record occurrences for red parts), and link strings (example: a string connecting a SUPPLIER record occurrence to PART occurrences for parts supplied by that supplier).

- *Encoding level.* Data objects and strings are mapped into linear address spaces, using a single simple representation primitive known as a basic encoding unit.

- *Physical device level.* Linear address spaces are allocated to formatted physical subdivisions of real recording media.

The aim of DIAM is to provide a framework in which a variety of system design problems can be addressed in a controlled and structured manner.

2.25 D. G. Severance and G. M. Lohman. "Differential Files: Their Application to the Maintenance of Large Databases." *ACM Transactions on Database Systems* **1**, No. 3 (September 1976).

This paper describes "differential files" and discusses their advantages. The basic idea is that updates are not made directly to the database itself—instead, they are recorded in a physically distinct file (the differential file) and are merged with the actual database at some suitable subsequent time. The following advantages are claimed for this approach. Note that the first six of these relate to database integrity and recovery, whereas the remaining four are operational advantages.

- Database dumping costs are reduced.
- Incremental dumping is facilitated.
- Dumping and reorganization may both be performed concurrently with updating operations.
- Recovery after a program error is fast.
- Recovery after a hardware failure is fast.
- The risk of a serious data loss is reduced.
- "Memo files" are supported efficiently.
- Software development is simplified.
- The main file software is simplified.
- Future storage costs may be reduced.

One problem not discussed is that of supporting key-sequenced access to the data when some records are in the real database and some are in the differential file.

2.26 B. J. Dzubak and C. R. Warburton. "The Organization of Structured Files." *CACM* **8**, No. 7 (July 1965).

Compares and contrasts ten methods of storing and accessing a "structured file" (i.e., a collection of information in the form of a linear graph, for example, a parts explosion).

2.27 E. Wong and T. C. Chiang. "Canonical Structure in Attribute Based File Organization." *CACM* **14**, No. 9 (September 1971).

A novel storage structure that has a number of advantages is proposed. It is assumed that all retrieval requests are expressed as a Boolean combination of elementary "field = value" conditions, and that these elementary conditions are known. Then the file can be partitioned into disjoint subsets for storage purposes; the subsets are the atoms of the Boolean algebra which is the set of all sets of record occurrences retrievable via the Boolean access requests. The advantages of this technique include the following.

a) Set intersection (of atoms) is never necessary.

b) An arbitrary request can easily be converted into a request for (the union of) one or more atoms.

c) Such a union never involves elimination of duplicates.

2.28 R. Fagin, J. Nievergelt, N. Pippenger, and H. R. Strong. "Extendible Hashing—A Fast Access Method for Dynamic Files." *ACM Transactions on Database Systems* **4**, No. 3 (September 1979).

A disadvantage of hashing schemes in general is that as the size of the data file increases, so the number of collisions also increases, and the average access time increases correspondingly (because more and more time is spent performing sequential searches through sets of collisions). This paper describes an elegant variation on the basic hashing technique, in which it is guaranteed that no more than two secondary storage accesses are ever needed to locate the record corresponding to a given key. An outline description of this scheme follows.

1. Let the basic hash function be *h,* and let the primary key value of some record *R* be *K*. Hashing *K*—i.e., evaluating *h(K)*—we obtain a value *K'*, which we call the *pseudokey* of *R*. Pseudokeys are not interpreted directly as addresses but instead lead to stored records in a somewhat indirect fashion as described below.

2. The stored file has a *directory* associated with it (also held in secondary storage). The directory consists of a header, containing a value *d* called the *depth* of the directory, and a list of 2^d pointers. The pointers are pointers to data blocks, which contain the actual stored records (multiple records per block). If we consider the leading *d* bits of a pseudokey as an unsigned binary integer *b*, then the *i*th pointer in the directory ($1 \leq i \leq 2^d$) points to a data block that contains all records for which *b* takes the value $i - 1$. In other words, the first pointer points to that block containing all records for which *b* is all zeros, the second points to that block containing all records for which *b* is 0 . . . 01, and so on. (These 2^d pointers are typically not all distinct; that is, there will typically be fewer than 2^d distinct data blocks.) Thus, to find the record having key *K,* we hash *K* to find the pseudokey *K'* and take the first *d* bits of that pseudokey; if these bits have the numeric value $i - 1$, we go to the *i*th entry in the directory (one secondary storage access) and follow the pointer we find there, which will take us to the data block containing the required record (also one secondary storage access). Note that the internal arrangement of records within a data block is independent of the extendible hashing scheme. It may very well involve an internal hashing operation of its own. But finding a record *within* a block does not require any additional secondary storage accesses, once that block has been fetched into main storage.

3. Each data block also has a header giving the *local depth p* of that block ($p \leq d$). Suppose, for example, that $d = 3$, and that the first pointer in the directory (the 000 pointer) points to a data block for which the local depth *p* is 2. Local depth 2 means in this case that, not only does this data block contain all records with pseudokeys starting 000, it contains *all* records with pseudokeys starting 00 (i.e., those starting 000 and also those starting 001). In other words, the 001 directory pointer also points to this data block.

4. Continuing the example from (3) above, suppose that the data block is full, and now we wish to insert a new record having a pseudokey that starts 000 (or 001). At this point the data block is split into two; that is, a new, empty

block is obtained, and all 001 records are moved out of the old block and into the new one. The 001 pointer in the directory is changed to point to the new block (the 000 pointer still points to the old block).

5. Again continuing the example, suppose that the data block for 000 becomes filled again and has to split again. The existing directory cannot handle this split, because the local depth of the block to be split is already equal to the directory depth. Therefore we "double the directory": that is, we increase d by 1 and replace each pointer by a pair of adjacent, identical pointers. The data block can now be split; 0000 records are left in the old block and 0001 records go in the new block; the first pointer in the directory is left unchanged (i.e., still points to the old block) and the second pointer is changed to point to the new block. We note that doubling the directory is a fairly inexpensive operation, since it does not involve any access to the data blocks.

3

Data Structures and Corresponding Operators

3.1 INTRODUCTION

In this chapter we examine the problem of what the database should look like to the user. As we explained in Chapter 1, it is normal to present the user with a view of the data in which details of how that data is represented in storage are deliberately omitted. This view is the *external view*. (In most systems today the external view and the conceptual view are rather similar, if not identical; for systems that do distinguish between the two, the points made in what follows are applicable to both levels.)

The range of data structures supported at the user level (external or conceptual) is a factor that critically affects many components of the system. In particular, it dictates the design of the corresponding data manipulation language(s), since each DML operation must be defined in terms of its effect on those data structures. Thus the question "What data structures and associated operators should the system support?" is a crucial one. We may conveniently categorize database systems according to the approach they adopt in answering this central question. The three best known approaches are

- the relational approach;
- the hierarchical approach; and
- the network approach.

This fact accounts for the overall structure of this book—Parts 2, 3, and 4 consist of detailed examinations of each of these three approaches. The purpose of the present chapter is to pave the way for these later chapters by

63

providing a brief introduction to, and comparison of, the three approaches. This chapter may accordingly be viewed as the key to the entire book; however, the reader is cautioned that we make no attempt at rigor or completeness until we reach the later chapters.

3.2 THE RELATIONAL APPROACH

This section and the following two are based on a sample database concerning suppliers, parts, and shipments. Figure 3.1 shows the sample data in relational form; that is, it represents a *relational view* of the data.

It can be seen that the data is organized into three tables: S (suppliers), P (parts), and SP (shipments). The S table contains, for each supplier, a supplier number, name, status code, and location; the P table contains, for each part, a part number, name, color, weight, and location where the part is stored; and the SP table contains, for each shipment, a supplier number, a part number, and the quantity shipped. The S table, incidentally, consists of the first three rows of the table in Fig. 2.2, which we can now see is a relational view of the data used as the basis of the examples in Chapter 2. We make the same assumptions regarding suppliers that we made in Chapter 2, namely, that each supplier has a unique supplier number and exactly one name, status value, and location. Likewise we assume that each part has a unique part number and exactly one name, color, weight, and location; and that, at any given time, no more than one shipment exists for a given supplier/part combination.

Each of the three tables closely resembles a conventional sequential file, with rows of the table corresponding to records of the file and columns corresponding to fields of the records. The table P, for example, contains

S	S#	SNAME	STATUS	CITY
	S1	Smith	20	London
	S2	Jones	10	Paris
	S3	Blake	30	Paris

P	P#	PNAME	COLOR	WEIGHT	CITY
	P1	Nut	Red	12	London
	P2	Bolt	Green	17	Paris
	P3	Screw	Blue	17	Rome
	P4	Screw	Red	14	London

SP	S#	P#	QTY
	S1	P1	300
	S1	P2	200
	S1	P3	400
	S2	P1	300
	S2	P2	400
	S3	P2	200

Fig. 3.1 Sample data in relational form.

four rows or records, each consisting of five fields. However, there are certain significant differences—to be explained in detail in Chapter 4—between tables such as those in Fig. 3.1 and traditional sequential files. Each of these tables is actually a special case of the construct known in mathematics as a *relation*—a term that has a much more precise definition than the more traditional data processing term "file," or "table" for that matter. (However, in this book we shall frequently use "table" as if it were synonymous with "relation.") The relational approach to data is based on the realization that files that obey certain constraints may be considered as mathematical relations, and hence that elementary relation theory may be brought to bear on various practical problems of dealing with data in such files.

In much of the relational literature, therefore, tables such as those of Fig. 3.1 are referred to as relations. Rows of such tables are generally referred to as *tuples* (usually pronounced to rhyme with "couples"), again because the term has a more precise definition than "row" or "record." In this book, however, we shall tend to use the terms "tuple" and "row" interchangeably. Likewise, columns are usually referred to as *attributes;* again we shall use the two terms interchangeably.

One concept that relational theory emphasizes and for which there does not seem to be an established data processing term is the concept of the *domain.* A domain is a pool of values from which the actual values appearing in a given column are drawn. For example, the values appearing in the P# column of both the P table and the SP table are drawn from the underlying domain of all valid part numbers. This domain itself, while it may not be explicitly recorded in the database as an actual set of values, will be defined in the appropriate schema and will have a name of its own; columns based on this domain may or may not have the same name. (Obviously they must have a different name if any ambiguity would otherwise result; e.g., if two columns in the same table were drawn from the same domain. An example of such a situation is given in Chapter 4.)

Observe that relations S and SP have a domain (supplier numbers) in common; so do P and SP (part numbers), and so do S and P (locations). A crucial feature of relational data structure is that *associations between tuples (rows) are represented solely by data values in columns drawn from a common domain.* The fact that supplier S3 and part P2 are located in the same city, for example, is represented by the appearance of the same value in the CITY column for the two tuples concerned. It is a characteristic of the relational approach, in fact, that all information in the database—both "entities" and "relationships," to use the terminology of Section 1.2—is represented in a single uniform manner, namely, in the form of tables. As we shall see later, this characteristic is not shared by the hierarchical and network approaches.

We shall not discuss any further aspects of relational structure at this point; a more complete treatment will be found in Chapter 4. It is clear, however, that relational structure is very easy to understand. But simplicity of data representation is not the end of the story. From the user's point of view the data manipulation language—i.e., the set of operators provided to manipulate data that is represented in relational form—is naturally at least as important. Before discussing relational operators in any detail, we observe that the uniformity of data representation leads to a corresponding uniformity in the operator set: Since information is represented in one and only one way, we need only one operator for each of the basic functions (insert, delete, etc.) that we wish to perform. This contrasts with the situation with more complex structures, where information may be represented in several ways and hence several sets of operators are required. As we shall see in Part 4 of this book, for example, the network-based DBTG system provides two "insert" operators: STORE to create a record occurrence, and CONNECT to create a "link" between two record occurrences.

Now let us consider some specific operations. For retrieval the basic operator we need is "get next where," which will fetch the next row of a table satisfying some specified condition. "Next" is interpreted relative to the *current position* (normally the row most recently accessed; for the initial case we assume it to be just prior to the first row of the table). This operator is illustrated in the examples given in Fig. 3.2, which show in outline the code required to handle two specific queries against the database of Fig. 3.1. The two queries are intentionally symmetric (each is the inverse of the other).

As for the other operations, we content ourselves with considering three simple problems, one for each of the basic functions insert, delete, and update,[1] and indicating briefly in each case a possible relational operation to handle it.

Insert Given information concerning a new supplier S4 in area W, insert this information into the database.

■   Insert tuple from W into relation S.

Delete Delete the shipment connecting part P2 and supplier S3.

■   Delete SP tuple where P# = P2 and S# = S3.

---

1. Here "update" is being used as a synonym for "modify," rather than as a general term that includes "insert" and "delete" also. Database literature is highly inconsistent in its use of the term "update," and this book is no exception. Henceforth we shall rely on context to make our meaning clear.

Q1: Find supplier numbers for suppliers who supply part P2.	Q2: Find part numbers for parts supplied by supplier S2.

do until no more shipments;
　　get next shipment
　　　　where P# = P2;
　　print S#;
end;
	do until no more shipments;
	　　get next shipment
	　　　　where S# = S2;
	　　print P#;
	end;

Fig. 3.2 Two sample queries against the relational view.

Update Supplier S1 has moved from London to Amsterdam.

■ Update S tuple where S# = S1 setting CITY to Amsterdam.

We shall return to the question of relational operators in Section 3.5. Before then, however, let us consider the hierarchical and network approaches.

3.3 THE HIERARCHICAL APPROACH

Figure 3.3 shows a possible *hierarchical view* for the suppliers-and-parts database. In this view the data is represented by a simple tree structure, with parts superior to suppliers. The user sees four individual trees, or hierarchical occurrences, one for each part. Each tree consists of one part record occurrence, together with a set of subordinate supplier record occurrences, one for each supplier of the part. Each supplier occurrence includes the corresponding shipment quantity. Note that the set of supplier occurrences for a given part occurrence may contain any number of members, including zero (as in the case of P4).

The record type at the top of the tree—the part record type in our example—is usually known as the "root." Figure 3.3 is an example of the simplest possible hierarchical structure (other than the degenerate case of a hierarchy consisting of a root only), with a root and a single dependent record type. In general, the root may have any number of dependents, each of these may have any number of lower-level dependents, and so on, to any number of levels. Examples of more complex hierarchies will be found in Part 3 of this book.

In the previous section we likened the relational view of Fig. 3.1 to three simple files. We may similarly liken the hierarchical view of Fig. 3.3 to a *single* file, containing records arranged into four individual trees. The hierarchical DML discussed below may be thought of as a collection of operations on such files. Note, however, that such a file is a more complex object than the tables in Fig. 3.1. In the first place, it contains several types

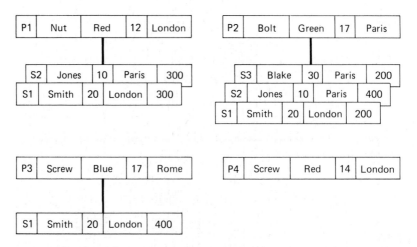

Fig. 3.3 Sample data in hierarchical form (parts superior to suppliers).

of record, not just one; in our example there are two, one for parts and one for suppliers. Second, it also contains *links* connecting occurrences of these records; in our example there are links between part occurrences and supplier occurrences, representing the associated shipments.

It is fundamental to the hierarchical view of data that any given record occurrence takes on its full significance only when seen in context—indeed, no dependent record occurrence can even exist without its superior. In the DML, therefore, the analogue of the relational "get next where" must include an additional operand (shown below via an "under" clause) to specify this context, i.e., to identify the superior of the target occurrence (unless the target occurrence is a root). Figure 3.4 shows in outline the code required to handle the two queries of Fig. 3.2 with the hierarchical view of Fig. 3.3. We have placed square brackets around "next" in those statements where we expect at most one occurrence to satisfy the specified conditions. Also, we have assumed that "where" may be omitted if we do not wish to specify any particular condition to be satisfied.

Although the original queries are symmetric, the two procedures shown in Fig. 3.4 are certainly not. (Contrast the relational case—Fig. 3.2—where the original symmetry is retained.) The loss of symmetry is a direct consequence of the view (Fig. 3.3), which is itself asymmetric, with parts being treated as superiors and suppliers as dependents. This asymmetry is a major drawback of the hierarchical approach, because it leads to unnecessary complications for the user. Specifically, the user is forced to devote time and effort to solving problems that are introduced by the hierarchical data structure and are not intrinsic to the questions being asked. It is clear that

Q1: Find supplier numbers for suppliers who supply part P2.	Q2: Find part numbers for parts supplied by supplier S2.

get [next] part where P# = P2;
do until no more suppliers
    under this part;
  get next supplier
    under this part;
  print S#;
end;
	do until no more parts;
	  get next part;
	  get [next] supplier
	    under this part
	    where S# = S2;
	  if found
	    then print P#;
	  end;

Fig. 3.4 Two sample queries against the hierarchical view.

matters will rapidly become worse as more types of record are introduced into the structure and the hierarchy becomes more complex. This is not a trivial matter. It means that programs are more complicated than they need be, with the consequence that program writing, debugging, and maintenance will all require more programmer time than they should.

On the other hand, hierarchies are obviously a natural way to model truly hierarchical structures from the real world. The suppliers-and-parts example is not such a case, since there is a many-to-many correspondence between suppliers and parts. Departments and employees afford an example of a genuine hierarchical structure (if it is true that each employee belongs to exactly one department). But even in a genuine hierarchical structure the problem of asymmetry in retrieval still arises—consider the queries "Find employees in a given department" and "Find the department for a given employee," for example. Moreover, even genuine hierarchical structures tend to develop into more complex many-to-many structures with time. We shall return to the question of presenting a hierarchical view of a many-to-many structure in Part 3 of this book.

Turning now to update operations, we find that the hierarchical structure in Fig. 3.3 possesses certain further undesirable properties. Anomalies arise in connection with each of the three basic operations (insert, delete, update). Unlike the retrieval problems discussed earlier, however, these anomalies are directly due to the fact that we are dealing with a many-to-many situation; they would not arise in a one-to-many situation. The difficulties are illustrated by the three simple problems from the end of the previous section.

Insert It is not possible, without introducing a special dummy part, to insert data concerning a new supplier—S4, say—until that supplier supplies some part.

Delete   Since shipment information is incorporated into the supplier record type, the only way to delete a shipment is to delete the corresponding supplier occurrence. It follows that if we delete the only shipment for a given supplier, we lose all information on that supplier. (The insert and delete anomalies are really two sides of the same coin.) For example, deleting the shipment connecting P2 and S3 is handled by deleting the occurrence for S3 under part P2, which—since it is the only occurrence for S3—causes all information on S3 to be lost.

Incidentally, a similar problem arises if we want to delete a part that happens to be the only part supplied by some supplier, because deletion of any record occurrence automatically deletes all dependent occurrences too, in keeping with the hierarchical philosophy.

Update   If we need to change the description of a supplier—e.g., to change the city for supplier S1 to Amsterdam—we are faced with either the problem of searching the entire view to find every occurrence of supplier S1, or the possibility of introducing an inconsistency (supplier S1 might be shown as being in Amsterdam at one point and London at another).[2]

3.4   THE NETWORK APPROACH

Figure 3.5 shows a *network view* for the suppliers-and-parts database. In this view, as in the hierarchical approach, the data is represented by *records* and *links*. However, a network is a more general structure than a hierarchy because a given record occurrence may have *any number* of immediate superiors (as well as any number of immediate dependents)—we are not limited to a maximum of one as we are with a hierarchy. The network approach thus allows us to model a many-to-many correspondence more directly than does the hierarchical approach, as Fig. 3.5 illustrates. In addition to the record types representing the suppliers and parts themselves, we introduce a third type of record, which we will call the connector. A connector occurrence represents the association (shipment) between one supplier and one part, and contains data describing that association (in the example, the quantity of the part supplied). All connector occurrences for a given supplier are placed on a chain[3] starting at and returning to that supplier. Simi-

---

2. This problem is a consequence of the redundancy in the data structure. If the redundancy were *controlled,* however (see Chapter 1), it would be a problem for the system rather than the user.

3. These chains may be physically represented in storage by actual chains of pointers or by some functionally equivalent method. However, the user may always *think* of the chains as physically existing, regardless of the actual implementation.

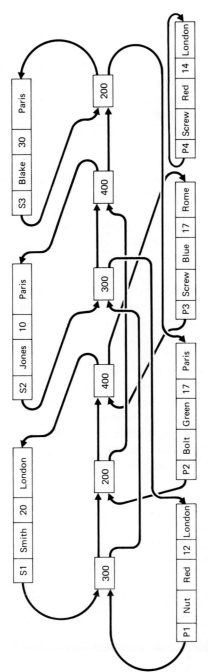

Fig. 3.5 Sample data in network form.

larly, all connector occurrences for a given part are placed on a chain starting at and returning to that part. Each connector occurrence is thus on exactly two chains, one supplier chain and one part chain. For example, Fig.
3.5 shows that supplier S2 supplies 300 of part P1 and 400 of part P2; similarly, it shows that part P1 is supplied in a quantity of 300 by supplier S1
and a quantity of 300 by supplier S2. Note, incidentally, that the correspondence between, say, one supplier and the associated connector records is
one-to-many, which shows that hierarchies may easily be represented in a
network system.

Again we may liken the view to a file of records and links; the internal
structure of this file is more complex than in the hierarchical case. As Fig.
3.6 illustrates, in the DML we now need not only the "get next under
where" operator, but also a "get over" operator to fetch the unique superior in a specified chain of a specified connector occurrence. (Actually
"get over" is required for hierarchies too, but in a hierarchy it is not necessary to specify what chain to follow.)

The network structure of Fig. 3.5 is more symmetric than the hierarchical structure of Fig. 3.3; and the symmetry is reflected in the two procedures
of Fig. 3.6. However, these procedures are significantly more complicated
than both (a) their relational analogues (Fig. 3.2), on the one hand, and (b)
the hierarchical solution to query Q1, at least (Fig. 3.4), on the other. Thus
symmetry is not everything.

Another complication, not illustrated by Fig. 3.6, arises in connection
with queries such as "Find the quantity of part P2 supplied by supplier S2."
To answer this query we must fetch the (unique) connector occurrence that
lies on both the chain for S2 and the chain for P2. The problem is that there
are two strategies for locating this occurrence, one that starts at the supplier
and scans its chain looking for a connector linked to the part, and one that
starts at the part and scans *its* chain looking for a connector linked to the

Q1: Find supplier numbers for suppliers who supply part P2.	Q2: Find part numbers for parts supplied by supplier S2.

get [next] part where P# = P2;
do until no more connectors
under this part;
get next connector
under this part;
get supplier over this
connector;
print S#;
end;
	get [next] supplier where S# = S2;
	do until no more connectors
	under this supplier;
	get next connector
	under this supplier;
	get part over this
	connector;
	print P#;
	end;

Fig. 3.6 Two sample queries against the network view.

supplier. How does the user decide which strategy to adopt? The choice could be significant.

Similar remarks apply to update operations. We find that the anomalies discussed in Section 3.3 for hierarchies do not arise with the network of Fig. 3.5.[4] However, the programming involved is not always as straightforward as it might be. In the delete case below, for example, we encounter precisely the strategy problem described in the previous paragraph.

Insert To insert data concerning a new supplier—S4, say—we simply create a new supplier record occurrence. Initially there will be no connector records for the new supplier; its chain will consist of a single pointer from the supplier to itself.

Delete To delete the shipment connecting P2 and S3 we delete the connector record occurrence linking this supplier and this part. The two chains concerned will need to be adjusted appropriately (such adjustments will probably be performed automatically).

Update We can change the city for supplier S1 to Amsterdam without search problems and without the possibility of inconsistency, because the city for S1 appears at precisely one place in the structure.

We contend, therefore, that the prime disadvantage of the network approach is undue complexity, both in the data structure itself and in the associated DML. The source of the complexity lies in the range of information-bearing constructs supported in the network structure (two have been illustrated in this chapter, namely, records and links, but network systems typically support others as well). In general, the more such constructs there are, the more operators are needed to handle them, and hence the more complicated the DML becomes. We shall discuss these points at greater length later in this book.

3.5 HIGHER-LEVEL OPERATORS

So far in our discussion of data manipulation languages we have tacitly assumed that, as in conventional file programming, all operators should deal with essentially one record at a time. However, many problems are most naturally expressed, not in terms of individual records, but rather in terms

---

4. The difficulties do not disappear simply because of the network approach per se, but rather because of the particular form the network takes. A similar qualification applies to our discussion of update operations in the relational approach (Section 3.2). The problem is really one of database design and normalization, details of which are beyond the scope of the present chapter; see Chapter 14.

of *sets* (consider queries Q1 and Q2 of Fig. 3.2, for example). In this section we introduce the possibility of more powerful languages—languages in which the operators are capable of manipulating entire sets as single objects, instead of being restricted to one record at a time.

We consider retrieval operations first, and begin by looking at some sample queries against the relational structure of Fig. 3.1.

3.5.1   Find CITY for supplier S1.

S	S#	SNAME	STATUS	CITY
	S1	Smith	20	London
	S2	Jones	10	Paris

RESULT

CITY
London

The answer is "London." To be more specific, the answer is a *table* (relation) with one row and one column, this column being based on the domain of locations (cities) and containing the single value "London."

3.5.2   Find S# and STATUS for suppliers in Paris.

S	S#	SNAME	STATUS	CITY
	S2	Jones	10	Paris
	S3	Blake	30	Paris

RESULT

S#	STATUS
S2	10
S3	30

The result is again a table, this time with two rows and two columns.

3.5.3   Find PNAME for parts supplied by supplier S1.

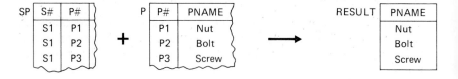

Once again the result is a table. In fact the result of *any* retrieval operation may be considered as a table, and this point is of considerable significance as we shall see later (e.g., in Chapter 12). In this particular example the result table is a subset of a single table, as it was in the two preceding examples, but *two* tables must be examined in constructing this result.

3.5.4   For each part supplied, find P# and names of all cities supplying the part.

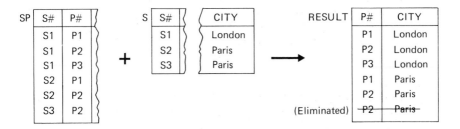

In this final example, not only is it necessary, again, to examine two tables, but the values in the result are actually derived from two tables. Note, incidentally, that a redundant duplicate row is eliminated from the final result; the reason for this is that, mathematically speaking, a table (relation) is a set—a set of rows—and sets by definition cannot contain duplicate elements. We shall discuss this point in more detail in Chapter 4.

In general, then, the result of any retrieval is a table, derived in some way from the tables in the database; any number of tables may be involved in forming the result, both in conditioning selection and in actually supplying result values. In other words, *the process of retrieval is, precisely, a process of table construction.* Recognizing this fact, we can define a set of *table construction operators* for use in retrieval. We will discuss briefly three such operators: SELECT, PROJECT, and JOIN.

The SELECT operator constructs a new table by taking a *horizontal subset* of an existing table, that is, all rows of an existing table that satisfy some condition. The PROJECT operator, in contrast, forms a *vertical* subset of an existing table by extracting specified columns and removing any redundant duplicate rows in the set of columns extracted. Using these two operators we may immediately write programs for the first two examples above.

3.5.1   Find CITY for supplier S1.

Step 1. `SELECT S WHERE S#='S1' GIVING TEMP`

This step gives us the following table (basically a copy of the "supplier S1" row from table S).

TEMP	S#	SNAME	STATUS	CITY
	S1	Smith	20	London

Step 2. `PROJECT TEMP OVER CITY GIVING RESULT`

This step extracts (i.e., makes a copy of) the CITY column from TEMP, giving the desired result.

3.5.2 Find S# and STATUS for supplies in Paris.

```
SELECT S WHERE CITY='PARIS' GIVING TEMP
PROJECT TEMP OVER (S#, STATUS) GIVING RESULT
```

This example is very similar to Example 3.5.1.

The remaining two examples—the ones involving two tables—require the use of the JOIN operator. If two tables each have a column defined over some common domain, they may be *joined* over those two columns; the result of the join is a new, wider table in which each row is formed by concatenating two rows, one from each of the original tables, such that the two rows have the same value in those two columns. For example, tables S and P may be joined over their CITY columns; the result is shown in Fig. 3.7.

We have renamed the two CITY columns SCITY and PCITY to avoid ambiguity. Note that if a row in one of the original tables has no counterpart in the other, it simply does not participate in the result; for example, P3 (stored in Rome) does not appear in the join in Fig. 3.7.

[The table in Fig. 3.7 contains two identical columns. This fact necessarily follows from the definition we gave for the join operation. Actually that definition corresponds to only one of many possible joins—namely, that join in which the "joining condition" is based on *equality* between values in the common column. That join is accordingly known as the *equijoin*. It is also possible to define, for example, a "greater than" join, a "not equal" join, and so on—though the equijoin is far and away the most frequently used. Only the equijoin necessarily contains two identical columns. It is of course always possible to eliminate one of those two columns via the PROJECT operation; an equijoin with one of the two identical columns eliminated is called a *natural join*. The natural join is important in the context of *further normalization* (to be discussed in Chapter 14). For the time being, however, we shall use the unqualified term "join" to mean the equijoin.]

S#	SNAME	STATUS	SCITY	P#	PNAME	COLOR	WEIGHT	PCITY
S1	Smith	20	London	P1	Nut	Red	12	London
S1	Smith	20	London	P4	Screw	Red	14	London
S2	Jones	10	Paris	P2	Bolt	Green	17	Paris
S3	Blake	30	Paris	P2	Bolt	Green	17	Paris

Fig. 3.7 Join of S and P over CITY.

Now we can program the other two examples.

3.5.3   Find PNAME for parts supplied by supplier S1.

```
SELECT SP WHERE S#='S1' GIVING TEMP1
JOIN TEMP1 AND P OVER P# GIVING TEMP2
PROJECT TEMP2 OVER PNAME GIVING RESULT
```

3.5.4   For each part supplied, find P# and names of all cities supplying the part.

```
JOIN SP AND S OVER S# GIVING TEMP
PROJECT TEMP OVER (P#, CITY) GIVING RESULT
```

In this last example the definition of PROJECT ensures that no duplicate rows will appear in the result.

The operators SELECT, PROJECT, and JOIN, along with others that will be discussed in Chapter 12, together constitute the *relational algebra.* Each operation of the relational algebra takes either one or two relations as its operand(s) and produces a new relation as its result. As we have illustrated, it is clearly possible to provide the user with a data manipulation language in which these operators are directly available; hence a higher-level (set-handling) DML is perfectly feasible, at least so far as retrieval is concerned. As for the other operations, we content ourselves at this point with the claim that it is indeed possible to define insert, delete, and update operators that, like the operators of the relational algebra, deal with entire sets as single operands. Examples of such operators will be shown in Part 2 of this book. Thus, for relational systems at least, a set-level DML is definitely achievable, and many relational systems do actually provide a language of this level. Indeed, it is one of the strengths of the relational approach that languages such as the relational algebra, which are simple and yet very powerful, can so readily be defined.

What about the hierarchical and network approaches? It would be misleading to suggest that set-level languages cannot be defined for such systems. Once again, however, the fact that there is more than one way to represent information in the data structure leads to the need for more than one set of operators in the DML. This statement is true regardless of language level. Without going into details, therefore, we claim that a set-level hierarchical or network language is necessarily more complex than a set-level relational language. Again we shall discuss this question in more detail later in the book.

In this section we have concentrated on relational algebra. Several relational systems provide a DML that is directly based on such an algebra. Since the algebra was first developed, however, a number of other languages have been designed for operating on relations, all at least as powerful as the algebra and many of them even easier to use. These languages include ALPHA and QUEL, both based on *relational calculus;* SQUARE and SEQUEL (later renamed SQL), based on an operation known as a "mapping"; and at least two graphic languages, Query By Example and CUPID, which are intended primarily for use with a visual display terminal. We shall describe some of these languages in subsequent chapters.

3.6 SUMMARY

In Section 1.2 we pointed out that a database system must be able to represent two types of object, namely, "entities" and "relationships." We also pointed out that fundamentally there is no real difference between the two; a relationship is merely a special kind of entity. The three approaches (relational, hierarchical, network) differ in the way in which they permit the user to view and manipulate *relationships.*

In the relational approach relationships are represented in the same way as other entities, i.e., as tuples in relations. In the hierarchical and network approaches certain relationships[5] are represented by means of "links." Basically such links are capable of representing one-to-many associations; the difference between the network and hierarchical approaches is that with the former links may be combined to model more complex many-to-many associations, whereas this is not possible with the latter. Another difference, not emphasized in the present chapter, is that links are generally named in a network and anonymous in a hierarchy, for reasons that are beyond the scope of this chapter.

We conclude this chapter by identifying some systems that may be considered representative of the three approaches. Some of the longest-established systems are *hierarchical;* as examples we may point to IBM's Information Management System, IMS; Informatics' Mark IV; MRI's System 2000; and the latter's forerunner, the Time-Shared Data Management System, TDMS, of SDC. IMS provides a record-at-a-time DML known as DL/I (Data Language/I), which we shall deal with in some detail in Part 3 of this book. System 2000 provides a set-oriented language, which, however, does not possess the full generality of the relational algebra introduced in Section 3.5.

---

5. Not all, however. In the hierarchical structure in Fig. 3.3, for example, the relationship "shipments having a given part number" is represented by links, whereas the relationship "suppliers having a given location" is represented by equality of CITY values in the record occurrences concerned. This latter method of representing relationships is the only method supported in the relational approach. We shall return to this topic in Chapter 28.

The most important example of a *network* system is provided by the specifications of the CODASYL Data Base Task Group (DBTG) and its various successor committees. Several commercially available systems are based on these proposals, among them UNIVAC's DMS 1100 and Cullinane's IDMS. Other network systems include Cincom's TOTAL; IBM's DBOMP; and Honeywell's Integrated Data Store, IDS, from which many of the DBTG ideas are derived. We shall discuss DBTG in depth in Part 4 of this book.

As for *relational* systems, we can identify Tymshare's MAGNUM and IBM's Query By Example (already mentioned) among commercially available systems. MAGNUM provides a record-at-a-time language, including full computational and report generation facilities, which can be used both in a command mode from an on-line terminal and in a more traditional batch programming mode. Query By Example is dealt with in detail in Chapter 11. Mention should also be made of the NOMAD system of NCSS, which supports both hierarchies and relations and includes several relational algebra operators—in particular, several forms of the join—among its report generation features. In addition to these (comparatively recent) commercial systems, a large number of experimental systems have been, and continue to be, developed at universities and similar institutions. In particular we mention System R, from IBM Research, and INGRES, from the University of California at Berkeley. System R is described in depth in Part 2 of this book, and INGRES is also mentioned at many points, in Chapter 13 in particular. Both of these systems provide set-handling languages that are actually *more* powerful than the relational algebra.

EXERCISES

A database is to contain information about persons and skills. At a particular time the following persons are represented in the database, and their skills are as indicated.

Person	Skills
Arthur	Programming
Bill	Operating and Programming
Charlie	Engineering, Programming, and Operating
Dave	Operating and Engineering

For each person the database contains various personal details, such as address. For each skill it contains an identification of the appropriate basic training course, an associated job grade code, and other information. The database also contains the date each person attended each course, where applicable (the assumption is that attendance at the course is essential before the skill can be said to be acquired).

3.1 Sketch a relational structure for this data.

3.2 Sketch *two* hierarchical structures for this data.

3.3 Sketch a network structure for this data.

3.4 For each of your answers to the first three questions, give an outline procedure for finding the names of all persons (a) having a specified skill; (b) having at least one skill in common with a specified person. In the relational case you should give solutions using both levels of language (record-at-a-time, set-at-a-time) introduced in this chapter.

REFERENCES AND BIBLIOGRAPHY

In addition to the references listed below, the reader's attention is drawn to *ACM Computing Surveys* **8,** No. 1 (special issue on database management systems), which includes tutorials on each of the three approaches.

3.1 R. E. Bleier. "Treating Hierarchical Data Structures in the SDC Time-Shared Data Management System (TDMS)." *Proc. ACM National Meeting* (1967).

Includes examples of the TDMS DML and DDL.

3.2 R. E. Bleier and A. H. Vorhaus. "File Organization in the SDC Time-Shared Data Management System (TDMS)." *Proc. IFIP Congress* (1968).

Describes the TDMS storage structure (an inverted organization).

3.3 C. W. Bachman and S. B. Williams. "A General Purpose Programming System for Random Access Memories." *Proc. FJCC,* AFIPS Press (1964).

One of the earliest descriptions of IDS (forerunner of DBTG). Bachman was the original architect of IDS.

Part 2
The Relational Approach

The basic concepts of the relational approach were introduced in Chapter 3. Part 2 consists of a more detailed treatment of some of those ideas. Chapter 4 deals more thoroughly with relational data structures, discussing such fundamental notions as domain, key, and normalized form in some depth. Chapters 5–10 examine a particular system, System R, in considerable detail. These chapters serve, not only as a comprehensive introduction to System R specifically, but also as an illustration of various aspects of relational systems in general. Chapter 11 describes another system, Query By Example, in somewhat less detail. Chapter 12 provides an expanded treatment of the relational algebra introduced in Chapter 3, and stresses the fundamental nature of the algebra as a component of the *relational model*. Chapter 13 discusses an alternative approach to the design of relational languages, based on the *relational calculus*. Finally, Chapter 14 (Further Normalization) is concerned with the problem of choosing the most appropriate set of relations to represent a given collection of data, i.e., the problem of relational database design.

4
Relational
Data Structure

4.1 RELATIONS

Definition Given a collection of sets $D_1, D_2, \ldots, D_n$ (not necessarily distinct), R is a *relation* on those n sets if it is a set of ordered n-tuples $\langle d_1, d_2, \ldots, d_n \rangle$ such that d_1 belongs to D_1, d_2 belongs to D_2, $\ldots$, d_n belongs to D_n. Sets $D_1, D_2, \ldots, D_n$ are the *domains* of R. The value n is the *degree* of R.

Figure 4.1 illustrates a relation called PART, of degree 5. The five domains are sets of values representing, respectively, part numbers, part names, part weights, part colors, and locations in which parts are stored. The "part color" domain, for example, is the set of all valid part colors; note that there may be colors included in this domain that do not actually appear in the PART relation at this particular time.

As the figure illustrates, it is convenient to represent a relation as a table. (The table in Fig. 4.1 is actually an extended version of the table P in

PART	P#	PNAME	COLOR	WEIGHT	CITY
	P1	Nut	Red	12	London
	P2	Bolt	Green	17	Paris
	P3	Screw	Blue	17	Rome
	P4	Screw	Red	14	London
	P5	Cam	Blue	12	Paris
	P6	Cog	Red	19	London

Fig. 4.1 The relation PART.

Fig. 3.1.) Each row of the table represents one *n*-tuple (or simply one *tuple*) of the relation. The number of tuples in a relation is called the *cardinality* of the relation; e.g., the cardinality of the PART relation is six.

Relations of degree one are said to be *unary;* for examples, see the result relations in Examples 3.5.1 and 3.5.3 (Section 3.5). Similarly, relations of degree two are *binary* (for examples, see the result relations in Examples 3.5.2 and 3.5.4), relations of degree three are *ternary,* . . . , and relations of degree *n* are *n-ary.*

We give another, equivalent, definition of relation that is sometimes useful. First we define the notion of a *Cartesian product.* Given a collection of sets $D_1, D_2, \ldots, D_n$ (not necessarily distinct), the Cartesian product of these *n* sets, written $D_1 \times D_2 \times \cdots \times D_n$, is the set of all possible ordered *n*-tuples $\langle d_1, d_2, \ldots, d_n \rangle$ such that d_1 belongs to D_1, d_2 belongs to $D_2, \ldots, d_n$ belongs to D_n. For example, Fig. 4.2 shows the Cartesian product of two sets S# and P#.

Now we define R to be a relation on the sets $D_1, D_2, \ldots, D_n$ if it is a subset of the Cartesian product $D_1 \times D_2 \times \cdots \times D_n$.

Strictly speaking, there is no ordering defined among the tuples of a relation, since a relation is a set and sets are not ordered. In Fig. 4.1, for example, the tuples of the relation PART could just as well have been shown in the reverse sequence—it would still have been the same relation. However, there are situations where it is very convenient to be able to guarantee some particular ordering, so that we know, for example, that the "get next" operator will fetch PART tuples in ascending part number sequence. In a database context, therefore, we do frequently consider relations to have an ordering—in fact, we must do so if "get next" is to have a meaning—but *either* (a) the ordering is system-defined, i.e., the user does not care what the ordering is (just so long as it remains stable), *or* (b) it is defined in terms of the values appearing within the relation, e.g., as ascending sequence by part number (*value-controlled* ordering). All other types of ordering, e.g., first-

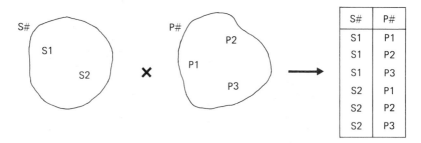

Fig. 4.2 An example of a Cartesian product.

in/first-out or program-controlled, are specifically excluded. We shall return to this subject in Chapter 28.

Referring back to the original definition, we can see that, by contrast,
the domains of a relation do have an ordering defined among them (a relation is a set of *ordered* n-tuples, with the *j*th element in each *n*-tuple being
drawn from the *j*th domain). If we were to rearrange the five columns of the
PART relation (Fig. 4.1) into some different order, the resulting table
would be a different relation, mathematically speaking. However, since
users normally refer to columns by name rather than by their relative position, many systems relax this restriction and treat column order as if it were
just as irrelevant as row order. In this book we shall generally assume that
column ordering is insignificant unless we explicitly state otherwise.

4.2 DOMAINS AND ATTRIBUTES

It is important to appreciate the difference between a domain, on the one
hand, and columns—or *attributes*—which are drawn from that domain, on
the other. An attribute represents the *use* of a domain within a relation. To
emphasize the distinction we may give attributes names that are distinct
from those of the underlying domains; for example, see Fig. 4.3.

```
DOMAIN   PART_NUMBER   CHARACTER  (6)
DOMAIN   PART_NAME     CHARACTER  (20)
DOMAIN   COLOR         CHARACTER  (6)
DOMAIN   WEIGHT        NUMERIC    (4)
DOMAIN   LOCATION      CHARACTER  (15)

RELATION   PART
           (P#      :   DOMAIN  PART_NUMBER,
            PNAME   :   DOMAIN  PART_NAME,
            COLOR   :   DOMAIN  COLOR,
            WEIGHT  :   DOMAIN  WEIGHT,
            CITY    :   DOMAIN  LOCATION)
```

Fig. 4.3 Domains vs. attributes.

In this figure we have part of a relational schema, in which five domains (PART_ NUMBER, PART_ NAME, etc.) and one relation (PART)
have been declared. The relation is defined with five attributes (P#,
PNAME, etc.), and each attribute is specified as being drawn from a corresponding domain. The schema is written in a hypothetical data definition
language.

We shall very often make use of a convention that allows us to omit the
specification of the domain from an attribute declaration if the attribute

COMPONENT	MAJOR_P#	MINOR_P#	QUANTITY
	P1	P2	2
	P1	P4	4
	P5	P3	1
	P3	P6	3
	P6	P1	9
	P5	P6	8
	P2	P4	3

Fig. 4.4 The relation COMPONENT.

bears the same name. However, it is not always possible to do this, as the example in Fig. 4.4 shows.

In this example we have a relation with three attributes but only two distinct domains. (Note in the original definition, in Section 4.1, that domains are "not necessarily distinct.") The meaning of a tuple of the relation COMPONENT is that the major part includes the minor part, in the indicated quantity, as an immediate component. The two distinct domains are P# (part numbers) and QUANTITY. The example illustrates another common convention, that of generating distinct attribute names by prefixing a common domain name with distinct *role names* to indicate the distinct roles being played by that domain in each of its appearances.

At this point we introduce the idea of *normalization*. All relations in a relational database are required to satisfy the following condition.

■   Every value in the relation—i.e., each attribute value in each tuple—is *atomic* (i.e., nondecomposable so far as the system is concerned).

To put it another way, at every row-and-column position in the table there always exists precisely one value, never a set of values. (We allow the possibility of *null* values—i.e., special values representing "unknown" or "inapplicable," as in the case of "hours worked" for an employee on vacation.) A relation satisfying the foregoing condition is said to be *normalized*.[1]

It is a trivial matter to cast an unnormalized relation into an equivalent normalized form. We give a simple example here; for further discussion of this process see Chapter 14, especially Section 14.6 and Exercise 14.1. Relation BEFORE (see Fig. 4.5) is defined on domains S# (supplier number)

---

1. Equivalently, such a relation is said to be in *first normal form*. Additional normal forms are described in Chapter 14.

BEFORE	S#	PQ		AFTER	S#	P#	QTY
		P#	QTY				
	S1	P1	300		S1	P1	300
		P2	200		S1	P2	200
		P3	400		S1	P3	400
		P4	200		S1	P4	200
		P5	100		S1	P5	100
		P6	100		S1	P6	100
	S2	P1	300		S2	P1	300
		P2	400		S2	P2	400
	S3	P2	200		S3	P2	200
	S4	P2	200		S4	P2	200
		P4	300		S4	P4	300
		P5	400		S4	P5	400

Fig. 4.5 An example of normalization.

and PQ (part-quantity); the elements of PQ are themselves relations defined on domains P# (part number) and QTY (quantity), and thus BEFORE is unnormalized. Relation AFTER is an equivalent normalized relation. (The meaning of each of these relations is that the indicated suppliers supply the indicated parts in the indicated quantities.)

Mathematically speaking, BEFORE *is* a relation, of degree two, but it is a relation for which not all the underlying domains are *simple*. (A simple domain is one in which all elements are atomic.) AFTER is a semantically equivalent relation of degree three, with the property that all its domains *are* simple—in other words, AFTER is normalized. We choose to support only normalized relations in the relational approach because (a) as the example shows, this choice imposes no real restriction on what can be represented, and (b) the resulting simplification in data structure leads to corresponding simplifications in numerous other areas—in particular, in the operators of the DML. Hereafter we shall assume that relations are always normalized.

4.3 KEYS

It is frequently the case that within a given relation there is one attribute with values that are unique within the relation and thus can be used to identify the tuples of that relation. For example, attribute P# of the PART relation has this property—each PART tuple contains a distinct P# value, and this value may be used to distinguish that tuple from all others in the relation. P# is said to be the *primary key* for PART.

Not every relation will have a single-attribute primary key. However, every relation *will* have some combination of attributes that, when taken together, have the unique identification property; a "combination" consisting of a single attribute is merely a special case. In the relation AFTER of Fig. 4.5, for example, the combination (S#,P#) has this property; so does the combination (MAJOR_P#, MINOR_P#) in the relation COMPONENT in Fig. 4.4. The existence of such a combination is guaranteed by the fact that a relation is a set: Since sets do not contain duplicate elements, each tuple of a given relation is unique with respect to that relation, and hence at least the combination of *all* attributes has the unique identification property. In practice it is not usually necessary to involve all the attributes—some lesser combination is normally sufficient. Thus every relation does have a (possibly composite) primary key. We shall assume that the primary key is nonredundant, in the sense that none of its constituent attributes is superfluous for the purpose of unique identification; for example, the combination (P#,COLOR) is not a primary key for PART.

Occasionally we may encounter a relation in which there is more than one attribute combination possessing the unique identification property, and hence more than one *candidate key*. Figure 4.6 illustrates such a relation (SUPPLIER). Here the situation is that, for all time, each supplier has a unique supplier number *and* a unique supplier name. In such a case we may arbitrarily choose one of the candidates, say S#, as *the* primary key for the relation. A candidate key that is not the primary key, such as SNAME in the example, is called an *alternate key*.

So far we have considered the primary key from a purely formal point of view, that is, purely as an identifier for tuples in a relation, without paying any heed to how those tuples are interpreted. Typically, however, those tuples represent *entities* in the real world, and the primary key really serves

SUPPLIER	S#	SNAME	STATUS	CITY
	S1	Smith	20	London
	S2	Jones	10	Paris
	S3	Blake	30	Paris
	S4	Clark	20	London
	S5	Adams	30	Athens

Fig. 4.6 The SUPPLIER relation.

as a unique identifier for those entities. For example, the tuples in the SUP-PLIER relation represent individual suppliers, and values of the S# attribute actually identify those suppliers, not just the tuples that represent them. This interpretation leads us to impose the following rule.

Integrity Rule 1 (Entity integrity)

No component of a primary key value may be null.

The rationale behind this rule is as follows. By definition all entities must be distinguishable—that is, they must have a unique identification of some kind. Primary keys perform the unique identification function in a relational database. An identifier (primary key value) that was wholly null would be a contradiction in terms; in effect, it would be saying that there was some entity that did not have any unique identification—i.e., was not distinguishable from other entities (and if two entities are not distinguishable from each other, then by definition there are not two entities but only one). Analogous arguments suggest that *partially* null identifiers should also be prohibited.

Similar considerations lead us to a second integrity rule. It is common for one relation to include references to another. For example, relation AFTER (Fig. 4.5) includes references to both the SUPPLIER relation and the PART relation, via its S# and P# attributes. It is clear that if a tuple of AFTER contains a value for S#, say *s*, then a tuple for supplier *s* should exist in SUPPLIER (otherwise, the AFTER tuple would apparently be referring to an nonexistent supplier); and similarly for parts. We can make these notions precise as follows.

First, we introduce the notion of *primary domain*. A given domain may optionally be designated as *primary* if and only if there exists some single-attribute primary key defined on that domain. For example, we may designate domain PART_NUMBER as primary, by extending its definition (see Fig. 4.3) as follows:

```
DOMAIN PART_NUMBER   CHARACTER (6) PRIMARY
```

Second, any relation including an attribute that is defined on a primary domain (for example, relation AFTER) must obey the following constraint.

Integrity Rule 2 (Referential integrity)

Let D be a primary domain, and let R_1 be a relation with an attribute A that is defined on D. Then, at any given time, each value of A in R_1 must be either (a) null, or (b) equal to V, say, where V is the primary key value of some tuple in some relation R_2 (R_1 and R_2 not necessarily distinct) with primary key defined on D.

(We note that R_2 must exist, by definition of primary domain. We also note that the constraint is trivially satisfied if A is the primary key of R_1.)

An attribute such as A is sometimes called a *foreign key*.[2] For example, attribute P# of relation AFTER is a foreign key, since its values are values of the primary key of the PART relation. Keys, primary and foreign, provide a means of representing relationships between tuples; note, however, that not all such "relationship" attributes are keys. For example, there is a relationship ("colocation") between parts and suppliers, represented by the CITY attributes of relations PART and SUPPLIER (see Figs. 4.1 and 4.6), but CITY is not a foreign key. (It could *become* a foreign key if a relation with a "CITY" primary key were added to the database.)

To conclude our discussion of keys we should point out that access to a relation from a relational DML should not be restricted to "access by primary key." This point has already been illustrated in the examples in Chapter 3 (see, for example, Fig. 3.2 and Example 3.5.2).

4.4 EXTENSIONS AND INTENSIONS

A relation in a relational database actually has two components, an extension and an intension, although it is common to gloss over this fact in informal discussion and to use the term "relation" to mean now one component, now the other.[3]

The *extension* of a given relation is the set of tuples appearing in that relation at any given instant. The extension thus varies with time (that is, it changes as tuples are created, destroyed, and updated). In other words, an extension is the same as what we have previously been calling a view. The tables in Figs. 4.1 and 4.6 are examples of extensions (except that those tables also show the intensional naming structure, discussed below).

The *intension* of a given relation, by contrast, is independent of time. Basically it is the *permanent* part of the relation; in other words, it corresponds to what is specified in the relational schema. The intension thus defines all permissible extensions. More precisely, the intension is the combination of two things: a naming structure and a set of integrity constraints.

- The *naming structure* consists of the relation name plus the names of the attributes (each with its associated domain name).

- The *integrity constraints* can be subdivided into key constraints, referential constraints, and other constraints.

---

2. This definition of foreign key is not identical to that given in earlier writings on the topic (including the second edition of this book).

3. If we think of a relation as a variable in the ordinary programming sense, then the intension is the type of that variable and the extension is its value.

Key constraints

Key constraints are constraints implied by the existence of candidate keys. The intension includes a specification of the attribute(s) constituting the primary key and also specifications of the attribute(s) constituting alternate keys, if any. Each of these specifications implies a uniqueness constraint (by the definition of candidate key); in addition, the primary key specification implies a no-nulls constraint (by Integrity Rule 1).

Referential constraints

Referential constraints are constraints implied by the existence of foreign keys. The intension includes (indirectly) a specification of all foreign keys in the relation. Each of these specifications implies a referential constraint (by Integrity Rule 2).

Other constraints

Many other constraints are possible in theory. An example might be "If the city is London then the status value must be 20" (for the SUPPLIER relation).

4.5 SUMMARY

We can define a *relational database* as a database that is perceived by the user as a collection of time-varying, normalized relations of assorted degrees. (By "time-varying relations" we mean that the extensions of the relations are time-varying.) In other words, the term "relational database" means a database for which the operators available to the user are ones that operate on relational structures. It does *not* necessarily mean that the data is stored in the form of physical tables. Figure 4.7 shows a sample relational database (extension); it consists of three relations, S (the SUPPLIER relation from Fig. 4.6), P (PART from Fig. 4.1), and SP (AFTER from Fig. 4.5). This database is an expanded version of the sample data in Fig. 3.1. We shall base most of our examples in the next few chapters on this database.

Figure 4.8 shows a schema for the database of Fig. 4.7. Attributes have been given the same name as the underlying domain throughout (e.g., the specification shown for the attribute S# of relation S is a shorthand for the specification "S# : DOMAIN S#"). Note that the schema includes explicit specifications of all primary and alternate keys; these specifications enable the DBMS to enforce the key constraints. The schema also specifies, indirectly (how?), that attributes S# and P# of relation SP are foreign keys, and thus enables the DBMS to enforce the referential constraints. This particular schema does not include any other constraints.

S	S#	SNAME	STATUS	CITY
	S1	Smith	20	London
	S2	Jones	10	Paris
	S3	Blake	30	Paris
	S4	Clark	20	London
	S5	Adams	30	Athens

SP	S#	P#	QTY
	S1	P1	300
	S1	P2	200
	S1	P3	400
	S1	P4	200
	S1	P5	100
	S1	P6	100
	S2	P1	300
	S2	P2	400
	S3	P2	200
	S4	P2	200
	S4	P4	300
	S4	P5	400

P	P#	PNAME	COLOR	WEIGHT	CITY
	P1	Nut	Red	12	London
	P2	Bolt	Green	17	Paris
	P3	Screw	Blue	17	Rome
	P4	Screw	Red	14	London
	P5	Cam	Blue	12	Paris
	P6	Cog	Red	19	London

Fig. 4.7 The suppliers-and-parts database: Relational view.

```
DOMAIN   S#       CHARACTER (5)  PRIMARY
DOMAIN   SNAME    CHARACTER (20)
DOMAIN   STATUS   NUMERIC   (3)
DOMAIN   CITY     CHARACTER (15)
DOMAIN   P#       CHARACTER (6)  PRIMARY
DOMAIN   PNAME    CHARACTER (20)
DOMAIN   COLOR    CHARACTER (6)
DOMAIN   WEIGHT   NUMERIC   (4)
DOMAIN   QTY      NUMERIC   (5)

RELATION   S   (S#,SNAME,STATUS,CITY)
               PRIMARY KEY  (S#)
               ALTERNATE KEY(SNAME)
RELATION   P   (P#,PNAME,COLOR,WEIGHT,CITY)
               PRIMARY KEY  (P#)
RELATION   SP  (S#,P#,QTY)
               PRIMARY KEY  (S#,P#)
```

Fig. 4.8 The suppliers-and-parts database: Relational schema.

To sum up, we can say that, in traditional terms, a relation resembles a *file,* a tuple a *record* (occurrence, not type), and an attribute a *field* (type, not occurrence). These correspondences are at best approximate, however. To put it another way, relations may be thought of as *highly disciplined* files—the discipline concerned being one that results in a considerable simplification in the data structures with which the user must deal, and hence in a corresponding simplification in the operators needed to manipulate them (as Chapter 3 has demonstrated). We conclude by summarizing informally the major features of relational "files" that distinguish them from traditional, undisciplined files.

1. Each "file" contains only one record type.

2. Every record occurrence in a given "file" has the same number of fields (in COBOL terms, OCCURS DEPENDING ON is outlawed—i.e., repeating groups are not allowed).

3. Each record occurrence has a unique identifier.

4. Within a "file," record occurrences either have an unspecified ordering or are ordered according to values contained within those occurrences. (The ordering field [combination] is not necessarily the primary key.) The relations defined in Fig. 4.8 have unspecified ordering.

EXERCISES

4.1 A large number of new terms have been introduced in this chapter. In many cases the underlying concept will already be reasonably familiar to you, but in general the relational terms for these concepts have a more precise definition than do many more traditional data processing terms. We have arranged the new terms below in two columns; you should be able to provide definitions for at least those in the left-hand column.

relation	degree
domain	cardinality
attribute	unary relation
tuple	binary relation
normalized relation	Cartesian product
primary key	simple domain
relational database	candidate key
foreign key	alternate key
extension	value-controlled ordering
intension	null value

4.2 Define a schema for your solution to Exercise 3.1 (relational structure for the persons-and-skills database).

4.3 Summarize the major differences between a relation and a traditional file.

4.4 State Integrity Rules 1 and 2.

4.5 How would you implement null values? *Note:* Very few systems, relational or otherwise, actually do support null. Why do you think this is?

REFERENCES AND BIBLIOGRAPHY

4.1 E. F. Codd. "A Relational Model of Data for Large Shared Data Banks." *CACM* **13,** No. 6 (June 1970).

The current interest in the relational approach is largely due to Codd's work, and this is the paper that triggered much of the subsequent activity in the field. It contains an explanation of relational structure, definitions of some relational algebra operations, and a discussion of redundancy and consistency. A seminal paper. The explanation of relational structure given in the present chapter is of course based on [4.1], but includes a large number of refinements that have been incorporated since 1970.

4.2 E. F. Codd. "Derivability, Redundancy, and Consistency of Relations Stored in Large Data Banks." IBM Research Report RJ 599 (August 1969).

An early version of [4.1].

4.3 E. F. Codd. "Understanding Relations." Continuing series of articles in *FDT* (quarterly bulletin of ACM Special Interest Group on Management of Data [SIG-MOD, formerly SIGFIDET]), beginning with Vol. 5, No. 1 (June 1973).

4.4 E. F. Codd (ed.). "Relational Data Base Management: A Bibliography." IBM Research Laboratory, San Jose, CA 95193 (August 1975).

A comprehensive (but not annotated) list of references pertaining to the relational approach as of 1975. The references are organized under the following headings.

- Models and theory
- Languages and human factors
- Implementations
- Implementation technology
- Authorization, views, and concurrency
- Integrity control
- Applications
- Deductive inference and approximate reasoning
- Natural language support
- Sets and relations prior to 1969

4.5 D. D. Chamberlin. "Relational Data Base Management: A Survey." *ACM Comp. Surv.* **8,** No. 1 (March 1976).

A tutorial. The paper is organized around the bibliography [4.4], which is included as an appendix.

4.6 E. F. Codd. "Extending the Database Relational Model to Capture More Meaning." *ACM Transactions on Database Systems* **4,** No. 4 (December 1979).

4.7 W. Kim. "Relational Database Systems." *ACM Comp. Surv.* **11,** No. 3 (September 1979).

A description of about 30 relational systems, most of them of an experimental nature, under the following headings.

- Survey
- Storage structures and access paths
- Relational interface optimizer
- User views and snapshots
- Selective access control
- Integrity control
- Concurrency control
- Recovery
- User response and performance monitoring

5
The Architecture
of System R

5.1 BACKGROUND

There have been many implementations of the relational approach since the publication of Codd's original papers [4.1, 4.2] in 1969 and 1970. Until about 1974, however, the only implemented systems were to some degree experimental, and were not available commercially (although a few commercial systems did provide certain relational features). Moreover, most of these early implementations tended to concentrate on specific aspects of the system, such as support for unanticipated queries, to the exclusion of other aspects; for example, few of these systems, if any, supported database recovery.

Today the situation is changing in at least two ways. First, software vendors have begun to include relational systems in their product line; examples include NOMAD, MAGNUM, and Query By Example. Second, the prototype activity has continued, but the prototypes have become considerably more ambitious, in that they have attempted to address much more of the total problem; examples include INGRES and System R. We choose System R as our primary example of a relational system, since it embodies so many of the principles we wish to discuss. The next few chapters therefore give a fairly comprehensive description of System R; the reader should bear in mind, however, that the purpose of these chapters is to discuss relational ideas in general as well as to cover System R specifically. Individual features of other systems will be described where appropriate—e.g., to illustrate a relational concept not supported in System R.

System R was designed and developed over the period 1974 to 1979 at the IBM San Jose Research Laboratory [5.1, 5.2, 5.3]. It is a prototype, not a product. However, the overall objective throughout development was to make the system "operationally complete"; that is, the purpose of the prototype was "to demonstrate that it is possible to build a relational system that can be used in a real environment to solve real problems, with performance at least comparable to that of existing systems" [5.1]. Accordingly, System R provides, not only the basic relational database facilities (as in earlier prototypes), but also many additional features, including

- database recovery management,
- automatic concurrency control,
- a flexible authorization mechanism,
- data independence,
- dynamic database definition,
- tuning and usability features.

(See the references, especially [5.1] and [5.3].) Although it would be absurd to suggest that only a relational system could possess all these desirable characteristics, it is fair to claim that a system that is built on a relational foundation does have a significant advantage over its competitors: If nothing else, the relational formalism provides a conceptual framework in which problems take on a more comprehensible formulation and generally become easier to manage.

System R runs on the IBM System/370, using either VM/CMS or MVS as the underlying operating system. It supports a relational database, i.e., a database in which all data is perceived by users in the form of tables. (System R generally refers to tables rather than relations; records or rows rather than tuples; and fields or columns rather than attributes. We shall do the same in System R contexts.) All access to this database is via a data sublanguage called SQL (previously spelled SEQUEL, and usually pronounced as though it still were). The original version of SQL [5.4] was based on an earlier language called SQUARE [5.6]. The two languages are essentially the same, in fact, but SQUARE uses a rather mathematical syntax whereas SQL is much more English-like. A prototype implementation of the original version of SQL was also built at the IBM San Jose Research Laboratory [5.7, 5.8]. In addition, experiments were carried out on the usability of the language, using college students as subjects [5.9]. A number of improvements were made to the language as a result of this work.

SQL is an acronym for "structured query language" [5.5]. But SQL is more than just a query language, the "query" in its name notwithstanding. First, it provides not only retrieval functions but also a full range of update operations, and also many other facilities that will be discussed in subsequent chapters. Second, it can be used both from an on-line terminal and, in the form of "embedded SQL," from an application program, batch or on-line, written in either COBOL or PL/I. The general level of the language is comparable to that of the relational algebra; in other words, its operators generally function in terms of sets rather than individual records, and do not include any reference to explicit access paths.

5.2 ARCHITECTURE

It is possible to establish a correspondence between functions provided in System R and components of the ANSI/SPARC architecture. The correspondence is not entirely clear-cut, as we shall see, but it is still useful as an aid to understanding. Figure 5.1 is an attempt to show this correspondence; it represents System R, *as perceived by one individual user,* from an ANSI/SPARC perspective.

We explain Fig. 5.1 as follows.

1. The closest equivalent to the ANSI/SPARC "conceptual record type" is the *base table*. A base table is a table that has independent existence—that is, it is not a "view" derived from other base tables (see below). Each base table is represented in storage by a distinct stored file.

2. A table that is seen by the user may be a base table or it may be a *view*. The term "view" is used in System R with a very specific meaning: A view is a table that does not have any existence in its own right but is instead derived from one or more base tables. For example, if the database includes a base table S, with fields S#, SNAME, STATUS, and CITY, then we may define a view called LONDON_SUPPLIER, say, with fields S#, SNAME, and STATUS, derived from S by selecting those records having CITY = 'LONDON' and then projecting out the CITY field. Note the distinction between a System R view and an external view as defined in Chapter 1—in System R the user will typically be interacting with several views (and base tables) at the same time, whereas in Chapter 1 we defined an external view as the *totality* of data seen by some user. We shall use "view" in the System R sense, rather than in the ANSI/SPARC sense, whenever we are specifically concerned with System R. Elsewhere we shall generally rely on context to indicate our meaning.

3. At the internal level, as stated earlier, each base table is represented in storage by a distinct stored file, i.e., by a named set of stored record occurrences, all of the same type. ("Stored file" is not a System R term.) One row in the base table corresponds to one stored record occurrence in the stored file. A given stored file may have any number of *indexes* associated with it.

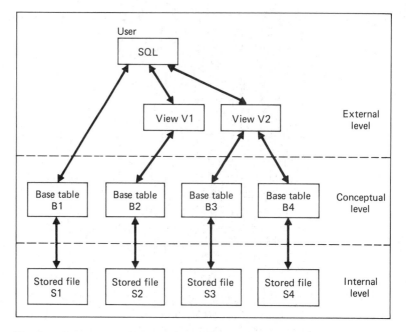

Fig. 5.1 System R as seen by an individual user.

Users above the internal level may be aware of the existence of such indexes but they cannot directly refer to them in data access requests. Indexes can be created and destroyed at any time without affecting users (other than in performance).

4. SQL is the System R data sublanguage. As such, it includes both a data definition language (DDL) and a data manipulation language (DML). As already indicated, the DML can operate at both the external and the conceptual level. Similarly, the DDL can be used to define objects at the external level (views), the conceptual level (base tables), and even the internal level (indexes). Moreover, SQL also provides "data control" facilities, that is, facilities that cannot really be classified as belonging to either the DDL or the DML. An example of such a facility is a statement to GRANT certain access rights to another user.

5. Application programming users can access the database from either PL/I or COBOL by means of "embedded SQL" statements. Embedded SQL represents a "loose coupling" of SQL and the host language (see Chapter 1). Almost any statement of the SQL language can be embedded.

In addition, certain special statements (to be discussed in Chapter 8) are provided for use in the embedded environment only.

6. One particular on-line application, supplied with the system, is the User-Friendly Interface, or UFI. UFI allows the on-line user to access the database using SQL as an interactive query language. That is, UFI accepts SQL statements from the terminal, passes them to System R for execution, and then returns the result to the terminal if appropriate. UFI also provides various special commands to control the output display, to modify and re-execute previously entered SQL statements, and so on.

In most of our discussions of the SQL language we shall assume a UFI environment—that is, we shall assume that the SQL statements are being entered from an on-line terminal. However, the "embedded SQL" environment is discussed in detail in Chapter 8.

Components of System R

System R consists of two major subsystems: the Research Storage System, or RSS, and the Relational Data System, or RDS. Basically, the RDS provides the external user interface, supporting tabular data structures and operators on those structures (the SQL language), and the RSS provides a stored record interface to the RDS (compare this system structure with the structure illustrated in Fig. 2.1). We consider each of the two components in slightly more detail below.

Research storage system (RSS)

The RSS is essentially a powerful access method. Its primary function is to handle all details of the physical level and to present its user with an interface called the Research Storage Interface, or RSI (this is the stored record interface just mentioned). The user of the RSS is normally not a direct user, however, but code generated by the RDS in compiling some SQL statement (see below). The RSI was specifically designed to be a good target for the SQL compiler.

The basic data object supported at the RSI is the stored file, i.e., the internal representation of a base table. Rows of the table are represented by records of the file; the stored records within one stored file need not be physically adjacent in storage, however. The RSS also supports an arbitrary number of indexes over any given stored file. Operators are provided at the RSI to search through a stored file in "system" (i.e., RSS-defined) sequence and in sequence according to any specified index. (By system sequence we mean a sequence that is not specified externally but is determined by the way in which the RSS represents the stored file on the physical medium.) The user of the RSI needs to know what stored files and indexes exist, and must specify the access path (index or system sequence) to be used in any given RSI access request.

The RSS also provides additional functions, which will be discussed in Chapter 10.

Relational data system (RDS)

The RDS in turn consists of two components, a precompiler and a run-time control system.

The *precompiler* is a compiler for the SQL language. Suppose the application programmer has written a program P that includes some embedded SQL statements. To fix our ideas let us assume that P is written in PL/I (the picture is essentially similar for COBOL). Before P can be compiled by the PL/I compiler in the usual way, it must first be processed by the RDS precompiler. The precompilation process is illustrated in Fig. 5.2. The statement "$SELECT . . . ;" in that figure is an example of a SQL statement embedded in PL/I.

Precompilation proceeds as follows.

1. The precompiler scans the source program P and locates the embedded SQL statements (those statements having a $-sign prefix).

2. For each statement it finds, the precompiler decides on a strategy for implementing that statement in terms of RSI operations. This process is referred to as *optimization*. Optimization is based on the precompiler's knowledge of access paths available at the RSI. (Remember that SQL statements such as SELECT do not include any reference to such access paths.) Having made its decisions, the precompiler generates a System/370 machine language routine (including calls to the RSS) that will implement the chosen strategy. The set of all such routines together constitutes the *access module* for the given program P. The access module is itself stored in the database.

3. The precompiler replaces each of the original embedded SQL statements by an ordinary PL/I statement to CALL XRDI (XRDI is the name of the run-time control component of the RDS).

The modified source program P can now be compiled by the PL/I compiler in the normal way.

The foregoing explanation applies to the case of *embedded* SQL. The process is essentially similar for the case of the on-line language (submitted via the User-Friendly Interface, UFI), except that execution occurs as soon as precompilation is complete. In other words, UFI reads the SQL statement from the terminal, passes it to the precompiler, and then immediately executes the compiled access module (via XRDI, of course). The PL/I compiler is not involved, since (a) the original statement stands alone (i.e., it

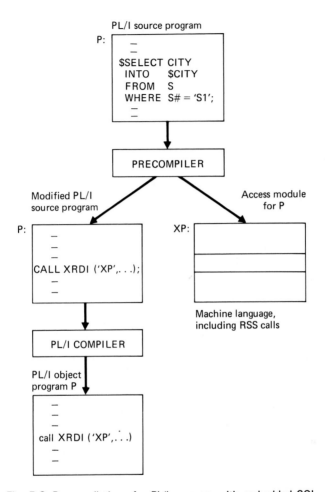

Fig. 5.2 Precompilation of a PL/I program with embedded SQL.

does not have any surrounding PL/I statements) and also (b) the precompiler generates machine code directly (it does *not* "cascade" through PL/I).

  The *run-time control system* (XRDI) provides the environment for executing an application program that has been through the precompilation process just described. Consider Fig. 5.2 again. When the object program P is executed, it will eventually reach the statement "call XRDI" that replaced the embedded SQL statement. Control will go to the RDS run-time control system, which will fetch the access module for P (if necessary), then call the

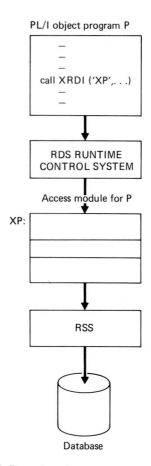

Fig. 5.3 Execution of a precompiled program.

appropriate section of that access module, namely, the section that was generated to correspond to the original SQL SELECT statement. This section will in turn invoke various RSS operations to perform the actions required for that original SELECT statement. See Fig. 5.3.

The run-time control system performs a number of other functions that will be touched on in later chapters.

REFERENCES AND BIBLIOGRAPHY

5.1 M. M. Astrahan et al. "System R: Relational Approach to Database Management." *ACM Transactions on Database Systems* **1**, No. 2 (June 1976).

5.2 M. M. Astrahan et al. "System R, A Relational Database Management System." *IEEE Computer Society: Computer* **12**, No. 5 (May 1979).

5.3 M. W. Blasgen et al. "System R: An Architectural Update." IBM Research Report RJ2581 (July 1979).

5.4 D. D. Chamberlin and R. F. Boyce. "SEQUEL: A Structured English Query Language." *Proc. 1974 ACM SIGMOD Workshop on Data Description, Access and Control.*

5.5 D. D. Chamberlin et al. "SEQUEL 2: A Unified Approach to Data Definition, Manipulation, and Control." *IBM J. R&D* **20**, No. 6 (November 1976).

5.6 R. F. Boyce, D. D. Chamberlin, W. F. King III, and M. M. Hammer. "Specifying Queries as Relational Expressions: SQUARE." Versions of this paper have appeared in *Proc. ACM SIGPLAN/SIGIR Interface Meeting on Programming Languages and Information Retrieval* (November 1973); *Proc. IFIP TC-2 Working Conference on Data Base Management Systems* (eds., Klimbie and Koffeman) (North-Holland, 1974); and *CACM* **18**, No. 11 (November 1975).

5.7 M. M. Astrahan and R. A. Lorie. "SEQUEL-XRM, a Relational System." *Proc. ACM Pacific Conference, San Francisco* (April 1975). Available from ACM Golden Gate Chapter, P.O. Box 24055, Oakland, California 94623.

5.8 M. M. Astrahan and D. D. Chamberlin. "Implementation of a Structured English Query Language." *CACM* **18**, No. 10 (October 1975).

5.9 P. Reisner, R. F. Boyce, and D. D. Chamberlin. "Human Factors Evaluation of Two Data Base Query Languages—SQUARE and SEQUEL." *Proc. NCC* **44** (May 1975).

5.10 D. D. Chamberlin. (ed., S. M. Deen and P. Hammersley). "A Summary of User Experience with the SQL Data Sublanguage." *Proc. International Conference on Data Bases, Aberdeen, Scotland* (July 1980). Also available as IBM Research Report RJ2767 (April 1980).

5.11 M. M. Astrahan et al. "A History and Evaluation of System R." IBM Research Report RJ2843 (June 1980).

6
System R
Data Structure

6.1 INTRODUCTION

The primary data structure in System R is the base table. In this chapter we consider base tables in detail; we show how base tables are created and destroyed using the SQL DDL facilities, and we compare and contrast the tabular structure with the relational structure defined in Chapter 4. For purposes of reference we show in Fig. 6.1 a System R equivalent of the suppliers-and-parts schema of Fig. 4.8. (The term "schema" is not used in System R.)

```
CREATE TABLE  S  ( S#      (CHAR(5), NONULL),
                   SNAME   (CHAR(20)),
                   STATUS  (SMALLINT),
                   CITY    (CHAR(15)) )

CREATE TABLE  P  ( P#      (CHAR(6), NONULL),
                   PNAME   (CHAR(20)),
                   COLOR   (CHAR(6)),
                   WEIGHT  (SMALLINT),
                   CITY    (CHAR(15)) )

CREATE TABLE  SP ( S#      (CHAR(5), NONULL),
                   P#      (CHAR(6), NONULL),
                   QTY     (INTEGER) )
```

Fig. 6.1 SQL definition for tables S, P, and SP.

107

6.2 BASE TABLES

As we explained in Chapter 5, a base table is a table that has its own independent existence. It is represented in the physical database by a stored file. A base table can be created at any time by executing the SQL DDL statement CREATE TABLE, which takes the general form

```
CREATE TABLE base-table-name
       ( field-definition [, field-definition ] ... )
       [ IN SEGMENT  segment-name ]
```

where a field-definition, in turn, takes the form

```
            field-name ( data-type [,NONULL] )
```

(Barring explicit statements to the contrary, square brackets are used throughout this book within syntax definitions to indicate that the material enclosed in those brackets may be omitted.)

Successful execution of a CREATE TABLE statement causes a new, empty base table to be created in the specified segment with the specified base-table-name and specified field-definitions. (We explain segments and field-definitions below.) The user may now proceed to enter data into that table using the SQL INSERT statement (part of the SQL DML). Alternatively the user may invoke the System R loader, a system-supplied utility program, to perform this function; details of the loader utility are beyond the scope of this text.

Segments A System R database is partitioned into a set of disjoint *segments*. (This partitioning is discussed further in Chapter 10.) Segments provide a mechanism for controlling the allocation of storage and the sharing of data among users. Any given base table is wholly contained within a single segment; any indexes on that base table are also contained in that same segment. However, a given segment may contain several base tables (plus their indexes).

A *public* segment contains shared data that can be simultaneously accessed by multiple users. A *private* segment contains data that can be used by only one user at a time (or data that is not shared at all). The CREATE TABLE statement optionally specifies the segment that is to contain the new base table; if no segment is specified, the base table will go in a *private* segment belonging to the user that issued the CREATE TABLE. Thus, in Fig. 6.1, each CREATE TABLE should include the specification "IN SEGMENT SHARED_SEG" (say), where SHARED_SEG is a public segment, if the suppliers-and-parts database is to be concurrently available to multiple users.

Fields Each *field-definition* in CREATE TABLE includes three items: a field-name, a data-type for the field, and (optionally) a NONULL specification. The field-name must, of course, be unique within the base table. The permissible data-types are as follows:

CHAR (*n*):	fixed-length character string,
CHAR (*n*) VAR:	variable-length character string,
INTEGER:	fullword binary integer,
SMALLINT:	halfword binary integer,
FLOAT:	doubleword floating-point number.

System R supports the concept of *null* field values. In fact, any field can contain a null value *unless* the definition of that field in CREATE TABLE explicitly includes the specification NONULL. Null is a special value that is used to represent "value unknown" or "value inapplicable." For example, a shipment record might contain a null QTY value (we know that the shipment exists but we do not know the quantity shipped); or a supplier record might contain a null STATUS value (perhaps "status" does not apply to suppliers in Paris for some reason). We do not discuss the properties of null in detail here, but content ourselves with noting that (a) arithmetic expressions in which one of the operands is null evaluate to null, and (b) comparisons in which one of the comparands is null evaluate to the "unknown" truth value [see Example 7.2.22 for an illustration of (b)].

Just as a new base table can be created at any time, so an existing base table can be *expanded* at any time by adding a new column (field) at the right:[1]

```
EXPAND TABLE   base-table-name
         ADD FIELD   field-name   ( data-type )
```

For example,

```
EXPAND TABLE SP
         ADD FIELD   DATE   ( CHAR (6) )
```

This statement adds a DATE field to the SP table. All existing SP records are expanded from three fields to four; the value of the new field is null in every case (the specification NONULL is not permitted in EXPAND TABLE). Note, incidentally, that the expansion of existing records just described does not mean that the records in the database are actually up-

---

1. In System R the left-to-right order of columns in a table *is* significant (contrast the last paragraph of Section 4.1).

dated at this time; only their stored description changes. (This description is stored in the System R dictionary—see Chapter 1. We shall discuss the System R dictionary in slightly more detail in Chapter 7.)

It is also possible to *destroy* an existing base table at any time:

```
DROP TABLE base-table-name
```

All records in the specified base table are deleted, all indexes and views on that table are destroyed, and the table itself is then also destroyed (that is, its description is removed from the dictionary and its storage space is released).

6.3   INDEXES

Like base tables, indexes are created and dropped using the SQL DDL. However, CREATE INDEX and DROP INDEX, and certain data control statements, are the *only* statements in the SQL language that refer to indexes at all; other statements—in particular, data accessing statements such as SELECT—deliberately do not include any such references. The decision as to whether to use an index or not in responding to a particular data request is made not by the user but by System R (actually by the optimizer component of the RDS precompiler).

CREATE INDEX takes the general form

```
CREATE [ UNIQUE ] INDEX index-name ON base-table-name
        ( field-name [ order ] [ , field-name [ order ] ] ...
```

where "order" is either ASC (ascending) or DESC (descending). If neither ASC nor DESC is specified, then ASC is assumed by default. The left-to-right sequence of naming fields in the CREATE INDEX statement corresponds to major-to-minor ordering in the usual way. For example, the statement

```
CREATE INDEX  X  ON  T  ( A, B, C )
```

will create an index called X on base table T in which entries are ordered by ascending C-value within ascending B-value within ascending A-value.[2]

Once created, an index is automatically maintained (by the RSS) to reflect updates on the indexed base table, until such time as the index is dropped.

The UNIQUE option in CREATE INDEX specifies that no two records in the indexed base table will be allowed to take on the same value for

---

2. For indexing purposes, null values are considered to be (a) all equal to each other and (b) greater than any nonnull value.

the indexed field or field combination (at the same time). This is the only way to specify that duplicate values are not allowed for some field or field combination. Thus if we wish to enforce uniqueness of the primary keys in the suppliers-and-parts database, we should add statements such as the following to Fig. 6.1:

```
CREATE UNIQUE INDEX   XS    ON  S  ( S# )
CREATE UNIQUE INDEX   XP    ON  P  ( P# )
CREATE UNIQUE INDEX   XSP   ON  SP ( S#, P# )
```

(Indexes, like base tables, can be created and dropped at any time. In the example we must ensure that indexes XS, XP, and XSP are created before any data is placed in base tables S, P, and SP; otherwise the uniqueness constraints might already have been violated. An attempt to create a unique index on a table that does not currently satisfy the uniqueness constraint will fail.)

The statement to drop an index is

```
DROP INDEX index-name
```

The index is destroyed; that is, its description is removed from the dictionary and its storage space is released. If a precompiled program has an access module (see Chapter 5) that depends on the dropped index, that access module is automatically marked "invalid" by the RDS run-time control system. When that access module is next invoked, System R will automatically re-precompile the original program, generating a replacement access module that supports the original SQL statements without using the now-vanished index. This process is completely hidden from the user.

6.4 DISCUSSION

The fact that SQL DDL statements can be executed at any time makes System R very flexible. In more conventional systems, adding new types of object to the database is not an operation to be undertaken lightly; typically it involves bringing the entire system to a halt, executing some special utility to compile the modified database definition (schema), and dumping and restoring the entire database, or at least some portion thereof. In such a system it becomes highly desirable to perform the data definition process once and for all before starting to load and use the database, which means that (a) it can take a long time to get the system installed and operational, and (b) it can be difficult and costly to remedy early design errors.

In System R, by contrast, it is possible to create and load just a few base tables and then to begin using them immediately. It is also possible to experiment with the effects of having or not having particular indexes, and to add new base tables and new fields in a piecemeal fashion, both without affecting existing applications at all (other than in performance, of course). Moreover, as we shall see in Chapter 9, it is even possible under certain circumstances to replace an existing base table by two or more (smaller) tables, again without affecting existing users, by providing those users with a *view* that is identical to the original base table but is defined in terms of the new smaller tables. In a nutshell, it is not necessary to go through the total database design process before any useful work can be done with the system, nor is it necessary to get everything right the first time.

We conclude this chapter by comparing the data structure of System R with the relational structure defined in Chapter 4. It should be clear that there are certain differences between the two. We summarize the points of difference here, then discuss them in detail below. In System R,

- domains are not supported;
- enforcement of candidate key uniqueness is optional;
- enforcement of Integrity Rule 1 (entity integrity) is optional;
- Integrity Rule 2 (referential integrity) is not enforced.

This list is not intended as a criticism of System R. (In fact, these features are omitted in most existing relational systems.) The definitions of Chapter 4 incorporate several refinements (especially the integrity rules) that were not widely published at the time System R was being designed, so the omissions are hardly surprising. The question is, how important are they? Any attempt to answer this question is certain to be branded as subjective; despite this fact, we suggest that the first three items in the list are not too important but that the last item (lack of support for Integrity Rule 2) is significant.[3]

Domains are not supported.

The relationship between a given supplier (say) and the shipments for that supplier is established by the appearance of the same value in the S# field of the S record concerned and the S# field of the corresponding SP records. However, this relationship is not explicitly defined in System R; it is in exactly the same category as the "relationship" between, say, a part having

---

3. On the other hand, a case can be made against supporting Integrity Rule 2 on the grounds that it leads to additional complexities for both the system and the user. For example, the system must be prepared to check for and reject certain kinds of update, and the user must be prepared to handle certain additional error situations.

a weight of 25 pounds and a shipment having a shipped quantity of 25 items, so far as System R is concerned. A practical consequence is that the system is unable to detect the fact that a request for, say, shipments where the quantity shipped is equal to the weight of the part is probably meaningless.

Domains are also relevant to Integrity Rule 2; see the end of this section.

Enforcement of candidate key uniqueness is optional.

System R has no knowledge of keys (candidate, primary, alternate, or foreign). In the absence of specifications to the contrary, fields and field combinations do *not* have the uniqueness property; a base table in general is thus not the same as a relation, since it may contain duplicate rows. But System R does provide a mechanism, the unique index, by which uniqueness can be enforced if desired. Note, however, that such enforcement is bundled together with the provision of an access path. It would be architecturally cleaner to split the two specifications apart. It is true that, if an index is provided on a candidate key, then that index must be "unique"; but, after all, the fact that a field is a candidate key does not necessarily mean that an ordered access path is required on that field, nor is a unique index the only way to enforce uniqueness. Moreover, in the case of base table SP (Fig. 6.1), key uniqueness could be enforced by either an index on (S#, P#), in that order, or an index on (P#, S#), in the reverse order; on what grounds do we choose one over the other?

Enforcement of Integrity Rule 1 (entity integrity) is optional.

Integrity Rule 1 prohibits null values in primary key fields (for details see Chapter 4). System R will enforce this constraint provided NONULL is specified for the field(s) in question. (As an aside, we note that if nulls are allowed for a field on which a unique index is defined, exactly one occurrence of that field may be null at any given time.)

Integrity Rule 2 (referential integrity) is not enforced.

Integrity Rule 2 prohibits references to nonexistent records (again, for details see Chapter 4). For example, if a given SP record contains a value s for the S# field, then there should also exist an S record having that value s for the S# field. The SQL language defined in [5.5] and [6.1] did include a general *assertion* mechanism that would permit the optional specification of constraints such as Rule 2 (and more general constraints), but assertions are not supported in System R.

EXERCISES

6.1 Define a schema for your solution to Exercise 3.1 (relational structure for the persons-and-skills database), using the SQL DDL.

6.2 Figure 6.2 shows a sample extension for a database containing information concerning suppliers (S), parts (P), and projects (J). Suppliers, parts, and projects are uniquely identified by supplier number (S#), part number (P#), and project number (J#), respectively. The significance of an SPJ record is that the specified supplier supplies the specified part to the specified project in the specified quantity (and the

S

S#	SNAME	STATUS	CITY
S1	Smith	20	London
S2	Jones	10	Paris
S3	Blake	30	Paris
S4	Clark	20	London
S5	Adams	30	Athens

P

P#	PNAME	COLOR	WEIGHT	CITY
P1	Nut	Red	12	London
P2	Bolt	Green	17	Paris
P3	Screw	Blue	17	Rome
P4	Screw	Red	14	London
P5	Cam	Blue	12	Paris
P6	Cog	Red	19	London

J

J#	JNAME	CITY
J1	Sorter	Paris
J2	Punch	Rome
J3	Reader	Athens
J4	Console	Athens
J5	Collator	London
J6	Terminal	Oslo
J7	Tape	London

SPJ

S#	P#	J#	QTY
S1	P1	J1	200
S1	P1	J4	700
S2	P3	J1	400
S2	P3	J2	200
S2	P3	J3	200
S2	P3	J4	500
S2	P3	J5	600
S2	P3	J6	400
S2	P3	J7	800
S2	P5	J2	100
S3	P3	J1	200
S3	P4	J2	500
S4	P6	J3	300
S4	P6	J7	300
S5	P2	J2	200
S5	P2	J4	100
S5	P5	J5	500
S5	P5	J7	100
S5	P6	J2	200
S5	P1	J4	1000
S5	P3	J4	1200
S5	P4	J4	800
S5	P5	J4	400
S5	P6	J4	500

Fig. 6.2 The suppliers-parts-projects database.

combination S#–P#–J# uniquely identifies such a record). Define a schema for this database using the SQL DDL. *Note:* This database will be used in numerous exercises in subsequent chapters.

6.3 How could the SQL DDL be extended to incorporate domains?

REFERENCES AND BIBLIOGRAPHY

See also all references in Chapter 5.

6.1 R. F. Boyce and D. D. Chamberlin. "Using a Structured English Query Language as a Data Definition Facility." IBM Research Report RJ1318 (December 1973).

7
System R Data Manipulation

7.1 INTRODUCTION

In this chapter we consider the data manipulation aspects of System R. In particular we present the DML portions of the SQL language. The SQL DML operates on both base tables and views, as explained in Chapter 5, but for the time being we concern ourselves with base tables only; also we continue to assume that operations are entered and results displayed at an on-line terminal (embedded SQL is discussed in Chapter 8). As usual, all examples will be based on the suppliers-and-parts database of Fig. 4.7.

The language defined in reference [5.5] includes a number of SQL DML features that are not supported in System R. We ignore these features in this chapter.

Note: Many of these examples, especially the later ones, are quite complex. The reader should not infer that it is the SQL DML itself that is complex. Rather, the point is that common operations are so simple in SQL (and comparable languages) that examples of such operations tend to be rather uninteresting, and do not illustrate the full power of the language. Of course we do show some simple examples first.

7.2 RETRIEVAL OPERATIONS

The fundamental operation in SQL is the *mapping,* represented syntactically as a SELECT-FROM-WHERE block. For example, the query "Get supplier numbers and status for suppliers in Paris" may be expressed as follows.

```
SELECT  S#, STATUS
FROM    S
WHERE   CITY = 'PARIS'
```

Result:

S#	STATUS
S2	10
S3	30

From this example we can see that the "mapping" operation is effectively a horizontal subsetting (find all rows where CITY = 'PARIS') followed by a vertical subsetting (extract S# and STATUS from these rows). In algebraic terms it may be considered as a SELECT followed by a PROJECT, except that, as we shall see, the horizontal subsetting operation may be considerably more sophisticated than the simple algebraic SELECT of Chapter 3. (Do not confuse the algebraic SELECT with the SQL SELECT.)

We now proceed to illustrate the major features of the retrieval language by means of a carefully developed set of examples.

7.2.1 Simple retrieval   Get part numbers for all parts supplied.

```
SELECT  P#
FROM    SP
```

Result:

P#
P1
P2
P2
P2
P4
P5

We suggested above that a mapping (SELECT-FROM-WHERE) may be thought of as a horizontal subsetting followed by a projection. In this example the horizontal subset is the entire table (no WHERE clause). As for the projection, we remind the reader that PROJECT as formally defined (see Chapter 3) operates by extracting specified columns and then *eliminating redundant duplicate rows* from the columns extracted (the result is a *relation,* with no duplicate rows). However, SQL does not generally eliminate duplicates from the result of a SELECT statement unless the user explicitly requests it to do so via the keyword UNIQUE, as in the following example.

```
SELECT  UNIQUE P#
FROM    SP
```

Result:

P#
P1
P2
P3
P4
P5
P6

The justification for requiring the user to specify UNIQUE in such cases is that (a) duplicate elimination may be a costly operation, and (b) users will frequently not be bothered by the presence of duplicates in their output. A similar philosophy is adopted in INGRES, incidentally (see Chapter 13).

7.2.2 Simple retrieval Get full details of all suppliers.

```
SELECT  *
FROM    S
```

Result: A copy of the entire S table.

The asterisk is shorthand for an ordered list of all field-names in the FROM table (as specified by the System R dictionary at the time the SELECT is precompiled; any new fields subsequently added to the table via EXPAND TABLE will *not* be included). The SELECT statement shown is thus equivalent to

```
SELECT  S#, SNAME, STATUS, CITY
FROM    S
```

7.2.3 Qualified retrieval Get supplier numbers for suppliers in Paris with status > 20.

```
SELECT  S#
FROM    S
WHERE   CITY = 'PARIS'
AND     STATUS > 20
```

Result:

S#
S3

The condition or *predicate* following WHERE may include the comparison operators $=$, $\neg=$ (not equal), $>$, $>=$, $<$, and $<=$; the Boolean operators AND, OR, and NOT; and parentheses to indicate a desired order of evaluation.

7.2.4 Retrieval with ordering Get supplier numbers and status for suppliers in Paris, in descending order of status.

```
SELECT  S#, STATUS
FROM    S
WHERE   CITY = 'PARIS'
ORDER   BY STATUS DESC
```

Result:

S#	STATUS
S3	30
S2	10

In general, the result of SELECT is not guaranteed to be in any particular sequence. Here, however, the user has specified that the result is to be ordered in a particular way before being displayed. Ordering may be specified in the same manner as in CREATE INDEX (Section 6.3)—that is,

```
field-name [order] [,field-name [order]] ...
```

7.2.5 Retrieval from more than one table For each part supplied, get part number and names of all cities supplying the part.

```
SELECT  UNIQUE P#,CITY
FROM    SP,S
WHERE   SP.S#=S.S#
```

Result:

P#	CITY
P1	London
P1	Paris
P2	London
P2	Paris
P3	London
P4	London
P5	London
P6	London

This example shows how a join is expressed in SQL. The user may name several tables in the FROM clause, and may use the table-names as qualifiers in the SELECT and WHERE clauses to resolve ambiguities if necessary (or for clarity). The SELECT clause in the foregoing example could have been written

```
SELECT  UNIQUE SP.P#, S.CITY
```

if desired.

Conceptually, the SELECT statement in this example operates as follows: (a) The Cartesian product of SP and S is formed; (b) rows not satisfying the "join condition" SP.S# = S.S# are eliminated from the result of step (a); (c) columns P# and CITY are extracted from the result of step (b); (d) redundant duplicate rows are eliminated from the result of step (c). (We do not mean to imply that System R actually implements the query like this—there are more efficient ways to do it—but you should convince yourself that this procedure does indeed produce the desired result. Also, "Cartesian product" here really refers to an *extended* Cartesian product, to be discussed in Chapter 12, rather than to the simple form defined in Chapter 4.)

7.2.6 Retrieval involving a join of a table with itself   Get all pairs of supplier numbers such that the two suppliers are located in the same city.

```
SELECT  FIRST.S#, SECOND.S#
FROM    S FIRST, S SECOND
WHERE   FIRST.CITY = SECOND.CITY
AND     FIRST.S# < SECOND.S#
```

Result:

S#	S#
S1	S4
S2	S3

This example involves a join of table S with itself; the join condition is that the two cities are the same and the first supplier number is less than the second. Table S appears twice in the FROM clause. To distinguish between the two appearances, we introduce arbitrary names FIRST and SECOND, and use them as qualifiers in the SELECT and WHERE clauses. (The reason for requiring the first supplier number to be less than the second is twofold: (a) it eliminates pairs of the form (x,x); (b) it guarantees that at most one of the pairs (x,y), (y,x) will appear.)

7.2.7 Retrieval using ANY   Get supplier names for suppliers who supply part P2.

SQL actually provides several ways of handling this query. One way is to use a join:

```
SELECT  UNIQUE SNAME
FROM    S, SP
WHERE   S.S# = SP.S#
AND     SP.P# = 'P2'
```

Result:

SNAME
Smith
Jones
Blake
Clark

(Note that UNIQUE is needed because the join of S and SP over S# will contain duplicate SNAMEs, in general.)

However, this example differs from the two previous examples in that the result is entirely extracted from a single table, table S—though it is true that two tables, S and SP, must be inspected to determine that result. It should therefore be possible to express the query in the form

```
SELECT  SNAME
FROM    S
WHERE   condition involving P2
```

where "condition involving P2" represents the condition that any supplier whose SNAME we extract must satisfy. What is this condition? Basically it is that that supplier must be one of those suppliers who supply part P2—in other words, that that supplier's S# value must be one of the S# values matching P# 'P2' in the shipment table. This condition can be expressed as follows (we repeat the SELECT and FROM clauses for clarity).

```
SELECT  SNAME
FROM    S
WHERE   S# =ANY (SELECT S#
                 FROM    SP
                 WHERE   P# = 'P2')
```

The expression in parentheses is a *subquery*. In the case at hand it evaluates to the set of supplier numbers that correspond to part number P2 in table SP, i.e., the set {'S1', 'S2', 'S3', 'S4'}. The condition

```
S# =ANY ( {'S1', 'S2', 'S3', 'S4'} )
```

then evaluates to *true* if and only if S# has one of the values S1, S2, S3, S4; thus the entire query produces the result shown earlier.

In general, the operator = ANY is interpreted as follows. The condition

```
f =ANY (SELECT F FROM ...)
```

evaluates to *true* if and only if the value *f* is equal to at least one value in the result of evaluating the "SELECT F FROM ...". Similarly, the condition

```
f <ANY (SELECT F FROM ...)
```

evaluates to *true* if and only if *f* is less than at least one value in the result of evaluating the SELECT. The operators < = ANY, > ANY, > = ANY, and ¬ = ANY are analogously defined.

We give an example of the use of < ANY.

7.2.8 Retrieval using <ANY   Get supplier numbers for suppliers with status value less than the current maximum status value in the S table. (A simpler solution to this problem is given later as Example 7.3.5.)

```
SELECT   S#
FROM     S
WHERE    STATUS <ANY (SELECT STATUS
                      FROM    S)
```

Result:

S#
S1
S2
S4

The purpose of showing this example is to warn the reader of a possible trap. The WHERE clause does *not* mean that the status of selected suppliers is less than any current status value, in the sense that that (admittedly ambiguous) expression would normally be understood in English; rather, it means that the status of selected suppliers is less than *some* current status value (and is therefore less than the current maximum). The intuitive interpretation of < ANY as "less than any" (i.e., less than *every*) is misleading. SOME might have been a better keyword than ANY.

Of the various ANY comparisons, easily the most useful is = ANY. This form may equivalently (and more clearly) be written as IN, as the following example illustrates.

7.2.9 Retrieval using IN   Get supplier names for suppliers who supply part P2 (the same as Example 7.2.7).

```
SELECT   SNAME
FROM     S
WHERE    S# IN
         (SELECT S#
          FROM    SP
          WHERE   P# = 'P2')
```

"IN" and " = ANY" are completely interchangeable. They may each be thought of as the set membership operator ∈. We shall generally use IN rather than = ANY from this point on.

7.2.10 Retrieval with multiple levels of nesting Get supplier names for suppliers who supply at least one red part.

```
SELECT   SNAME
FROM     S
WHERE    S# IN
          (SELECT   S#
           FROM     SP
           WHERE    P# IN
                     (SELECT P#
                      FROM    P
                      WHERE   COLOR = 'RED'))
```

Result:

SNAME
Smith
Jones
Clark

Subqueries can be nested to any depth.

7.2.11 Retrieval with a subquery, with interblock reference Get supplier names for suppliers who supply part P2 (the same as Examples 7.2.7 and 7.2.9).

   We show another solution to this problem to illustrate another new point.

```
SELECT   SNAME
FROM     S
WHERE    'P2' IN
          (SELECT P#
           FROM    SP
           WHERE   S# = S.S#)
```

In the last line here the unqualified reference to S# is implicitly qualified by the table-name SP. To refer to an S# from the outer block within the inner block, an explicit qualifier (S) is needed.

7.2.12 Retrieval with a subquery, with same table involved in both blocks Get supplier numbers for suppliers who supply at least one part supplied by supplier S2.

```
SELECT   UNIQUE S#
FROM     SP
WHERE    P# IN
         (SELECT P#
          FROM    SP
          WHERE   S# = 'S2')
```

Result:

S#
S1
S2
S3
S4

Again the unqualified reference to S# in the last line is implicitly qualified by table-name SP. In fact, the reference is entirely local to the inner block: It does not have the same meaning as a reference to S# (or SP.S#) in the outer block (first line). The question arises, how then *can* we reference the outer S# in the inner block, since the same table is involved in both blocks? The answer is that we introduce another name in the outer block and use that as a qualifier, as Example 7.2.13 illustrates (compare Example 7.2.6).

7.2.13 Retrieval with a subquery, with interblock reference and same table involved in both blocks Get part numbers for all parts supplied by more than one supplier. (A simpler solution to this problem is given later as Example 7.3.7.)

```
SELECT   UNIQUE P#
FROM     SP SPX
WHERE    P# IN
         (SELECT P#
          FROM    SP
          WHERE   S# ¬= SPX.S#)
```

Result:

P#
P1
P2
P4
P5

SPX is an arbitrary name used to link the reference SPX.S# in the inner block to the table of the outer block. The operation of the query may be explained as follows: "For each row in turn, say SPX, of table SP, extract the

P# value if that P# value is in the set of P# values whose corresponding S# value is *not* that in row SPX—i.e., if that part is supplied by some supplier distinct from that identified by row SPX.''

7.2.14 Retrieval using ALL Get supplier names for suppliers who do not supply part P2.

Once again there are many possible solutions; the one shown is chosen to illustrate an ALL comparison (defined analogously to an ANY comparison).

```
SELECT  SNAME
FROM    S
WHERE   'P2' ¬=ALL
        (SELECT P#
         FROM    SP
         WHERE   S# = S.S#)
```

Result:

SNAME
Adams

In general, the operator *ALL (where * is any one of =, ¬=, >, >=, <, <=) is defined as follows. The condition

```
        f  *ALL  (SELECT F FROM ...)
```

evaluates to *true* if and only if the comparison "*f* * *V*" evaluates to *true* for all values *V* in the result of evaluating the "SELECT F FROM . . .". In the example above, therefore, suppliers are selected if and only if the value 'P2' is not equal to any of the part numbers they supply. (As with ANY, there is a trap here for the unwary.)

Just as = ANY may be written IN, so ¬= ALL may be written NOT IN.

Sometimes the user may know that a given subquery should return exactly one value. In such a case = ANY, >ALL, etc., may be abbreviated to the unqualified forms =, >, etc. An example follows.

7.2.15 Retrieval with subquery and unqualified comparison operator Get supplier numbers for suppliers who are located in the same city as supplier S1.

```
SELECT  S#
FROM    S
WHERE   CITY =
        (SELECT CITY
         FROM    S
         WHERE   S# = 'S1')
```

Result:

S#
S1
S4

7.2.16 Retrieval using EXISTS Get supplier names for suppliers who supply part P2 (the same as Examples 7.2.7, 7.2.9, and 7.2.11).

```
SELECT   SNAME
FROM     S
WHERE    EXISTS
         (SELECT  *
         FROM     SP
         WHERE    S# = S.S#
         AND      P# = 'P2')
```

EXISTS here represents the *existential quantifier*. The expression "EXISTS (SELECT . . .)" evaluates to *true* if and only if the result of evaluating the "SELECT . . ." is not empty, that is, if and only if there exists a record in the indicated table (the SP table in the example) satisfying the WHERE condition specified in the "SELECT . . .". One way to think about this example is to take each SNAME in turn and see whether it causes the existence test to evaluate to *true*. Thus the first SNAME value in Fig. 4.7 is 'Smith'; the corresponding S# value is 'S1'; does there exist an SP record with S# equal to 'S1' and P# equal to 'P2'? If the answer is yes, 'Smith' is one of the values retrieved. Similarly for each of the remaining SNAME values.

7.2.17 Retrieval using NOT EXISTS Get supplier names for suppliers who do not supply part P2 (the same as Example 7.2.14).

```
SELECT   SNAME
FROM     S
WHERE    NOT EXISTS
         (SELECT  *
         FROM     SP
         WHERE    S# = S.S#
         AND      P# = 'P2')
```

The query may be paraphrased as follows: "Select supplier names for suppliers such that there does not exist a shipment relating them to part P2."

7.2.18 Retrieval using NOT EXISTS Get supplier names for suppliers who supply all parts.

```
SELECT SNAME
FROM    S
WHERE   NOT EXISTS
        (SELECT *
         FROM    P
         WHERE   NOT EXISTS
                 (SELECT *
                  FROM    SP
                  WHERE   S# = S.S#
                  AND     P# = P.P#))
```

Result:

SNAME
Smith

The query may be paraphrased: "Select supplier names for suppliers such that there does not exist a part that they do not supply."

7.2.19 Retrieval using NOT EXISTS   Get supplier numbers for suppliers who supply at least all those parts supplied by supplier S2.

One way to tackle this problem is to break it down into smaller queries. Thus we can first discover the set of part numbers for parts supplied by supplier S2:

```
SELECT P#
FROM    SP
WHERE   S# = 'S2'
```

Result:

P#
P1
P2

Using CREATE TABLE and INSERT (discussed in Section 7.4), it is possible to store this result in a temporary table in the database, say TEMP. Then we can go on to discover the set of supplier numbers for suppliers who supply all parts listed in TEMP (compare Example 7.2.18):

```
SELECT UNIQUE S#
FROM    SP SPX
WHERE   NOT EXISTS
        (SELECT *
         FROM    TEMP
         WHERE   NOT EXISTS
                 (SELECT *
                  FROM    SP
                  WHERE   S# = SPX.S#
                  AND     P# = TEMP.P#))
```

Result:

S#
S1
S2

[Note, however, that we must introduce another name (SPX), since here we are extracting S# values from table SP, not SNAME values from table S.] Table TEMP can now be dropped.

It is also possible to express the entire query as a single SELECT, eliminating the need for TEMP:

```
SELECT  UNIQUE  S#
FROM    SP SPX
WHERE   NOT EXISTS
        (SELECT *
        FROM    SP SPY
        WHERE   S# = 'S2'
        AND     NOT EXISTS
                (SELECT *
                FROM    SP
                WHERE   S# = SPX.S#
                AND     P# = SPY.P#))
```

7.2.20 Retrieval using UNION Get part numbers for parts that either weigh more than 18 pounds or are currently supplied by supplier S2 (or both).

```
SELECT  P#
FROM    P
WHERE   WEIGHT > 18

UNION

SELECT  P#
FROM    SP
WHERE   S# = 'S2'
```

Result:

P#
P1
P2
P6

UNION is the union operator of traditional set theory; in other words, A UNION B (where A and B are sets) is the set of all objects x such that x is a member of A or x is a member of B (or both). Redundant duplicates are always eliminated from the result of a UNION.

7.2.21 Retrieval of computed values For all parts, get the part number and the weight of the part in grams. Weights are given in table P in pounds.

```
SELECT P#, WEIGHT * 454
FROM    P
```

Result:

P#	
P1	5448
P2	7718
P3	7718
P4	6356
P5	5448
P6	8626

The SELECT clause (and the WHERE clause) can include arithmetic expressions involving fields as well as simple field-names.

7.2.22 Retrieval involving NULL Suppose for the sake of the example that supplier S5 has a status value of null, rather than 30. Get supplier numbers for suppliers with status greater than 25.

```
SELECT S#
FROM   S
WHERE  STATUS > 25
```

Result:

S#
S3

Supplier S5 does not qualify. When a null value is compared with some other value in evaluating a predicate, regardless of the comparison operator involved, the result of the comparison is *never* true, even if that other value is also null. In other words, none of the following yields *true:*[1]

```
null > 25
null < 25
null = 25
null ¬= 25
null = null
```

A special predicate, of the form "field IS [NOT] NULL", is provided for testing to see if a given field is or is not null. For example,

---

1. Actually, as indicated in Chapter 6, they all yield the *unknown* truth value. Predicates are evaluated using a three-valued logic (*true, false, unknown*). WHERE clauses designate records for which the predicate evaluates to *true,* i.e., not *false* and not *unknown.*

```
SELECT  S#
FROM    S
WHERE   STATUS > 25
OR      STATUS IS NULL
```

Result:

S#
S3
S5

We have now reached the end of our retrieval examples. It is clear that the retrieval language is very powerful. It is in fact *relationally complete* [12.1]. Relational completeness is a basic measure of the selective power of a language. A language is said to be relationally complete if any relation derivable from the given relations (i.e., the database) by means of an expression of the *relational calculus* (see Chapter 13) can be retrieved using that language. What makes SQL (and similar languages) so powerful is the economy with which this completeness is achieved: Any derivable relation can be retrieved using a *single statement* of the language. In fact, the term "relational completeness" is frequently taken to include this additional constraint (namely, that any derivable relation be retrievable via a single statement), and in this book we shall generally use the term in this more demanding sense. Most of the set-level relational languages discussed in this book are at least this powerful; lower-level languages, relational or otherwise, are certainly not. What relational completeness means to the user is that, *very* loosely speaking, if the information wanted is in the database, then it can be retrieved by means of a single self-contained request. (But see Section 7.3.) In lower-level languages the user must write quite complicated procedures to answer all but the simplest questions. Of course, most queries will be fairly simple in practice; but we know from the underlying theory that the user *can* ask arbitrarily complex questions if necessary.

7.3 BUILT-IN FUNCTIONS

Although "complete" as just explained, the retrieval language described so far is still inadequate for many practical problems. For example, even a query as simple as "How many suppliers are there?" cannot be expressed using only the constructs given in Section 7.2. SQL therefore provides a number of special *built-in functions* to enhance its basic retrieval power. The functions currently supported are COUNT, SUM, AVG, MAX, and MIN. Apart from the special case of "COUNT(*)" (see below), each of these functions operates on the collection of values in one column of some table, and produces a result as follows:

COUNT: number of values,

SUM: sum of the values,

AVG: average of the values,

MAX: largest value,

MIN: smallest value.

For SUM and AVG the column concerned must contain numeric values. In general, the argument of the function may optionally be preceded by the keyword UNIQUE to indicate that redundant duplicate values should be eliminated before the function is applied. UNIQUE *must* be specified for COUNT; however, the special function COUNT(*) is provided to count all rows in a table without any duplicate elimination.

Any null values in the argument are always eliminated before the function is applied, regardless of whether UNIQUE is specified, *except* for the case of COUNT(*), where rows are counted even if they are all null (i.e., consist entirely of null fields).

If the argument happens to be an empty set, COUNT returns a result of zero; the other functions all return null.

7.3.1 Function in the SELECT clause   Get the total number of suppliers.

```
SELECT COUNT (*)
FROM    S
```

Result:

5

7.3.2 Function in the SELECT clause   Get the total number of suppliers currently supplying parts.

```
SELECT COUNT (UNIQUE S#)
FROM    SP
```

Result:

4

7.3.3 Function in the SELECT clause, with a predicate   Get the number of shipments for part P2.

```
SELECT COUNT(*)
FROM    SP
WHERE   P# = 'P2'
```

Result:

7.3.4 Function in the SELECT clause, with a predicate

Get the total quantity of part P2 supplied.

```
SELECT  SUM(QTY)
FROM    SP
WHERE   P# = 'P2'
```

Result:

1000

7.3.5 Function in a subquery

Get supplier numbers for suppliers with status value less than the current maximum status value in the S table (the same as Example 7.2.8).

```
SELECT S#
FROM   S
WHERE  STATUS  <
       (SELECT  MAX(STATUS)
        FROM    S)
```

7.3.6 Use of GROUP BY

For each part supplied, get the part number and the total quantity supplied of that part.

```
SELECT P#, SUM(QTY)
FROM   SP
GROUP  BY P#
```

Result:

P#	
P1	600
P2	1000
P3	400
P4	500
P5	500
P6	100

The GROUP BY operator conceptually rearranges the FROM table into partitions or *groups,* such that within any one group all rows have the same value for the GROUP BY field. (Of course, this does not mean that the table is physically rearranged in the database.) In the example, table SP is grouped such that the first group contains the rows for part P1, the second contains the rows for part P2, and so on. The SELECT clause is then applied to each group of the partitioned table (rather than to each row of the original table). Each expression in the SELECT clause must be *single-valued* for each group; that is, it can be either the GROUP BY field itself, or a function such as SUM that operates on all values of a given field within a group and reduces those values to a single value.

A table can be grouped by any combination of its fields.

7.3.7 Use of GROUP BY with HAVING   Get part numbers for all parts supplied by more than one supplier (the same as Example 7.2.13).

```
SELECT  P#
FROM    SP
GROUP   BY P#
HAVING  COUNT(*) > 1
```

HAVING is to groups what WHERE is to rows. (If HAVING is specified, GROUP BY should also have been specified.) Expressions in a HAVING clause must be single-valued for each group.

Note that the SELECT clause no longer requires a UNIQUE specification (contrast Example 7.2.13).

7.3.8 A comprehensive example   For all parts such that the total quantity supplied is greater than 300 (excluding from the total all shipments for which the quantity is less than or equal to 200), get the part number and the maximum quantity of the part supplied; and order the result by descending part number within those maximum quantity values.

```
SELECT  P#, MAX(QTY)
FROM    SP
WHERE   QTY > 200
GROUP   BY P#
HAVING  SUM(QTY) > 300
ORDER   BY 2, P# DESC
```

Result:

P#	
P1	300
P5	400
P3	400
P2	400

The FROM, WHERE, GROUP BY, and HAVING clauses are applied in the order suggested by that in which they must be written. Thus, in the example, we can imagine the result being formed as follows.

1. (FROM)   A copy is made of table SP.
2. (WHERE)   Rows not satisfying "QTY > 200" are eliminated.
3. (GROUP BY)   The remaining rows are grouped by P#.
4. (HAVING)   Groups not satisfying "SUM(QTY) > 300" are eliminated.
5. (SELECT)   Part numbers and maximum quantities are extracted from the remaining groups.
6. (ORDER BY)   The table so formed is ordered as specified. In the example, since we wish to order the result (in part) by values of the second field of that result and that field does not have its own field-name, we use its ordinal position within the result (2) in the ORDER BY specification.

7.4 UPDATE OPERATIONS

The SQL DML includes three update operations: UPDATE (modify), INSERT, and DELETE.

7.4.1 Single-record update   Change the color of part P2 to yellow, increase its weight by 5, and set its city to "unknown" (NULL).

```
UPDATE P
SET     COLOR = 'YELLOW',
        WEIGHT = WEIGHT + 5,
        CITY = NULL
WHERE   P# = 'P2'
```

Within a SET clause, any reference to a field on the right-hand side of an equals sign refers to the value of that field before any updating has been done.

7.4.2 Multiple-record update   Double the status of all suppliers in London.

```
UPDATE S
SET     STATUS = 2 * STATUS
WHERE   CITY = 'LONDON'
```

7.4.3 Update with a subquery   Set the quantity to zero for all suppliers in London.

```
UPDATE SP
SET     QTY = 0
WHERE   'LONDON' =
        (SELECT CITY
         FROM    S
         WHERE   S# = SP.S#)
```

7.4.4 Multiple-table update Change the supplier number for supplier S2 to S9.

```
UPDATE S
SET    S# = 'S9'
WHERE  S# = 'S2'

UPDATE SP
SET    S# = 'S9'
WHERE  S# = 'S2'
```

It is not possible to update more than one table in a single UPDATE statement; to put it another way, the UPDATE clause must specify exactly one table. In this example, therefore, we have an *integrity problem:* The database becomes inconsistent after the first UPDATE and remains so until the second. Reversing the sequence of the two UPDATEs does not solve the problem. In this particular example, in fact, Integrity Rule 2 (referential integrity) is temporarily violated, because it is a primary key that is being changed. In fact, some systems (but not System R) prohibit primary key updates because of such complications (changing a primary key in such a system thus involves a deletion followed by an insertion). However, multiple-table updates—that is, performing linked update operations on multiple tables—can still cause inconsistency problems even if Integrity Rule 2 per se is not involved.

7.4.5 Single-record insertion Add part P7 (name 'WASHER', color 'GREY', weight 2, city 'ATHENS') to table P.

```
INSERT INTO P:
        <'P7','WASHER','GREY',2,'ATHENS'>
```

(Note that the operation relies on the left-to-right order of columns within the table.) It is also possible to insert a new record in which not all fields have known values. For example,

```
INSERT INTO P (P#, WEIGHT, PNAME):
        <'P7',2,'WASHER'>
```

A new P record is created with the specified number, weight, and name, and with null values for COLOR and CITY. Of course, these fields must not have been defined with the NONULL option. The order in which fields are named in this format of INSERT need not be the same as their order within the table.

INSERT may be used to insert a single record, as in the example just shown, or a whole set of records resulting from the evaluation of an inner query, as in the next example.

7.4.6 Multiple-record insertion Table TEMP has one column, called P#. Enter into TEMP part numbers for all parts supplied by supplier S2 (see Example 7.2.19).

```
INSERT INTO TEMP:
       SELECT P#
       FROM   SP
       WHERE  S# = 'S2'
```

It is not necessary for the target table to be initially empty for a multiple-record INSERT, though for Example 7.2.19 it would be.

7.4.7 Single-record deletion Delete supplier S1.

```
DELETE S
WHERE  S# = 'S1'
```

If table SP currently has any shipments for supplier S1, this DELETE will cause Integrity Rule 2 to be violated.

7.4.8 Multiple-record deletion Delete all shipments.

```
DELETE SP
```

SP is still a known table but is now empty.

7.4.9 Multiple-record, multiple-table deletion Delete all shipments from suppliers in London and also the suppliers concerned.

```
DELETE SP
WHERE  'LONDON' =
       (SELECT CITY
        FROM   S
        WHERE  S# = SP.S#)

DELETE S
WHERE  CITY = 'LONDON'
```

7.5 THE SYSTEM R DICTIONARY

Recall from Chapter 1 that the dictionary is that component of the system that contains "data about the data"—that is, *descriptions* of other objects in the system. In a relational system the objects to be described are, or course, relations, attributes, and so forth. If these descriptions are themselves presented to the user in the form of relations—in other words, if the user views the dictionary itself as a collection of relations—then in principle the same data sublanguage may be used for the dictionary as for the rest of the data, a very nice conceptual simplification.

Let us now consider System R explicitly. In System R the dictionary *is* represented to the user as a set of relations. We mention only two of these relations here, TABLES and COLUMNS (not the actual System R names). TABLES contains a row for each table defined to the system, giving TNAME (table-name; this is the primary key), CREATOR (identification of the creator of this table), NCOLS (number of columns in this table), and other information. COLUMNS contains a row for every column of every table defined to the system, giving TNAME and CNAME (table-name and column-name; this combination is the primary key), COLTYPE (data-type for this column, e.g., character or numeric), LENGTH (number of bytes), and other information.

The SQL DML can be used to interrogate these dictionary tables. For example, the query

```
SELECT  TNAME
FROM    COLUMNS
WHERE   CNAME = 'S#'
```

will result in a list of table-names for all tables having a column called S#. Similarly, the query

```
SELECT  CNAME
FROM    COLUMNS
WHERE   TNAME = 'S'
```

will give a list of all column-names for table S. Hence a user who wishes to retrieve information concerning suppliers but who initially knows only that suppliers are identified by an attribute called S# could use the two "dictionary" queries above as preliminaries to a "data" query, such as

```
SELECT  S#, STATUS, CITY
FROM    S
```

It should be clear that the system is crucially dependent on the correctness of the tables in the dictionary; in particular, it must be able to rely on those tables being mutually consistent. For example, every TNAME mentioned in COLUMNS must also appear in TABLES. Thus it would be very dangerous to allow users to perform uncontrolled INSERT, DELETE, or UPDATE operations on the dictionary, using the ordinary SQL DML. Instead, users normally use "bundled" DDL operations such as CREATE TABLE. CREATE TABLE, for example, makes an entry in TABLES for the new table and also entries in COLUMNS for all columns of that table, and *guarantees* that TABLES and COLUMNS will be consistent at the end of the operation. It *is* possible to use direct INSERT, DELETE, and UPDATE operations on the dictionary, but only if the user has "DBA authority," and then only in very exceptional circumstances.

Finally, the DDL operations CREATE TABLE, DROP TABLE, etc., are *not* generally applicable to the objects in the dictionary. Consider CREATE TABLE, for example. The function of CREATE TABLE is to build a new table (obtaining the necessary storage space) and, as we have just seen, to construct appropriate definitions (entries in the dictionary) for that new table. There is no need to issue CREATE TABLE for the dictionary tables themselves, because those tables already exist; they were built when the system was initialized, and their definitions are already in the dictionary (they are "hardwired" into the system). For instance, the TABLES table already contains an entry for every dictionary table—including the TABLES table itself—at the time the system is initialized.

7.6 DISCUSSION

To conclude this chapter we present a brief discussion of the advantages of the SQL DML when compared with lower-level DMLs (such as the record-at-a-time DMLs presented in Chapter 3). Many of the following points apply equally well to other set-level relational DMLs, as we shall see in later chapters.

■ Simplicity

Many problems can be expressed in SQL more easily and concisely than in lower-level languages. Simplicity in turn means increased productivity. In the case of embedded SQL, this applies both to the person who produces the original program and to the person who must maintain that program.

■ Completeness

The language is relationally complete, as indicated in Section 7.2. This means that, for a very large class of queries, the user need never resort to loops or branching. (This statement is not quite true for embedded SQL. Application programmers *will* frequently have to use some form of loop construct. However, those loops will usually fall into one particular stylized pattern. See Chapter 8.)

■ Nonprocedurality

Languages such as the SQL DML are frequently described as "nonprocedural." A SELECT statement, for example, specifies only what data is wanted, not a procedure for obtaining that data. To put it another way, such a statement is a high-level *statement of intent* on the part of the user. This is significant because it means that the implementation is able to *capture* the user's intent—that is, it can understand what the user is trying to do, at a reasonably high level. Capturing the user's intent, in turn, makes search optimization a practical proposition. Search optimization would be very difficult with a lower-level DML.

Capturing intent is also important in the implementation of other aspects of the system, such as authorization checking.

- Data independence

SQL DML statements include no reference to explicit access paths such as indexes or physical sequence. (They may insist on a *logical* sequence.) Thus the SQL DML provides total "physical" data independence [7.8]—that is, independence of the way in which the data is physically stored. As we shall see in Chapter 9, it also provides a certain amount of "logical" data independence—that is, independence of the way in which the data is logically structured. (Record-level DMLs could also provide physical data independence in theory, but in practice they have tended not to.)

- Ease of extension

Section 7.3 shows that the retrieval power of the basic language can be easily extended by the provision of built-in functions. Some systems (for example, PRTV [12.5]) permit users to define their own built-in functions.

- Support for higher-level languages

We do not mean to suggest that all users should have to use SQL or something like it. On the contrary, it will often be preferable to provide a variety of special-purpose languages, each such language being tailored to some particular application area and supporting terminology and operations specific to that area. Indeed, some "casual" users may have no formal language at all for accessing the system other than their own unrestricted natural language [7.3–7.5]. However, languages like SQL provide a common core of features that will be required in some shape or form in all such higher languages. SQL, or some other language of comparable power, can therefore conveniently be used as a common target for those higher languages—i.e., as an intermediate step in the translation of those languages to the language of the underlying machine.

EXERCISES

All the questions in this section are based on the suppliers-parts-projects database (see the exercises in Chapter 6). Some sample data values were shown in Fig. 6.2. You may find it helpful to interpret the questions in terms of that sample data; the process of working out the result by hand may give you some insight into how to formulate an appropriate SQL statement. For convenience we repeat the table-names and field-names here. Primary keys are shown by underlining.

```
S    (S#, SNAME, STATUS, CITY)
P    (P#, PNAME, COLOR, WEIGHT, CITY)
J    (J#, JNAME, CITY)
SPJ  (S#, P#, J#, QTY)
```

The questions are in approximate order of increasing complexity. You probably will not want to tackle them all, at least not on a first reading; a representative sample is all even-numbered exercises from 7.2 to 7.20, inclusive, plus all exercises from 7.30 to the end. Numbers 7.21 to 7.28 are quite difficult.

As an additional exercise, you are strongly recommended to try converting the answers provided for some of the more complex questions back into English.

7.1 Get full details of all projects.

7.2 Get full details of all projects in London.

7.3 Get the part number for parts such that no other part has a smaller weight value.

7.4 Get S# values for suppliers who supply project J1.

7.5 Get S# values for suppliers who supply project J1 with part P1.

7.6 Get JNAME values for projects supplied by supplier S1.

7.7 Get COLOR values for parts supplied by supplier S1.

7.8 Get S# values for suppliers who supply both projects J1 and J2.

7.9 Get S# values for suppliers who supply project J1 with a red part.

7.10 Get P# values for parts supplied to any project in London.

7.11 Get S# values for suppliers who supply a London or Paris project with a red part.

7.12 Get P# values for parts supplied to any project by a supplier in the same city.

7.13 Get P# values for parts supplied to any project in London by a supplier in London.

7.14 Get J# values for projects supplied by at least one supplier not in the same city.

7.15 Get J# values for projects not supplied with any red part by any London supplier.

7.16 Get S# values for suppliers supplying at least one part supplied by at least one supplier who supplies at least one red part.

7.17 Get J# values for projects using at least one part available from supplier S1.

7.18 Get all pairs of CITY values such that a supplier in the first city supplies a project in the second city.

7.19 Get all ⟨CITY,P#,CITY⟩ triples such that a supplier in the first city supplies the specified part to a project in the second city.

7.20 Repeat Exercise 7.19, but do not retrieve triples in which the two CITY values are the same.

7.21 Get S# values for suppliers who supply the same part to all projects.

7.22 Get J# values for projects supplied entirely by supplier S1.

7.23 Get P# values for parts supplied to all projects in London.

7.24 Get J# values for projects supplied with at least all parts supplied by supplier S1.

7.25 Get J# values for projects which use only parts which are available from supplier S1.

7.26 Get J# values for projects supplied by supplier S1 with all parts that supplier S1 supplies.

7.27 Get J# values for projects which obtain at least some of every part they use from supplier S1.

7.28 Get J# values for projects supplied by all suppliers who supply some red part.

7.29 Change the name of project J6 to 'VIDEO'.

7.30 Change the color of all red parts to orange.

7.31 Delete all red parts and the corresponding SPJ records.

7.32 Get the total number of projects supplied by supplier S3.

7.33 Get the total quantity of part P1 supplied by supplier S1.

7.34 For each part being supplied to a project, get the part number, the project number, and the corresponding total quantity.

REFERENCES AND BIBLIOGRAPHY

7.1 Relational Software, Inc. ORACLE Introduction—Version 1.3 (1978, 1979). Available from RSI, 3000 Sand Hill Road, Menlo Park, California 94025.

> The language SEQUEL/2 [5.5] is used essentially unchanged as the user interface to ORACLE.

7.2 Honeywell Information Systems, Inc. Series 60 (Level 68) MULTICS Logical Inquiry and Update System (LINUS). Reference Manual, Preliminary Edition (October 1978).

> LINUS is a database access and report generation system for the Honeywell MULTICS Relational Data Store (MRDS). It includes an interactive "selection language" called LILA (Linus Language) that is similar to the SELECT statement of SQL. It also provides update operations that are rather less SQL-like.

7.3 E. F. Codd. "Seven Steps to Rendezvous with the Casual User." In *Data Base Management* (eds., Klimbie and Koffeman). *Proc. IFIP TC-2 Working Conference on Data Base Management Systems* (April 1974). North-Holland (1974).

7.4 E. F. Codd. "How About Recently? (English Dialog with Relational Data Bases Using RENDEZVOUS Version 1)." In *Databases: Improving Usability and Responsiveness* (ed., B. Shneiderman). New York: Academic Press (1978).

7.5 E. F. Codd, R. S. Arnold, J.-M. Cadiou, C. L. Chang, and N. Roussopoulos. "RENDEZVOUS Version 1: An Experimental English-Language Query Formulation System for Casual Users of Relational Data Bases." IBM Research Report RJ2144 (January 1978).

These papers [7.3–7.5] are concerned with a system called RENDEZVOUS that permits on-line "casual" users—i.e., users having no knowledge of computers, programming, or artificial languages—to make queries against a relational database, using only their unrestricted natural language. Where necessary the system interrogates the user about the query, until it is able to synthesize an internal representation of that query in the form of an expression in a language called DEDUCE [7.6] (a language at a level comparable to that of SQL), which it can then execute. The conversation between the system and the user includes the use of multiple-choice interrogation (menu selection) as a fallback, and a precise restatement in natural language of the user's query as the system understands it before any data is actually retrieved.

7.6 C. L. Chang. "DEDUCE—A Deductive Query Language for Relational Data Bases." In *Pattern Recognition and Artificial Intelligence* (ed., C. H. Chen). New York: Academic Press (1976).

7.7 F. Antonacci, P. Dell'Orco, and V. N. Spadavecchia. "AQL: An APL-Based System for Accessing and Manipulating Data in a Relational Database System." *Proc. APL 76 Conference, Ottawa* (September 1976). Available from ACM.

Describes a SQL-like query language implemented as an extension to APL.

7.8 C. J. Date and P. Hopewell. "Storage Structure and Physical Data Independence." *Proc. 1971 ACM SIGFIDET Workshop on Data Description, Access and Control.*

An investigation into possible storage structures to support a relational database. A given storage structure is said to be a "conformable representation" of a given relational structure if there exists a 1–1 onto mapping between the two. Several examples of conformable and nonconformable representations are given, and it is demonstrated by example that (a) the class of conformable representations is very large, and (b) it is difficult to implement even very simple relational operations in terms of a nonconformable representation. It is therefore suggested that in practice only conformable representations should be considered.

8
Embedded
SQL

8.1 INTRODUCTION

Chapters 6 and 7 have been concerned with the SQL DML and (parts of) the SQL DDL, and have shown how SQL statements can be used in an interactive environment. In this chapter we turn our attention to the application programming environment, and consider *embedded* SQL, i.e., SQL as it appears to the application programmer. To fix our ideas we assume that the host programming language is PL/I; most of the ideas translate into COBOL with only minor changes.

We start by giving a few preliminary details, all of which are illustrated in the program fragment shown in Fig. 8.1. First, embedded SQL statements are prefixed by a $-sign (so that they can be easily recognized by the RDS precompiler), and terminated, like ordinary PL/I statements, by a semicolon (lines 1, 2, 3, and 8–11). Second, an executable SQL statement (from now on we shall usually drop the word "embedded") can appear wherever an executable PL/I statement can appear (lines 8–11). Third, SQL statements can include references to PL/I variables—that is, they may include the names of ordinary PL/I variables—but all such references must be prefixed by a $-sign (lines 9 and 11), and the variables concerned must be "$-declared" (i.e., defined by a $DCL statement rather than an ordinary PL/I declaration—lines 1, 2, and 3).

We make the following additional comments.

1. The $SELECT statement includes an INTO clause (line 9) specifying variables to which values retrieved from the database are to be assigned.

2. $-declared variables are $-referenced inside SQL statements (lines 9 and 11), but referenced normally in PL/I statements (line 12). "$-references"

```
1        $DCL GIVENS# CHAR(5);
2        $DCL RANK FIXED BIN(15);
3        $DCL CITY CHAR(15);
4         DCL ALPHA ... ;
5         DCL BETA   ... ;
          . . . . . . .
6         IF ALPHA > BETA THEN
7 GETSC:
8         $SELECT STATUS, CITY
9          INTO    $RANK, $CITY
10         FROM    S
11         WHERE   S# = $GIVENS#;
           . . . . . . .
12         PUT SKIP LIST (RANK, CITY);
```

Fig. 8.1 Fragment of a PL/I program with embedded SQL.

can be used to specify target variables (INTO clause in SELECT), comparands (WHERE clause in SELECT, UPDATE, and DELETE), new field values (data list in INSERT), and update values (SET clause in UPDATE).

3. $-declared variables should have a PL/I data-type compatible with the System R data-type of fields they are compared with (line 11) or assigned to or from (line 9). (The System R data-type of a field is specified in the CREATE TABLE or EXPAND TABLE that defines that field.) Data-type compatibility is defined as follows: (a) The System R CHAR data-type is compatible with the PL/I CHAR data-type, regardless of length and regardless of whether VAR is specified in either case; (b) the System R numeric data-types (INTEGER, SMALLINT, FLOAT) are each compatible with each of the PL/I data-types FIXED BIN(15), FIXED BIN(31), FLOAT BIN(53). If data is lost on assignment (either to or from the database) because the target is too small, an error indication is returned to the program.

4. PL/I variables and database fields can have the same name. The SQL objects—tables, fields, etc.—in terms of which SQL statements are compiled are not declared in the PL/I program, but rather in the System R dictionary. In fact, these objects are not known in the PL/I program per se and cannot be referenced other than in the embedded SQL statements.

5. After any SQL statement has been executed, a numeric status indicator is returned to the program in a system variable called SYR_CODE. A value of zero indicates that the statement executed successfully; a value of +100 indicates that no data was found in the database that satisfied the request; and a negative value indicates an error. Thus the programmer should follow

every SQL statement with a test of the value of SYR_CODE, taking appropriate action if the value is not what was expected. This step is not shown in Fig. 8.1.

6. Finally, we stress the point that *any* SQL statement can be used within an application program—not just DML statements but DDL statements as well, if desired. In practice, as one would expect, it is DML statements that appear most often, but it is easy to find uses for DDL statements too; for example, CREATE TABLE might be used to create a table to save an intermediate result. However, the remainder of the chapter concentrates on DML statements only.

Most of the SQL DML statements can be embedded in PL/I and COBOL in a fairly straightforward fashion (i.e., with only minor alterations in their syntax). However, SELECT statements require special treatment. Executing a SQL SELECT statement causes a *table* to be returned to the user—a table that, in general, contains multiple records. Languages such as PL/I, however, are not well equipped to handle more than one record at a time. It is therefore necessary to provide some form of bridge between the two functional levels, and embedded SQL provides such a bridge by means of a new type of object called a *cursor*. We defer detailed discussion of cursors to Section 8.3, and consider first (Section 8.2) those statements that have no need of them.

8.2   OPERATIONS NOT INVOLVING CURSORS

The DML statements that do not need cursors are as follows:

- "singleton SELECT",
- UPDATE (except the "current" form—see Section 8.3),
- INSERT,
- DELETE (again, except the "current" form).

We give examples of each of these statements in turn.

8.2.1 Singleton SELECT   Retrieve status and city for the supplier whose supplier number is given by the program variable GIVENS#.

```
$SELECT STATUS, CITY
  INTO   $RANK, $CITY
  FROM   S
  WHERE  S# = $GIVENS#;
```

We use the term "singleton SELECT" to mean a SELECT statement for which the retrieved table contains at most one row. In the example, if there exists exactly one (STATUS, CITY) pair satisfying the SELECT, then that pair of values will be delivered to the program variables RANK and CITY as requested, and SYR_CODE will be set to zero. If no (STATUS, CITY) pair satisfies the SELECT, SYR_CODE will be set to +100. If more than one (STATUS, CITY) pair satisfies the SELECT, the program is in error; SYR_CODE will be set to a negative value (actually −810).

8.2.2 UPDATE   Increase the status of all London suppliers by the amount given in the program variable RAISE.

```
$UPDATE S
 SET     STATUS = STATUS + $RAISE
 WHERE   CITY = 'LONDON';
```

If no S records satisfy the WHERE clause, SYR_CODE will be set to +100.

8.2.3 INSERT   Insert a new part (part number, name, and weight given by program variables PNO, PNAME, PWT, respectively; color and city unknown) into table P.

```
$INSERT INTO P (P#, PNAME, WEIGHT):
        <$PNO, $PNAME, $PWT>;
```

8.2.4 DELETE   Delete all shipments for suppliers whose city is given by the program variable CITY.

```
$DELETE SP
 WHERE   S# IN
         (SELECT S#
          FROM   S
          WHERE  CITY = $CITY);
```

Again SYR_CODE will be set to +100 if no records satisfy the WHERE clause.

8.3   OPERATIONS INVOLVING CURSORS

Now let us consider the case of a SELECT that selects a whole set of records, not just one. What is needed is a mechanism for accessing the records in the set one by one; and *cursors* provide such a mechanism. The process is outlined in the example given in Fig. 8.2, which is intended to retrieve supplier information (S#, SNAME, and STATUS) for all suppliers in the city given by the program variable Y.

```
$LET  X  BE                    /*     define cursor X    */
       SELECT  S#, SNAME, STATUS
       INTO    $S#, $SNAME, $STATUS
       FROM    S
       WHERE   CITY = $Y;

$OPEN  X;                      /*      activate X        */
  DO  WHILE  more-to-come;
       $FETCH X;               /* fetch next supplier */
        . . . . .
  END;
```

Fig. 8.2 Retrieving multiple records.

Now we consider cursor operations in more detail. A cursor is *defined* by means of a LET statement, which takes the general form

```
$LET  cursor-name  BE  embedded-SELECT-statement;
```

For an example, see Fig. 8.2. The LET statement is declarative, not executable. The LET statement in Fig. 8.2 declares X to be a cursor, with associated SELECT statement as specified (note that the SELECT can include "$-references"). A program can contain any number of LET statements, each of which must be for a different cursor.

Three executable statements are provided to operate on cursors: OPEN, FETCH, and CLOSE.

1. The statement

```
$OPEN  X;
```

makes cursor X *active*. In effect, the SELECT statement associated with X is executed (using the current value of the program variable Y); a set of records is thus identified, and cursor X is associated with that set. Cursor X also identifies a *position* in that set, namely, the position just before the first record in the set. (Sets of records that are associated with a cursor are always considered to have an ordering—either an ordering defined by an ORDER BY clause in the LET statement, or a system-determined ordering in the absence of such a clause.)

2. The statement

```
$FETCH  X;
```

advances cursor X and positions it "on" the next record in the associated set, and then assigns fields from that record to program variables in accordance with the SELECT and INTO clauses of the LET statement for X.

(After the OPEN, X is positioned just before the first record, so the first FETCH will position it on, and will fetch fields from, that first record.) The FETCH statement is normally executed within a program loop, as shown in Fig. 8.2.

   3. The statement

```
$CLOSE X;
```

deactivates cursor X; that is, X is no longer associated with the set of records selected when it was opened. It is still associated with the same SELECT statement, however, and if it is opened again it will again become associated with some set (probably not exactly the same set as before, particularly if the value of the program variable Y has changed in the meantime).

   If there is no "next" record when FETCH is executed, SYR_CODE is set to +100, and the cursor is closed automatically. This explains why no CLOSE statement was shown in Fig. 8.2.

   Note, incidentally, that changing the value of the program variable Y while cursor X is in the active state has no effect on the set of records accessible via X (the set with which X is currently associated).

   Two further statements can include references to cursors. These are the "current" forms of UPDATE and DELETE. If a cursor, X say, is positioned on a particular record in the database, then it is possible to UPDATE or DELETE the "current of X," i.e., the record on which X is positioned. For example,

```
$UPDATE S
   SET     STATUS = STATUS + $RAISE
   WHERE   CURRENT OF X;
```

UPDATE and DELETE are subject to certain restrictions, of which the most important is that the record to be updated or deleted—that is, the record as seen by the user—must be essentially identical to a real record in the database (for example, it cannot be a join).[1] Moreover, the LET statement for the cursor concerned (a) must not include an ORDER BY clause, and (b) in the case of UPDATE, must include a clause of the form

```
FOR UPDATE OF field-name [, field-name ] ...
```

identifying all the fields that may be a target of a SET clause in an "UPDATE CURRENT" statement for that cursor.

---

1. It can omit fields of the underlying record, however. This question of update restrictions will be considered in detail in Chapter 9.

A Comprehensive Example

We present a comprehensive example (Fig. 8.3) to illustrate the use of cursors in full detail. The program accepts four input values: a part number (GIVENP#), a city name (GIVENCIT), a status increment (GIVENINC), and a status level (GIVENLVL). The program scans all suppliers of the part identified by GIVENP#. For each such supplier, if the supplier city is GIVENCIT, then the status is increased by GIVENINC; otherwise, if the status is less than GIVENLVL, the supplier is deleted, together with all shipments for that supplier. In all cases supplier information is listed on the printer, with an indication of how that particular supplier was handled by the program.

```
SQLEX: PROC OPTIONS (MAIN);

   $DCL GIVENP# CHAR(6);
   $DCL GIVENCIT CHAR(15);
   $DCL GIVENINC FIXED BIN(15);
   $DCL GIVENLVL FIXED BIN(15);
   $DCL S# CHAR(5);
   $DCL SNAME CHAR(20);
   $DCL STATUS FIXED BIN(15);
   $DCL CITY CHAR(15);
    DCL DISP CHAR(7);
    DCL MORE_SUPPLIERS BIT(1);

   $SYR;
   /* expands into System R feedback structure SYR */

   $LET Z BE SELECT * INTO $S#, $SNAME, $STATUS, $CITY
            FROM S WHERE S# IN
                  (SELECT S# FROM SP WHERE P# = $GIVENP#)
            FOR UPDATE OF STATUS;
   /*   ORDER BY not allowed because of UPDATE/DELETE  */

     ON CONDITION (DBERROR)
        BEGIN;
           PUT SKIP LIST (SYR_CODE);
           /* in practice would probably print additional   */
           /* debugging information, e.g., selected program */
           /* variables                                     */
           GO TO QUIT;
        END;
```

Fig. 8.3 Embedded SQL—a complete example (first part).

```
    GET LIST (GIVENP#, GIVENCIT, GIVENINC, GIVENLVL);

  $BEGIN TRANSACTION;

  $OPEN Z;
   IF SYR_CODE ¬= 0 THEN SIGNAL CONDITION (DBERROR);
   MORE_SUPPLIERS = '1'B;
   DO WHILE (MORE_SUPPLIERS);
     $FETCH Z;
     SELECT;
   /* NB: SELECT - WHEN - WHEN - ... - END is a PL/I */
   /* ''case'' statement, not a SQL SELECT statement */
     WHEN (SYR_CODE = 100)
         /* Z automatically CLOSED */
         MORE_SUPPLIERS = '0'B;
     WHEN (SYR_CODE < 0)
         SIGNAL CONDITION (DBERROR);
     WHEN (SYR_CODE = 0)
         DO;
            DISP = '';
            IF CITY = GIVENCIT THEN
               DO;
                 $UPDATE S
                  SET STATUS = STATUS + $GIVENINC
                  WHERE CURRENT OF Z;
                  IF SYR_CODE ¬= 0
                  THEN SIGNAL CONDITION (DBERROR);
                  DISP = 'UPDATED';
               END;
            ELSE
            IF STATUS < GIVENLVL THEN
               DO;
                 $DELETE SP
                  WHERE S# = $S#;
                  IF SYR_CODE < 0
                  THEN SIGNAL CONDITION (DBERROR);
                 $DELETE S
                  WHERE CURRENT OF Z;
                  IF SYR_CODE ¬= 0
                  THEN SIGNAL CONDITION (DBERROR);
                  DISP = 'DELETED';
               END;
            PUT SKIP LIST (S#, SNAME, STATUS, CITY, DISP);
         END; /* WHEN (SYR_CODE = 0) */
     END; /* SELECT */
   END; /* DO loop */

  $END TRANSACTION;
QUIT:
   END; /* SQLEX */
```

Fig. 8.3 Embedded SQL—a complete example (second part).

Note the special statements $BEGIN TRANSACTION and $END TRANSACTION in Fig. 8.3. $BEGIN TRANSACTION *must* be the first SQL statement executed in a program; and $END TRANSACTION must be the last, unless the program terminates abnormally. The term "transaction" refers to the unit of work that the program performs between these two statements. If $END TRANSACTION is not executed, System R will automatically cancel all changes the program has made to the database since $BEGIN TRANSACTION.

Note also the statement "$SYR;" (after the PL/I declarations). This statement causes the precompiler to generate a PL/I structure called SYR, which is used to receive feedback information after a SQL statement has been executed. The return code variable SYR_CODE is a field in this structure. Details of the other fields are beyond the scope of this book.

8.4 DYNAMIC STATEMENTS

As we mentioned in Chapter 5, embedded SQL provides certain features to facilitate the writing of on-line application programs—that is, programs to support on-line access to the database from an end-user at a terminal. Consider what such a program must do. In outline, the steps it must go through are as follows:

1. Accept a command from the terminal;

2. Analyze the command;

3. Issue appropriate SQL statements;

4. Return a message and/or results to the terminal.

If the set of commands the program can accept is fairly small, as in the case of (e.g.) a program handling airline reservations, then the set of possible SQL statements to be issued may also be small and can be "hardwired" into the program. In this case, steps 2 and 3 above will consist simply of logic to examine the input command and then branch to the piece of the program that issues the predefined SQL statement(s). If, on the other hand, there can be great variability in the input, then it may not be practical to predefine and "hardwire" SQL statements for every possible command. Instead, it is probably much more convenient to *construct* SQL statements dynamically (and then to execute those dynamically constructed statements).[2] The "dynamic statements" of embedded SQL are provided to assist in this process.

---

2. This is exactly the way that UFI works. UFI is an on-line application program that accepts a wide variety of input, namely, any valid (or invalid!) SQL statement. It uses the dynamic statement facility to construct embedded SQL statements corresponding to its input and to execute them.

The two principal dynamic statements are PREPARE and EXECUTE. The use of these two statements is illustrated in the following example.[3]

```
DCL SQLSOURCE CHAR(256);
. . . . . . .
SQLSOURCE = 'DELETE SP WHERE QTY < 100';
$PREPARE SQLOBJ FROM SQLSOURCE;
$EXECUTE SQLOBJ;
```

We explain this example as follows. The assignment statement assigns to the character string variable SQLSOURCE the character string representation of a SQL statement. (In practice the process of building this character string representation would probably be rather more complicated.) The PREPARE statement then passes this string to the RDS precompiler, which goes through its normal process of parsing, optimization, and code generation, and builds a machine language version of the statement, called SQLOBJ. (This name is arbitrary and is specified in the PREPARE.) Finally, the EXECUTE statement causes this machine language routine to be executed, and thus (in the example) causes the actual deletions to occur.

Note, incidentally, that SQLSOURCE in the PREPARE statement is an ordinary variable reference, not a "$-reference."

Once PREPAREd, a given dynamically generated SQL statement can be EXECUTEd many times. The generated statement can be replaced by another by issuing PREPARE again with the same target and a different source.

The procedure just illustrated is adequate for the dynamic generation and execution of all "regular" SQL statements *except* SELECT. (By the term "regular" we mean to exclude the cursor statements, such as OPEN and CLOSE, and the dynamic statements themselves that we describe in this section.) The reason that SELECT is different is that it returns data to the user; all the other statements return only a status indicator (SYR_CODE value).

A program using SELECT needs to know something about the data that will be retrieved; after all, it has to specify a set of target variables in the INTO clause of that SELECT. In other words, it needs to know at least how many fields will be retrieved and what their data-types are. If the SELECT is generated dynamically in response to a command from the terminal, the program cannot in general know this information in advance. What it does, therefore, is the following:

1. It builds and PREPAREs the SELECT statement *without* an INTO clause.

---

3. SQL actually uses the keyword AS in place of FROM in the PREPARE statement. We use FROM for clarity.

2. It then interrogates System R about the results it can expect from that SELECT, using another "dynamic" statement called DESCRIBE.

3. Next, it makes available a set of target variables to receive the results in accordance with what it has just learned from DESCRIBE.

4. Finally, it uses OPEN, FETCH, and CLOSE to retrieve the result records one at a time, supplying an INTO clause on the FETCH (since it was not specified in the SELECT).

We make the process just outlined slightly more concrete by sketching a PL/I procedure to perform steps 1 through 4 in sequence (Fig. 8.4). The

```
DCL SQLSOURCE CHAR(100);

SQLSOURCE = 'SELECT * FROM SP WHERE QTY > 100';
$PREPARE SQLOBJ FROM SQLSOURCE;
$DESCRIBE SQLOBJ INTO D;

   /* D is a PL/I pointer that designates a structure */
   /* that will be filled in by DESCRIBE. After the   */
   /* DESCRIBE, the structure contains the following  */
   /* information (slightly simplified):              */
   /*    number of fields SELECTed;                   */
   /*    for each field -                             */
   /*         data-type                               */
   /*         length                                  */
   /* Using the information returned by DESCRIBE, the */
   /* program can allocate a target variable for each */
   /* field to be returned, using (e.g.) the normal   */
   /* PL/I storage allocation facilities. The program */
   /* then builds another structure, giving the       */
   /* following information (slightly simplified):     */
   /*    for each target variable -                   */
   /*         data-type                               */
   /*         length                                  */
   /*         address                                 */
   /* The program sets a pointer, say pointer E, to   */
   /* point to this structure.                        */

$OPEN SQLOBJ;
   DO WHILE more-to-come;
     $FETCH SQLOBJ INTO E;
     /* Note that E identifies a description of the   */
     /* INTO variables, not the variables themselves. */
     .......
   END;
```

Fig. 8.4 Handling a dynamic SELECT.

specific SELECT shown and the names SQLSOURCE, SQLOBJ, D, and E are all arbitrary. Note that OPEN and FETCH are used against the prepared SELECT, just as if it were a cursor.

Dynamically generated statements cannot contain "$-references." However, they can contain *parameters,* denoted in the character string representation of the statement by question marks. Parameters can appear wherever "$-references" can appear. For example,

```
SQLSOURCE = 'DELETE SP WHERE QTY > ? AND QTY < ?';
$PREPARE SQLOBJ FROM SQLSOURCE;
```

Arguments to replace the parameters are specified when the dynamically prepared statement is executed; for example,

```
$EXECUTE SQLOBJ USING $LOW, $HIGH;
```

Arguments and parameters are matched by their ordinal position. Thus, in the example, the DELETE that is actually executed is equivalent to

```
$DELETE SP WHERE QTY > $LOW AND QTY < $HIGH;
```

As usual, SELECT requires special treatment. If the prepared statement is a SELECT—for example,

```
SQLSOURCE = 'SELECT * FROM SP WHERE QTY > ? AND QTY < ?';
$PREPARE SQLOBJ FROM SQLSOURCE;
```

then arguments are specified on the OPEN (remember that EXECUTE is not used in this case)—for example,

```
$OPEN SQLOBJ USING $LOW, $HIGH;
```

8.5 DISCUSSION

We conclude our discussion of embedded SQL by offering a number of observations on the System R approach to database application programming.

1. The use of essentially the same language for both on-line access via UFI and access from application programs has a number of advantages. For one thing, it greatly eases communication between UFI users and application programmers. For another, it provides a convenient program development and debugging tool; it is easy to generate simple test databases using UFI and to try out the database portions of the program—at least the noncursor operations—at the terminal. Moreover, the language is essentially the same regardless of whether the host is PL/I or COBOL.

2. The fact that System R database requests—i.e., SQL statements—are compiled (or, rather, precompiled) means that System R can have a significant run-time performance advantage over systems that adopt a more conventional interpretive approach [8.1, 8.2]. The operations of analyzing the request, binding source-level names to internal system identifiers, selecting access paths (optimization), and checking authorization can all be performed at precompilation time, and can thus be removed from the run-time path. (The run-time path is the sequence of instructions needed to perform the actual database operations at execution time.) Since the run-time path must be executed on every request, and such requests frequently occur within program loops, the savings can be considerable.

3. Even in the case of dynamically constructed statements, where everything is necessarily in the run-time path, the compilation approach can still pay off. This is because the generated code is tailored to the specific request instead of being generalized (and thus partly interpretive). In fact, it is claimed that compilation is faster than interpretation as soon as it becomes necessary to access more than some fairly small number of stored records in the database [8.1].

4. A disadvantage of SQL as an application programming language is that it is only very loosely coupled to the host. In fact, of course, it is a totally different language. SQL objects (e.g., tables, fields, cursors) are not known and cannot be referenced in the host environment; and host objects can be referenced in the SQL environment only in an ad hoc manner ("$-references"). The rules for such things as name formation, name resolution, name qualification, expression evaluation, and so forth all change slightly as the programmer crosses the boundary between SQL and the host. Perhaps more significant, SQL does not take advantage of constructs that already exist in the host language for such things as loop control, data structures, exception handling, and argument passing. As a consequence, SQL programs tend to be rather unstructured and not very concise.

EXERCISES

8.1 Using the suppliers-parts-projects database, write a program with embedded SQL statements to list all supplier records in supplier number order. Each supplier record should be immediately followed in the listing by all part records for parts supplied by that supplier in part number order.

8.2 Why do you think the FOR UPDATE clause is required?

8.3 Given the table

COMPONENT (MAJORP#, MINORP#, QTY)

(compare Fig. 4.4), write a SQL program to list all component parts of a given part to all levels (the "parts explosion" problem).

8.4 What do you think should happen if a FETCH or singleton SELECT attempts to retrieve a null value?

REFERENCES AND BIBLIOGRAPHY

8.1 R. A. Lorie and B. W. Wade. "The Compilation of a Very High Level Data Language." IBM Research Report RJ2008 (May 1977).

Describes the precompilation approach.

8.2 D. D. Chamberlin et al. "Support for Repetitive Transactions and Ad-Hoc Query in System R." IBM Research Report RJ2551 (May 1979).

Gives more details of the precompiler and some information on performance.

8.3 R. A. Lorie and J. F. Nilsson. "An Access Specification Language for a Relational Data Base System." *IBM J. R & D.* **23**, No. 3 (May 1979).

For any given SQL statement, the optimizer component of the RDS generates a program in an internal language called ASL (Access Specification Language). This language serves as the interface between the optimizer and the code generator, which converts an ASL program into machine code (including calls on the RSS). ASL consists of operators such as "scan" and "insert" on objects such as indexes and stored files. ASL makes the total translation process more manageable, by breaking it down into well-defined subprocesses.

8.4 P. G. Selinger, M. M. Astrahan, D. D. Chamberlin, R. A. Lorie, and T. G. Price. "Access Path Selection in a Relational Database System." *Proc. 1979 ACM SIGMOD International Conference on Management of Data* (May 1979).

Gives details of the optimizer.

9

The External
Level of
System R

9.1 INTRODUCTION

At the external level of the ANSI/SPARC architecture, the database is perceived as an "external view," defined by an external schema. Different users can have different external views. As we explained in Chapter 5, however, the term *view* is reserved in System R to mean a *derived table* (as opposed to a base table); the System R version of an ANSI/SPARC "external view" is thus, typically, a collection of tables, some of them base tables and some of them views. The "external schema" consists of definitions of those base tables and views. In this chapter we examine the System R view construct in some detail.

The ANSI/SPARC framework is very general and allows for great variability between the external and conceptual levels. In principle even the *types* of data structure supported at the two levels could be different; for example, the conceptual level could be based on *n*-ary relations, while a given user could have an external view of the database as a hierarchy. In practice, however, most implemented systems use the same structure type as the basis for both levels, and System R is no exception—a view is still a table, like a base table. And since the same type of object is supported at both levels, the same manipulative language (i.e., the SQL DML) applies to both levels also.

9.2 VIEWS

A view may be thought of as a *virtual* table, that is, a table that does not really exist in its own right but is instead derived from one or more underlying base tables. In other words, there is no stored file that directly represents the view per se. Instead, a *definition* of the view is stored in the dictionary. The view definition shows how the view is derived from the underlying base tables.

In principle, any derivable table can be defined as a view. The derivation process might involve projecting some base table over certain fields, or joining two base tables together, or indeed performing any sequence of projections, joins, and similar operations on any collection of base tables. A view is created by executing the SQL DDL statement DEFINE VIEW, which takes the general form[1],

```
DEFINE VIEW   view-name
           [ ( field-name [ , field-name ] ... ) ]
             AS  SELECT-statement
```

For example,

```
DEFINE VIEW   LONDON_SUPPLIERS
           AS   SELECT S#, SNAME, STATUS
                FROM   S
                WHERE  CITY = 'LONDON'
```

This example defines a view that is a projection of a horizontal subset of the base table S. The view is called LONDON_SUPPLIERS, and has three fields, with names S#, SNAME, and STATUS inherited from the names in table S. We could if we liked have given the fields new names by specifying "(LS#, LSNAME, LSTAT)", say, after the view-name LONDON_SUPPLIERS in the DEFINE VIEW. Field-names *must* be specified if the inherited names are not unique—for example, if the view is a join of two tables and those tables have some field-names in common—or if some selected "field" is the result of an arithmetic expression or a built-in function. We give an example of each of these cases.

```
DEFINE VIEW   CITY_PAIRS ( SCITY, PCITY )
           AS   SELECT UNIQUE S.CITY, P.CITY
                FROM   S, SP, P
                WHERE  S.S# = SP.S#
                AND    SP.P# = P.P#

DEFINE VIEW   PQ ( P#, SUMQTY )
           AS   SELECT P#, SUM(QTY)
                FROM   SP
                GROUP  BY P#
```

---

1. In ANSI/SPARC terms, DEFINE VIEW combines the external schema function (describing the external object) and the mapping definition function (specifying the mapping to the conceptual level).

The SELECT statement in a view definition cannot include ORDER BY, nor can it contain references to program variables ("$-references").

Once a view is defined, the user can go on to use it just as if it were a real base table, subject to certain constraints (to be discussed). For example,

```
SELECT  *
FROM    LONDON_SUPPLIERS
WHERE   STATUS < 50
ORDER   BY S#
```

Successful execution of a DEFINE VIEW statement causes the view definition to be stored away in the System R dictionary. The SELECT statement within that definition is *not* executed at this time. Instead, what happens is that when the user does a SELECT (or UPDATE or DELETE) against the view, that operation and the SELECT in the view definition are *combined* to form a modified statement that operates on the underlying data.[2] For example, the SELECT statement above will be combined with the definition of LONDON_SUPPLIERS to produce

```
SELECT  S#, SNAME, STATUS
FROM    S
WHERE   STATUS < 50
AND     CITY = 'LONDON'
ORDER   BY S#
```

The modified statement is then processed in the normal way.

Since view definitions are expressed by means of SELECT statements, and SELECT statements can select data from views as well as base tables, it is possible to define one view in terms of others. For example,

```
DEFINE VIEW  LONDON_NAMES
             AS   SELECT SNAME
                  FROM    LONDON_SUPPLIERS
```

It is also possible to drop an existing view at any time:

```
DROP VIEW   view-name
```

The definition of the view is removed from the dictionary. The underlying base tables are not affected in any way; but if any other views are defined in terms of this view, then they will automatically be dropped too. Likewise, if a base table is dropped, all views defined on it are also dropped automatically.

---

2. The combination process is performed by the RDS precompiler prior to the optimization step.

We conclude this section by noting that, in System R, fields in a view inherit their data-type from the underlying base table. Field STATUS of LONDON_SUPPLIERS, for example, has data-type SMALLINT, as in table S. A more general mechanism would permit view fields to have data-types that differ from those in the base table.

9.3 DML OPERATIONS ON VIEWS

A view is a "window" on the real data, not a separate copy of that data. Changes to the real data are visible through the view; and, as we explained in the previous section, operations against the view are converted into operations on the real data. For SELECT operations, such a conversion is always possible; that is, the statement that a view can be any derivable table is certainly true so far as retrieval is concerned. But the situation is different for update operations, as we now explain.

In System R, a view that is to accept updates must be derived from a single base table. Moreover, it must satisfy the following constraints.

C1. Each distinct row of the view must correspond to a distinct and uniquely identifiable row of the base table.

C2. Each distinct column of the view must correspond to a distinct and uniquely identifiable column of the base table.

In other words, the only differences permitted between the view and the base table are that in the view, (a) individual rows (those not satisfying the defining predicate) can be omitted, and/or (b) individual columns can be omitted. The view *cannot* be a genuine projection (with duplicates eliminated), nor a join, nor a union; also, it cannot involve GROUP BY, and it cannot contain computed fields.[3]

It should be clear that, if a view does satisfy constraints C1 and C2, then any update against it can easily be mapped into an update on the corresponding base table; in other words, such views are "updatable." To show the converse—that views violating C1 and C2 are not updatable and that therefore the constraints are reasonable—we consider some examples.

Example 1

```
DEFINE VIEW  V1  AS
        SELECT UNIQUE COLOR, CITY
        FROM    P
```

---

3. An exception to these constraints is that DELETE operations are allowed on a view that includes computed fields (violating C2 but not C1), and UPDATE operations are allowed on the other (noncomputed) fields in such a view.

V1 is a projection of table P, with duplicates eliminated. If table P is as given in Fig. 4.7, the value (extension) of V1—that is, the subset of P visible via V1—is as shown in Fig. 9.1. Alongside each row of this extension we show the P# value(s) corresponding to that row.

V1	COLOR	CITY	
	Red	London	P1, P4, P6
	Green	Paris	P2
	Blue	Rome	P3
	Blue	Paris	P5

Fig. 9.1 Extension of view V1.

It should be clear that V1 cannot support INSERT operations. (Insertions on the underlying table P require the user to specify a P# value.) DELETE and UPDATE operations could theoretically be defined (to delete or update *all* corresponding rows in P), but those operations could equally well be expressed directly in terms of P anyway, or at least a view of P that does include P#; and a user who is updating or deleting parts should probably be interested in exactly which parts are affected.

Example 2

```
DEFINE VIEW   V2   AS
         SELECT P#, CITY
         FROM    SP, S
         WHERE   SP.S# = S.S#
```

V2 involves a join of tables SP and S over S#. The extension corresponding to Fig. 4.7 is shown in Fig. 9.2; S# values corresponding to each row are shown alongside.

V2 cannot support any update operations at all. Inserting a new (P#, CITY) pair would involve the insertion of a new SP row, for which an S# value is required. Deleting a (P#, CITY) pair would require the deletion of some SP row, but which one is not always clear; for example, the pair (P2, Paris) might correspond to either S2 or S3. Updating a (P#, CITY) pair—say, changing (P2, Paris) to (P2, London)—might mean either that the supplier concerned (which one?) has changed location, or that the part is now supplied by a different supplier (again, which one?). The situation would be even worse if the SELECT in the DEFINE VIEW had specified UNIQUE.

V2	P#	CITY				
	P1	London	S1	P1	Paris	S2
	P2	London	S1	P2	Paris	S2
	P3	London	S1	P2	Paris	S3
	P4	London	S1	P2	London	S4
	P5	London	S1	P4	London	S4
	P6	London	S1	P5	London	S4

Fig. 9.2 Extension of view V2.

Example 3

```
DEFINE VIEW  V3 ( P#, SUMQTY ) AS
      SELECT P#, SUM(QTY)
      FROM   SP
      GROUP  BY P#
```

V3 involves both GROUP BY and a built-in function. Without having to look at any extension, it should be obvious that INSERT cannot be handled; nor can UPDATE if it is the SUMQTY field that is to be changed. DELETE operations, and UPDATE operations on the P# field, *could* be defined (to delete or update *all* corresponding rows in SP), but the remarks under Example 1 on this topic apply again here.

Example 4

```
DEFINE VIEW  REDPARTS  AS
      SELECT P#, PNAME, WEIGHT, COLOR
      FROM   P
      WHERE  COLOR = 'RED'
```

REDPARTS does satisfy the constraints and is thus updatable.[4] However, it serves to illustrate three further points. First we show (in Fig. 9.3) the extension of REDPARTS corresponding to the tabulation of P in Fig. 4.7.

4. This statement would still be true even if P# were excluded from the view, since System R does not eliminate duplicate rows unless UNIQUE is specified. But it is not clear that users *should* be allowed to update such a view, since there is no guarantee that a given row in the view corresponds to any particular part—that is, the user is not able to specify exactly which part is to be updated. (See the comments on view V1 [Example 1]. V1 would also be updatable in System R if "UNIQUE" were omitted from the V1 definition.) It would be preferable to replace constraint C1 by a constraint that the view must include the primary key of the base table. Unfortunately, as we pointed out in Chapter 6, System R has no knowledge of keys.

REDPARTS

P#	PNAME	WEIGHT	COLOR
P1	Nut	12	Red
P4	Screw	14	Red
P6	Cog	19	Red

Fig. 9.3 Extension of view REDPARTS.

The first point is that a successful INSERT against REDPARTS will have to generate a null value for the missing field CITY (of course, this field must not have been defined with the NONULL option). Second, it appears from Fig. 9.3 that the user should be able to create a row via the view RED-PARTS that has a P# value of, say, P3, which is not a duplicate so far as the view is concerned but *is* a duplicate with respect to the underlying base table. Such an operation clearly cannot be allowed; it must be rejected, just as if it had been applied directly to table P.

Last, consider the following UPDATE:

```
UPDATE  REDPARTS
SET     COLOR = 'BLUE'
WHERE   P# = 'P1'
```

Should this UPDATE be accepted? If it is, it will have the effect of removing part P1 from the view, since it no longer satisfies the defining predicate. (On the other hand, checking every update via a view for such a violation could be very expensive.) In System R such updates *are* accepted and the record does vanish. Likewise, an INSERT on a view may be accepted even if the new record does not satisfy the view predicate, but the inserted record will not be visible through that view.

It is clear that the System R philosophy on the updating of views is rather ad hoc; there exist situations in which System R prohibits an update that theoretically could be supported. The difficulty is in stating precisely what those situations are. Various researchers have attempted to define a more systematic and precise set of rules [9.4, 9.5, 9.6]. Others have suggested that the system should not have any fixed rules but that the DBA (or whoever is responsible for defining views) should define the effect of each type of update on each view [9.7, 9.8]. Each of these approaches has its drawbacks. The System R approach of having a single, simple, fixed rule probably gains by its simplicity more than it loses by its slight lack of function—though, as we shall see in the next section, there are some situations in which the rule could profitably be relaxed a little.

9.4   VIEWS AND DATA INDEPENDENCE

In this section we consider the contribution made by views to the provision of data independence—not so much in System R specifically as in database systems in general, though we continue to use System R as an example where appropriate. As we suggested in Chapter 1, there are many levels of data independence. Separation of the conceptual and internal layers of the system provides one major level, namely, independence from physical storage details (sometimes called physical data independence). Similarly, the separation between the external and conceptual layers—the view mechanism, in System R—provides another major level, namely, independence from changes in the conceptual schema (sometimes called logical data independence [9.1]). We consider two broad classes of change that can occur in the conceptual schema: growth and restructuring.

Growth

As the scope of the database grows—that is, as new types of information are added to it—so the conceptual schema must grow accordingly. There are two possible types of growth that can occur in the conceptual schema:

1. The expansion of an existing base table to include a new field (corresponding to the addition of new information concerning an existing type of entity); and

2. The inclusion of a new base table (corresponding to the addition of a new type of entity).

Neither of these changes should have any effect on existing views, however; by definition, those views can contain no reference to the new fields or tables.[5] Thus the view mechanism can insulate users from the effects of growth in the database. We refer to this insulation—possibly the single most important aspect of data independence—as *immunity to growth*.

Restructuring

Occasionally it becomes necessary to restructure the conceptual schema in such a way that, although the overall information content remains the same, the placement of information within the schema does change—that is, the allocation of fields to tables is altered. Such restructuring is generally troublesome but sometimes desirable. One important class of restructuring, and the only one that we discuss (but see Exercise 9.4), is the replacement of a given table by two of its projections, in such a way that the original table

---

5. Actually, most SQL statements are impervious to such changes, even if directed at base tables rather than views, *except* for the case of "SELECT * " (the meaning of which can change if the table concerned acquires a new field).

can be recovered by taking a join of those projections. For example, the supplier table S might be replaced by the following two tables:

```
SX (S#, SNAME, CITY)
SY (S#, STATUS)
```

(The original table S is the natural join of SX and SY over S#. One possible reason for the change could be to simplify authorization control.) What effect will this change have on existing users? The answer so far as retrieval is concerned will be *none,* if we define the old table S as a *view* as follows:

```
DEFINE VIEW  S (S#, SNAME, STATUS, CITY) AS
        SELECT SX.S#, SNAME, STATUS, CITY
        FROM   SX, SY
        WHERE  SX.S# = SY.S#
```

Then any existing SELECT operation on S will continue to work exactly as before (although it will require additional analysis during precompilation and additional run-time overhead). However, as we explained in Section 9.3, update operations on S will no longer work (in other words, a user performing updates is not immune to this type of change)—although, as a matter of fact, the restrictions on updating views could be relaxed in this case, since there is a one-to-one correspondence between table SX and table SY, and the effect of all possible updates on S is clearly defined in terms of SX and SY. (Do you agree with this statement?)

As another example, suppose the database originally included the table

```
SPT (S#, P#, QTY, STATUS)
```

(probably not a very good design, as we shall see in Chapter 14, but the designer must be allowed to make mistakes sometimes), and suppose that SPT is subsequently replaced by its two projections

```
SP (S#, P#, QTY)
ST (S#, STATUS)
```

Again the original table SPT can be defined as a view, obtained by joining the new tables SP and ST over S#, and again retrieval operations will still work. This time, however, the two projections are not in one-to-one correspondence with each other, and there is no chance of automatically handling arbitrary updates expressed in terms of SPT.

9.5 SUMMARY

We conclude this chapter by summarizing in general terms the advantages of separating the individual user's view of the data (defined by an external schema) from the community view (defined by the conceptual schema).

Most of these points apply to any system that includes this separation, not just to System R.

- Users are immune to growth in the database.
- Users may be immune to restructuring in the database.
- The user's perception is simplified.

It is obvious that the external schema allows the user to focus on just the data that is of concern to that user. What is perhaps not so obvious is that, for retrieval at least, the external schema can also considerably simplify the user's DML operations. In particular, because the user can be provided with a view in which all underlying tables are joined together, the need for DML operations to step from table to table is greatly reduced. As an example, consider view V2 of Section 9.3, and contrast the SELECT needed to find part numbers for parts available from London using that view with the SELECT needed to obtain the same result from the underlying base tables. In effect the complex selection process is moved out of the DML and into the DDL (though the distinction between the two is rather blurred in a language like SQL).

- The same data can be viewed by different users in different ways.

This consideration is important when there are many different categories of user all interacting with a single integrated database.

- Automatic security is provided for hidden data.

"Hidden data" refers to tables and fields not included in the external schema. Such data should clearly be secure from all access by users of that particular schema. Thus forcing users to access the database via an external schema is a simple but effective mechanism for authorization control.

EXERCISES

9.1 Define relation SP (Fig. 4.8) as a System R view of relation SPJ (see Exercise 6.2).

9.2 Design a mechanism for defining *hierarchical* external views, given a relational conceptual schema.

9.3 In order to be able to accept updates, relations at the external level are generally required to be essentially the same as the corresponding relation at the conceptual level. Interpret this constraint for the case of a hierarchical external view (defined, again, in terms of a relational conceptual schema).

9.4 Suppose the conceptual schema is restructured in such a way that relations A and B are replaced by their natural join C. To what extent can the view mechanism conceal this restructuring from existing users?

REFERENCES AND BIBLIOGRAPHY

9.1 C. J. Date and P. Hopewell. "File Definition and Logical Data Independence." *Proc. 1971 ACM SIGFIDET Workshop on Data Description, Access and Control.*

This paper presents a number of ideas similar to those in this chapter in a somewhat different form.

9.2 E. F. Codd. "Recent Investigations into Relational Data Base Systems." *Proc. IFIP Congress 1974.* Also in *Proc. ACM Pacific Conference, San Francisco* (April 1975), available from ACM Golden Gate Chapter, P.O. Box 24055, Oakland, California 94623.

Includes a preliminary discussion of a theory for multiple view support. The other topics discussed are "Boyce/Codd Normal Form" (see Chapter 14), data sublanguages, data exchange, and needed investigations. The most urgent "needed investigations" are said to be (paraphrasing):

1. Development of concurrency control techniques;

2. Ascertaining the performance attainable on really large relational systems with concurrent access and update;

3. Development of a theory of views;

4. Development of storage, access, and update theory; and

5. Development of the viability of RENDEZVOUS-like subsystems [7.3–7.5].

9.3 D. D. Chamberlin, J. N. Gray, and I. L. Traiger. "Views, Authorization, and Locking in a Relational Data Base System." *Proc. NCC* **44** (May 1975).

Includes a brief rationale for the overall approach to view updating in System R.

9.4 S. J. P. Todd. "Automatic Constraint Maintenance and Updating Defined Relations." *Proc. IFIP Congress 1977.*

9.5 U. Dayal and P. A. Bernstein. "On the Updatability of Relational Views." Aiken Computation Laboratory, Harvard University, Cambridge, Mass. 02136 (1978).

9.6 A. L. Furtado and K. C. Sevcik. "Permitting Updates Through Views of Data Bases." Departamento de Informatica, Pontificia Universidade Catolica, Rio de Janeiro, Brazil (1977).

9.7 K. C. Sevcik and A. L. Furtado. "Complete and Compatible Sets of Update Operations." Departamento de Informatica, Pontificia Universidade Catolica, Rio de Janeiro, Brazil (1977).

9.8 A. L. Furtado. "A View Construct for the Specification of External Schemas." Departamento de Informatica, Pontificia Universidade Catolica, Rio de Janeiro, Brazil (1978).

10
The Internal
Level of
System R

10.1 THE RESEARCH STORAGE SYSTEM

The Research Storage System (RSS) is the System R access method or storage subsystem. It supports the stored form of a SQL base table, which we refer to as a stored file (the RSS calls it simply a relation or table). It is always possible to access a stored file in "system" (RSS-defined) sequence; in addition, any number of indexes may be defined over any given stored file, thus providing additional access paths to that file.[1] These RSS objects (stored files, indexes, etc.) and the associated operators together constitute the Research Storage Interface, or RSI, which is the interface used as the target by the RDS in precompiling SQL requests. In this chapter we shall take a closer look at the RSI in order to give some idea as to what must go on "under the covers" of a working system. However, our discussion is very much simplified and we intentionally omit a great deal of low-level detail.

In addition to the functions outlined here, the RSS also provides support for concurrency control, transaction management, and system checkpoint/restart. References [5.1, 5.3] give details.

---

1. The RSS also provides another type of access path called a *link,* but links are not currently used by the RDS. Links in the RSS are basically pointer chains as described in Chapter 2; that is, a link is a mechanism for chaining together a record of one type and a set of related records of another type.

10.2 SEGMENTS AND PAGES

The stored database is logically divided into a set of disjoint *segments*. Each segment consists of an integral number of 4096-byte *pages* (the number of pages in a given segment varies dynamically, as we shall see). The page is the unit of transfer between the database and primary storage. When a page is required from the database, the RSS fetches it into a slot within a main storage buffer that is shared among all current users, and returns the address of that slot to the component requesting the page. Using a single fixed-size page as the unit for all input/output simplifies buffer management and provides a clean interface for device independence [10.1].

Segments provide a basis for controlling the allocation of data objects to storage. As we explained in Chapter 6, any given base table (stored file), together with all indexes on that base table, must be wholly contained within a single segment. Any given page can contain either base-table data or index data, but not both. More significantly, a given base table (plus all its indexes) can be stored in a segment of the appropriate *type*. System R provides three different types of segment, with properties that are appropriate to public, private, and temporary data, respectively. Basically, data in *public* segments is recoverable and sharable; data in *private* segments is recoverable but not sharable; and data in *temporary* segments is neither recoverable nor sharable. (By "recoverable" we mean that the data will not be lost in the event of a failure; by "sharable" we mean that the data is concurrently available to multiple users.) Thus, for example, the overhead associated with full support of concurrent sharing, needed for public data, can be avoided for private and temporary data (which do not require such support). Note, however, that the type of a segment is fixed at the time of system installation and cannot be changed.

Each segment has a predetermined maximum size (usually very large), but at any given time occupies only as much physical storage as it actually needs for the data objects it currently contains. Pages are allocated to segments as necessary (e.g., when a table grows sufficiently large), and are released when the segment shrinks again (e.g., when an index is dropped). A *page map* is maintained for each segment, giving the physical location in secondary storage of each page currently allocated to the segment.

At the RSI, segments are identified by a numeric *segment identifier* or SID. Pages are identified by page number within segment. The symbolic segment-names used in CREATE TABLE and certain other SQL operations are mapped to SIDs by the RDS, using the System R dictionary. Pages are never directly referenced in SQL.

10.3 **FILES AND RECORDS**

Each base table is represented as a stored file. Like a segment, a stored file is identified at the RSI by a numeric identifier called an RID (R for relation). The RDS is responsible for mapping SQL table-names to RIDs.

Records in the stored file represent rows of the table. Each record is stored as a byte string. The byte string consists of a prefix (containing control information, such as the RID of the containing file), followed by the stored representation of each field in the record. For a variable-length field the stored representation includes an indication of the field length. (Note that all fields are considered simply as byte strings by the RSS; any interpretation of such a string as, for example, a floating-point number, is performed above the RSI by the RDS.)

Like segments and files, individual records have their own numeric identifier, called a TID (T for tuple). TIDs are the RSS equivalent of the stored record address (SRA) discussed in Chapter 2; they are used within the RSS to build indexes (and links), and are also exposed at the RSI so that the "user"—normally compiled code generated by the RDS—can obtain fast access to specific records (by specifying the TIDs of those records). They are *not* exposed in SQL. Figure 10.1 shows how TIDs are implemented.

The TID for a record R consists of two parts: the page number of the page P containing R, and a byte offset from the bottom of P identifying a slot that contains, in turn, the byte offset of R from the top of P. This scheme represents a good compromise between the speed of direct addressing and the flexibility of indirection: Records can be rearranged within their page—e.g., to close up the gap when a record is deleted—without hav-

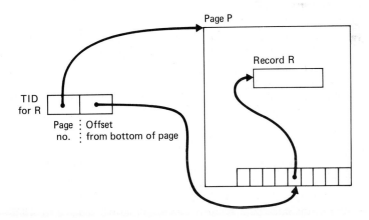

Fig. 10.1 Implementation of TIDs.

ing to change TIDs (only the local offsets at the bottom of the page must be changed); yet access to a record given the TID is fast, involving only a single page access.[2]

Note, incidentally, that RIDs and TIDs are unique only within their containing segment.

RSI operations on records include the following.

- FETCH sid tid field-list target-list

The specified fields of the record identified by "sid" and "tid" are fetched into the specified target locations.

- INSERT sid rid source-list [tid]

A record is created in the file specified by "sid" and "rid," taking its field values from the specified source locations. An attempt is made to place the new record near the record identified by "tid" (if specified); thus it is possible to arrange for records that are frequently used together (e.g., a department and its employees) to be stored close together. The TID for the new record is returned.

- DELETE sid tid

The record specified by "sid" and "tid" is deleted.

- UPDATE sid tid field-list source-list

The specified fields of the record identified by "sid" and "tid" are updated, taking their new values from the specified source locations.

10.4   ACCESS PATHS

It is always possible to access a record *directly* by its TID, as explained in Section 10.3. However, it is often necessary to access records *sequentially* (according to some particular ordering), or directly by value rather than by TID. The RSS provides three types of access path to support such requirements: "system sequence," indexes, and links. In this section we discuss only the "system" and index cases.

---

2. In rare cases it might involve two page accesses (but never more than two). This can happen if a record is updated such that it is longer than before (e.g., the value in some variable-length field has expanded), and there is not enough free space on the page to accommodate the increase. In such a situation, the updated record is placed on another ("overflow") page, and the original record is replaced by a pointer to the new location. If the same thing happens again, so that the updated record must be moved to still a third page, the pointer record in the original page is changed to point to this newest location.

System Sequence

Every stored file has a system sequence. Initially (i.e., just after the file is first loaded), system sequence is the same as "chronological" sequence—in other words, it is the sequence in which the records of the file were created. However, system sequence will gradually diverge from chronological sequence as subsequent changes (insertions and deletions) are made to the file.

To perform an exhaustive search on a file according to system sequence, the RSS will look in turn at every data page (as opposed to index page) in the segment that contains the file. For each such page, it will examine each record on the page, inspecting the prefix to see if that record belongs to the file in question. (A given page can contain records from several different files.) Thus each data page in the segment will be accessed exactly once in the search. The sequence in which records are returned will appear random to the user, in general.

Indexes

Any stored file may have an arbitrary number of additional sequences imposed on it by means of appropriate indexes. A given index defines an ordering for the underlying file in terms of values of one or more fields in that file. Ascending or descending sequence may be specified separately for each indexed field within a given index. (A special encoding scheme is used so that, regardless of how many fields are indexed by a given index and regardless of whether any of those fields are variable-length, the index behaves as if it were on a single, fixed-length field [10.2]. The advantage of this scheme is that it greatly speeds up the fundamental comparison operation on which all uses of the index are based.)

Internally, indexes are organized as *B*-trees (see Chapter 2), with each block of the index occupying one page in storage (this is why a page can be either a data page or an index page but not both). The index pages are in the same segment as the data pages of the indexed file.

At the RSI, indexes are identified by a numeric index identifier (IID); the index-name specified in the SQL DDL statements CREATE INDEX and DROP INDEX is mapped to an IID by the RDS.

To perform an exhaustive search on a file according to a given index, the RSS will access all records in the file in the sequence defined by that index. Since this sequence may be quite different from the system sequence, individual data pages may be accessed many times. (On the other hand, data pages not containing any records of the file will not be accessed at all, even though they are in the same segment.) Thus exhaustive search via an index could potentially be much slower than exhaustive search using system sequence, *unless* the index concerned is a "clustering" index. A clustering index is one for which the sequence defined by the index *is* the same as, or close to, the system sequence. A clustering index can be created for a given stored file only at the time that file is initially loaded; moreover, records of the file must be presented for loading in the sequence corresponding to that index (since their order of presentation determines the initial system sequence). Clustering indexes are important to the RDS in its process of optimization.

An index can also provide direct access to records by values of the indexed field(s). (Sequential search must be used to simulate this function in the absence of a suitable index.) The RSI operation for direct *retrieval* by value is as follows.

- `FETCH sid rid iid value-list field-list target-list`

The parameters "sid" and "rid" identify a file, and "iid" identifies an index on that file (on certain fields). The fields specified by "field-list" are fetched into the locations specified by "target-list" from the record having the values specified by "value-list" for the indexed fields.

Operations to DELETE and UPDATE by value are analogously defined.

Scans

We have now seen how to perform *direct* access by TID (Section 10.3) and by value (above). To perform *sequential* access we need another RSS object—the scan. Scans are similar to cursors in embedded SQL; in other words, they provide a means for moving through a set of records, one record at a time, in some particular sequence. At any given time, a scan designates a particular *access path* (e.g., a stored file, in system sequence) and a *position* along that path (e.g., a record within that file).

Scans are created and destroyed dynamically. Any number of scans can exist simultaneously. A scan is identified at the RSI by means of a unique SCANID.

The RSI operations involving scans are as follows.

- `OPEN sid pathid [ value-list ]`

The parameter "pathid" is either an RID or an IID. A scan is created for the file (using system sequence) or the index (using that index sequence), as appropriate. In the case of an index scan, values may optionally be specified for the indexed fields. The scan is positioned on the first record in the path, or the first record in the path having the specified values for the indexed fields (if applicable). The SCANID for the new scan is returned.

- NEXT scanid field-list target-list [predicate]

The scan identified by "scanid" is moved to the next record along its path that satisfies the predicate, and the specified fields of that record are fetched into the specified target locations. (The predicate is restricted to a simple Boolean combination of comparisons involving fields of the record-type concerned and program variables. If the predicate is omitted, the effect is as though a predicate of *true* were specified.) A parameter in the NEXT specifies whether the search is to start at the record on which the scan is currently positioned or at the next record along the path.

- DELETE scanid

The record identified by "scanid" is deleted.

- UPDATE scanid field-list source-list

The specified fields of the record identified by "scanid" are updated, taking their new values from the specified source locations.

- CLOSE scanid

The scan identified by "scanid" is destroyed.

10.5 AN EXAMPLE

We present an example to show in outline how the RDS might make use of the RSS operators in implementing a SQL statement. Consider the query "Find supplier numbers for suppliers in London who supply part P1," for which one possible SQL formulation is

```
SELECT  S#
FROM    S
WHERE   CITY = 'LONDON'
AND     S# IN
        (SELECT  S#
        FROM    SP
        WHERE   P# = 'P1')
```

Suppose that the database includes the following three indexes (for clarity we use symbolic rather than numeric identifiers):

- XSS (index on suppliers by supplier number);
- XSPS (index on shipments by supplier number);
- XSPP (index on shipments by part number).

We show two possible procedures for implementing the query (with numerous details elided). The RDS will choose one of these procedures, or possibly some other procedure, according to such criteria as the cardinality of the tables and its knowledge as to whether any of the indexes is a clustering index.

Procedure 1 For each London supplier, check to see whether there is a shipment for part P1.

```
OPEN scan on file S;
let returned SCANID be SCAN1;
DO while more-to-come on SCAN1;
   NEXT using SCAN1, CITY = 'LONDON'
                       fetch S# into W1;
   /* start search at ''current'' record on 1st iteration, */
   /* at ''next'' record on subsequent iterations          */
   IF found THEN
      DO;
          OPEN scan on index XSPS, S# = W1;
          let returned SCANID be SCAN2;
          NEXT using SCAN2, S# = W1, P# = 'P1';
          /* start search at ''current'' record */
          IF found THEN output W1;
          CLOSE scan SCAN2;
      END;
END;
CLOSE scan SCAN1;
```

Procedure 2 For each P1 shipment, check to see whether the supplier is located in London.

```
OPEN scan on index XSPP, P# = 'P1';
let returned SCANID be SCAN3;
DO while more-to-come on SCAN3;
   NEXT using SCAN3, P# = 'P1',
                     fetch S# into W2;
   /* start search at ''current'' record on 1st iteration, */
   /* at ''next'' record on subsequent iterations          */
   IF found THEN
      DO;
          OPEN scan on index XSS, S# = W2;
          let returned SCANID be SCAN4;
          NEXT using SCAN4, S# = W2, CITY = 'LONDON';
          /* start search at ''current'' record */
          IF found THEN output W2;
          CLOSE scan SCAN4;
      END;
END;
CLOSE scan SCAN3;
```

10.6   THE RSS DIRECTORY

Just as the RDS maintains the System R dictionary for objects defined at the SQL interface (base tables, views, etc.), so the RSS maintains an internal directory of the objects defined at the RSI (stored files, indexes, etc.). Using this directory, the RSS is able (for example) to locate all indexes for a given stored file, and is thus able to ensure that updates to that file are reflected in those indexes.

The directory is physically distributed across the segments of the database. Each segment includes a set of predefined tables (stored files) containing descriptions of the segment and all objects within that segment. Special RSI operators are provided to fetch, insert, delete, and update directory records. These operators (or at least the last three) are the RSS analogues of the DDL statements of SQL. For example, creating a new index involves the insertion of appropriate descriptor records into the directory; dropping the index involves the deletion of those records.

REFERENCES AND BIBLIOGRAPHY

Most of the material in this chapter is taken from [5.1] and [5.3].

10.1 R. A. Lorie. "Physical Integrity in a Large Segmented Database." *ACM Transactions on Database Systems* **2,** No. 1 (March 1977).

> This paper is concerned with the Storage Component of the RSS. The Storage Component is that component that is responsible for handling physical devices, providing other components with a view of the database in terms of segments and pages. As the title implies, the paper is primarily concerned with techniques for recovering the database after failure (when the failure damages either the database itself or the buffer in main storage). However, the paper also gives details of segments and pages per se.

10.2 M. W. Blasgen, R. G. Casey, and K. P. Eswaran. "An Encoding Method for Multifield Sorting and Indexing." *CACM* **20,** No. 11 (November 1977).

10.3 D. Bjørner, E. F. Codd, K. L. Deckert, and I. L. Traiger. "The GAMMA-0 *n*-ary Relational Data Base Interface: Specifications of Objects and Operations." IBM Research Report RJ1200 (April 1973).

> GAMMA-0 was a hypothetical low-level interface to a relational system (intended for use in the implementation of a higher-level language such as SQL). Although it was never implemented, many of its ideas were incorporated into the RSI.

10.4 R. A. Lorie. "XRM—An Extended (*n*-ary) Relational Memory." IBM Technical Report G320-2096 (January 1974).

XRM (another forerunner of the RSS) was used as the access method for the original SEQUEL prototype [5.7, 5.8]. XRM in turn was a development of an earlier system called RAM [10.5].

10.5 M. F. Crick and A. J. Symonds. "A Software Associative Memory for Complex Data Structures." IBM Technical Report G320-2060 (1972).

11
Query By Example

11.1 INTRODUCTION

In this chapter we examine another relational system, Query By Example (originally developed by M. M. Zloof at the IBM Yorktown Heights Research Laboratory [11.3–11.9], and now available from IBM as an "Installed User Program" running on the VM/CMS operating system [11.1, 11.2]). The name "Query By Example" (or QBE) is used to refer both to the system itself and to the user language the system supports, and we shall follow this practice, relying on context to make it clear which we mean. The functional level of QBE is approximately the same as that of SQL. But QBE differs from SQL in that it is specifically designed for use with a visual display terminal: Not only are results presented in the form of displayed tables (as with the User-Friendly Interface of System R), but all requests from the user are also specified by filling in tables on the screen. These tables are constructed partly by the system and partly by the user (we shall examine this process in slightly more detail below). Since operations are specified in tabular form, we say that QBE has a *two-dimensional syntax*. Most traditional computer languages, by contrast, have a linear syntax.[1]

Like SQL, QBE has undergone a certain amount of usability testing, with very encouraging results [11.11, 11.12].

The name "Query By Example" derives from the fact that *examples* are used in the specification of queries (and also in most other operations;

---

1. Although intended primarily for interactive use, QBE can be invoked via a subroutine call interface from PL/I and APL. For this purpose a linear version of the QBE syntax has been defined [11.2]. But the linear syntax is not nearly so appealing as the two-dimensional form.

for the moment we consider retrieval only). The basic idea is that the user formulates the query by entering an example of a possible answer in the appropriate place in an empty table. For example, consider the query "Get supplier numbers for suppliers in Paris." First, by pressing a certain *function key* on the terminal, the user can have a blank "skeleton" table displayed on the screen. Then, knowing that the answer to the query can be found in table S, the user enters S as the table-name, and, in a manner to be described (Example 11.6.2), gets QBE to respond by filling in the column-names for S. Now the user can express the query by making entries in two positions in this table, as follows.

S	S#	SNAME	STATUS	CITY
	P.S7			PARIS

The "P." stands for "print"; it indicates the target of the query, i.e., the values that are to appear in the result. S7 is an "example element," i.e., an example of a possible answer to the query; example elements are indicated by underlining. PARIS (not underlined) is a "constant element." The query may be paraphrased: "Print all S# values, such as S7 (say), where the corresponding city is Paris." Note that S7 need not actually appear in the resulting set, or even in the original set; the example element is completely arbitrary, and we could have equally well used PIG, 7, or X without changing the meaning of the query.[2]

Later we shall see that example elements are used to establish links between rows in more complicated queries. If no links are necessary, as in the simple query above, it is possible to omit example elements entirely (so that "P.S7" would reduce to just "P."), but for clarity we shall generally include them.

We now present the major features of the QBE language by means of a number of examples. We treat DML operations before DDL operations because, as we shall see, the DDL operations are essentially special cases of the DML operations. The language as originally defined [11.3] includes certain features that are not supported in the IBM implementation; we ignore most of these features in this chapter. (We should also point out that the IBM implementation includes certain additional features, especially in the realm of authorization, which we do not discuss here.)

---

2. The IBM implementation of QBE uses a single prefix underscore character rather than underlining to indicate an example element (e.g., S7 appears as _S7).

11.2 RETRIEVAL OPERATIONS

11.2.1 Simple retrieval Get part numbers for all parts supplied. (Example 7.2.1)

SP	S#	P#	QTY
		P.P̲X̲	

Unlike SQL, QBE automatically eliminates redundant duplicates from a query result. To suppress such elimination, the user can specify the keyword "ALL." (QBE operators always terminate in a period). For example,

SP	S#	P#	QTY
		P.ALL.P̲X̲	

Incidentally if a column is too narrow on the screen to contain the entry desired, the user can widen it first by means of another function key. Function keys are also provided to add columns, add rows, delete columns, delete rows, and so on.

11.2.2 Simple retrieval Get full details of all suppliers. (Example 7.2.2)

S	S#	SNAME	STATUS	CITY
	P.S̲X̲	P.S̲N̲	P.S̲T̲	P.S̲C̲

The following is a shorthand representation of the same query.

S	S#	SNAME	STATUS	CITY
P.				

Here the print operator is applied to the entire row.

11.2.3 Qualified retrieval Get supplier numbers for suppliers in Paris with status > 20. (Example 7.2.3)

S	S#	SNAME	STATUS	CITY
	P.S̲X̲		> 20	PARIS

Observe how the condition "status > 20" is specified. In general, any of the comparison operators =, ¬=, <, <=, >, >= can be used in this way (except that = is normally omitted, as in the CITY column above, and ¬= is usually abbreviated to simply ¬). Also, any of these operators can be preceded by "P." if we desire to print the value concerned. For example, we could have specified "P. > 20" under STATUS above, if we had wanted to print the status values too.

11.2.4 Qualified retrieval Get supplier numbers for suppliers who are located in Paris or have status > 20 (or both).

S	S#	SNAME	STATUS	CITY
	P.SX			PARIS
	P.SY		> 20	

Conditions specified within a single row are considered to be "ANDed" together. To "OR" two conditions, therefore, it is necessary to specify them in separate rows. The query above is effectively asking for the *union* of all supplier numbers SX for suppliers in Paris and all supplier numbers SY with status > 20. Two different example elements are needed, because if we had used the same one twice it would have meant that the *same* supplier had to be in Paris and to have status > 20.

When a query involves more than one row, as in the present example, the rows may be entered in any order.

11.2.5 Qualified retrieval Get supplier numbers for suppliers who supply both part P1 and part P2.

SP	S#	P#	QTY
	P.SX	P1	
	SX	P2	

Here the same example element *must* be used twice; we need two rows to express the query because we need to "AND" together two conditions on the same column.

11.2.6 Retrieval with ordering Get supplier numbers and status for suppliers in Paris, in descending order of status. (Example 7.2.4)

S	S#	SNAME	STATUS	CITY
	P.SX		P.DO.ST	PARIS

The "DO." stands for "descending order." "AO." is used for ascending order. When ordering is required in terms of several fields, then the major field is indicated by "AO(1)." [or "DO(1)."], the next by "AO(2)." [or "DO(2)."], and so on.

11.2.7 Retrieval using a link   Get supplier names for suppliers who supply part P2. (Examples 7.2.7, 7.2.9, 7.2.11, and 7.2.16)

S	S#	SNAME	STATUS	CITY
	SX	P.SN		

SP	S#	P#	QTY
	SX	P2	

The example element SX is used as a link between S and SP. The query may be paraphrased: "Print supplier names (such as SN) where the corresponding supplier number, say SX, appears in the SP table matched with part number P2." Generally speaking, links are used in QBE where SQL would use a nested SELECT or an existential quantifier, or where the algebra would use a join. As a matter of fact, SX in Example 11.2.5 was also acting as a link, but the rows being linked were in the same table.

11.2.8 Retrieval using links   Get supplier names for suppliers who supply at least one red part. (Example 7.2.10)

S	S#	SNAME	STATUS	CITY
	SX	P.SN		

SP	S#	P#	QTY
	SX	PX	

P	P#	PNAME	COLOR	WEIGHT	CITY
	PX		RED		

11.2.9 Retrieval using negation   Get supplier names for suppliers who do not supply part P2. (Examples 7.2.14 and 7.2.17)

S	S#	SNAME	STATUS	CITY
	SX	P.SN		

SP	S#	P#	QTY
¬	SX	P2	

Notice the NOT operator (¬) against the query row in table SP. The query may be paraphrased: "Print supplier names for suppliers SX such that it is not the case that SX supplies part P2."

11.2.10 Retrieval using a link within a single table Get supplier numbers for suppliers who supply at least one part supplied by supplier S2. (Example 7.2.12; compare also Example 11.2.5)

SP	S#	P#	QTY
	P.SX	PX	
	S2	PX	

11.2.11 Retrieval using a link within a single table Get part numbers for all parts supplied by more than one supplier. (Examples 7.2.13 and 7.3.7)

SP	S#	P#	QTY
	SX	P.PX	
	¬ SX	PX	

This query may be paraphrased: "Print part numbers PX such that PX is supplied by some supplier SX and also by some supplier distinct from SX."

11.2.12 Retrieval from more than one table For each part supplied, get part number and names of all cities supplying the part. (Example 7.2.5)

The result of this query is not a projection of an existing table; rather, it is a projection of a join of two existing tables. In order to formulate such a query in Query By Example, the user must first create a skeleton table the same shape as the expected result (i.e., with the appropriate number of columns). This table and its columns may be given any names that the user desires—they may even be left unnamed. The user can then express the query using the "result" table and the two existing tables, as follows.

S	S#	SNAME	STATUS	CITY
	SX			SC

SP	S#	P#	QTY
	SX	PX	

RESULT	P#	CITY
	P.PX	P.SC

11.2.13 Retrieval using the condition box Get all pairs of supplier numbers such that the two suppliers are located in the same city. (Example 7.2.6)

S	S#	SNAME	STATUS	CITY
	SX			CZ
	SY			CZ

RESULT	FIRST	SECOND
P.	SX	SY

CONDITIONS
SX < SY

Occasionally it is difficult to express some desired condition within the framework of the query table(s). In such a situation, QBE allows the user to enter the condition in a separate "condition box," as this example illustrates. The condition box is obtained using yet another function key on the terminal. (We remind the reader that the reason for requiring the first supplier number to be less than the second is to eliminate pairs of the form (x, x) and to ensure that at most one of the pairs (x, y), (y, x) will appear.)

11.3   RETRIEVAL OPERATIONS ON TREE-STRUCTURED RELATIONS

The QBE operations described in this section are not supported in the current IBM implementation. However, they are worth some examination because they address an interesting application area, one that few languages, relational or otherwise, deal with elegantly. Further details of these operations can be found in [11.5].

Consider the relation RS (reporting structure) shown in Fig. 11.1. This relation has two attributes, EMP # and MGR#, both drawn from an underlying domain of employee numbers. The meaning of a given tuple of RS is that the indicated employee (EMP#) reports directly to the indicated manager (MGR#).

We assume that the reporting structure represented by relation RS satisfies the following constraints (at all times).

1. No employee is his or her own manager.

2. No employee has more than one immediate manager.

3. If EX (for example) is the immediate manager of EY, then EY cannot be the manager at any level of EX.

RS	MGR#	EMP#
	E1	E6
	E1	E7
	E1	E8
	E6	E18
	E8	E15
	E8	E16
	E15	E20
	E15	E24
	E24	E32

Fig. 11.1 The reporting structure relation RS.

The reader will observe that the sample tabulation of Fig. 11.1 does satisfy these constraints. Because of this fact we may represent the relation as a tree structure, as Fig. 11.2 illustrates.

We shall refer to a relation possessing two attributes defined on a common domain and satisfying constraints analogous to those above as a *tree-structured relation*. In Query By Example the user is able to formulate certain queries on a tree-structured relation that less powerful languages such as the relational algebra are unable to express. Let us consider some examples.

11.3.1 Retrieval going down one level   Get employee numbers for employees reporting to employee E8 at the first level.

RS	MGR#	EMP#
	E8	P.<u>EX</u>

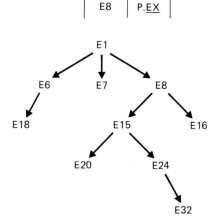

Fig. 11.2 Relation RS represented as a tree.

By "at the first level" we mean that E8 is the immediate manager of the employees we want. The answer to the query is employees E15 and E16. This example is straightforward and does not illustrate any new points.

11.3.2 Retrieval going down two levels Get employee numbers for employees reporting to employee E8 at the second level.

RS	MGR#	EMP#
	E8	E͟Y͟
	E͟Y͟	P.E͟X͟

Again the solution is straightforward—but observe that we have had to introduce a link, E͟Y͟, and have had to enter the link into the table twice. In general, if we wanted to go down n levels in the tree, we would have to enter each of $n - 1$ links twice, a rather tedious process. Accordingly, Query By Example provides a convenient shorthand, which is illustrated in the following alternative formulation of the above query.

RS	MGR#	EMP#
	E8	P.E͟X͟(2L)

The "(2L)" stands for "second level." In general, a level entry may consist of any integer followed by the letter L, the whole enclosed in parentheses. Whenever a level entry is used, Query By Example includes relative levels in the tabulated result, for example, as follows.

EMP#
E20(2L)
E24(2L)

11.3.3 Retrieval going up two levels Get the employee number of the manager two levels above employee E20.

RS	MGR#	EMP#
	P.M͟X͟(2L)	E20

Here the level entry appears in the MGR# column. In general, the direction of search (up or down the tree) is indicated by the column in which the level entry appears. In certain situations this rule could lead to an ambiguity, however [11.5]; to avoid this problem, Query By Example imposes the restriction that not more than two entries may appear in any given row in the formulation of a query involving levels.

11.3.4 Retrieval going down to all levels   Get employee numbers for employees reporting to employee E8 at *any* level.

RS	MGR#	EMP#
	E8	P.EX(6L)

Result:

EMP#
E15(1L)
E20(2L)
E24(2L)
E32(3L)
E16(1L)

This is an example of a query that cannot be expressed in the relational algebra or languages of equivalent power. Note the underline in the level entry.

11.3.5 Retrieval going down to lowest level   Get employee numbers for employees reporting to employee E8 at the *lowest* level.

RS	MGR#	EMP#
	E8	P.EX(MAX.6L)

MAX is a built-in function (see Section 11.4). The meaning of this query is "Get employee numbers for employees whose relative level below E8 is greatest." The result is the single employee E32(3L).

11.3.6 Retrieval going down to terminal levels   Get employee numbers for employees reporting to employee E8 who do not have anyone reporting to them.

RS	MGR#	EMP#
	E8	P.EX(LAST.L)

We are looking for employees at terminal nodes of the tree below E8. Since these employees will be at different relative levels, in general, we cannot enter either a constant integer or an example integer (a constant would mean a fixed level, an example would mean all levels); therefore, Query By Example provides the special function LAST.

11.3.7 Retrieval of level At what level is employee E20 below employee E1?

RS	MGR#	EMP#
	E1	P.E20(7L)

Result:

EMP#
E20(3L)

11.4 BUILT-IN FUNCTIONS

Like SQL, QBE provides a set of built-in functions, as follows.

```
CNT.ALL.     CNT.UNQ.ALL.
SUM.ALL.     SUM.UNQ.ALL.
AVG.ALL.     AVG.UNQ.ALL.
MAX.ALL.
MIN.ALL.
```

Note that "ALL." is always specified. The optional "UNQ." means "eliminate redundant duplicates before applying the function" (CNT., SUM., and AVG. only). The meanings of the other keywords are obvious. Null values are always eliminated, except for CNT.

11.4.1 Simple retrieval using a function Get the total number of suppliers. (Example 7.3.1)

S	S#	SNAME	STATUS	CITY
	P.CNT.ALL. SX			

11.4.2 Simple retrieval using a function Get the total number of suppliers currently supplying parts. (Example 7.3.2)

SP	S#	P#	QTY
	P.CNT.UNQ.ALL.SX		

11.4.3 Qualified retrieval using a function Get the number of shipments for part P2. (Example 7.3.3)

SP	S#	P#	QTY
	P.CNT.ALL.<u>SX</u>	P2	

11.4.4 Qualified retrieval using a function Get the total quantity of part P2 supplied. (Example 7.3.4)

SP	S#	P#	QTY
		P2	P.SUM.ALL.<u>Q</u>

11.4.5 Function in the condition box Get supplier numbers for suppliers with status value less than the current maximum status value in the S table (Examples 7.2.8 and 7.3.5); also get that maximum value.

S	S#	SNAME	STATUS	CITY	CONDITIONS
	P.<u>SX</u>		<u>ST</u> P.MAX.ALL.<u>SS</u>		<u>ST</u> < MAX.ALL.<u>SS</u>

11.4.6 Retrieval with grouping For each part supplied, get the part number and the total quantity supplied of that part. (Example 7.3.6)

SP	S#	P#	QTY
		P.G.<u>PX</u>	P.SUM.ALL.<u>QX</u>

The "G." is the QBE equivalent of the SQL GROUP BY operator.

11.4.7 Retrieval using grouping and the condition box Get part numbers for all parts supplied by more than one supplier (the same as Example 11.2.11); also get the corresponding supplier counts.

SP	S#	P#	QTY	CONDITIONS
	P.CNT.ALL.<u>SX</u>	P.G.<u>PX</u>		CNT.ALL.<u>SX</u> > 1

11.5 UPDATE OPERATIONS

11.5.1 Single-record update Change the color of part P2 to yellow.

P	P#	PNAME	COLOR	WEIGHT	CITY
	P2		U. YELLOW		

Or:

P	P#	PNAME	COLOR	WEIGHT	CITY
U.	P2		YELLOW		

The update operation is "U." The record to be updated is identified by its primary key value. Primary key values cannot be updated.

11.5.2 Single-record update based on previous value Increase the weight of part P2 by 5.

P	P#	PNAME	COLOR	WEIGHT	CITY
	P2			WT	
U.	P2			$WT + 5$	

To update a record based on its old value, the user enters a row representing the old version and another representing the new version. The "U." indicates which is the new one.

11.5.3 Multiple-record update Double the status of all suppliers in London. (Example 7.4.2)

S	S#	SNAME	STATUS	CITY
	SX		ST	LONDON
U.	SX		$2*ST$	

Here the primary key value (supplier number) is specified as an example element, not a constant.

11.5.4 Multiple-record update   Set the quantity to zero for all suppliers in London. (Example 7.4.3)

SP	S#	P#	QTY
U.	SX		0

S	S#	SNAME	STATUS	CITY
	SX			LONDON

11.5.5 Multiple-table update   Set the quantity and status to zero for all suppliers in London.

SP	S#	P#	QTY
U.	SX		0

S	S#	SNAME	STATUS	CITY
	SX			LONDON
	SY			LONDON
U.	SY		0	

Since the unit of input to QBE is the entire screen, several updates can be entered simultaneously.

11.5.6 Single-record insertion   Add part P7 (name 'WASHER', color 'GREY', weight 2, city 'ATHENS') to table P. (Example 7.4.5)

P	P#	PNAME	COLOR	WEIGHT	CITY
I.	P7	WASHER	GREY	2	ATHENS

"I." is the insert operator. The new record must have a primary key value that is nonnull and distinct from all existing primary key values in the table. Other fields may be left blank in the skeleton table, in which case they will be set to null in the database.

11.5.7 Multiple-record insertion   Table TEMP has one column, called P#. Enter into TEMP part numbers for all parts supplied by supplier S2 (see Example 7.4.6).

TEMP	P#
I.	PX

SP	S#	P#	QTY
	S2	PX	

11.5.8 Single-record deletion Delete supplier S1. (Example 7.4.7)

S	S#	SNAME	STATUS	CITY
D.	S1			

"D." is the delete operator. If table SP currently has any shipments for supplier S1, this deletion will cause Integrity Rule 2 to be violated. (But see Example 11.5.11.)

11.5.9 Multiple-record deletion Delete all suppliers in London.

S	S#	SNAME	STATUS	CITY
D.				LONDON

Again this deletion may cause Integrity Rule 2 to be violated.

11.5.10 Multiple-record deletion Delete all shipments. (Example 7.4.8)

SP	S#	P#	QTY
D.			

11.5.11 Multiple-record, multiple-table deletion Delete all suppliers in London and also all shipments for those suppliers. (Example 7.4.9)

S	S#	SNAME	STATUS	CITY
	SX			LONDON
D.				LONDON

SP	S#	P#	QTY
D.	SX		

QBE will delete the shipments first and then the suppliers in this example.

11.6 THE QBE DICTIONARY

Like System R, Query By Example features a primitive built-in dictionary that is represented to the user as a collection of tables. The dictionary includes, for example, a TABLE table and a DOMAIN table, giving details of all tables and all domains currently known to the system. As in System R, the dictionary tables can be interrogated using the ordinary retrieval operations of the DML. However, QBE goes a little further than System R in this respect, in that operators for querying *and updating* the dictionary are actually built into the language, in a style that is consistent with the other (nondictionary) operators. In particular, QBE does not really include a DDL per se, but instead uses special forms of the DML update operators to provide equivalent function.

We begin by showing two retrieval examples.

11.6.1 Retrieval of table-names Get names of all tables known to the system.

P.				

Instead of having to build a skeleton for the TABLE table and entering "P." in the NAME column of that skeleton, the user can formulate this query by simply entering the "P." in the *table-name* position of a blank table.

11.6.2 Retrieval of column-names for a given table Get names of all columns in table S.

S	P.				

To formulate this query, the user enters the table-name (S) followed by "P." against the row of (blank) column-names. QBE responds by filling in those blanks appropriately. This function is commonly used in building up to the "real" query. (*Note:* If the result contains column-names that are not required for the expression of the "real" query, they can be eliminated via a function key before the user proceeds.)

Now we move on to the data definition functions.

11.6.3 Creation of a new table Create table S (assuming it does not yet exist).

I. S I.	S#	SNAME	STATUS	CITY

The first "I." creates a dictionary entry for table S; the second "I." creates dictionary entries for the four columns of table S. However, the table creation process is not yet complete; certain additional information must be specified for each column. The additional information includes (for each column) the name of the underlying domain; the data-type of the domain, if that domain is not already known to QBE; an indication as to whether or not the column participates in the primary key; and a specification as to whether or not an index ("inversion") is to be built on the column. (QBE assumes that every column is part of the key and that every column is to be indexed, unless informed to the contrary.) We show in outline how this information can be specified for table S; for further details of the specification process and for details of other information that must be specified, the reader is referred to [11.2].

S		S#	SNAME	STATUS	CITY
DOMAIN	I.	S#	SNAME	STATUS	CITY
TYPE	I.	CHAR (5)	CHAR (20)	FIXED	CHAR (15)
KEY		Y	U.N	U.N	U.N
INVERSION		Y	U.N	U.N	U.N

In this example, DOMAIN and TYPE information is supplied by inserting an entire row of specifications; KEY and INVERSION information is supplied by updating the QBE default values. Note that we have now defined certain *domains* to QBE as well as the S table and columns; CITY, for example, is now known to QBE as a domain of character strings of length 15. The data-types supported in QBE are CHAR (i.e., varying length character strings), CHAR (*n*), FIXED, FLOAT, DATE, and TIME.

11.6.4 Creating a snapshot For each part supplied, get part number and names of all cities supplying the part (Example 11.2.12), and save the result in the database.

S	S#	SNAME	STATUS	CITY		SP	S#	P#	QTY
	SX			SC			SX	PX	

			I.	RESULT	I.	P#	CITY
					P.I.	PX	SC

RESULT is evaluated as in Example 11.2.12 and displayed (because of the "P." in the last row). Also, a copy of this table, with table-name RESULT and column-names P# and CITY, is stored in the database (because of the "I." operators). Domain (and thus data-type) specifications for the columns of this table are inherited from the underlying tables; other specifications (e.g., KEY, INVERSION) are taken by default (but can be changed if desired, using "U."; however, such changes can be specified only at the time the table is created, not in a subsequent operation). The newly stored table is said to be a *snapshot* of the underlying tables. Once created, however, it is quite independent of those tables—that is, those tables and the snapshot can be independently updated; a snapshot is not a view (in the System R sense).

11.6.5 Dropping a table   Drop table SP.

A table can be dropped only if it is currently empty.

Step 1: Delete all shipments. (Example 11.5.10)

SP	S#	P#	QTY
D.			

Step 2: Drop the table.

D. SP	S#	P#	QTY

11.6.6 Expanding a table   Add a DATE column to table SP.

Unlike System R, QBE does not directly support the dynamic addition of a new column to an existing table, unless that table is currently empty. Therefore, it is necessary to do the following:

1. Define a new table the same shape as the existing table plus the new column.
2. Load the new table from the old, using a multiple-record insert.
3. Delete all data from the old table.
4. Drop the old table.
5. Change the name of the new table to that of the old table.

Steps 1 and 2:

SP	S#	P#	QTY
	SX	PX	QX

I. SPCOPY I.	S#	P#	QTY	DATE
DOMAIN				U. DATES
TYPE				U. DATE
KEY			U.N	U.N
INVERSION			U.N	U.N
I.	SX	PX	QX	

Step 3:

SP	S#	P#	QTY
D.			

Step 4:

D. SP	S#	P#	QTY

Step 5:

SPCOPY U. SP	S#	P#	QTY	DATE

All DATE values in the new SP table are initially null.

11.7 DISCUSSION

One significant advantage of QBE, compared to most other query languages, is the amount of *freedom* the user enjoys—freedom, that is, to construct the query in whatever manner seems most natural. Specifically, the query may be built up in any *order* the user likes: The order of rows within a query table is entirely immaterial; moreover, the order in which the user fills in all the entries constituting these rows is also completely arbitrary. Take Example 11.2.8, for instance ("Get supplier names for suppliers supplying red parts"). The user may think about this query as follows: "Pick out red parts, then pick out numbers of suppliers supplying these parts, then pick out the corresponding names"—in which case he or she will probably complete the query tables in the order P, SP, S. Alternatively, the user may think about it as: "Pick out supplier names such that the corresponding suppliers supply a part that is red"—in which case he or she will probably fill in the tables in the order S, SP, P. Either way the final query is the same. In other words, Query By Example is a highly nonprocedural language that is capable of supporting several different ways of thinking about a problem; it does not force every user to perceive the problem in exactly the same way.

For interest, we offer some functional comparisons between the QBE product and System R. (Of course, most of these comparisons reflect characteristics of the implementations, rather than intrinsic properties of the QBE and SQL languages.)

- *Dynamic sharing.* A QBE database can be concurrently shared by any number of read-only users *or* can be dedicated to a single update user. In System R, by contrast, the database is normally available to any number of simultaneous updaters.

- *Dynamic database definition.* QBE is not quite as flexible as System R in this regard. See Example 11.6.6.

- *Views.* Although the full QBE language does include views (in the System R sense), they are not supported in the current IBM implementation.

- *Compilation vs. interpretation.* QBE uses the traditional interpretive approach. There is no QBE precompiler.

- *Application programming interface.* Like SQL, QBE is available from both an on-line terminal and a batch application program. The interface for "embedded QBE" is rather rudimentary, however.

- *Data structure.* QBE tables really are relations, unlike the base tables of System R. Moreover, QBE provides explicit support for the concepts of *domain* and *primary key* (but not alternate key); primary keys are required to be unique and nonnull. The user is not required to create an index to obtain this uniqueness checking. Integrity Rule 2 is not enforced, however. (Again, like SQL, the full QBE language does include a means of specifying arbitrary integrity constraints, but it is not supported in the current implementation.)

- *Relational completeness.* The full QBE language is complete in the sense of Section 7.2, but the implemented subset is not. (Some SQL queries cannot be expressed in this subset.)

- *IMS Extract.* QBE provides a utility to copy data from an IMS database (see Part 3 of this book) into a QBE database, thus making it available for query through the normal QBE interface.

EXERCISES

Give QBE solutions to Exercises 7.1–7.20 and 7.29–7.34.

REFERENCES AND BIBLIOGRAPHY

Some alternative approaches to formal interactive languages that exploit display terminals are presented in [11.13] and [11.14]. Reference [11.15] includes a comparative evaluation of a large number of query languages, including QBE and SQL. Reference [11.16] reports on a system called the System for Business Automation that is actually a superset of QBE.

11.1 IBM Corporation. "Query-by-Example: Program Description/Operations Manual." IBM Form No. SH20–2077.

11.2 IBM Corporation. "Query-by-Example: Terminal User's Guide." IBM Form No. SH20–2078.

11.3 M. M. Zloof. "Query By Example." *Proc. NCC* **44** (May 1975).

11.4 M. M. Zloof. "Query By Example: The Invocation and Definition of Tables and Forms." *Proc. 1st International Conference on Very Large Data Bases* (September 1975).

11.5 M. M. Zloof. "Query-by-Example: Operations on the Transitive Closure." IBM Research Report RC5526 (July 1975).

11.6 M. M. Zloof. "Query-by-Example: Operations on Hierarchical Data Bases." *Proc. NCC* **45** (1976).

Describes a version of QBE based on hierarchies rather than tables. Also introduces a linear syntax.

11.7 M. M. Zloof. "Query-by-Example: A Data Base Management Language." IBM Research Report (in preparation).

11.8 M. M. Zloof. "Query-by-Example: A Data Base Language." *IBM Sys. J.* **16**, No. 4 (1977).

11.9 M. M. Zloof. "Design Aspects of the Query-by-Example Data Base Management Language." In *Databases: Improving Usability and Responsiveness* (ed., B. Shneiderman). New York: Academic Press (1978).

11.10 K. E. Niebuhr and S. E. Smith. "Implementation of Query-by-Example on VM/370." IBM Research Report (in preparation).

11.11 J. C. Thomas and J. D. Gould. "A Psychological Study of Query By Example." *Proc. NCC* **44** (May 1975).

11.12 D. Greenblatt and J. Waxman. "A Study of Three Database Query Languages." In *Databases: Improving Usability and Responsiveness* (ed., B. Shneiderman). New York: Academic Press (1978).

A comparative study of QBE, SQL, and relational algebra from the standpoint of usability.

11.13 M. E. Senko. "DIAM II with FORAL LP: Making Pointed Queries with Light Pen." *Proc. IFIP Congress* (1977).

11.14 N. McDonald and M. R. Stonebraker. "CUPID—The Friendly Query Language." *Proc. ACM Pacific Conference, San Francisco* (April 1975). Available from ACM Golden Gate Chapter, P.O. Box 24055, Oakland, California 94623.

A short introduction to the CUPID language, which is implemented on top of QUEL (see Chapter 13). CUPID is a graphic language in which the user can construct queries of arbitrary complexity by simple light-pen manipulation of a small number of standard symbols. In Fig. 11.3, we give a possible CUPID representation of Example 11.2.8 to illustrate the language's ready comprehensibility.

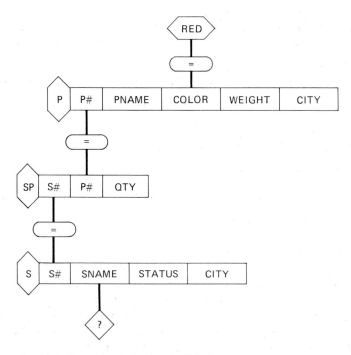

Fig. 11.3 Example of a query in CUPID.

11.15 R. N. Cuff. "Database Query Systems for the Casual User." Man-Machine Systems Laboratory, Dept. of Electrical Engineering, University of Essex, Colchester, England CO4 3SQ (March 1979).

11.16 M. M. Zloof and S. P. de Jong. "The System for Business Automation (SBA): Programming Language." *CACM* **20**, No. 6 (June 1977).

12
Relational
Algebra

12.1 INTRODUCTION

We discussed relational algebra briefly in Section 3.5 as the basis for a high-level data sublanguage. In that section we also pointed out that several other languages, such as SQL and QBE, have been developed since the algebra was first defined, and that most relational systems support one of these newer languages rather than the algebra per se. But the algebra is still important, nevertheless, and in this chapter we shall describe it in some detail.

Relational algebra is a collection of operations on relations. Each operation takes one or more relations as its operand(s) and produces another relation as its result.[1] Codd originally defined a set of such operations in [12.1], and showed that those operations were "relationally complete," in the sense that they provided at least the retrieval power of the relational calculus (see Chapter 13). Numerous variations on the original algebra have been proposed since the publication of [12.1]; see, for example, references [12.7, 12.12, 12.14, 12.15]. In this chapter we present a variation of our own—one that does not, however, depart too far from the original—and

---

1. Since the result of a relational algebra operation is a relation, that relation in turn may be subjected to further algebraic operations. Operands of any given operation can thus be specified either as simple relation names or as *expressions* that evaluate to relations. In other words, relational algebra expressions can be nested to any depth. (There is an obvious analogy with nested arithmetic expressions in ordinary programming languages.) In mathematical terms we express the fact that the result of any algebraic operation is another relation by saying that relations form a *closed system* under the algebra. Of course, similar remarks apply to SQL, QBE, and other high-level relational languages.

use it to introduce several other concepts, including, in particular, that of the *relational database model.*

The algebra as we present it consists of two groups of operators: the traditional set operators union, intersection, difference, and Cartesian product (all modified somewhat to operate on relations rather than arbitrary sets); and the special relational operators selection, projection, join, and division. For reference, we give a complete BNF syntax for our version of the algebra in Fig. 12.1. The syntax is deliberately less wordy than that of Section 3.5. We then discuss the two groups of operators in detail, with examples, in subsequent sections. As usual, all examples are based on the suppliers-and-parts database. We remark that our version of the algebra includes rules for naming the attributes of results, an aspect that is frequently ignored.

Note: We assume throughout this chapter that the order of attributes within a relation *is* significant—not because it is necessary to do so, but because it simplifies the definitions.

Note: Square brackets are not used in the following syntax to indicate optional material, but are instead symbols in the language being defined.

A1.	alg-stmt	::=	alias-def | assignment
A2.	alias-def	::=	alias ALIASES rel-name ;
A3.	assignment	::=	rel-name [attr-spec-commalist] := alg-exp ;
A4.	attr-spec-commalist	::=	attr-spec | attr-spec, attr-spec-commalist
A5.	attr-spec	::=	attr-name | rel-name . attr-name | alias . attr-name
A6.	alg-exp	::=	selection | projection | infix
A7.	selection	::=	primitive WHERE bool-exp
A8.	primitive	::=	rel-name | alias | (alg-exp)
A9.	projection	::=	primitive | primitive [attr-spec-commalist]
A10.	infix	::=	projection infix-op projection
A11.	infix-op	::=	UNION | INTERSECT | MINUS | TIMES | JOIN | DIVIDEBY
A12.	bool-exp	::=	.....
A13.	comparison	::=	attr-spec comp-op value-spec

Fig. 12.1 A syntax for the relational algebra.

Some Notes on The Syntax

1. An assignment operation is included (A3) to permit the saving of results. Relations shown on the left-hand side of an assignment are assumed
to have been suitably declared, like all named relations (as opposed to derived relations), but for clarity their attribute-names are mentioned explicitly in the assignment itself. No syntax is shown for relation declaration.

2. The categories *alias, rel-name,* and *attr-name* are all defined to be *identifiers* (a terminal category with respect to this syntax).

3. The category *bool-exp* represents a Boolean expression (that is, a
Boolean combination of *comparisons,* formed in accordance with the normal rules). The category *comparison* represents a simple comparison between an attribute value (represented by an *attr-spec,* i.e., a qualified or
unqualified attribute-name) and a constant or another attribute value
(represented by a *value-spec*).

12.2   TRADITIONAL SET OPERATIONS

The traditional set operations are union, intersection, difference, and Cartesian product. For all except Cartesian product, the two operand relations
must be *union-compatible:* that is, they must be of the same degree, n say,
and the jth attributes of the two relations (j in the range 1 to n) must be
drawn from the same domain (they need not have the same name).

Union

The union of two (union-compatible) relations A and B, A UNION B, is the
set of all tuples t belonging to either A or B (or both).

Example. Let A be the set of supplier tuples for suppliers in London, and
B the set of supplier tuples for suppliers who supply part P1. Then A
UNION B is the set of supplier tuples for suppliers who *either* are located in
London *or* supply part P1 (or both).

Intersection

The intersection of two (union-compatible) relations A and B, A INTER-
SECT B, is the set of all tuples t belonging to both A and B.

Example. Let A and B be as in the example under "Union" above. Then A
INTERSECT B is the set of supplier tuples for suppliers who are located in
London *and* supply part P1.

Difference

The difference between two (union-compatible) relations A and B (in that order), A MINUS B, is the set of all tuples t belonging to A and not to B.

Example. Let A and B again be as in the example under "Union." Then A MINUS B is the set of supplier tuples for suppliers who are located in London and who do *not* supply part P1. (What is B MINUS A?)

Extended Cartesian Product

The extended Cartesian product of two relations A and B, A TIMES B, is the set of all tuples t such that t is the concatenation of a tuple a belonging to A and a tuple b belonging to B. The *concatenation* of a tuple $a = (a_1, \ldots, a_m)$ and a tuple $b = (b_{m+1}, \ldots, b_{m+n})$—in that order—is the tuple $t = (a_1, \ldots, a_m, b_{m+1}, \ldots, b_{m+n})$.

Example. Let A be the set of all supplier numbers, and B the set of all part numbers. Then A TIMES B is the set of all possible supplier-number/part-number pairs.

It is easy to verify that UNION is associative—that is, if X, Y, and Z are arbitrary *projections* (in the sense of Fig. 12.1), then the expressions (X UNION Y) UNION Z and X UNION (Y UNION Z) are equivalent. For convenience, therefore, we allow a sequence of UNIONs to be written without any embedded parentheses; for example, each of the foregoing expressions can unambiguously be simplified to X UNION Y UNION Z. Similar remarks apply to INTERSECT and TIMES, but not to MINUS.

12.3   ATTRIBUTE-NAMES FOR DERIVED RELATIONS

Despite the fact that we are considering attributes to be ordered left to right within a relation, we still rely on attribute-names for purposes of reference, and we still require that no relation have two attributes with the same name. We assume that this constraint is automatically enforced for the declared or "base" relations. In this section we introduce a rule for generating attribute-names for *derived* relations—that is, relations represented by expressions rather than by name or alias (see below)—in accordance with the unique naming constraint.

First, let R be the name of a declared relation, and let A be the name of an attribute within R. A is said to be the *unqualified* name for this attribute. For a declared relation, no two attributes can have the same unqualified name. Let S be an alias for R, introduced by the alias definition

```
S ALIASES R;
```

(S is simply another name for the relation R). When the given relation is referenced by the name R, attribute A is considered to have the *qualified* name R.A. When the given relation is referenced by the alias S, attribute A is considered to have the *qualified* name S.A. Thus an attribute of a declared relation always has a qualified name, since an attribute can be referenced only in the context of its containing relation, and its containing relation must be referenced either by name or by alias; but the attribute may be referenced by its unqualified name if no ambiguity results.

Attributes of derived relations also always have qualified names, generated as described below. (Again, however, they may be referenced by their unqualified names if no ambiguity results.) As stated earlier, a derived relation is a relation that is represented by an expression, rather than by its name or an alias. In considering such derivations, we can obviously restrict our attention to expressions involving exactly one of the algebraic operators (since the operand(s) of that operator can in turn be derived relations).

Union, Intersection, Difference

The result has the same qualified attribute-names as the first operand.

Extended Cartesian Product

Consider the product A TIMES B. Let the qualified attribute-names for A and B, in their left-to-right order, be

$$A.A_1, \ldots, A.A_m \quad \text{and} \quad B.B_{(m+1)}, \ldots, B.B_{(m+n)},$$

respectively. Then the attributes of A TIMES B have exactly these qualified attribute-names (in left-to-right order).

Example. Let A(S#), B(P#), and D(S#, P#) be three relations. A TIMES B has attributes (A.S#, B.P#). If we call this product C, then C TIMES D has attributes (A.S#, B.P#, D.S#, D.P#).

As the example shows, attributes of a derived relation can have non-unique unqualified names, but their qualified names must be unique. Suppose we need to form the extended Cartesian product of a relation R with itself. The expression R TIMES R is illegal, because it would violate the unique naming rule. Therefore, we must introduce an alias, R1 say:

```
R1 ALIASES R;
```

Now we can write R1 TIMES R, or R TIMES R1, thus generating the required product without violating the unique naming rule.

Special Relational Operations

See the following section.

12.4   SPECIAL RELATIONAL OPERATIONS

Selection

The algebraic selection operator (not to be confused with the SQL SE-LECT) yields a "horizontal" subset of a given relation—that is, that subset of tuples within the given relation for which a specified predicate is satisfied. The predicate is expressed as a Boolean combination of terms, each term being a simple comparison that can be established as true or false for a given tuple by inspecting that tuple in isolation. (If a term involves a comparison between values of two attributes within the tuple, then those attributes must be defined on the same domain.) If X denotes the relation on which the selection is performed, then the result of the selection has exactly the same qualified attribute-names as X (note that X may be an expression).

Some examples of selection are shown in Fig. 12.2.

The syntax of Fig. 12.1 permits the "given relation" of a selection to be specified by name (or alias), or as any relational algebra expression enclosed in parentheses. Further examples are given in Section 12.5.

Projection

The projection operator yields a "vertical" subset of a given relation—that is, that subset obtained by selecting specified attributes, in a specified left-to-right order, and then eliminating duplicate tuples within the attributes selected. Since we are assigning significance to the order of attributes within a relation, projection provides us with a way to permute (reorder) the attributes of a given relation. If X denotes the relation to be projected, then the

S WHERE CITY = 'LONDON'

S#	SNAME	STATUS	CITY
S1	Smith	20	London
S4	Clark	20	London

P WHERE WEIGHT < 14

P#	PNAME	COLOR	WEIGHT	CITY
P1	Nut	Red	12	London
P5	Cam	Blue	12	Paris

SP WHERE S# = 'S1'
       AND P# = 'P1'

S#	P#	QTY
S1	P1	300

Fig. 12.2 Three sample selections.

result of the projection has the same qualified attribute-names as X (again, X may be an expression). No attribute may be specified more than once in a projection operation. Omitting the list of attribute-names is equivalent to specifying a list containing all attribute-names of the given relation, in their correct left-to-right order (in other words, such a projection is identical to the given relation).

Some examples of projection are shown in Fig. 12.3.

The syntax of Fig. 12.1 permits the "given relation" in a projection to be specified by name or alias, or as any relational expression enclosed in parentheses. Again, further examples are given in Section 12.5.

Join

In Section 3.5 we introduced the *equijoin,* and mentioned that it was only one of many possible join operators. As an example, we may define the *greater-than* join of relation A on attribute X with relation B on attribute Y as the set of all tuples t such that t is the concatenation of a tuple a belonging to A and a tuple b belonging to B, where $x > y$ (x being the X-component of A and y the Y-component of B). It should be clear, however, that such joins are not essential; by definition, they are equivalent to taking the extended Cartesian product of the two given relations and then performing a suitable selection on that product. The greater-than join above, for instance, produces the same result as the expression

```
(A TIMES B) WHERE A.X > B.Y
```

One particular join is so common, however, that it is useful to have an explicit shorthand for it. That join is the *natural* join. Recall from Section 3.5 that a natural join is an equijoin with the column duplication eliminated. The syntax of Fig. 12.1 provides for an important special case of natural

S [CITY]

CITY
London
Paris
Athens

S [SNAME, CITY, S#, STATUS]

SNAME	CITY	S#	STATUS
Smith	London	S1	20
Jones	Paris	S2	10
Blake	Paris	S3	30
Clark	London	S4	20
Adams	Athens	S5	30

Fig. 12.3 Two sample projections.

join, that in which common attributes of the two relations have the same unqualified names. The expression A JOIN B is defined if and only if, for every unqualified attribute-name that is common to A and B, the underlying domain is the same for both relations. Assume that this condition is satisfied. Let the qualified attribute-names for A and B, in their left-to-right order, be

$$A.A_1, \ldots, A.A_m \quad \text{and} \quad B.B_{(m+1)}, \ldots, B.B_{(m+n)},$$

respectively; let $C_i, \ldots, C_j$ be the unqualified attribute-names that are common to A and B; and let $B_r, \ldots, B_s$ be the unqualified attribute-names remaining for B (with their relative order undisturbed) after removal of $C_i, \ldots, C_j$. Then A JOIN B is defined to be equivalent to

```
(A TIMES B)[A.A1,  . . . , A.Am,B.Br, . . . , B.Bs]
                    WHERE A.Ci=B.Ci
                    AND   . . . . . . . .
                    AND   A.Cj=B.Cj
```

Henceforth we take "join" to mean this natural join, unless we explicitly state otherwise. For convenience, we allow a sequence of JOINs to be written without any embedded parentheses; for example, the expressions (X JOIN Y) JOIN Z and X JOIN (Y JOIN Z) can both be unambiguously simplified to X JOIN Y JOIN Z, since JOIN is associative. (*Exercise:* Prove this last statement.) We remark that, if A and B have no attribute-names in common, then A JOIN B is identical to A TIMES B. Figure 12.4 shows the natural join of relations S and SP (including the qualified names generated for the result).

S.S#	S.SNAME	S.STATUS	S.CITY	SP.P#	SP.QTY
S1	Smith	20	London	P1	300
S1	Smith	20	London	P2	200
S1	Smith	20	London	P3	400
S1	Smith	20	London	P4	200
S1	Smith	20	London	P5	100
S1	Smith	20	London	P6	100
S2	Jones	10	Paris	P1	300
S2	Jones	10	Paris	P2	400
S3	Blake	30	Paris	P2	200
S4	Clark	20	London	P2	200
S4	Clark	20	London	P4	300
S4	Clark	20	London	P5	400

Fig. 12.4 Join of S and SP over S# (S JOIN SP).

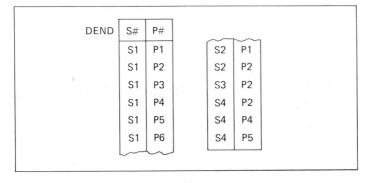

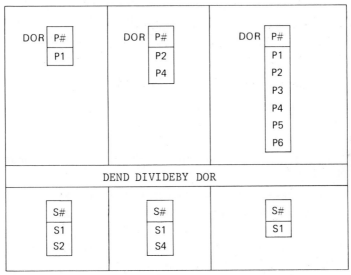

Fig. 12.5 Three sample divisions.

Division

The division operator divides a dividend relation A of degree $m + n$ by a divisor relation B of degree n, and produces a result relation of degree m. The $(m + i)$th attribute of A and the ith attribute of B (i in the range 1 to n) must be defined on the same domain. Consider the first m attributes of A as a single composite attribute X, and the last n as another, Y; A may then be thought of as a set of pairs of values $\langle x, y \rangle$. Similarly, B may be thought of as a set of single values, $\langle y \rangle$. Then the result of dividing A by B—that is, A DIVIDEBY B—is the set of values x such that the pair $\langle x, y \rangle$ appears in A for *all* values y appearing in B. The attributes of the result have the same qualified names as the first m attributes of A.

Figure 12.5 shows some examples of division. The dividend in each case (DEND) is the projection of SP over (S#, P#); the divisors (DOR) are indicated in the figure.

12.5 EXAMPLES

12.5.1 Get supplier names for suppliers who supply part P2. (Example 7.2.7)

We show a step-at-a-time solution first:

```
TEMP1 [S#, SNAME, STATUS, CITY, P#, QTY]
                 :=  S JOIN SP ;
TEMP2 [S#, SNAME, STATUS, CITY, P#, QTY]
                 :=  TEMP1 WHERE P# = 'P2' ;
RESULT [SNAME]   :=  TEMP2 [SNAME] ;
```

Using a nested expression:

```
((S JOIN SP) WHERE P# = 'P2')[SNAME]
```

The result of this expression has one attribute, with qualified name S.SNAME.

12.5.2 Get supplier numbers for suppliers who supply at least one red part. (Example 7.2.10)

```
((P WHERE COLOR = 'RED')[P#] JOIN SP) [S#]
```
Result attribute-name: SP.S#.

12.5.3 Get supplier names for suppliers who supply all parts. (Example 7.2.18)

```
((SP[S#,P#] DIVIDEBY P[P#]) JOIN S) [SNAME]
```
Result attribute name: S.SNAME.

12.5.4 Get supplier numbers for suppliers who supply at least all those parts supplied by supplier S2. (Example 7.2.19)

```
SP[S#,P#] DIVIDEBY (SP WHERE S# = 'S2') [P#]
```
Result attribute-name: SP.S#.

12.5.5 Get supplier names for suppliers who do not supply part P2. (Example 7.2.14)

```
((S[S#] MINUS (SP WHERE P# = 'P2')[S#]) JOIN S) [SNAME]
```
Result attribute-name: S.SNAME.

12.5.6 Get all pairs of supplier numbers such that the two suppliers are located in the same city. (Example 7.2.6)

```
FIRST   ALIASES S;
SECOND ALIASES S;
((FIRST TIMES SECOND)
        WHERE FIRST.CITY = SECOND.CITY
          AND FIRST.S#   < SECOND.S#  )
                               [FIRST.S#, SECOND.S#]
```

Result attribute-names: FIRST.S#, SECOND.S#.

We conclude this section with a note on update operations. The relational algebra is basically a retrieval language. UNION and MINUS *could* be used to handle insert and delete operations; for example,

```
P  := P UNION {<'P7','WASHER','GREY',2,'ATHENS'>} ;
SP := SP MINUS {<'S1',?,?>} ;
```

(The first of these assignments inserts the tuple for P7 into relation P; the second removes all tuples for S1 from relation SP.) However, UNION and MINUS are not really a satisfactory substitute for INSERT and DELETE, because they do not handle error situations appropriately (by "error situations" we mean conditions that are customarily treated as errors by INSERT and DELETE). UNION, for example, will not reject an attempt to "insert" a tuple that is a duplicate of one that already exists; and MINUS will not reject an attempt to "delete" a nonexistent tuple. In practice, therefore, a system that supports a DML based on relational algebra should provide explicit INSERT and DELETE (and UPDATE) operators as well.

12.6   DISCUSSION

We stated at the beginning of this chapter that the algebra is still important, even though it is less "user-friendly" than languages such as QBE and SQL. The basic reason for its importance is that it provides a yardstick against which other languages can be measured. Since the algebra is relationally complete, to show that some other language L is also complete in this sense, it is sufficient to show that L includes equivalents of the algebraic operators. (See Exercise 12.2.) The algebra also lays a foundation for research into several other aspects of database management, such as database design, view definition, and restructuring. We have already touched on some of these topics in Chapter 9 (in that chapter we were talking in terms of SQL rather than the algebra, but most of the SQL operators have direct algebraic equivalents); and Chapter 14 will show the fundamental role played by projection and natural join in the area of database design. References [12.8–12.11] also use the algebra as a basis for important work on optimization techniques. (See also the book by Ullman [13.6], which includes a survey chapter on query optimization.)

We are now in a position to define the *relational database model.*[2] The relational model consists of two principal components:

- the relational data structure defined in Chapter 4; and

- the relational algebra.

A database system may be called *fully relational* [4.6] if it supports

- relational databases (including the concepts of domain and key and the two integrity rules); and

- a language that is at least as powerful as the relational algebra (and that would remain so even if all facilities for loops and recursion were to be deleted).[3]

A system that supports relational databases but has a language that is less powerful than the algebra may be called *semirelational* [4.6].

We observe that there are probably no systems today (1981) that are fully relational, or even semirelational, according to these definitions! Relational definitions have changed somewhat over the past ten years; criticisms that "relational system" is a moving target are not unfounded. But it would be more accurate to say that the concepts have *evolved,* not changed wildly or unpredictably. Very few, if any, of the original principles have actually been superseded. For example, the initial definition of the relational database model is still basically valid today; but more recent research has resulted in various additions and clarifications to that original definition (the two integrity rules are a case in point).

We can also predict with certainty that the concepts will continue to evolve. One area currently receiving much attention is the treatment of null values. Several investigators have already proposed enhancements to the algebra to deal with nulls [12.17, 12.18, 4.6]. Reference [4.6], for example, suggests (among other things) two variants of the join operator: the "maybe join," in which tuples are joined not on the basis of some condition being *true* but on the basis of its having the *unknown* (null) truth value; and the "outer join," in which tuples in one relation having no counterpart in the other appear in the result concatenated with an all-null tuple. However, all such proposals are best regarded as preliminary at this time.

---

2. Our usage of this term differs from that in previous editions of this book.

3. This condition is tantamount to insisting that the language is relationally complete in the more demanding sense of the term (see the remarks at the end of Section 7.2).

EXERCISES

12.1 We have already pointed out that join is not an essential operation but can be defined in terms of more primitive operators. The same is true for intersection and division (thus the true primitives are union, difference, product, selection, and projection). Give definitions of intersection and division in terms of these five primitives.

12.2 Show that SQL is relationally complete, by showing that it includes analogues of the five algebraic primitives.

12.3 Given the database in Fig. 4.7, evaluate the expression

```
        S  JOIN  SP  JOIN  P
```

(*Warning:* There is a trap here.)

12.4 Give algebraic solutions to Exercises 7.1–7.28.

REFERENCES AND BIBLIOGRAPHY

References [12.1–12.18] are specifically concerned with the relational algebra. The remaining references describe languages and systems that are only loosely connected with the algebra as such, but are relevant nevertheless.

12.1 E. F. Codd. "Relational Completeness of Data Base Sublanguages." In *Data Base Systems,* Courant Computer Science Symposia Series, Vol. 6. Englewood Cliffs, N.J.: Prentice-Hall (1972).

This paper includes a formal definition of the relational calculus (see Chapter 13), and introduces the concept of relational completeness. A language is said to be relationally complete if it possesses the property that any relation definable by means of calculus expressions may be retrieved via suitable statements in that language. (As already indicated, our definition of relational completeness in Section 7.2 is more demanding than this: It stipulates that any relation definable via a *single* calculus expression be retrievable via a *single* statement of the language.)

The paper also provides a formal definition of a relational algebra, and proves the completeness of this algebra by giving an algorithm ("Codd's reduction algorithm") for converting an arbitrary calculus expression into a semantically equivalent algebraic expression (and thus demonstrating a possible approach to implementing the calculus). The paper concludes with a brief section comparing and contrasting the calculus and algebra as candidates for a data sublanguage.

12.2 R. C. Goldstein and A. J. Strnad. "The MacAIMS Data Management System." *Proc. 1970 ACM SICFIDET Workshop on Data Description and Access.*

12.3 A. J. Strnad. "The Relational Approach to the Management of Data Bases." *Proc. IFIP Congress 1971.*

MacAIMS [12.2, 12.3] appears to have been the earliest example of a system supporting both *n*-ary relations and a set-oriented data sublanguage. The language is algebraic. Two particularly interesting features of MacAIMS are the following.

- The storage structure may vary from relation to relation (thus allowing each relation to be stored in the form most suited to it). For each structure a "relational strategy module" maintains the relations appropriately and permits the user to view them in the simple tabular form.

- Attributes are stored as "data element sets." Each data element (attribute value) is assigned a unique fixed-length reference number, and all reference to the data element within a relation is via the reference number. The algorithm for assigning reference numbers is such that, if A and B belong to the same data element set, the reference number for A will be greater than that for B if and only if A is greater than B. As a result, any comparison operation between two data elements (from the same data element set) can be made directly on the corresponding reference numbers; moreover, the actual comparison itself will probably be more efficient, because reference numbers are fixed-length whereas data elements may be variable-length. This is particularly significant in view of the fact that such comparisons are the operations most frequently performed in the system.

The system RDMS [12.4], which is currently in use within the administrative departments at M.I.T., is apparently an upgraded form of MacAIMS.

12.4 J. Stewart and J. Goldman. "The Relational Data Management System: A Perspective." *Proc. 1974 ACM SIGMOD Workshop on Data Description, Access and Control.*

12.5 S. J. P. Todd. "The Peterlee Relational Test Vehicle—A System Overview." *IBM Sys. J.* **15**, No. 4 (1976).

PRTV is an experimental system developed at the IBM UK Scientific Centre in Peterlee, England. It is based on an earlier prototype called IS/1 [12.6]. It supports *n*-ary relations and a version of the algebra based on proposals documented in [12.7]. Three significant aspects of PRTV are the following.

1. It incorporates some interesting high-level optimization techniques [12.9].

2. It includes a "delayed evaluation" feature, which is important both for optimization [12.9] and for the provision of views. That is, a relational assignment statement can be treated as a view definition, instead of being executed immediately.

3. It provides "function extensibility"—i.e., the ability for the user to extend the system to include an arbitrary set of built-in functions.

12.6 M. G. Notley. "The Peterlee IS/1 System." IBM (UK) Scientific Centre Report UKSC-0018 (March 1972), IBM (UK) Scientific Centre, Neville Rd., Peterlee, Co. Durham, England HA2 7HH.

12.7 P. A. V. Hall, P. Hitchcock, and S. J. P. Todd. "An Algebra of Relations for Machine Computation." *Conference Record of the Second ACM Symposium on Principles of Programming Languages* (1975).

12.8 J. M. Smith and P. Y.-T. Chang. "Optimizing the Performance of a Relational Algebra Database Interface." *CACM* **18**, No. 10 (October 1975).

An extremely clear paper explaining the algorithms used in the "Smart Query Interface for a Relational Algebra" (SQUIRAL). The optimization techniques employed include the following.

- Transforming the original algebraic expression into an equivalent but more efficient sequence of operations.

- Assigning distinct operations in the transformed expression to distinct tasks and exploiting concurrency and pipelining among them.

- Coordinating the sort orders of the temporary relations passed between these tasks.

SQUIRAL also seeks to exploit any indexes that may exist and to localize stored page references.

12.9 P. A. V. Hall. "Optimisation of a Single Relational Expression in a Relational Data Base System." *IBM J. R & D.* **20**, No. 3 (1976).

This paper describes some of the optimizing techniques used in the system PRTV [12.5]. PRTV, like SQUIRAL [12.8], attempts to transform a given algebraic expression into a more efficient form before evaluating it. A feature of PRTV is that the system does not automatically evaluate each expression as soon as it receives it; rather, it combines each new expression with those it has already accepted to build a larger and more complex expression, and defers actual evaluation until the last possible moment. Thus the "single relational expression" of the paper's title may represent an entire sequence of end-user operations. The optimizations described resemble those of SQUIRAL but go further in some respects; briefly they are as follows (in order of application).

- Move SELECT operations so that they are performed as early as possible.

- Combine sequences of PROJECT operations.

- Eliminate redundant operations; simplify expressions involving empty relations and trivial predicates.

- Eliminate common subexpressions.

The paper concludes with some experimental results and some suggestions for further investigations.

12.10 F. P. Palermo. "A Data Base Search Problem." *Information Systems: COINS IV* (ed., J. T. Tou). New York: Plenum Press (1974).

This paper presents a method of implementation for an arbitrary retrieval statement of the relational calculus. The method is based on Codd's reduction algorithm [12.1], but introduces a number of interesting optimization techniques. Specifically, the following improvements (among others) are made to the basic algorithm. (It is assumed that the tuple is the unit of access to the stored database.)

- No tuple is ever retrieved more than once.

- Unnecessary values are discarded from a tuple as soon as that tuple is retrieved ("unnecessary values" being either values corresponding to attributes not referenced in the query or values used solely for selection purposes—e.g., values of SP.P# in Example 12.5.1). This is equivalent to projecting the relation over the attributes concerned, and therefore not only reduces the space required for each tuple but may also reduce the number of tuples that must be retained.

- The method used to build up the result relation is based on a "least growth principle," so that the result tends to grow slowly. This has the effect of reducing both the number of comparisons involved and the amount of intermediate storage necessary.

- An efficient technique is employed in the construction of joins, involving the dynamic factoring out of values used in "join terms" (such as S.S# = SP.S#) into "semijoins" (which are effectively a kind of secondary index) and the use of an internal representation of each join called an "indirect join" (which makes use of internal tuple reference numbers to represent the tuples involved). These techniques are designed to reduce the amount of scanning necessary in the construction of a join, by ensuring for each join term that the tuples concerned are (logically) ordered on the values in the relevant attributes. They also permit the dynamic determination of a "best" sequence in which to access the required database relations.

12.11 M. W. Blasgen and K. P. Eswaran. "On the Evaluation of Queries in a Relational Data Base System." IBM Research Report RJ 1745 (April 1976).

Several techniques for handling queries involving projection, join, and selection operations are compared on the basis of their cost in secondary storage access. The conclusions are that physical clustering of logically related items is a critical performance parameter, and that, in the absence of such clustering, methods that depend on sorting seem to be the most generally satisfactory.

12.12 R. M. Pecherer. "Efficient Evaluation of Expressions in a Relational Algebra." *Proc. ACM Pacific Conference, San Francisco* (April 1975). Available from ACM Golden Gate Chapter, P.O. Box 24055, Oakland, California 94623.

This paper begins by introducing a slightly revised version of the algebra of [12.1]. The revisions are motivated by efficiency considerations. The implementation of individual operators of this algebra is then discussed; it is assumed that relations are stored as sorted tables and may only be accessed according to their stored sequence. Performance bounds are given for each operator. Under the stated assumptions the operators requiring the most care-ful attention are projection and division. For these two it is concluded that the best approach is to sort the data before the operation; the paper shows that, for a large class of algebraic expressions, intermediate results can be obtained in the desired order at no extra cost. The paper also considers the transformation of expressions into an equivalent, more efficient form, using some of Palermo's techniques [12.10].

12.13 L. R. Gotlieb. "Computing Joins of Relations." *Proc. 1975 ACM SIGMOD International Conference on the Management of Data.*

Presents and compares a number of algorithms for implementing the natural join.

12.14 A. L. Furtado and L. Kerschberg. "An Algebra of Quotient Relations." *Proc. 1977 ACM SIGMOD International Conference on Management of Data* (August 1977).

Presents a revised relational algebra for operating directly on "quotient re-lations." Given an *n*-ary relation *R,* a corresponding quotient relation may be derived from *R* by grouping tuples on the basis of the values of some attribute of *R* (see the description of GROUP BY in Chapter 7). For example, the quo-tient relation derived from relation SUPPLIER (Fig. 4.6) on the basis of CITY values is a set of three groups of tuples: one containing two London tuples, one containing two Paris tuples, and one containing a single Athens tuple. The au-thors claim that operating directly on quotient relations leads both to more nat-ural query formulation and to a potential for more efficient implementation.

12.15 T. H. Merrett. "The Extended Relational Algebra, A Basis for Query Lan-guages." In *Databases: Improving Usability and Responsiveness* (ed., B. Shneider-man). New York: Academic Press (1978).

Proposes the introduction of quantifiers into the algebra—not just the existen-tial and universal quantifiers of the calculus (Chapter 13), but the more general quantifiers "the number of" and "the proportion of." These quantifiers allow the expression of such conditions as "at least three of," "not more than half of," "an odd number of."

12.16 A. V. Aho, C. Beeri, and J. D. Ullman. "The Theory of Joins in Relational Databases." *ACM Transactions on Database Systems* **4,** No. 3 (September 1979).

The definition of natural join given in Section 12.3 is based on one given in this paper.

12.17 I. J. Heath. Private communication (April 1971).

12.18 M. Lacroix and A. Pirotte. "Generalized Joins." *SIGMOD Record* (bulletin of ACM SIGMOD) **8,** No. 3 (September 1976).

12.19 CODASYL Development Committee. "An Information Algebra." *CACM* **5,** No. 4 (April 1962).

The Information Algebra is an interesting precursor of the relational algebra.

12.20 D. L. Childs. "Description of a Set-Theoretic Data Structure." *Proc. FJCC* **33** (1968).

STDS is a system in which the emphasis is on general sets rather than on relations as such. The STDS language includes the traditional set operations (union, intersection, etc.), but not the special relational operations such as join.

12.21 J. A. Feldman and P. D. Rovner. "An Algol-Based Associative Language." *CACM* **12,** No. 8 (August 1969).

This paper describes the LEAP language and its implementation. LEAP is essentially an extension of Algol 60 that provides set-manipulation operations (not only union, intersection, etc., but also a powerful loop operation, which allows the user to manipulate the individual set elements one by one). The set elements may be either simple items or "associations," i.e., triples of the form ⟨attribute, object, value⟩. A set of "associations" corresponds to a binary relation in which "attribute" is the relation name (all triples in one such set have the same "attribute" component) and within each triple, "object" and "value" are the two items that are associated. Association sets are implemented via a complex hashing scheme that, by means of data redundancy, enables any "associative operation" to be handled in a reasonably efficient manner.

12.22 W. Ash and E. H. Sibley. "TRAMP: An Interpretive Associative Processor with Deductive Capabilities." *Proc. ACM 23rd Nat. Conf.* (1968).

TRAMP is a system that, like LEAP [12.21], is designed for associative processing. Like LEAP, it works in terms of ⟨attribute, object, value⟩ triples; i.e., it stores binary relations. The storage structure is again based on hashing; however, there is no data redundancy—instead, a complex system of pointers is used to provide the required flexibility. The really significant difference between TRAMP and LEAP, however, is that TRAMP permits the user to state the definition of a (binary or unary) relation in terms of stored (binary) relations, using the "converse" and "composition" operators; for example, the relation "parent of" can be defined as the converse of "child of." Requests in terms of such a defined relation are then dynamically interpreted in terms of the relations actually stored.

12.23 R. E. Levein and M. E. Maron. "A Computer System for Inference Execution and Data Retrieval." *CACM* **10,** No. 11 (November 1967).

This paper describes the "Relational Data File" and a language for retrieving data from it. The Relational Data File is essentially a collection of binary relations, stored with a high degree of data redundancy to provide efficient response to retrieval operations. As in TRAMP [12.22], the user can define rules for deriving further relations from the ones actually stored.

12.24 P. J. Titman. "An Experimental Data Base System Using Binary Relations." *Proc. IFIP TC-2 Working Conference on Data Base Management Systems* (eds., Klimbie and Koffeman) (April 1974). North-Holland, 1974.

The major objective of the prototype described in this paper was to evaluate a particular storage structure and an associated access strategy; thus the emphasis was on those aspects of a database system that lie below the user interface. The "binary relations" of the title would more accurately be described as ordered binary *arrays:* Each value pair in the "relation" could be addressed via (a coded form of) its position in the sequence. Thus each value pair had an implicit identifier. Domains were represented by "value sets," i.e., ordered unary arrays in which, again, each element had an implicit identifier, namely, its position. The data values in a given pair within any one of the binary arrays were identifiers, either of elements in value sets or of other pairs. Thus, for example, the triple $\langle$ 'S1', 'P1', 300$\rangle$ of relation SP might be represented as the value pair $\langle a, b\rangle$, where b is the identifier of the value 300 in the QTY value set and a is the identifier of the pair $\langle c, d\rangle$ in the S#-P# binary array, and c and d are in turn identifiers of S1 and P1, respectively, in the S# and P# value sets. Both value sets and binary arrays employed some simple yet effective compression techniques—a space reduction of about 70 percent was achieved in the benchmark application (a bill of materials structure). Differential file techniques [2.24] were also used. To access the database, the system provided a collection of set operations, principally "collate," which may be considered as a join followed by a projection. Access times seemed to be reasonably acceptable. The paper concludes with some interesting observations on the reliability, security, and integrity aspects of such a system.

12.25 E. H. Beitz. "A Set-Theoretic View of Data-Base Representation." *Proc. 1974 ACM SIGMOD Workshop on Data Description, Access and Control.*

12.26 E. H. Beitz. "Sets as a Model for Data Base Representation: Much Ado About Something." *Proc. ACM Pacific Conference, San Francisco* (April 1975). Available from ACM Golden Gate Chapter, P.O. Box 24055, Oakland, California 94623.

These two papers [12.25, 12.26], like [12.24], are not really concerned with the user's view of a database but rather with the conceptual and internal levels of the system. However, the conceptual structure proposed could well prove suitable for supporting relational views. Every entity and every "property" (such as WEIGHT = 17) is given a unique system identifier; the conceptual model then consists of (a) the set of all entity identifiers, (b) the set of all property identifiers, and (c) a binary relation defined over (a) and (b). At the stored level this binary relation is represented twice, once in each direction, giving symmetry of access and incidentally an automatic backup copy. Each of the two representations actually consists of an index into the appropriate one of (a) or (b). Many advantages are claimed for such an approach.

13
Relational
Calculus

13.1 INTRODUCTION

The idea of using predicate calculus as the basis for a query language appears to have originated in a paper by Kuhns [13.1]. The concept of a *relational* calculus—that is, an applied predicate calculus specifically tailored to relational databases—was first proposed by Codd in [12.1]; a language explicitly based on this calculus, Data Sublanguage ALPHA (DSL ALPHA), was also presented by Codd [13.2]. DSL ALPHA itself was never implemented, but a language very similar to it in spirit, called QUEL, was used as the query language in the system INGRES [13.7–13.16]. We shall examine QUEL in a little more detail later. We note also that SQL and QBE both incorporate certain elements of the calculus.

A fundamental aspect of the calculus of [12.1], and of languages based on it, is the notion of the *tuple variable*. A tuple variable is a variable that "ranges over" some named relation[1]—i.e., a variable whose only permitted values are tuples of that relation. (In other words, if tuple variable T ranges over relation R, then, at any given time, T represents some individual tuple of R.) For example, the query "Get supplier numbers for suppliers in London" can be expressed in QUEL as follows:

```
RANGE OF SX IS S
RETRIEVE (SX.S#) WHERE SX.CITY = 'LONDON'
```

The tuple variable here is SX, which ranges over relation S. The query may be paraphrased: "For each possible value of the variable SX, retrieve the

---

1. More accurately, a tuple variable ranges over either a named relation or the *union* of two or more (union-compatible) named relations. To simplify the discussion we ignore the union case for most of this chapter.

S# component of that value, if and only if the CITY component has the value 'LONDON'.''

[As an aside, we note that the SQL formulation of this query—SELECT S# FROM S WHERE CITY = 'LONDON'—does not require the explicit introduction of a tuple variable, but instead allows the relation-name S to play the role implicitly. But the underlying concept is the same. To understand how the SQL query is evaluated, it is necessary to imagine the *tuple variable* S ranging over the *relation* S. In effect, SQL simply has a default rule for the automatic definition of tuple variables that is adequate in simple cases. In more complex cases the user still has to introduce tuple variables explicitly; see, for instance, Examples 7.2.6, 7.2.13, and 7.2.19.]

Because of its reliance on tuple variables (and to distinguish it from the domain calculus discussed below), the original relational calculus of [12.1] has come to be known as the *tuple* calculus. The tuple calculus is described in detail in Section 13.2.

More recently, Lacroix and Pirotte [13.3] have proposed an alternative relational calculus, the *domain* calculus, in which tuple variables are replaced by domain variables—i.e., variables that range over the underlying domains instead of over relations. A language called ILL based on this calculus is presented by the same authors in [13.4]. Query by Example can also be considered as an implementation of the domain calculus. (In the QBE version of the QUEL example above,

S	S#	SNAME	STATUS	CITY
	P.SX			LONDON

the example element SX is a variable that ranges over the supplier-number domain.) DEDUCE [7.6] is another domain-oriented language. We shall discuss domain calculus in Section 13.3.

13.2   TUPLE-ORIENTED RELATIONAL CALCULUS

The primary construct of the tuple-oriented relational calculus (tuple calculus for short) is the *tuple calculus expression*. A tuple calculus expression is essentially a nonprocedural definition of some relation in terms of some given set of relations. Such an expression can thus clearly be used to define the result of a query, or the target of an update, or a view (in the System R sense), and so on. In this section we present a fairly formal definition of the tuple calculus, along the lines of [12.1] (but simplified), then follow it with a number of examples.

The expressions of the tuple calculus are constructed from the following elements.

- *Tuple variables* T, U, V, ... Each tuple variable is constrained to range over some named relation.[2] If tuple variable T represents tuple t (at some given time), then the expression T.A represents the A-component of t (at that time), where A is an attribute of the relation over which T ranges.

- *Conditions* of the form $x * y$, where $*$ is any one of $=$, $\neg=$, $<$, $<=$, $>$, or $>=$, and at least one of x and y is an expression of the form T.A (see the previous paragraph) and the other is either a similar expression or a constant.

- *Well-formed formulas* (WFFs). A WFF is constructed from conditions, Boolean operators (AND, OR, NOT), and quantifiers (∃, ∀) according to rules F1–F5 below.

  F1. Every condition is a WFF.

  F2. If f is a WFF, then so are (f) and NOT (f).

  F3. If f and g are WFFs, then so are $(f$ AND $g)$ and $(f$ OR $g)$.[3]

  F4. If f is a WFF in which T occurs as a free variable (see below), then ∃T(f) and ∀T(f) are WFFs.

  F5. Nothing else is a WFF.

Free and Bound Variables

Each occurrence of a tuple variable within a WFF is either *free* or *bound*. [An "occurrence" of a tuple variable is an appearance of the variable name within the symbol string that is the WFF under consideration. A tuple variable occurs within a WFF in the context of an expression of the form T.A (where T is a tuple variable and A is an attribute of the associated relation), or as the variable following one of the quantifier symbols ∃, ∀.]

1. Within a condition all tuple variable occurrences are free.

2. Tuple variable occurrences in the WFFs (f), NOT (f) are free/bound according as they are free/bound in f. Tuple variable occurrences in the WFFs $(f$ AND $g)$, $(f$ OR $g)$ are free/bound according as they are free/bound in f or g (whichever of f, g they appear in).

---

2. Or over a union (see footnote 1, p. 223). In the union case the relations concerned must not only be union-compatible but must also have identical attribute-names.

3. The usual conventions are adopted for eliminating unnecessary parentheses.

3. Occurrences of T that are free in f are bound in the WFFs $\exists T(f)$, $\forall T(f)$. Other tuple variable occurrences in f are free/bound in these WFFs according as they are free/bound in f.

Finally, a *tuple calculus expression* is an expression of the form

```
T.A,U.B,...,V.C [ WHERE f ]
```

where T,U, . . . ,V are tuple variables; A,B, . . . ,C are attributes of the associated relations; and f is a WFF containing exactly T,U, . . . ,V as free variables. The value of this expression is a projection of that subset of the Cartesian product $T \times U \times \cdots \times V$ (where T,U, . . . ,V range over all their possible values) for which f evaluates to *true*—or, if "WHERE f" is omitted, a projection of that entire Cartesian product. The projection in question is of course taken over the components (attributes) indicated by the entries in the list T.A,U.B, . . . ,V.C (the "target list").

Examples

In these examples we use as tuple variables SX, SY, . . . for relation S; PX, PY, . . . for relation P; SPX, SPY, . . . for relation SP.

Some valid conditions

```
SX.S# = 'S1'
SX.S# =  SPY.S#
SPY.P# ¬= PZ.P#
```

Some valid WFFs

```
NOT (SX.CITY = 'LONDON')
SX.S# = SPY.S# AND SPY.P# ¬= PZ.P#
∃SPX (SPX.S# = SX.S# AND SPX.P# = 'P2')
```

The existential quantifier $\exists$ is read "there exists." Thus the last example here can be read: "There exists an SP tuple with S# value equal to the S# component of SX [whatever that is] and P# value equal to P2."

```
∀PZ (PZ.COLOR = 'RED')
```

The symbol $\forall$ represents the *universal* quantifier ("for all"). This WFF can therefore be read "For all P tuples, the COLOR is RED." The universal quantifier is included purely for convenience; it is not essential—the identity

$$\forall x(f) \equiv NOT \; (\exists x \; (NOT \; f))$$

shows that any WFF involving $\forall$ can always be replaced by an equivalent WFF involving $\exists$ instead. For example, the (true) statement "for all integers x, there exists an integer y such that $y > x$" is equivalent to the statement "there does not exist an integer x such that there does not exist an integer y such that $y > x$." But it is frequently easier to think in terms of ∀ rather than in terms of ∃ and a double negative.

Free and bound variables

SX, SPY, and PZ are all free in the first two WFFs above. In the third WFF, SX is free and SPX is bound. Similarly, PZ is bound in the fourth WFF. To examine the concept of bound variables a little more closely, let us take a simpler example:

$$∃ x \ (x > 3)$$

(where x ranges over the set of integers). The bound variable x in this formula is a sort of *dummy*—it serves only to link the expression in parentheses to the quantifier outside. The formula states simply that there exists some integer, say x, that is greater than three. The meaning of the formula would remain unchanged if all occurrences of x were replaced by some other variable y [to yield $∃y(y > 3)$].

Now consider

$$∃ x \ (x > 3) \ \text{AND} \ x < 0$$

Here there are three occurrences of x, *referring to two different variables.* The first two occurrences are bound, and could be replaced by some other variable without changing the meaning. The third occurrence is free, and *cannot* be replaced with impunity. Thus, of the two expressions below, the first is equivalent to the one above and the second is not:

```
∃ y (y > 3) AND x < 0
∃ y (y > 3) AND y < 0
```

Tuple calculus expressions

```
SX.S#
SX.S# WHERE SX.CITY = 'LONDON'
SX.S#, SX.CITY WHERE ∃SPX (SPX.S# = SX.S# AND
                            SPX.P# = 'P2')
```

The first of these denotes the set of all supplier numbers in relation S; the second denotes that subset of those supplier numbers for which the city is London. The third is a tuple calculus representation of the query: "Get supplier numbers and cities for suppliers who supply part P2."

The tuple calculus was used as the basis for the definition of relational completeness given in [12.1]. That paper also gave an algorithm for converting an arbitrary calculus expression into an equivalent expression of the relational algebra (and hence showed that the algebra is complete).

Conversely, Ullman [13.6] shows that any algebraic expression can be converted into an expression of the tuple calculus, so the two languages are formally equivalent.

QUEL

We conclude this section with a number of examples of the tuple calculus language QUEL. First we give definitions of all the tuple variables we shall need.

```
RANGE OF SX  IS S
RANGE OF PX  IS P
RANGE OF SPX IS SP
RANGE OF SPY IS SP
```

13.2.1 Get supplier numbers for suppliers in Paris with status > 20. (Example 7.2.3)

```
RETRIEVE (SX.S#) WHERE SX.CITY = 'PARIS' AND
                       SX.STATUS > 20
```

Attributes of the result can be given user-specified names if desired. For example,

```
RETRIEVE (FOURNISSEUR = SX.S#)
             WHERE SX.CITY = 'PARIS' AND
                   SX.STATUS > 20
```

13.2.2 Get supplier numbers and cities for suppliers who supply part P2.

```
RETRIEVE (SX.S#, SX.CITY) WHERE SX.S# = SPX.S# AND
                                SPX.P# = 'P2'
```

We saw earlier that SPX needs to be existentially quantified in this example. In QUEL, however, all tuple variables appearing after the WHERE but not in the target list before the WHERE are simply *assumed* to be existentially quantified. That is, the formula following the WHERE is assumed to be in prenex normal form (see Example 13.2.3 below) with all quantifiers omitted. Quantifiers are never explicitly stated in QUEL.

13.2.3 Get supplier names for suppliers who supply at least one red part. (Example 7.2.10)

In "pure" tuple calculus,

```
SX.SNAME WHERE ∃SPX (SX.S# = SPX.S# AND
                 ∃PX (SPX.P# = PX.P# AND
                      PX.COLOR = 'RED'))
```

Or equivalently (but in *prenex normal form*, in which all quantifiers appear at the front of the WFF),

```
SX.SNAME WHERE ∃SPX (∃PX (SX.S# = SPX.S# AND
                          SPX.P# = PX.P# AND
                          PX.COLOR = 'RED'))
```

In QUEL,

```
RETRIEVE (SX.SNAME) WHERE SX.S# = SPX.S# AND
                          SPX.P# = PX.P# AND
                          PX.COLOR = 'RED'
```

13.2.4 Get supplier names for suppliers who supply at least one part supplied by supplier S2. (Example 7.2.12)

```
RETRIEVE (SX.SNAME) WHERE SX.S# = SPX.S# AND
                          SPX.P# = SPY.P# AND
                          SPY.S# = 'S2'
```

13.2.5 For each part supplied, get part number and names of all cities supplying the part. (Example 7.2.5)

```
RETRIEVE (SPX.P#, SX.CITY) WHERE SPX.S# = SX.S#
```

In SQL the user can specify UNIQUE to eliminate duplicates. In QUEL duplicates are eliminated if the user saves the result of the RETRIEVE in the database (by specifying "INTO relation-name" after the keyword RETRIEVE), but not if the result is simply displayed at the terminal.

13.2.6 Get supplier names for suppliers who do not supply part P2. (Examples 7.2.14 and 7.2.17)

In "pure" tuple calculus,

```
SX.SNAME WHERE NOT (∃SPX (SPX.S# = SX.S# AND
                          SPX.P# ='P2'))
```

Or equivalently,

```
SX.SNAME WHERE ∀SPX (SPX.S# ¬= SX.S# OR
                     SPX.S# ¬= 'P2')
```

In QUEL,

```
RETRIEVE (SX.SNAME) WHERE
         COUNT(SPX.S# WHERE SPX.S# = SX.S# AND
                            SPX.P# = 'P2')
                                        = 0
```

QUEL does not support the universal quantifier. However, it does provide the usual array of built-in functions, so that the effect of universal quantification can be achieved as indicated in the example. (The statement "For all x, f is true" is equivalent to the statement "The count of the number of x's where f is false is zero.")

Note that the QUEL statement

```
RETRIEVE SX.SNAME WHERE NOT (SPX.S# = SX.S# AND
                             SPX.P# = 'P2')
```

does *not* achieve the desired result. (Why not? What *does* it do?)

13.2.7 Increase the shipment quantity by 100 for all suppliers in London.

```
REPLACE SPX (QTY = QTY + 100) WHERE SPX.S# = SX.S# AND
                              SX.CITY = 'LONDON'
```

13.2.8 Add part P7 (name 'WASHER', city 'ATHENS', other attribute values unknown) to table P (see Example 7.4.5).

```
APPEND TO P (P# = 'P7', PNAME = 'WASHER', CITY = 'ATHENS')
```

In the new tuple, WEIGHT is set to zero and COLOR is set to the empty (zero-length) string.

13.2.9 Delete all shipments for supplier S1.

```
DELETE SPX WHERE SPX.S# = 'S1'
```

Further details of INGRES and the QUEL language are given in references [13.7–13.16].

13.3 DOMAIN-ORIENTED RELATIONAL CALCULUS

As we indicated in Section 13.1, the domain-oriented relational calculus (domain calculus for short) differs from the tuple calculus in that its variables range over domains rather than relations. Expressions of the domain calculus are constructed from the following elements.

- *Domain variables* D, E, F, ... Each domain variable is constrained to range over some specified domain. ("Element variable" would be a better name, since the values are domain *elements,* not domains.)

- *Conditions,* which can take two forms: (a) simple comparisons of the form $x * y$, as for the tuple calculus, except that x and y are now domain variables (or constants); and (b) membership conditions, of the form R(term, term, . . .). Here R is a relation, and each "term" is a pair A:V, where A in turn is an attribute of R and V is either a domain variable or a constant. For example, SP(S#:'S1',P#:'P1') is a membership condition (which evaluates to *true* if and only if there exists an SP tuple having S# = 'S1' and P# = 'P1').

■ *Well-formed formulas* (WFFs), formed in accordance with rules F1–F5 of Section 13.2 (but with the revised definition of "condition").

Free and Bound Variables

The rules concerning free and bound variables given for the tuple calculus apply to the domain calculus also, mutatis mutandis. Note in particular that the variable x in "$\exists x$" and "$\forall x$" is now a *domain* variable.

A *domain calculus expression* is then an expression of the form

```
D,E,...,F [ WHERE f ]
```

where D,E, . . . ,F are domain variables, and f is a WFF containing exactly D,E, . . . ,F as free variables. The value of this expression is that subset of the Cartesian product $D \times E \times \cdots \times F$ (where D,E, . . . ,F range over all their possible values) for which f evaluates to *true*—or, if "WHERE f" is omitted, that entire Cartesian product.

Examples

In these examples we use domain variables with names formed by appending X,Y,Z, . . . to the appropriate domain-name—except that, for domains whose names end in "#", we drop that "#". We remind the reader that in the suppliers-and-parts database each attribute has the same name as its underlying domain.

Some valid conditions

```
CITYX ¬= 'LONDON'
S (CITY : 'LONDON')
S (CITY : CITYX)
SP (S# : SY, P# : PZ)
```

As we indicated earlier, a membership condition evaluates to *true* if and only if there exists a tuple of the specified relation having the specified values for the specified attributes.

Some valid WFFs

```
NOT S (CITY : 'LONDON')
```

This is *true* if and only if there is no S tuple having a CITY value of 'LONDON'. Contrast

```
S (CITY : CITYX) AND CITYX ¬= 'LONDON'
```

This is *true* if and only if there exists an S tuple having a CITY value not 'LONDON'.

```
S (S# : SX, CITY : CITYX) AND SP (S# : SX, P# : 'P2')
```

This WFF can be read "SX and CITYX are supplier number and city for a supplier who supplies part P2."

```
∃CITYX (S (CITY : CITYX) AND P (CITY : CITYX))
```

"There exists at least one city having both a supplier and a part located therein."

```
∀CITYX (S (CITY : CITYX))
```

"Every city known to the system has at least one corresponding supplier."

Domain calculus expressions

```
SX
SX WHERE S (S# : SX)
SX WHERE S (S# : SX, CITY : 'LONDON')
SX, CITYX WHERE S (S# : SX, CITY : CITYX) AND
                SP (S# : SX, P# : 'P2')
```

The first of these denotes the set of all supplier numbers; the second denotes the set of all supplier numbers in relation S; and the third denotes the set of all supplier numbers from relation S for suppliers located in London. The fourth is a domain calculus representation of the query: "Get supplier numbers and cities for suppliers who supply part P2" (note that the tuple calculus version of this query required an existential quantifier).

```
SX, CITYX WHERE S (S# : SX, CITY : CITYX) AND
                ∃PX (SP (S# : SX, P# : PX) AND
                     P (P# : PX, COLOR : 'RED'))
```

"Get supplier numbers and cities for suppliers who supply at least one red part."

For examples of a language that is at least partially an implementation of the domain calculus, see Chapter 11 (Query By Example). The language ILL of Lacroix and Pirotte [13.3, 13.4] is not discussed here: ILL is much further from the basic domain calculus than QUEL is from the tuple calculus, and examples would require considerably more preliminary explanation. We recommend that the interested reader study the references.

The difference between tuple calculus and domain calculus lies basically in how the user perceives the database. For the suppliers-and-parts database, the tuple calculus encourages the user to think in terms of three entity types (suppliers, parts, shipments), each having various properties. The domain calculus, by contrast, encourages the user to think in terms of rather more entity types (suppliers, parts, cities, colors, quantities, . . .), and to see the three relations S, P, and SP as representing various associations among those entity types. The domain calculus formulation of a given query tends to be somewhat simpler than the tuple calculus formulation (particularly if we allow quantifiers to be omitted, as in QUEL) for the following reason: If a given entity, say a supplier, occurs several times in the English statement of the query, then the domain calculus formulation will contain several occurrences of some corresponding domain variable; the tuple calculus formulation, by contrast, will contain occurrences of several distinct tuple variables (such as SX, SPX), with "join conditions" (such as SX.S# = SPX.S#) connecting those occurrences together.

Finally, it is easy to see that the domain calculus is relationally complete. We have already mentioned Ullman's proof [13.6] that any relational algebra expression is equivalent to an expression of the tuple calculus. He also shows in [13.6] that any tuple calculus expression can be converted to an equivalent domain calculus expression, and that any domain calculus expression can be converted to an equivalent algebraic expression. The three languages are thus all equivalent to each other in their selective power.

EXERCISES

13.1 Let $f(x, y)$ be an arbitrary formula with free variables x and y. Which of the following are true statements?

a) $\exists x \ (\exists y \ (f(x,y))) \equiv \exists y \ (\exists x \ (f(x,y)))$

b) $\forall x \ (f(x,y)) \equiv \text{NOT} \ \exists x \ (\text{NOT} \ f(x,y))$

c) $\exists x \ (\forall y \ (f(x,y))) \equiv \forall y \ (\exists x \ (f(x,y)))$

d) $\forall x \ (\forall y \ (f(x,y))) \equiv \forall y \ (\forall x \ (f(x,y)))$

13.2 Give tuple calculus and domain calculus solutions to Exercises 7.1–7.28. *Note:* To simplify some of the solutions it is convenient to introduce the *logical implication* operator "IF . . . THEN . . .". "IF A THEN B" is defined to be equivalent to "(NOT A) OR B".

13.3 Suppose a rule is introduced that is similar (but not identical) to that of QUEL, to the following effect: In the formula following WHERE, an existential quantifier is assumed (at the left-hand end) for any variable not appearing in the target list and not already *explicitly* quantified. Revise your solutions to Exercise 13.2 to take advantage of this rule.

13.4 Show that every expression of the tuple calculus has a domain calculus equivalent (and the converse).

13.5 Give tuple calculus and domain calculus equivalents for each of the five primitive algebraic operators.

REFERENCES AND BIBLIOGRAPHY

13.1 J. L. Kuhns. "Answering Questions by Computer; A Logical Study." Report RM-5428-PR, Rand Corp., Santa Monica, Calif. (1967).

13.2 E. F. Codd. "A Data Base Sublanguage Founded on the Relational Calculus." *Proc. 1971 ACM SIGFIDET Workshop on Data Description, Access and Control.*

13.3 M. Lacroix and A. Pirotte. "Domain-Oriented Relational Languages." *Proc. 3rd International Conference on Very Large Data Bases* (October 1977).

13.4 M. Lacroix and A. Pirotte. "ILL: An English Structured Query Language for Relational Data Bases." In *Architecture and Models in Data Base Management Systems* (ed., G. M. Nijssen). North-Holland (1977).

13.5 A. Pirotte and P. Wodon. "A Comprehensive Formal Query Language for a Relational Data Base." *R.A.I.R.O. Informatique/Computer Science* **11**, No. 2 (1977).

> FQL, like ILL, is based on the domain calculus, but is much more formal (less "English-like") than ILL.

13.6 J. D. Ullman. *Principles of Database Systems.* Washington, D.C.: Computer Science Press (1979).

13.7 G. D. Held, M. R. Stonebraker, and E. Wong. "INGRES—A Relational Data Base System." *Proc. NCC* **44** (May 1975).

> Gives a high-level description of the system; includes a definition of QUEL.

13.8 M. R. Stonebraker, E. Wong, and P. Kreps. "The Design and Implementation of INGRES." *ACM Transactions on Database Systems* **1**, No. 3 (September 1976).

> An expanded version of [13.7].

13.9 M. R. Stonebraker. "Getting Started in INGRES—A Tutorial." Berkeley: University of California, Electronics Research Laboratory Memorandum ERL-M518 (April 1975).

13.10 R. Epstein. "Creating and Maintaining a Database Using INGRES." Berkeley: University of California, Electronics Research Laboratoy Memorandum UCB/ERL M77/71 (December 1977).

13.11 E. Allman, G. D. Held, and M. R. Stonebraker. "Embedding a Data Manipulation Language in a General Purpose Programming Language." *Proc. 1976 ACM SIGPLAN/SIGMOD Conference on Data Abstraction* (March 1976).

> Describes an operational precompiler for EQUEL (QUEL embedded in the programming language C).

13.12 G. D. Held and M. R. Stonebraker. "Storage Structures and Access Methods in the Relational Data Base Management System INGRES." *Proc. ACM Pacific Conference, San Francisco* (April 1975). Available from ACM Golden Gate Chapter, P. O. Box 24055, Oakland, California 94623.

> Like System R, INGRES includes an internal "stored record interface" called the AMI (analogous to the RSI). At this level relations are represented as stored

files, with each tuple represented as a stored record. Tuples have TIDs as in the RSS. A given stored file can have any one of the following storage structures: (1) *heap* (an unsorted table); (2) *hash;* (3) *isam* (index on the primary key). Various forms of (2) and (3), including some involving compression techniques, are discussed in the paper. The specific storage structure used for a given relation is hidden from higher-level components of the system; the AMI provides generic operators INSERT, REPLACE/DELETE/GET (given a TID), FIND (to establish start and end conditions for a sequential scan), and GET (within scan), that operate on any structure. In addition the higher-level component of the system can create secondary indexes over any relation; a secondary index is itself treated as a relation (stored as an *isam* file), in which one field gives pointers (TIDs) to records in the indexed relation (but of course these TIDs are not accessible to the INGRES user). The AMI itself is unaware of the relationship between a secondary index relation and the corresponding indexed relation.

13.13 E. Wong and K. Youssefi. "Decomposition—A Strategy for Query Processing." *ACM Transactions on Database Systems* **1,** No. 3 (September 1976).

Describes the strategy for processing queries in INGRES. The general procedure is to break a query involving more than one tuple variable down into a sequence of queries involving one such variable each, using *reduction* and *tuple substitution* alternately to achieve the desired decomposition. *Reduction* is the process of removing a component of the query that has just one variable in common with the rest of the query. *Tuple substitution* is the process of substituting for one of the variables a tuple at a time. The paper gives algorithms for reduction and for selecting the variable for tuple substitution.

13.14 P. Hawthorne and M. R. Stonebraker. "The Use of Technological Advances to Enhance Data Management System Performance." *Proc. 1979 ACM SIGMOD International Conference on Management of Data* (May 1979).

13.15 R. Epstein. "Techniques for Processing of Aggregates in Relational Database Systems." Berkeley: University of California, Electronics Reseach Laboratory Memorandum UCB/ERL M79/8 (February 1979).

The "aggregates" of the title refer to the built-in functions such as COUNT.

13.16 M. R. Stonebraker. "Requiem for a Data Base System." Berkeley: University of Califonia, Electronics Research Laboratory Memorandum UCB/ERL M79/4 (January 1979).

An account of the history of the INGRES project (to January 1979). The emphasis is on mistakes and lessons learned, rather than on successes.

13.17 J. B. Rothnie, Jr. "Evaluating Inter-Entry Retrieval Expressions in a Relational Data Base Management System." *Proc. NCC* **44** (1975).

13.18 J. B. Rothnie, Jr. "An Approach to Implementing a Relational Data Management System." *Proc. 1974 ACM SIGMOD Workshop on Data Description, Access and Control.*

These two papers [13.17, 13.18] describe some techniques used in the experimental system DAMAS (built at M.I.T.) for implementing a calculus-based retrieval language. [13.17] is more tutorial in nature; [13.18] gives some experimental results and more internal details. The papers discuss, specifically, the implementation of retrieval expressions involving a single existentially quantified tuple variable in terms of simpler expressions known as "primitive Boolean conditions" or PBCs. A PBC is a predicate that can be established as true or false for a given tuple by examining that tuple in isolation—i.e., it is a predicate involving no quantifiers. The "storage modules" of DAMAS, which are responsible for managing the stored database, support the following operations directly:

- get next tuple where P is true,

- test the existence of a tuple such that P is true,

- eliminate from consideration all tuples where P is true,

where P is a PBC. Using these operations, DAMAS handles a retrieval involving R1 (unquantified) and R2 (existentially quantified) as follows. Note that the target of the query must be some projection of R1.

Step 1. In the original predicate, set all terms involving R2 to true and simplify. The result is a PBC, PBC1, say. Tuples of R1 not satisfying PBC1 may be eliminated from further consideration.

Step 2. Get a (noneliminated) tuple from R1. Substitute values from this tuple in original predicate and simplify, yielding PBC2. Does there exist a tuple in R2 such that PBC2 is true?

Step 3. (Yes) Fetch identified R2 tuple. Extract target values from the R1 tuple and add to result relation. Build PBC3, selecting all R1 tuples containing the same values for target attributes, and use it to eliminate from consideration all R1 tuples that would generate duplicates. (This elimination can be performed whenever a tuple is added to the result.) Also, substitute values from fetched R2 tuple in original predicate and simplify, yielding PBC4. Get all R1 tuples satisfying PBC4 and add target values to result.

Step 4. (No) Build PBC5, selecting all R1 tuples that would yield (in Step 2) a PBC for which there cannot exist an R2 tuple to make it true (because no R2 tuple made PBC2 true). Eliminate these R1 tuples.

Step 5. Repeat from Step 2 until no R1 tuples remain.

The design of the foregoing algorithm is based on the principle that as much information as possible should be derived from each database access. In practice, however, it may prove *more* expensive to eliminate tuples from consideration (for example) than simply to examine and reject them. For this reason certain steps of the algorithm may or may not be applied in a given situation. In DAMAS the choice of whether or not to apply them is left to the user, but some suggestions are given for automating this choice.

14
Further
Normalization

14.1 INTRODUCTION

By now we have examined several aspects of database systems in general and relational systems in particular. We have looked at the overall structure of such systems, at languages for defining and manipulating data in relational form, at methods for implementing those languages, at techniques for representing relations in storage, and more. But we have not yet considered a very fundamental question, namely: Given a body of data to be represented in a database, how do we decide on a suitable logical structure for that data? In other words, how do we decide what relations are needed and what their attributes should be? This is the *database design* problem.

Consider the suppliers-and-parts database once again. The relational schema in Fig. 4.7 does have a feeling of rightness about it; it is "obvious" that three relations (S, P, SP) are necessary, that (for example) COLOR belongs in relation P, STATUS in relation S, QTY in relation SP, and so on. But what is it that tells us that these things are so? Some insight into this question can be gained by seeing what happens if we change the design. Suppose that STATUS is moved out of relation S and into relation SP (intuitively the wrong place for it, since STATUS concerns suppliers, not shipments). Figure 14.1 shows a partial tabulation of this revised SP relation (which we refer to as SP' to avoid confusion).

It is clear from Fig. 14.1 that relation SP' involves a lot of redundancy—the fact that a given supplier has a certain status is stated as many times as there are shipments for that supplier. This redundancy can lead to problems. For example, after an update, supplier S1 may be shown as having a status of 20 in one tuple and a status of 30 in another. So perhaps a

SP'	S#	P#	QTY	STATUS
	S1	P1	300	20
	S1	P2	200	20
	S1	P3	400	20
	S1	P4	100	20

Fig. 14.1 Partial tabulation of relation SP'.

good design principle is "one fact in one place" (i.e., avoid redundancy if possible). The topic of this chapter, normalization theory, is basically a formalization of simple ideas such as this one—a formalization that has practical application in the area of database design.

Before going any further, we should stress the fact that designing a database can be an extremely complex task. Normalization theory is a useful aid in the design process, but it is *not* a panacea. Anyone designing a relational database is advised to be familiar with the basic techniques of normalization as described in this chapter, but we certainly do not suggest that the design should be based on normalization principles alone.

Recall from Chapter 4 that relations in a relational database are always normalized, in the sense that they are defined over simple domains (domains that contain atomic values only). In Section 4.2 we showed by example how an unnormalized relation can be reduced to an equivalent normalized form. Normalization theory takes this basic concept much further. The fundamental point is that a given relation, even though it is normalized, may still possess certain undesirable properties (relation SP' in Fig. 14.1 is a case in point); normalization theory allows us to recognize such cases and shows how such relations can be converted to a more desirable form.

Normal Forms

Normalization theory is built around the concept of *normal forms.* A relation is said to be in a particular normal form if it satisfies a certain specified set of constraints. For example, a relation is said to be in *first normal form* (abbreviated 1NF) if and only if it satisfies the constraint that it contains atomic values only (thus every normalized relation is in 1NF, which accounts for the "first").

Numerous normal forms have been defined (see Fig. 14.2). Codd originally defined first, second, and third normal form (1NF, 2NF, 3NF) in reference [14.1]. Briefly, as Fig. 14.2 suggests, all normalized relations are in 1NF; some 1NF relations are also in 2NF; and some 2NF relations are also in 3NF. The motivation behind the definitions was that 2NF was "more

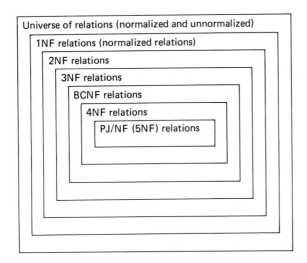

Fig. 14.2 Normal forms.

desirable'' than 1NF, in a sense to be explained, and 3NF in turn was more desirable than 2NF. That is, the designer should generally choose 3NF relations in designing a database, rather than 2NF or 1NF relations.[1]

Codd's original definition of 3NF [14.1] suffered from certain inadequacies, as we shall see in Section 14.4. A revised (stronger) definition, due to Boyce and Codd, was given in [9.2]—stronger in the sense that any relation that was 3NF by the new definition was certainly 3NF by the old, but a relation could be 3NF by the old definition and not by the new. The new 3NF is sometimes called Boyce/Codd Normal Form (BCNF) to distinguish it from the old form. Subsequently, Fagin [14.4] defined a new "fourth" normal form (4NF) and, more recently, another normal form which he called "projection-join normal form" (PJ/NF, also known as 5NF) [14.5]. As Fig. 14.2 shows, some BCNF relations are also in 4NF, and some 4NF relations are also in 5NF.

The reader may very well be wondering by now whether there is a 6NF, a 7NF, . . . , ad infinitum. Although this is a good question to ask, we are obviously not in a position to give it any detailed consideration yet. We content ourselves with the rather equivocal statement that there are indeed additional normal forms not shown in Fig. 14.2, but that 5NF is actually the

---

1. This statement should *not* be construed as law. Sometimes there are good reasons for flouting the principles of normalization (see Section 14.8). The only hard requirement is that relations be in at least first normal form.

"final" normal form in a special (but important) sense. We shall return to this topic at the end of the chapter.

The reader is warned that we make little attempt at rigor in what follows; rather, we rely to a considerable extent on plain intuition. Indeed, part of the argument is that concepts such as 4NF, despite the somewhat esoteric terminology, are essentially very simple and commonsense ideas. Most of the references treat the material in a more formal and rigorous manner.

14.2 FUNCTIONAL DEPENDENCE

We begin by introducing the fundamental notion of *functional dependence* (FD).

- Given a relation R, attribute Y of R is *functionally dependent* on attribute X of R if and only if each X-value in R has associated with it precisely one Y-value in R (at any one time).

In the suppliers-and-parts database, for example, attributes SNAME, STATUS, and CITY of relation S are each functionally dependent on attribute S# because, given a particular value for S#, there exists precisely one corresponding value for each of SNAME, STATUS, and CITY (provided that the S# value occurs in relation S, of course). In symbols, we have

```
S.S# → S.SNAME
S.S# → S.STATUS
S.S# → S.CITY
```

or, more succinctly,

```
S.S# → S.(SNAME, STATUS, CITY)
```

The statement "S.S# → S.CITY" (for example) is read as "attribute S.CITY is functionally dependent on attribute S.S#", or, equivalently, "attribute S.S# *functionally determines* attribute S.CITY". The statement "S.S# → S. (SNAME, STATUS, CITY)" can be similarly interpreted if we agree to consider the combination (SNAME, STATUS, CITY) as a composite attribute of relation S.

Note that there is no requirement in the definition of functional dependence that a given X-value appear in only one tuple of R. We give an alternative definition that makes this point explicit.

- Given a relation R, attribute Y of R is *functionally dependent* on attribute X of R if and only if, whenever two tuples of R agree on their X-value, they also agree on their Y-value.

For example, relation SP′ in Fig. 14.1 satisfies the FD

$$\mathtt{SP'.S\# \ \rightarrow \ SP'.STATUS}$$

We have already seen that attribute Y in the definition can be composite. The same applies to attribute X. For example, attribute QTY of relation SP is functionally dependent on the composite attribute (S#, P#):

$$\mathtt{SP.(S\#, \ P\#) \ \rightarrow \ SP.QTY}$$

(Given a particular combination of S# and P# values, there exists precisely one corresponding QTY value—assuming, of course, that the particular (S#, P#) combination occurs within SP.)

A functional dependence is a special form of *integrity constraint*. When we say, for example, that relation S satisfies the FD S.S# → S. CITY, we mean that *every legal extension* (tabulation) of that relation satisfies that constraint; in other words, we are saying something about the *intension* of the relation (see Chapter 4). Database design, by definition, is concerned with intensions rather than extensions. In this chapter, therefore, we shall generally take "relation" to mean the intensional part of the relation rather than the extensional part.

It is convenient to represent the FDs in a given set of relations by means of a functional dependency diagram.[2] An example is shown in Fig. 14.3. Note in relation S that we have both S.S# → S.SNAME and S.SNAME → S.S# (because SNAME is an alternate key for relation S).

We also introduce the concept of *full* functional dependence. Attribute Y is fully functionally dependent on attribute X if it is functionally depen-

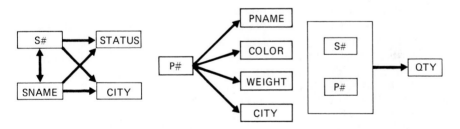

Fig. 14.3 Functional dependencies in relations S, P, SP.

---

2. All dependencies considered in this chapter, functional or otherwise, are defined within the context of a single relation. Dependencies that span relations also exist; for example, the constraint that any S# value appearing in relation SP should also appear in relation S is such a dependency. Current normalization theory says little about such interrelational dependencies.

dent on X and *not* functionally dependent on any proper subset of X (in other words, there does not exist a proper subset X′ of the attributes constituting X such that Y is functionally dependent on X′). For example, in the relation S, the attribute CITY is functionally dependent on the composite attribute (S#, STATUS); however, it is not *fully* functionally dependent on this composite attribute because, of course, it is also functionally dependent on S# alone. (If Y is functionally dependent on X but not fully so, then X must be composite). Throughout this book we shall take "functional dependence" to mean full functional dependence unless explicitly stated otherwise.

We conclude this section by noting that recognizing functional dependencies is an essential part of understanding the meaning or semantics of the data. The fact that CITY is functionally dependent on S#, for example, means that each supplier is located in precisely one city. In other words, we have a constraint in the real world that the database represents, namely, that each supplier is located in precisely one city. Since it is part of the semantics of the situation, this constraint must somehow be observed in the database; the way to ensure that it is so observed is to specify the constraint in the database definition (i.e., the conceptual schema), so that the DBMS can enforce it; and the way to specify it in the conceptual schema is to declare the functional dependency. Later we shall see that the concepts of normalization lead to a simple means of declaring such functional dependencies.

14.3   FIRST, SECOND, AND THIRD NORMAL FORMS

We are now in a position to describe 1NF, 2NF, and 3NF. We present a preliminary, *very* intuitive, definition of 3NF first in order to give some idea of the point we are aiming for. We then consider the process of reducing an arbitrary relation to an equivalent collection of 3NF relations, giving somewhat more precise definitions of the three forms as we go. However, we note at the outset that 1NF, 2NF, and 3NF are not very significant in themselves except as stepping-stones to BCNF (and beyond).

■   A relation R is in third normal form (3NF) if and only if, for all time, each tuple of R consists of a primary key value that identifies some entity, together with a set of mutually independent attribute values that describe that entity in some way.[3]

---

3. For simplicity we assume throughout this section that each relation has a single candidate key (i.e., a primary key and no alternate keys). In particular, we ignore attribute SNAME. This assumption is reflected in our definitions, which (we repeat) are not totally rigorous. The case of a relation having two or more candidate keys is discussed in Section 14.4.

For example, relation P is in 3NF: Each P tuple consists of a P# value, identifying some particular part, together with four pieces of descriptive information concerning that part—name, color, weight, and location. Moreover, each of the four descriptive items is independent of the other three (two attributes are mutually independent if neither is functionally dependent on the other; as usual we allow the attributes to be composite). Relations S and SP are also in 3NF; the entities in these cases are suppliers and shipments, respectively. In general, the entities identified by the primary key values are the fundamental entities about which data is recorded in the database (Section 1.2).

Now we turn to the reduction process. First we give a definition of first normal form.

■ A relation R is in *first normal form* (1NF) if and only if all underlying domains contain atomic values only.

This definition merely states that *any* normalized relation is in 1NF, which is of course correct. A relation that is only in first normal form (that is, a 1NF relation that is not also in 2NF, and therefore not in 3NF either) has a structure that is undesirable for a number of reasons. To illustrate the point, let us suppose that information concerning suppliers and shipments, rather than being split into two separate relations (S and SP), is lumped together into a single relation FIRST(S#, STATUS, CITY, P#, QTY). The attributes here have their usual meanings; however, for the sake of the example, we introduce an additional constraint, namely, that STATUS is functionally dependent on CITY. (The meaning of this constraint is that a supplier's status is determined by the corresponding location; e.g., all London suppliers *must* have a status of 20.) Also we ignore the attribute SNAME for simplicity. The primary key of FIRST is the combination (S#, P#). Figure 14.4 is the functional dependency diagram for this relation; note that the diagram is "more complex" than a 3NF diagram.

We see from Fig. 14.4 that (a) STATUS and CITY are not fully functionally dependent on the primary key, and (b) STATUS and CITY are not mutually independent. It is these two conditions that make the diagram

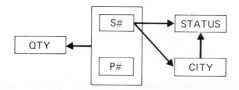

Fig. 14.4 Functional dependencies in the relation FIRST.

more complex than a 3NF diagram; and each of the two leads to problems. To illustrate some of the difficulties, we consider a sample tabulation (extension) of FIRST (Fig. 14.5). The data values shown are basically those of Fig. 4.7, except that the status of supplier S3 has been changed from 30 to 10 to be consistent with the new constraint that STATUS is dependent on CITY.

The relation FIRST suffers from anomalies with respect to update operations that are very similar to those encountered in certain hierarchies (as described in Section 3.3). To fix our ideas we concentrate on the association between suppliers and cities—that is, on the functional dependency of CITY on S#. Problems occur with each of the three basic operations.

Inserting We cannot enter the fact that a particular supplier is located in a particular city until that supplier supplies at least one part. Indeed, the tabulation in Fig. 14.5 does not show that supplier S5 is located in Athens. The reason is that, until S5 supplies some part, we have no appropriate primary key value. (Remember that, by Integrity Rule 1 (Section 4.3), no component of a primary key value may be null; in relation FIRST, primary key values consist of a supplier number and a part number.)

Deleting If we delete the only FIRST tuple for a particular supplier, we destroy not only the shipment connecting that supplier to some part but also the information that the supplier is located in a particular city. For example, if we delete the FIRST tuple with S# value S3 and P# value P2, we lose the information that S3 is located in Paris. (As in Section 3.3, the insertion and deletion problems are really two sides of the same coin.)

FIRST	S#	STATUS	CITY	P#	QTY
	S1	20	London	P1	300
	S1	20	London	P2	200
	S1	20	London	P3	400
	S1	20	London	P4	200
	S1	20	London	P5	100
	S1	20	London	P6	100
	S2	10	Paris	P1	300
	S2	10	Paris	P2	400
	S3	10	Paris	P2	200
	S4	20	London	P2	200
	S4	20	London	P4	300
	S4	20	London	P5	400

Fig. 14.5 Sample tabulation of FIRST.

Updating The city value for a given supplier appears in FIRST many times, in general. This redundancy causes update problems. For example, if supplier S1 moves from London to Amsterdam, we are faced with *either* the problem of searching the FIRST relation to find every tuple connecting S1 and London (and changing it) *or* the possibility of producing an inconsistent result (the city for S1 may be given as Amsterdam in one place and London in another).

The solution to these problems is to replace the relation FIRST by the two relations SECOND (S#, STATUS, CITY) and SP(S#, P#, QTY). Figure 14.6 shows the functional dependency diagrams for these two relations; Fig. 14.7 shows sample tabulations corresponding to the data values of Fig. 14.5, except that information for supplier S5 has now been incorporated into relation SECOND (but not SP). Relation SP is now in fact exactly as given in Fig. 4.7.

Fig. 14.6 Functional dependencies in the relations SECOND and SP.

SECOND

S#	STATUS	CITY
S1	20	London
S2	10	Paris
S3	10	Paris
S4	20	London
S5	30	Athens

SP

S#	P#	QTY
S1	P1	300
S1	P2	200
S1	P3	400
S1	P4	200
S1	P5	100
S1	P6	100
S2	P1	300
S2	P2	400
S3	P2	200
S4	P2	200
S4	P4	300
S4	P5	400

Fig. 14.7 Sample tabulations of SECOND and SP.

It should be clear that this revised structure overcomes all the problems that we had with update operations involving the S#–CITY association.

Inserting We can enter the information that S5 is located in Athens, even though S5 does not currently supply any parts, by simply inserting the appropriate tuple into SECOND (as in Fig. 14.7).

Deleting We can delete the shipment connecting S3 and P2 by deleting the appropriate tuple from SP; we do not lose the information that S3 is located in Paris.

Updating In the revised structure, the city for a given supplier appears once, not many times (the redundancy has been eliminated). Thus we can change the city for S1 from London to Amsterdam by changing it once and for all in the relevant SECOND tuple.

Comparing Figs. 14.6 and 14.4, we see that the effect of our structural revision has been to eliminate the *nonfull* functional dependencies, and it is this elimination that has resolved the difficulties. Intuitively we may say that in relation FIRST the attributes STATUS and CITY did not describe the entity identified by the primary key, namely, a supplier–part shipment; instead they described the supplier alone. Mixing the two types of information in the same relation was what caused the problems.

We now give a definition of second normal form.[4]

■ A relation R is in *second normal form* (2NF) if and only if it is in 1NF and every nonkey attribute is fully dependent on the primary key.

(An attribute is *nonkey* if it does not participate in the primary key.)[5] Relations SECOND and SP are both 2NF [the primary keys are S# and the combination (S#, P#), respectively]. Relation FIRST is not 2NF. A relation that is in first normal form and not in second can always be reduced to an equivalent collection of 2NF relations. (Note, incidentally, that a 1NF relation that is not also 2NF must have a composite primary key.) The reduction consists of replacing the relations by suitable *projections*; the collection of these projections is equivalent to the original relation, in the sense that the original relation can always be recovered by taking the *natural join* of these projections, so no information is lost in the process (which is highly important, of course). In other words, the process is reversible. In our example, SECOND and SP are projections of FIRST, and FIRST is the natural join of SECOND and SP over S#.

4. See footnote 3 on p. 242.
5. See footnote 3 on p. 242.

The reduction of FIRST to the pair (SECOND, SP) is an example of a *nonloss decomposition.*[6] In general, given a relation R with possibly composite attributes A, B, C satisfying the FD R.A → R.B, R can always be "nonloss-decomposed" into its projections R1(A, B) and R2(A, C) (this theorem was first proved by Heath [14.3]). Since no information is lost in the reduction process, any information that can be derived from the original structure can also be derived from the new structure. The converse is not true, however: The new structure may contain information (such as the fact that S5 is located in Athens) that could not be represented in the original. In this sense, the new structure is a slightly more faithful reflection of the real world.

The SECOND/SP structure still causes problems, however. Relation SP is satisfactory; as a matter of fact, relation SP is now in third normal form, and we shall ignore it for the remainder of this section. Relation SECOND, on the other hand, still suffers from a lack of mutual independence among its nonkey attributes. The dependency diagram for SECOND is still "more complex" than a 3NF diagram. To be specific, the dependency of STATUS on S#, though it *is* functional, is *transitive* (via CITY): Each S# value determines a CITY value, and this in turn determines the STATUS value. This transitivity leads, once again, to difficulties over update operations. (We now concentrate on the association between cities and status values—i.e., on the functional dependency of STATUS on CITY.)

Inserting We cannot enter the fact that a particular city has a particular status value—for example, we cannot state that any supplier in Rome must have a status of 50—until we have some supplier located in that city. The reason is, again, that until such a supplier exists we have no appropriate primary key value.

Deleting If we delete the only SECOND tuple for a particular city, we destroy not only the information for the supplier concerned but also the information that that city has that particular status value. For example, if we

---

6. "Nonloss decomposition" is actually rather a strange term. The decomposition per se cannot lose information; the projection of a relation R onto some possibly composite attribute A contains exactly the same information as the original attribute R.A. However, joining the projections back together may cause the original relation R to reappear *together with some additional "spurious" tuples.* It can never produce anything *less* than R. (*Exercise:* Prove this statement.) A nonloss decomposition guarantees that the join produces exactly the original relation R. A decomposition that is not nonloss loses information in the sense that the join may produce a superset of the original R, and there is no way of knowing which tuples in the superset are spurious and which genuine.

delete the SECOND tuple for S5, we lose the information that the status for Athens is 30. (Once again, the insertion and deletion problems are two sides of the same coin.)

Updating The status value for a given city appears in SECOND many times, in general (the relation still contains some redundancy). Thus, if we need to change the status value for London from 20 to 30, we are faced with *either* the problem of searching the SECOND relation to find every tuple for London *or* the possibility of producing an inconsistent result (the status for London may be given as 20 in one place and 30 in another).

Again the solution to the problems is to replace the original relation (SECOND) by two projections, in this case SC(S#, CITY) and CS(CITY, STATUS). Figure 14.8 shows the corresponding functional dependency diagram and Fig. 14.9 the tabulation corresponding to the data values of the original SECOND (Fig. 14.7). The process is reversible, once again, since SECOND is the join of SC and CS over CITY.

It should be clear that this new structure overcomes all the problems over update operations concerning the CITY-STATUS association. Detailed consideration of these problems is left to the reader. Comparing Figs. 14.8 and 14.6, we see that the effect of the further restructuring has been to eliminate the transitive dependence of STATUS on S#.

We now give a definition of third normal form.[7]

- A relation R is in *third normal form* (3NF) if and only if it is in 2NF and every nonkey attribute is nontransitively dependent on the primary key.

Fig. 14.8 Functional dependencies in the relations SC and CS.

SC	S#	CITY
	S1	London
	S2	Paris
	S3	Paris
	S4	London
	S5	Athens

CS	CITY	STATUS
	Athens	30
	London	20
	Paris	10

Fig. 14.9 Sample tabulations of SC and CS.

---

7. See footnote 3 on p. 242.

Relations SC and CS are both 3NF; relation SECOND is not. (The primary keys for SC and CS are S# and CITY, respectively.) A relation that is in second normal form and not in third can always be reduced to an equivalent collection of 3NF relations. We have already indicated that the process is reversible, and hence that no information is lost in the reduction; however, the 3NF collection may contain information, such as the fact that the status for Rome is 50, that could not be represented in the original 2NF relation. Just as the SECOND/SP structure was a slightly better representation of the real world than the 1NF relation FIRST, so the SC/CS structure is a slightly better representation than the 2NF relation SECOND.

We conclude this section by repeating that the level of normalization of a given relation is a matter of *semantics,* not a matter of the data values that happen to appear in that relation at some particular time. It is not possible just to look at the tabulation (extension) of a given relation at a given time and to say whether or not that relation is 3NF—it is necessary to know the meaning of the data, i.e., the dependencies involved, before such a judgment can be made. In particular, the DBMS cannot ensure that a relation is maintained in 3NF (or any other given form, except 1NF) without being informed of all relevant dependencies. For a relation in 3NF, however, all that is needed to inform the DBMS of those dependencies is an indication of the attribute(s) constituting the primary key. The DBMS will then know that all other attributes are functionally dependent on this attribute or attribute combination, and will be able to enforce this constraint.[8] For a relation that is not in 3NF, additional specifications would be necessary.

14.4 RELATIONS WITH MORE THAN ONE CANDIDATE KEY

As we mentioned in Section 14.1, the original definition of 3NF was subsequently replaced by a stronger definition. The new definition is due to Boyce and Codd; hence the term "Boyce/Codd Normal Form" (BCNF) is often used to distinguish the new 3NF from the old. The definition of BCNF is conceptually simpler than that of 3NF, in that it makes no explicit reference to first and second normal form as such, nor to the concepts of full and transitive dependence. Let us agree to call an attribute, possibly composite, on which some other attribute is fully functionally dependent a (functional) *determinant.* Then we can define BCNF as follows.

- A relation R is in Boyce/Codd Normal Form (BCNF) if and only if every determinant is a candidate key.

Observe that we are now talking in terms of *candidate* keys, not just the primary key. The motivation for introducing BCNF is that the original 3NF

---

8. See footnote 3 on p. 242.

definition does not satisfactorily handle the case of a relation possessing two or more composite and overlapping candidate keys (see below). Although BCNF is stronger (more restrictive) than 3NF, it is still true that any relation can be decomposed in a nonloss way into an equivalent collection of BCNF relations.

Before considering examples involving more than one candidate key, let us convince ourselves that relations FIRST and SECOND, which were not 3NF under the old definition, are not BCNF either; also that relations SP, SC, and CS, which *were* 3NF under the old definition, are also BCNF. Relation FIRST contains three determinants: S#, CITY, and the combination (S#, P#). Of these, only (S#, P#) is a candidate key; hence FIRST is not BCNF. Similarly, SECOND is not BCNF, because the determinant CITY is not a candidate key. Relations SP, SC, and CS, on the other hand, are each BCNF, because in each case the primary key is the only determinant in the relation.

We now look at an example involving two disjoint (nonoverlapping) candidate keys. Let us consider relation S(S#, SNAME, STATUS, CITY) once again. We now assume, as earlier in the book, that STATUS and CITY are mutually independent, and also that supplier *names,* as well as supplier numbers, are unique (for all time)—in other words, we assume that SNAME is a candidate key. See Fig. 14.3 for the dependency diagram.

Relation S is BCNF. However, it is desirable to specify *both* keys in the definition of the relation: (a) to inform the DBMS, so that it may enforce the constraints implied by the two-way dependency between the two keys—namely, that corresponding to each supplier number there exists a unique supplier name, and conversely; and (b) to inform the users, since of course the uniqueness of the two attributes is an aspect of the semantics of the relation and is therefore of interest to people using it. See Fig. 4.8 (Chapter 4).

Now we present some examples in which the candidate keys overlap. Two candidate keys overlap if they involve two or more attributes each and have an attribute in common. For our first example, we suppose again that supplier names are unique, and we consider the relation SSP(S#, SNAME, P#, QTY). The keys are (S#, P#) and (SNAME, P#). Is this relation BCNF? The answer is no, because we have two determinants, S# and SNAME, which are not keys for the relation (S# determines SNAME, and conversely). But the relation *is* 3NF under the original definition[14.1]; the original definition did not require an attribute to be fully dependent on the primary key if it was itself a component of some other key in the relation, and so the fact that SNAME is not fully dependent on (S#, P#)—assuming the latter to be the primary key—was ignored. However, this fact gives rise to redundancy, and hence to update problems, in the relation SSP. For instance, updating the name of supplier S1 from Smith to Robinson leads (once again) either to search problems or to possibly inconsistent results. The solution to the problems, as usual, is to decompose the relation SSP into two projections, in this case SS(S#, SNAME) and SP(S#, P#, QTY) [or SP(SNAME, P#, QTY)]. These projections are both BCNF.

As a second example, we consider the relation SJT with attributes S (student), J (subject), and T (teacher). The meaning of an SJT tuple is that the specified student is taught the specified subject by the specified teacher. The semantic rules follow.

- For each subject, each student of that subject is taught by only one teacher.
- Each teacher teaches only one subject.
- Each subject is taught by several teachers.

Figure 14.10 shows a sample tabulation of this relation.

What are the functional dependencies in SJT? From the first semantic rule we have a functional dependency of T on the composite attribute (S, J). From the second semantic rule we have a functional dependency of J on T. The third semantic rule tells us that there is *not* a functional dependency of T on J. Hence we have the situation shown in Fig. 14.11.

Again we have two overlapping candidate keys: the combination (S, J) and the combination (S, T). Once again the relation is 3NF and not BCNF; and once again the relation suffers from certain anomalies in connection

SJT	S	J	T
	Smith	Math	Prof. White
	Smith	Physics	Prof. Green
	Jones	Math	Prof. White
	Jones	Physics	Prof. Brown

Fig. 14.10 Sample tabulation of the relation SJT.

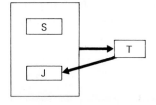

Fig. 14.11 Functional dependencies in the relation SJT.

with update operations. For example, if we wish to delete the information that Jones is studying physics, we cannot do so without at the same time losing the information that Professor Brown teaches physics. The difficulties are caused by the fact that T is a determinant but not a candidate key. Again we can get over the problem by replacing the original relation by two BCNF projections, in this case ST(S, T) and TJ(T, J). It is left as an exercise for the reader to give tabulations of these two relations corresponding to the data in Fig. 14.10, to draw a corresponding dependency diagram, to ensure that the two projections are indeed BCNF (what are the keys?),[9] and to check that this solution does indeed avoid the problems. (However, it introduces different problems. See the next section.)

Our third and final example of overlapping keys concerns a relation EXAM with attributes S (student), J (subject), and P (position). The meaning of an EXAM tuple is that the specified student was examined in the specified subject and achieved the specified position in the class list. For the purposes of the example, we suppose that the following semantic rule holds.

- There are no ties; that is, no two students obtained the same position in the same subject.

Then the functional dependencies are as illustrated in Fig. 14.12.

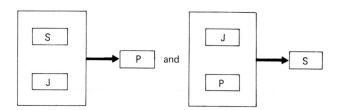

Fig. 14.12 Functional dependencies in the relation EXAM.

Again we have two candidate keys, (S, J) and (J, P). The relation is BCNF, despite the fact that the keys overlap, because the keys are the only determinants. The reader should check that difficulties over update operations such as those discussed earlier in this chapter do not occur with this relation. A possible declaration is

```
RELATION EXAM(S, J, P)
         PRIMARY KEY (S, J)
         ALTERNATE KEY (J, P)
```

---

9. As a matter of fact *any* binary relation must be in BCNF. (Why?)

We see, therefore, that the concept of BCNF eliminates certain problem cases that could occur under the old definition of 3NF. Moreover, BCNF is conceptually simpler than 3NF, in that it involves no reference to the concepts of primary key, transitive dependence, and full dependence. The reference to candidate keys can also be replaced by a reference to the more fundamental notion of functional dependence (the definition given in [9.2] actually makes this replacement). On the other hand, the concepts of full and transitive dependence are useful in practice, since they give some idea of the actual step-by-step process the designer must go through in order to reduce an arbitrary relation to an equivalent collection of BCNF relations. We summarize this process in Section 14.8.

14.5 GOOD AND BAD DECOMPOSITIONS

During the reduction process it is frequently the case that a given relation can be decomposed in a variety of different ways. Consider the relation SECOND (S#, STATUS, CITY) given in Section 14.3 once again, with functional dependencies (FDs)

```
SECOND.S#   → SECOND.CITY
SECOND.CITY → SECOND.STATUS
```

and therefore also (by transitivity)

```
SECOND.S#   → SECOND.STATUS
```

(see Fig. 14.13, in which the transitive FD is shown as a broken arrow). We showed in Fig. 14.3 that the update problems encountered with SECOND could be overcome by replacing it by its decomposition into the two 3NF projections

```
SC(S#, CITY)   and   CS(CITY, STATUS)
```

(in fact, SC and CS are not only 3NF but BCNF). Let us call this decomposition A. As suggested at the beginning of the section, decomposition A is not the only one possible. An alternative is decomposition B:

```
SC(S#, CITY)   and   SS(S#, STATUS)
```

(projection SC is the same for both A and B). Decomposition B is also nonloss, and the two projections are again BCNF. But decomposition B is less satisfactory than decomposition A, for several reasons. For example, it is still not possible (in B) to insert the fact that a particular city has a particular status value unless some supplier is located in that city.

Let us examine this example a little more closely. First, note that the projections in decomposition A correspond to the *solid* arrows in Fig.

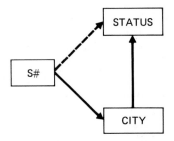

Fig. 14.13 Functional dependencies in the relation SECOND.

14.13, whereas one of the projections in decomposition B corresponds to the *broken* arrow. In decomposition A the two projections are *independent* of each other, in the sense that updates can be made to either one without regard for the other; providing such an update is legal within the context of the projection concerned—i.e., does not violate the FD constraint applying to that projection—then *the join of the two projections remains a legal extension for relation SECOND.* That is, such a join cannot possibly violate the FD constraints on SECOND. In decomposition B, by contrast, updates to either of the two projections must be monitored to ensure that the FD SECOND.CITY → SECOND.STATUS is not violated. (If two suppliers have the same city in projection SC, they must have the same status in projection SS.) Thus projections SC and SS are *not* independent of each other.

The basic problem is that, in decomposition B, the FD CITY → STATUS has become an *interrelational constraint.* In decomposition A, on the other hand, it is the *transitive* FD S# → STATUS that is the interrelational constraint, and this constraint is enforced automatically if the two *intra*relational constraints S# → CITY and CITY → STATUS are enforced. (We drop the "SECOND." prefixes for clarity.)

The concept of independent projections provides a guideline for choosing a particular decomposition when there is more than one possibility. Specifically, a decomposition in which the projections are independent in the sense described is generally preferable to one in which they are not. Rissanen [14.6] shows that projections R1 and R2 of a relation R are independent in this sense if and only if (a) every FD in R can be logically deduced from those in R1 and R2, *and* (b) the common attributes of R1 and R2 form a candidate key for at least one of the pair. This theorem makes checking for independence a very simple operation. Consider decompositions A and B. In A the two projections are independent, because their common attribute CITY is the primary key for CS, and every FD in SECOND either appears in one of the two projections or is a logical consequence of those that do. In B, by contrast, the two projections are not independent, because the FD CITY → STATUS cannot be deduced from the FDs in those projections (though their common attribute S# is actually the primary key for both).

As an aside, we note that the third possibility, replacing SECOND by its two projections

SS(S#, STATUS)   and   CS(CITY, STATUS),

is not a valid decomposition because it is not nonloss. (*Exercise:* Prove this statement.)

A relation that cannot be decomposed into independent components is said to be *atomic* [14.6]. We do not mean to suggest that a nonatomic relation should necessarily be decomposed into atomic components; for example, relations S and P of the suppliers-and-parts database are not atomic, but there seems little point in decomposing them further. (Relation SP, by contrast, *is* atomic.)

The fact that an atomic relation cannot be decomposed into independent components does not mean that it cannot be decomposed at all. Consider relation SJT of Section 14.4, with FDs:

$$(S, J) \rightarrow T$$
$$T \rightarrow J$$

(again we ignore the relation-name prefixes). As we saw, this relation (which is 3NF but not BCNF) can be nonloss-decomposed into its projections ST(S, T) and TJ(T, J). However, these projections are not independent, by Rissanen's theorem; the FD $(S, J) \rightarrow T$ cannot be deduced from the FD $T \rightarrow J$ (the only FD represented in the two projections). As a result, the two projections cannot be independently updated (*exercise:* prove this statement); in fact, relation SJT is atomic. We are forced to the unpleasant conclusion that the two objectives of decomposing a relation into BCNF components and decomposing it into independent components may occasionally be in conflict.

14.6 FOURTH NORMAL FORM

Suppose we are given an *unnormalized* relation containing information about courses, teachers, and texts. Each record in the relation consists of a course name, plus a repeating group of teacher names, plus a repeating group of text names. Figure 14.14 shows two such records.

The meaning of a given record in this unnormalized relation is that the indicated course can be taught by any of the indicated teachers, and uses all the indicated texts. We suppose that, for a given course, there may exist any number of corresponding teachers and any number of corresponding texts;

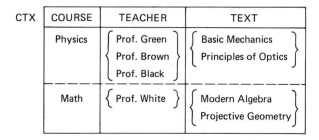

Fig. 14.14 Sample tabulation of CTX (unnormalized).

moreover, we assume—perhaps not very realistically—that teachers and texts are quite independent of each other (that is, no matter who actually teaches any particular offering of the given course, the same texts are used). We also assume that a given teacher or text can be associated with any number of courses.

Now let us convert this structure into an equivalent normalized form. Observe first that there are no functional dependencies in the data at all (apart from trivial ones such as COURSE → COURSE). The theory we have developed in this chapter so far therefore provides us with no formal basis by which to decompose the structure into projections; the only operation of a normalizing nature is the elementary one of "flattening" the structure (as in Chapter 4), which for the data of Fig. 14.14 yields the tabulation shown in Fig. 14.15.

The meaning of the normalized relation CTX is as follows: A tuple ⟨c, t, x⟩ appears in CTX if and only if course c can be taught by teacher t and uses text x as a reference. Note that, for a given course, all possible

CTX	COURSE	TEACHER	TEXT
	Physics	Prof. Green	Basic Mechanics
	Physics	Prof. Green	Principles of Optics
	Physics	Prof. Brown	Basic Mechanics
	Physics	Prof. Brown	Principles of Optics
	Physics	Prof. Black	Basic Mechanics
	Physics	Prof. Black	Principles of Optics
	Math	Prof. White	Modern Algebra
	Math	Prof. White	Projective Geometry

Fig. 14.15 Sample tabulation of CTX (normalized).

combinations of teacher and text appear—that is, CTX satisfies the constraint

if tuples $\langle c, t_1, x_1 \rangle$, $\langle c, t_2, x_2 \rangle$ both appear,

then tuples $\langle c, t_1, x_2 \rangle$, $\langle c, t_2, x_1 \rangle$ both appear also.

It is apparent that relation CTX contains a good deal of redundancy, leading as usual to problems over update operations. For example, to add the information that the physics course uses a new text called *Advanced Mechanics,* it is necessary to create *three* new tuples, one for each of the three teachers.[10] Nevertheless, CTX *is* in BCNF, since it is "all key" and there are no other functional determinants.

The existence of such "problem" BCNF relations has been recognized for some time; see, for example, Schmid and Swenson [14.23]. So far as relation CTX is concerned, it is intuitively clear that the difficulties are caused by the fact that teachers and texts are independent of each other; it is also easy to see that matters would be improved if CTX were replaced by its two projections CT(COURSE, TEACHER) and CX(COURSE, TEXT). See Fig. 14.16. (CT and CX are both "all key" and are thus both BCNF.)

We have already said that the decomposition of Fig. 14.16 cannot be made on the basis of functional dependencies, however. Instead, it is made on the basis of a new type of dependency, the *multivalued* dependency. Multivalued dependencies (MVDs) are a generalization of functional depen-

CT	COURSE	TEACHER
	Physics	Prof. Green
	Physics	Prof. Brown
	Physics	Prof. Black
	Math	Prof. White

CX	COURSE	TEXT
	Physics	Basic Mechanics
	Physics	Principles of Optics
	Math	Modern Algebra
	Math	Projective Geometry

Fig. 14.16 Sample tabulation of CT and CX.

---

10. The reader may object that it is not necessary to include all teacher-text combinations for a given course; for example, three tuples are sufficient to show that the physics course has three teachers and two texts. The problem is, *which* three? Any particular choice leads to a relation having a very unobvious interpretation and very strange update behavior. To see that this is so, the reader should try the experiment of making such a choice and then stating the meaning of the relation that results—i.e., stating the criteria for deciding whether a given tuple is or is not acceptable as a member of that relation.

dencies (i.e., an FD is a special case of an MVD). There are two MVDs in relation CTX:

$$\text{CTX.COURSE} \rightarrow\rightarrow \text{CTX.TEACHER}$$
$$\text{CTX.COURSE} \rightarrow\rightarrow \text{CTX.TEXT}$$

(The MVD statement "R.A $\rightarrow\rightarrow$ R.B" is read as "attribute R.B is *multidependent* on attribute R.A", or, equivalently, "attribute R.A *multidetermines* attribute R.B".) For the moment we concentrate on the first of the two MVDs above, which means intuitively that, although a course does not have a *single* corresponding teacher (i.e., TEACHER is not functionally dependent on COURSE), nevertheless, each course does have a well-defined *set* of corresponding teachers. By "well-defined" we mean, more precisely, that for a course *c* and a text *x*, the set of teachers *t* matching the pair (*c, x*) in CTX depends on *c* alone—it makes no difference what value of *x* we choose, provided only that *c* and *x* appear together in some CTX tuple. The second MVD (of TEXT on COURSE) is interpreted analogously.

We now give a definition of MVD.

■ Given a relation R with attributes A, B, and C, the *multivalued dependence*

$$\text{R.A} \rightarrow\rightarrow \text{R.B}$$

holds in R if and only if the set of B-values matching a given (A-value, C-value) pair in R depends only on the A-value and is independent of the C-value. As usual A, B, and C may be composite.

Note that MVDs as we have defined them can exist only if the relation R has at least three attributes.[11]

It is easy to show (see [14.4]) that, given the relation R(A, B, C), the MVD R.A $\rightarrow\rightarrow$ R.B holds if and only if the MVD R.A $\rightarrow\rightarrow$ R.C also holds. MVDs always go together in pairs in this way. For this reason it is common to express both in a single statement, using the notation

$$\text{R.A} \rightarrow\rightarrow \text{R.B} \mid \text{R.C}$$

For example,

$$\text{COURSE} \rightarrow\rightarrow \text{TEACHER} \mid \text{TEXT}$$

(dropping the relation-name prefixes).

---

11. The definition given in [14.4] does not require the relation R to have at least three attributes. For simplicity we are ignoring certain special cases: for example, the "trivial" MVD R.X $\rightarrow\rightarrow$ R.Y which always holds in the binary relation R(X, Y), and certain nontrivial MVDs in which the left-hand side is the empty set. See [14.4] for details; see also Exercise 14.5.

An FD is an MVD in which the "set" of dependent values actually consists of a single value. Returning to our normalization problem, we can see that the trouble with relations such as CTX is that they involve MVDs that are not also FDs. The two projections CT and CX do not involve any such MVDs, which is why they represent an improvement over the original relation. We would therefore like to replace CTX by these two projections. A theorem proved by Fagin in [14.4] allows us to make this replacement.

■ Relation R, with attributes A, B, and C, can be nonloss-decomposed into its two projections R1(A, B) and R2(A, C) if and only if the MVD A →→ B | C holds in R.

[This is a stronger version of Heath's theorem (see Section 14.3).]

We can now define *fourth normal form* (4NF).

■ A relation R is in fourth normal form (4NF) if and only if, whenever there exists an MVD in R, say A →→ B, then all attributes of R are also *functionally* dependent on A (i.e., A → X for all attributes X of R).

In other words, the only dependencies (FDs or MVDs) in R are of the form K → X (i.e., a functional dependency from a candidate key K to some other attribute X).

We can now see that relation CTX is not in 4NF, since it involves an MVD that is not an FD at all, let alone an FD in which the determinant is a candidate key. The two projections CT and CX are in 4NF, however. Thus 4NF is an improvement over BCNF, in that it eliminates another form of undesirable structure.

Fagin proves two further important results in [14.4] that enable us to incorporate 4NF into the overall normalization procedure that we are gradually building up in this chapter:

1. 4NF is strictly stronger than BCNF—i.e., any 4NF relation is necessarily in BCNF;

2. Any relation can be nonloss-decomposed into an equivalent collection of 4NF relations.

In other words, 4NF is always achievable—though the results of Section 14.5 show that it may not be desirable in some cases to carry the decomposition that far (or even as far as BCNF). It is worth noting, incidentally, that Rissanen's work on independent projections [14.6], though couched in terms of FDs, is applicable to MVDs also. Remember that a relation R(A, B, C) satisfying the FDs A → B, B → C is better decomposed into its projections on (A, B) and (B, C), rather than into those on (A, B) and (A, C). The same is true if the FDs are replaced by the MVDs A →→ B, B →→ C.

14.7 FIFTH NORMAL FORM

So far in this chapter we have tacitly assumed that the sole operation necessary or available in the decomposition process is the replacement of a relation by two of its projections. This assumption has successfully carried us as
far as 4NF. It comes perhaps as a surprise to discover that there exist relations that cannot be nonloss-decomposed into two projections but *can* be
nonloss-decomposed into three (or more). This phenomenon was first noted
by Aho, Beeri, and Ullman [12.16], and was also studied by Nicolas [14.9].
Consider relation SPJ (Fig. 14.17). This relation is "all key" and involves
no nontrivial FDs or MVDs, and so is 4NF. Figure 14.17 also shows (a) the
three projections SP, PJ, and JS of SPJ, and (b) the effect of joining SP
and PJ over P# and then joining the result and JS over (J#, S#). Note that

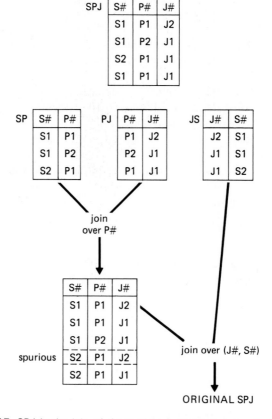

Fig. 14.17 SPJ is the join of three of its projections but not of any two.

the result of the first join is to produce a copy of the original SPJ plus one spurious tuple, and that the effect of the second join is to eliminate that tuple. (The net result is the same whatever pair of projections we choose for the first join, though the intermediate result is different in each case.)

The example in Fig. 14.17 is of course expressed in terms of *extensions*. However, the "three-decomposability" (to coin an ugly but convenient term) of SPJ could be a more fundamental *intensional* property—i.e., a property satisfied by all legal extensions—if the relation satisfies a certain time-independent constraint. To understand what this constraint must be, observe first that the statement that SPJ is equal to the join[12] of its three projections SP, PJ, and JS is equivalent to the statement:

> *if*   the pair $\langle s_1, p_1 \rangle$ appears in SP
> *and* the pair $\langle p_1, j_1 \rangle$ appears in PJ
> *and* the pair $\langle j_1, s_1 \rangle$ appears in JS
> *then* the triple $\langle s_1, p_1, j_1 \rangle$ appears in SPJ

(because the triple $\langle s_1, p_1, j_1 \rangle$ obviously appears in the join of SP, PJ, and JS).[13] Since $\langle s_1, p_1 \rangle$ appears in SP if and only if s_1 and p_1 appear together in SPJ, and similarly for $\langle p_1, j_1 \rangle$ and $\langle j_1, s_1 \rangle$, we can rewrite this latter statement as a *constraint* on SPJ:

> *if* $\langle s_1, p_1, j_2 \rangle$, $\langle s_2, p_1, j_1 \rangle$, $\langle s_1, p_2, j_1 \rangle$ appear in SPJ
> *then* $\langle s_1, p_1, j_1 \rangle$ also appears in SPJ.

This *is* a constraint (albeit rather a bizarre one), just like an FD or an MVD. Because it is satisfied if and only if the relation concerned is the join of certain of its projections, such a constraint is called a *join dependency* (JD). In the example, we say that SPJ satisfies the join dependency "∗(SP, PJ, JS)". In general, relation R satisfies the JD ∗(X, Y, . . . , Z) if and only if it is the join of its projections on X, Y, . . . , Z, where X, Y, . . . , Z are subsets of the set of attributes of R.

We have seen that relation SPJ, with its join dependency ∗(SP, PJ, JS), can be "three-decomposed." The question is, *should* it be? The answer is probably yes. Relation SPJ suffers from a number of problems over update operations, problems that are removed when it is "three-decomposed." Some examples are shown in Fig. 14.18. Consideration of what happens after "three-decomposition" is left as an exercise for the reader.

---

12. Aho, Beeri, and Ullman [12.16] give a generalized definition of "join" that allows us to speak unambiguously of the join of any number of relations. The generalized join of an ordered list of relations is formed by repeatedly replacing the first and second relations in the list by their natural join, until the entire list has been reduced to a single relation.
13. The converse of this statement, that if $\langle s_1, p_1, j_1 \rangle$ appears in SPJ then $\langle s_1, p_1 \rangle$ appears in its projection SP (etc.), is obviously true for any degree-3 relation SPJ.

SPJ	S#	P#	J#
	S1	P1	J2
	S1	P2	J1

SPJ	S#	P#	J#
	S1	P1	J2
	S1	P2	J1
	S2	P1	J1
	S1	P1	J1

- if ⟨S2, P1, J1⟩ inserted, ⟨S1, P1, J1⟩ must also be inserted

- yet converse is not true

- can delete ⟨S2, P1, J1⟩ without side effects

- if ⟨S1, P1, J1⟩ deleted, another tuple must also be deleted (which?)

Fig. 14.18 Examples of update problems in SPJ.

Fagin's theorem (Section 14.6) that R(A, B, C) can be nonloss-decomposed into R1 (A, B) and R2 (A, C) if and only if A $\rightarrow \rightarrow$ B | C holds in R is equivalent to the statement that R(A, B, C) satisfies the JD *(AB, AC) if and only if it satisfies the MVD A $\rightarrow \rightarrow$ B | C. Since the theorem can be taken as a *definition* of MVD, it follows that an MVD is just a special case of a JD, or that JDs are a generalization of MVDs (just as MVDs are a generalization of FDs). What is more, it is immediate from the definition that JDs are the *most* general form of dependency possible—i.e., there does not exist a still higher form of dependency such that JDs are in turn merely a special case of that higher form—so long as we restrict our attention to dependencies that deal with a relation being decomposed via projection and reconstructed via join. (However, if we allow additional types of operator in the decomposition and reconstruction processes, then additional types of dependency will come into play. We discuss this possibility very briefly at the end of the chapter.)

Returning now to our example, the problem with relation SPJ is that, although it is 4NF, it still involves a JD (one that is not an FD nor an MVD). We have seen, therefore, that it is possible, and probably desirable, to decompose such a relation into smaller components—namely, into the projections specified by the join dependency. The decomposition process can be repeated until all projections are in *fifth normal form* (5NF).

- A relation R is in fifth normal form (5NF)—also called projection-join normal form (PJ/NF)—if and only if every join dependency in R is implied by the candidate keys of R. (We amplify the notion of a JD being "implied by candidate keys" below.)

Relation SPJ is not 5NF; its single candidate key, the combination (S#, P#, J#), certainly does not imply that the relation can be nonloss-decomposed into its projections SP, PJ, and JS. The projections SP, PJ, and JS are in 5NF, since they do not involve any JDs at all.

We note that, since an MVD is a special case of a JD, any 5NF relation is automatically 4NF also. (Fagin shows in [14.5] that an MVD that is implied by a candidate key must in fact be an FD in which that key is the determinant.) As indicated earlier, any relation can be nonloss-decomposed into an equivalent collection of 5NF relations.

Referring back to the question of a JD being "implied" by keys, we first consider a simple example. The supplier relation S (S#, SNAME, STATUS, CITY), with candidate keys S# and SNAME, satisfies several join dependencies, for example the JD:

    * ((S#, SNAME, STATUS), (S#, CITY))

That is, relation S is equal to the join of its projections on (S#, SNAME, STATUS) and (S#, CITY). This JD is implied by the fact that S# is a candidate key (by Heath's theorem). Relation S also satisfies the JD:

    * ((S#, SNAME), (S#, STATUS), (SNAME, CITY))

This JD is implied by the fact that S# and SNAME are *both* candidate keys. Fagin [14.5] gives an algorithm by which it is possible, given a JD and a set of candidate keys, to test whether that JD is implied by those keys (it is not immediately obvious, in general—witness the second example above). Thus, given a relation R, we can tell if R is in 5NF, provided we know the candidate keys *and all JDs* in R. However, discovering all the JDs is itself a nontrivial operation. That is, whereas it is relatively easy to find FDs and MVDs (because they have a fairly straightforward real-world interpretation), the same cannot be said for a JD that is not an MVD (because the intuitive meaning of such a JD is far from straightforward). Hence the process of determining when a given relation is 4NF but not 5NF (and so could probably be decomposed to advantage) is still unclear. It is tempting to suggest that such relations are pathological cases and likely to be rare in practice.

In conclusion, we note that it follows from the definition that 5NF is the *ultimate* normal form with respect to projection and join. For, if a relation is in 5NF, the only valid decompositions are those that are based on candidate keys (so that each projection consists of one or more candidate keys, plus zero or more other attributes). For example, the supplier relation S is 5NF. It *can* be nonloss-decomposed in several ways, as we saw above, but every projection will still contain at least one of the two keys, and so there does not seem to be any advantage to such a decomposition.

14.8 SUMMARY

This chapter has been concerned with the technique of *nonloss decomposition* as an aid to relational database design. The basic idea is that we start with some given relation, together with a statement of certain constraints (FDs, MVDs, and JDs), and we systematically reduce that relation to a collection of relations that are equivalent to the original and yet are in some way preferable to it, using the constraints to guide us in the reduction process. We may summarize this reduction process informally as follows.

a) Take projections of the original 1NF relation to eliminate any nonfull functional dependencies. This will produce a collection of 2NF relations.

b) Take projections of these 2NF relations to eliminate any transitive dependencies. This will produce a collection of 3NF relations.

c) Take projections of these 3NF relations to eliminate any remaining functional dependencies in which the determinant is not a candidate key. This will produce a collection of BCNF relations. [*Note:* Steps (a)–(c) can be condensed into the single guideline "Take projections of the original relation to eliminate FDs in which the determinant is not a candidate key."]

d) Take projections of these BCNF relations to eliminate any multivalued dependencies that are not also functional dependencies. This will produce a collection of 4NF relations. (*Note:* In practice it is usual to eliminate these MVDs *before* applying the other steps above.)

e) Take projections of these 4NF relations to eliminate any join dependencies that are not implied by the candidate keys (though perhaps we should add "if you can find them").

At each step in the process the concept of independent components (Section 14.5) can be used to guide the choice of which projections to take.

The general objective of the reduction process is to reduce redundancy, and hence to avoid certain problems over update operations. But it should be stressed once again that the normalization guidelines are only guidelines; sometimes there are good reasons for not normalizing "all the way" (though the designer should document and justify any departures from that extreme position). The classic example is the name-and-address relation

NADDR (NAME, STREET, CITY, STATE, ZIP)

in which we assume that, in addition to the FDs implied by NAME (the primary key), we also have the FD

ZIP → (CITY, STATE)

This relation is certainly not in 5NF (what form *is* it in?), and the reduction process outlined above would suggest that we decompose it into projections on (NAME, STREET, ZIP) and (ZIP, CITY, STATE). However, since STREET, CITY, and STATE are invariably required together, and since zipcodes do not change very often, it seems unlikely that such a decomposition would be worthwhile. (As a matter of fact, the dependency structure of relation NADDR is even worse than just indicated, since it also involves the FD (STREET, CITY, STATE) → ZIP.)

We observe that the topic of this chapter is different in kind from that of the last few chapters. The notions of dependency and normalization are concerned with the *meaning* of data. By contrast, languages such as the relational algebra and relational calculus are concerned only with actual data values—any interpretation of those values is imposed from outside, and plays no part in the languages per se. In particular, these languages have no requirement that the relations they operate on be in any particular normal form other than 1NF. Normalization can be regarded primarily as a *discipline*—a discipline by which the database designer can capture a part, albeit a small part, of the semantics of the real-world enterprise that the database represents.

We conclude this chapter by referring back to the remark in Section 14.1 to the effect that there do exist other normal forms, over and above those shown in Fig. 14.2. We discuss two additional normal forms very briefly here, in order to give some idea as to how normalization research is continuing. First, Smith [14.25] has examined the possibility of reducing a relation by splitting it apart "horizontally" (instead of "vertically," which is what projection does), in such a way that the original relation can be recovered via a union operation; these considerations have led him to define a normal form that he calls (3,3)NF. (3,3)NF implies BCNF; however, a (3,3)NF relation need not be 4NF, nor need a 4NF relation be (3,3)NF, so that reduction to (3,3)NF is "orthogonal" to reduction to 4NF and 5NF. Second, Fagin [14.26] has defined "domain-key normal form" (DK/NF), in which the notions of FD, MVD, and JD are not mentioned at all. A relation is in DK/NF if and only if every constraint on the relation is a logical consequence of *key constraints* and *domain constraints*. (A key constraint is a statement that a certain attribute or attribute combination is a candidate key; a domain constraint is a statement that values of a certain attribute lie within some prescribed set of values.) Enforcing constraints in a DK/NF relation is thus conceptually simple. Fagin also shows that any DK/NF relation is automatically 5NF (and therefore 4NF, etc.), and indeed also (3,3)NF. However, DK/NF is not always achievable, nor has the question "Exactly when *can* it be achieved?" been answered.

EXERCISES

14.1 Figure 14.19 represents a hierarchical structure (see Chapter 3) that contains information about departments of a company. For each department the database contains a department number (unique), a budget value, and the department manager's employee number (unique). For each department the database also contains information about all employees working in the department, all projects assigned to the department, and all offices occupied by the department. The employee information consists of employee number (unique), the number of the project on which he or she is working, and his or her office number and phone number; the project information consists of project number (unique) and a budget value; and the office information consists of an office number (unique) and the area of that office (in square feet). Also, for each employee the database contains the title of each job the employee has held, together with date and salary for each distinct salary received in that job; and for each office it contains the numbers (unique) of all phones in that office.

Convert this hierarchical structure to an appropriate collection of normalized relations. Make any assumptions you deem reasonable about the dependencies involved.

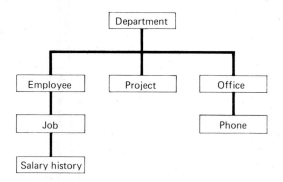

Fig. 14.19 A company database (hierarchical structure).

14.2 A database used in an order-entry system is to contain information about *customers, items,* and *orders.* The following information is to be included.

- For each *customer:*
  Customer number (unique)
  Valid "ship-to" addresses (several per customer)
  Balance
  Credit limit
  Discount

- For each *order:*
  Heading information: customer number, "ship-to" address, date of order
  Detail lines (several per order), each giving item number, quantity ordered
- For each *item:*
  Item number (unique)
  Manufacturing plants
  Quantity on hand at each plant
  Stock danger level for each plant
  Item description

For internal processing reasons a "quantity outstanding" value is associated with each detail line of each order. [This value is initially set equal to the quantity of the item ordered and is (progressively) reduced to zero as (partial) shipments are made.]

Design a database for this data. As in the previous question, make any semantic assumptions that seem necessary.

14.3 Suppose that in Exercise 14.2 only a very small number of customers, say one percent, actually have more than one ship-to address. (This is typical of real-life situations, in which frequently just a very few exceptions—usually rather important ones—fail to conform to a general pattern.) Can you see any drawbacks to your solution to Exercise 14.2? Can you think of any improvements?

14.4 A relation TIMETABLE is defined with the following attributes.

D   Day of the week (1–5)
P   Period within day (1–8)
C   Classroom number
T   Teacher name
S   Student name
L   Lesson identifier

A tuple $\langle d, p, c, t, s, l \rangle$ is an element of this relation if at time $\langle d, p \rangle$ student s is taught lesson l by teacher t in classroom c. You may assume that lessons are one period in duration and that every lesson has an identifier that is unique among all lessons taught in the week. Reduce TIMETABLE to a more desirable structure.

14.5 Which of the following statements are true? For those that are false, produce a counterexample.

a) Any binary relation is in 3NF.

b) Any binary relation is in BCNF.

c) Any binary relation is in 4NF.

d) Any binary relation is in PJ/NF.

e) Relation R (A, B, C) is equal to the join of its projections Rl (A, B) and R2 (A, C) if and only if the FD A → B holds in R.

f) If R.A → R.B and R.B → R.C, then R.A → R.C.

g) If R.A → R.B and R.A → R.C, then R.A → R. (B, C).

h) If R.B → R.A and R.C → R.A, then R. (B, C) → R.A.

14.6 A database is to contain information concerning sales representatives, sales areas, and products. Each representative is responsible for sales in one or more areas; each area has one or more responsible representatives. Similarly, each representative is responsible for sales of one or more products, and each product has one or more responsible representatives. Every product is sold in every area; however, no two representatives sell the same product in the same area. Every representative sells the same set of products in every area for which that representative is responsible. Design a suitable relational structure for this data.

REFERENCES AND BIBLIOGRAPHY

14.1 E. F. Codd. "Further Normalization of the Data Base Relational Model." In *Data Base Systems,* Courant Computer Science Symposia Series, Vol. 6. Englewood Cliffs, N.J.: Prentice-Hall (1972).

14.2 E. F. Codd. "Normalized Data Base Structure: A Brief Tutorial." *Proc. 1971 ACM SIGFIDET Workshop on Data Description, Access and Control.*

14.3 I. J. Heath. "Unacceptable File Operations in a Relational Database." *Proc. 1971 ACM SIGFIDET Workshop on Data Description, Access and Control.*

14.4 R. Fagin. "Multivalued Dependencies and a New Normal Form for Relational Databases." *ACM Transactions on Database Systems* **2,** No. 3 (September 1977).

14.5 R. Fagin. "Normal Forms and Relational Database Operators." *Proc. 1979 ACM SIGMOD International Conference on Management of Data.*

14.6 J. Rissanen. "Independent Components of Relations." *ACM Transactions on Database Systems* **2,** No. 4 (December 1977).

14.7 W. W. Armstrong. "Dependency Structures of Data Base Relationships." *Proc. IFIP Congress 1974.*

The paper that first formalized the theory of FDs. The theory provides a set of axioms that characterize precisely all possible FD structures within a relation. The axioms can be stated as follows:

1. $A_1 A_2 \cdots A_m \rightarrow A_i$, for $i = 1, 2, \ldots, m$.
2. $A_1 A_2 \cdots A_m \rightarrow B_1 B_2 \cdots B_r$
   if and only if
   $A_1 A_2 \cdots A_m \rightarrow B_i$, for each i in $1, 2, \ldots, r$.
3. If $A_1 A_2 \cdots A_m \rightarrow B_1 B_2 \cdots B_r$
   and $B_1 B_2 \cdots B_r \rightarrow C_1 C_2 \cdots C_p$,
   then $A_1 A_2 \cdots A_m \rightarrow C_1 C_2 \cdots C_p$.

These axioms are *complete* in the sense that, given a set S of FDs, all FDs implied by S can be derived from S using the axioms, and *sound*, in the sense that no additional FDs (i.e., FDs not implied by S) can be so derived. The paper also gives a complete characterization of candidate keys.

14.8 C. Beeri, R. Fagin, and J. H. Howard. "A Complete Axiomatization for Functional and Multivalued Dependencies." *Proc. 1977 ACM SIGMOD International Conference on Management of Data.*

Extends the work of Armstrong [14.7] to include MVDs as well as FDs.

14.9 J. M. Nicolas. "Mutual Dependencies and Some Results on Undecomposable Relations." *Proc. 4th International Conference on Very Large Data Bases* (1978).

Introduces the concept of "mutual dependency" (actually a special case of the general join dependency—i.e., a JD that is not an MVD or an FD—involving exactly three projections). This notion has nothing to do with the concept of mutual dependency mentioned in Section 14.3.

14.10 J. Rissanen and C. Delobel. "Decomposition of Files, a Basis for Data Storage and Retrieval." IBM Research Report RJ 1220 (May 1973).

One of the earliest formal treatments.

14.11 R. G. Casey and C. Delobel. "Decomposition of a Data Base and the Theory of Boolean Switching Functions." *IBM J. R & D* **17,** No. 5 (September 1973).

Shows that for any given 1NF relation the set of functional dependencies (called functional relations in this paper) may be represented by a Boolean function, and moreover that this function is unique in the following sense: The original dependencies may be specified in many (superficially) different ways, each one in general giving rise to a (superficially) different Boolean function—but all such functions may be reduced by the laws of Boolean algebra to the same canonical form. The problem of decomposing the 1NF relation is then shown to be logically equivalent to the well-understood Boolean algebra problem of finding a covering set of prime implicants for the Boolean function corresponding to the original relation together with its functional dependencies. Hence the original problem can be transformed into a problem in Boolean algebra, which has several potential advantages. For example, it should be possible to use analytic modeling techniques to evaluate alternative decompositions.

14.12 C. Delobel and D. S. Parker. "Functional and Multivalued Dependencies in a Relational Database and the Theory of Boolean Switching Functions." Tech. Report No. 142, Dept. Maths. Appl. et Informatique, Univ. de Grenoble, France (November 1978).

Extends the results of [14.11] to incorporate MVDs.

14.13 D. S. Parker and C. Delobel. "Algorithmic Applications for a New Result on Multivalued Dependencies." *Proc. 5th International Conference on Very Large Data Bases* (1979).

Applies the results of [14.12] to various problems, such as the problem of testing for a nonloss decomposition.

14.14 R. Fagin. "Functional Dependencies in a Relational Database and Propositional Logic." *IBM J. R & D.* **21,** No. 6 (November 1977).

Shows that Armstrong's axioms [14.7] are strictly equivalent to the system of implicational statements in propositional logic: That is, a given dependency statement is a consequence of a given set of dependency statements if and only if the corresponding implicational statement is a consequence of the corresponding set of implicational statements.

14.15 Y. Sagiv and R. Fagin. "An Equivalence Between Relational Database Dependencies and a Subclass of Propositional Logic." IBM Research Report RJ2500 (March 1979).

Extends the results of [14.14] to include MVDs.

14.16 P. A. Bernstein. "Synthesizing Third Normal Form Relations from Functional Dependencies." *ACM Transactions on Database Systems* **1**, No. 4 (December 1976).

This chapter has presented the *decomposition* approach to the design problem. Bernstein proposes a converse approach: Given a set of attributes and a set of functional dependencies over them, it should be possible to *synthesize* an appropriate set of relations. Algorithms are presented for performing this task. However, since attributes (and hence functional dependencies) have no meaning outside the framework of a relation that contains them, it would be more accurate to regard the primitive construct not as a functional dependency but as a binary relation. The synthesis process is thus one of constructing *n*-ary relations from binary relations, with the constraint that all constructed relations be in third normal form. (The higher normal forms were not defined when this work was done.) A more serious objection (recognized by the author) is that the manipulations performed by the synthesis algorithm are purely syntactic in nature and take no account of semantics. For instance, given the functional dependencies

$$R.A \rightarrow R.B$$
$$S.B \rightarrow S.C$$
$$T.A \rightarrow T.C$$

the third may or may not be redundant (deducible from the first and second), depending on the meaning of R, S, T. As an example of where it is not, take A as employee number, B as office number, C as department number; take R as "office of employee," S as "department owning office," T as "department of employee"; and consider the case of an employee working in an office belonging to a department not his or her own. The synthesis algorithm effectively assumes that S.C and T.C are one and the same; it relies on the existence of some external mechanism (i.e., human intervention) for avoiding semantically invalid manipulations. In the case at hand, it would be the responsibility of the person defining the original FDs to use distinct attribute names (C and D, say) in place of S.C and T.C. (In fact, relation-names such as S and T are not recognized by the algorithm at all.)

14.17 J. Biskup, U. Dayal, and P. A. Bernstein. "Synthesizing Independent Database Schemas." *Proc. 1979 ACM SIGMOD International Conference on Management of Data.*

An extension of the work of [14.16].

14.18 R. Fagin. "The Decomposition Versus the Synthetic Approach to Relational Database Design." *Proc. 3rd International Conference on Very Large Data Bases* (1977).

14.19 R. Fadous and J. Forsyth. "Finding Candidate Keys for Relational Data Bases." *Proc. 1975 ACM SIGMOD International Conference on the Management of Data.*

Presents an algorithm for finding all candidate keys in a 1NF relation, given the set of all functional dependencies in that relation.

14.20 J. Rissanen. "Theory of Relations for Databases—A Tutorial Survey." *Proc. 7th Symposium on Mathematical Foundations of Computer Science,* Lecture Notes in Computer Science 64. New York: Springer-Verlag (1978).

14.21 C. Beeri, P. A. Bernstein, and N. Goodman. "A Sophisticate's Introduction to Database Normalization Theory." *Proc. 4th International Conference on Very Large Data Bases* (1978).

14.22 J.-M. Cadiou. "On Semantic Issues in the Relational Model of Data." *Proc. International Symposium on Mathematical Foundations of Computer Science,* Gdansk, Poland (September 1975). New York: Springer-Verlag, Lecture Notes in Computer Science.

14.23 H. A. Schmid and J. R. Swenson. "On the Semantics of the Relational Data Model." *Proc. 1975 ACM SIGMOD International Conference on Management of Data.*

Starting with the premise that the real world may be modeled as "complex independent objects" (entities) and associations between them, this paper presents an insertion/deletion theory for relational databases. In terms of the suppliers-and-parts example, the theory formalizes such constraints as: (a) An SP tuple may be created only if the indicated supplier and part already exist, and (b) an S or P tuple may be deleted only if the indicated supplier or part does not participate in any SP association. The authors emphasize the distinction between "associations" (such as SP) and "characteristics." A characteristic may be represented by a simple attribute—for example, STATUS is a simple characteristic of suppliers—or by a subordinate relation—for example, in a personnel database, we may have the relations:

```
EMP (EMP#,DESCRIPTION)
EC  (EMP#,CAR#)
CAR (CAR#,DESCRIPTION)
```

Here employees are the "complex independent objects" (we are assuming for the sake of the example that the system has no interest in cars other than as employee possessions); each employee is represented by one EMP tuple, n EC tuples, and n CAR tuples. Cars are "complex characteristics" of employees. Using these ideas, the authors categorize 3NF relations into five different types, and suggest that this categorization should be reflected in the conceptual schema.

14.24 W. Kent. "Consequences of Assuming a Universal Relation." To appear in *ACM Transactions on Database Systems.*

The decomposition approach (see, e.g., [14.18]) assumes that it is possible to define an initial "universal relation" (involving all attributes relevant to the database under consideration), and then shows how that relation can be replaced by successively smaller and smaller projections until some "good" structure is reached. This paper suggests that this initial assumption is unrealistic and difficult to justify on both practical and theoretical grounds.

14.25 J. M. Smith. "A Normal Form for Abstract Syntax." *Proc. 4th International Conference on Very Large Data Bases* (1978).

14.26 R. Fagin. "A Normal Form for Relational Databases That Is Based on Domains and Keys." IBM Research Report RJ2520 (revised version, November 1980). To appear in *ACM Transactions on Database Systems.*

14.27 Y. Sagiv, C. Delobel, D. S. Parker, and R. Fagin. "An Equivalence Between Relational Database Dependencies and a Subclass of Propositional Logic." *JACM* (to appear).

Combines [14.12] and [14.15].

Part 3
The Hierarchical
Approach

Many present-day database systems are based on the hierarchical approach. In Part 3 we examine one such system, IMS, in considerable detail. Chapter 15 describes the overall structure of an IMS system. Chapters 16, 17, and 18 describe the IMS data structure (at both the "conceptual" and the external level) and the IMS data manipulation language DL/I. Chapter 19 is concerned with those parts of an IMS system that lie below the user interface, i.e., the storage structure and the mapping between the conceptual and internal levels. Chapters 20 and 21 provide introductions to two special IMS features, namely, "logical databases" (Chapter 20) and secondary indexing (Chapter 21). Finally, Chapter 22 discusses the database aspects of the IMS Fast Path feature. Although not really part of the hierarchical approach as such, being very definitely special features of IMS, these latter topics have been included as interesting examples of how the hierarchical approach may be extended and also of its limitations.

Many other hierarchical systems are described in the references in Chapter 1.

15

The Architecture
of an IMS
System

15.1 BACKGROUND

The name IMS is an acronym for Information Management System. IMS is an IBM program product that is designed to support both batch and on-line application programs. During its evolution several distinct versions of IMS and related products have been made available by IBM; the principal ones are IMS/360 Version 1, IMS/360 Version 2, and the version current at the time of writing, IMS/VS (Information Management System/Virtual Storage), Version 1, which runs under the IBM operating system OS/VS (Operating System/Virtual Storage). We shall generally be discussing only this most recent version; IBM manuals invariably refer to this version as IMS/VS, but we shall use the abbreviated form "IMS" throughout this book. We choose IMS as our main example of the hierarchical approach since at the time of this writing it is one of the most widely used of all database systems, hierarchical or otherwise.

In its basic form an IMS system provides facilities for the running of batch applications only. It is possible to extend such a system, via the data communications feature, to permit the development of on-line applications (that is, applications that support access to the database from a remote terminal); however, such an application will use the same facilities as a batch application for actually accessing the database—the data communications feature provides the facilities required to access the terminal, not the database. For the most part, therefore, we shall ignore the on-line aspects of IMS, since they do not form part of an IMS *database* system as such.

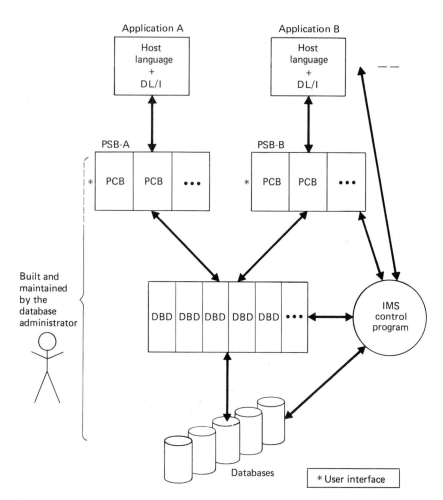

Fig. 15.1 Architecture of an IMS system.

15.2 ARCHITECTURE

The architecture of an IMS system is illustrated in Fig. 15.1. Note first of all that the stored data consists of several databases, not just one. An IMS database is a stored representation of a "physical database," and a physical database, to use relational terminology, is simply an unnormalized relation (more or less)—i.e., it consists of a collection of hierarchical records.

The "conceptual view" (not an IMS term) consists then of a collection of physical databases. The term "physical" is somewhat misleading in this context, since the user does *not* see such a database exactly as it is stored; indeed, IMS provides a fairly high degree of insulation of the user from the storage structure (and hence a fairly high degree of data independence), as we shall see in Chapter 19. Each physical database is defined by a *database description* (DBD). The mapping of the physical database to storage is also specified (at least in part; see Chapter 19) in the DBD. Hence the set of all DBDs corresponds to the conceptual schema plus (part of) the associated conceptual/internal mapping definition.

As in the general architecture of Chapter 1, the user does not operate directly at the physical database level but rather on an "external view" (not an IMS term) of the data. A particular user's external view consists of a collection of "logical databases," where each logical database is a subset (in a sense to be explained) of the corresponding physical database.[1] Each logical database is defined, together with its mapping to the corresponding physical database, by means of a *program communication block* (PCB). The set of all PCBs for one user, corresponding to the external schema plus the associated mapping definition, is called a *program specification block* (PSB).

Finally, as we indicated in Section 15.1, the users are ordinary application programmers, using a host language (PL/I, COBOL, or System/370 Assembler Language) from which the IMS data manipulation language DL/I—"Data Language/I"—may be invoked by subroutine call. ("Data manipulation language" is not an IMS term.) *End-users* are supported (in a system with the data communications feature) via user-written on-line application programs. IMS does not provide an integrated query language.

REFERENCES AND BIBLIOGRAPHY

15.1 IBM Corporation. Information Management System/Virtual Storage General Information Manual. IBM Form No. GH20-1260.

15.2 D. C. Tsichritzis and F. H. Lochovsky. "Hierarchical Data Base Management: A Survey." *ACM Comp. Surv.* **8,** No. 1 (March 1976).

Includes a brief tutorial not only on IMS but also on System 2000.

---

1. The term "logical database" actually has two distinct meanings in IMS. The meaning presented here is probably the less important of the two. The second meaning is introduced in Chapter 20. It must be emphasized that logical databases in this second sense are not really considered at all prior to Chapter 20; this has the effect of simplifying the presentation of much of the material in Chapters 15–19. Several of the topics introduced in these chapters are given an extended interpretation in Chapter 20.

Secondary indexing also has a significant effect on the external level. For tutorial reasons, again, we shall substantially ignore all aspects of this topic until we reach Chapter 21.

15.3 W. C. McGee. "The IMS/VS System." *IBM Sys. J.* **16,** No. 2 (June 1977).

An extensive tutorial on both database and data communications aspects.

15.4 D. Kapp and J. F. Leben. *IMS Programming Techniques: A Guide to Using DL/I.* New York: Van Nostrand Reinhold (1978).

16

IMS Data
Structure

16.1 PHYSICAL DATABASES

In the previous chapter the IMS conceptual view was defined as a collection
of *physical databases* (PDBs). A physical database is an ordered set, the elements of which consist of all occurrences of one type of *physical database
record* (PDBR). A PDBR occurrence in turn consists of a hierarchical
arrangement of fixed-length *segment* occurrences;[1] and a segment occurrence consists of a set of associated fixed-length *field* occurrences. The
smallest unit of data that can be accessed in a single DL/I operation is the
field occurrence (though most DL/I operations deal with segments containing several fields, not just with a single field).

As an example we consider a PDB that contains information about the
internal education system of a large industrial company. The hierarchical
structure of this PDB—that is, the PDBR *type*—is illustrated in Fig. 16.1.

In this example we are assuming that the company maintains an education department whose function is to run a number of training courses.
Each course is offered at a number of different locations within the company. The PDB contains details both of offerings already given and of
offerings scheduled to be given in the future. The details are as follows:

- For each course: course number (unique), course title, course description, details of prerequisite courses (if any), and details of all offerings
  (past and planned);

---

1. Variable-length segments are also permitted, but the details are beyond the scope
of this text.

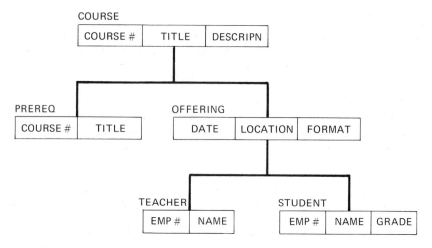

Fig. 16.1 PDBR type for the education database.

- For each prerequisite course for a given course: course number and title;
- For each offering of a given course: date, location, format (e.g., full-time or half-time), details of all teachers, and details of all students;
- For each teacher of a given offering: employee number and name;
- For each student of a given offering: employee number, name, and grade.

As Fig. 16.1 shows, we have here five types of segment: COURSE, PREREQ, OFFERING, TEACHER, and STUDENT, each one consisting of the field types indicated. COURSE is the *root* segment type; the others are dependent segment types. Each dependent (segment type) has a *parent* (segment type)—the parent of TEACHER (and STUDENT) is OFFERING, for example. Similarly, each parent (segment type) has at least one *child* (segment type); COURSE, for example, has two.

It is important to understand that for one occurrence of any given segment type there may be any number of occurrences (possibly zero) of each of its child segment types. Figure 16.2 illustrates this point.

Here we have one occurrence of the root (COURSE), and hence, by definition, one occurrence of the education PDBR type. The complete PDB will contain many PDBR occurrences, representing information about many courses. In the particular PDBR occurrence shown in Fig. 16.2, we

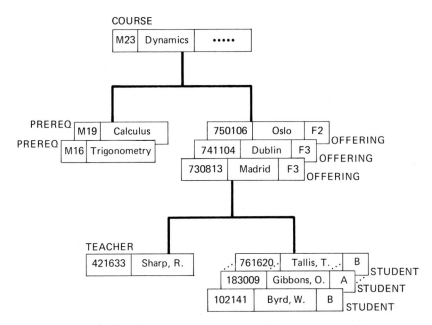

Fig. 16.2 Sample PDBR occurrence for the education database.

have dependent on the COURSE occurrence two occurrences of PREREQ and three of OFFERING. The first OFFERING occurrence in turn has one TEACHER occurrence and several STUDENT occurrences (only three shown) dependent on it. The other OFFERINGs have no teachers or students assigned to them as yet.

The parent-child nomenclature, introduced earlier for segment types, applies also to segment occurrences. Thus each dependent segment occurrence has a parent (segment occurrence)—the parent of the TEACHER occurrence (and the STUDENT occurrences) is the first OFFERING occurrence, for example. Conversely, the TEACHER and STUDENT occurrences are considered as children (child segment occurrences) of this OFFERING occurrence. In addition, all occurrences of a particular type of child segment that share a common parent occurrence are said to be *twins*. Thus the OFFERING occurrences in Fig. 16.2, for example, are twins (even though there are three of them).

To sum up, then:

- A PDBR type contains a single type of root segment.
- The root may have any number of child segment types.

- Each child of the root may also have any number of child segment types, and so on (up to a maximum of 15 segment types in any one hierarchical path and a maximum of 255 segment types in the complete PDBR type).[2]

- For one occurrence of any given segment type there may be any number of occurrences (possibly zero) of each of its children.

- No child segment occurrence can exist without its parent.

The last point is essentially a restatement of the hierarchical philosophy. It means, for example, that if a given segment occurrence is deleted, so are all its children (as we explained in Chapter 3).

From this point on we shall drop the terms "type" and "occurrence" if there is no possibility of confusion; indeed, we have already started to do so, as the reader may have noticed.

16.2   THE DATABASE DESCRIPTION

Each physical database is defined, together with its mapping to storage, by a database description (DBD). The source form of the DBD is written using special System/370 Assembler Language macro statements. (These macros thus constitute the "conceptual DDL" for IMS.) Once written, the DBD is assembled and the object form is stored away in a system library, from which it may be extracted when required by the IMS control program.

We shall ignore for now that part of the DBD concerned with the mapping to storage. We shall also ignore a few statements concerned purely with housekeeping details (such as error message generation). The remainder—what we may call the "conceptual schema part"—for the education database example is shown in Fig. 16.3. The statements have been numbered as reference points for the explanations that follow.

Explanation

Statement 1 merely assigns the name EDUCPDBD ("education physical database description") to the DBD. All names in IMS are limited to a maximum length of eight characters.

Statement 2 defines the root segment type as having the name COURSE and as being 256 bytes in length.

Statements 3–5 define the field types that go to make up COURSE. Each is given a name, a length in bytes, and a start position within the

---

2. These figures are of course characteristics of IMS, not a fundamental part of the hierarchical approach.

```
 1  DBD     NAME=EDUCPDBD
 2  SEGM    NAME=COURSE,BYTES=256
 3  FIELD   NAME=(COURSE#,SEQ),BYTES=3,START=1
 4  FIELD   NAME=TITLE,BYTES=33,START=4
 5  FIELD   NAME=DESCRIPN,BYTES=220,START=37
 6  SEGM    NAME=PREREQ,PARENT=COURSE,BYTES=36
 7  FIELD   NAME=(COURSE#,SEQ),BYTES=3,START=1
 8  FIELD   NAME=TITLE,BYTES=33,START=4
 9  SEGM    NAME=OFFERING,PARENT=COURSE,BYTES=20
10  FIELD   NAME=(DATE,SEQ,M),BYTES=6,START=1
11  FIELD   NAME=LOCATION,BYTES=12,START=7
12  FIELD   NAME=FORMAT,BYTES=2,START=19
13  SEGM    NAME=TEACHER,PARENT=OFFERING,BYTES=24
14  FIELD   NAME=(EMP#,SEQ),BYTES=6,START=1
15  FIELD   NAME=NAME,BYTES=18,START=7
16  SEGM    NAME=STUDENT,PARENT=OFFERING,BYTES=25
17  FIELD   NAME=(EMP#,SEQ),BYTES=6,START=1
18  FIELD   NAME=NAME,BYTES=18,START=7
19  FIELD   NAME=GRADE,BYTES=1,START=25
```

Fig. 16.3 DBD (conceptual schema part) for the education PDB.

segment. The first field, COURSE#, is defined (via the SEQ specification) to be the sequence field for the segment. This means that within the education PDB, PDBR occurrences will be sequenced in ascending course number order.

Statement 6 defines PREREQ as a 36-byte segment dependent on COURSE.

Statements 7–8 define the fields of PREREQ. The first field, COURSE# (again), is defined as the sequence field for PREREQ. This means that for each occurrence of the parent (COURSE), occurrences of this child (PREREQ) will be sequenced in ascending course number order. (In other words, the sequence field for a child segment type defines "twin sequence" for that child type. The same can be said for the root segment type, if we agree to consider all root occurrences as twins of each other.)

Statement 9 defines OFFERING as a child of COURSE.

Statements 10–12 define the fields of OFFERING. DATE is defined as the sequence field for OFFERING. The specification M (multiple) means that twin OFFERING occurrences may contain the *same* date value (implying in this case that two offerings of the same course are being taught concurrently).

Statements 13–15 define the TEACHER segment (a child of OFFER-ING) and its fields.

Statements 16–19 define the STUDENT segment (a child of OFFER-ING) and its fields.

The sequence of statements in the DBD is ignificant. Specifically, SEGM statements must appear in the sequence that reflects the hierarchical structure (top to bottom, left to right);[3] also, each SEGM statement must be immediately followed by the appropriate FIELD statements. As we shall see, the first of these points has a very definite effect on the user. It means that the sequence, not only of segment occurrences but also of segment *types,* is built into the data structure, so that, for example, the user can issue a DL/I "get next" operation to step from a TEACHER occurrence to a STUDENT occurrence.

A few additional points:

- Specification of a sequence field is optional, except as noted below.

- The sequence field, if specified, is taken to be *unique* unless M (multiple) is specified. By "unique" here we mean that no two occurrences of the given segment type under a common parent occurrence—or, in the case of the root, no two occurrences of the given segment type in the database—may have the same value for the sequence field.

- A unique sequence field is required for the root segment in HISAM and HIDAM (see Chapter 19).

- The simple rule given earlier for twin sequence (ascending values of the sequence field) does not specify what happens if the sequence field is omitted or is nonunique. In such a case additional specifications (not shown in Fig. 16.3) are needed in the DBD, and additional programming may be required on the part of the user when a new segment is to be inserted. In certain situations, moreover, the lack of a unique sequence field can lead to serious logical difficulties [19.1]; the details are beyond the scope of this text, but for reasons such as these we shall generally restrict ourselves to unique sequence fields throughout this book.

- The FIELD statement for the sequence field, if there is one, must be the first such statement for the segment.

- Overlapping fields may be defined; for example, the COURSE segment may be defined to contain a field COURSE#N (BYTES = 2, START = 2), representing the second and third (numeric) characters of the COURSE# field. [Note that this permits the combination of several (contiguous) fields to be defined as the sequence field.]

---

3. Internally IMS identifies each type of segment by its position in the hierarchical structure. Thus, in the education PDB, COURSE has type code 1, PREREQ has type code 2, OFFERING 3, TEACHER 4, and STUDENT 5.

- The FIELD statement may optionally include the specification "TYPE = datatype," where "datatype" is C (character), X (hexadecimal), or P (packed decimal). C is the default. However, IMS does *not* check field values for validity (except as noted in Chapter 22), and DL/I operations always perform comparisons bit by bit from left to right (again, except as noted in Chapter 22).

16.3   HIERARCHICAL SEQUENCE

The concept of hierarchical sequence within a database is a very important one in IMS. We may formally define it as follows.[4]

- For each segment occurrence, we define the "hierarchical sequence key value" to consist of the sequence field value for that segment, prefixed with the type code for that segment (see footnote 3), prefixed with the hierarchical sequence key value of its parent, if any. For example, the hierarchical sequence key value for the STUDENT occurrence for "Byrd, W." (see Fig. 16.2) is

$$1M2337308135102141$$

Then the hierarchical sequence for an IMS database is that sequence of segment occurrences defined by ascending values of the hierarchical sequence key.

The reason for the importance of this notion is that IMS databases are stored in hierarchical sequence,[5] in general; hence certain DL/I operations—essentially those concerned with sequential retrieval and with loading the database—are defined in terms of this sequence. (This statement is not quite true for HDAM; see Chapter 19.)

16.4   SOME REMARKS ON THE EDUCATION DATABASE

Before we leave the subject of IMS data structure, there are a few additional points to be made in connection with the education example. They arise from the various redundancies deliberately introduced into that example.

Consider students, first of all. For every course offering attended by a particular student, the PDB will contain that student's employee number

---

4. We do not consider the case where sequence fields are omitted or are nonunique.
5. This statement should not be taken to mean that the data is *physically* stored in this sequence. Several techniques—chaining, indexing, and so on—are actually used to represent the hierarchical sequence. See Chapter 19 for details.

and his or her name. Hence the association between a particular number and the corresponding name will appear many times, in general. This in turn introduces the possibility that a given employee number may have different names associated with it at different points, i.e., that the PDB may be inconsistent.

Similar remarks apply to teachers, where again the redundancy concerns employee numbers and names, and to prerequisite courses. For the latter, the redundancy concerns the relationship between a course number and a title; not only will a given instance of this association appear every time the particular course is a prerequisite for some other course, but it will also appear in the root for the PDBR occurrence for the particular course itself.

However, it may actually be desirable to provide the user with a data structure containing redundancies such as these. The "logical database" feature of IMS allows redundancy to be built into the data as viewed by the user *without* necessarily entailing a corresponding redundancy in the data as stored, and hence *without* the possibility of inconsistency. ("Logical database" is being used here in the sense of Chapter 20.) To see why redundancy may be desirable, let us consider what would happen if it were removed in the example.

To remove the employee name redundancy, we can eliminate the employee name field from the TEACHER and STUDENT segments and introduce another PDB containing a single type of segment—EMP, say—with fields EMP# and NAME. This PDB represents the required association between employee numbers and names. Similarly, we can eliminate the course title field from the PREREQ segment; the association between course numbers and titles is already represented in the education PDB (in the COURSE segment). However, the effect of removing the redundancies in this way is to make more work for the user, as the following paragraphs explain.

Observe first that the data structure seen by the user is made more complicated, in that it now contains two (interconnected) PDBs instead of one. The nature of DL/I is such that within one operation the user can process only one database. Hence the programming required in many cases will be more complex than before. Consider, for example, the query "Find the names of all students on a specified offering of a specified course." With the original structure this task is comparatively straightforward, involving only a simple scan of all STUDENT occurrences subordinate to the specified OFFERING of the specified COURSE. With the revised structure the user must still scan the same set of STUDENT occurrences; in addition, however, the user must extract the EMP# value from each such STUDENT and use it to retrieve an EMP occurrence from the second database.

As another example, take the query "Find the titles of all prerequisites of a specified course." With the original structure, this query requires only a simple scan of all PREREQ occurrences subordinate to the specified COURSE. With the revised structure, it requires such a scan, followed by the extraction of prerequisite COURSE# values and additional retrieval operations (on the same database)—with further complications arising from the IMS notion of current position (to be explained in Chapter 18).

For reasons such as these, it is quite usual to choose a data structure in IMS that does involve a certain amount of redundancy. As mentioned above, this does not necessarily imply redundancy in the data as stored.

EXERCISES

16.1 Write down the segment occurrences of Fig. 16.2 in hierarchical sequence.

16.2 Figure 16.4 represents the hierarchical structure of a physical database that contains information about publications in a number of selected subject areas.

For the purposes of this database, we assume that publications are of two types: articles and monographs. An article is a paper appearing in a journal or magazine that will also, in general, contain other articles (by different authors). A monograph is a publication devoted entirely to the work of one author or one team of authors. Note that a publication may appear in several different places; for example, the same article may be published in both *Communications of the ACM* and the *BCS Computer Bulletin* (reference [1.3] is an example).

The segments contain the following fields.

- Subject: subject classification number (unique), name of subject
- Publication: type flag (A = article, M = monograph), title

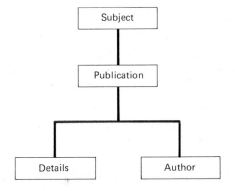

Fig. 16.4 PDBR type for the publications database.

- Details: date of publication, publishing house (if a monograph), journal name plus volume number and issue number (if an article)
- Author: author name and address

Write (the conceptual schema part of) an appropriate DBD.

REFERENCES AND BIBLIOGRAPHY

16.1 IBM Corporation. Information Management System/Virtual Storage Utilities Reference Manual. IBM Form No. SH20-9029.

This manual includes full details of DBD specification (also PSB specification; see Chapter 17).

17

The External
Level of IMS

17.1 LOGICAL DATABASES

In Chapter 15 a particular user's external view was defined as a collection of logical databases, and a logical database, in turn, was defined as a subset of the (unique) corresponding physical database. We can now amplify these ideas. A logical database (LDB) is an ordered set, the elements of which consist of all occurrences of one type of logical database record (LDBR). An LDBR type is a hierarchical arrangement of segment types; this hierarchy is derived from the corresponding PDBR hierarchy in accordance with the following rules.

1. Any segment type of the PDBR hierarchy, together with all its dependents (at all levels), can be omitted from the LDBR hierarchy.[1]

2. The fields of an LDBR segment type can be a subset of those of the corresponding PDBR segment type, and can be rearranged within that LDBR segment type.

Rule 1 implies that the LDB root must be the same as the PDB root. Consider the education PDB shown in Fig. 16.1. If we ignore Rule 2, there are basically ten distinct LDBs that can be derived from that PDB. One is illustrated in Fig. 17.1. What are the others?

---

1. It is also possible to reorder child segment types under a given parent type (e.g., to have OFFERINGs appear to the left of PREREQs under COURSEs), if those children are connected to their parent in storage via "child/twin pointers" (see Chapter 19).

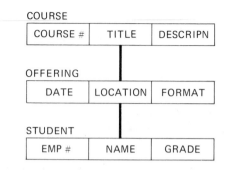

Fig. 17.1 Sample LDBR type for the education database.

Sensitive Segments

Those PDB segment types included in the LDB—segments COURSE, OFFERING, and STUDENT in Fig. 17.1—are said to be "sensitive." A user of this LDB will not be aware of the existence of any other segments; for example, the DL/I "get next" operation, which in general is used for sequential retrieval, will simply skip over any segments not sensitive for that user. The only exception is that if the user deletes a sensitive segment (occurrence), all children of that segment will be deleted, too, regardless of whether they are sensitive or not. In practice, a user should presumably not be given the authority to delete a segment if it permits the deletion of other hidden segments as well (see the discussion of PROCOPT in Section 17.2).

The sensitive-segment concept protects the user from certain types of growth in the PDB. Specifically, a new type of segment may be added (as the child of an existing segment) at any point, provided only that it does not affect any existing parent-child relationship in any way.[2] The new segment will simply not be sensitive for any existing user. In the case of the education PDB, a new segment may be added at any of the following points.

1. Subordinate to PREREQ
2. Subordinate to TEACHER
3. Subordinate to STUDENT

---

2. Of course, a new DBD will have to be created, and in most cases the PDB will have to be unloaded and reloaded according to the new DBD. (Reloading is unnecessary if the new segment appears after all existing segments in the top-to-bottom, left-to-right sequence.)

4. Subordinate to COURSE (at the same level as PREREQ and OFFERING)

5. Subordinate to OFFERING (at the same level as TEACHER and STUDENT)

However, introducing a new segment between COURSE and OFFERING would definitely affect current users of that particular hierarchical path.

The sensitive-segment concept also provides a degree of control over data security, inasmuch as users can be prevented from accessing particular segment types by the omission of those segments from the LDB (except as noted above for deletions).

Sensitive Fields

Sensitive fields are those fields (i.e., field *types*) of the PDB that are included in the LDB. By definition, every sensitive field must be contained within a sensitive segment. A given LDB may include or exclude any combination of fields from the PDB, in general, except that if the program intends to insert new occurrences of a given segment type, then it must be "sensitive to" the sequence field for that segment type.

Field sensitivity, like segment sensitivity, protects the user from certain types of growth in the database and provides a simple level of data security.

17.2   THE PROGRAM COMMUNICATION BLOCK

Each logical database is defined by a program communication block (PCB). The PCB includes a specification of the mapping between the LDB and the corresponding PDB (which is of course very simple). Like a DBD, a PCB is written using special System/370 Assembler Language macro statements. These statements constitute the "external DDL" for IMS. The set of all PCBs for a given user forms that user's program specification block (PSB); the object form of the PSB is stored in a system library, from which it may be extracted when required by the IMS control program.

Figure 17.2 shows the PCB for the LDB of Fig. 17.1. The statements are again numbered as reference points for the explanations that follow.

```
1 PCB       TYPE=DB,DBDNAME=EDUCPDBD,KEYLEN=15
2 SENSEG    NAME=COURSE,PROCOPT=G
3 SENSEG    NAME=OFFERING,PARENT=COURSE,PROCOPT=G
4 SENSEG    NAME=STUDENT,PARENT=OFFERING,PROCOPT=G
```

Fig. 17.2 PCB for the LDB of Fig. 17.1.

Explanation

Statement 1 specifies (a) that this is a database PCB as opposed to a terminal PCB;[3] (b) that the DBD for the underlying physical database is called EDUCPDBD; and (c) that the length of the key feedback area is 15 bytes. The last point requires some explanation. When the user accesses an LDB, the corresponding PCB is held in storage and acts as a communication area between the user's program and IMS. One of the fields in the PCB is the key feedback area. When the user retrieves a segment from the LDB (via a DL/I "get" operation), IMS not only fetches the requested segment but also places a "fully concatenated key" into the key feedback area. The fully concatenated key consists of the concatenation of the sequence field values of all segments in the hierarchical path from the root down to the retrieved segment. For example, if the user retrieves the STUDENT occurrence for "Byrd, W." (see Fig. 16.2), IMS will place the value

M23730813102141

in the key feedback area. In order for IMS to be able to reserve a sufficiently large key feedback area within the PCB, the maximum length for a fully concatenated key (considering all hierarchical paths in the LDB) must be calculated and quoted in the KEYLEN entry of the PCB statement. In our example the value is 15 (3 for COURSE# plus 6 for DATE plus 6 for EMP#).

Note that the fully concatenated key of a segment is not quite the same as the "hierarchical sequence key" of Section 16.3—it does not include the segment type code information.

Statement 2 specifies the first sensitive segment (the root) in the LDB. Note that the name of a sensitive segment must be the same as the name assigned to the segment in the DBD. The PROCOPT ("processing options") entry specifies the types of operation that the user will be permitted to perform on this segment. In the example the entry is G ("get"), indicating retrieval only. Other possible values are I ("insert"), R ("replace"), and D ("delete"); any or all of G, I, R, and D may be specified, in any order. Some other entries are explained in reference [16.1].

Statement 3 defines the next sensitive segment in the LDB. As in the DBD, segments are specified in hierarchical sequence (top to bottom, left to right). The PARENT entry specifies the appropriate parent segment (which must be as defined in the DBD). Again PROCOPT has been quoted as G.

Statement 4 defines the last sensitive segment. In our example statements 3 and 4 are very similar. In the PCB in Fig 17.1 the PROCOPT entry is the same for each of the three sensitive segments. In such a situation we

---

3. Terminal PCBs are used in connection with the data communications feature.

may specify PROCOPT in the PCB statement instead of in each SENSEG statement. If PROCOPT is specified in both the PCB statement and in a SENSEG statement, the SENSEG entry overrides the PCB entry, in general. However, there is one entry, L ("load"—i.e., create the initial version of the database), which may be specified only in the PCB statement and which cannot be overridden. Also, there is one entry, K, which may be specified only in the SENSEG statement. K ("key sensitivity") is used when the designer of the PCB is forced by the hierarchical structure of the underlying physical database to include a segment that the user of the PCB does not really require (or perhaps is not allowed to access). Suppose, for example, that a particular application is interested only in courses and students, not in offerings. The PCB for this user must include the OFFERING segment, because it forms part of the hierarchical path from COURSE to STUDENT. However, if PROCOPT = K is specified in the SENSEG statement for OFFERING, the user may largely ignore the presence of OFFERINGs in the hierarchy. For most purposes, in other words, the user may think of the logical database as if it had the structure shown in Fig. 17.3; the main difference is that when a STUDENT occurrence is retrieved, the fully concatenated key in the key feedback area will include the date value from the parent OFFERING. To be more precise, the user may issue DL/I retrieval requests exactly as if key-sensitive segments were *not* absent—in the case at hand, in particular, the user may refer to the OFFERING segment and to fields within it in the usual way—and IMS will handle such requests in exactly the normal manner,[4] right up to the point at which the retrieved data (if any) is due to be delivered to the program. At that point, delivery will be suppressed for any segment for which key sensitivity was specified (although the segment's sequence field value will be placed in the key feedback area). A key-sensitive segment may not be the direct target of a DL/I update operation (insert,

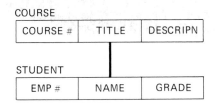

Fig. 17.3 Effect of specifying PROCOPT = K for OFFERING.

---

4. An exception to this statement is that retrieval requests without SSAs—see Examples 18.3.6 and 18.3.9 in the following chapter—will skip over key-sensitive segments.

delete, or replace), although of course it is possible to delete such a segment by deleting its parent.

The LDB in Fig. 17.1 (as defined by the PCB in Fig 17.2) is sensitive to all fields in segments COURSE, OFFERING, and STUDENT of the underlying PDB. Suppose we wished to exclude the LOCATION field of the OFFERING segment from the LDB, while still remaining sensitive to all other fields shown in Fig. 17.1. The PCB in Fig. 17.2 must be extended to include the statements

```
SENFLD NAME=FORMAT,START=1
SENFLD NAME=DATE,START=3
```

immediately following the SENSEG statement for OFFERING. These statements specify the fields to be included in the LDB segment and their start position within that segment. (Purely for the sake of the example we have interchanged the two sensitive fields within the segment.) Name and length for such fields are inherited from the DBD. If no SENFLD statements are given for a particular SENSEG statement, then by default that segment is taken to be identical to the underlying PDB segment (unless PROCOPT = K).

EXERCISE

17.1 Write a PCB (all segments and fields sensitive) for the publications PDB (see Exercise 16.2). This PCB is to be used for retrieval operations only.

REFERENCES AND BIBLIOGRAPHY

See [16.1].

18
IMS Data
Manipulation

18.1 DEFINING THE PROGRAM COMMUNICATION BLOCK (PCB)

The IMS data manipulation language (DL/I) is invoked from the host language (PL/I, COBOL, or System/370 Assembler Language) by means of ordinary subroutine calls. As we mentioned in Section 17.2, when an application program is operating on a particular logical database (LDB), the PCB for that LDB is kept in storage to serve as a communication area between the program and IMS; in fact, when the program calls DL/I, it has to quote the storage address of the appropriate PCB to identify to DL/I which LDB it is to operate on (remember that one program may be accessing many LDBs, in general).

How, then, does the program know the PCB address? The answer is that it is supplied to the program by IMS when the program is first entered. What actually happens is this. When a database application is to be run, IMS is given control first. IMS determines which PSB and DBD(s) are required, fetches them from their respective libraries, and loads them into storage. IMS then fetches the application program and gives it control, passing it the PCB addresses as parameters.

In order for the application program to be able to access the information in the PCB for a particular LDB, it must contain a definition of that PCB. The definition will not reserve any storage space but will act as a mask to fit over the real PCB (which will not physically reside within the application's own storage area). A reference to a field within the PCB definition will be interpreted as a reference to the corresponding field in the real PCB.

```
DLITPLI: PROCEDURE(COSPCB_ADDR) OPTIONS(MAIN);
            .
            .
            .
        DECLARE 1 COSPCB    BASED(COSPCB_ADDR),
                2 DBDNAME   CHARACTER(8),
                2 SEGLEVEL  CHARACTER(2),
                2 STATUS    CHARACTER(2),
                2 PROCOPT   CHARACTER(4),
                2 RESERVED  FIXED BINARY(31),
                2 SEGNAME   CHARACTER(8),
                2 KEYFBLEN  FIXED BINARY(31),
                2 #SENSEGS  FIXED BINARY(31),
                2 KEYFBAREA CHARACTER(15);
```

Fig. 18.1 Example of program entry and PCB definition (PL/I).

For example, suppose that we have a PL/I application that operates on the course–offering–student LDB in Fig. 17.1, and suppose also that this is the only LDB used in this application. Then part of the program might look like Fig. 18.1.

Explanation

The PROCEDURE statement (labeled DLITPLI) is the program entry point. The name DLITPLI is mandatory (for PL/I); all other names shown (COSPCB, DBDNAME, SEGLEVEL, etc.) are arbitrary. The expression in parentheses following the keyword PROCEDURE represents the parameters to be passed to the program by IMS; in general, it will consist of a list of pointers, one for each PCB in the PSB, where the first pointer gives the address of the first PCB, and so on. In the example there is only one PCB and hence only one pointer in the list.

The rest of Fig. 18.1 consists of a DECLARE statement that defines a structure (named COSPCB) to represent the single PCB used in this application. This structure is based on the pointer COSPCB_ADDR. The fields of the structure are used to hold various IMS-supplied information, as follows.

The field DBDNAME contains the name of the underlying DBD (in our example, EDUCPDBD) throughout execution of the program.

The SEGLEVEL field is set after a DL/I operation to contain the segment level number of the segment just accessed (where the root segment is considered to be level 1, its children level 2, and so on).

The STATUS field is easily the most important field in the PCB so far as the user is concerned. After each and every DL/I call, a two-character value is placed in this field to indicate the success or otherwise of the requested operation. A blank value indicates that the operation was completed satisfactorily; any other value represents an exceptional or error condition (for example, a value of GE means "segment not found").

The PROCOPT field contains the PROCOPT value as specified in the PCB statement when the PCB was originally defined.

RESERVED is a field reserved for IMS's own use.

The SEGNAME field contains the name of the segment last accessed.

The KEYFBLEN field contains the current significant length of the fully concatenated key in the key feedback area (see KEYFBAREA below).

The #SENSEGS field contains a count of the number of sensitive segments. In our example the value would be 3 throughout execution.

The field KEYFBAREA is the key feedback area; as we explained in Section 17.2, it contains the fully concatenated key (left-justified) of the segment last accessed.

The reader will appreciate that these programming details have very little to do with the hierarchical approach as such. However, it is necessary to have a general comprehension of this material in order to understand the IMS data manipulation language (DL/I). The DL/I operations *can* reasonably be regarded as typical of the hierarchical approach although again, of course, they do involve a certain amount of IMS-specific detail.

18.2   THE DL/I OPERATIONS

Figure 18.2 summarizes the DL/I operations. As explained before, the application invokes a DL/I operation by means of a subroutine call, one of the parameters of which consists of the address of the appropriate PCB. The other parameters include the operation required (e.g., GU), the address

GET UNIQUE (GU)	Direct retrieval
GET NEXT (GN)	Sequential retrieval
GET NEXT WITHIN PARENT (GNP)	Sequential retrieval under current parent
GET HOLD (GHU, GHN, GHNP)	As above but allow subsequent DLET/REPL
INSERT (ISRT)	Add new segment
DELETE (DLET)	Delete existing segment
REPLACE (REPL)	Replace existing segment

Fig. 18.2 DL/I operations (summary).

of the input/output area, and (in some cases) one or more qualification conditions, referred to as "segment search arguments" (SSAs). The name of the subroutine is fixed by IMS; for a PL/I application it is PLITDLI. To simplify the examples we shall not normally use genuine DL/I syntax in this book, but rather the hypothetical syntax illustrated by the example in Fig. 18.3, which shows a GU operation with three SSAs. (However, one "genuine" example is given in Fig 18.5.)

```
GU  COURSE    (TITLE='DYNAMICS')
    OFFERING  (FORMAT='F1'|FORMAT='F3')
    STUDENT   (GRADE='A')
```

Fig. 18.3 Example of simplified DL/I syntax.

If we assume that the data is as shown in Fig. 16.2 the result of the DL/I operation in Fig 18.3 is to retrieve the STUDENT segment for "Gibbons, O." The explanation is as follows. "Get unique" (GU) always causes a sequential scan forward from the start of the database[1] (at least conceptually, although beneath the user interface indexing or hashing is normally used; see Chapter 19). The segment retrieved will be the first encountered that satisfies the three SSAs. SSAs are considered in more detail below; in this example the three SSAs specify the hierarchical path to the desired segment—that is, they specify the segment type at each level from the root down, together with an occurrence-identifying condition for each type. The effect of these SSAs is to cause IMS to search in a forward direction for the first COURSE occurrence containing a TITLE value of 'DYNAMICS', then to scan that COURSE's subordinate OFFERING occurrences for the first containing a FORMAT value of 'F1' or 'F3', then to scan that OFFERING's subordinate STUDENT occurrences for the first containing a GRADE value of 'A'. If no such STUDENT exists for that OFFERING, the STUDENTs of the next F1 or F3 format OFFERING of this COURSE will be scanned, and so on. If no further F1 or F3 format OFFERINGs of this COURSE exist, IMS will search for the next COURSE occurrence containing a TITLE value of 'DYNAMICS' and repeat the process (of course, there may not be another such, in which case the retrieval operation will fail and a nonblank status value will be returned to the user).

---

1. This is true provided an SSA has been specified for the root. See [18.1] for details of what happens if this is not the case.

Note that only the segment at the bottom of the hierarchical path is returned to the user. Note, too, that in our simplified syntax we have completely omitted the specification of the input/output area and of the PCB (the course–offering–student logical database was tacitly assumed to be the relevant LDB).

In general, an SSA consists of a segment name, optionally followed by a condition. If the condition is omitted, any occurrence of the indicated segment will satisfy this SSA (provided that it forms part of a hierarchical path as defined by any associated SSAs). If the condition is included, it must consist of a set of comparison expressions connected by means of the Boolean operators "and" and "or"; each comparison expression consists of a ⟨field, comparison operator, value⟩ triple, where the field must belong to the specified segment and the comparison operator may be any one of the usual set ($=$, $\neg=$, $<$, $<=$, $>$, $>=$). All comparison operations are performed by IMS bit by bit from left to right (i.e., no particular data representation is assumed for the values concerned).[2]

To simplify the IMS rules somewhat, we may say that "get unique" and "insert" operations require SSAs specifying the entire hierarchical path, from the root down; "get next" and "get next within parent" operations may or may not involve SSAs, and if they do, the SSAs must again specify a hierarchical path, but one that may start at any hierarchical level, not just at the root; and "delete" and "replace" operations do not involve SSAs at all. We now give examples of all these possibilities. For these examples we shall assume that the LDB is identical to the PDB of Chapter 16 (i.e., all segments and all fields are sensitive).

18.3   DL/I EXAMPLES

For convenience, the structure of the sample database is shown again as Fig. 18.4.

18.3.1 Direct retrieval   Get the first OFFERING occurrence where the location is Stockholm.

```
GU COURSE
   OFFERING (LOCATION='STOCKHOLM')
```

This illustrates (a) the use of an SSA without a condition and (b) a hierarchical path stopping short of a lowest-level segment. Incidentally, this "get unique," like all other DL/I operations, should in practice be followed by an appropriate test on the status value returned; we shall generally ignore

---

2. Except as noted in Chapter 22.

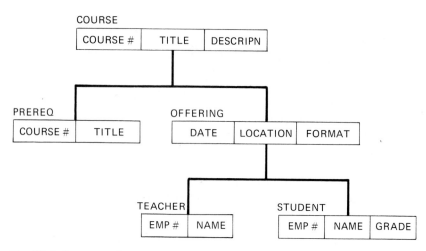

Fig. 18.4 Structure of the education database.

this step in our examples. Note that "get unique" is something of a misnomer—the operation is really "get first."

18.3.2 Sequential retrieval with an SSA Get all STUDENT occurrences in the LDB, starting with the first student for the offering found in Example 18.3.1.

```
      GU COURSE
         OFFERING (LOCATION='STOCKHOLM')
         STUDENT
   NS GN STUDENT
      go to NS
```

The "get unique" retrieves the first student for the first offering in Stockholm. This establishes a current position within the database. The first time "get next" is executed, it retrieves the first student following this position (in a forward direction), and establishes a new current position; the second time it is executed, it retrieves the next one following *this* position, and so on. All other segment types will be ignored. Eventually a status value indicating "segment not found" will be returned.

In general, the operation of "get next" is defined in terms of the current position, and the current position is defined as the segment last accessed via a "get" operation (of any type) or an "insert" operation.

18.3.3 Sequential retrieval with a conditional SSA Like Example 18.3.2, except that only STUDENT occurrences with a grade of A are to be retrieved.

```
      GU COURSE
         OFFERING (LOCATION='STOCKHOLM')
         STUDENT  (GRADE='A')
NSA GN STUDENT  (GRADE='A')
      go to NSA
```

18.3.4 Sequential retrieval with an SSA Like Example 18.3.3, except that the search is to start at the beginning of the database.

```
      GU COURSE
NX GN STUDENT (GRADE='A')
      go to NX
```

The "get unique" is used here merely to establish the first segment in the database (the first occurrence of the root) as the initial position. Note that it also retrieves that segment, which is not really required.

18.3.5 Sequential retrieval with multiple conditional SSAs Like Example 18.3.3, except that only STUDENT occurrences with a grade of A for Stockholm offerings are to be retrieved.

```
      GU COURSE
         OFFERING (LOCATION='STOCKHOLM')
         STUDENT  (GRADE='A')
NY GN OFFERING (LOCATION='STOCKHOLM')
         STUDENT  (GRADE='A')
      go to NY
```

18.3.6 Sequential retrieval without SSAs Get all segments.

```
      GU COURSE
NZ GN
      go to NZ
```

The user can determine the type of each segment after it is retrieved by inspecting the PCB.

18.3.7 Sequential retrieval with an SSA within a parent Get all students for the offering on 13 August 1973 of course M23. (See Fig. 16.2. We assume that there is only one offering of this course on this date.)

```
      GU  COURSE   (COURSE#='M23')
          OFFERING (DATE='730813')
NP GNP STUDENT
      go to NP
```

The operation of "get next within parent" is the same as that of "get next," except that when all segments satisfying the SSAs have been retrieved for the current parent, the next attempt to execute the GNP will return a status value indicating this fact. The current parent is the segment last accessed by means of "get unique" or "get next" (*not* "get next within parent").

18.3.8 Sequential retrieval with a conditional SSA within a parent Get all students who achieved a grade of A on (any offering of) course M23.

```
      GU   COURSE   (COURSE#='M23')
NQ GNP STUDENT  (GRADE='A')
      go to NQ
```

In this case the "parent" for the GNP operation is not the immediate parent of the segment to be retrieved but rather its "grandparent." Any ancestor segment can serve as the "parent" for a GNP operation.

18.3.9 Sequential retrieval without SSAs within a parent Get all subordinate segments (of all types) for course M23.

```
      GU   COURSE   (COURSE#='M23')
NN GNP
      go  to  NN
```

As in Example 18.3.6, the user can determine the type of each segment after it is retrieved by inspecting the PCB.

18.3.10 Segment insertion Add a new STUDENT occurrence for the offering on 13 August 1973 of course M23. (Again we assume that there is only one offering of this course on this date.)

```
      build new segment in I/O area
ISRT    COURSE   (COURSE#='M23')
        OFFERING (DATE='730813')
        STUDENT
```

When a segment occurrence is to be inserted, the parent occurrence must already exist in the database. The "insert" operation specifies the complete hierarchical path to this parent (note the conditions in the COURSE and OFFERING SSAs in the example) and also the type of the segment to be inserted. IMS will enter the new occurrence at the correct position, as defined by the value of its sequence field (in this case EMP#).

It is in fact possible to omit the specification of the hierarchical path and to quote just the type of the new segment. In this case IMS will use the current position—i.e., the segment last accessed via a "get" or "insert operation—to determine where to insert the new segment. Consider, for example, the "insert" operation

```
ISRT STUDENT
```

If the current segment is an OFFERING, the new STUDENT will be inserted beneath it; if it is a TEACHER or a STUDENT, it will be inserted beneath the OFFERING above that TEACHER or STUDENT. In all cases the sequence field value will be used to determine the position of the new segment with respect to any existing twins.

"Insert" is also used to perform the initial loading of the database. Since segment occurrences to be loaded must be presented in hierarchical sequence,[3] specifying just the segment type in the ISRT is the normal method of operation in this case. (Basically each new segment has to be loaded immediately following the current segment.)

Any nonsensitive fields in the PDB segment are set to binary zeros by ISRT.

18.3.11 Segment deletion Delete the offering of course M23 on 13 August 1973.

```
GHU COURSE    (COURSE#='M23')
    OFFERING (DATE='730813')
DLET
```

The segment to be deleted must first be retrieved via one of the "get hold" operations—"get hold unique" (GHU), "get hold next" (GHN), or "get hold next within parent" (GHNP). The "delete" operation may then be issued (unless the user decides not to delete the segment after all, in which case he or she may simply continue processing as usual, e.g., issue another "get hold"). Note that the "delete" operation has no SSAs; however, it does specify the I/O area (not shown in our simplified syntax), and the retrieved segment remains in the I/O area after the deletion has been performed. Remember that a successful "delete" operation deletes the specified segment occurrence and also all its children.

18.3.12 Segment replacement Change the location of the 13 August 1973 offering of course M23 to Helsinki.

```
GHU COURSE    (COURSE#='M23')
    OFFERING (DATE='730813')
change location to 'HELSINKI' in I/O area
REPL
```

As with "delete," the segment to be replaced must first be retrieved via one of the "get hold" calls. It is then modified in the I/O area, and the "replace" operation is issued. The sequence field cannot be modified, however; its value must remain unchanged in the I/O area (incidentally, this applies to "delete" as well). Again, if the user decides not to replace the segment after all, he or she may simply continue processing in the usual way; and again there are no SSAs involved.

---

3. Not quite true for HDAM; see Chapter 19.

18.4   CONSTRUCTING THE SEGMENT SEARCH ARGUMENT (SSA)

The process of constructing a segment search argument is a detail of IMS, not a part of the hierarchical approach as such. However, a little should be said about the subject here in order to avoid leaving the reader with a false impression. The simple syntax we have been using has concealed the fact that an SSA is actually a character string, forming one of the parameters of a subroutine call. A typical value for this character string might be

```
'STUDENTb(GRADEbbb=bA)'
```

(We now show genuine IMS syntax, in which blank padding characters—shown as b above—must be used to make each portion of the SSA a predefined fixed length, and the comparison value is not enclosed in quotation marks.) The point about this example is that the comparison value is a constant, whereas in practice it is far more likely that the value of a variable would be required. Consequently, before issuing the DL/I subroutine call, the programmer must dynamically *construct* the SSA character string by actually moving the value of the comparison variable into the appropriate position. (In general, of course, the programmer may dynamically vary any portion of the SSA in this way.) As an illustration, we show in Fig. 18.5 part of a PL/I program that is using genuine IMS syntax. The code shown corresponds to the first DL/I call (GU) of Example 18.3.3.

18.5   SSA COMMAND CODES

An SSA may optionally include one or more "command codes." Each command code is represented by a single character (e.g., F, for "first"); command codes are specified by writing an asterisk followed by the appropriate character(s) immediately after the segment name in the SSA. We give examples of the use of command codes D (probably the most useful of the set), F, and V. Note in the case of command code D that PROCOPT in the PCB must include the entry P [16.1]. For details of the remaining codes (C, L, P, Q, U, N, −), see reference [18.1].

18.5.1 Path retrieval Get the first OFFERING occurrence where the location is Stockholm, together with its parent COURSE occurrence (cf. Example 18.3.1).

```
GU    COURSE*D
      OFFERING (LOCATION='STOCKHOLM')
```

The "D" stands for data. The effect of this "get unique" is to locate the first Stockholm offering (as in Example 18.3.1), and then to retrieve the entire hierarchical path of segments to that point—in this case, two segments.

```
DLITPLI: PROC(EDPCB_ADDR) OPTIONS(MAIN);

  DCL 1 EDPCB BASED(EDPCB_ADDR), . . . ;
  DCL STUDENT_AREA CHAR(25); /* input area */

  DCL 1 CSSA,
        2 CSEGNAME CHAR(8)   INITIAL('COURSEbb'),
        2 CSSAEND  CHAR(1)   INITIAL('b');

  DCL 1 OSSA,
        2 OSEGNAME CHAR(8)   INITIAL('OFFERING'),
        2 OLPAREN  CHAR(1)   INITIAL('('),
        2 OFLDNAME CHAR(8)   INITIAL('LOCATION'),
        2 OCOMPOP  CHAR(2)   INITIAL('=b'),
        2 OFLDVAL  CHAR(12),
        2 ORPAREN  CHAR(1)   INITIAL(')');

  DCL 1 SSSA,
        2 SSEGNAME CHAR(8)   INITIAL('STUDENTb'),
        2 SLPAREN  CHAR(1)   INITIAL('('),
        2 SFLDNAME CHAR(8)   INITIAL('GRADEbbb'),
        2 SCOMPOP  CHAR(2)   INITIAL('=b'),
        2 SFLDVAL  CHAR(1),
        2 SRPAREN  CHAR(1)   INITIAL(')');

  DCL GU CHAR(4) INITIAL('GUbb');
  DCL SIX FIXED BIN(31) INITIAL(6);
  ........
    OFLDVAL='STOCKHOLMbbb';   /* would be variables in practice, */
    SFLDVAL='A';                 /* not constants                */
    CALL PLITDLI (SIX, GU, EDPCB, STUDENT_AREA, /* call DL/I     */
                  CSSA, OSSA, SSSA);
    IF EDPCB.STATUS='GE' THEN.../* segment not found */
  ........
END DLITPLI;
```

Fig. 18.5 Example of IMS syntax.

In general, command code D may be specified at some levels and not at others; the effect is to retrieve just the indicated segments from the hierarchical path and to concatenate them in the I/O area. Note that it is not necessary to specify *D at the lowest level in the path, since this segment is retrieved anyway.

The reader should consider how this example could be handled without the path retrieval facility. (One possibility: Retrieve the OFFERING occurrence as in Example 18.3.1; extract the number of the COURSE from the key feedback area in the PCB; using this value, construct an SSA and hence retrieve the COURSE directly, via another "get unique.")

If the "get hold" preceding a "delete" or "replace" operation is a path retrieval, the DLET/REPL operation is normally taken to apply to the

entire path. However, it is possible to be more selective than this; for details
see reference [18.1].

18.5.2   Path insertion   Insert a new course (M40), together with an offering at Brussels on 4 January 1976, for which the teacher is employee number
876225.

```
      build three segments concatenated in I/O area
      ISRT COURSE*D
           OFFERING
           TEACHER
```

Note that *D is required only for the first segment in the path. This segment is inserted (in this example it is a root, so it has no parent); the second
segment in the path may now be inserted, since its parent exists; and similarly for the third.

18.5.3   Use of command code F   Get the teacher (we assume that there is
only one) of the first offering (of any course) attended by student 183009.

```
         GU    COURSE
      NO GN    OFFERING
         GNP   STUDENT    (EMP#='183009')
         if not found go to NO
         GNP   TEACHER*F
```

The "get unique" positions us to the start of the database. The "get next"
establishes an offering as the current parent, and the "get next within parent" for STUDENT searches to see whether the specified student has
attended this offering. These two operations are repeated until an offering
attended by this student has been found. We now wish to retrieve the corresponding teacher. However, "get next within parent" (without the *F) will
return "segment not found," since it will search in a forward direction, and
teachers precede students in the hierarchical sequence. Similarly, "get next"
(not within parent) will retrieve a teacher, but it will be the teacher of some
subsequent offering. What we require is a means of stepping *backward*
under the current parent, and this is what the *F does; it causes IMS to start
the search at the first occurrence of the specified segment type under the current parent. In this example, since the TEACHER SSA is unconditional, the
first occurrence is in fact the one that satisfies the search, and is hence the one
retrieved.

18.5.4   Use of command code V   Get all students for the offering on 13
August 1973 of course M23 (the same as Example 18.3.7).

```
         GU COURSE    (COURSE#='M23')
            OFFERING (DATE='730813')
      NP GN OFFERING*V
            STUDENT
         go to NP
```

This sequence of operations produces exactly the same result as that in Example 18.3.7. Before explaining it in detail, it is necessary to amplify slightly the concept of "current position." Basically, current position is defined as the segment last accessed via a "get" or "insert" operation. In addition, however, each *ancestor* of the current segment—that is, each segment in the path from the current segment to the root—is considered as the current of the relevant segment type. For example, if the segment last retrieved is a STUDENT, then that STUDENT is the current segment; also, that STUDENT's parent is the current OFFERING, and that OFFERING's parent is the current COURSE. This OFFERING and this COURSE are the current segments of their respective types, but they are not *the* current segment.

An SSA with a V command code directs IMS not to move away from the current segment of the type named in the SSA in searching for a segment to satisfy the request. Returning now to the example, let X be the OFFERING occurrence located by the GU. The GN operation may then be paraphrased as "Get the next STUDENT under X" (because of the *V in the OFFERING SSA). In other words, it is equivalent to a "get next within parent" for STUDENTs under X. It follows that the code above has the same effect as that in Example 18.3.7.

This example does not illustrate the true value of *V. The advantage in using *V in preference to GNP is that the "parent" referenced by *V need not be the "current parent" as defined under Example 18.3.7—rather, it can be any ancestor of the current segment. The following example demonstrates this point.

18.5.5 Use of command code V Get the teacher of the first offering attended by student 183009 (the same as Example 18.5.3).

```
GU    STUDENT    (EMP#='183009')
GN    OFFERING*V
      TEACHER*F
```

The GU retrieves the first STUDENT occurrence in the database for employee 183009. This retrieval has the effect (among other things) of making the parent of this STUDENT the current OFFERING. The GN then retrieves the first TEACHER under this OFFERING (note that the *F on TEACHER is still necessary).

Comparing this example with Example 18.5.3, we see that (a) we now do not need a special GU to position us at the start of the database, (b) nor do we need to retrieve OFFERINGs—we had to do this before simply to establish a "current parent"—and finally (c) we have eliminated a loop, since we are able to go directly to the desired STUDENT occurrence.

The V command code may not be used at the lowest level in a sequence of SSAs, nor may it be used in an SSA that includes qualification conditions on the fields of the segment. However, since it provides almost all the function of GNP and more besides, it might be desirable always to use it in preference to GNP wherever possible.

18.6   USING MORE THAN ONE PCB

Consider the problem "Given a course number (say M23), print a report listing all offerings of all prerequisite courses of that given course." A solution to this problem runs in outline as follows:

```
DO until no more PREREQs for given COURSE
   get next PREREQ for given COURSE
   get COURSE where COURSE# = course# of PREREQ
   DO until no more OFFERINGs for latter COURSE
      get next OFFERING for latter COURSE
      print OFFERING
   END
END
```

It should be clear that this logic requires the ability to maintain two positions in the database simultaneously—the outer loop relies on a position that moves through the PREREQs of the given course; the inner loop relies on a second position that moves through the OFFERINGs of the course corresponding to the PREREQ identified by the first position. The first position must not change while the inner loop is executed.

How can such a problem be programmed in DL/I? The answer is by using two PCBs. Remember that each DL/I operation has as one of its parameters the address of a PCB (see Fig. 18.5 for an example). The specified PCB identifies the appropriate database to IMS *and also a current position within that database.* That is, IMS remembers "current position" (see Example 18.3.2) by recording it in a "hidden" field of the PCB (i.e., a field that is not accessible to the user), and operations such as GN implicitly make use of this hidden field. For the problem at hand, therefore, the application's PSB should include two PCBs, both corresponding to the education database. Let us refer to these two PCBs as PPCB and OPCB. Then the problem can be coded as follows (still using a simplified syntax):

```
GU    COURSE(COURSE# = given course#) [USING PPCB]
DO until 'not found' on PPCB
      GN    COURSE*V
            PREREQ    [USING PPCB]
      GU    COURSE(COURSE# = PREREQ course#) [USING OPCB]
      DO until 'not found' on OPCB
            GN    COURSE*V
                  OFFERING    [USING OPCB]
            print OFFERING
      END
END
```

It can be seen that there are similarities between the PCBs of DL/I and the cursors of embedded SQL (though a PCB carries much more information than a cursor does).

EXERCISES

The following exercises are based on the publications database (see Exercise 16.2). You may assume that all segments and all fields are sensitive. Ignore status value testing as far as possible.

18.1 Get all authors of publications on the subject of "information retrieval" (you may assume that this subject name is unique).

18.2 Get the names of all publications for which Grace or Hobbs is (one of) the author(s).

18.3 Get the names of all subjects on which Bradbury has published a monograph.

18.4 Get the name of the article and date of first publication for all articles published by Owen.

18.5 Get the names of all authors who have had a monograph published by the Cider Press since 1 January 1970.

18.6 A monograph on the subject of science fiction, entitled "Computers in SF," was published on 1 January 1973 by the Galactic Publishing Corporation. The author's name is Hal. Add this information to the database. (You may assume that the subject "science fiction" is already represented.)

18.7 For all publications currently available from more than one source, delete all details segments except the most recent. (You may ignore the possibility that two segments may include the same date and hence both be "most recent.")

18.8 For each of the foregoing questions (where applicable), determine whether the use of *V instead of GNP offers any advantages.

REFERENCES AND BIBLIOGRAPHY

18.1 IBM Corporation. Information Management System/Virtual Storage Application Programming Reference Manual. IBM Form No. SH20-9026.

19

The Internal
Level
of IMS

19.1 INTRODUCTION

Continuing our study of IMS as an example of the hierarchical approach, we now take a look below the user interface and consider the IMS storage structure. IMS actually provides four different storage structures, known as HSAM, HISAM, HDAM, and HIDAM,[1] and a stored database (i.e., the stored representation of a physical database) may be in any one of the four.

In Chapter 2 we drew a distinction between the DBMS on the one hand and the access method it used on the other. The function of the access method was to present a "stored record interface" to the DBMS. Such an interface does in fact exist within an IMS system, although the picture is rather more complicated than the one given in Chapter 2. See Fig. 19.1.

The first point is that IMS actually uses several access methods below the stored record interface, not just one. They are as follows:

- The OS/VS Sequential Access Methods (QSAM and BSAM, collectively known as SAM);

- The OS/VS Indexed Sequential Access Method (ISAM);

- The OS/VS Virtual Storage Access Method (VSAM);

- A special IMS access method called the Overflow Sequential Access Method (OSAM).

1. We follow the standard IMS usage here, although strictly speaking it would be more accurate to reserve these names for the corresponding sets of routines within the IMS control program; see the subsequent explanation of the acronyms.

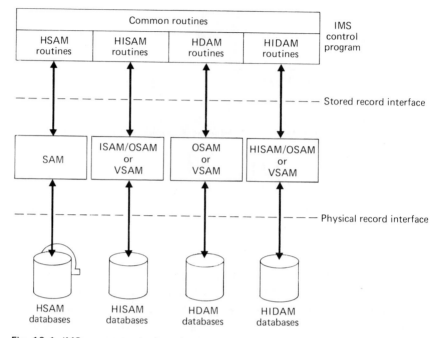

Fig. 19.1 IMS access methods and storage structures.

For example, the HISAM routines—those routines within the IMS control program that process HISAM databases—use either VSAM or a combination of ISAM and OSAM, and the function of these access methods is to enable the HISAM routines to consider the underlying data as being in the HISAM structure. The HISAM routines are thus not involved in any details of (for example) the indexing required to support this particular structure. It is not our purpose here to describe the access methods below the stored record interface in any detail; such descriptions can be found in [19.2] (for SAM and ISAM), [19.4] (for VSAM), and [19.1] (for OSAM).

The term "access method" is also used for the routines within the IMS control program that process the four different structures. These "access methods" are as follows:[2]

---

2. In addition to these four, IMS also provides an access method known as GSAM (Generalized Sequential Access Method), which allows a very restricted set of DL/I operators to be used on ordinary OS/VS sequential (SAM or VSAM) data sets. Using GSAM could mean that the progam is not involved in conventional input/output at all—all such operations could be handled via DL/I. However, GSAM is not really a *database* access method as such, and we ignore it from this point on.

- The Hierarchical Sequential Access Method (HSAM);
- The Hierarchical Indexed Sequential Access Method (HISAM);
- The Hierarchical Direct Access Method (HDAM);
- The Hierarchical Indexed Direct Access Method (HIDAM).

The situation is complicated slightly by the fact that the HISAM routines also appear below the stored record interface as one of the access methods used for HIDAM. This does not really affect the overall picture, however. In what follows we shall generally restrict ourselves to discussion at the level of the stored record interface.

As we have said, each physical database (PDB) is represented as a stored database in one of the four structures. Within the stored database each PDB segment occurrence is represented by means of a *stored* segment occurrence, which contains the data—exactly as the user sees it[3]—together with a *prefix* that the user does not see.[4] The prefix contains control information for the segment: deletion flags, segment type code, pointers, and so on. PDB segments as such, then, are represented in essentially the same way in each of the four structures. Where the four structures differ is in the means used (a) to tie PDB segment occurrences together to form PDBR occurrences, and (b) to tie PDBR occurrences together to form the PDB. In other words, the difference lies in the manner in which the hierarchical sequence of the PDB is represented.

We now proceed to investigate each of the four structures in some detail.

19.2 HSAM

The adjective that best describes HSAM is *tapelike*. Indeed, as can be seen from Fig 19.1, an HSAM database may actually be on tape. The hierarchical sequence is represented entirely by physical contiguity. For an example, see Fig. 19.2 (where we assume that course M27 is the next in sequence after course M23 in the education database—there is no M24, M25, or M26).

An HSAM database, then, is represented by means of a single SAM *data set* [19.2] containing fixed-length stored records.[5] Each stored record may contain any number of stored segments; however, each stored segment must be contained entirely within one stored record (i.e., stored segments

---

3. For HDAM and HIDAM, a PDB segment consisting of an odd number of bytes is extended to an even number by the addition of a single pad byte, which the user does not see.

4. Segments in "simple HSAM" and "simple HISAM" do not have a prefix. See Section 19.8.

5. The OS/VS term for stored record is "logical record."

COURSE	PREREQ	PREREQ	OFFERING	TEACHER	STUDENT	STUDENT	
M23	M16	M19	730813	421633	102141	183009	...

STUDENT	OFFERING	OFFERING	COURSE	PREREQ	OFFERING	TEACHER	TEACHER	
761620	741104	750106	M27	L02	740602	421633	502417	...

Fig. 19.2 Part of the education database (HSAM).

may not "span" stored records), which means that bytes at the end of a stored record may be left unused—depending on the stored record length chosen by the DBA. (In fact, none of the four structures permits segments to span stored records.) Apart from the occasional gaps this may cause, however, each stored segment is immediately followed by its successor in hierarchical sequence.

An HSAM database is created by means of a series of "insert" operations; note that the segments to be loaded must be presented in hierarchical sequence. Once created, the database may be used only for input; that is, only the "get" operations are valid (GU, GN, and GNP, not the "get hold" operations). It follows that the most common use of HSAM involves the "old master/new master" technique familiar from sequential file processing. In other words, updates are applied to an existing version of the database to generate a new (physically separate) version. The DL/I operations "delete" and "replace" may not be used. Instead, the user can delete an existing segment by not inserting it into the new database, and can replace an existing segment by modifying it before inserting it into the new database.

19.3 HISAM

We may characterize HISAM, a little inaccurately, by saying that it provides indexed access to the root segments, sequential access to the subordinate segments. (The index is on the root segment sequence field.) At least, this statement is true of a HISAM database just after it has been loaded; as we shall see, however, the picture may become somewhat distorted after insertions and deletions have occurred. The picture is also slightly different if secondary data set groups are used; we defer discussion of this case to Section 19.7.

As we indicated in Section 19.1, HISAM uses either VSAM or a combination of ISAM and OSAM as its supporting access method. We consider first the ISAM/OSAM case, then describe the differences for VSAM.

HISAM Using ISAM/OSAM

A HISAM database under ISAM/OSAM consists of two data sets, an ISAM data set and an OSAM data set. Each is divided up into fixed-length stored records. In both data sets, stored records are created sequentially and may be retrieved either sequentially or directly—for ISAM via the ISAM index (generally nondense, incidentally; see Section 2.3) and for OSAM via the relative address of the record within the data set (compare the SRA of Section 2.1). Figure 19.3 shows the structure of one of these stored records.

When the database is initially loaded (remember that loading must be done in hierarchical sequence), each root segment presented causes a new ISAM stored record to be created; the root segment is placed at the front of this record, and as many dependent segments as will fit are placed after the root. If the ISAM record is filled before all dependents of the current root have been loaded, then a new OSAM record is created and the next dependent is placed at the front of that; also the relative address of the OSAM record is placed in the "next dependent pointer" position in the ISAM record.[6] Subsequent dependents follow this one in the OSAM record. If the OSAM record is in turn filled, another is created (and its address is placed in the previous one), and so on. Thus each physical database record occurrence is represented as a chain containing one ISAM record together with zero or more OSAM records; any free space at the end of a record in the chain is considered as belonging to the PDBR occurrence concerned (it may assist with subsequent "insert" operations).

Figure 19.4 shows part of the education database as it might appear in HISAM just after loading.

Deletion of a segment in HISAM is accomplished by setting a flag in the segment prefix. Dependents of the deleted segment are automatically

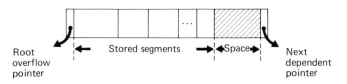

Root
overflow
pointer
← Stored segments →◄Space► Next
dependent
pointer

Fig. 19.3 Structure of a stored record in HISAM (using ISAM/OSAM).

---

6. In practice, the last stored segment in the record is followed by a byte of zeros (effectively a zero segment type code), and the "next dependent" pointer immediately follows this byte. Figure 19.3 and others show the pointer at the far end of the stored record, for clarity.

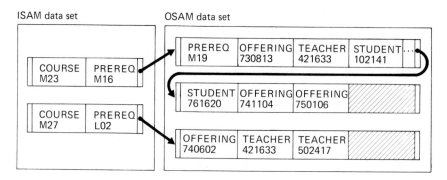

Fig. 19.4 Part of the education database (HISAM, using ISAM/OSAM).

considered as deleted; it is not normally necessary to set their deletion flags, since any attempt to access them must be via the deleted segment anyway. (This is *not* necessarily true for an HDAM or HIDAM database; see Chapter 20.) The deleted segment continues to occupy space in the database; this space is not available for reuse.

As for insertion, the method of operation depends on whether the new segment is a root or a subordinate. If it is a root, a new OSAM record is automatically created and the new segment is placed at the front of it. Let Y be the sequence field value for the new root, and let X and Z be the sequence field values of the roots that immediately precede and immediately follow the new root, respectively, in the hierarchical sequence.[7] Suppose that the X and Z roots are in (consecutive stored records in) the ISAM data set; i.e., this is the first insertion that has occurred at this position. Then, as explained above, the Y root is placed in a new OSAM record; also, a pointer to this OSAM record is placed in the "root overflow pointer" position in the ISAM record containing the Z root. If now a new root is inserted, with sequence field value Y', such that X < Y' < Z, then again a new OSAM record will be created. If Y < Y', then a pointer to the new OSAM record will be set in the Y record; but if Y' < Y, then the pointer in the ISAM record will be changed to point to the Y' record, and in turn a pointer in the Y' record will be set to point to the Y record. In general, the Z record may point to a chain of any number of OSAM records, each containing one inserted root segment, and this chain will be maintained in ascending root sequence. Figure 19.5 shows the situation after (a) root M26 and then (b) root

---

7. The Z segment always exists, because IMS automatically places a dummy root in the database at the end of the loading process with a sequence field value greater than any possible real value. The X segment may not exist, but this does not really matter, as the subsequent explanation makes clear.

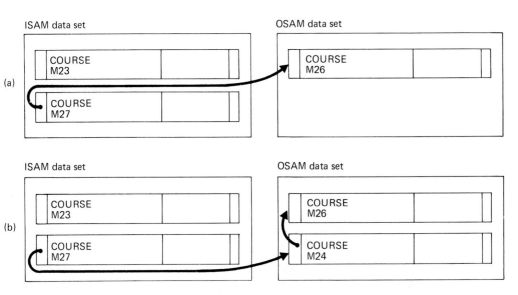

Fig. 19.5 Root segment insertion examples (HISAM, using ISAM/OSAM).

M24, in that order, have been inserted into the HISAM database of Fig. 19.4 (only the root segments are shown). Note, incidentally, that as a result of the technique used for root insertion, no new key is ever entered into the ISAM index once the database has been loaded.

Dependent segments are inserted at the correct point in hierarchical sequence. This involves scanning the chain of stored records representing the relevant PDBR occurrence to find the record containing the predecessor of the new segment. Segments following this predecessor (if any) are then shifted right within the stored record to make room for the new segment.[8] Provided there is sufficient free space to accommodate both the new segment and the shifted segments, no further processing is necessary. However, it will frequently be the case that one or more segments will no longer fit into the record; indeed, there may not even be room for the new segment itself (this situation will arise if the length exceeds the number of bytes between the predecessor and the end of the record). All such overflow segments are placed into the OSAM data set, occupying one or possibly two OSAM records. The "next dependent" pointer chain is adjusted appropriately to maintain the required sequence. Figure 19.6 illustrates the situation after the insertion of a PREREQ segment (L01) subordinate to root M27 (only relevant stored records are shown).

---

8. Deleted segments are treated just like other segments in this process.

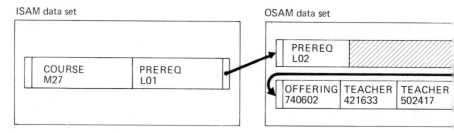

Fig. 19.6 Dependent segment insertion example (HISAM, using ISAM/OSAM).

HISAM Using VSAM

We summarize below the most important ways in which HISAM using VSAM differs from HISAM using ISAM/OSAM.

- The ISAM and OSAM data sets are replaced by a VSAM key-sequenced and a VSAM entry-sequenced data set, respectively.

- All root segments reside in the key-sequenced data set, even insertions. When a new root is inserted, it is placed in its proper position in this data set and the VSAM index is updated if necessary. The root over-flow pointer shown in Fig. 19.3 for ISAM/OSAM does not exist for VSAM. (As a matter of fact, the "next dependent" pointer appears in place of it, i.e., at the front of the record, instead of after all stored segments in the record as with ISAM/OSAM.)

- Under certain circumstances—see [19.1] for details—deleting a root segment will free the storage space for the record containing it (in the key-sequenced data set) for later reuse.

To conclude our discussion of HISAM, we amplify the remarks made at the beginning of the section. Access to the root segments in a HISAM database is by means of an (ISAM or VSAM) index on the root segment sequence field. However, the indexing is generally only partial for the following reasons.

- The index is nondense, so that in general there will be many roots for each index entry—basically N per entry, where N is the number of ISAM records per track or VSAM records per control interval.[9]

- In addition, some roots (insertions) may exist in the OSAM data set rather than the ISAM data set if the ISAM/OSAM combination is being used.

---

9. However, the DBA may arrange that $N = 1$.

Access to dependent segments is sequential, inasmuch as to access the
Nth dependent (in hierarchical sequence) of a particular root, it is necessary
to traverse all the (N–1) dependents that precede it. This may involve traversing deleted segments. It may also involve traversing chains from one
stored record to another.

19.4 HD STRUCTURES: POINTERS

The two hierarchical direct structures, HDAM and HIDAM, both involve
the use of pointers to link segments together. If VSAM is the underlying
access method, all data in the database is stored in one or more VSAM entry-sequenced data sets; otherwise it is stored in one or more OSAM data
sets. In either case the pointers just mentioned consist of byte offsets within
the relevant data set. Physically they are stored as part of the segment prefix. They are used (a) to represent the hierarchical sequence of segments
within a PDBR occurrence, and (b) to represent the sequence of PDBR
occurrences—at least to some extent. We shall consider these pointers in
some detail before moving on to discuss HDAM and HIDAM as such.

Let us consider first the hierarchical sequence of segments within a
PDBR occurrence. Basically this may be represented in two ways, either by
means of "hierarchical" pointers or by means of "child/twin" pointers.
Figure 19.7 shows a PDBR occurrence in which hierarchical pointers are
used.

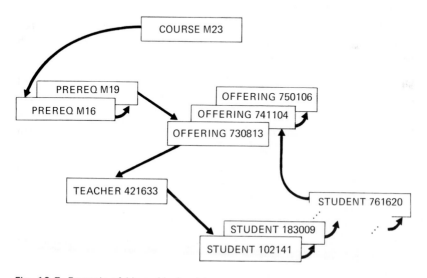

Fig. 19.7 Example of hierarchical pointers.

Observe that within the stored PDBR occurrence, each segment includes a pointer to the next in hierarchical sequence. (However, the last segment does *not* contain a pointer to the next root.) As an option, the hierarchical pointers can be made two-way; that is, each segment can additionally include a pointer to its predecessor (again, within one PDBR occurrence).

Figure 19.8 shows how the same PDBR occurrence would appear if child/twin pointers were used instead. Here each parent segment occurrence includes a pointer to the first occurrence of each of its child segment types, and each child segment occurrence includes a pointer to the next occurrence—if there is one—of that child under the current parent (i.e., to the next twin). Like the hierarchical pointers, these twin pointers may optionally be made two-way. In addition, each parent may include a pointer to the last (as well as the first) occurrence of any or all of its child segment types.

Now let us consider the sequence of PDBR occurrences within the database, which may also be represented, in whole or in part, by means of pointers. The pointers concerned are actually the twin pointer(s) in the root prefix. The possibilities are as follows.

- In HDAM all roots that collide at a position K (see Section 19.5) are kept on a chain (one-way or two-way) that starts at record K and is maintained in ascending root sequence. (This is only a partial representation of the sequence of PDBR occurrences, as we shall see in Section 19.5.)

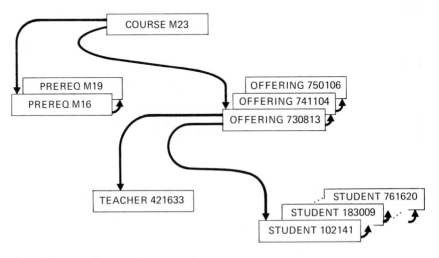

Fig. 19.8 Example of child/twin pointers.

- In HIDAM, if the one-way option is selected, all roots within one stored record are chained, but in reverse chronological sequence, not in proper root sequence; i.e., the most recently inserted root will be at the start of the chain. In this case it is the HIDAM index that defines the sequence of PDBR occurrences (see Section 19.6); the chain is provided for IMS's own use and is in no way directly accessible to the user.

- In HIDAM, if the two-way option is selected, all roots in the database are maintained in proper root sequence on the two-way chain, thus permitting sequential retrieval of the roots without reference to the index (see Section 19.6).

Each of the chains mentioned here uses the root segment twin pointer(s). This is true regardless of whether hierarchical or child/twin pointers are specified (in the mapping portion of the DBD; see Section 19.8).

Finally, we observe that it is possible to mix the two types of pointer within one PDBR type; that is, hierarchical pointers may be specified for some segments in the hierarchy, child/twin pointers for others. It is beyond the scope of this book to describe in detail all the relative performance advantages and disadvantages that influence the choice of a particular arrangement of pointers. However, since access to subordinate segments must obviously be sequential with hierarchical pointers, whereas it is (relatively) direct with child/twin pointers, we may say that, as a general rule, hierarchical pointers would be chosen if most processing were sequential in nature, and child/twin pointers would be chosen otherwise. Note, however, that child/twin pointers will normally occupy more space than hierarchical pointers.

19.5 HDAM

HDAM provides direct access (by sequence field value) to the root segments, via a hashing and chaining technique, together with pointer access to the subordinate segments (as we have seen). In its simplest form, an HDAM database consists of a single OSAM data set or a single VSAM entry-sequenced data set, divided up into fixed-length stored records. The stored records are numbered from 1; records 1 to N form the "root segment addressable area," and the remaining records form an overflow area. (The value of N is specified in the DBD; see Section 19.8.) Figure 19.9 shows the structure of an HDAM database.

HDAM differs from the other three structures in that the initial loading of the database need not be performed in sequence. More accurately, *root* segments may be presented for loading in any order; however, all depen-

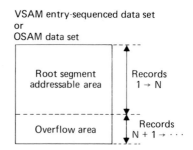

Fig. 19.9 Structure of an HDAM database.

dents of a given root must be presented in strict hierarchical sequence before the next root is loaded. When a root segment is presented for loading, the value of its sequence field is passed to a DBA-supplied hashing routine, which hashes the value and generates the address, K, of a record within the root segment addressable area (hence $1 \leq K \leq N$). The new root will be placed in record K, provided record K contains sufficient space for it. If it does not, the new root will be placed in the nearest record in the root segment addressable area that does contain sufficient space. If no space exists anywhere in the root segment addressable area, the new root will be placed in the next available position in the overflow area. (This description is somewhat simplified; see reference [19.1] for more details.)

The procedure just described is followed in exactly the same way when new roots are presented for insertion into an existing database.

Two root segments whose sequence field values hash to the same value K are said to *collide* at K (not IMS terminology). All such K-collisions are maintained in ascending root sequence on a chain that starts at an "anchor point" within record K (actually, this is the twin chain; see Section 19.4). Note that, in general, some of these K-collisions will actually be in record K, some will be in other records within the root segment addressable area, and some will be in overflow records. Note, too, that each of the N collision chains is entirely separate from all the rest—they are not linked to one another in any way. (Thus in HDAM—depending on the hashing routine supplied by the DBA—the logical sequence of root segment occurrences may not be completely represented, inasmuch as two roots that are consecutive in hierarchical sequence will probably be on different collision chains. Underneath any one root, however, the hierarchical sequence of subordinate segment occurrences is always represented completely by means of the appropriate pointers.)

As an example, suppose that $N = 100$ and the hashing algorithm is "Divide the root sequence field value by N, and let $K =$ remainder plus 1." Suppose that the following sequence of events occurs.

- Root 322 is presented for insertion.
  $K = 23$; record 23 has space available.

- Root 522 is presented for insertion.
  $K = 23$; record 23 has space available.

- Root 222 is presented for insertion.
  $K = 23$; record 23 is full; nearest record with space is record 25.

- Root 422 is presented for insertion.
  $K = 23$; root segment addressable area is full; next available position in overflow area is in record 144.

Then the collision chain will appear as shown in Fig. 19.10.

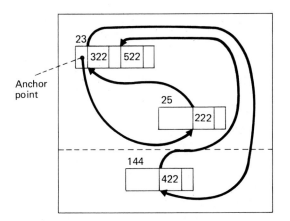

Fig. 19.10 Example of a collision chain (HDAM).

We can see that access to the root segments in HDAM will be very fast, provided the collision chains do not get too long. Indeed, this is one of the major objectives of the HDAM structure. As for the subordinate segments, an attempt is made to provide fast access to these, too, by placing them physically near the corresponding root (thus minimizing the amount of seeking involved with a moving-head device). Suppose that the root resides in record K. When the first dependent is inserted (either during loading or subsequently), it will be placed as close as possible to the root, possibly even in record K; the method used to search for space is exactly the same as that used for a root that hashes to K. If the next DL/I operation is the insertion of another dependent of this root, that dependent will also be placed as close as possible to the root. The process continues until either (a) the series of insertions under the current root comes to an end—i.e., some other DL/I operation is performed, perhaps an insertion involving another PDBR occurrence; or (b) placing another dependent in the root segment addressable area would mean that more than M bytes of this area had been assigned to this PDBR occurrence during this series of insertions, in which case all further dependents inserted in this series will be placed in the overflow area. (The value M, which is specified in the DBD, acts as a safety limit to prevent an unusually large PDBR occurrence from swamping the root segment addressable area during loading.) The whole process is repeated the next time a series of insertions involving this PDBR occurrence is performed.

Note that inserting a new segment does not cause any existing segments to be moved in HDAM—a significant performance advantage over HISAM. This is made possible by the pointers, of course, which allow the space allocation routines to place an inserted segment at any convenient position while still maintaining both the hierarchical sequence and the ability to access the segment directly. The deletion of segments is also performed differently in the two structures. In HISAM, deletions are indicated merely by setting a flag in the segment prefix. In HDAM, however, the space occupied by the deleted segment is made available for reuse, so that a subsequent insertion may cause the segment to be physically overwritten.

19.6   HIDAM

HIDAM provides indexed access to the root segments, pointer access to the subordinate segments. As in HISAM, the indexing is on the root segment sequence field. However, in HIDAM the index is controlled by IMS, not by the access method (see the remarks on DBMS-controlled indexing in Chapter 2). A HIDAM database actually consists of *two* databases: a "data" database, which contains the actual data, and an associated INDEX database, which provides the (dense) index.

The "data" database consists in its simplest form of a single OSAM data set or a single VSAM entry-sequenced data set, divided up into fixed-length stored records. The initial loading of the database must be performed in hierarchical sequence. As each segment is presented, it is placed in the data set at the next available position in sequence, exactly as if this were an HSAM database. In addition, of course, the appropriate pointer values are placed in relevant prefixes. Subsequent deletions are handled exactly as in HDAM; that is, the space is freed and may be used for segments added later. The subsequent insertion of a root segment will cause the new root to be placed as near as possible to the root that precedes it in hierarchical sequence. Subsequent insertion of a dependent segment will cause the new segment to be placed as near as possible to its immediate predecessor in hierarchical sequence. (As in HDAM, segments never move once they have been stored.) For further details of the method used to search for space, see reference [19.1].

The INDEX database is actually a special form of HISAM database—that is, either an ISAM–OSAM data set pair or a single VSAM key-sequenced data set (no entry-sequenced data set is needed). It contains just one type of segment, the index segment.[10] There is one occurrence of the index segment for each root occurrence in the "data" database; it contains the root sequence field value, together with a pointer to that root. This pointer forms part of the index segment prefix (it is in fact a logical child pointer; see Chapter 20).

Figure 19.11 shows how the example in Fig. 19.5(a) would appear in HIDAM, using HISAM/OSAM. Using VSAM the "data" database would consist of a VSAM entry-sequenced data set; the INDEX database would consist of a VSAM key-sequenced data set (only), and all index segments would be contained in it, including the one for M26. (The pointer from the M27 index segment to this index segment would not exist.)

19.7   SECONDARY DATA SET GROUPS

So far we have assumed that each stored database consists of a single "data set group" (DSG). However, a HISAM, HDAM, or HIDAM database—not an INDEX or HSAM database—may be split into one *primary* data set group and from one to nine *secondary* data set groups. Each DSG consists of an ISAM–OSAM data set pair (for HISAM),[11] or a single OSAM data set or single VSAM entry-sequenced data set (for HDAM and HIDAM). In each case all occurrences of any one type of segment are contained entirely within one DSG (on the other hand, several different segment types may all be contained in the same DSG). The primary DSG is the one containing the roots.

In HISAM the basic advantage (not the only one) of splitting a database into a number of DSGs is that each secondary DSG will provide indexed access, via the ISAM index in that DSG, to certain dependent segments. This will have the effect of improving the response time for some direct-access operations (e.g., a "get unique" for a segment near the bottom right-hand corner of the hierarchy need not involve traversing all segments that precede it in the hierarchy). Other advantages may accrue from the fact that the database may be spread across several devices, thus allowing (for example) the concentration of highly active portions of the database into comparatively small areas, and the possibility of greater concurrency in access to different portions. On the other hand, response time for some

10. The INDEX database is thus "root segment only," which is why no entry-sequenced data set is necessary in the VSAM case.

11. Secondary DSGs may not be used in HISAM if VSAM is the supporting access method.

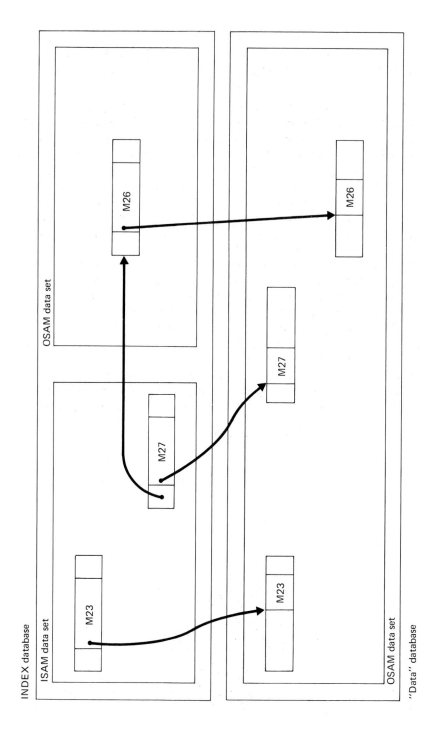

Fig. 19.11 Root segment insertion example (HIDAM, using HISAM/OSAM).

operations may be increased, owing (for example) to the additional space required for the extra indexes.

Figure 19.12 shows how the education database in Fig. 16.1 might be split into two DSGs, the primary one containing COURSE and PREREQ segments and the (single) secondary one containing OFFERING, TEACHER, and STUDENT segments. Figure 19.13 shows part of this database as it might appear just after loading (cf. Fig. 19.4).

In general, the split into multiple DSGs is performed under HISAM as follows.

1. Choose a second-level segment type (i.e., an immediate child of the root).

2. Assign that segment and all segments following it in the hierarchical structure to a secondary DSG.

3. Remove these segments from the hierarchy and repeat steps 1–3 on the hierarchy that remains (if desired).

Note that each secondary DSG starts off with a second-level segment. What happens when the database is loaded is this. Segments in the primary DSG (COURSEs and PREREQs in the example) are loaded exactly as if they were the only segments in a single-DSG situation. Segments in a secondary DSG (OFFERINGs, TEACHERs, and STUDENTs in the example) are loaded into their DSG in exactly the same way, except that the segments belonging to a single PDBR occurrence are preceded in their DSG by a copy of

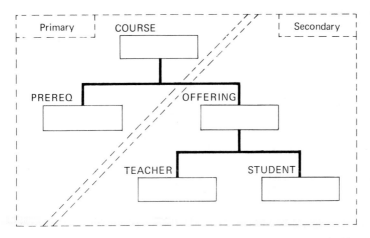

Fig. 19.12 Splitting the education database into two DSGs (HISAM).

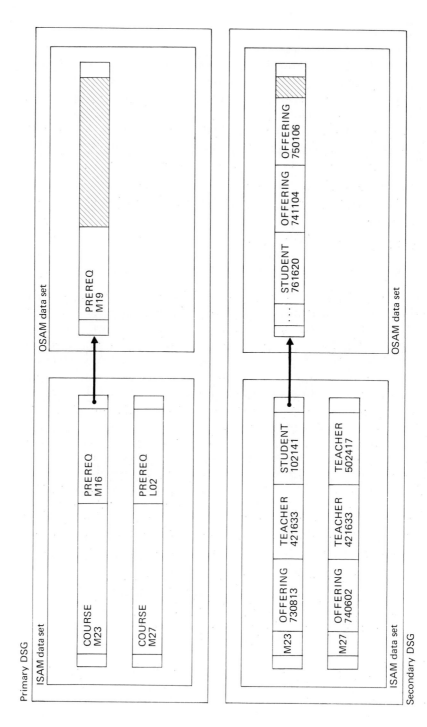

Fig. 19.13 Part of the education database (HISAM, two DSGs).

the sequence field from the corresponding root occurrence. This effectively acts as the "root" for the secondary DSG (see Fig. 19.13). The ISAM index in the secondary DSG is an index on this "root."

For HDAM and HIDAM there is another reason for splitting a database into several DSGs (in addition to the advantages already mentioned that derive from spreading the data across several devices): It may help to reduce the amount of storage fragmentation. As a somewhat simplified example, suppose that an HD database contains two types of segment, A (100 bytes) and B (60 bytes), and suppose also that the database consists of a single DSG. Suppose that an A segment is deleted, thus making a space of 100 bytes available for subsequent insertions. Suppose now that a B segment is inserted and is stored in this space. This insertion will leave 40 bytes that cannot be used at all, i.e., 40 bytes totally wasted. If, on the other hand, A segments and B segments are assigned to different DSGs, this problem cannot arise: Only an A segment will be allowed to use the space freed by the deletion of an A segment, and B segments will always be inserted in the other DSG.

There is no restriction in HDAM/HIDAM on the assignment of segment types to DSGs (contrast the situation with HISAM). For example, if the education database were stored in HDAM or HIDAM, COURSEs could be assigned to one DSG (the primary one), OFFERINGs could be assigned to another (a secondary DSG), and PREREQs, TEACHERs, and STUDENTs to a third (another secondary DSG). In the case of HDAM, only the primary DSG contains a root segment addressable area; all others consist entirely of overflow area. One restriction that does exist is that segments in different DSGs cannot be connected by hierarchical pointers; child/twin pointers *must* be used in this case.

Insertions and deletions in a secondary DSG are handled in essentially the same way as for the primary DSG. For further details see [19.1].

19.8 THE MAPPING DEFINITION

As mentioned in Section 16.2, the mapping of a PDB into storage is defined as part of the DBD. We can now investigate this in more detail. The mapping definition involves additional entries in the DBD and SEGM statements and two additional statements (the LCHILD and DATASET statements).

The additional entries in the DBD statement are as follows.

■ `ACCESS=HSAM or HISAM or HDAM or HIDAM or INDEX`

This entry specifies the relevant structure. Note that INDEX is one of the possibilities; for HIDAM *two* DBDs are required, one for the "data" database (for which ACCESS = HIDAM must be specified) and one for the

INDEX database. The two DBDs will be referred to as the HIDAM DBD and the INDEX DBD, respectively. These two DBDs are cross-referenced. (Note, however, that the user need not be aware of the existence of the INDEX database; the INDEX DBD is not part of the "conceptual schema"—it is part of the mapping definition solely.)

Other parameters in the ACCESS entry, not shown above, specify the underlying access method (e.g., OSAM or VSAM). In addition, a variation of HSAM, known as "simple HSAM" (SHSAM), may be specified; a simple HSAM database is an HSAM database containing only one type of segment, and does not contain any stored prefixes. HISAM has an analogous "simple" form known as SHISAM (available only with VSAM, not with ISAM/OSAM).

■   RMNAME=

This entry is required only if ACCESS = HDAM. It specifies the name of the DBA-supplied hashing routine (which must exist in a system library available to IMS). It also specifies the values N and $M,$ which are, respectively, the number of stored records in the root segment addressable area and the maximum number of bytes within the root segment addressable area that may be assigned to one PDBR occurrence during one series of insertions (see Section 19.5).

The additional entries in the SEGM statement are concerned with the pointer options available in HDAM and HIDAM; they do not apply to HSAM, HISAM, or INDEX databases. The first and more important of the additional entries is the POINTER operand.

■   POINTER=HIER or HIERBWD or TWIN or TWINBWD

HIER specifies that each occurrence of this segment is to contain a pointer to the next segment occurrence (of any type) in hierarchical sequence, except that the last dependent segment occurrence under a given root does *not* contain a pointer to the next root. In addition, if the segment being defined is the root, each occurrence will also include a pointer to the next[12] root occurrence. HIERBWD is the same as HIER, except that the pointers are two-way. TWIN specifies that each occurrence of this segment is to contain a pointer to the next occurrence (if there is one) of the same type of segment under the same parent occurrence *and* a pointer to the first occurrence of each type of child under this occurrence. If the segment being defined is the root, each occurrence's twin pointer will actually point to the next[13] root occurrence. TWINBWD is the same as TWIN, except that the twin pointers are two-way.

---

12. See Section 19.4 for details of what "next" means in this context.
13. See Section 19.4 for details of what "next" means in this context.

The second new entry in the SEGM statement consists of a new parameter in the PARENT operand. It is required only if child/twin pointers are being used (POINTER = TWIN/TWINBWD for the parent) and a pointer from each occurrence of the parent to the last (as well as the first) occurrence of this particular type of child under that parent occurrence is desired. The entry is specified for the particular child segment concerned, and it is written as follows (the double parentheses are required):

- `PARENT=((parent,DBLE))`

The LCHILD statement is primarily used in connection with logical databases (to be discussed in Chapter 20). However, it is also used in HIDAM to link the index segment in the INDEX database with the segment being indexed in the corresponding "data" database; the data segment is considered as a "logical child" of the INDEX segment. The INDEX DBD will contain one SEGM statement and one FIELD statement. For example, part of the INDEX DBD for the database of Fig. 19.11 might look as follows:

```
SEGM   NAME=XSEG,BYTES=3
FIELD  NAME=(COURSE#,SEQ),BYTES=3,START=1
```

(Incidentally, the field name need not be the same as the field name specified in the HIDAM DBD, although it is in this example.) In addition to these two statements, the INDEX DBD must include an LCHILD statement (either before or after the FIELD statement) to specify the data segment and the field within it on which the indexing is to be performed (which must be the sequence field). For example,

```
LCHILD NAME=(COURSE,EDUCPDBD),INDEX=COURSE#
```

An LCHILD statement must also be included in the HIDAM DBD, preceding or following the FIELD statements for the HIDAM root. In our example it might be

```
LCHILD NAME=(XSEG,XDBD),POINTER=INDX
```

where XDBD is the name of the INDEX DBD. The "POINTER = INDX" entry is required.

The other additional statement is the DATASET statement. DATASET statements are used for two main purposes. First, they specify, by their positioning with respect to the SEGM statements in the DBD, which segments are to be assigned to which data set groups. Second, they specify the names of the OS/VS Job Control Language statements that will be required when an application is scheduled to operate on the database. We shall consider each of these functions in turn.

For HISAM, one DATASET statement must be supplied for each data set group. Each must immediately precede the SEGM statements for the segments in that DSG. Figure 19.14 shows the sequence of statements required to define the database of Fig. 19.12 (only the relevant statements and entries are shown).

```
DBD        NAME=EDUCPDBD,ACCESS=HISAM
DATASET    ...
SEGM       NAME=COURSE,...
SEGM       NAME=PREREQ,...
DATASET    ...
SEGM       NAME=OFFERING,...
SEGM       NAME=TEACHER,...
SEGM       NAME=STUDENT,...
```

Fig. 19.14 Example of DATASET statement positioning (HISAM).

For HDAM and HIDAM, more than one DATASET statement may be required for a given DSG, because segments do not have to be adjacent to each other in the hierarchical structure (which is defined by the sequence of SEGM statements) in order to be placed in the same DSG. In such a situation *labeled* DATASET statements are used. As with HISAM, each segment is assigned to the DSG identified by the nearest preceding DATASET statement; however, two (or more) DATASET statements with the same label are considered as referring to the same DSG. Figure 19.15 shows the statements required to define an HDAM structure for the education database consisting of three DSGs, one containing COURSEs, one containing OFFERiNGs, and one containing PREREQs, TEACHERs, and STUDENTs. PRIME, SECONDA, and SECONDB are labels.

```
            DBD        NAME=EDUCPDBD,ACCESS=HDAM,...
PRIME       DATASET    ...
            SEGM       NAME=COURSE,...
SECONDA     DATASET    ...
            SEGM       NAME=PREREQ,...
SECONDB     DATASET    ...
            SEGM       NAME=OFFERING,...
SECONDA     DATASET    (blank)
            SEGM       NAME=TEACHER,...
            SEGM       NAME=STUDENT,...
```

Fig. 19.15 Example of DATASET statement positioning (HD).

A DATASET statement containing a label that is the same as that in a preceding DATASET statement may not contain any other entries.

The second function performed by the DATASET statement is the specification of the appropriate Job Control Language "ddnames." When an application is to be run against the database, OS/VS requires "DD statements," identified by ddnames, for each data set in each DSG. A DD statement defines the final details of the mapping of a data set into physical storage. For example, it may specify the device on which the storage volume containing the data set is mounted (which can in general vary from run to run). Broadly speaking, these details form (at least part of) the definition of the mapping from the stored to the physical record interface, and we shall not concern ourselves with them any further here. The interested reader is referred to [19.3]. We content ourselves with pointing out that, when an IMS application is to be run, either the user or the DBA must supply all appropriate DD statements, with ddnames as specified in the DATASET statements. The relevant DATASET entries are as follows.

- DD1=ddname

For HSAM this is the ddname for the input data set (SAM) which forms an existing ("old master") database. For a HISAM DSG or an INDEX database it is the ddname for the ISAM data set or VSAM key-sequenced data set. For an HDAM or HIDAM DSG it is the ddname for the OSAM data set or VSAM entry-sequenced data set.

- DD2=ddname

For HSAM (the only case in which the entry is needed), this is the ddname for the output data set (SAM) which forms a new ("new master") database.

- OVFLW=ddname

For a HISAM DSG or INDEX database using ISAM/OSAM (the only cases in which the entry is used) this is the ddname for the OSAM data set.

The DATASET statement also contains a few other entries concerned with such details as stored record length, blocking factors, and so on. See reference [19.1].

19.9 REORGANIZATION

From Sections 19.3–19.6 it is apparent that, as time progresses and more and more insertions and deletions are performed on a database, the organization of that database in storage will become more and more untidy. For example, with HISAM, more and more space may be taken up by unwanted (deleted) segments. (Of course, IMS is not alone in this respect; similar problems arise in most systems.) As the stored database organization degenerates, so also will the overall performance of the system, in terms of both space utilization and response time. Eventually a point will be reached where it is necessary to reorganize the database in order to prevent performance—particularly space utilization—from degenerating to an unacceptable level. Reorganization is the process of unloading the database and reloading it. More accurately, it involves retrieving all (nondeleted) segments from the existing database and loading them into a new database. (In practice, because of limitations on the number of available devices, it is usual to unload the old database to tape—probably in the form of an HSAM database—and then to reload it from there, overwriting the old database with the new one. This technique has the additional advantage of providing a back-up copy of the database.)

In practice an IMS utility program is normally used to perform the reorganization. For explanatory purposes, however, let us assume that the user actually has to write such a program. In general, all that is required is a series of unqualified "get next" operations on the old database and a corresponding series of "insert" operations on the new database. This will retrieve all existing segments in hierarchical sequence (not quite true for HDAM, where the sequence will be hierarchical only within each PDBR occurrence) and load them in the same sequence into the new database.

For HISAM, this process will recover the space occupied by deleted segments, since the deletions will not be written to the new database. Under ISAM/OSAM, it will also move any root segments in the OSAM data set (insertions) into their correct position within the ISAM data set of the new database.

For HDAM, reorganization will normally have the effect of moving root segments from the overflow area into the root segment addressable area. It will also recover space lost through fragmentation.

For HIDAM, reorganization will arrange all segments into a physical sequence that reflects the hierarchical sequence. Again, space lost through fragmentation will be recovered.

As a general rule it should not be necessary to reorganize an HDAM or HIDAM database as often as a HISAM database, because of the differences in the techniques employed in the two cases for insertion and deletion.

19.10 DATA INDEPENDENCE

In the previous section we tacitly assumed that when reorganization is performed, the DBD for the new database is essentially the same as the DBD for the old one. In practice many differences between the two are possible; i.e., the storage structure for the new database may differ considerably from that of the old one. In other words, IMS does provide a fair degree of data independence. Below are some of the possible variations.

- New segment types may be added at certain points in the hierarchy (see Section 17.1).
- New fields may be added to existing segment types.
- Stored record size may be changed.
- Different pointer options may be chosen in HDAM or HIDAM.
- The division of a database into data set groups may be changed.
- For HDAM the values of N (number of stored records in the root segment addressable area) and M (maximum number of bytes in the root segment addressable area to be allocated to a single PDBR occurrence in one series of insertions) may be changed.
- The HDAM hashing routine may be changed.
- The underlying access method may be changed (e.g., in HDAM, OSAM may be replaced by VSAM).

In addition, it is possible to convert a database from one of the four basic structures to another—from HISAM to HIDAM, say—subject to certain restrictions. The possibilities are summarized in Fig. 19.16.

From \ To	HSAM	HISAM	HDAM	HIDAM
HSAM		OK	Note 3	OK
HISAM	Note 1		Note 3	OK
HDAM	Note 1 Note 2	Note 2		Note 2
HIDAM	Note 1	OK	Note 3	

Fig. **19.16** Stored database transformations in IMS.

Notes

1. These transformations are extremely unlikely in practice, since HSAM will not permit "delete," "replace," or "insert" operations (except for initial loading, when "insert" is the only valid operation).

2. The new database must be loaded in hierarchical sequence. This requirement may cause difficulties if the root segment "twin" sequence—i.e., the sequence defined by ascending values of the root segment sequence field—is not properly represented in the old (HDAM) database. See Section 19.5.

3. The new (HDAM) database will probably contain no representation of the root segment "twin" sequence (see note 2). Hence "get next" operations at the root level will not in general function in terms of this sequence. (Details of how they do function are beyond the scope of this book.)

19.11   SUMMARY

Figure 19.17 constitutes an attempt to summarize Sections 19.2–19.6, which form the major part of the present chapter. Note that pointers are used in HISAM as well as HDAM and HIDAM, but that in HISAM they are used to link stored records, not segments. Section 19.7 explained an extension of the basic storage structures, namely, the concept of the secondary data set group (not applicable to HSAM). Section 19.8 showed how the storage structure for a given PDB is defined (via the DBD). Sections 19.9 and 19.10 discussed the concept of reorganization and the types of change that may be made when a database is reorganized. Finally, the advantages and disadvantages of the various possible structures have been mentioned at several points throughout the chapter.

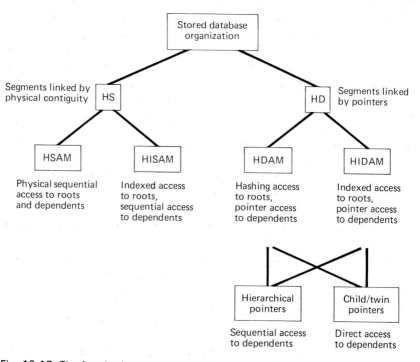

Fig. 19.17 The four basic storage structures.

EXERCISES

19.1 Suppose that the education PDB is to be stored as an HDAM database, with pointer options as indicated below.

```
DBD  NAME=EDUCPDBD,ACCESS=HDAM,...
SEGM NAME=COURSE,POINTER=TWIN,BYTES=256,...
SEGM NAME=PREREQ,POINTER=HIER,BYTES=36,...
SEGM NAME=OFFERING,POINTER=TWINBWD,BYTES=20,...
SEGM NAME=TEACHER,POINTER=TWIN,BYTES=24,...
SEGM NAME=STUDENT,POINTER=HIER,BYTES=25,...
```

Draw a diagram showing all pointers involved in the PDBR occurrence in Fig. 16.2.

19.2 Each prefix in HDAM/HIDAM consists of a 1-byte type code, a delete byte, a 4-byte counter, and a number of pointers (4 bytes each). On the basis of the DBD in Exercise 19.1, work out the relative amounts of storage space required for prefixes and for data. You may assume that on average there are two PREREQs and eight OFFERINGs for any given course, and 1.5 TEACHERs and 16 STUDENTs for each OFFERING.

19.3 Again on the basis of the DBD in Exercise 19.1, would it be possible to divide the database into data set groups as follows?

a) COURSE, PREREQ (primary); OFFERING, TEACHER, STUDENT (secondary).

b) COURSE, OFFERING, STUDENT (primary); PREREQ, TEACHER (secondary).

c) COURSE, TEACHER (primary); PREREQ, OFFERING (secondary); STUDENT (another secondary).

For those cases where it is possible, show the DATASET statements required to effect the division. Which of these divisions would be permissible if HISAM were used instead?

REFERENCES AND BIBLIOGRAPHY

See also [16.1].

19.1 IBM Corporation. Information Management System/Virtual Storage System/Application Design Guide. IBM Form No. SH20-9025.

19.2 IBM Corporation. Operating System/Virtual Storage Access Method Services. IBM Form No. GC26-3836.

19.3 IBM Corporation. Operating System/Virtual Storage Job Control Language Reference Manual. IBM Form No. GC28-0618.

19.4 IBM Corporation. Operating System/Virtual Storage VSAM Programmers' Guide. IBM Form No. GC26-3838.

20
IMS Logical
Databases

20.1 LOGICAL DATABASES (LDBs)

We have already mentioned several times that the term "logical database" has two distinct meanings in IMS. The first meaning was dealt with in Chapter 17. The present chapter is concerned with the second, and perhaps more important, of the two. However, it is an introduction only; more details will be found in references [16.1] and [19.1].

A logical database (LDB), then—second meaning—is an ordered set of logical database record (LDBR) occurrences. Like a PDBR, an LDBR is a hierarchical arrangement of fixed-length segments.[1] Like a PDB, an LDB is defined by means of a DBD. However, an LDB differs from a PDB in that it has no existence in its own right; instead, it is defined in terms of one or more existing PDBs. Specifically, each LDBR occurrence consists of segments from several distinct PDBR occurrences (from one PDB or several). Thus the LDB imposes a (hierarchical) structure on the data that is different from the (hierarchical) structure represented by the underlying PDB(s); in other words, it provides the user with an alternative view of the data.

We can see that logical databases are to some extent the IMS equivalent of the "views" of System R,[2] and indeed, the overall objectives are similar for the two constructs. However, in IMS the LDB is really part of the conceptual level rather than the external level. The storage structure, in fact, does represent the LDB directly, inasmuch as it contains additional pointers

---

1. See footnote 1, Chapter 16, p. 279.
2. The same can also be said for logical databases in the first meaning of the term, of course.

linking stored segments together into the desired structure (over and above the pointers already discussed in the previous chapter). Thus it is not entirely true to say that the LDB as such does not exist (but the point is that the *data* really belongs to one or more PDBs rather than to the LDB). Since it is part of the conceptual level, an LDB should ideally look exactly like a PDB to the user, and so it does, at least so far as retrieval is concerned. The situation with respect to update operations is not quite so straightforward, however, for reasons that will be discussed in Sections 20.5 and 20.6.

20.2 AN EXAMPLE

The ornithological section of a nature conservation institute is conducting a survey of the bird life of a particular region. The region is divided up into areas, and for each area, observations are to be recorded in a survey database. The information recorded for an area is to consist of area number (a unique identifier), area name, area description, and, for each type of bird observed in the area, the common name, date of observation, observer's remarks, the bird's scientific name, and a set of descriptive information. Thus the database record, as seen by the user, is to appear (approximately) as shown in Fig. 20.1.

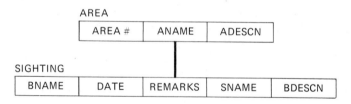

Fig. 20.1 Required record structure for the survey database.

The institute already maintains a PDB of bird information, however. This PDB is a "root segment only" database with a record structure as shown in Fig. 20.2. Here BNAME (common name) is the sequence field.

Therefore, if a new PDB were built with the structure shown in Fig. 20.1, much of the data it contained would be a repetition of the data in this bird database. Also, the new PDB would have a high degree of internal redundancy, in that many PDBR occurrences would contain identical infor-

BIRD

BNAME	SNAME	BDESCN

Fig. 20.2 Record structure of the bird database.

mation—specifically, the scientific name and description would be recorded once for each sighting of a particular type of bird, instead of once only.

These inefficiencies can be avoided by means of a logical database, as follows. First, a *physical* database is defined with a structure similar to that shown in Fig. 20.1. However, the SIGHTING segment contains only the fields DATE and REMARKS, together with a *pointer* to the appropriate BIRD segment in the bird PDB. (This pointer is part of the segment prefix[3] and is not seen by the user.) Thus we have the situation illustrated in Fig. 20.3.

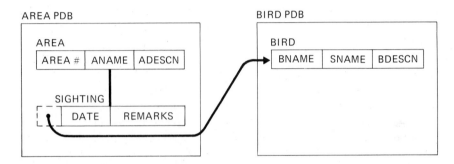

Fig. 20.3 AREA and BIRD PDBs.

Second, a *logical* database can now be defined with the structure shown in Fig. 20.4, which shows what the user does see (contrast Fig. 20.1). The user can now process this LDB as if it were a PDB—within certain limits (to be discussed).

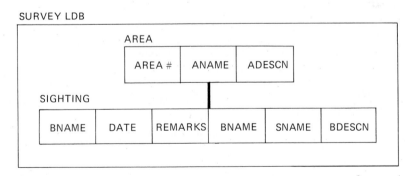

Fig. 20.4 The SURVEY LDB.

---

3. This assumes "direct pointing." See Section 20.4.

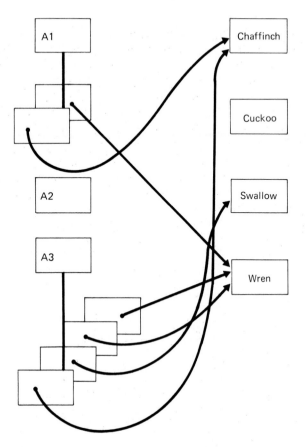

Fig. 20.5 Sample PDBs (AREA and BIRD).

For example, suppose that Fig. 20.5 represents the actual data in the PDBs at some particular time. Then the LDB seen by the user is as shown in Fig. 20.6. (Only the sequence fields are shown, but the reader should understand that each dependent segment occurrence includes all the fields given in SIGHTING in Fig. 20.4. Note that there are *two* SIGHTINGs for 'WREN' under area A3.)

Actually the foregoing explanation is slightly oversimplified. In order that an LDB may be defined in terms of one or more existing PDBs, those PDBs must be appropriately defined; that is, their DBDs must specify that they are involved in the LDB concerned. In other words, the DBA must be aware that the PDBs are to be involved in an LDB at the time that their DBDs are written. Thus, in the example, either it must have been foreseen

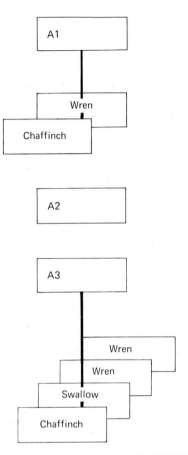

Fig. 20.6 Corresponding LDB (SURVEY).

that the BIRD PDB was eventually to participate in the SURVEY LDB, or else it will be necessary to unload the BIRD PDB and then to reload it in accordance with a revised DBD. The latter tends to be the method most often used in practice. See Section 20.4.

20.3 TERMINOLOGY

The "pointer segment" SIGHTING of Fig. 20.3 is of course a child of the AREA segment. It is also considered a child of the BIRD segment (the segment it points to). Thus SIGHTING has two parent segments. To distinguish between the two, we refer to AREA as the *physical* parent, BIRD as the *logical* parent; also, we refer to SIGHTING both as the physical child of

AREA and as the logical child of BIRD. The pointer is a "logical parent" pointer. A given segment can have at most one physical parent and at most one logical parent.

The terminology of logical-parent/logical-child, like that of physical-parent/physical-child, applies to both types and occurrences. Thus the BIRD segment 'CHAFFINCH', for example, is the logical parent of two SIGHTING segments, whose physical parents are, respectively, the 'A1' AREA segment and the 'A3' AREA segment. Moreover, these two SIGHT-INGs are considered as "logical twins"; by analogy with physical twins, all occurrences of one type of logical child with a common logical parent occurrence are known as logical twins.

As the example of the previous section illustrates, it is permitted —though not required—for the "pointer segment" to contain data fields in addition to the pointer. These fields contain "intersection data"— that is, data that describes the physical-parent/logical-parent *combination*. The intersection data would normally be functionally dependent on the combination of the physical parent and logical parent fully concatenated keys (see Chapter 14).

We are now in a position to explain Fig. 20.4. The SIGHTING segment in that diagram is a concatenation of the following three items.

1. The fully concatenated key of the logical parent

2. The intersection data

3. The logical parent (including the logical parent sequence field value)

This is in general how a logical child always appears to the user. (Actually, it is possible to omit *either* the first two of these *or* the third, but we shall never do so in our examples. What is *not* possible is to see the intersection data without the fully concatenated key of the logical parent.)

20.4   THE DATABASE DESCRIPTIONS (DBDs)

A logical database, like a physical database, is defined by means of a data-base description (DBD). This DBD is said to be a "logical" DBD, as opposed to a "physical" DBD, which is a DBD for a physical database. Each logical DBD is defined in terms of one or more underlying physical DBDs, which must already exist. Thus in our example we shall require (a) a physical DBD for the BIRD PDB, (b) a physical DBD for the AREA PDB, and (c) a logical DBD for the SURVEY LDB. We consider each of these in turn.

Figure 20.7 illustrates in outline the DBD for the BIRD PDB. The only thing to note here is that the SEGM statement for the BIRD segment is fol-

```
DBD    NAME=BIRDPDBD,...
SEGM   NAME=BIRD,POINTER=TWIN,...
LCHILD NAME=(SIGHTING,AREAPDBD)
(FIELD statements for BIRD)
```

Fig. 20.7 DBD for the BIRD PDB (outline).

lowed by an LCHILD statement specifying the SIGHTING segment—defined in the DBD for the AREA PDB (Fig. 20.8)—as a logical child of BIRD. (As an aid to memory, it may be helpful to point out that LCHILD appears as part of the logical *parent* description. In other words, if the SEGM statement for segment type S is followed by an LCHILD statement, it means that S *possesses* a logical child—not that S *is* a logical child.)

```
DBD    NAME=AREAPDBD,...
SEGM   NAME=AREA,POINTER=TWIN,...
(FIELD statements for AREA)
SEGM   NAME=SIGHTING,POINTER=(LPARNT,TWIN),
       PARENT=((AREA),(BIRD,VIRTUAL,BIRDPDBD)),...
FIELD  NAME=BNAME,...
FIELD  NAME=DATE,...
FIELD  NAME=REMARKS,...
```

Fig. 20.8 DBD for the AREA PDB (outline).

Figure 20.8, which illustrates in outline a possible DBD for the AREA PDB, requires rather more explanation. Consider first the POINTER entry for the SIGHTING segment, which specifies that the SIGHTING prefix is to contain the following pointers.

■   A logical parent pointer (as explained in Section 20.2)

This of course provides the basic linkage necessary to construct the LDB. However, LPARNT may be specified only if the logical parent resides in HDAM or HIDAM; if instead it resides in HISAM (HSAM cannot be used) then symbolic pointers must be used (see below).

■   A physical twin pointer (explained in Chapter 19)

TWIN (or TWINBWD or HIER or HIERBWD) may be specified, provided that the SIGHTING segment resides in HDAM or HIDAM; if instead it resides in HISAM, then of course physical twin sequence will be represented by physical position. But what is the physical twin sequence? Clearly BNAME is the field we would like as the sequence field for SIGHTING (see

Fig. 20.6).[4] However, this raises additional problems, since BNAME is physically part of the BIRD segment, not the SIGHTING segment. We shall return to this point in a moment.

Consider next the PARENT entry for the SIGHTING segment, which specifies (a) that the physical parent of this segment is AREA, and (b) that the logical parent of this segment is BIRD, which is defined in the DBD for the BIRD PDB. VIRTUAL specifies tht the fully concatenated key of the logical parent is a virtual field—field BNAME—so far as this segment is concerned; i.e., it is not physically stored as part of the segment. Note, however, that a FIELD statement for BNAME *is* provided.

The alternative to VIRTUAL is PHYSICAL, which means that a copy of the BNAME field is to be physically stored as part of the SIGHTING segment. If PHYSICAL is specified, then (and only then) BNAME may be specified (in the FIELD statement) as the sequence field for this segment. Thus, if this sequencing is required, PHYSICAL *must* be specified in the PARENT entry. (The fully concatenated key returned in the PCB when a SIGHTING is retrieved will then consist of an AREA# value followed by a BNAME value.)

But if PHYSICAL is specified, the logical parent pointer in the prefix is conceptually redundant. If the logical parent resides in HDAM or HIDAM, this pointer may still be included for performance reasons, although it is perfectly valid to omit it; however, if the logical parent resides in HISAM, the pointer *must* be omitted (and PHYSICAL must be specified). It is never possible to use pointers to point to segments in HISAM, since in HISAM the insertion of a new segment may cause existing segments to be moved.

In general, therefore, we have two distinct ways of representing the link from a logical child to its logical parent (except when the logical parent resides in HISAM): either via a "direct" pointer (i.e., including a logical parent pointer in the logical child prefix) or via a "symbolic" pointer (i.e., physically recording the logical parent fully concatenated key as the first field of the logical child). The relative advantages of the two are essentially as discussed in Section 2.4: Direct pointers provide faster access; symbolic pointers need no adjustment if the database they point to is reorganized. Some other considerations affecting the choice are discussed in reference [19.1]. It is also possible to use both techniques in combination. However,

---

4. We will have to specify NAME = (BNAME,SEQ,M) to allow for multiple sightings of one type of bird within one area (see Section 16.2). Alternatively, if (say) no more than one sighting per day of each type of bird within each area is to be recorded in the database, the combination of BNAME and DATE could be defined as the sequence field (and values would then be unique).

the choice of method in no way affects the contents of the logical child segment as seen by the user. For simplicity, we shall assume for the rest of this chapter that all physical databases are in HDAM or HIDAM, and that symbolic pointers are not being used (unless it is explicitly stated otherwise). We are now in a position to examine the logical DBD (Fig. 20.9).

```
DBD       NAME=SVEYLDBD,ACCESS=LOGICAL
DATASET   LOGICAL
SEGM      NAME=AREA,SOURCE=((AREA,,AREAPDBD))
SEGM      NAME=SIGHTING,PARENT=AREA,
          SOURCE=((SIGHTING,,AREAPDBD),(BIRD,,BIRDPDBD))
```

Fig. 20.9 DBD for the SURVEY LDB.

Observe first that ACCESS = LOGICAL must be specified in the DBD statement, and that LOGICAL must also be specified in the DATASET statement. The remaining statements define the segments of the LDB; note that FIELD statements may not be included. The first SEGM statement states that the root segment of the LDB, AREA, is in fact the AREA segment defined in the DBD for the AREA PDB (the segment could be given a different name within the LDB if desired). The double comma indicates an omitted operand; see reference [16.1] for details. The second SEGM statement states that within this LDB, SIGHTING is dependent on AREA, and it consists of the concatenation of the SIGHTING segment defined in the DBD for the AREA PDB together with the BIRD segment defined in the DBD for the BIRD PDB. (As seen by the user, of course, the segment also includes as its first field the BIRD fully concatenated key.)

20.5 LOADING THE LOGICAL DATABASE

The process of loading a logical database consists essentially of loading the underlying physical database(s) and setting up the required pointers. For a number of reasons, this operation is performed directly on the underlying PDB(s), not on the LDB as such. To see why this is necessary, suppose for a moment that the SURVEY LDB were to be loaded via an appropriate series of ISRT operations issued directly against that LDB. Several problems would arise. For example, the insertion of a SIGHTING occurrence would sometimes have to cause the creation of a BIRD occurrence, sometimes not, depending on whether the BIRD occurrence already existed in the BIRD PDB. Also, what about a BIRD for which there are no SIGHTINGs (e.g., 'CUCKOO' in Fig. 20.5)? How would it get loaded? What about the restriction that PDBs must be loaded in hierarchical sequence (at least in HISAM and HIDAM)? And again considering the data in Fig. 20.5, what if the

BDESCN value for 'CHAFFINCH' (say) were given differently for the A1 and A3 SIGHTINGs?

For reasons such as these, the procedure actually followed is to load the LDB by inserting segments directly into the underlying PDB(s), i.e., by loading each of the underlying PDBs as a separate operation. Let us assume, therefore, that the BIRD PDB has already been loaded (in the form shown in Fig. 20.5), and let us consider what is involved in loading the AREA PDB.

AREA A1 is loaded (inserted) in the usual way. A SIGHTING segment, containing fields BNAME (with value 'CHAFFINCH'), DATE, and REMARKS may then be loaded, followed by a similar SIGHTING segment for 'WREN'. Then follow AREA A2, AREA A3, a SIGHTING for 'CHAFFINCH' under A3, and similar SIGHTINGs for 'SWALLOW' and 'WREN'. Note, however, that at this stage the SIGHTING segments do not contain the logical parent pointers. These are inserted subsequently by a special utility program, which must be executed before the loading process can be considered complete. Moreover, the logical parent prefixes must also be adjusted; this is also handled by a special utility program, which operates on the BIRD PDB.

For further details of the loading process see reference [16.1].

20.6   PROCESSING THE LOGICAL DATABASE

Once the LDB has been loaded, the user can process it exactly as though it were a PDB, at least so far as retrieval operations are concerned.[5] Update operations are more complicated, however. In general, the effect of an update operation on a segment that participates in a logical relationship—that is, a logical child, a logical parent, or a physical parent of a segment that also has a logical parent—is defined by the *rule* specified by the DBA for that operation and that segment. The DBA is required to specify, in the SEGM statement in the appropriate *physical* DBD, an insert rule, a delete rule, and a replace rule for each such segment. Each of these rules, in general, may be specified as "physical," "logical," or "virtual."[6] It is not our intention here to go into full details of these rules (see [16.1]), but we shall consider their significance with respect to the SURVEY LDB. Note that the specified rules govern *all* update operations on the segment; the operation in question may actually be issued either (a) directly against the relevant PDB or (b) "indirectly" against some LDB built on top of the PDB.

---

5. A PCB is required for the LDB, just as if it were a PDB.
6. In the case of delete there is a fourth possibility: "bidirectional virtual."

Consider ISRT operations first. It is always possible to insert an AREA, and the effect is simply to insert that AREA into the AREA PDB. What about SIGHTINGs? The problem here, as mentioned in the previous section, is that the BIRD to which the SIGHTING refers may or may not already exist in the BIRD PDB. If it does, the ISRT is accepted (that is, the SIGHTING is inserted into the AREA PDB); moreover, if the insert rule for BIRD is "virtual," the SNAME and BDESCN values from the SIGHTING segment as presented by the user actually replace the previous values in the corresponding BIRD segment. If, on the other hand, the BIRD does not currently exist in the BIRD PDB, the ISRT will be (a) rejected if the insert rule for BIRD is "physical"; (b) accepted otherwise, in which case the effect will be not only to insert the SIGHTING into the AREA PDB but also to insert the BIRD into the BIRD PDB (again, remember that the SIGHTING as presented by the user includes SNAME and BDESCN).

(Of course, it is always possible to insert new BIRDs into the BIRD PDB, independently of the SURVEY LDB.)

Now consider DLET operations. Deletion of an AREA will remove that AREA and its subordinate SIGHTINGs from the AREA PDB. Deletion of a SIGHTING (either directly or via deletion of its parent AREA) will remove that SIGHTING from the AREA PDB, and if this is the last SIGHTING for the BIRD concerned and BIRD has a delete rule of "virtual," it will also remove the BIRD from the BIRD PDB.

As for an attempt to delete a BIRD directly from the BIRD PDB, the effect depends on the delete rule for BIRD. "Physical" will permit the deletion of a BIRD only if no SIGHTINGs refer to it. "Logical" and "virtual" will permit the deletion of a BIRD from the BIRD PDB while at the same time keeping it available via the SURVEY LDB so long as any SIGHTING refers to it (this effect is achieved via appropriate flags in the BIRD prefix). Such a BIRD will be removed entirely when the last SIGHTING referring to it is deleted.

Finally, consider REPL operations. Replacement of an AREA simply causes the corresponding replacement to occur in the AREA PDB. Replacement of the intersection data (DATE and REMARKS) in a SIGHTING also simply causes the corresponding replacement to occur in the AREA PDB. Replacement of the logical parent data (SNAME and BDESCN) in a SIGHTING is permitted only if the replace rule for BIRD is "virtual"; the effect in this case is to replace the BIRD segment, which in turn causes the logical parent data to change accordingly in all other SIGHTINGs for that BIRD. (Of course, a BIRD may always be replaced directly by means of a REPL operation on the BIRD PDB.)

To sum up, therefore, the SURVEY LDB may be made to look more or less like a PDB, provided that the DBA specifies rules as shown in Fig. 20.10 (P, L, and V stand for "physical," "logical," and "virtual").

Segment Rule	AREA	SIGHTING	BIRD
Insert	P, L, or V	V (Note 1)	L or V (Note 3)
Delete	V (Note 2)	P, L, or V	P or L (Note 4)
Replace	P, L, or V	P, L, or V	V (Note 3)

Fig. 20.10 Rules for AREA and BIRD PDBs.

Notes

1. The insert rule for a logical child segment is always given as V.[7]

2. The delete rule for a physical parent segment is always given as V.[7]

3. Observe that the structure of the SURVEY LDB makes it appear that (for example) to change the BDESCN value for an existing BIRD, it would be necessary to make the change in every SIGHTING for that BIRD, whereas, in fact, this is not required; that is, the LDB structure permits redundancy in the user's view of the data without requiring a corresponding redundancy in what is actually stored.

4. The delete rule for BIRD could be V without affecting the behavior of the LDB as such, but this would allow operations on the LDB (or the AREA PDB) to have possibly undesirable side effects on the BIRD PDB. For example, deletion of an AREA might cause deletion of a BIRD (if there are now no SIGHTINGs for that BIRD).

We can see that it is only the BIRD segment for which the rules are critical (in this example). However, bear in mind that so far we have discussed only the simplest possible type of LDB, that is, one involving a "unidirectional relationship," with one physical parent, one logical parent, and one logical child. The effect of the rules in more complicated situations is beyond the scope of this book.

20.7   BIDIRECTIONAL LOGICAL RELATIONSHIPS

The SURVEY LDB, being hierarchical, represents the association between AREAs and BIRDs as if it were a one-to-many correspondence. In fact, of course, the correspondence is really many-to-many: Not only are there many BIRDs for a given AREA, there are also many AREAs for a given BIRD. Thus (as was pointed out in Chapter 3) an operation such as "Find all areas in which a particular bird has been sighted" is comparatively diffi-

---

7. Actually IMS will always assume V in these cases, regardless of what is specified, in order to prevent certain inconsistencies that might otherwise be allowed to occur.

cult with the SURVEY LDB. We may overcome this difficulty by means of another LDB—BASURVEY, say—in which AREA is viewed as subordinate to BIRD. (For consistency, let us rename the original LDB, in which BIRD is subordinate to AREA, as ABSURVEY.) Thus we have a "bidirectional logical relationship" between AREAs and BIRDs.

Bidirectional logical relationships may be implemented in IMS in two ways, known respectively as physical and virtual pairing.

Physical Pairing

Physical pairing involves the introduction of a new type of segment— BASIGHT, say—as a physical child of BIRD and a logical child of AREA. (Again for consistency, let us rename the original SIGHTING segment as ABSIGHT.) See Fig. 20.11.

The purpose of the BASIGHT segment is exactly analogous to that of the ABSIGHT segment; that is, it contains a pointer (in its prefix) to its logical parent (AREA), together with intersection data (DATE and REMARKS, as in ABSIGHT). This enables us to define the BASURVEY LDB (as well as the ABSURVEY LDB). A BASIGHT occurrence as seen by the user will consist of the concatenation of the logical parent fully concatenated key (an AREA # value), the intersection data, and the logical parent data (including the AREA# value again). ABSIGHT and BASIGHT are "paired segments" and are declared as such to IMS in the DBDs for the AREA and BIRD PDBs; see Figs. 20.12 and 20.13.

Figure 20.12 shows (in the lines with asterisks) the changes involved in the DBD for the AREA PDB (compare Fig. 20.8). The SEGM statement for the AREA segment is followed by an LCHILD statement specifying the BASIGHT segment—defined in the DBD for the BIRD PDB (Fig. 20.13)—as a logical child of AREA. The LCHILD statement also specifies

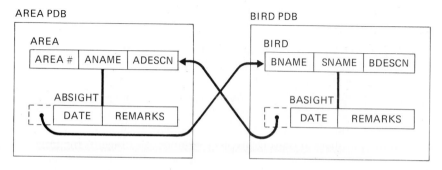

Fig. 20.11 AREA and BIRD PDBs (with physical pairing).

```
DBD     NAME=AREAPDBD,...
SEGM    NAME=AREA,POINTER=TWIN,...
*  LCHILD NAME=(BASIGHT,BIRDPDBD),PAIR=ABSIGHT
   (FIELD statements for AREA)
*  SEGM    NAME=ABSIGHT,POINTER=(LPARNT,TWIN,PAIRED),
*          PARENT=((AREA),
*                  (BIRD,PHYSICAL,BIRDPDBD)),...
   FIELD   NAME=(BNAME,SEQ,M),...
   FIELD   NAME=DATE,...
   FIELD   NAME=REMARKS,...
```

Fig. 20.12 DBD for the AREA PDB (outline)—physical pairing.

that the logical child (BASIGHT) is paired with the ABSIGHT segment, defined subsequently in the current DBD. The other change to this DBD is in the POINTER entry for ABSIGHT, which specifies PAIRED (among other things); this specification is required.

Note, incidentally, that BNAME has been physically included in the ABSIGHT segment. This permits the sightings within one area to be sequenced on bird name.

Figure 20.13 shows the changes involved in the DBD for the BIRD PDB (compare Fig. 20.7).

```
DBD     NAME=BIRDPDBD,...
SEGM    NAME=BIRD,POINTER=TWIN,...
*  LCHILD NAME=(ABSIGHT,AREAPDBD),PAIR=BASIGHT
   (FIELD statements for BIRD)
*  SEGM    NAME=BASIGHT,POINTER=(LPARNT,TWIN,PAIRED),
*          PARENT=((BIRD),
*                  (AREA,PHYSICAL,AREAPDBD)),...
*  FIELD   NAME=(AREA#,SEQ,M),...
*  FIELD   NAME=DATE,...
*  FIELD   NAME=REMARKS,...
```

Fig. 20.13 DBD for the BIRD PDB (outline)—physical pairing.

The BIRD DBD is essentially similar to the DBD for AREA. Note again that the logical parent fully concatenated key field—AREA#—has been physically included in the logical child segment (BASIGHT), to permit the sightings of one bird to be sequenced on area number.

The DBD for the ABSURVEY LDB is the same as before (Fig. 20.9). The DBD for the BASURVEY LDB is essentially similar.

Note that physical pairing involves redundant storage of the intersection data; that is, every item of intersection data will be physically recorded twice, once in an ABSIGHT occurrence and once in the paired BASIGHT occurrence. (For example, the ABSIGHT occurrence that links area A1 to 'CHAFFINCH' for a particular date will contain precisely the same inter-section data as the BASIGHT occurrence that links 'CHAFFINCH' to area A1 for that date.) However, since the segments are paired, when the user in-serts an occurrence of either one, IMS will automatically create the corre-sponding occurrence of the other (except during loading, when it is the user's responsibility to create both). Similarly, if the user deletes or replaces an occurrence of one of the pair, IMS will automatically make the appropri-ate change to the other.

Virtual Pairing

Virtual pairing avoids the redundancy of physical pairing. The idea is that one of the two paired segment types may be eliminated; for example, the BASIGHT segment need not physically exist, since its data may be found from the ABSIGHT segment. The directed relationship from BIRD to AREA is then represented, not via a logical parent pointer from BASIGHT to AREA but via a logical child pointer from BIRD to ABSIGHT *plus* a physical parent pointer[8] from ABSIGHT to AREA. (Logical twin pointers are also required; see below.) Figure 20.14 illustrates this organization.

The first point to be made is that virtual pairing looks almost exactly like physical pairing to the user. In the example, although the segment BASIGHT no longer exists, IMS makes it look as if it did; for this reason

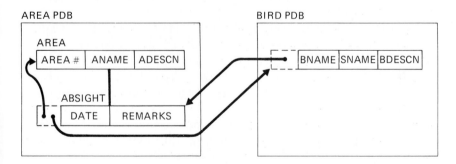

Fig. 20.14 AREA and BIRD PDBs (with virtual pairing).

---

8. This is not the only situation in which physical parent pointers are required. They are also necessary if a logical child points via a direct pointer to a logical parent that is not a root. In such a situation each segment in the physical hierarchical path to the logical parent will include a physical parent pointer, to allow the construction of the logical parent fully concatenated key.

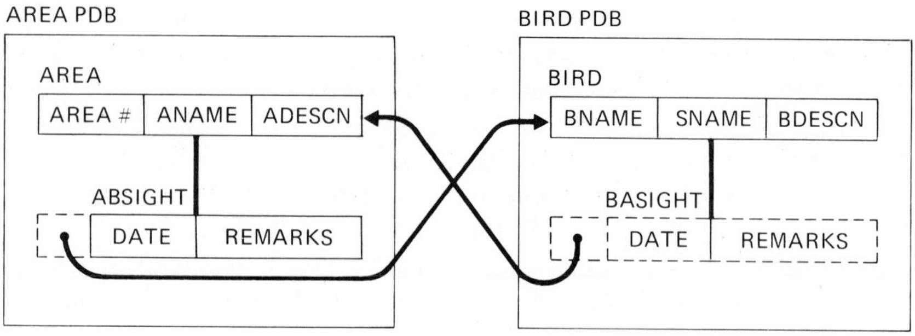

AREA PDB   BIRD PDB

Fig. 20.15 AREA and BIRD PDBs (with virtual pairing) — conventional representation.

BASIGHT is said to be a virtual segment. (There is one very minor difference between a virtual segment and a real one as seen by the user: A virtual segment cannot be "loaded" as part of the process of loading the PDB that contains it; instead it is "created" when the real segment is loaded.) The conventional representation of a virtual pairing situation is shown in Fig. 20.15 (but bear in mind that Fig. 20.14 represents the true picture).

A second general point is that the real member of the pair (ABSIGHT in the example) must reside in HDAM or HIDAM, since the logical parent segment prefix contains a direct pointer to it, namely, the logical child pointer. (Logical parent pointers are the only ones that may be symbolic.)

Now consider the sequencing involved in this example. The sightings within one area are sequenced on bird name; this is done by physically including the BNAME field in the ABSIGHT segment and specifying POINTER = TWIN (which links all ABSIGHTs for one AREA on a physical twin chain). What about the sequence of sightings of one bird? That is represented by another chain, the logical twin chain, which links all ABSIGHTs that point to the same BIRD in physical parent fully concatenated key sequence. Hence the sightings of one bird are sequenced on area number, as required.

Conceptually, however, this second sequencing is achieved by making AREA# the SEQ field for the (virtual) segment BASIGHT, and this is what is specified in the DBD. See Figs. 20.16 and 20.17.

Figure 20.16 shows (see asterisks) the changes involved in the DBD for the AREA PDB (compare Fig. 20.12). An LCHILD statement for the virtual segment BASIGHT is *not* supplied. Also, the POINTER entry for ABSIGHT no longer specifies PAIRED but instead requests a logical twin pointer to be included in the prefix. The sequencing for this logical twin chain is specified in the *other* DBD; see below. (It is also possible to request a two-way logical twin chain by specifying LTWINBWD.) Note that there is

```
    DBD      NAME=AREAPDBD,...
    SEGM     NAME=AREA,POINTER=TWIN,...
*   (LCHILD statement for BASIGHT must not be included)
    (FIELD statements for AREA)
*   SEGM     NAME=ABSIGHT,POINTER=(LPARNT,TWIN,LTWIN),
*            PARENT=((AREA),
*                    (BIRD,PHYSICAL,BIRDPDBD)),...
    FIELD    NAME=(BNAME,SEQ,M),...
    FIELD    NAME=DATE,...
    FIELD    NAME=REMARKS,...
```

Fig. 20.16 DBD for the AREA PDB (outline) — virtual pairing.

```
    DBD      NAME=BIRDPDBD,...
    SEGM     NAME=BIRD,POINTER=TWIN,...
*   LCHILD   NAME=(ABSIGHT,AREAPDBD),PAIR=BASIGHT,
*            POINTER=SNGL
    (FIELD statements for BIRD)
*   SEGM     NAME=BASIGHT,POINTER=PAIRED,
*            PARENT=BIRD,
*            SOURCE=((ABSIGHT,,AREAPDBD))
    FIELD    NAME=(AREA#,SEQ,M),...
    FIELD    NAME=DATE,...
    FIELD    NAME=REMARKS,...
```

Fig. 20.17 DBD for the BIRD PDB (outline) — virtual pairing.

no mention here of the physical parent pointer, which IMS provides automatically.

Figure 20.17 shows the changes involved in the DBD for the BIRD PDB (compare Fig. 20.13). The LCHILD statement includes the additional entry POINTER = SNGL, which is a request for each occurrence of BIRD to include a logical child pointer in its prefix to the first ABSIGHT occurrence on the logical twin chain corresponding to this BIRD occurrence. (It is also possible to request each BIRD to point to both the first and the last of its logical children, by specifying POINTER = DBLE.) The SEGM statement for the virtual segment BASIGHT specifies (a) POINTER = PAIRED, (b) the physical parent (only), (c) a new entry— SOURCE—which refers to the corresponding real segment; this statement contains no other entries (not even BYTES). Lastly, there is *no* change in the FIELD statements for BASIGHT; in particular, the first defines "BASIGHT sequence," i.e., logical twin sequence for ABSIGHT.

The logical DBDs are the same as before.

20.8   A NOTE ON THE STORAGE STRUCTURE

From the foregoing sections we can see that, although the user sees an LDB as a hierarchical structure—at least so far as retrieval is concerned—the underlying stored representation is somewhat more complex. It is in fact a *network,* inasmuch as certain segments, namely, the logical parents, may be pointed at by any number of (logical parent) pointers and hence may participate in any number of LDBR occurrences. However, since IMS does not support "*n*-directional logical relationships" for any value of $n > 2$, such networks are not completely general. Instead, they are essentially limited (at their most complex) to what we may call "two-entity nets." In the networks of Section 17.7, for example, the two types of entity are of course AREA and BIRD.[9] The supplier-part-project problem (see Part 2 of this book) is an example of a situation in which a "three-entity net" would be required, and thus one that would have to be handled in a somewhat indirect fashion in IMS (see Exercise 20.7).

20.9   LOGICAL DATABASES INVOLVING
A SINGLE PHYSICAL DATABASE

In the introduction to this chapter we stated that the segments constituting an LDBR occurrence are drawn from several distinct PDBR occurrences, and that the PDBR occurrences, in turn, may belong to one or more distinct PDBs. As an example involving only one PDB, consider the hierarchical structure illustrated in Fig. 16.1 (the education database), in which the root segment COURSE (fields COURSE#, TITLE, DESCRIPN) has a dependent segment PREREQ (fields COURSE#, TITLE). Clearly, we can avoid the redundancy that this PDB structure entails by replacing PREREQ by a "pointer segment," so that each COURSE occurrence has a set of dependent pointer segment occurrences that point to the appropriate COURSEs. Figures 20.18 and 20.19 show, respectively, the conventional way of representing such a situation on paper and the hierarchical structure seen by the user[10] (for simplicity we ignore the OFFERING, TEACHER, and STUDENT segments, as well as any intersection data that may exist).

---

9. But see Exercise 24.5.

10. On the basis of the same PDB, it would also be possible to define an LDB of three levels, consisting of COURSE (root), PREREQ1 (first dependent level), and PREREQ2 (second dependent level). PREREQ1 would represent the immediate prerequisites of COURSE, and PREREQ2 would represent the immediate prerequisites of PREREQ1. Similarly, LDBs of four, five, . . . levels may be defined (up to a maximum of 15 levels). In practice this is an extremely useful facility, but for simplicity we shall stick to two levels in our examples.

EDUC PDB

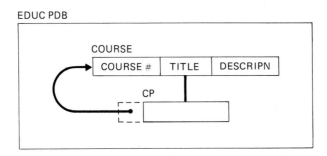

Fig. 20.18 The EDUC PDB.

EDCP LDB

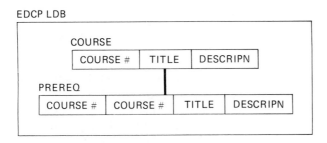

Fig. 20.19 The EDCP LDB.

The segment CP is both a physical child and a logical child of COURSE. Conversely, COURSE is both the physical parent and the logical parent of CP. We should stress, however, that no CP *occurrence* would have the same COURSE *occurrence* as both physical and logical parent (Fig. 20.18 notwithstanding). The DBD for the education PDB will include an LCHILD statement for CP (following the SEGM statement for COURSE), and in addition the SEGM statement for CP will specify COURSE as both physical and logical parent.

The education PDB of Fig. 20.18 involves a unidirectional logical relationship (from CP to COURSE) which, as we have just seen, enables us to find all PREREQs for a given COURSE. It is also possible to add a logical relationship in the other direction (thus converting it into a bidirectional relationship), so that, in addition, we can find all COURSEs that have a given PREREQ. This is done by including a second type of pointer segment—PC, say—physically dependent on COURSE, such that each COURSE occurrence has a set of PC occurrences that point to occurrences of COURSEs for which the original course is actually a PREREQ. PC and CP will be paired segments. If we assume that virtual pairing is used (and that PC is the virtual member of the pair), Figs. 20.20, 20.21, and 20.22 show,

EDUC PDB

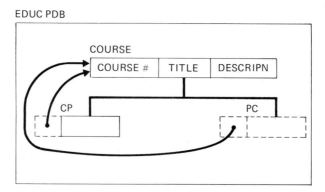

Fig. 20.20 The EDUC PDB (with virtual pairing) — conventional representation.

respectively, the conventional way of representing such a situation, the structures that actually exist, and the two LDBs that can be seen by the user.

Once again, let it be emphasized that no child *occurrence* would have the same segment *occurrence* as both physical parent and logical parent. The two pointers in Fig. 20.21 from CP to COURSE are, respectively, a logical parent and a physical parent pointer; for one CP occurrence they will point to *different* COURSE occurrences. Referring now to Fig. 20.22, the user will employ the EDCP LDB to find PREREQs for a given COURSE, the EDPC LDB to find COURSEs for a given PREREQ. (The segment names in these LDBs are of course arbitrary; the significant point is that EDCP must be defined in terms of the CP logical child, and EDPC must be defined in terms of the PC logical child.)

See Exercises 20.3, 20.4, and 20.5.

EDUC PDB

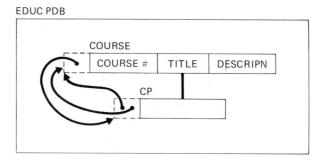

Fig. 20.21 The EDUC PDB (with virtual pairing).

EDCP LDB

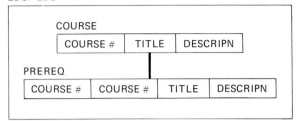

Fig. 20.22 The EDCP and EDPC LDBs.

20.10   SOME RULES AND RESTRICTIONS

The definition of an LDB is subject to a number of rules and restrictions, documented in detail in [19.1]. In this section we shall examine some of these rules, probably the most important ones from a practical point of view. Development of suitable diagrams to illustrate these points has been left as an exercise for the reader.

1. The root of an LDB must also be a root of a PDB.

2. A logical child segment must have one physical parent and one logical parent. It follows that (a) a root cannot be a logical child; (b) IMS cannot directly support "*n*-directional relationships" for $n > 2$.

3. A physical child of a logical child may appear as a dependent of the concatenated (logical-child/logical-parent) segment in the LDB. For example, consider the databases of Section 20.2. Suppose that in the AREA PDB (Fig 20.3) REMARKS actually consists of a character string that varies in length between (say) 100 and 1000 characters. Instead of including REMARKS as a field within the SIGHTING segment, it might be preferable in such a situation to have a REMARKS segment physically dependent on the SIGHTING segment (if the REMARKS segment is 100

bytes long, there would be from 1 to 10 occurrences of it for each SIGHTING occurrence). The SURVEY LDB (Fig. 20.4) could then consist of three levels, with AREA at the root level, the concatenated SIGHTING segment at the second level, and REMARKS at the third level. This is an example of how "variable intersection data" is handled in IMS ("variable" here meaning "variable-length"). Incidentally, the REMARKS segment would probably not include a sequence field (see the end of Section 16.2).

4.   A physical child of a logical parent may appear as a dependent of the concatenated (logical-child/logical-parent) segment in the LDB, provided that the logical parent is the first logical parent encountered in the definition of the LDB hierarchical path.[11] To continue with the example of Section 20.2, suppose that BDESCN is represented as a segment physically dependent on BIRD (like REMARKS, it may actually consist of a character string that is highly variable in length). Then BDESCN may appear as a child of the concatenated SIGHTING segment in the SURVEY LDB. (Also, if BDESCN has a physical child called SUBDESCN, say, then SUBDESCN may appear as a child of BDESCN in the SURVEY LDB.) However, if BIRD also has a physical child—X, say—that in turn has a logical parent, Y, so that X is a logical child as well as a physical child, then although the concatenation of X and Y *could* be included in SURVEY (as a child of the SIGHTING segment), no physical child of Y could be so included.

5.   A physical parent of a logical parent may appear as a dependent of the concatenated (logical-child/logical-parent) segment in the LDB. Suppose that BIRD has a physical parent segment GENUS. Then GENUS may be seen as a *child* of the concatenated SIGHTING segment in the SURVEY LDB. Moreover, if GENUS in turn has a physical parent segment FAMILY, then FAMILY may be seen as a child of GENUS in the SURVEY LDB, and so on, up to 15 levels (always the overall limit in IMS). In other words, it is possible to invert the hierarchical structure of the PDB, at least to a certain extent. For further details the reader is referred to [19.1].

6.   If X and Y are two segments in an LDB hierarchical path, all segments traversed in the path between X and Y in the underlying PDB(s) must also be included (in the same relative positions) in that LDB hierarchical path.

20.11   SUMMARY

The logical database facility of IMS makes it possible to overcome some of the "retrieval complexity" problems mentioned in the section on hierarchies (Section 3.3) in Chapter 3. It provides a method of reducing

---

11. This restriction is relaxed for an LDB defined in terms of a single PDB, as described in footnote 9.

redundancy in the data as stored, while at the same time permitting redundancy in the user view where this is considered desirable. More important, perhaps, it provides a means of allowing users to view the data in many different ways (although each individual user view is still hierarchical). These objectives are achieved by means of an extended storage structure which is in effect a (limited) network, although once again we must emphasize that the user does not actually *see* a network structure. In conclusion, however, we should perhaps point out that logical databases provide an essentially *static* restructuring of the data. There is no means of *dynamically* creating a structure not previously known to the system, as was done in many examples in Parts 1 and 2 of this book—see Example 3.5.4, for instance.

EXERCISES

20.1 Restructure the publications database of Exercise 16.1 as two PDBs, so that LDBs can be defined that are specifically suited to responding to both of the following requests.

Find the authors of a given publication.

Find all publications for a given author.

What LDBs may the user see with your design? Write all relevant DBDs (in outline); for simplicity you may assume that both PDBs use hierarchical direct organization.

20.2 Assuming the sample data in Fig. 20.5, draw a diagram of the storage structure (showing all relevant pointers) corresponding to the following.

a) The SURVEY LDB (Figs. 20.7, 20.8, and 20.9)

b) The ABSURVEY and BASURVEY LDBs with physical pairing (Figs. 20.12 and 20.13)

c) The ABSURVEY and BASURVEY LDBs with virtual pairing (Figs. 20.16 and 20.17)

20.3 Sketch all segment occurrences together with their logical parent pointers for the EDUC PDB (Fig. 20.18), assuming the sample data in Fig. 20.23.

COURSE #	PREREQ COURSE #s
L02	—
M16	—
M19	—
M23	M16, M19
M27	L02
M30	L02, M23, M27

Fig. 20.23 Sample data for the EDUC PDB.

20.4 Sketch all segment occurrences together with their logical parent, logical child, and physical parent pointers for the EDUC PDB (Fig 20.21), assuming the same sample data as in the previous exercise.

20.5 Define in reasonable detail DBDs for the EDUC PDB of Fig. 20.21 and the LDBs of Fig. 20.22.

20.6 What is involved in loading the EDUC PDB of Fig. 20.21?

20.7 How would you handle the supplier-part-project problem in IMS?

20.8 The bidirectional logical relationship of Section 20.7 can be implemented in three ways: via physical pairing, via virtual pairing with ABSIGHT virtual, or via virtual pairing with BASIGHT virtual. To what extent can the DBA switch between these three techniques without affecting existing users?

REFERENCES AND BIBLIOGRAPHY

See [16.1] and [19.1].

21
IMS
Secondary
Indexing

21.1 INTRODUCTION

As explained in Chapter 19, the root sequencing in a HISAM or HIDAM database is supported by means of an *index* on the root segment sequence field. For HISAM the indexing is provided by a standard OS/VS access method (either ISAM or VSAM); for HIDAM the index is actually an IMS database in its own right, with either VSAM or a combination of ISAM and OSAM as the underlying access method. Since these indexes are on the root segment sequence field, we may refer to them as *primary* indexes (the root segment sequence field, which must take unique values in HISAM and HIDAM, may be thought of as the primary key for the physical database record); and the corresponding root ordering, namely, by ascending values of the sequence field, may be referred to as the primary processing sequence. In this chapter we present an introduction to IMS *secondary* indexing and the associated notion of secondary processing sequence.

In Chapter 2 we defined a secondary index as an index on a field other than the primary key. At that point, however, we were tacitly assuming that the file to be indexed was no more complex than a conventional sequential file. In IMS, of course, the file (database) to be indexed is hierarchical in structure, and the concept of secondary indexing must be extended accordingly. In fact, a secondary index in IMS can be used:

■ to index a given segment, root or dependent, on the basis of any field of that segment;

- to index a given segment, root or dependent, on the basis of any field in a dependent (not necessarily an immediate child) of that segment.[1]

In all cases the "field" on which the index is based may actually be a concatenation of up to five fields, not necessarily contiguous, taken in any order. The index is implemented as an INDEX database, rather like the primary index in HIDAM, except that the underlying access method for this INDEX database *must* be VSAM, not ISAM/OSAM. The database to be indexed must be in HISAM, HDAM, or HIDAM, not in HSAM (nor may it be an INDEX itself). It is also possible to index a logical database, but details of this case are beyond the scope of this book.

To illustrate the possibilities, we consider once again the education database of Fig. 16.1 (shown again here as Fig. 21.1). The following list outlines some of the many possible indexes that could be constructed for this database.

- An index to COURSEs on the TITLE field
- An index to COURSEs on the LOCATION field from the OFFERING segment
- An index to OFFERINGs on the LOCATION field
- An index to OFFERINGs on the EMP# field from the TEACHER segment

We now proceed to consider each of these four examples in detail.

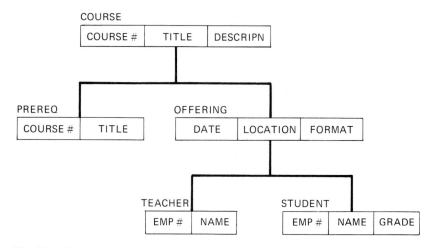

Fig. 21.1 Structure of the education database.

---

1. By "dependent of that segment" here we mean a dependent of the segment in its *physical* database.

21.2 INDEXING THE ROOT ON A FIELD NOT THE SEQUENCE FIELD

As our first example, we consider an index on COURSEs based on values of the TITLE field. We shall assume initially that TITLE values are unique. In order to establish *any* secondary index we need a DBD for that index—much like the DBD for the INDEX database in HIDAM—together with entries in the DBD for the database being indexed to indicate the field(s) the index is to be based on and other details. The index will then automatically be constructed by IMS as the database is loaded, and it will automatically be maintained as the database is subsequently updated. In the case at hand we need the following two additional statements in the DBD for the education database:

```
LCHILD   NAME=(TPTR,TXDBD),POINTER=INDX
XDFLD    NAME=XTITLE,SRCH=TITLE
```

These two statements must appear together as shown. They may appear anywhere after the SEGM statement for COURSE (and before the next SEGM statement), except that they may not precede the FIELD statement for the sequence field (COURSE#), and if the education database is HIDAM then they may not precede the LCHILD statement connecting COURSE to the primary index (see Section 19.8).

The LCHILD statement specifies that the COURSE segment is indexed by the segment TPTR in the database defined in the DBD called TXDBD. As we show below, TXDBD is the DBD that defines the secondary index database, and TPTR is the "index segment"—i.e., it is the (single) segment type in the index database. The "POINTER = INDX" entry specifies that the link between COURSE and TPTR is really an index connection rather than a logical-child/logical-parent connection. The XDFLD ("indexed field") statement specifies the field on which the secondary index is to be built. In the example this field is TITLE—see the SRCH entry. However, an SSA that includes a condition on the field-name TITLE—e.g., TITLE = 'DYNAMICS'—will *not* cause IMS to use the index in searching for the required segment occurrence. Rather, the user must *force* use of the index (when required) by using the field-name XTITLE, specified in the NAME entry of the XDFLD statement. To force IMS to use the secondary index in searching for the COURSE with TITLE 'DYNAMICS', for example, the user could write

```
GU COURSE (XTITLE='DYNAMICS')
```

This GU will cause IMS to fetch the 'DYNAMICS' index segment and then to fetch the COURSE segment this index segment points to. Note that the retrieved segment (in the I/O area) is exactly as usual—specifically, it does not include an extra field corresponding to XTITLE.

We turn now to the DBD for the secondary index.

```
DBD     NAME=TXDBD,ACCESS=INDEX
SEGM    NAME=TPTR,BYTES=33
FIELD   NAME=(TITLE,SEQ),BYTES=33,START=1
LCHILD  NAME=(COURSE,EDUCPDBD),INDEX=XTITLE
```

As mentioned earlier, the DBD for a secondary index is very similar to that for a primary index in HIDAM (see Section 19.8 for details). The only significant difference in the example above is that the INDEX entry in the LCHILD statement refers to XTITLE rather than to TITLE, i.e., to the "XD field" rather than to the actual field. Some other possible differences are discussed later in this section.

The secondary index on COURSEs just defined will contain one index segment occurrence for each COURSE occurrence. Each index segment will contain a TITLE value and a pointer to the corresponding COURSE. Given this index, the user can now choose to see the education database in a *secondary processing sequence,* namely, by ascending values of the course title field. (The *primary* processing sequence is by ascending values of the course number field.) To specify that this secondary sequence is required, the user simply includes the entry

```
PROCSEQ=TXDBD
```

in the PCB statement of the PCB (see Section 17.2). "Get unique" and "get next" operations using this PCB will now operate in terms of this sequence; note, however, that if such operations include an SSA involving a condition on the title field, the condition should be expressed in terms of XTITLE rather than TITLE.

If the PCB does not include a PROCSEQ entry, the *primary* processing sequence is used by default. In this case SSAs may still include references to "XD fields" such as XTITLE, but normally they should not, for reasons of efficiency. For example, the operation

```
GU COURSE (XTITLE='DYNAMICS')
```

will be implemented as follows if the primary processing sequence is used:

```
       get to start of primary sequence
loop:  get next COURSE in primary sequence
       get index segment for DYNAMICS
       if index segment points to current COURSE, go to ex
       go to loop
```

The reason is that the "get unique" (which is really a "get first") must locate that COURSE which is the first to satisfy the SSA according to the *primary* sequence. IMS therefore scans COURSEs in this sequence, testing each in turn against the SSA; and since the SSA involves an XD field, each such test causes an access to the secondary index. Using TITLE rather than XTITLE would mean that each such test could be performed directly on the data in the COURSE segment and would not involve any index access at all.

Remarks similar to those above apply to the use of an XD field in an SSA in conjunction with a *secondary* processing sequence, if that secondary sequence is not the one associated with that XD field. For instance, the "get unique" in the example above (using XTITLE) would result in similarly poor performance if the processing sequence were based on values of the DESCRIPN field. It follows that a single SSA should usually not include references to two distinct XD fields, since at least one of them must fail to match the processing sequence. There *are* some situations when it could be advantageous to use a secondary index in conjunction with a processing sequence not based on that index, but the details are beyond the scope of this text; for further information see [19.1]. From this point on we shall restrict our attention to the case where the processing sequence is the one associated with the XD field concerned.

We list below some additional points the user must be aware of when using a secondary processing sequence.

- Values of the indexed field need not be unique. In our illustration, for example, courses need not have unique titles. If they do not, the FIELD statement in the DBD for the index (TXDBD in the example) must include the specification M (multiple) in the NAME entry:

      FIELD NAME=(TITLE,SEQ,M),...

  If *n* COURSEs all have the same title there will be *n* index segments for that title in the INDEX database; i.e., each COURSE occurrence will have an index entry pointing to it. See [19.1] for details of how "duplicates" are ordered with respect to the secondary processing sequence.

- The fully concatenated key returned in the key feedback area (in the PCB) will contain a TITLE value in place of a COURSE# value. In effect the indexed field is being treated as the sequence field for COURSE segments.

- Notwithstanding the previous point, the user is allowed to update TITLE fields (using REPL) and is not allowed to update COURSE# fields. In other words, the rules for REPL are unaffected by the use of a secondary index. Note that updating the TITLE field for a particular COURSE may cause that COURSE to change position in the secondary sequence; for example, changing the title of course M19 from 'CALCULUS' to 'INTEGRAL CALCULUS' will move it from before 'DYNAMICS' to after 'DYNAMICS'. (IMS automatically maintains all secondary indexes to reflect such updates, by deleting the old index segment and creating a new one.) A subsequent "get next" operation may therefore retrieve the same COURSE again.

- The "index target segment" (i.e., the segment pointed to by the index—COURSE in our example) may not be the object of ISRT or DLET operations when processing is via the secondary sequence. If the index target is a dependent rather than the root, this restriction applies not only to it but also to all its ancestors (see Sections 21.4 and 21.5).

- If the database to be indexed resides in HISAM rather than in HDAM or HIDAM, the pointers in the index must be symbolic rather than direct (cf. the situation with logical parent pointers when the logical parent is in HISAM, as described in Chapter 20). In this case, the "POINTER = INDX" entry in the LCHILD statement for the database to be indexed must be replaced by "POINTER = SYMB" *and* "POINTER = SYMB" must also be specified in the LCHILD statement for the INDEX database itself.

- A secondary index cannot be defined over a HISAM database that includes any secondary data set groups.

The foregoing points, suitably modified where appropriate, apply whenever a secondary processing sequence is being used, not merely to the particular case considered in this section.

21.3   INDEXING THE ROOT ON A FIELD IN A DEPENDENT

Suppose we wish to find course numbers for all COURSEs that have an OFFERING in Stockholm. The following code (using a path call) represents a possible solution to the problem.

```
NC  GN      COURSE*D
            OFFERING (LOCATION='STOCKHOLM')
      if not found, go to exit
      add COURSE# to result list
      go to NC
```

(We assume that we are initially positioned at the start of the database. Also we ignore the question of eliminating duplicate course numbers from the result.) This code is not particularly efficient, however, since it consists essentially of a sequential scan of the entire database (though some segments may be skipped over if the stored database contains child/twin pointers). Also, the user is forced to retrieve OFFERING segments although they are not really wanted.

A more efficient solution to the problem can be achieved using a secondary index, indexing COURSE segments on the basis of LOCATION values—i.e., indexing the root on a field in a dependent. The necessary DBDs are basically as in Section 21.2, except that: (a) for the COURSE segment, the XDFLD statement is

```
XDFLD NAME=XLOC,SRCH=LOCATION,SEGMENT=OFFERING
```

(specifying that the XD field XLOC is derived from the LOCATION field in the OFFERING segment); and (b) in the INDEX database DBD, the LCHILD statement is

```
LCHILD NAME=(COURSE,EDUCPDBD),INDEX=XLOC
```

Incidentally we could have given the XD field the name LOCATION without risk of ambiguity, but for clarity we choose the distinct name XLOC.

The secondary index will contain one index segment for each OFFERING occurrence in the education database. Each such index segment will point to the corresponding COURSE occurrence (the parent of the OFFERING concerned). If the education database contains m COURSEs and an average of n OFFERINGs per COURSE, the index will contain mn index segments, with an average of n index segments pointing at any given COURSE. The secondary processing sequence for the education database is defined by the sequence of these index segments, i.e., by ascending values of LOCATION (again, see [19.1] for details of ordering within duplicates). Note that, on average, each individual COURSE (together with all its dependents) will appear n times in this sequence, and that all occurrences of a given COURSE will *not* appear together, in general. In other words, when seen via the secondary index, the database appears to contain n times as many database records—though these records are not all independent of each other: For example, changing the title in a given COURSE occurrence will cause the same change in all other COURSE occurrences for the course concerned.

Assuming that the PCB specifies the secondary processing sequence (PROCSEQ = index-DBD-name), we can now write

```
NC GN    COURSE (XLOC='STOCKHOLM')
   if not found, go to exit
   add COURSE# to result list
   go to NC
```

(Note that the syntax makes it look as if XLOC is a field within the COURSE segment.) Each iteration of this code causes IMS to fetch the next index segment for 'STOCKHOLM' and then to fetch the COURSE segment that this index segment points to. It is thus more efficient than the code given earlier, since basically it involves only $2N$ database accesses (where N is the number of Stockholm offerings) instead of a scan of the entire database. Again, however, we have ignored the problem of eliminating duplicate course numbers.

Note that the fully concatenated key returned in the key feedback area when this secondary sequence is used will contain a LOCATION value in place of a COURSE# value (true for all segment types in the hierarchy).

The Independent AND

When a segment is indexed on the basis of a field in some dependent of that segment, it is possible to write an SSA for that segment involving two or more distinct conditions on the XD field, separated by the special operator # ("independent AND")—for example,

```
GU      COURSE (XLOC='STOCKHOLM'#XLOC='OSLO')
```

To understand what this means, the reader must realize first of all that for a given occurrence of the indexed segment (COURSE in the example), there is really a *set* of values of the XD field (XLOC in the example). An SSA such as the one above is considered as satisfied if, for each of the distinct conditions separated by # operators, there exists at least one value in the set for which the condition is true. In the example, therefore, the GU will retrieve the first COURSE that has both a Stockholm offering and an Oslo offering—first, that is, according to the specified processing sequence.

Note that if the # were replaced by the ordinary ("dependent") AND operator, the SSA would be requesting a COURSE with some *single* offering in both Stockholm and Oslo. IMS would not recognize any contradiction in the request but would search the database and eventually return a "not found" status code.

As another example, suppose that COURSEs were indexed on the basis of DATE values from the OFFERING segment, and consider the following operation:

```
GU      COURSE (XDATE>'691231'#XDATE<'710101')
```

(where XDATE is the XD field name). As written, this operation will retrieve the first course with an offering later than 1969 and an offering—not necessarily the same one—earlier than 1971. If the independent AND were replaced by the dependent AND, the operation would retrieve the first course with an offering in 1970.

21.4   INDEXING A DEPENDENT ON A FIELD IN THAT DEPENDENT

As indicated in Section 21.1, the index target segment—the segment pointed to by the index—does not have to be the root. However, if it is not, the effect is to restructure the hierarchy so that it *becomes* the root in the structure seen by the user.[2] As an example we consider the case of indexing OFFERINGs on the basis of LOCATION field values.

The DBDs are again essentially the same as in Section 21.2. The education DBD will include appropriate LCHILD and XDFLD statements for OFFERING; the index DBD will refer to the appropriate XD field name (XLOC, say; we *cannot* use the name LOCATION this time, because the genuine field and the XD field must be uniquely named with respect to all fields of OFFERING). Note once again that, syntactically, XD fields are always considered as fields of the target segment. The index will contain one index segment for each OFFERING occurrence in the education database; in fact, it is exactly the same as the index in Section 21.3, except that the index segments point to OFFERINGs instead of COURSEs.

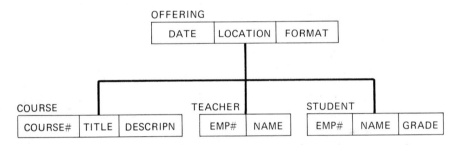

Fig. 21.2 Indexing OFFERINGs on LOCATION: Secondary data structure.

Figure 21.2 shows the *secondary data structure* that results when the user specifies this secondary processing sequence in the PCB. Figure 21.3 shows the corresponding PCB (relevant details only; LXDBD is the name of the DBD for the LOCATION index).

---

2. We are assuming, as usual, that the secondary processing sequence is used. As indicated earlier, there may be situations in which a secondary index can profitably be used with the primary processing sequence; in such a situation the restructuring of the hierarchy does not occur.

```
PCB       TYPE=DB,...,KEYLEN=12,PROCSEQ=LXDBD
SENSEG    NAME=OFFERING
SENSEG    NAME=COURSE,PARENT=OFFERING
SENSEG    NAME=TEACHER,PARENT=OFFERING
SENSEG    NAME=STUDENT,PARENT=OFFERING
```

Fig. 21.3 PCB for secondary data structure (Fig. 21.2).

The rules for defining a secondary data structure are as follows.

- The index target segment becomes the root.

- Ancestors of the index target segment become the leftmost dependents of this root, in reverse order. (If COURSE were to have a parent CATEGORY in the education database, CATEGORY would be a *dependent* of COURSE in the secondary structure.)

- Dependents of the index target segment appear exactly as in the original database, except that they are to the right of the dependent segment(s) introduced as explained in the previous paragraph.

- No other segments are included. (In the example, the secondary structure does not include PREREQs.)

The PCB of Fig. 21.3 defines a structure in accordance with these rules.

There are some similarities between a secondary data structure such as that of Fig. 21.2 and a logical database; in particular, the reader is invited to compare the foregoing rules with the notes in Section 20.10. "Get unique" and "get next" operations function in terms of the secondary structure (and secondary sequence). Fully concatenated keys (for the structure of Fig. 21.2) consist of a LOCATION value followed, if appropriate, by a COURSE# or EMP# value. ISRT/DLET operations may be used for TEACHER and STUDENT but not for OFFERING or COURSE.

As an illustration of a possible use for such a structure, we extend our Stockholm courses example as follows. Suppose we wish to find not only course numbers, but also corresponding teacher employee numbers, for all courses with an offering in Stockholm. To keep matters simple we assume that each offering has exactly one teacher. In other words, we wish to produce a report containing one line for each Stockholm offering, giving course number and teacher number (possibly other information too, such as the offering date). The index of Section 21.3 is not particularly helpful here: It will enable us to find a qualifying course, but we have no immediate way of knowing which of the several dependent teachers is the one we want.

With the structure of Fig. 21.2, however, we can write

```
NC GN     OFFERING (XLOC='STOCKHOLM')
          COURSE
   if not found, go to exit
   GN     TEACHER
   print COURSE# and teacher EMP#
   go to NC
```

The point is that once we have found a Stockholm offering, we know that there must be exactly one corresponding course and one corresponding teacher, and these are the ones we want.

It is interesting to observe, incidentally, how a slight variation in the problem statement (find teacher numbers too) leads to a major change in the solution (a restructured hierarchy becomes desirable, with the consequence that the accessing procedure needs revision also). In other words, a small perturbation in the query leads to a large perturbation in the solution. This perturbation effect may be attributed to the fact that secondary indexes represent an attempt to provide symmetry of access (access to the database via an indexed field should be similar to access via the "primary key," i.e., the root sequence field), whereas a hierarchy is a fundamentally asymmetric structure (providing access via an indexed field therefore requires a restructuring so that the indexed field *becomes* the root sequence field).

21.5   INDEXING A DEPENDENT ON A FIELD IN A LOWER-LEVEL DEPENDENT

This, the last of the four possible combinations, does not really illustrate any new points, but we include it for completeness. As our example we consider the case of indexing OFFERINGs on the basis of TEACHER employee numbers.

Once again the DBDs are essentially the same as before. The education DBD will include appropriate LCHILD and XDFLD statements for OFFERING; the XDFLD statement must include the entry "SEGMENT = TEACHER" (since the XD field is derived from a field of the TEACHER segment, not the OFFERING segment). The index DBD will refer to the XD field name (XEMP#, say). The index will contain one index segment for each TEACHER occurrence, and each such index segment will point to the corresponding OFFERING. The user will see the same secondary structure as in Fig. 21.2; however, OFFERINGs may now be accessed via the XD field XEMP#, and sequencing and fully concatenated keys will be defined in terms of XEMP#. We present a single coding example. The problem is: "Find the date of all offerings taught by employee number 876225 in Stockholm."

```
NO GN    OFFERING (LOCATION='STOCKHOLM'&XEMP#='876225')
         if not found, go to exit
         print DATE
         go to NO
```

21.6 ADDITIONAL FEATURES

The secondary indexing feature of IMS includes a number of facilities in addition to those discussed so far. We outline two of these additional facilities below. For information on the remainder—user data in the index, the use of subsequence fields, shared index databases, and the use of "system-related fields"—the reader is referred to [19.1].

■   Sparse indexing

It is possible to suppress the creation of index segments for particular values of the XD field (see the discussion of selective indexing in Chapter 2). It is assumed that suppressed values are of no interest so far as that index is concerned; an attempt to find a segment via an SSA specifying a suppressed value for the XD field will simply cause a "not found" condition, even if a qualifying segment exists. In other words, nonindexed segments simply do not appear in the secondary processing sequence.

■   Duplicate data

A secondary index is a database in its own right and may be processed independently of the database it indexes. To enhance the usefulness of this feature, the database administrator may specify that certain fields from the index source segment (the segment from which values of the XD field are derived) are to be duplicated in the corresponding segment in the index. IMS will automatically maintain these duplicate fields when an update is made to the source segment. An application for which high performance is a necessity and which requires only data that has been duplicated in the index may then actually use the index in place of the original database.

21.7 SUMMARY

We may summarize the major points introduced in this chapter as follows.

■   In general, a secondary index in IMS can be used to index a given segment on the basis of any field in that segment or in any physical dependent of that segment. (There are some exceptions to this statement: Certain types of segment, for example, logical child segments, cannot be indexed; for details, see [19.1].) The field or field combination on which the index is built is represented by an "XD field" which is made to look like an additional field of the index target segment. SSAs must be expressed in terms of this XD field if IMS is to make use of the index in responding to a DL/I request.

■ Given the existence of a secondary index, the user may choose to process the corresponding database in the secondary sequence defined by that index. If the index target segment is not the physical root, selecting the secondary sequence will cause a restructuring of the hierarchy as explained in Section 21.4; in particular, the index target segment will become the root in this restructuring. In the secondary sequence, the indexed field acts as the root segment sequence field: The user sees exactly as many database records as there are occurrences of the indexed field in the physical database, and these records are sequenced on ascending values of that field. Values of the indexed field are returned as the root portion of the fully concatenated key in the key feedback area. Secondary sequence and secondary structure (if applicable) are specified in the PCB; note that here we have a situation in which the view defined in the PCB is not just a simple subset of the view defined in the underlying DBD.

■ The reader is also reminded of the independent AND, which can be useful if the XD field corresponds to a field in a physical dependent of the target segment.

In conclusion, let us attempt to relate the concepts of secondary indexing as implemented in IMS to the ANSI/SPARC architecture presented in Chapter 1. At the *external* level the user is no longer restricted to the primary processing sequence, nor to the primary hierarchical structure (where "primary" refers to what is defined at the *conceptual* level). However, secondary sequence and secondary structure are supported at the external level—i.e., an appropriate external schema and mapping to the conceptual schema can be defined—only if an appropriate index exists, so that the index must be considered as part of the conceptual level, not just the storage (internal) level. To be more explicit, the user at the external level must effectively be aware of the existence of the secondary index—use of the index is not automatic but must be *forced* by reference to the XD field. In other words, the decision as to whether or not to use the index is in the hands of the application programmer, instead of being under the control of the system. This is unfortunate, since not only do programs that use a secondary index therefore lose some measure of data independence, but also, as we have seen, system performance may be critically dependent on a judicious choice of when and when not to use a particular index.

EXERCISES

The following exercises are based on the publications database (see Exercise 16.2). The segment and field names are those defined in the answer to Exercise 16.2.

21.1 A secondary index is to be built for this database. What structure does the user see:

a) if segment SUB is indexed on the field AUTHNAME (in segment AUTHOR);

b) if segment PUB is indexed on this field;

c) if segment AUTHOR is indexed on this field?

21.2 For case (b) above, show the DBD for the index and the additions needed in PUBDBD (the publications database DBD). You may assume that the publications database is HDAM or HIDAM, not HISAM. Show also a corresponding PCB.

21.3 Using the secondary structure of case (b) above, get names of all publications for a given author (Adams, say).

21.4 For the same structure, show the form of the fully concatenated key returned on retrieval for each of the segment types involved.

21.5 What restrictions apply to the use of the DL/I operators against this structure?

21.6 If the publications database contains:

100 SUB segments,

average of 100 PUB segments per SUB,

average of 1.5 DETAILS segments per PUB,

average of 1.2 AUTHOR segments per PUB,

how many segments of each type are seen in the secondary structure of case (b) in Exercise 21.1?

21.7 Can you think of a situation in which it could be useful to build a secondary index on the root segment *primary* sequence field?

21.8 Referring back to Exercise 21.3 above, compare and contrast the use of a logical database (see Exercise 20.1) to obtain the same result.

REFERENCES AND BIBLIOGRAPHY

See [19.1].

22
IMS
Fast Path
Databases

22.1 THE FAST PATH FEATURE

Fast Path is an optional feature of IMS that is specifically designed for certain types of on-line system. By "on-line system" we mean a system that is driven by the end-users—a system, that is, that operates by reacting to commands entered by end-users from on-line terminals. As an example, consider a banking system, in which the end-users are bank clerks and the commands they can issue are, for instance, "display balance of account A," "deposit x dollars in account A," "withdraw x dollars from account A," and so on. The application program to handle such commands is usually rather simple in structure: Basically, all it has to do is interpret the message (command) from the terminal, perform the desired operations on the database, send a response back to the originating terminal, and then wait for the next input message to start the cycle again. The processing carried out on behalf of one input message is called a *transaction*.[1] Note, incidentally, that the portion of a transaction concerned with the database is often very simple indeed, sometimes involving no more than a single read or a single update.

Although individual transactions themselves may be very simple, the system may be required to handle a very high transaction *rate* (say, several thousand transactions a minute). Again the banking environment provides a good example, where many hundreds of terminals in the bank's branch

---

1. IMS documentation generally uses "transaction" to mean the input message itself rather than the processing triggered by that message. Other systems—for example, System R—use the term in our sense.

offices may each communicate with the central system many hundreds of times during the working day, initiating a transaction every time. The Fast Path feature is intended for applications having just this combination of requirements (high transaction rate, comparatively simple database processing).[2]

The Fast Path feature provides both special data communications facilities (beyond the scope of this book) and two special database structures, the Main Storage database (MSDB) and the Data Entry database (DEDB). Main Storage and Data Entry databases have a simpler structure than other IMS databases and provide better performance for certain kinds of operation. Briefly, a Main Storage database is a root-only database that is kept in (virtual) main storage throughout system operation; and a Data Entry database is a restricted form of hierarchy that is kept on secondary storage in the usual way but is partitioned into *areas* for enhanced availability and other reasons. Sections 22.2 and 22.3 discuss these new types of database in more detail.

22.2 MAIN STORAGE DATABASES

As we indicated in the previous section, a Main Storage database (MSDB) is a root-only database that resides in primary storage throughout system execution (thus reducing I/O activity and access times). Small tables of reference information—e.g., timetables, currency conversion tables, interest rate tables—are good candidates for implementation as an MSDB. As an option, it is possible to establish a one-to-one relationship (for a given MSDB) between the segment occurrences of that MSDB and the terminals on the system, in which case a given segment occurrence can be updated only by transactions whose input message originated at the corresponding terminal. Such an arrangement is appropriate when each terminal requires its own dedicated storage area; an example is a cash-issuing system, in which a record must be kept for each terminal of the cash on hand at that terminal. In what follows, however, we restrict our attention to the case where no such relationship is established.

---

2. This statement should not be construed to mean that more conventional applications cannot use the Fast Path feature. On the contrary, it is common to find Fast Path databases being used by comparatively long-running batch applications as well as by short, simple transactions of the kind we have been discussing (or even instead of them). For instance, the banking system mentioned earlier might very well run simple clerical transactions (such as "deposit," "withdraw," etc.) during the working day and long batch applications (such as "print account statements") overnight.

Figure 22.1 shows an example of a DBD for a "bank account" MSDB. Note:

1. the ACCESS entry (MSDB) in the DBD statement;
2. the entry REL = NO in the DATASET statement, which indicates that there is no specified segment-terminal relationship for this MSDB;
3. the TYPE entry (F) for the field BALANCE. Fields in an MSDB may have type F (fullword fixed-point binary) or H (halfword fixed-point binary) in addition to the usual IMS types C, X, and P. Moreover, SSA comparisons involving a numeric field (types F, H, and P) are true arithmetic comparisons rather than the usual IMS byte-string (bit by bit, left to right) comparisons.

```
DBD        NAME=ACCOUNTS,ACCESS=MSDB
DATASET    REL=NO
SEGM       NAME=ACCOUNT,BYTES=56
FIELD      NAME=(ACCNO,SEQ),BYTES=6,START=1
FIELD      NAME=NADDR,BYTES=46,START=7
FIELD      NAME=BALANCE,BYTES=4,START=53,TYPE=F
```

Fig. 22.1 DBD for the ACCOUNTS MSDB.

PCBs for an MSDB follow essentially the same rules as PCBs for any other type of database, except that the only valid PROCOPTs are G (get) and R (replace). R must be specified if the FLD/CHANGE operation is used (see below). The DL/I operations ISRT and DLET are not allowed for an MSDB with REL = NO. (When not in primary storage an MSDB resides in an ordinary sequential data set. This data set is created by a special utility, *not* via DL/I ISRT operations.)

We turn now to the DL/I operations that can be used with an MSDB. We have already indicated that ISRT and DLET do not apply. GNP is obviously invalid also. The remaining "get" operations (GU, GN, GHU, and GHN) and "replace" (REPL) are allowed—though SSAs are restricted to at most one comparison (no ANDs and ORs), and command codes cannot be used. Moreover, the "get hold" operations, and REPL, should be avoided if possible, since they can cause delays for concurrently running transactions and thus reduce overall system throughput. In order to explain this remark we need to introduce the concept of *synchronization point* (usually abbreviated as "synchpoint").

Loosely speaking, a synchpoint corresponds to the *end of the transaction.*[3] It is signaled to IMS either by the special DL/I operation SYNC or by the DL/I operation, not discussed in this book, that requests the next input message from the terminal. (Which of these two possibilities applies in a given situation depends on an externally specified parameter that we do not discuss here.)

When a transaction T1 successfully executes a "get hold" on a given segment, that segment becomes *locked.* Locking is a mechanism for protecting transactions from interference on the part of other, concurrently executing transactions—i.e., the presence of one transaction in the system should not cause some other transaction to produce incorrect results. The purpose of the lock in the example is basically to guarantee that no other transaction T2 can update the segment (in particular, to guarantee that, if T1 updates the segment, then no other transaction T2 can destroy that update by overwriting it). The rule is that a transaction must hold a lock on a segment in order to be able to update that segment. If T1 itself updates the segment, via REPL, then concurrent transactions will not even be allowed to *get* that segment, let alone update it, until the lock is released. For an MSDB segment, locks are not released until the transaction holding the lock reaches its next synchpoint.[4] Any concurrent transaction attempting to access such a segment will simply have to wait until that synchpoint occurs. It is these waits that lead to the reduction in throughput mentioned above.

The FLD operation is intended to avoid the delays caused by such waits. In a nutshell, FLD allows a transaction to *request* an update on an MSDB segment, but does not actually perform the update until the transaction reaches its next synchpoint,[5] *and does not lock the segment.* (The problem of interference between transactions is handled differently, in a manner to be discussed.) Thus concurrent transactions are not locked out of the segment and the delays caused by locking do not occur.

A FLD operation logically consists of two or more suboperations, one suboperation to select (but not retrieve) the segment concerned and one or

---

3. The synchpoint concept applies to any transaction, not just to one operating under Fast Path on an MSDB.

4. In other types of database the lock is released earlier than the next synchpoint, provided the segment has not been updated.

5. For an MSDB the REPL operation also does not actually update the segment until the next synchpoint. One reason for deferring the update is that IMS may decide during synchpoint processing that the whole transaction has to be run again from the beginning (see later in this section). The semantics of the sequence GHU-REPL-GU, where all three operations refer to the same segment, thus depend on whether the database concerned is an MSDB or one of the other types (in an MSDB the GU sees the segment exactly as it was before the REPL was issued.)

more CHANGE and/or VERIFY suboperations against the segment. For example, the FLD operation

```
FLD     ACCOUNT (ACCNO='729835'):
                CHANGE (BALANCE=0)
```

which changes the balance to zero in the segment for account 729835, may be thought of as a "get unique" suboperation[6] followed by a "replace" suboperation—except that (a) the segment is not retrieved as it would be in a genuine GU, and (b) the change does not actually take place until the next synchpoint. (The expression "CHANGE (BALANCE = 0)" is an example of a *field search argument* (FSA). As usual we use a simplified version of the actual DL/I syntax.)

Execution of a FLD operation results in several status codes being returned to the transaction—one code for each distinct CHANGE or VERIFY suboperation, plus an overall summary code. The summary code is returned in the PCB in the usual way. The other codes are returned in special slots within the field search arguments; for details, see [22.1].

In general, a FLD/CHANGE operation can update a specified field by setting it to a specified value, as in the example above, or by increasing or decreasing it by a specified amount. The three cases are represented by the operators = , + , and − , respectively. For example, to subtract $60 from the balance of account 729835:

```
FLD     ACCOUNT (ACCNO='729835'):
                CHANGE (BALANCE-60)
```

FLD/VERIFY is used to verify that the segment satisfies some specified condition. For example:

```
FLD     ACCOUNT (ACCNO='729835'):
                VERIFY (BALANCE>60)
```

(Of course, FLD/VERIFY should be followed by a test of the appropriate return code.) It is clear that a VERIFY of the form just shown ought to have preceded the "decrease balance" CHANGE shown earlier. In practice the two steps would normally be combined into a single FLD operation:

```
FLD     ACCOUNT (ACCNO='729835'):
                VERIFY (BALANCE>60),
                CHANGE (BALANCE-60)
```

---

6. If the SSA specifies an equality condition on the key (which must be unique, incidentally; nonunique keys are not allowed in an MSDB), IMS will use a binary search to locate the required segment.

A single FLD operation can include any number of VERIFYs and/or CHANGES. The VERIFYs are done first. If any VERIFY fails, *none* of the CHANGEs in that FLD operation is performed. If every VERIFY succeeds, the CHANGEs are performed in sequence as written.

Now consider the following situation. Suppose that the current balance for account 729835 is $100, and suppose that two distinct transactions A and B are initiated (from two different terminals) at approximately the same time, both trying to withdraw $60 from this same account. Two copies of the withdrawal application program will be started up and will execute concurrently for these two transactions. Suppose that the sequence of events is as shown as Fig. 22.2.

Figure 22.2 is interpreted as follows.

- Transaction A: balance > 60? (Yes)

- Transaction A: subtract 60 from balance. (OK, but the update is not actually performed at this time)

- Transaction B: balance > 60? (Yes, because it is still 100, despite the previous step)

- Transaction B: subtract 60 from balance. (OK, but the update is not actually performed at this time)

- Transaction A completes.

- Transaction B completes.

- Transaction A synchpoint processing begins. During this processing locks are obtained on all segments to be updated, and all VERIFYs in the transaction are repeated—successfully, in the case at hand. The CHANGEs in the transaction are then applied (so that the account balance now becomes 40), locks are released, and the synchpoint processing terminates. *Note that synchpoint processing for B cannot be done until A's synchpoint processing is complete;* if B attempts synchpoint processing before A has finished, as in Fig. 22.2, then B is make to wait (because A holds a lock on the account segment and B needs it). In other words, although transactions A and B themselves are "interleaved" (i.e., they execute in parallel), synchpoint processing for these two transactions is effectively not interleaved but is performed one transaction at a time.

- Transaction B synchpoint processing resumes. The account segment is locked. All VERIFYs are repeated. If any VERIFY fails—which it does in the case at hand—then the system "rolls back" the transaction and tries it again. The rollback process consists of throwing away all the

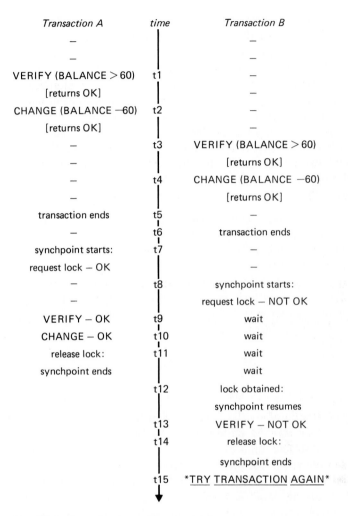

Transaction A	time	Transaction B
—		—
—		—
VERIFY (BALANCE > 60)	t1	—
[returns OK]		—
CHANGE (BALANCE −60)	t2	—
[returns OK]		—
—	t3	VERIFY (BALANCE > 60)
—		[returns OK]
—	t4	CHANGE (BALANCE −60)
—		[returns OK]
transaction ends	t5	—
—	t6	transaction ends
synchpoint starts:	t7	—
request lock — OK		—
—	t8	synchpoint starts:
—		request lock — NOT OK
VERIFY — OK	t9	wait
CHANGE — OK	t10	wait
release lock:	t11	wait
synchpoint ends		wait
	t12	lock obtained:
		synchpoint resumes
	t13	VERIFY — NOT OK
	t14	release lock:
		synchpoint ends
	t15	*TRY TRANSACTION AGAIN*

Fig. 22.2 Example of need for transaction retry.

deferred CHANGE and REPL updates[7], throwing away any message the transaction has generated for transmission back to the terminal, and executing the program over again from the beginning, giving it its original input message to process again. In the example, this second

---

7. Rolling back a transaction that has made updates to a non-MSDB database is more complicated; since such updates are not deferred but are applied at the time of the request, they must actually be undone, not just "forgotten."

execution will receive a failure code from the VERIFY (because the balance is now 40). The program can now take whatever action it deems appropriate—e.g., it can send an "INSUFFICIENT FUNDS" message back to the terminal. (If the program has already performed or requested any database updates [on any database, MSDB or otherwise] it may need to cancel those updates at this point. The special DL/I operation ROLB is provided to allow for such program-initiated rollbacks. Note that it is the responsibility of the application to issue ROLB if necessary—the system will *not* automatically cancel the updates during synchpoint processing, because it has to assume, by definition, that all update requests from the transaction actually mean what they say.)

From the foregoing explanations it can be seen that, from the point of view of a single transaction, the fact that a certain condition (e.g., BALANCE > 60) is satisfied in an MSDB at time t does *not* guarantee that that same condition will still be satisfied at a later time t'. If the logic of the transaction requires such a guarantee, "get hold" can be used instead of VERIFY. "Get hold" will ensure that no concurrent transaction can change the segment concerned before this transaction completes. However, as indicated earlier, "get hold" should generally be used as little as possible on an MSDB.

22.3   DATA ENTRY DATABASES

A Data Entry database (DEDB) is similar in some ways to an HDAM database—but an HDAM database that is both extended and restricted in various ways. The main extensions are as follows: (a) A DEDB provides special support for "sequential dependent" segments; (b) a DEDB can be partitioned into up to 240 *areas*. The main restriction is that the hierarchic structure of the database is limited to a root segment type (unique key required), plus from zero to seven immediate child segment types. (Thus the hierarchy has at most two levels.) Of these child segment types, at most one, the leftmost, is a "sequential dependent" segment type; the rest, which behave essentially as ordinary HDAM segments, are referred to as "direct dependent" segment types.

Sequential dependent segments are intended to support "data capture" applications, in which large amounts of data are entered from terminals for use in later batch processing. They can also be useful in providing an audit trail, particularly since they cannot be updated (see later). Typically, each terminal corresponds to a particular root segment in the database, and all data entered from that terminal is stored as sequential dependents of that root. Sequential dependents are chained from their root in last-in/first-out sequence (see below); thus inserting a new segment is fast. A special scan utility is provided to perform mass retrieval of sequential dependent segments and to copy them to a sequential data set for subsequent batch processing.

Partitioning into areas provides a number of operational advantages. Each area is a separate VSAM data set, and each database record (root plus all its dependents) is wholly contained within one area. The area corresponding to a particular record is determined by a DBA-supplied hashing routine; thus, for example, one area might contain corporate customer records, another individual customer records. The partitioning is not seen by the application programmer. We give some examples of the advantages that the area concept offers.

- Different areas can be assigned to different device types (in the customer example above, if corporate customers account for 90 percent of all processing, then it might be advantageous to keep those records on a faster device).

- Space allocation parameters can vary from area to area (e.g., some areas might have proportionately more space for sequential dependents than others).

- Reorganization and recovery operations can be performed on individual areas, or rather on *subsets* of individual areas, instead of on the entire database; thus it is not necessary to make the whole database unavailable while such operations are going on.

- Large databases (bigger than the capacity of a single VSAM data set) can be supported.

- Not all areas need be on-line simultaneously.

As already indicated, access to the roots in a DEDB is provided by a DBA-supplied hashing routine, as in HDAM. Access from a given root to its dependents is provided by child/twin pointers. Sequential dependents of a given root are chained in last-in/first-out sequence (i.e., the most recent insertion appears at the front of the chain, closest to the root); no sequence field can be defined for such segments. Direct dependents (of a given type) either have a unique sequence field, in which case IMS maintains twin sequence in the usual way, or do not have a sequence field at all, in which case twin sequence must be maintained by program (see [22.1] for details).

Each area of a DEDB is divided into three parts: a *root addressable part,* an *independent overflow part,* and a *sequential dependent part.* The first two of these are analogous to the root segment addressable area and overflow area in HDAM (see Chapter 19), except that in a DEDB the hashing routine must generate an area number as well as a record address within that area. The sequential dependent part holds all sequential dependent segments for all roots in the area, chained to their roots as explained earlier but physically stored in time-of-arrival sequence (thus physically adjacent segments may belong to different roots).

We consider the DBD for a DEDB very briefly. First, the DBD statement itself must specify ACCESS = DEDB and a hashing routine (via the RMNAME entry, as in HDAM). Second, the DBD statement must be immediately followed by from 1 to 240 AREA statements, each one containing a DD1 entry (similar to a DATASET DD1 entry—see Chapter 19) and various details of the area itself, such as the size of its component parts. Third, SEGM and FIELD statements are basically as usual, except that the SEGM statement for the sequential dependent, if there is one, must include the entry TYPE = SEQ.

Turning now to the PCB, we note that the only valid PROCOPTS for a sequential dependent segment are G (get) and I (insert). REPL and DLET cannot be used on such segments. (Deleting a root in a DEDB does not necessarily cause all sequential dependents of that root to be deleted. See [22.1] for further explanation.) We also note that a PROCOPT of P has a special interpretation for a DEDB; again, see [22.1] for details.

Finally, we consider DL/I operations. Apart from the restrictions on sequential dependent segments noted above, all the usual DL/I operations are valid—except that, as with Main Storage databases, SSAs are restricted to at most one comparison (no ANDs or ORs), and command codes cannot be used. However, sequential retrieval operations (GN or GNP) against sequential dependents should be avoided if possible, since they tend to be rather slow (a consequence of the storage structure, which, as already explained, is specifically designed for fast insertion). A special operation, POS, is provided to allow the user to find out how much space has been used within the sequential-dependent part of a given area.

REFERENCES AND BIBLIOGRAPHY

See also [16.1], [18.1], and [19.1].

22.1 IBM Corporation. IMS Version 1 Release 1.5 Fast Path Feature Description and Design Guide. IBM Form No. G320-5775.

Part 4
The Network Approach

Most of the current interest in the network approach can be traced back to the publication in April 1971 of the DBTG Report [23.1]. In Part 4 we take a detailed look at the DBTG specifications. As in Part 3, therefore, much of the detail here is somewhat system-specific, but the underlying concepts may be regarded as typical of any network-based system. In any case, DBTG is easily the most important single example of this approach. Chapter 23, then, describes the overall structure of a DBTG system; Chapters 24 and 25 discuss the DBTG data structure (at both "conceptual" and external levels); and Chapter 26 introduces the DBTG data manipulation language.

A number of other network systems are described in the references in Chapter 1.

23
The
Architecture
of a
DBTG System

23.1 BACKGROUND

The acronym DBTG refers to the Data Base Task Group of the CODASYL COBOL Committee (CC). The CC is the body responsible for development of the COBOL language; its activities are documented in the *COBOL Journal of Development,* which is published every two or three years and which serves as the official COBOL language specification. The Data Base Task Group, though a task group of the CC, did not confine its attention to COBOL alone, however. In fact, the DBTG final report [23.1], which appeared in April 1971, contained proposals for three distinct languages: the schema data description language (schema DDL), a subschema data description language (subschema DDL), and a data manipulation language (DML). The second and third of these did consist basically of extensions to COBOL, but the first was definitely a distinct and self-contained language, albeit one having a certain COBOL flavor.

The purpose of these three languages is as follows. The schema DDL is a language for describing a network-structured database; the DBTG "schema" is thus analogous to the ANSI/SPARC conceptual schema. The schema DDL is intended to meet the requirements of many distinct programming languages, not just COBOL—as with IMS, the "user" in a DBTG system is considered to be an ordinary application programmer—and the language therefore is not biased toward any single specific programming language. A subschema DDL, on the other hand, is a language for defining an external view (the DBTG "subschema" corresponds to the ANSI/SPARC external schema), and therefore it must have a

389

syntax compatible with that of some particular programming language, as explained in Chapter 1. Similarly, a data manipulation language must have a syntax compatible with that of some particular host language. The DML and subschema DDL defined in [23.1] were intended for use with COBOL; it was the hope of the Task Group that other responsible bodies would define DMLs and subschema DDLs for use with other programming languages such as PL/I.

Toward the end of 1971 a new CODASYL committee was established, the Data Description Language Committee (DDLC). The DDLC was formed to serve the same function with respect to the schema DDL as the CC does with respect to COBOL; in other words, it is responsible for the continued development of the schema DDL and for producing a corresponding *Journal of Development* documenting the current status of that language. The first version of this journal appeared in 1973.

The COBOL DML and subschema DDL of DBTG now form part of the current (1978) *COBOL Journal of Development* [23.3] (under the name of "The COBOL Data Base Facility"). This version of COBOL is under consideration by the American National Standards COBOL Committee (X3J4) as the basis for the next COBOL standard. Similarly, the schema DDL documented in the 1978 *DDL Journal of Development* [23.4] is under consideration by the ANS Data Description Committee (X3H2) as the basis for a data description standard. It is thus possible that some form of the DBTG specifications will become a standard in the near future. (We continue to use "DBTG" as a convenient label, though all language details in the next few chapters are based on the 1978 Journals of Development and the current ANS working documents rather than on the original report. We note that these more recent specifications differ quite markedly from the original 1971 proposal.)

Henceforth we shall use "DDL" to mean the schema DDL, unless otherwise qualified, and "COBOL" to mean the version of COBOL documented in [23.3], which includes the Data Base Facility.

23.2   ARCHITECTURE

The architecture of a DBTG system is illustrated in Fig. 23.1.

The "conceptual view" (not a DBTG term) is defined by the *schema*. The schema consists essentially of definitions of the various types of *record* in the database, the *data-items* they contain, and the *sets* into which they are grouped. (The DBTG set concept is explained in detail in Chapter 24. Broadly speaking, it is the means by which relationships are represented in a DBTG system.)

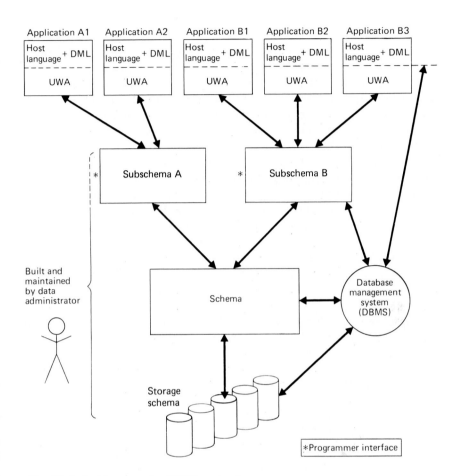

Fig. 23.1 Architecture of a DBTG system.

The storage structure (internal view) of the database is described by the *storage schema,* written in a Data Storage Description Language (DSDL). The 1978 *DDL Journal of Development* includes an appendix containing proposals for a possible DSDL [24.6].

An external view (not a DBTG term) is defined by a *subschema.* A subschema consists essentially of a specification of which schema record types the user is interested in, which schema data-items he or she wishes to see in those records, and which schema relationships (sets) linking those records he or she wishes to consider. By default, all other types of record, data-item, and set are excluded. It is not possible, at least in the subschema

DDL as currently specified, to define any structuring in the subschema —e.g., a new type of relationship (set) or a record that spans two or more schema records—that does not explicitly exist in the schema.

Finally, as we explained in Section 23.1, the users are application programmers, writing in an ordinary programming language, such as COBOL, that has been extended to include the DBTG data manipulation language. Each application program "invokes" the corresponding subschema; using the COBOL Data Base Facility, for example, the programmer simply specifies the name of the required subschema in the Data Division of the program. This invocation provides the definition of the "user work area" (UWA) for that program. The UWA contains a distinct location for each type of record (and hence for each type of data-item) defined in the subschema. The program may refer to these data-item and record locations by the names defined in the subschema. (The term "user work area" is not used in COBOL; instead, each record-type has a distinct "record area." The concept is the same, however.)

The DBTG terms for "DBA" and "user interface" are "data administrator" and "programmer interface," respectively. "DBMS" is a DDL term in its own right. COBOL uses "DBCS" (Data Base Control System) to refer to the runtime component of the DBMS.

REFERENCES AND BIBLIOGRAPHY

23.1 Data Base Task Group of CODASYL Programming Language Committee. *Report* (April 1971). Available from ACM, BCS, and IAG.

> The CODASYL COBOL Committee was known as the Programming Language Committee (PLC) at the time of this report.

23.2 R. W. Engles. "An Analysis of the April 1971 DBTG Report—A Position Paper Presented to the Programming Language Committee by the IBM Representative to the Data Base Task Group." *Proc. 1971 ACM SIGFIDET Workshop on Data Description, Access and Control.*

> Engles was the IBM representative on the Data Base Task Group at the time the final report [23.1] was produced. This paper—the so-called IBM position paper—documents a number of major objections to the proposals of [23.1].

23.3 CODASYL COBOL Committee. *COBOL Journal of Development* (1978).

23.4 CODASYL Data Description Language Committee. *DDL Journal of Development* (1978).

23.5 G. G. Dodd. "APL—A Language for Associative Data Handling in PL/I." *Proc. FJCC.* Montvale, N.J.: AFIPS Press (1966).

> Dodd's Associative Programming Language was one of the two major original influences on DBTG (the other was IDS [3.3]).

23.6 R. W. Taylor and R. L. Frank. "CODASYL Data Base Management Systems." *ACM Computing Surveys* **8,** No. 1 (March 1976).

23.7 R. W. Engles. "A Description of the COBOL Data Base Facility." *Proc. GUIDE* **47** (November 1978). Available from GUIDE International.

23.8 T. W. Olle. *The CODASYL Approach to Data Base Management.* New York: Wiley Interscience (1978).

23.9 CODASYL Fortran Data Base Committee. Fortran Data Base Facility (1980).

A proposal for a Fortran DML and subschema DDL.

24
DBTG Data
Structure

24.1 INTRODUCTION

The plan of this chapter is as follows. Sections 24.2, 24.3, and 24.4 are concerned with "DBTG sets," the most obviously distinctive feature of the DBTG data structure. Specifically, Section 24.2 shows how DBTG sets can be used to build hierarchical structures; Section 24.3 performs the same function for network structures; and Section 24.4 deals with a special type of set known as a "singular" set. Section 24.5 then presents a complete schema for a DBTG version of the suppliers-and-parts database discussed in earlier chapters.

Section 24.6 is concerned with the problem of "membership class." Since membership class is specified in the schema, an explanation of it has been included in this chapter. However, the reader will probably find it necessary to refer back to this section after reading in Chapter 26 the descriptions of those DML statements that membership class affects. Section 24.7 discusses SET SELECTION. Again the reader may find it desirable to review this section after working through Chapter 26, since SET SELECTION also depends to some extent on certain aspects of the DML.

24.2 THE SET CONSTRUCT: HIERARCHICAL EXAMPLES

24.2.1 Hierarchy with one dependent level Figure 24.1 shows a database that contains information about departments and employees.

This database contains two types of record: DEPT (department) and EMP (employee). In general, each of these records would include several

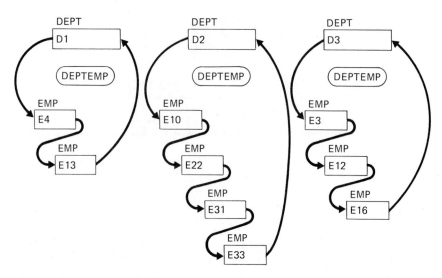

Fig. 24.1 The department-employee database.

data-items,[1] although in the diagram only one has been shown in each, namely, DNO (department number) for DEPT and ENO (employee number) for EMP. There are three occurrences of DEPT and nine of EMP. These record occurrences are grouped into three occurrences of a *set* called DEPTEMP. As already indicated, the set is the primary distinguishing feature of the DBTG data structure. Each set *type* is defined in the schema to have a certain type of record as its *owner* and some other type of record as its *member;* in the example, set type DEPTEMP would be declared in the schema with DEPT as its owner and EMP as its member.[2] Each *occurrence* of a given set type consists of precisely one occurrence of its owner together with zero or more occurrences of its member. (The zero case would arise if, for example, some department currently had no employees. In such a situation the set occurrence still exists—it consists of an owner occurrence only—but is said to be empty.) Within a given set, no occurrence of the member record can belong to more than one occurrence of that set at any one time (though it may belong to different occurrences at different times, in general). For example, no EMP occurrence can belong to more than one DEPTEMP occurrence at any given time.

---

1. DBTG allows records to contain repeating groups. We restrict our attention to normalized records throughout this part of the book.

2. We ignore the possibility of sets that contain more than one type of member. See [23.4] for details of such sets.

Each occurrence of a set represents a hierarchical relationship between the owner occurrence and the corresponding member occurrences. In the example, of course, the relationship is the normal one of departments to employees. The means by which each owner occurrence is connected to the corresponding member occurrences is irrelevant so far as the user is concerned. One way of making these connections (not the only way) is via a chain of pointers that originates at the owner occurrence, runs through all the member occurrences, and finally returns to the owner occurrence (as shown in Fig. 24.1). For simplicity this method will be assumed throughout this part of the book; if some other method is adopted in practice, it must be functionally equivalent to the pointer chain method, so this simplification is a reasonable one. (The point is that the user may always think of the pointer chains as physically existing, even if they are not actually represented as pointers in storage. See Chapter 3.)

Drawing set occurrences as chains of pointers, as in Fig. 24.1, has come to be an accepted convention. An equally widely accepted convention for the representation of set *types* is the "data structure diagram" technique of Bachman [24.1]; for an illustration see Fig. 24.2, where the structure of DEPTEMP has been shown rather as if it were an IMS structure. The differences between Bachman's symbolism and that used in IMS are that (a) the link between the owner and the member is *labeled* with the set name, whereas such links are anonymous in IMS, and (b) the link is *directed* to indicate which is the owner and which the member. (Specifying the direction of the link becomes necessary in more complex situations, where it is not always possible to show the owner as being "above" the member.) It is usually clearer to sketch some sample set occurrences rather than simply to show the set type, however, and we shall generally do this in our examples.

The reader will have realized by now that the DBTG "set" is rather different from a set as the term is commonly understood in mathematics. The DBTG terminology is somewhat unfortunate, since one often needs to refer (for example) to the set of member records—normal meaning—belonging

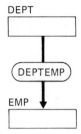

Fig. 24.2 Structure of the set DEPTEMP.

to a particular set—DBTG meaning. To avoid such confusions, some writers use special terminology to refer to the DBTG construct; among the terms that have been used are "DBTG set," "CODASYL set," "database set," "data structure set," "owner-coupled set," and "fanset." In this book we shall continue to use the unqualified term "set" for the most part, except where this usage may lead to ambiguity.

24.2.2   Hierarchy with more than one dependent level   Figure 24.3 shows (part of) a database that contains information about divisions, departments, and employees.

This example illustrates the fact that a particular type of record (DEPT in the example) can be declared in the schema to be a member of one type of set (DIVDEPT) and the owner of another (DEPTEMP). Two occurrences of DIVDEPT and three of DEPTEMP are shown in Fig. 24.3. (It is *always* true, by definition, that the number of occurrences of a set is precisely the same as the number of occurrences of the owner.) Hence we have a hierarchical structure with two dependent levels (see Fig. 24.4). In general, of course, we can build up a hierarchy in this way with any number of dependent levels.

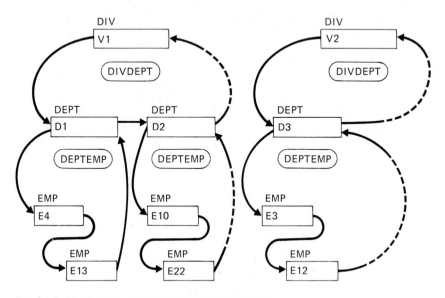

Fig. 24.3 The division-department-employee database.

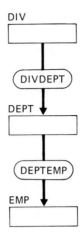

Fig. 24.4 Structure of the sets DIVDEPT and DEPTEMP.

24.2.3 Hierarchy with more than one type of record at a dependent level

Figure 24.5 shows (part of) a database that contains information about employees, their job history, and their education history.

Here each EMP occurrence is the owner of two set occurrences: an occurrence of EMPJOB, in which the members represent jobs the employee has held, and an occurrence of EMPCOURSE, in which the members represent courses the employee has attended. In general, a given type of record (EMP in the example) can be declared in the schema to be the owner

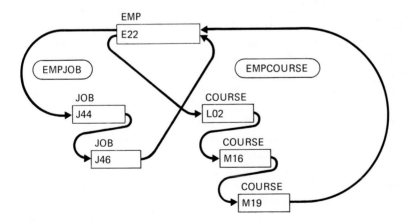

Fig. 24.5 The employee-history database.

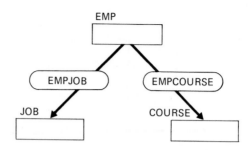

Fig. 24.6 Structure of the sets EMPJOB and EMPCOURSE.

of any number of types of set. Hence we can build hierarchical structures that not only have any number of levels but also have any number of types of record at each dependent level. See Fig. 24.6.

Incidentally, there is a significant difference between the DBTG structure of Fig. 24.6 and the corresponding IMS structure. In DBTG the two branches of the hierarchy could be interchanged without in any way affecting the structure, whereas in IMS such a change would affect the hierarchical sequence (in which the user sees JOBs as preceding COURSEs, for example, if the JOB branch is to the left of the COURSE branch).

24.2.4 Hierarchy with the same type of record at more than one level Figure 24.7 shows (part of) a database that contains information about the managerial structure of a company.

It is not permitted for the same type of record to be both owner and member of the same type of set. To represent a hierarchical relationship between different occurrences of the same type of record, therefore, it is necessary to introduce a level of indirection, as Fig. 24.7 illustrates. Here the relationship to be represented is the normal one of manager to employees (where a manager is also considered as an employee and in turn has a manager, and so on). We introduce a second record type (LINK), and define two types of set: EL (owner EMP, member LINK) and LE (owner LINK, member EMP). Each EMP occurrence representing a manager is the owner of an EL occurrence containing precisely one LINK;[3] this LINK in turn is the owner of an LE occurrence whose members are the EMP occurrences representing the manager's immediate subordinates. Thus, for example, employee E1 is the manager of employees E6, E8, . . . ; E6 is the manager of E18, . . . ; and so on. Figure 24.8 is the data structure diagram. Note that there is no requirement for the LINK record to contain any data-items at all.

---

3. Maintaining this 1–1 correspondence between EMPs and LINKs is the responsibility of the application program, not the DBMS.

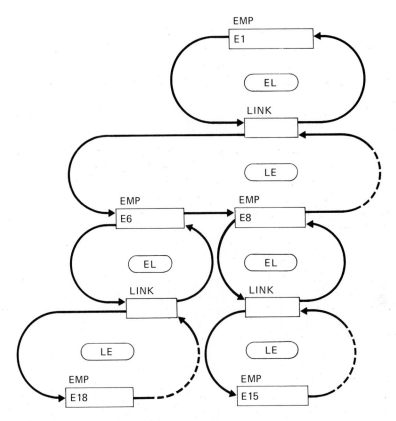

Fig. 24.7 The managerial-structure database.

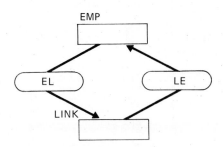

Fig. 24.8 Structure of the sets EL and LE.

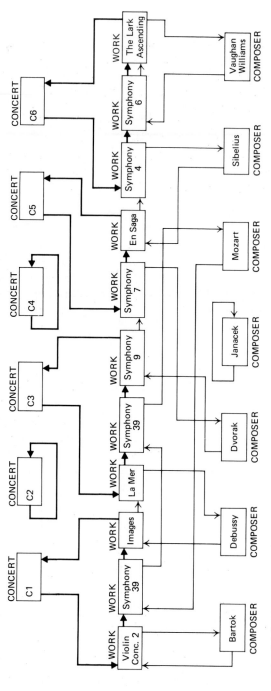

Fig. 24.9 The orchestral-concerts database.

24.3   THE SET CONSTRUCT: NETWORK EXAMPLES

24.3.1   Network involving two types of entity   Figure 24.9 represents a database that contains the current plans for a series of orchestral concerts.

We have here a typical network situation since, in general, each concert will include works by several composers and each composer will have works in several concerts. We can represent this situation in DBTG by introducing a "connection" record type (WORK), whose function is to connect the two basic types of entity (represented by the record types CONCERT and COMPOSER, respectively). Each WORK occurrence connects one concert and one composer; it represents the inclusion in the concert concerned of a work by the composer concerned. We also introduce two types of set: CONCW (owner CONCERT, member WORK) and COMPW (owner COMPOSER, member WORK).[4] To establish a connection between a particular concert and a particular composer, we must ensure that the appropriate WORK occurrence is entered into the CONCW set occurrence for the concert and the COMPW set occurrence for the composer. For example, there is a connection between the concert C1 and the composer Bartok (see Fig. 24.9). In general, then, the CONCW set occurrence for a given concert contains WORK occurrences for all the works in that concert, and the COMPW set occurrence for a given composer contains WORK occurrences for all performances of all works by that composer in any concert.

Figure 24.9 shows six occurrences of the set CONCW (two are empty, representing concerts whose programs have not been planned yet) and seven of the set COMPW (one is empty, representing a composer who is intended for inclusion in some concert when program plans are completed). For reasons of space the set names are not shown. Note that each WORK occurrence contains data describing the connection it represents, i.e., the name of the appropriate work.

Figure 24.10 is the corresponding data structure diagram.

24.3.2   Networks involving more than two types of entity   The previous example illustrates the general method of constructing a network database in DBTG. Specifically, if n types of entity (represented by n record types) are to be connected, we introduce a connection record type and n set types; each of the n "entity" record types is made the owner of one of the set types, and the connection record type is made the member of all of them; and each connection record occurrence is made a member of exactly one occurrence of each of the n types of set and thus represents the connection between the corresponding n entities.

---

4. Do not be misled by Fig. 24.9 into thinking that WORK is the *owner* of COMPW.

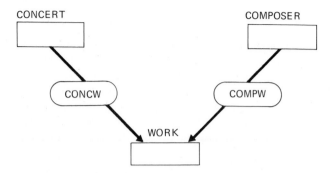

Fig. 24.10 Structure of the sets CONCW and COMPW.

Example 24.3.1 can be extended in many ways to illustrate this technique. A few outline examples follow.

- A new type of entity, SOLOIST, is introduced. A soloist may play at several concerts, and some concerts may have several soloists.

- A new type of entity, CONDUCTOR, is introduced. Each conductor may conduct several concerts. (This by itself is a hierarchical relationship, but if more than one conductor may appear at the same concert, as sometimes occurs, we have a network situation.)

- A new type of entity, ORCHESTRA, is introduced.

- A new type of entity, WORK-CATEGORY, is introduced (possible work categories are symphony, overture, tone poem, violin concerto, and so on). Each concert includes works in several categories, and each category is represented at many concerts. Furthermore, each composer produces works in several categories, and each category includes works by many composers.

The reader is urged to invent some sample data and to sketch the corresponding set occurrences for some of these examples.

24.3.3   Network involving only one type of entity   Figure 24.11 represents a database containing information about parts and components (where a component is itself a part and may have further components, and so on).

Here we have a network involving only one type of entity, parts. However, each part, in general, is playing two roles: It is the *assembly* of certain immediate components, and it is also a *component* of certain immediate assemblies. Hence this is merely a special case of the "two-entity" situation in which the two types of entity are in fact one and the same, and we tackle

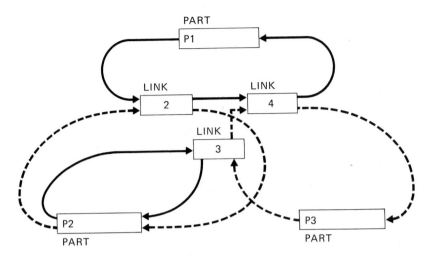

Fig. 24.11 The parts database.

it in the same way. First we introduce a connection record, LINK. Then we define two types of set: BM (bill of materials) and WU (where used), both with PART as owner, LINK as member. In Fig. 24.11 BM set occurrences are indicated by solid arrows, WU set occurrences by broken arrows. The BM set occurrence for a given part contains a link for each part that is an immediate component of that part; the WU set occurrence for a given part contains a link for each part that contains that part as an immediate component. Thus, in Fig. 24.11, we see that P1 contains P2 and P3 as immediate components, and P2 in turn also contains P3 as an immediate component; conversely, P3 is an immediate component of P1 and P2, and P2 in turn is also an immediate component of P1. The numbers within the LINK occurrences represent the corresponding quantities (e.g., each "P1" part includes as components two "P2" parts and four "P3" parts).[5]

The reader is urged to take the data of relation COMPONENT (Fig. 4.4) and to sketch an equivalent DBTG structure. (Incidentally, what is the relational representation of the data in Fig. 24.11?) Note that we have here an example of two distinct types of set having the same owner and the same member (the two set types represent two different hierarchical relationships, of course). The structure diagram is shown in Fig. 24.12.

---

5. Remember that a given type of set may not have the same type of record as both owner and member. Thus declaring the set BM (say) to have owner PART and member PART would not be an allowable approach in this example. (Such an approach would be unsuitable in any case, since it would not provide any obvious place for the quantity information.)

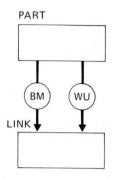

Fig. 24.12 Structure of the sets BM and WU.

24.4 SINGULAR SETS

The set construct introduced in the previous two sections provides a way of grouping member records such that the records in any one group are logically related in some way. For instance, consider the departments-and-employees example once again (Fig. 24.1). In that example, each group represents the collection of all employees in some given department. A "find next within group" operator in the data manipulation language (more accurately, a Format 3 FIND statement—see Chapter 26) will allow a group to be used as an access path to the corresponding records; in Fig. 24.1, for example, each occurrence of the set DEPTEMP provides an access path from a DEPT occurrence to the related EMP occurrences, and user programs will exploit these access paths.

With Fig. 24.1 as it stands, however, there is no access path connecting *all* EMP record occurrences together; nor is there one connecting all DEPT record occurrences together. Let us restrict our attention to departments only, for the moment. If some program needs an access path linking all DEPT occurrences, then of course such a path can be added. Using the set construct as described so far for this purpose turns out to be rather clumsy, however. We would have to introduce another record type, DEPTS-OWNER say, and make it the owner of a set type, DEPTSET say, with DEPT as member. There would exist exactly one occurrence of DEPTS-OWNER—possibly with no data-items in it—and one occurrence of DEPTSET, and every DEPT record occurrence would be a member of this single DEPTSET occurrence.

Singular sets provide a more convenient solution to the problem. A singular set may be thought of as a set having exactly one occurrence and having no owner record (in the schema, the set owner is actually declared as

SYSTEM instead of as some named record type). In the example, therefore, we could gather all DEPT occurrences together into a singular set DEPTSET, and thus avoid having to introduce the DEPTS-OWNER record type. Similarly, we could gather all EMP occurrences together into another singular set called EMPSET. These two singular sets are very similar to ordinary sequential files. EMPSET, for example, provides sequential access to the set of all EMP occurrences, according to the ordering—probably employee number ordering—specified for EMPSET in the schema. However, it is possible, though perhaps unusual, for a singular set to contain some *subset* of the occurrences of its member record type (unlike a normal sequential file). We shall discuss this possibility in Section 24.6.

24.5 A SAMPLE SCHEMA

In this section we present a possible schema for the suppliers-and-parts database of Chapter 4. We return to that example in order to facilitate a direct comparison between the relational approach and the network approach. Figure 24.13 shows the sample data (cf. Fig. 4.7), redrawn to

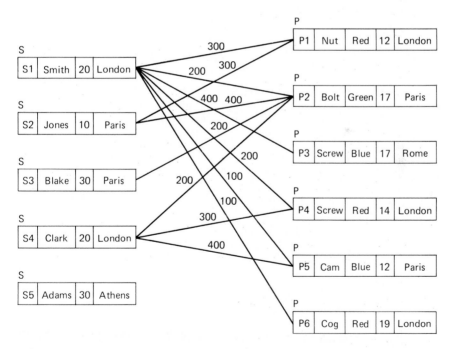

Fig. 24.13 Sample data (suppliers and parts).

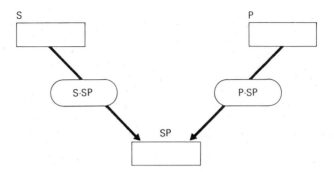

Fig. 24.14 Structure of the sets S-SP and P-SP.

emphasize the network structure. The lines represent supplier-part connections (SP tuples in relational terminology), and the numbers alongside them are the appropriate quantities.

We choose a network structure to represent this information, introducing a connection record, SP (data-items SNO, PNO, and QTY), and two sets: S-SP (owner S, member SP) and P-SP (owner P, member SP).[6] A data structure diagram for this network is shown in Fig. 24.14. Part of the actual database corresponding to the sample data is shown in Fig. 24.15.

Rather than attempt to draw the entire database in the style of Fig. 24.15, we shall take Fig. 24.13 as a simplified representation of it from this point on. The lines in that diagram must therefore be considered as SP record occurrences. Note that each SP record occurrence explicitly includes the appropriate SNO and PNO values; that is, the structure includes a degree of redundancy (the SNO value for a given SP occurrence could always be found from the owner of the S-SP set occurrence in which that SP occurrence appears, and similarly for the PNO value). This redundancy has been introduced deliberately, to allow us to order the SP occurrences on PNO within each S-SP occurrence and on SNO within each P-SP occurrence. (It would be possible to avoid the redundancy, i.e., to exclude SNO and PNO from record type SP, but it would not then be possible to have the DBMS automatically maintain these orderings.)

The schema is shown in Fig. 24.16.

Explanation

Line 1 assigns a name to the schema.

Line 3 defines the existence of a record type S.

Lines 4 and 5 specify that no two occurrences of the S record type may contain the same value for the data-item SNO (at any given time). We could

---

6. We use SNO, PNO rather than S#, P# because # is not a valid character in the schema DDL.

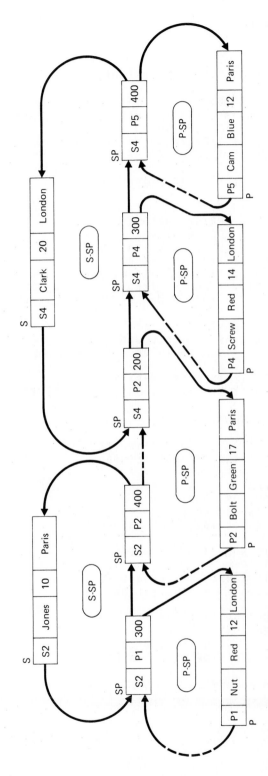

Fig. 24.15 (Part of) the suppliers-and-parts database.

```
 1 SCHEMA NAME IS SUPPLIERS-AND-PARTS.
 2
 3 RECORD NAME IS S;
 4    DUPLICATES ARE NOT ALLOWED
 5                 FOR SNO IN S.
 6       SNO    ; TYPE IS CHARACTER 5.
 7       SNAME  ; TYPE IS CHARACTER 20.
 8       STATUS ; TYPE IS FIXED DECIMAL 3.
 9       CITY   ; TYPE IS CHARACTER 15.
10
11 RECORD NAME IS P;
12    DUPLICATES ARE NOT ALLOWED
13                 FOR PNO IN P.
14       PNO    ; TYPE IS CHARACTER 6.
15       PNAME  ; TYPE IS CHARACTER 20.
16       COLOR  ; TYPE IS CHARACTER 6.
17       WEIGHT ; TYPE IS FIXED DECIMAL 4; DEFAULT IS -1.
18       CITY   ; TYPE IS CHARACTER 15.
19
20 RECORD NAME IS SP;
21    DUPLICATES ARE NOT ALLOWED
22                 FOR SNO IN SP, PNO IN SP.
23       SNO    ; TYPE IS CHARACTER 5.
24       PNO    ; TYPE IS CHARACTER 6.
25       QTY    ; TYPE IS FIXED DECIMAL 5.
26
27 SET NAME IS S-SP;
28    OWNER IS S;
29    ORDER IS SORTED BY DEFINED KEYS
30        DUPLICATES ARE NOT ALLOWED.
31    MEMBER IS SP;
32       INSERTION IS AUTOMATIC
33       RETENTION IS FIXED;
34       KEY IS ASCENDING PNO IN SP;
35       SET SELECTION IS BY VALUE OF SNO IN S.
36
37 SET NAME IS P-SP;
38    OWNER IS P;
39    ORDER IS SORTED BY DEFINED KEYS
40        DUPLICATES ARE NOT ALLOWED.
41    MEMBER IS SP;
42       INSERTION IS AUTOMATIC
43       RETENTION IS FIXED;
44       KEY IS ASCENDING SNO IN SP;
45       SET SELECTION IS BY VALUE OF PNO IN P.
```

Fig. 24.16 The schema SUPPLIERS-AND-PARTS.

additionally specify that DUPLICATES ARE NOT ALLOWED FOR SNAME IN S, if desired. Data-items for which DUPLICATES ARE NOT ALLOWED are frequently used as the basis for locating specific records. For example, to locate the S record occurrence for supplier S1, the programmer can supply the applicable value (i.e., 'S1') for the data-item SNO IN S, by moving that value into the data-item location with that name in the User Work Area, and can then issue (an appropriate form of) the DML FIND statement:

```
MOVE 'S1' TO SNO IN S
FIND ANY S USING SNO IN S
```

(Other ways of locating record occurrences will be discussed in Chapter 26. Note that in the DML statement "FIND ANY *r* USING *x*" it is not *required* that data-item *x* be declared with DUPLICATES NOT ALLOWED, though it very often will be. See Section 26.11.1 for a more detailed discussion of this point.)

Lines 6–9 define the types of data-item constituting S.

Lines 11–18 define record type P similarly. Note in line 17 the phrase "DEFAULT IS −1" for the data-item WEIGHT. The meaning of this specification is that if WEIGHT is omitted from a subschema record corresponding to schema record P, and if a program creates an occurrence of record P using that subschema, then the WEIGHT value in that occurrence will be set to −1. In general, if R is a subschema record type and occurrences of R are to be created by some program using that subschema, then R must include every data-item of the underlying schema record type not having a DEFAULT specification.

Lines 20–25 define record type SP similarly; notice in this case that DUPLICATES NOT ALLOWED has been specified for the *combination* of two distinct data-items.

Line 27 defines the existence of a set type S-SP.

Line 28 specifies the owner record type for S-SP, namely, S.

Line 29 defines the sequence of SP occurrences within each S-SP set occurrence to be SORTED BY DEFINED KEYS. The "sort control key" is defined by the KEY clause—line 34—to be ASCENDING PNO IN SP. In other words, for each S record occurrence the SP record occurrences in the corresponding S-SP set occurrence are in ascending part number sequence. The DBMS is responsible for maintaining this sequence throughout the life of the database. (Several other forms of ordering are permitted; for details see [23.4].) Line 30 (DUPLICATES ARE NOT ALLOWED) specifies that no two SP occurrences within a given S-SP occurrence may contain the same PNO value.

Line 31 specifies the member record type for S-SP, namely, SP.

Lines 32–33 specify the class of membership for SP within S-SP. An explanation of membership class is deferred to Section 24.6.

Line 34 has already been explained. In general, the KEY clause may specify ASCENDING or DESCENDING, and the "key" concerned may be the combination of any number of data-items in the record; a mixture of ascending and descending keys may be specified by a sequence of ASCENDING/DESCENDING entries within the KEY clause. The left-to-right order of specifying data-items (within one ASCENDING/DESCENDING entry or across several) signifies major-to-minor sorting in the usual way.

Line 35 concerns SET SELECTION, an explanation of which is deferred to Section 24.7.

Lines 37–45 define set type P-SP similarly.

24.6   MEMBERSHIP CLASS

Each MEMBER subentry in the schema must include a specification of the *membership class* for the record type concerned in the set type concerned. Membership class is specified by means of the INSERTION/RETENTION entry, and may therefore be thought of as a combination of an insertion class and a retention class. The insertion class is AUTOMATIC or MANUAL. The retention class is FIXED, MANDATORY, or OPTION-AL. A given record type may have any combination of insertion class and retention class with respect to a given set type; moreover, it may have different combinations—that is, different classes of membership—in different set types. Broadly speaking, the membership class of a record in a set affects programs concerned with the maintenance of that set—that is, programs that create, modify, or delete instances of the hierarchical relationship which that set represents. Specifically, the interpretation of the DML statements CONNECT, DISCONNECT, RECONNECT, STORE, and ERASE (and possibly MODIFY) is affected.

To fix our ideas, let us consider a typical set OM (owner O, member M). Figure 24.17 shows a sample occurrence of this set.

■   Retention class (FIXED or MANDATORY or OPTIONAL)

If the membership of M in OM is FIXED, then once an occurrence of M (*m*, say) has been entered into an occurrence of OM, it can never have any existence in the database *not* as a member of that occurrence of OM. Specifically, it can never be taken out of the OM occurrence by means of a DISCONNECT operation, nor may it be transferred from one OM occurrence to another by means of a RECONNECT operation. The only way to

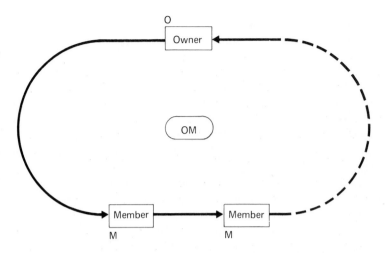

Fig. 24.17 Typical set occurrence.

destroy the association between *m* and OM is by deleting *m* entirely from the database by means of an ERASE operation. Note the implication here that if an occurrence of O is deleted (erased), all corresponding occurrences of M must also be deleted.

If the membership of M in OM is MANDATORY, then once an occurrence of M (*m*, say) has been entered into an occurrence of OM, it can never have any existence in the database not as a member of *some* occurrence of OM. Specifically, it can never be taken out of the OM occurrence by means of a DISCONNECT operation, but it may be transferred from one OM occurrence to another by means of a RECONNECT operation.

Finally, if the membership of M in OM is OPTIONAL, an occurrence of M *can* be removed from an occurrence of OM (e.g., by means of a DIS-CONNECT operation) without being entirely erased from the database.

As an example, consider the singular set EMPSET, the set of all employees given in Section 24.4. Since, by definition, we should never have an employee in the database *not* a member of this set, it seems reasonable to make the membership FIXED (or MANDATORY—the two are equivalent in the case of a singular set). On the other hand, consider the set CONCW (owner CONCERT, member WORK) in Example 24.3.1. An occurrence of this set represents the planned program for a particular concert. If the program for that concert changes, a WORK occurrence may have to be taken out of that CONCW occurrence and not entered into any other (i.e., if the work is now not scheduled to be played at all). However, it may still be desirable to retain the WORK occurrence in the database, on the grounds that it may be entered into another CONCW occurrence at a later time. It therefore seems reasonable in this case to make the membership OPTIONAL.

- Insertion class (AUTOMATIC or MANUAL)

If the membership of M in OM is AUTOMATIC, then when an occurrence of M (*m,* say) is first created and placed in the database (by means of a STORE operation), the DBMS will automatically connect it into the appropriate occurrence of OM. (It is in general up to the program that stores *m* to specify the OM occurrence concerned; see Section 24.7.) On the other hand, if the membership of M in OM is MANUAL, storing an occurrence *m* does not cause this automatic connection; to connect *m* into an OM occurrence, the program must issue an explicit CONNECT operation.

As an example, consider again the singular set EMPSET in Section 24.4. Since, as stated before, we should never have an employee in the database *not* a member of this set, it seems reasonable to make the membership AUTOMATIC. On the other hand, consider again the set CONCW (owner CONCERT, member WORK) of Example 24.3.1. Here it may well be a requirement to be able to store a particular WORK occurrence in the database without immediately connecting it to some CONCERT occurrence, and to be able later to connect it into a CONCW set occurrence when the work is added to the program for that concert. Hence it seems reasonable in this case to make the membership MANUAL.

Figure 24.18 represents a partial summary of the foregoing. The apparent anomaly in this table—that CONNECT is valid when the membership is OPTIONAL AUTOMATIC[7]—is explained by the fact that, even though automatic connection will occur when the STORE is executed, the record occurrence may later be DISCONNECTed and subsequently CONNECTed again (possibly into a different occurrence of the set). The point is that, whereas retention class (FIXED/MANDATORY/OPTIONAL) is a time-independent property, insertion class (AUTOMATIC/MANUAL) has meaning only when the record occurrence concerned is actually being created (i.e., at STORE time); it is irrelevant thereafter.

---

7. Actually this is not the only anomaly. The table would be more strictly accurate if it showed RECONNECT as valid even when membership is FIXED. RECONNECT *is* a legal operation in this case, but only if the set occurrence from which the record occurrence is being disconnected and the set occurrence to which it is being transferred are one and the same (a run-time check).

	AUTOMATIC		MANUAL	
FIXED	CONNECT	X	CONNECT	√
	DISCONNECT	X	DISCONNECT	X
	RECONNECT	X	RECONNECT	X
MANDATORY	CONNECT	X	CONNECT	√
	DISCONNECT	X	DISCONNECT	X
	RECONNECT	√	RECONNECT	√
OPTIONAL	CONNECT	√	CONNECT	√
	DISCONNECT	√	DISCONNECT	√
	RECONNECT	√	RECONNECT	√

Fig. 24.18 Effect of membership class on CONNECT, DISCONNECT, and RECONNECT.

24.7 SET SELECTION

There are certain situations in which the DBMS needs to be able to select a particular occurrence of a set automatically. One such situation has already been touched on in Section 24.6: A new record occurrence is to be stored in the database, and the record type concerned is an AUTOMATIC member of one or more set types. In this example the DBMS must select the appropriate occurrence of each applicable set type so that it can connect the new record into that set occurrence. We shall meet other situations requiring this automatic selection process in Chapter 26.

To permit the DBMS to perform this automatic selection of a set occurrence when necessary, the DBA must define a SET SELECTION clause within the (MEMBER subentry of the) set entry in the schema. The present section consists of a somewhat simplified explanation of this clause. To fix our ideas, let us restrict our attention to the set S-SP (see Section 24.5), and let us consider the situation where it is required to store the new SP occurrence 'S5/P6/700'. (SP is declared in the schema—Fig. 24.16—to be an AUTOMATIC member of S-SP; of course, it is also an AUTOMATIC member of P-SP, but we ignore this set for simplicity.)

In the simplest case the SET SELECTION clause for set S-SP (member SP) is

SET SELECTION IS BY APPLICATION

This simply means that the application program is responsible for procedurally selecting the correct occurrence of S-SP before storing the new SP occurrence. It will normally do this by FINDing the correct occurrence of the owner (record type S), but this step may not be necessary if the current S-SP occurrence is already the one required. In other words, the DBMS will simply assume that the current occurrence of S-SP is the correct one. To store the SP occurrence 'S5/P6/700', therefore, a possible code sequence is as follows.

```
build SP occurrence 'S5/P6/700' in UWA
MOVE 'S5' TO SNO IN S
FIND ANY S USING SNO IN S
STORE SP
```

Of course, this is only one of many possible ways of establishing the required occurrence of S-SP as the current such occurrence.[8]

The second case is the one illustrated in the schema of Fig. 24.16:

```
SET SELECTION IS BY VALUE OF SNO IN S
```

This means that when the DBMS is to select an S-SP occurrence, it is to do so by locating the corresponding occurrence of its owner (S), using the data-item SNO IN S (which must have been specified with DUPLICATES NOT ALLOWED in the definition of that owner). This in turn means that the programmer must correctly initialize the corresponding UWA data-item before storing the new SP occurrence, e.g., as follows:

```
build SP occurrence 'S5/P6/700' in UWA
MOVE 'S5' TO SNO IN S
STORE SP
```

We mention the third form of SET SELECTION only for completeness. It is clear in our example that set type S-SP must satisfy the *structural constraint* that, for any given occurrence of the set, the value of SNO IN SP in all members in that occurrence must be identical to the value of SNO IN S in the owner of that occurrence. (In fact, it is possible to declare such a constraint, and thus have the DBMS enforce it, by means of a special CHECK clause within the set entry. However, no such clause appears in Fig. 24.16.) Because set S-SP satisfies this constraint (regardless of whether the constraint is declared via the CHECK clause), we can specify SET SELECTION as

```
SET SELECTION IS BY STRUCTURAL SNO IN SP = SNO IN S
```

meaning (in the case at hand) that the DBMS will select an S-SP set occurrence by selecting the S record occurrence having an SNO value equal to the

---

8. The most recent ANS working document on the DDL does not in fact allow an explicit SET SELECTION clause that specifies BY APPLICATION. Instead, BY APPLICATION is simply assumed if nothing is specified in the schema *and* nothing is specified in the subschema either (see Chapter 25).

value in the SP record being stored—that is, equal to the value of SNO IN SP within the UWA. (The data-item SNO IN S must have DUPLICATES NOT ALLOWED for this form of SET SELECTION to be legal.) The code to create the SP occurrence 'S5/P6/700' now reduces to

```
build SP occurrence 'S5/P6/700' in UWA
   STORE SP
```

We do not discuss the STRUCTURAL case, or structural constraints in general, any further in this book.[9] For details see [23.3], [23.4].

Finally, we observe that a SET SELECTION clause is neither required nor allowed if the set concerned is singular. In effect, the single occurrence of the set is always considered to be the current occurrence.

The process of SET SELECTION has no effect on the currency indicators for the run-unit (currency indicators are discussed in Chapter 26).

EXERCISES

24.1 Define a schema for a DBTG version of the publications database of Exercise 16.2. (Retain the hierarchical structure; i.e., do not attempt to convert it to a network.)

24.2 Define a schema (in outline) for the "managerial structure" database of Section 24.2.4.

24.3 Define a schema for a DBTG version of the supplier-part-project database. *Note:* Several of the exercises in Chapter 26 will be based on this schema.

24.4 Define a schema (in outline) for the parts-and-components database of Section 24.3.3.

24.5 Consider the areas-and-birds database of Section 20.7. Define a schema for a DBTG version (a) as a "two-entity net," involving AREAs and BIRDs; (b) as a "three-entity net" involving AREAs, BIRDs, and DATEs. (Observe that the situation is fundamentally a "three-entity" one, since a given AREA-BIRD combination may recur on many DATEs. You may assume that no more than one sighting per day of each type of bird within each area is to appear within the database.)

---

9. A set with a declared structural constraint is an approximation to what in Chapter 28 we will refer to as an "inessential set." As the example illustrates, the general intent of inessential sets is to make it easier to maintain the database in a proper state of integrity, so that, for example, a member record does not get connected to the wrong owner. But the full extent of the interaction between the concept of inessentiality, on the one hand, and SET SELECTION, membership class, and the semantics of the update operators (STORE, ERASE, MODIFY, CONNECT, DISCONNECT, RECONNECT), on the other, is quite complex. (As a simple example, consider the effect of MODIFYing an instance of the data-item SNO-IN SP if the set S-SP is inessential.) Moreover, as we shall argue in Chapter 28, and as the name suggests, there are good reasons for not including inessential sets in the schema at all.

24.6 Design a DBTG database to represent a transportation network. You may base your design on any network with which you are familiar—for example, the New York subway system.

REFERENCES AND BIBLIOGRAPHY

See also [23.4].

24.1 C. W. Bachman. "Data Structure Diagrams." *Data Base* (journal of ACM SIGBDP) **1**, No. 2 (Summer 1969).

24.2 C. W. Bachman. "Implementation Techniques for Data Structure Sets." In reference [1.12].

Describes a number of possible techniques for mapping the DBTG set construct into storage. Comparative performance characteristics are included.

24.3 B. C. M. Douqué and G. M. Nijssen (eds.). "Data Base Description." *Proc. IFIP TC-2 Special Working Conference on Data Base Description* (January 1975). North-Holland (1975).

The major objective of this conference was to perform a critical evaluation of the CODASYL schema DDL. At the end of the conference, the participants formulated a set of recommendations for improving the DDL. These recommendations are summarized below.

- Allow a given set type to have the same record type as both owner and member.

- Eliminate repeating groups.

- Allow the specification of any number of identifiers for a given record type. (This feature has since been incorporated into the DDL, via the DUPLICATES NOT ALLOWED clause.)

- Allow the specification of a SEARCH KEY for a given record type, to allow optimization of access to record occurrences on the basis of specified data-item values.

- Allow access (from the DML) to record occurrences on the basis of specified data-item values. (The FIND statement now provides this function.)

- Allow SET SELECTION to be based on identifiers other than CALC-keys. (This feature has now effectively been incorporated into the DDL. Also CALC-keys have been dropped.)

- Allow only one member record type per set type.

- Consolidate SEARCH KEY and SORTED INDEXED. (Effectively done.)

- Improve the selective power of SET SELECTION—in particular, support existential quantification.

- Allow cardinality constraints (number of member occurrences per owner occurrence) to be specified in the set declaration.

24.4 H. Schenk. "Implementational Aspects of the CODASYL DBTG Proposal." In "Data Base Management" (eds., Klimbie and Koffeman), *Proc. IFIP TC-2 Working Conference on Data Base Management Systems* (April 1974). North-Holland (1974).

Includes a description of how records and sets are implemented in a DBTG system called PHOLAS. Also discusses the handling of the UWA, system buffers, and the object forms of the schema and subschema.

24.5 R. Gerritsen. "A Preliminary System for the Design of DBTG Data Structures." *CACM* **18**, No. 10 (October 1975).

Describes an automatic method (implemented in the form of a program called the Designer) of generating a DBTG database design given a set of anticipated queries. This technique is referred to as the functional approach to database design, and is contrasted with the "existential" approach of modeling the enterprise in a manner that is independent of the uses to be made of the information. As a simple example, the query "list all suppliers who supply part P1" will cause the Designer to generate the assertion "ABOVE (SUPPLIER PART)"—meaning that supplier records should probably be hierarchically above part records in the resulting structure.

24.6 BCS/CODASYL DDLC Data Base Administration Working Group. "Draft Specification of a Data Storage Description Language." Appendix to [23.4].

Proposes a language (DSDL) for defining a storage schema. The major concepts of this language are summarized below.

- The total storage space is partitioned into disjoint *storage areas,* each consisting of an integral number of *pages.* Page size is fixed within any given storage area but may vary from one storage area to another. Area size can be fixed or variable.

- A record type defined at the schema level is represented by one or more *storage record types* at the storage schema level. For example, the supplier record type S might map to two storage record types SX and SY, with SX containing data-items SNO, SNAME, and CITY, and SY containing SNO and STATUS. The SX and SY occurrences corresponding to a given S occurrence will be chained together (the duplication of SNO is optional). It is also possible to partition occurrences of the schema record type; for example, some S occurrences (say those with CITY = 'LONDON') might map to one storage record type, others to another.

  All occurrences of a given storage record type are stored in the same storage area. Placement within the area may be sequential, "CALC" (hashed), or "clustered" in accordance with a specified set type (e.g., shipment records could be stored close to the corresponding supplier record).

- Schema set types are represented by embedded pointer chains or by indexes. In the index case, the index actually consists of a collection of "subindexes" (not a DSDL term), one for each occurrence of the set being represented, and each such subindex consists of an index for the member record occurrences within that set occurrence. Each owner record occurrence points to the corresponding subindex.

- Indexes can also be used to provide additional access paths not exposed in the schema. Index placement within storage areas is under the control of the storage schema designer.

25

The External
Level
of DBTG

25.1 INTRODUCTION

As we explained in Chapter 23, an external view in DBTG is defined by means of a *subschema*. In this chapter we examine the COBOL subschema DDL. Broadly speaking, a subschema is a simple subset of the corresponding schema; more specific details of differences that may exist between a given subschema and the corresponding schema are given in Section 25.2.

Any number of subschemas can be defined on a given schema; any number of programs may share a given subschema; different subschemas can overlap. Remember that it is the "invocation" of the subschema by a program which provides that program with the definition of its User Work Area (UWA). An example of such an invocation is

```
DB SUPPLIERS WITHIN SUPPLIERS-AND-PARTS.
```

This statement (which appears in the Data Division of the COBOL program) invokes the subschema called SUPPLIERS, which is derived from the schema called SUPPLIERS-AND-PARTS. We show a possible definition of SUPPLIERS in Section 25.3.

25.2 DIFFERENCES BETWEEN THE SUBSCHEMA AND SCHEMA

First let us make precise the statement that a subschema is a subset of the schema. In general, any of the following schema entries may be omitted in a given subschema.

- The declaration of one or more sets
- The declaration of one or more records
- The declaration of one or more data-items

Of course, the subschema must be self-consistent. For example, a record declaration should not be omitted if a set declaration is included for a set type owned by that record type.

It follows from the foregoing that, as with IMS, users are protected from certain types of growth in the schema. For example, a new type of data-item can be added to an existing type of record. Similarly, new record types can be added. New types of set can be added under certain circumstances (see Exercise 25.1).

It also follows that the subschema automatically provides a level of data security, inasmuch as a program cannot possibly access any data not defined in the corresponding subschema (except in the case of ERASE; see Chapter 26).

Other important differences that may exist between the subschema and the schema are as follows.

- Private names ("aliases") may be defined for sets, records, and data-items.

- Data-items may be given different data types.

- The relative order of data-items within their containing record may be changed.

- Sets may be given different SET SELECTION clauses.

Of these, only the last one seems to require any explanation. The idea is that the SET SELECTION clause in the schema can be overridden by one in the subschema. For example, the schema could specify BY APPLICATION, implying that set occurrence selection is to be completely procedural, whereas an individual subschema could specify BY VALUE OF so that for programs invoking that particular subschema the operation could be slightly less procedural.[1]

25.3 A SAMPLE SUBSCHEMA

Figure 25.1 consists of a simple example of a COBOL subschema based on the schema of Fig. 24.16. Basically, this subschema includes supplier and shipment information from the underlying schema, but excludes part information.

---

1. See footnote 8 in Chapter 24, p. 416.

```
TITLE DIVISION.

SS SUPPLIERS WITHIN SUPPLIERS-AND-PARTS.

MAPPING DIVISION.

ALIAS SECTION.
AD SET SUPPLIES IS S-SP.

STRUCTURE DIVISION.

REALM SECTION.
RD SUPPLIES-REALM CONTAINS S, SP RECORDS.

RECORD SECTION.
01 S.
    02 SNO ; PICTURE IS X(5).
    02 CITY; PICTURE IS X(24).
01 SP.
    02 PNO ; PICTURE IS X(6).
    02 SNO ; PICTURE IS X(5).
    02 QTY ; PICTURE IS S9(5).

SET SECTION.
SD SUPPLIES.
```

Fig. 25.1 A sample subschema (COBOL).

In general, a COBOL subschema consists of a Title Division (which names the subschema and identifies the underlying schema), a Mapping Division (in which aliases are defined), and a Structure Division. The Structure Division in turn consists of three Sections: a Realm Section, a Record Section, and a Set Section. The Realm Section is explained below. The Record Section lists all schema record types of interest (in each case with just the data-items required). The Set Section lists all schema set types of interest (each one possibly with its own respecified SET SELECTION).

The Realm Section specifies the *realms* of interest. A realm is a logical subset of the total database view as defined by the subschema. It consists of all occurrences of records of one or more specified types (very often all types listed in the Record Section, as in Fig. 25.1). A given subschema can list any number of realms, and distinct realms can overlap (have record types in common). Each realm specifies a "processing scope"; before a program can access any part of the database defined by its subschema, it must first READY the appropriate realm (analogous to opening a conventional file), in order to inform the DBMS of its intent to access that part of the database. The READY statement also indicates whether access will be limited to RETRIEVAL-type operations only or will include UPDATE-type operations too. More details are given in Chapter 26.

From this point on—in Chapter 26 in particular—we shall generally assume that the subschema is identical in all major respects to the corresponding schema.

EXERCISE

25.1 Suppose that a new type of set OM (owner O, member M) is added to the schema. To what extent can existing programs remain unaffected by this addition? You should consider each of the following cases.

   a) O and M both new types of record (additions)

   b) O and M both old (existing) types of record

   c) O old and M new

   d) O new and M old

(*Note:* Membership class is important here; so also may be SET SELECTION. You may prefer to postpone detailed consideration of this exercise until after you have read Chapter 26 and reviewed Sections 24.7 and 24.8.)

REFERENCES AND BIBLIOGRAPHY

See [23.3] and [23.4].

25.1 M. H. Kay. "An Assessment of the CODASYL DDL for Use with a Relational Subschema." In "Data Base Description" (eds., Douqué and Nijssen), *Proc. IFIP TC-2 Working Conference on Data Base Description* (February 1975). North-Holland (1975).

> Presents some ideas on the support of a relational subschema on top of a DBTG schema. In general, such a subschema would be more than just a "simple subset of the schema." The paper identifies some problems that arise and criticizes the schema DDL in the light of these problems.

25.2 C. A. Zaniolo. "Multimodel External Schemas for CODASYL Data Base Management Systems." In "Data Base Architecture" (eds., Bracchi and Nijssen), *Proc. IFIP TC-2 Working Conference on Data Base Architecture* (June 1979). North-Holland (1979).

25.3 C. A. Zaniolo. "Design of Relational Views over Network Schemas." *Proc. 1979 ACM SIGMOD International Conference on Management of Data.*

25.4 L. I. Mercz. "Issues in Building a Relational Interface on a CODASYL DBMS." In "Data Base Architecture" (eds., Bracchi and Nijssen), *Proc. IFIP TC-2 Working Conference on Data Base Architecture* (June 1979). North-Holland (1979).

25.5 E. K. Clemons. "The External Schema and CODASYL." *Proc. 4th International Conference on Very Large Data Bases* (1978).

25.6 E. K. Clemons. "An External Schema Facility for CODASYL 1978." *Proc. 5th International Conference on Very Large Data Bases* (1979).

26
DBTG
Data
Manipulation

26.1 INTRODUCTION

As with the subschema DDL, we shall base our explanation of DBTG data manipulation on the DML defined for COBOL. The general plan of the chapter is as follows. Section 26.2 deals with the concept of currency, an understanding of which is prerequisite to an understanding of any of the DML statements. Section 26.3 discusses the handling of errors and exceptions. Sections 26.4–26.11 deal with all the major statements of the language; the FIND statement in particular is dealt with last, in Section 26.11, because, although it is easily the most important single statement in the DML, it is also the most complex. Section 26.12 gives a brief description of the remaining statements.

All examples will be based on the data of Fig. 24.13 and the schema of Fig. 24.16 (suppliers and parts). As noted before, we shall be assuming that the subschema is essentially the same as the schema; the subschema is actually invoked as indicated in Section 25.1. For convenience the sample data is shown again as Fig. 26.1.

26.2 CURRENCY

Before we examine the statements of the DML in any detail, it is essential to discuss the fundamental concept of currency. This concept is a generalization of the familiar notion of current position within a file. The basic idea is that, for each program operating under its control, the DBMS maintains a table of "currency indicators." A currency indicator is an object whose value (typically) is a *database key*. Database keys are system-generated

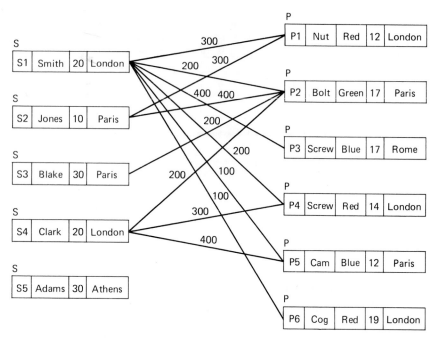

Fig. 26.1 Sample data (suppliers and parts).

values that uniquely identify records in the database (they may be thought of as stored record addresses, in the sense of Chapter 2). The currency indicators for a given run-unit[1] identify the record occurrence most recently accessed[2] by the run-unit for each of the following.

- Each realm

    For a realm R the most recently accessed record occurrence within R is referred to as the "current record of realm R."

- Each type of record

    For a record type T the most recently accessed T occurrence is referred to as the "current record of type T" or the "current T occurrence."

- Each type of set

    For a set type S the most recently accessed record occurrence that participates in an occurrence of S may be an occurrence of either the owner or a

---

1. "Run-unit" is a term meaning the execution of a program.
2. "Most recently accessed" is not strictly accurate here; see Section 26.11.7.

member. Whichever it is, it is referred to as the "current record of set S." Note that the "current record of set S" refers to a *record* occurrence, but that it also uniquely identifies a *set* occurrence, namely, the unique S occurrence containing it; this set occurrence is referred to as the "current S occurrence."

■ Any type of record

The most recently accessed record occurrence, no matter what its type is (and no matter what realms it belongs to and what sets it participates in), is referred to as the "current record of the run-unit" (usually abbreviated to just "current of run-unit"). This is the most important currency of all, as will shortly be made clear.

For example, consider the following sequence of statements.

```
MOVE 'S4' TO SNO IN S
FIND ANY S USING SNO IN S
FIND FIRST SP WITHIN S-SP
FIND OWNER WITHIN P-SP
```

The effect of these statements is as follows. The MOVE initializes the User Work Area data-item SNO IN S. The first FIND then locates the corresponding S record occurrence, namely, that for supplier S4. The next FIND locates the first SP occurrence within the S-SP set occurrence owned by supplier S4, namely, the SP occurrence 'S4/P2/200'; and the last FIND then locates the owner of this SP occurrence within the set P-SP, namely, the P occurrence for part P2. At the end of the sequence, therefore, this P occurrence is the current of run-unit. Now complete the rest of the table:

Current of run-unit	P 'P2'
Current S occurrence	
Current P occurrence	
Current SP occurrence	
Current record of set S-SP	
Current record of set P-SP	
Current S-SP occurrence	
Current P-SP occurrence	
Current record of realm S-SP-P	

(We assume that realm S-SP-P encompasses the entire database. The complete table is given in the answer section at the back of the book.)

The following summary of the major DML statements shows why currency—and in particular "current of run-unit"—are such important notions.

- **FIND**   locates an existing record occurrence and establishes it as the current of run-unit (also updating other currency indicators as appropriate).

- **GET**   retrieves the current of run-unit.

- **ERASE**   deletes the current of run-unit.

- **STORE**   creates a new record occurrence and establishes it as the current of run-unit (also updating other currency indicators as appropriate).

- **MODIFY**   updates the current of run-unit.

- **CONNECT**   connects the current of run-unit into a set occurrence.

- **DISCONNECT** disconnects the current of run-unit from a set occurrence.

- **RECONNECT**   disconnects the current of run-unit from a set occurrence and connects it into another set occurrence of the same set type.

The importance of the FIND statement is apparent from this summary: It is logically required before each of the other statements, except STORE. However, as mentioned in the introduction, we shall defer treatment of FIND until after the other statements have been dealt with, restricting ourselves to formats of the FIND statement already illustrated when a FIND is necessary.

26.3 EXCEPTION HANDLING

As the final step in executing any DML statement, the DBMS places a value in the "database special register" DB-STATUS to indicate the outcome of that statement; a zero value means the statement executed successfully, a nonzero value means some error or exceptional condition occurred. The programmer is required to supply one or more "declarative procedures" (via the USE FOR DB-EXCEPTION statement) to handle all nonzero cases. These procedures are specified at the start of the Procedure Division, prior to the main executable code. We present an example, using a simplified form of the actual COBOL syntax.

```
DECLARATIVES.

    USE FOR DB-EXCEPTION ON '0502100'.
EOF-PROC.
    MOVE 'YES' TO EOF.
```

```
          USE FOR DB-EXCEPTION ON '0502400'.
        NOTFOUND-PROC.
          MOVE 'YES' TO NOTFOUND.

          USE FOR DB-EXCEPTION ON OTHER.
        OTHER-PROC.

        END DECLARATIVES.
```

The first USE here specifies a procedure—consisting of the single statement MOVE 'YES' TO EOF—to be executed whenever DB-STATUS is set to 0502100 (which happens when the current position in a FIND NEXT operation is at end-of-set or end-of-realm). The second USE specifies a similar procedure for DB-STATUS value 0502400 ("record not found"). The third specifies a "do-nothing" (empty) procedure to be executed whenever any other nonzero DB-STATUS value occurs (i.e., one not handled by the more explicit USE statements already shown).

In general a given USE statement can specify either OTHER or a list of specific values. When a DML statement causes DB-STATUS to be set to a nonzero value, the corresponding declarative procedure is invoked. There must be exactly one such procedure (possibly empty) corresponding to each such value. After the procedure has been executed, control is returned to the statement following the original DML statement. (Specifying an empty procedure thus allows the corresponding condition to be handled in-line—that is, the original DML statement can be followed by an explicit test for the corresponding DB-STATUS value and explicit code to handle the corresponding condition, if necessary.)

In addition to DB-STATUS, certain other special registers (DB-SET-NAME, DB-RECORD-NAME, DB-DATA-NAME) are also set by the DBMS after executing certain DML statements. These registers, which have the obvious interpretation, can help in debugging and other situations.

In what follows we shall usually ignore the necessity of testing for exceptions.

26.4 GET

- **Get full details of supplier S4.**

```
          MOVE 'S4' TO SNO IN S
          FIND ANY S USING SNO IN S
          GET S
```

The effect of this code is to bring the S record occurrence for supplier S4 into the S location within the UWA. Note that the FIND statement itself does *not* retrieve any data. Incidentally, since GET (like most other statements) operates on the current of run-unit, it would be perfectly valid to write simply

```
GET
```

This would bring the current of run-unit, whatever its type, into the appropriate UWA location. However, by specifying a record name (S in the example), the programmer is enabling the DBMS to check that the current of run-unit is actually an occurrence of the appropriate type (and in any case such explicit specification is clearer). In the example, if for some reason the current of run-unit were not an S occurrence, the GET would fail and a nonzero value would be placed in DB-STATUS.

Most of the DML statements allow the specification of the record name to be omitted in the same way that GET does. However, the practice is not recommended, and we shall generally not adopt it in our examples.

It is also possible to get just specified data-items from the current of run-unit, as the following example illustrates.

- **Get supplier name and city for supplier S4.**

```
FIND S occurrence for S4
GET SNAME IN S, CITY IN S
```

In this example only the name and city for supplier S4 are brought into the UWA; other UWA data-items remain unchanged.

26.5   STORE

- **Create the SP occurrence 'S5/P6/700'.**

```
1. MOVE 'S5' TO SNO IN SP
   MOVE 'P6' TO PNO IN SP
   MOVE  700 TO QTY IN SP
2. MOVE 'S5' TO SNO IN S
   MOVE 'P6' TO PNO IN P
3. STORE SP
```

Step 1 consists of statements—three MOVEs—to construct the new SP occurrence in the UWA. It can now be stored in the database (step 3). However, SP is declared in the schema of Fig. 24.16 to be an AUTOMATIC member of both S-SP and P-SP; hence, when an SP occurrence is stored, the DBMS must automatically connect it into the appropriate occurrences of these two sets—in the example, the S-SP occurrence owned by S5 and the P-SP occurrence owned by P6. In general, the occurrences of S-SP and P-SP into which the new SP occurrence is to be connected are chosen by the

DBMS on the basis of the SET SELECTION clauses given in the schema for these two sets. A full explanation of this clause was given in Section 24.7; it is sufficient here to note that, in order for the process of SET SELECTION to pick the correct occurrences of the sets in this example, the programmer must first initialize—step 2—the UWA data-items SNO IN S and PNO IN P with the correct values.

After the STORE in the example, the new SP occurrence is the current of run-unit, the current SP occurrence, the current record of realm S-SP-P, and the current record of both S-SP and P-SP. (In general, a newly stored record occurrence becomes the current record of all sets for which it is the owner or an AUTOMATIC member, except as explained subsequently in Section 26.11.7.)

26.6   ERASE

■   **Delete the S occurrence for supplier S4.**

```
FIND S occurrence for S4
ERASE [ ALL ] S
```

As the example shows, there are two ERASE formats, one with and one without the specification ALL. Their meaning differs when the target record (the current of run-unit) is the owner of one or more nonempty set occurrences, as in the case at hand. Let us define the term "descendant of R," recursively, to mean a member record whose owner in some set is R or a descendant of R. The ERASE ALL statement deletes the current of run-unit and all its descendants; in the example, ERASE ALL would delete supplier S4 and all its shipments. The ERASE statement without ALL, on the other hand, operates according to the procedure described in steps 1–6 below. (The general intent of this procedure is that the ERASE fails if it requests the deletion of a record having MANDATORY members; otherwise, it causes OPTIONAL members to be disconnected and FIXED members to be deleted.)

1. Let R be the current of run-unit.

2. If there exists a record X that is a MANDATORY member of a set T with owner R, then the ERASE fails; any "deletable" and "disconnectable" marks set earlier during the operation (see steps 3 and 5 below) are removed, and the ERASE terminates unsuccessfully (DB-STATUS is nonzero). The database remains in exactly the state it was in before the ERASE.

3. For each record X that is an OPTIONAL member of a set T with owner R, X is marked "disconnectable from T."

4. For each record X that is a FIXED member of a set T with owner R, steps 2–5 are repeated with X replacing R.

5. R is marked "deletable."

6. All records marked "disconnectable" are disconnected from the indicated set. All records marked "deletable" are disconnected from all sets in which they are members and then destroyed. The ERASE operation terminates successfully (DB-STATUS is zero).

Note that descendants can be deleted or disconnected even if they are not visible through the subschema.

After a successful ERASE, the currency indicator for "current of rununit" is null (identifies no position). The effect on other currency indicators is as follows. Let the record to be erased be R, and suppose that R is the current record of some realm M, the current record of its record type, the current record of set T1 (in which it is an owner), and the current record of set T2 (in which it is a member); in other words, the currency indicators for M, the record type concerned, set type T1, and set type T2 all designate record R. Now suppose R is erased.

- The currency indicator for realm M is updated so that it no longer designates a record but instead identifies the "hole" left by R within the realm. An attempt to find the next record after R within the realm M (using a Format 3 FIND; see Section 26.11.3) will move the currency indicator for realm M along to the record following this hole within M.

- The currency indicator for the record type is updated similarly; that is, it is updated to identify the hole. An attempt to find the next record after R using a Format 1 FIND (Section 26.11.1) will move the currency indicator along to the record following the hole.

- The currency indicator for set type T1 is set to null.

- The currency indicator for set type T2 is updated to identify the hole. An attempt to find the next record after R within the set type T2 (using a Format 3 FIND) will move the currency indicator along to the record following the hole.

26.7 MODIFY

- **Add 10 to the status value for supplier S4.**

```
FIND S occurrence for S4
GET S
ADD 10 TO STATUS IN S
MODIFY S
```

The MODIFY statement replaces (portions of) the current of run-unit with values taken from the UWA. Thus, to add 10 to S4's status value, the user must retrieve it, increase it in the UWA, and then put it back. If the MODIFY specifies a record name, the entire record is replaced. If it specifies a list of data-items, just those items are replaced. In the example, therefore, the desired effect could equally well have been achieved by specifying STATUS IN S (instead of simply S) in both the GET and the MODIFY.

Under certain circumstances—for example, if a sort control key is changed—MODIFY may cause currency indicators to be updated. See [23.3] for details.

26.8   CONNECT

Just as STORE, ERASE, and MODIFY statements are provided to create, destroy, and change records, so CONNECT, DISCONNECT, and RE-CONNECT statements are provided to create, destroy, and change "set memberships"—i.e., connections between a member record and an owner record. For the sake of the examples, we introduce a new set type SETX (owner X, member S, SET SELECTION IS BY APPLICATION; here S is the supplier record type, as usual, and X is some arbitrary new record type).

■ **Connect the S occurrence for supplier S4 into the SETX occurrence owned by the X occurrence *x*.**

The connection process consists essentially of (1) locating the required occurrence of SETX, (2) locating the required occurrence of S, and (3) executing a CONNECT statement to connect the latter into the former. The procedure for step 1 can be any procedure that makes the required occurrence of SETX the *current* occurrence of SETX: typically, a procedure to FIND the appropriate occurrence (*x*) of its owner X.

1. FIND . . . x
2. FIND S occurrence for S4
3. CONNECT S TO SETX

The CONNECT statement connects the current of run-unit into an occurrence of the specified set. The occurrence concerned is determined according to the SET SELECTION criteria for the specified set. Note that the class of membership of S in SETX must not be AUTOMATIC unless it is also OPTIONAL (and the S occurrence for S4 must not currently be a member of any occurrence of SETX). Note too in the example that step 1 *must* be performed before step 2. (Why?) After the CONNECT, the S occurrence for S4 is the current record of set SETX.

26.9 DISCONNECT

■   **Disconnect the S occurrence for S4 from the SETX occurrence that contains it.** (See the example in Section 26.8.)

```
FIND S occurrence for S4
DISCONNECT S FROM SETX
```

The DISCONNECT statement disconnects the current of run-unit from the occurrence of the specified set containing it; the record occurrence still exists in the database but is no longer a member of the specified set. If the current of run-unit was previously the current record of the specified set, then the currency indicator for that set is adjusted so that it still identifies the position (the "hole") in the set previously occupied by the now disconnected record, but does *not* identify that record. Note that S must be an OPTIONAL member of SETX; note, too, that the S occurrence for S4 must currently be a member of some SETX occurrence.

26.10 RECONNECT

■   **Disconnect the S occurrence from the SETX occurrence that contains it and connect it into the SETX occurrence owned by the X occurrence x.** (See the examples in Sections 26.8 and 26.9.)

```
1. FIND . . . x
2. FIND S occurrence for S4
3. RECONNECT S WITHIN SETX
```

The RECONNECT statement disconnects the current of run-unit from the occurrence of the specified set containing it, and then connects it into some occurrence—possibly the same one—of that set. This latter occurrence is determined according to the SET SELECTION criteria for the specified set. The effect on currency indicators is exactly as for DISCONNECT, *except* that if during the connection stage of the operation the "hole" into which the record is connected happens to be identified by the currency indicator for the set, then that currency indicator is adjusted to identify the reconnected record. Note in the example that S must not be a FIXED member of SETX unless the SETX occurrence from which the record is disconnected and the SETX occurrence into which it is reconnected are one and the same.[3] Note, too, that (as in Section 26.8) steps 1 and 2 may not be interchanged.

---

3. Sometimes it is necessary to move records around within a set occurrence, instead of moving them from one set occurrence to another. In particular, this function may be required if the set concerned is singular. RECONNECT thus permits such movement, even if membership is FIXED (when DISCONNECT and CONNECT could not be used).

26.11 FIND

The basic format of the FIND statement is:

```
FIND record-selection-expression
```

where "record-selection-expression" (r-s-e for short) is an expression that designates some record occurrence in the database. The function of FIND is to locate the designated occurrence and to make it the current of run-unit—also the current record of all realms and all sets in which it participates, and the current record of its record type (but see Section 26.11.7). There are six general formats of r-s-e, and hence six FIND formats. (Originally there were seven, but Format 1 was later dropped. We have renumbered Formats 2-7 as Formats 1-6 in what follows. In any case we choose not to discuss them in numerical order, for pedagogical reasons.)

26.11.1 Access within record type (Format 1) The basic Format 1 FIND (FIND ANY) has already been illustrated many times. It provides direct access to a record occurrence by the value of some data-item (or data-item combination) for that occurrence. There is an important variation on the basic format, however, which is needed when the data-item concerned is nonunique (i.e., DUPLICATES NOT ALLOWED is not specified). For example, to find all S record occurrences where the city value is LONDON:[4]

```
MOVE 'LONDON' TO CITY IN S
FIND ANY S USING CITY IN S
MOVE 'NO' TO NOTFOUND
PERFORM UNTIL NOTFOUND = 'YES'
    GET S
    ....
    FIND DUPLICATE S USING CITY IN S
END-PERFORM
```

The effect of this code is as follows. The first two statements locate *some* S occurrence with city value LONDON (assuming one exists; which particular one is found is implementor-defined). The third statement initializes the data-item NOTFOUND to 'NO'. The PERFORM-loop then retrieves the S occurrence just found, processes it, and then attempts to find a "duplicate" of that S occurrence. A duplicate here is an S occurrence having the same value for CITY as the current record of type S. The loop is repeated until NOTFOUND is set to 'YES' (which we assume happens as the result of a "record not found" declarative procedure, as in Section 26.3). The code is guaranteed to find all required S occurrences and not to find

---

4. In this example we make use of the PERFORM/END-PERFORM construct introduced as part of the COBOL structured programming extensions in [23.3]. Later examples will also use the IF/END-IF construct, from the same source.

any occurrence twice, though the precise sequence in which those records are found is implementor-defined.

The USING clause can take the form "USING data-item, data-item, . . . ", in which case the search is for an occurrence containing the desired values for all specified data-items. It may be helpful to think of access via a Format 1 FIND as an abstraction of hashing.

26.11.2 Access to owner (Format 5)   Assume that the current record of set P-SP is a particular SP occurrence. Find the corresponding P occurrence.

```
FIND OWNER WITHIN P-SP
```

In general, "FIND OWNER" finds the owner in the specified set type of the current set occurrence of that type. Note that the current record of the set may in fact already be the owner.

26.11.3 Sequential access within set or realm (Format 3)   Find PNO values for parts supplied by supplier S4.

```
MOVE 'S4' TO SNO IN S
FIND ANY S USING SNO IN S
MOVE 'NO' TO EOF
FIND FIRST SP WITHIN S-SP
PERFORM UNTIL EOF = 'YES'
    GET SP
    (add PNO IN SP to result list)
    FIND NEXT SP WITHIN S-SP
END-PERFORM
```

Two versions of the Format 3 FIND are illustrated in this example. The FIND FIRST locates the first SP occurrence within the current occurrence of set S-SP (namely, the S-SP occurrence owned by supplier S4). Then, on each iteration of the loop, the FIND NEXT locates the next SP occurrence within the current occurrence of set S-SP (namely, the S-SP occurrence containing the SP occurrence most recently found), relative to the position identified by the S-SP currency indicator (namely, the position of the SP occurrence most recently found). We assume that data-item EOF is set to 'YES' when no next SP occurrence can be found.

The specification NEXT (or FIRST) in a Format 3 FIND can be replaced by PRIOR, LAST, an integer n, or the name of a data-item having an integer value. In the last two cases a positive integer represents the number of the desired record occurrence counting in the NEXT direction from the beginning of the set occurrence (1 = FIRST), a negative integer represents the number of the desired record occurrence counting in the PRIOR direction from the end of the set occurrence (−1 = LAST). Also, the set name can be replaced by a realm name, in which case NEXT, PRIOR, etc., are interpreted in terms of positions within the indicated realm. The sequence of records within a realm is implementor-defined.

26.11.4 Sequential access within set (Format 6) Find the quantity of part P5 supplied by supplier S1.

```
MOVE 'S1' TO SNO IN S
FIND ANY S USING SNO IN S
MOVE 'P5' TO PNO IN SP
FIND SP WITHIN S-SP CURRENT USING PNO IN SP
GET SP
(print QTY IN SP)
```

The fourth statement here is a Format 6 FIND. It operates by locating the first SP record occurrence within the current S-SP set occurrence having a PNO value equal to the value of PNO IN SP in the UWA (i.e., a PNO value of 'P5').

Note, incidentally, that we are faced with a strategy problem in this example: Instead of starting with the supplier and scanning the corresponding S-SP occurrence, we could have started with the part and scanned the corresponding P-SP occurrence.[5] If CURRENT is omitted from a Format 6 FIND, the set occurrence to be scanned is determined according to the SET SELECTION specification for the set concerned. In the foregoing procedure, therefore, the statement FIND ANY S USING SNO IN S could have been omitted, provided that CURRENT was also omitted from the other FIND. Thus there are not two but four possible procedures that can be used to answer the original question (starting with S1 or P5, including or omitting CURRENT). As an exercise, the reader might like to consider the effect on currency of each of the four (each one, of course, results in the same current of run-unit, but other resultant currency values are *not* the same in every case).

26.11.5 Sequential access within set (Format 2) Find all shipments for supplier S1 in which the quantity is 100.

```
MOVE 'S1' TO SNO IN S
FIND ANY S USING SNO IN S
MOVE 100 TO QTY IN SP
FIND SP WITHIN S-SP CURRENT USING QTY IN SP
MOVE 'NO' TO NOTFOUND
PERFORM UNTIL NOTFOUND = 'YES'
    GET SP
    ....
    FIND DUPLICATE WITHIN S-SP USING QTY IN SP
END-PERFORM
```

---

5. If the database included a singular set linking all SP occurrences, there would be a third possibility.

The first four statements locate the first SP occurrence for supplier S1 that contains a QTY value of 100 (i.e., the SP occurrence 'S1/P5/100'; the procedure is essentially the same as in the previous example and makes use of a Format 6 FIND). The next statement initializes NOTFOUND to 'NO'. Within the PERFORM loop, the Format 2 FIND (FIND DUPLICATE . . .) scans the current S-SP occurrence, in the NEXT direction, starting from the current record of set S-SP and looking for the next SP occurrence having the same QTY value as that current record. Note that the Format 6 FIND cannot be used at this point, since it would simply locate 'S1/P5/100' again; we need a statement to scan forward from the current position, as the Format 2 FIND does. The loop is repeated until a "not found" condition occurs.

It is important to understand that the effect of the clause 'USING QTY IN SP' in the Format 2 FIND is to cause the DBMS to search for the next SP occurrence with the same QTY value as the current record of the set—not the same value as the UWA data-item QTY IN SP. (Contrast the semantics of the same clause in the Format 6 FIND.) In the example above, the two values are in fact the same, but the statement "GET SP" could be replaced by the statement, say,

```
MOVE 400 TO QTY IN SP
```

without having the least effect on which SP occurrence is found by the Format 2 FIND.

The USING clause in both Format 2 and Format 6 FIND statements can take the form "USING data-item, data-item, ...", in which case the search is for an occurrence containing the desired values for all specified data-items.

26.11.6 Access by database key (Format 4)   The Format 4 FIND is used to "find" the record having a specified database key value. We place "find" in quotes to emphasize the fact that, in a sense, the record concerned must already have been found, since in the last analysis the only way the run-unit can discover a record's database key value is by making that record the current of run-unit. Format 4 differs from the other FIND formats in that its *only* function is to update the table of currency indicators; it does not require any access to the database.

The "record-selection-expression" in a Format 4 FIND takes the form of a *database key identifier*. A database key identifier, in turn, can take two forms; we discuss each one in turn.

Case 1

Establish the current record of set S-SP as the current of run-unit. (Note that this record is not necessarily the current of run-unit already.) We assume that the current record of set S-SP is an SP occurrence.

```
FIND CURRENT SP WITHIN S-SP
```

If a record name and "WITHIN set" are both specified, as in the example, then the current record of the indicated set must be of the indicated type. The WITHIN phrase can refer to a realm instead of a set, in which case the record to be found is the current record of that realm; again, that current record must be of the indicated type if a record name is specified. If the WITHIN phrase is omitted but the record name is specified, then the record to be found is the current record of the indicated record type. If both the record name and the WITHIN phrase are omitted, the record to be found is the current of run-unit. Thus the general form of "database key identifier" (case 1) is:

```
CURRENT [ record-name ] [ WITHIN name ]
```

where "name" is either a set name or a realm name.

Case 2

The second case relies on the notion of *keep lists*. Keep lists are discussed in detail in Section 26.12, and we therefore defer detailed discussion of this FIND format to that same section. For completeness, however, we give the syntax for the second case of "database key identifier" here:

```
position WITHIN keep-list-name
```

where "position" is either FIRST or LAST.

Example:

```
FIND LAST WITHIN LISTA
```

26.11.7 The RETAINING phrase For each supplier who supplies part P4, find another part supplied by the same supplier, and print supplier number, supplier name, and part number. For simplicity assume that each supplier that supplies part P4 does supply at least one other part.

In outline, the required procedure is as follows. Starting at part P4, we inspect each SP occurrence for that part. For each such SP occurrence, we extract SNO and SNAME from the corresponding S occurrence, and then search the SP occurrences for that supplier, looking for one linking the supplier to a part that is *not* P4. As soon as we find such an SP occurrence, we extract the relevant PNO. Thus, given the sample data of Fig. 26.1, a possible result from such a procedure would be

SNO	SNAME	PNO
S1	Smith	P1
S4	Clark	P2

The following represents a first attempt to code this problem using the COBOL DML.

```
 1 MOVE 'P4' TO PNO IN P
 2 FIND ANY P USING PNO IN P
 3 MOVE 'NO' TO EOF
 4 PERFORM UNTIL EOF = 'YES'
 5    FIND NEXT SP WITHIN P-SP
 6    IF EOF NOT = 'YES'
 7       FIND OWNER WITHIN S-SP
 8       GET S
 9       MOVE 'NO' TO FOUND
10       PERFORM UNTIL FOUND = 'YES'
11          FIND NEXT SP WITHIN S-SP
12          GET SP
13          IF PNO IN SP NOT = 'P4'
14             MOVE 'YES' TO FOUND
15          END-IF
16       END-PERFORM
17       (print SNO IN S, SNAME IN S, PNO IN SP)
18    END-IF
19 END-PERFORM
```

(In accordance with our simplifying assumption, we do not test for the end-of-set condition in the inner loop. Note that FIND NEXT is equivalent to FIND FIRST if the current record of the set is an owner.)

The code is not correct, however; it contains a logical error. Try finding the error before reading the explanation below; it is probably a good idea to "execute" the procedure on the sample data of Fig. 26.1. The result is

SNO	SNAME	PNO
S1	Smith	P1
S2	Jones	P1

It is interesting to observe that the procedure does not terminate abnormally in any way. It simply gives an answer that looks right but is in fact wrong.

The error is as follows. When the FIND in line 11 is executed, it establishes an SP occurrence as the current of run-unit. This occurrence, being the SP occurrence most recently accessed, also becomes the current record of all sets in which it participates—including, in particular, the set P-SP. This in turn makes the current P-SP occurrence the one containing this SP occurrence. Thus, when the FIND in line 5 is executed on the next iteration of the outer loop (in an attempt to find the next supplier of P4), the P-SP occurrence referenced in that statement will no longer be the one owned by

P4 (in general). To avoid this situation, the FIND in line 11 must be extended to include an appropriate RETAINING phrase:

```
FIND NEXT SP WITHIN S-SP
      RETAINING P-SP CURRENCY
```

The effect of this phrase is to prevent the updating of the currency indicator for set P-SP. In general, currency updating may be suppressed for all realms involved,[6] for the record type involved, for any or all set types involved, or for any combination of these; see [23.3] for details of syntax in each case. The only currency indicator for which updating can never be suppressed is that for "current of run-unit."

A RETAINING phrase may be specified in any FIND or STORE statement.

26.12   KEEP LISTS

■ **Let the current maximum status value for all suppliers in Paris be M. Set the status value equal to M for every supplier in Paris.**

It is clear that this problem requires two iterations over the set of Paris suppliers—one to determine the value M, and one to perform the updates. (The term "set" is used here in its usual sense, not in its special DBTG sense.) A possible procedure is as follows.

```
MOVE 'PARIS' TO CITY IN S
MOVE ZERO TO M
MOVE 'NO' TO NOTFOUND
FIND ANY S USING CITY IN S
PERFORM UNTIL NOTFOUND = 'YES'
   GET STATUS IN S
   IF STATUS IN S > M
      MOVE STATUS IN S TO M
   END-IF
   FIND DUPLICATE S USING CITY IN S
END-PERFORM

MOVE M TO STATUS IN S
MOVE 'NO' TO NOTFOUND
FIND ANY S USING CITY IN S
PERFORM UNTIL NOTFOUND = 'YES'
   MODIFY STATUS IN S
   FIND DUPLICATE S USING CITY IN S
END-PERFORM
```

---

6. Remember that a given record may belong to multiple realms. It is not possible to suppress currency updating for some realms and not others.

However, since both loops iterate over exactly the same set of records, it would be more efficient if we could somehow note the addresses (database key values) of the records found in the first loop, and then in the second loop go directly to those records via their addresses instead of having to search for them from scratch again. *Keep lists* provide a basis for such an approach. A keep list is a named object whose function is to hold an ordered list of database key values. A run-unit can have any number of keep lists; note that keep lists are not part of the database but are local to the run-unit using them. They are defined in the program's Data Division, following the statement that "invokes" the subschema. For example,

```
DB SUPPLIERS WITHIN SUPPLIERS-AND-PARTS.
LD LISTA LIMIT IS 15.
LD LISTB LIMIT IS 20.
```

During the execution of this program, keep lists LISTA and LISTB will each contain an ordered list of database key values, and will thus each designate a set of records in the database. LISTA can hold up to 15 such values and LISTB up to 20. Database key values are added to a keep list via the KEEP statement and removed via the FREE statement. These statements are discussed in detail later.

Returning now to the problem at hand, we show a solution using a keep list (LISTA, as defined above; we assume that there are no more than 15 Paris suppliers).

```
MOVE 'PARIS' TO CITY IN S
MOVE ZERO TO M
MOVE 'NO' TO NOTFOUND
FIND ANY S USING CITY IN S
PERFORM UNTIL NOTFOUND = 'YES'
   KEEP USING LISTA
   GET STATUS IN S
   IF STATUS IN S > M
      MOVE STATUS IN S TO M
   END-IF
   FIND DUPLICATE S USING CITY IN S
END-PERFORM

MOVE M TO STATUS IN S
MOVE 'NO' TO LISTEMPTY
PERFORM UNTIL LISTEMPTY = 'YES'
   FIND FIRST WITHIN LISTA
   FREE FIRST WITHIN LISTA
   MODIFY STATUS IN S
END-PERFORM
```

Each time the KEEP statement is executed, it adds the database key value for the current of run-unit (a Paris supplier in our example) to the end of the specified keep list (LISTA). On exit from the first loop, therefore, LISTA contains the database key values for all Paris suppliers, in the order in which they were found. The second loop then iterates over the records designated by these database key values; on each iteration it "finds" the record given by the first value in the list and then removes that value from the list. (Note, however, that the terminating condition for the loop is not "record not found" but "keep list empty." We do not show the details of handling this condition, but simply assume they follow our usual pattern.) As we mentioned in Section 26.11.6, the expression FIRST WITHIN LISTA is a "database key identifier."

The general format of KEEP is

```
KEEP [ database-key-identifier ] USING keep-list-name
```

where the possible formats for "database key identifier" are

```
CURRENT [ record-name ] [ WITHIN { set-name
                                   realm-name } ]
```

and

```
{ FIRST
  LAST  } WITHIN keep-list-name
```

(Vertical stacking of options within braces is intended to show that the options concerned are alternatives.) The effect of the KEEP statement is as follows. The database key value represented by the database key identifier—or, if no such identifier is specified, the database key value for the current of run-unit—is appended to the end of the specified keep list. The CURRENT form of database key identifier is as explained in Section 26.11.6; the FIRST/LAST forms should be self-explanatory. A given database key value may appear in several distinct keep lists, or several times in the same keep list, or both.

The general format of FREE is

```
FREE database-key-identifier
```

or

```
FREE ALL [ FROM keep-list-name ]
```

In the first format, if the database key identifier is one of the CURRENT forms, then the specified currency indicator is set to null; if it is one of the keep-list forms (FIRST or LAST), then the indicated value is removed from the indicated keep list. In the second format, all values in the indicated keep list (or, if the FROM phrase is omitted, in all keep lists) are removed; in other words, the indicated keep list becomes empty (or, if the FROM phrase is omitted, all keep lists become empty).

26.13 MISCELLANEOUS STATEMENTS

We conclude this chapter with a brief description of the remaining DML statements (READY and FINISH, COMMIT and ROLLBACK).

26.13.1 READY and FINISH The READY statement makes a realm available for processing—for example,

```
READY S-SP-P USAGE-MODE IS UPDATE
```

USAGE-MODE is either RETRIEVAL or UPDATE. Each of these may further be qualified as PROTECTED or EXCLUSIVE, indicating the run-unit's requirements with respect to the sharing of the realm with concurrent run-units; PROTECTED means that the realm can be shared with retrievers but not updaters, EXCLUSIVE means it cannot be shared at all.

FINISH makes an available realm unavailable—for example,

```
FINISH S-SP-P
```

26.13.2 COMMIT and ROLLBACK These two statements (neither of which has any operands) are the DBTG analogues of the DL/I SYNC and ROLB operations (Chapter 22). We discuss them here only very briefly.

The COMMIT statement establishes a "quiet point" (synchpoint) for the run-unit. (Run-unit initiation is also considered to be a quiet point.) All database changes made by the run-unit since the previous quiet point are "committed"—i.e., they are made visible to concurrent run-units, and are guaranteed never to be "rolled back" (see below). The last statement executed in the run-unit should normally be a COMMIT, since at run-unit termination the DBMS automatically rolls back any database changes made by the run-unit since its last quiet point. (This will frequently, but not invariably, be the only COMMIT in the run-unit.)

The ROLLBACK statement undoes all database changes made by the run-unit since its last quiet point. As indicated above, the DBMS automatically issues a ROLLBACK on the run-unit's behalf at run-unit termination. The run-unit itself may decide to issue ROLLBACK if, for example, it discovers some error in the middle of processing some batch of input. Note, however, that the run-unit is still executing after the ROLLBACK, and that therefore it can go on to make further updates that will not be rolled back.

EXERCISES

26.1 Using your answer to Exercise 24.3 (schema for the supplier-part-project data-base) as a basis, give DBTG solutions to the following questions (Exercises 26.1.1–26.1.9).

26.1.1 Get SNO values for suppliers who supply project J1.

26.1.2 Get SNO values for suppliers who supply project J1 with part P1.

26.1.3 Get SNO values for suppliers who supply project J1 with a red part.

26.1.4 Get PNO values for parts supplied to all projects in London.

26.1.5 Get JNO values for projects not supplied with any red part by any London supplier.

26.1.6 Get PNO values for parts supplied by at least one supplier who supplies at least one part supplied by supplier S1.

26.1.7 Get all pairs of CITY values such that a supplier in the first city supplies a project in the second city.

26.1.8 Change the color of all red parts to orange.

26.1.9 The quantity of P1 supplied to J1 by S1 is now to be supplied by S2 instead. Make all the necessary changes.

26.2 Suppose that the SPJ record in the supplier-part-project schema contains only the data-item QTY; i.e., the redundant recording of SNO, PNO, and JNO has been eliminated. It is still possible—procedurally—to maintain the desired ordering of SPJ occurrences within any given set occurrence, e.g., to maintain all SPJ occurrences for a given supplier in project number order within part number order. (Note, however, that this change will have considerable repercussions on the programs concerned with maintaining these sets.)

Suppose, therefore, that the redundancy has been eliminated but that the ordering within the sets has been maintained. What effect will this have on your solutions to Exercise 26.1? (*Note:* You will need to refer to [23.3] and [23.4] for the last of these to find out how to maintain ordering within a set when ORDER IS SORTED has not been specified.)

26.3 Consider the "managerial structure" schema in Exercise 24.2. Write statements to create an EMP occurrence for employee E15 and to place it at the appropriate point within the hierarchy. You may assume that EMP occurrences for employees E1 and E8 (see Fig. 24.7) already exist and that a LINK occurrence connecting them also exists; do not, however, assume that a LINK occurrence already exists subordinate to E8. State the assumptions you make with respect to membership class and SET SELECTION.

26.4 Consider the "parts and components" schema in Exercise 24.4.

26.4.1 For each part, print the part number, the numbers of its immediate components, and the numbers of parts for which it is an immediate component (immediate assemblies).

26.4.2 For a given part, print numbers of all its component parts, to all levels (the parts explosion problem).

Assume that the schema includes a singular set called PART-SET, containing as members all PART occurrences.

REFERENCES AND BIBLIOGRAPHY

26.1 C. W. Bachman. "The Programmer as Navigator." *CACM* **16,** No. 11 (November 1973).

Contains the lecture Bachman gave on the occasion of his receiving the 1973 Turing Award. Bachman contrasts the earlier view of data processing, in which the computer was central and data was considered as flowing through the machine as it was processed, with the more modern view, in which the database is the major resource and the computer is merely a tool for accessing it. The term "navigation" is used to describe the process of traveling through the database, following explicit paths from one record to the next in the search for some required piece of data.

Part 5
The Three Approaches Revisited

The purpose of this part of the book is to draw together some of the themes introduced in the preceding chapters and to analyze certain aspects of the three approaches in somewhat greater depth than before. Chapter 27 introduces the Unified Database Language (UDL), an application programming language that supports all three approaches and thus provides a convenient basis for comparing them at the external level. Chapter 28 then presents a detailed analysis and comparison of the relative merits of relations and networks as a basis for the conceptual level. However, we do not claim that our treatment of the material is in any way exhaustive.

27

The Unified
Database
Language

27.1 INTRODUCTION

As indicated earlier, the Unified Database Language (UDL) is a language that supports all three of the well-known approaches—relations, hierarchies, networks—in a uniform and consistent manner. It is not a self-contained language; rather, it is explicitly intended as a "tightly coupled" extension to existing programming languages (COBOL, PL/I, . . .), and can be incorporated, with suitable syntactic modifications, into a variety of such host languages. In addition to supporting all three approaches, UDL also provides both record-at-a-time and set-at-a-time operations for each of them, as we shall see. (The set level is desirable for reasons of productivity and ease of programming; the record level serves as a bridge to existing function in the host language. Also, there are some problems for which the record level is more suitable anyway [see, e.g., Exercise 27.2, second part].)

A general introduction to UDL is given in [27.1]; detailed specifications for COBOL and PL/I versions can be found in [27.3–27.6]. We shall use the PL/I version as the basis for most of our discussions. No implementation of UDL is available at the time of writing.

27.2 THE APPROACH TO COMMONALITY

UDL is designed, not only to support all three approaches, but to do so with as much commonality of language as possible across the different structures. The following observation is the key to meeting this objective.

- A relation may be considered as a special case of a hierarchy—namely, one that is "root only." Likewise, a hierarchy may be considered as a special case of a network—namely, one in which each child record has exactly one parent record.

It is by recognizing this pattern among the three data structures that the language is able to handle them in a unified fashion. Of course, the "key observation" is much too vague to be useful other than as a general statement of direction. We may make it a little more precise as follows.

1. We define a *record set* as a set of ordered pairs $\langle R_i, P_i \rangle$, such that all the records R_i in a given set are of the same type, and no two records have the same position (address) P_i.

2. The particular record set involving *all* records of a given type (in a given database) is the *baseset* for that record type.

3. A *database* is a collection of one or more basesets, together with zero or more fansets (see number 7 below).[1]

4. A *relation* is a record set for which $i \neq j$ (see number 1 above) implies $R_i \neq R_j$.

5. A *relational database* is a collection of one or more basesets, each of which is a relation.

6. A *fan* on basesets P and C, in that order, is an ordered pair $\langle$ parent, children $\rangle$, such that "parent" is a record of P and "children" is a subset (possibly empty) of the records of C.

7. A *fanset F* on basesets P and C, in that order, is a set of fans on P and C, in that order. Each record of P is the parent for exactly one fan of F (see number 6), and no other records are parents in F; each record of C is a child in at most one fan of F, and no other records are children in F. (Fansets correspond to DBTG's set types. The DBTG terms for parent and child are owner and member, respectively.)

8. A *network database* is simply a database as defined in number 3 above.

9. A *hierarchical database* is a network database that can be divided up into partitions *(hierarchies)* as follows: (a) Each baseset belongs to exactly one partition; (b) no fanset spans partitions; (c) if fanset F is defined on basesets P and C, in that order, then each record of C is a child in exactly—not "at most"—one fan of F; (d) within a partition, every baseset except one—the "root"—is the child set for exactly one fanset; (e) within a partition, there exists a path from the root to each

---

1. It may also include "sequences," which correspond to DBTG's singular sets, but we choose not to discuss these for reasons of space.

nonroot—where a path from baseset A to baseset B is a sequence of fansets F_1, F_2, . . . , F_n such that A is the parent set for F_1, the child set for F_1 is the parent set for F_2, . . . , and the child set for F_n is B.[2]

The reader is cautioned that the foregoing definitions are still very incomplete. Moreover, they do not cater for IMS's "hierarchical sequence," which is a total ordering of all records in the hierarchy, nor for those DBTG set types that have more than one type of member (child). These features are considered to be of rather minor importance. (It is true that hierarchical sequence is of more than minor importance in IMS today, but this is largely due to the way DL/I is defined. In most cases equivalent function could be provided without relying on this sequence, and indeed it is not hard to find situations where the concept is a positive hindrance.) If these restrictions are accepted, it can be seen from the definitions that, as stated earlier, a relation is a special case of a hierarchy, and a hierarchy is a special case of a network. These facts are reflected in the structure of the language we are describing. The entire language thus has an "onion-layer" structure, as illustrated in Fig. 27.1. To be specific:

- the language features required to declare a relational database are a subset of those required to declare a hierarchical database, and these in turn are a subset of those required to declare a network database;

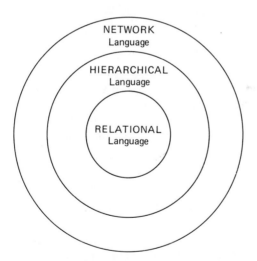

Fig. 27.1 The onion-layer language.

---

2. An IMS database consists of a single partition, in the sense of this definition. Also, IMS uses "segment" to refer to what we are calling a record.

- the language operators required to manipulate a relational database are a subset of those required to manipulate a hierarchical database, and these in turn are a subset of those required to manipulate a network database;

- (for a given operator, as applicable) the language operands required for a relational database are a subset of those required for a hierarchical database, and these in turn are a subset of those required for a network database.

27.3   DECLARATIVE LANGUAGE

The declarative features of UDL provide for a *programming language* declaration of a database—not to be confused with the "system" declaration, i.e., the declaration known to the underlying DBMS. (The system declaration is the external schema, in ANSI/SPARC terms.) Of course the two declarations must not be in conflict; at some point the UDL declaration must be mapped to the system declaration, but details of this process fall outside the UDL framework as such.[3] However, UDL programmers will *not* normally have to write UDL declarations themselves (at the very least, it should be possible to COPY or INCLUDE those declarations from some source library).[4] But conceptually the UDL declaration is part of the source program; it is used by the compiler in compiling UDL manipulative statements, it will appear in the program listing, and it must be understood by the UDL programmer.

   We present the declarative language by means of an example (based on a variation of the education database of Chapter 16). The education database contains information about an in-house company training scheme. For each training course the database contains details of all prerequisite courses for that course and all offerings of that course; and for each offering it contains details of all teachers and all students for that offering. The database also contains information about employees. A relational structure for this information is shown in Fig. 27.2; Figs. 27.3 and 27.4 show, respectively, a hierarchical and network structure for the same information. Note that two

---

3. As an analogy, consider the case of a conventional file, for which there will exist (a) a programming language declaration [in any source program referencing the file], (b) a "system declaration" [consisting, e.g., of entries in a system catalog], and (c) a mapping between the two [specified by means of job control statements].

4. In practice it may be possible to use the system declaration to generate the UDL declaration (or conversely).

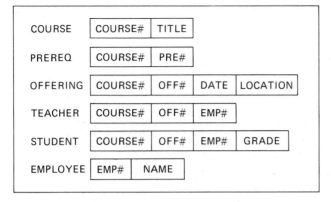

Fig. 27.2 Relational structure for the education database.

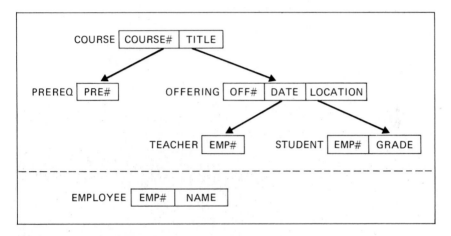

Fig. 27.3 Hierarchical structure for the education database.

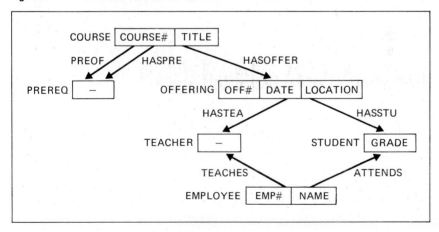

Fig. 27.4 Network structure for the education database.

hierarchies (one of them "root only") are required in Fig. 27.3 if redundancy is to be avoided.

The UDL declarations corresponding to Figs. 27.2, 27.3, and 27.4 define a *database* containing various *basesets* and *fansets*. We consider the basesets first. (For the sake of the example the basesets have all been named, although in practice names can be omitted if they are never referenced elsewhere in the program. Also, we assume for simplicity that all fields are of character string (CHAR) data type. In practice, of course, many other data types can also be supported.)

```
        DCL EDUC DATABASE
          BASESETS(
            CSET RECTYPE(1 COURSE BASED(C),
                           2 COURSE# CHAR(3),
                           2 TITLE CHAR(33))
                         UNIQUE(COURSE#),
            PSET RECTYPE(1 PREREQ BASED(P),
      **                 2 COURSE# CHAR(3),
      *                  2 PRE# CHAR(3))
      **                 UNIQUE,
            OSET RECTYPE(1 OFFERING BASED(O),
      **                 2 COURSE# CHAR(3),
                           2 OFF# CHAR(3),
                           2 DATE CHAR(6),
                           2 LOCATION CHAR(12))
      **                 UNIQUE((COURSE#,OFF#)),
            TSET RECTYPE(1 TEACHER BASED(T),
      **                 2 COURSE# CHAR(3),
      **                 2 OFF# CHAR(3),
      *                  2 EMP# CHAR(6))
      **                 UNIQUE,
            SSET RECTYPE(1 STUDENT BASED(S),
      **                 2 COURSE# CHAR(3),
      **                 2 OFF# CHAR(3),
      *                  2 EMP# CHAR(6),
                           2 GRADE CHAR(1))
      **                 UNIQUE((COURSE#,EMP#)),
            ESET RECTYPE(1 EMPLOYEE BASED(E),
                           2 EMP# CHAR(6),
                           2 NAME CHAR(18))
                         UNIQUE(EMP#)         )
```

Lines marked with a single asterisk are omitted for the network case (Fig. 27.4); lines marked with a double asterisk are omitted for both hierarchical and network cases (Figs. 27.3 and 27.4). (Such omissions will of course entail minor adjustments in the surrounding punctuation.) The omissions are possible because the relevant information is carried by the fanset structuring, instead of by foreign keys as in the relational case.[5] In the network case the omissions cause the record types PREREQ and TEACHER to contain no data fields at all (but the record types still exist, and corresponding occurrences still appear in the database).

Each record type has a *cursor* associated with it (specified by means of the BASED clause). A cursor in UDL is a "database pointer"—i.e., a pointer that points to database records. C, for example, is a cursor that will be used to point to individual COURSEs (only). Also, C serves as the default cursor for implicitly qualified references to COURSE in the manipulative part of the program (see the next section). Further cursors may be defined for a record type by means of explicit cursor declarations—for example,

```
DCL C1 CURSOR RECTYPE(COURSE);
```

Every individual cursor is constrained to a single record type.

For the relational case, each baseset has a UNIQUE clause, specifying that each record in the baseset has a unique value for the indicated field or field combination (at any given time). Omitting the field-name specification from a UNIQUE clause is equivalent to specifying the combination of all fields in the record type concerned (see, e.g., PREREQ). For the hierarchical and network cases UNIQUE is specified for COURSE and EMPLOYEE only—the other four basesets are not relations in these structures.

Any or all of the six basesets could be defined to have an *ordering:* For example, we could specify ORDER(UP COURSE#) for courses (and such an entry would imply UNIQUE(COURSE#) unless the ORDER entry also included the specification NONUNIQUE). For the relational case the only valid orderings are value-controlled and system-defined, for the other structures additional types of ordering can be specified; for details see [27.4] and [27.5]. For simplicity we have assumed default (system-defined) ordering in every case.

To impose a hierarchical or network structure on the database, the declaration must include a FANSETS specification as well as the BASESETS specification already shown. For the hierarchical structure of Fig. 27.3 this

---

5. It would be possible to include the foreign keys in the hierarchical and network cases (e.g., OFFERINGS could still include a COURSE# field), but then the fansets would become "inessential"—that is, they would be redundant from an information-bearing point of view. "Essentiality" is discussed in Chapter 28. In this chapter we do not consider inessential fansets at all.

could be as follows.

```
FANSETS
(RECORD(PREREQ)     UNDER(COURSE)      UNIQUE,
  RECORD(OFFERING)  UNDER(COURSE)      UNIQUE(OFF#),
  RECORD(TEACHER)   UNDER(OFFERING)    UNIQUE,
  RECORD(STUDENT)   UNDER(OFFERING)    UNIQUE(EMP#))
```

The four fansets are unnamed, though there is no reason why they should not be given a name if desired. The UNIQUE entries refer to uniqueness within each fan of the applicable fanset (e.g., each offering under a given course has a unique offering number). It is also possible to specify an ORDER for the children of each fan; again default (system-defined) ordering has been chosen for simplicity.

For the network structure in Fig. 27.4 the FANSETS entry could be as follows. This time the fansets have been named, although there is no reason why they should not remain unnamed if no name is required. Note, however, that the first two fansets *must* be named, since otherwise there would be no way to distinguish between them (they both consist of PREREQs under COURSEs). Note also that the UNIQUE clauses in many cases refer to fields in *ancestors* (parents, or parents of parents, or . . .) of the record type in question. Similar UNIQUE clauses could also have been specified at the baseset level, if desired.

```
FANSETS
(PREOF    RECORD(PREREQ)    UNDER(COURSE)
                            UNIQUE(COURSE# OVER PREREQ
                                           VIA HASPRE),
 HASPRE   RECORD(PREREQ)    UNDER(COURSE)
                            UNIQUE(COURSE# OVER PREREQ
                                           VIA PREOF),
 HASOFFER RECORD(OFFERING)  UNDER(COURSE)
                            UNIQUE(OFF#),
 HASTEA   RECORD(TEACHER)   UNDER(OFFERING)
                            UNIQUE(EMP# OVER TEACHER),
 HASSTU   RECORD(STUDENT)   UNDER(OFFERING)
                            UNIQUE(EMP# OVER STUDENT),
 TEACHES  RECORD(TEACHER)   UNDER(EMPLOYEE)
                            UNIQUE((COURSE# CVER TEACHER,
                                    OFF#    OVER TEACHER)),
 ATTENDS  RECORD(STUDENT)   UNDER(EMPLOYEE)
                            UNIQUE(COURSE# OVER STUDENT))
```

The fanset entries as shown are still not complete. For any given fanset, in general, the child record type may be (a) AUTOMATIC or MANUAL, and (b) FIXED, MANDATORY, or OPTIONAL, with respect to that fanset. (For a hierarchy only AUTOMATIC and FIXED are valid, and these are the defaults.) The meanings of these terms are as for DBTG.

27.4   MANIPULATIVE LANGUAGE

We base the major part of our discussion of the manipulative language on a single example, the enrollment example. Suppose that the structure GIVEN—declaration:

```
DCL 1 GIVEN,
      2 COURSE# CHAR(3),
      2 OFF#    CHAR(3),
      2 EMP#    CHAR(6);
```

contains a set of input values, representing an employee's application to enroll in a particular offering of a particular course. We wish to check that the employee has attended all appropriate prerequisite courses—if so, we will accept the application; otherwise we will reject it. We present relational, hierarchical, and network procedures for this problem, first using record-level operations and then set-level operations. (In practice our procedures should verify that the given course number, offering number, and employee number are all valid, by looking for corresponding records in the database, but for brevity we omit this step.)

Figure 27.5 shows a relational record-at-a-time solution, operating against the relational structure of Fig. 27.2 (only the PREREQ and STUDENT relations are needed for this problem). The logic of the procedure is as follows. We start by setting the flag APPLICATION_OK to true ('1'B); we then step through the PREREQs for the given course until the flag becomes false or until all such PREREQs have been processed. For each PREREQ examined, we check to see whether there exists a STUDENT record indicating that the given employee has attended the corresponding prerequisite course; if the check fails, we set APPLICATION_OK to false. If the check succeeds for all PREREQs, we enroll the employee in the speci-

```
APPLICATION_OK = '1'B;
DO PREREQ WHERE PREREQ.COURSE# = GIVEN.COURSE#
        WHILE (APPLICATION_OK);
   IF EXISTS (STUDENT WHERE STUDENT.EMP# = GIVEN.EMP#
                      & STUDENT.COURSE# = PREREQ.PRE#)
   THEN ;   /* employee has attended this prereq */
   ELSE APPLICATION_OK = '0'B;
END;
IF APPLICATION_OK THEN
   ALLOCATE STUDENT INITIAL (GIVEN, ' ');
```

Fig. 27.5 Record-at-a-time relational procedure.

fied offering by creating a new STUDENT record with the given COURSE#, OFF#, EMP#, and a blank grade. (ALLOCATE is used to create new records in the PL/I version of UDL.)

A few aspects of the code in Fig. 27.5 require some further explanation. First, the expression PREREQ WHERE . . . refers to a *set* of PREREQ records; the DO—END loop is executed once for each record in this set (assuming that the employee concerned has actually attended all prerequisite courses). On the ith iteration, cursor P (the cursor associated with PREREQs in the declaration of the PREREQ record type) is set to point to the ith PREREQ in the set. (Successful execution of a DO or FIND[6] statement causes a cursor to be set to point to a record. The cursor to be set is specified by means of the phrase "SET (cursor-name)"; if this phrase is omitted, as in Fig. 27.5, the cursor named in the declaration of the record type concerned is used by default.)

Second, we can refer to the ith PREREQ (on the ith iteration) by means of the *cursor-qualified reference* P→PREREQ. Cursor qualification is analogous to pointer qualification in PL/I today; the expression P→PREREQ is a reference to the individual PREREQ record identified by the current value of the cursor P. (It would be an error if P were not pointing at a PREREQ.) Similarly, the expression P→PREREQ.PRE# is a reference to the PRE# value within the PREREQ identified by P. The cursor-qualification portion "cursor-name→" may be omitted from such expressions, in which case (again) the cursor named in the declaration of the record type concerned is used by default; again we have made use of this default rule in the example (in the expression PREREQ.PRE# in the fifth line).

Third, the expression STUDENT WHERE . . . is also a reference to a set. The built-in function EXISTS returns the value *true* if its argument set is nonempty, *false* otherwise.

Note, incidentally, that setting a cursor to point to a record gives the programmer addressability to that record directly ("direct reference"). For example, once cursor P has been set to a particular PREREQ record, the programmer can refer directly to that record, and to fields within it, by means of cursor-qualified references in which P is the (explicit or implicit) cursor qualifier. It is *not* necessary to bring a private copy of the record into some program-local area, using some form of GET or READ statement. In other words, the database appears to the programmer as if it were all in main storage. For arguments in support of this approach see [27.1].

Now we turn to a hierarchical solution (Fig. 27.6; for the corresponding hierarchical structure, see Fig. 27.3). The logic is essentially the same as

---

6. FIND is used to locate a specific record. DO is shorthand for a sequence of FINDs.

```
APPLICATION_OK = '1'B;
FIND UNIQUE(COURSE WHERE COURSE.COURSE# = GIVEN.COURSE#);
DO PREREQ UNDER COURSE
            WHILE (APPLICATION_OK);
   IF EXISTS (STUDENT WHERE STUDENT.EMP# = GIVEN.EMP#
                & UNIQUE(COURSE.COURSE# OVER STUDENT)
                                        = PREREQ.PRE#)
   THEN ;   /* employee has attended this prereq */
   ELSE APPLICATION_OK = '0'B;
END;
IF APPLICATION_OK THEN
   DO;
        FIND UNIQUE(OFFERING UNDER COURSE
                WHERE OFFERING.OFF# = GIVEN.OFF#);
        ALLOCATE STUDENT INITIAL (GIVEN.EMP#, ' ')
                        CONNECT (UNDER OFFERING);
   END;
```

Fig. 27.6 Record-at-a-time hierarchical procedure.

before; however, for reasons of efficiency, we start by FINDing the given COURSE and setting cursor C (default) to point to it. This step is not required—we could replace each of the subsequent references to this COURSE by the entire expression "UNIQUE (COURSE WHERE . . .)," if desired. (UNIQUE is an operator whose function is to select the single record in a set containing exactly one record.) Then we iterate over the set of PREREQs under this COURSE. Note that the details of the EXISTS test have become more complex: We need to compare the COURSE# for the STUDENT under consideration with the value of PREREQ.PRE#; however, that COURSE# is no longer in the STUDENT record, as it was in the relational case, but is instead in the unique COURSE record *over* that STUDENT. Note also that, since the record to be created (ALLOCATEd) is not a root, we somehow have to identify the parent to which the new record is to be connected; in the example this is done by FINDing that parent (an OFFERING), setting cursor O (default) to point to it, and then specifying that OFFERING (via the cursor-qualified reference "O→OFFERING", with the "O→" assumed by default) in the CONNECT option of the ALLOCATE.

It can be seen that, compared with the relational procedure, the hierarchical procedure requires the following additional constructs; (a) UNDER, (b) OVER, and (c) CONNECT.

Figure 27.7 shows the corresponding network procedure. The additional constructs here, over and above those of Fig. 27.6, are (a) VIA, and (b) multiple UNDERs in the CONNECT option.

```
APPLICATION_OK = '1'B;
FIND UNIQUE(COURSE WHERE COURSE.COURSE# = GIVEN.COURSE#);
DO PREREQ UNDER COURSE VIA HASPRE
                    WHILE (APPLICATION_OK);
   IF EXISTS (STUDENT WHERE
                      UNIQUE(EMPLOYEE.EMP# OVER STUDENT)
                                          = GIVEN.EMP#
                    & UNIQUE(COURSE.COURSE# OVER STUDENT)
                                          =
                      UNIQUE(COURSE.COURSE# OVER PREREQ
                                            VIA PREOF))
      THEN ;  /* employee has attended this prereq */
      ELSE APPLICATION_OK = '0'B;
END;
IF APPLICATION_OK THEN
      DO;
         FIND UNIQUE(OFFERING UNDER COURSE
                      WHERE OFFERING.OFF# = GIVEN.OFF#);
         FIND UNIQUE(EMPLOYEE
                      WHERE EMPLOYEE.EMP# = GIVEN.EMP#);
         ALLOCATE   STUDENT INITIAL (' ')
                        CONNECT (UNDER OFFERING,
                                 UNDER EMPLOYEE);
      END;
```

Fig. 27.7 Record-at-a-time network procedure.

We also give a DBTG solution to the problem (Fig. 27.8). For this procedure we assume that SET SELECTION for both ATTENDS and HAS-STU is BY APPLICATION. It is interesting to compare Figs. 27.7 and 27.8, since they both represent record-at-a-time network procedures for the same problem. Admittedly, Fig. 27.7 uses PL/I whereas Fig. 27.8 uses COBOL, but this fact alone does not account for the differences between them. Figure 27.9 summarizes these differences, and also the differences between the two network solutions and the relational and hierarchical solutions shown earlier. (All figures are based on COBOL versions of the examples [shown for reference in the answer section at the back of the book], though actually the UDL figures are almost independent of whether PL/I or COBOL is the host language. Note, however, that the definition of "token" is slightly arbitrary, so that the token counts shown should be construed only as rough measures of relative procedure size, not as absolute figures of merit. The DBTG count does not include USE procedures for other exceptions, which are required but are not shown in Fig. 27.8.)

Incidentally, one of the primary reasons for the complexity of the DBTG solution is that the programmer has to handle the central existence test by means of procedural code. We note that there are at least two strategies for performing this test: (a) Check all student records for the given em-

```
DECLARATIVES.
USE FOR DB-EXCEPTION ON '0502100'.
EOF-PROC.
  MOVE 'YES' TO EOF.
   .....
  END DECLARATIVES.

  MOVE 'YES' TO APPLICATION-OK
  MOVE COURSENO OF GIVEN TO COURSENO IN COURSE
  FIND ANY COURSE USING COURSENO IN COURSE
  MOVE EMPNO OF GIVEN TO EMPNO IN EMPLOYEE
  FIND ANY EMPLOYEE USING EMPNO IN EMPLOYEE
  MOVE 'NO' TO EOF
  PERFORM UNTIL EOF = 'YES'
              OR APPLICATION-OK = 'NO'
    FIND NEXT PREREQ WITHIN HASPRE
    IF EOF = 'NO'
      FIND OWNER WITHIN PREOF
          RETAINING HASPRE, RECORD CURRENCY
      GET COURSENO IN COURSE
      MOVE COURSENO IN COURSE TO TEMP
      MOVE 'NO' TO APPLICATION-OK
      FIND CURRENT EMPLOYEE
      PERFORM UNTIL EOF = 'YES'
        FIND NEXT STUDENT WITHIN ATTENDS
        IF EOF = 'NO'
          FIND OWNER WITHIN HASSTU
          FIND OWNER WITHIN HASOFFER
              RETAINING HASPRE, RECORD CURRENCY
          GET COURSENO IN COURSE
          IF COURSENO IN COURSE = TEMP
            MOVE 'YES' TO APPLICATION-OK
            MOVE 'YES' TO EOF
          END-IF
        END-IF
      END-PERFORM
      MOVE 'NO' TO EOF
    END-IF
  END-PERFORM
  IF APPLICATION-OK = 'YES'
    FIND CURRENT COURSE
    MOVE OFFNO OF GIVEN TO OFFNO IN OFFERING
    FIND OFFERING WITHIN HASOFFER CURRENT USING OFFNO IN OFFERING
    FIND CURRENT EMPLOYEE
    MOVE SPACES TO GRADE IN STUDENT
    STORE STUDENT
  END-IF
```

Fig. 27.8 DBTG procedure.

ployee to see if any of them is for the current prerequisite course; (b) check all student records for the current prerequisite course to see if any of them is for the given employee. Which strategy is more efficient will depend on many parameters, including in particular the average number of students

	Relational	Hierarchical	Network	DBTG
Database as seen by user	6 basesets	6 basesets + 4 fansets	6 basesets + 7 fansets (2 names nec.)	6 record types + 7 (named) "sets"
Number of tokens in procedure (Note 1)	48	71	102	189
Manipulative language constructs (Note 2)	FIND WHERE	FIND WHERE FIND UNDER FIND OVER	FIND WHERE FIND UNDER [VIA] FIND OVER [VIA]	FIND ANY FIND NEXT WITHIN FIND OWNER WITHIN FIND CURRENT FIND WITHIN USING − SET SELECTION GET RETAIN CURRENCY
	ALLOCATE	ALLOCATE [CONNECT]	ALLOCATE [CONNECT [VIA]]	STORE − SET SELECTION

Note 1. A token is a "lexical" unit in the source program; e.g., "MOVE 'NO' TO EOF" consists of four tokens. All figures are based on COBOL.

Note 2. DO (PERFORM in COBOL) is equivalent to a sequence of FIND WHERE operators.

Fig. 27.9 Some comparisons.

per course and the average number of courses attended per employee. The choice of strategy is left to the system in UDL but must be made by the programmer in DBTG.

The reader's attention is also drawn to the complexities caused by the notion of currency in the DBTG procedure. Note in particular the necessity for the two RETAINING phrases ("RETAINING HASPRE, RECORD CURRENCY" means "do not update the currency indicators for the HASPRE fanset or for the record type that is to be found"). It is instructive to work through the entire procedure in detail. Finally, we note that matters would be considerably worse if STUDENTs were to be maintained in course number order within the ATTENDS fanset and in employee number order within the HASSTU fanset (this [reasonable] requirement can be specified in the declarations and handled by the system in UDL, but must be dealt with procedurally in DBTG).

We now present (Figs. 27.10, 27.11, and 27.12) "set level" UDL solutions to the enrollment problem. (We place "set-level" in quotes because actually the boundary between set- and record-levels is somewhat arbi-

trary.) Each of these solutions consists of a single IF statement. The basic
logic in each case is as follows: If there exists a prerequisite for the given
course that the given employee has not attended, then reject the application;
otherwise, perform the enrollment. We observe once again that the relational language features are a subset of the hierarchical features, and these
in turn are a subset of the network features.

We remark also that set-level procedures are not always easier to write
or read than record-level procedures!—though perhaps the enrollment
problem is unusual in this regard; earlier in the book we have seen plenty of
examples in which a set-level solution clearly *is* easier to understand. In any
case, even for the enrollment problem, the set-level solutions are at least no
worse than the record-level versions; and set-level operations do generally
offer advantages over record-level operations—in particular, the advantage
that the system has more freedom to choose a method for implementing
such operations (e.g., in selecting access paths). We note too that one particular implementation that is always available involves simply translating
the given set-level operation into an equivalent sequence of record-level
operations.

```
IF EXISTS (PREREQ WHERE PREREQ.COURSE# = GIVEN.COURSE#
            & ⌐ EXISTS (STUDENT WHERE
                            STUDENT.EMP# = GIVEN.EMP#
                          & STUDENT.COURSE# = PREREQ.PRE#))
THEN ; /* employee does not have some prereq */
ELSE ALLOCATE STUDENT INITIAL (GIVEN, ' ');
```

Fig. 27.10 Set-at-a-time relational procedure.

```
IF EXISTS (PREREQ UNDER
        UNIQUE (COURSE WHERE COURSE.COURSE# = GIVEN.COURSE#)
        WHERE ⌐ EXISTS (STUDENT WHERE
                            STUDENT.EMP# = GIVEN.EMP#
                          & UNIQUE (COURSE.COURSE# OVER STUDENT)
                                    = PREREQ.PRE#))
THEN ; /* employee does not have some prereq */
ELSE
        ALLOCATE STUDENT INITIAL (GIVEN.EMP#, ' ')
        CONNECT (UNDER UNIQUE (OFFERING UNDER
                        UNIQUE (COURSE WHERE
                                COURSE.COURSE# = GIVEN.COURSE#)
                        WHERE OFFERING.OFF# = GIVEN.OFF#));
```

Fig. 27.11 Set-at-a-time hierarchical procedure.

```
IF EXISTS (PREREQ UNDER
      UNIQUE (COURSE WHERE COURSE.COURSE# = GIVEN.COURSE#)
                                              VIA HASPRE
      WHERE ¬ EXISTS (STUDENT WHERE
                        UNIQUE (EMPLOYEE.EMP# OVER STUDENT)
                                    = GIVEN.EMP#
                      & UNIQUE (COURSE.COURSE# OVER STUDENT)
                                    =
                        UNIQUE (COURSE.COURSE# OVER PREREQ
                                              VIA PREOF)))
THEN ; /* employee does not have some prereq */
ELSE
      ALLOCATE STUDENT INITIAL (' ')
      CONNECT (UNDER UNIQUE (OFFERING UNDER
                      UNIQUE (COURSE WHERE
                              COURSE.COURSE# = GIVEN.COURSE#)
                      WHERE OFFERING.OFF# = GIVEN.OFF#),
                UNDER UNIQUE (EMPLOYEE
                      WHERE EMPLOYEE.EMP# = GIVEN.EMP#));
```

Fig. 27.12 Set-at-a-time network procedure.

27.5 ADDITIONAL FEATURES

In this section we briefly describe some of the features of the manipulative language not already discussed in Section 27.4.

Bound cursors We have already seen several examples of *set references* —i.e., expressions representing sets of records. Suppose we need to refer to the set of STUDENTs having a GRADE of 'A', which can be written

```
S→STUDENT WHERE S→STUDENT.GRADE = 'A'
```

—or, more intuitively, if S is the default cursor for STUDENT and if GRADE (unqualified) is unambiguous:

```
STUDENT WHERE GRADE = 'A'
```

Either way, the programmer can think of this expression as being evaluated as follows: Cursor S is used to run through the entire baseset of STUDENTs, one record at a time, in some sequence, and records not satisfying the predicate (the condition following the WHERE) are eliminated. However, cursor S itself is not really used; a system-supplied cursor is used instead. In fact the current value of cursor S is irrelevant, and is not changed; the symbol "S" is being used merely as a syntactic device to link field references in the predicate to specific instances of the record type concerned. S here is an example of a *bound cursor*.

As another example, the expression

```
S1→STUDENT WHERE S1→STUDENT.GRADE = S2→STUDENT.GRADE
```

is a reference to the set of students having the same grade as the student selected by cursor S2. Cursor S2 here is performing its normal selection function; cursor S1, by contrast, is acting as a bound cursor.

Set expressions In addition to expressions that designate sets of records as declared, the language also provides expressions representing projections and joins of such records. Some examples (all based on the relational version of the database) are as follows.

1. Employee numbers for students with a grade of 'A':

```
STUDENT.EMP# WHERE GRADE = 'A'
```

2. As (1), but with duplicates eliminated:

```
DISTINCT (STUDENT.EMP# WHERE GRADE = 'A')
```

3. Join of teachers and students on employee number:

```
(TEACHER, STUDENT) WHERE TEACHER.EMP# = STUDENT.EMP#
```

4. Teacher and student employee number pairs for teachers and students of the same offering of the same course (with duplicates eliminated):

```
DISTINCT ((TEACHER.EMP#, STUDENT.EMP#)
                WHERE TEACHER.COURSE# = STUDENT.COURSE#
                    & TEACHER.OFF#    = STUDENT.OFF#)
```

MATCHING MATCHING is a convenient shorthand for a commonly occurring form of WHERE. The DO statement in Fig. 27.5 (the relational record-level solution) could equivalently have been written

```
DO PREREQ MATCHING GIVEN;
```

MATCHING is defined to be equivalent to a WHERE clause specifying an ANDed set of equality comparisons between all pairs of fields having the same name in the two structures (or records) concerned. In the example the two structures are PREREQ and GIVEN, and the only pair of fields having the same name is the pair PREREQ.COURSE# and GIVEN.COURSE#.

It is also possible to specify the matching fields explicitly, by means of an ON clause. For example, the expression

```
STUDENT MATCHING TEACHER ON (COURSE#,OFF#)
```

is equivalent to the expression

```
STUDENT WHERE STUDENT.COURSE# = TEACHER.COURSE#
             & STUDENT.OFF#   = TEACHER.OFF#
```

Note that the comparison "STUDENT.EMP# = TEACHER.EMP# does *not* appear in the implied WHERE clause, even though STUDENT and TEACHER both include a field called EMP#. If ON is specified, the set of comparisons is restricted to the nominated fields. Omitting ON is equivalent to specifying an ON clause listing all field-names that are common to the two structures (or records) concerned.

A set expression can include both WHERE and MATCHING.

FOUND/NOTFOUND   The FIND statement can optionally include a FOUND/NOTFOUND specification (analogous to THEN/ELSE in an IF statement). For example,

```
FIND UNIQUE (COURSE MATCHING GIVEN)
FOUND    found-unit
NOTFOUND  notfound-unit
```

The found-unit and notfound-unit are each "executable-units," exactly as in IF—THEN—ELSE. The found-unit is executed if and only if the desired COURSE is found; the notfound-unit is executed if and only if the desired COURSE is not found. If FOUND/NOTFOUND is not specified and the desired record is not found, the NOTFOUND exception condition is raised (see "Exception handling" below).

Assignment   As pointed out earlier, *retrieval,* in the sense of bringing a copy of a record into some program-local area, is not usually necessary, because of the direct reference feature. On the rare occasions when it is needed, however, a record, or a field within a record, can be "retrieved" using an ordinary assignment statement—for example,

```
ASSIGN S→STUDENT TO STUDENT_AREA;
```

(for reasons beyond the scope of this chapter we use a keyword form of the assignment statement instead of the more familiar "target = expression;" form). Similarly, a record, or a field within a record, is *updated* by means of an assignment statement—for example,

```
ASSIGN STUDENT_AREA.GRADE TO S→STUDENT.GRADE;
```

FREE   Just as ALLOCATE is used to create new records (in PL/I), so FREE is used to destroy them—for example,

```
FREE S→STUDENT;
```

Cursor S is advanced to "preselect" the next STUDENT in sequence, so that a FIND NEXT following the FREE will operate as intuition would suggest—that is, it will select the STUDENT following the position of the one just FREEd. For more details see [27.1].

Fanset operations   CONNECT, DISCONNECT, and RECONNECT statements are provided to create, destroy, and modify the link between a given child record and a given parent record (via a given fanset). For example (assuming for the moment that STUDENTs are MANUAL and OPTIONAL with respect to OFFERINGs),

```
CONNECT S→STUDENT UNDER O→OFFERING;

DISCONNECT S→STUDENT FROM OFFERING;

RECONNECT S→STUDENT UNDER O→OFFERING;
```

Note that UNDER specifies the relevant parent record *occurrence* (CONNECT, RECONNECT), whereas FROM specifies the corresponding parent *type* (DISCONNECT). Each of these statements may additionally include a VIA option to specify the relevant fanset, if necessary or desired.

Transaction handling   A COMMIT statement is provided to establish a synchpoint and commit database updates. A ROLLBACK statement is provided to back out uncommitted updates. Program termination causes an implicit COMMIT or an implicit ROLLBACK (according as that termination is normal or abnormal).

Exception handling   Several exceptional conditions are defined in the language. In the PL/I version these are handled by means of various ON-conditions: NOTFOUND, NONUNIQUE, ADDREX (addressing exception—raised if, for example, the cursor in a cursor-qualified reference is not pointing to a record), and DBERROR (a catchall). Associated debugging functions, such as ONRECTYPE, are also provided. (ONRECTYPE, for example, has as its value the name of the record type on which the most recent exception occurred.) System action for DBERROR is to raise ERROR. System action for the other conditions is to raise DBERROR. The programmer is thus able to trap exceptions at a variety of different levels.

Built-in functions   In addition to EXISTS, the debugging functions (ONRECTYPE, etc.), and the "built-in references" such as UNIQUE, UDL provides functions to count the number of records in a set (SETCOUNT), to find the greatest value in a set (SETMAX), to eliminate duplicates from a set (DISTINCT), and so on.

27.6 CONCLUSION

The reader will appreciate that we have done little more than scratch the surface of UDL in this short description. However, sufficient examples have been given to illustrate the onion-layer structure and to demonstrate that both the declarative and the manipulative portions of the language necessarily become more complex as the database structure becomes more complex. We have also drawn a comparison between the proposed language and DBTG (which is of course a record-at-a-time network system). We conclude with the following observation: Although the relational approach seems the best candidate as a basis for a general-purpose database language in the long term, there is no question that networks and hierarchies will continue to be around for some time yet, for the very good reason that there is already a lot of investment in such systems. In other words, all three approaches will be used at the *external* level for some time to come. (We emphasize that in this chapter we are considering the external level only.) Given this fact, the idea of using a single, well-structured language as a common programming interface to a variety of distinct systems seems a very attractive one; it could greatly simplify problems of communication between users of different systems, it could ease education problems, and it could assist with migration of programs and programmers from one system to another (including, in particular, migration from a current system to some future system, say a relational system). Note, however, that we are *not* suggesting that (say) the relational portions of UDL should be implemented as an interface to (say) a hierarchical system such as IMS. What we are suggesting is that, for example, a relational UDL implementation (on a relational system) and a hierarchical implementation (on a hierarchical system) would provide a useful degree of commonality at the programming language level.

EXERCISES

27.1 We give UDL declarations (in outline) for a relational version and a network version of the suppliers-parts-projects database.

```
DCL RSPJ DATABASE     /* relational */
    BASESETS
    (SSET RECTYPE (1 S BASED(CS), 2 S# ...) UNIQUE(S#),
     PSET RECTYPE (1 P BASED(CP), 2 P# ...) UNIQUE(P#),
     JSET RECTYPE (1 J BASED(CJ), 2 J# ...) UNIQUE(J#),
     SPJSET RECTYPE (1 SPJ BASED(CSPJ),
                     2 (S# ..., P# ..., J# ..., QTY ...))
                                  UNIQUE ((S#,P#,J#)));
```

```
DCL NSPJ DATABASE    /* network */
   BASESETS
   (SSET RECTYPE (1 S BASED(CS), 2 S# ...) UNIQUE(S#),
    PSET RECTYPE (1 P BASED(CP), 2 P# ...) UNIQUE(P#),
    JSET RECTYPE (1 J BASED(CJ), 2 J# ...) UNIQUE(J#),
    SPJSET RECTYPE (1 SPJ BASED(CSPJ), 2  QTY ...)
                                    UNIQUE ((S# OVER SPJ,
                                             P# OVER SPJ,
                                             J# OVER SPJ)))

   FANSETS
   (S_SPJ RECORD(SPJ) UNDER(S)
                      UNIQUE((P# OVER SPJ, J# OVER SPJ)),
    P_SPJ RECORD(SPJ) UNDER(P)
                      UNIQUE((J# OVER SPJ, S# OVER SPJ)),
    J_SPJ RECORD(SPJ) UNDER(J)
                      UNIQUE((S# OVER SPJ, P# OVER SPJ)));
```

Using these declarations, give UDL solutions (both relational and network) to Exercises 26.1.1–26.1.9. For the network versions, note carefully that fansets S_SPJ, P_SPJ, J_SPJ are *essential* in the UDL network structure defined above (record SPJ does not include fields S#, P#, J#).

27.2 We give UDL declarations (in outline) for a relational version and a network version of the parts-and-components database.

```
DCL RPC DATABASE       /* relational */
   BASESETS
   (PART_SET RECTYPE (1 PART BASED(P), 2 P# ...)
                                UNIQUE(P#),
    COMPONENT_SET RECTYPE (1  COMPONENT BASED(C),
                           2  (MAJORP# ...,
                               MINORP# ...,
                               QTY ...))
                      UNIQUE((MAJORP#, MINORP#)));

DCL NPC DATABASE       /* network */
   BASESETS
   (PART_SET RECTYPE (1 PART BASED(P), 2 P# ...)
                                UNIQUE(P#),
    COMPONENT_SET RECTYPE (1  COMPONENT BASED(C),
                           2  QTY ...))
   FANSETS
   (WU RECORD(COMPONENT) UNDER(PART)
                UNIQUE(P# OVER COMPONENT VIA BM),
    BM RECORD(COMPONENT) UNDER(PART)
                UNIQUE(P# OVER COMPONENT VIA WU));
```

Using these declarations, give UDL solutions (both relational and network) to Exercises 26.4.1 and 26.4.2. For the second of these you may like to compare your solution with the SQL version (Exercise 8.4).

27.3 Give a UDL solution to the problem in Section 18.6 (given a course number, print a report listing all offerings of all prerequisite courses of that given course).

27.4 Consider the three record-at-a-time solutions given for the enrollment problem. For each one:

   a) Design a storage structure to represent the database, mapping each record to a single stored record but using indexes, pointer chains, etc., as you feel appropriate.

   b) Derive expressions representing the amount of storage space each of your solutions to (a) will require. State any assumptions you make.

   c) Derive expressions representing the number of stored records (both data records and index records) accessed in executing the three enrollment procedures. Again, state any assumptions you make.

REFERENCES AND BIBLIOGRAPHY

27.1 C. J. Date. "An Introduction to the Unified Database Language (UDL)." *Proc. 6th International Conference on Very Large Data Bases* (October 1980).

27.2 C. J. Date. "An Architecture for High-Level Language Database Extensions." *Proc. 1976 ACM SIGMOD International Conference on Management of Data* (June 1976).

   An earlier version of [27.1].

27.3 C. J. Date. "An Architecture for High-Level Language Database Extensions: PL/I Version. Part I: Record-at-a-time Operations." *Proc. SEAS Anniversary Meeting* (September 1977).

27.4 C. J. Date. "An Architecture for High-Level Language Database Extensions (Unified Database Language—UDL): PL/I Version." IBM Technical Report TR 03.099 (June 1980).

   A major revision of [27.3].

27.5 C. J. Date. "An Architecture for High-Level Language Database Extensions (Unified Database Language—UDL): COBOL Version" (December 1978).

27.6 C. J. Date. Relational subset of [27.4] (April 1979).

27.7 C. J. Date. Relational subset of [27.5] (April 1979).

27.8 SHARE DBMS Language Task Force. "An Evaluation of Three COBOL Data Base Languages—UDL, SQL, and CODASYL." *Proc. SHARE 53* (August 1979).

   In the opinion of the Task Force, any COBOL database language should:

- be a natural extension of COBOL;
- be easy to learn;
- conform to a standard;
- support relations, hierarchies, and networks;
- promote quality programming;
- be usable as a query language;

- provide set-level access;
- have a stable definition;
- increase programmer productivity;
- be data independent;
- reflect user input in its design.

27.9 M. H. H. Huits. "Requirements for Languages in Data Base Systems." In [24.3].

Includes some good examples of problems for which record-at-a-time solutions are more appropriate than set-at-a-time solutions.

28

A Comparison of the Relational and Network Approaches

28.1 INTRODUCTION

In this chapter we consider the relative merits of the relational and network approaches as a basis for the conceptual level of the system. (We do not deal explicitly with hierarchies, treating them for the purposes of this discussion as merely a restricted form of network.) We concentrate on relations and networks because they are clearly in direct competition as candidates for this role. However, we certainly do not mean to suggest that they are the *only* candidates. Indeed, there is widespread agreement that neither approach is adequate in itself for the task, but rather that some extended formalism, such as Chen's "entity-relationship model" [28.20], is needed. Notwithstanding this fact, it is still useful to examine the two approaches in some depth, because most such extended formalisms have their basis in one or the other.

Although our discussion is couched for the most part in terms of the conceptual level, several of the points made are also relevant at the external level.

28.2 THE CONCEPTUAL LEVEL

The conceptual schema is intended to serve as a solid and enduring foundation for the overall operation of the enterprise. It consists of an abstract description of the various types of entity that need to be processed in any way by that enterprise. By "solid and enduring" we mean that the schema should be *stable*. It should certainly not be dependent on the quirks of any individual DBMS (it may even have to survive the replacement of one underlying DBMS by another). More specifically, a given entry, say the description of a particular type of entity, should never have to change once it has been incorporated into the conceptual schema, *unless* a change occurs in the portion of the real world that that particular entry describes. If the conceptual schema is not stable in this sense, then applications and external schemas are likely to be unstable too, leading to user confusion, an increased need for reprogramming, and an increased chance of error.

To repeat: The conceptual schema should not have to be changed unless some adjustment in the real world requires some definition to be adjusted too, so that it may continue to reflect reality. Of course, one particular type of adjustment that is frequently necessary is the *expansion* of the conceptual schema to reflect a larger portion of reality; see the discussion of growth in the conceptual schema in Section 9.4. Such expansion does not conflict with the basic objective of stability, however. As an example of a change in the real world that would require alteration to, rather than merely expansion of, the conceptual schema, consider the following change in the rule associating employees and departments: Under the old rule each employee had to belong to exactly one department; under the new rule an employee may belong to any number of departments simultaneously.

Designing the conceptual schema is without any doubt the most important single step in the installation of a database system. Ideally it should be the *first* such step (though, as indicated in Section 6.4, it may be possible to perform the design in a piecemeal manner in some situations). In any case it should certainly not be unduly influenced by considerations of how the data is to be physically stored and accessed, on the one hand, or how it is going to be used in specific applications, on the other. In other words, the design of the conceptual schema should be undertaken quite independently of the design of the associated internal schema and external schemas—for if it is not, there is a danger that the design will not be stable but will continually be undergoing revisions, with consequent impacts on other components of the system. (Alternatively, if such revisions are not made, the installation will find itself locked into a conceptual schema that becomes increasingly unsuitable as more and more applications are brought into the system.)

Given the database management systems of today, however, the notion of designing the conceptual schema independently of the internal and external schemas is something of an ideal. Most systems currently marketed severely constrain the set of possibilities available to the designer at the conceptual level. Indeed, as we indicated in Chapter 1, most existing installations do not really have a conceptual schema at all; today's designers simply provide an internal schema and a set of external schemas, and the "conceptual schema" is then effectively nothing more than the union of all the external schemas. (Moreover, the amount of significant variation possible between the external and internal levels is usually quite limited.) But the fact that this is the way design has traditionally been done does not mean it is the right way. Experience has shown that the problems mentioned earlier (instability, unsuitability for new applications) do tend to arise after installations have been running for a while [1.12].

We would like to suggest, therefore, that it is still important to construct a conceptual schema, at a suitable level of abstraction, even if the database management system available is such that this schema will exist only in manuscript or typescript form. If the system does not support a true conceptual level, the schema designer—presumably the DBA—will then have to perform a manual mapping of the conceptual design into a form that the system does support. If the system does support the design directly, of course, so much the better. Either way, the enterprise will find itself immeasurably better off for having a self-contained, succinct description of its operational data, expressed ideally in terms that—albeit precise—are human-oriented rather than machine-oriented. (It is becoming increasingly recognized that the biggest obstacle of all to progress in the use of computers is the difficulty of *communication* among all the many people involved—end-users, enterprise management, programming specialists, the database administrator, and so on [26.1]. The role of the conceptual schema in overcoming such problems is obvious.)

We also express the hope that database management systems of the future will cater for conceptual schemas of an adequate level of abstraction, thus more directly supporting the independent design technique advocated above. At the same time, of course, the system should be able to support a wide variety of external schemas, and should do so, moreover, with an efficiency at least comparable to that of today's systems. For the remainder of this chapter we shall assume that such a system can and eventually will exist.

As we indicated at the beginning of the section, the conceptual schema should not be dependent on the peculiarities of any specific system. However, it must be based on *some* view of data, such as relations or networks. In the next section we describe some properties that the conceptual view of data should possess; then, in Sections 28.4 and 28.5, we examine relations and networks in turn to see to what extent they possess these desirable properties.

28.3 SOME CRITERIA FOR THE CONCEPTUAL SCHEMA

The two most important properties that the conceptual view of data should possess are the following.

1. It should be as simple as is practically possible.
2. It should have a sound theoretical base.

We consider each of these in turn.

Simplicity

When we say that the conceptual view should be simple, we really mean that it should be easy to understand and easy to manipulate. We do not necessarily mean that it should be minimal in any sense. (An analogy from arithmetic may help to clarify the distinction. When we represent a number in the familiar positional notation, we generally use decimal as the base, not binary, even though binary is logically sufficient. Binary is minimal, but decimal is simpler [more usable] from the user's point of view.)

The requirement that the view be easy to understand should not require any justification. Comprehensibility is obviously crucial if the communication problem mentioned earlier is to be addressed. Of course there are many aspects to comprehensibility; we list some of them below.

- The number of basic constructs should be small.

The conceptual schema will be built out of a set of basic building blocks. It is obviously desirable that the number of distinct building blocks be kept to a manageable and convenient size. (As already indicated, however, we certainly do not want to sacrifice *conciseness* in the interests of this objective. The key word here is "convenient.")

- Distinct concepts should be cleanly separated.

An individual construct (building block) should not "bundle together" two or more distinct concepts; for if it does, it becomes difficult to tell exactly what purpose that construct is serving in a given situation (and it may be used for a purpose for which it was not intended).

- Symmetry should be preserved.

It should not be necessary to represent a naturally symmetric structure in an asymmetric manner. Symmetry is important in aiding understanding. To quote Polya (writing in a different context): "Try to treat symmetrically what is symmetrical, and do not destroy wantonly any natural symmetry" [28.19].

- Redundancy should be carefully controlled.

Redundancy in the sense of the same fact appearing in two places should probably not be allowed at all. (By "fact" we mean the association between a given entity and some property of that entity—e.g., the association between an item and its price.) However, there are other types of redundancy [4.1] that cannot be eliminated, in general. In such cases the conceptual schema should include a statement of exactly what the redundancy is; see the discussion of controlled redundancy in Chapter 1. (We note in passing that we currently do not seem to have a good definition of redundancy; we have only a somewhat vague idea that it is bad in some situations and good in others.)

Likewise, the requirement that the conceptual view be easy to manipulate should also require little justification. Although users will not actually operate directly at the conceptual level, they must understand what operations are possible at that level, since these operations will be used to model the transactions of the enterprise. In an implementation in which the user's view is the same as or close to the conceptual view, of course, it becomes even more imperative that these operations be easy to understand. To paraphrase [28.3]: "The reader is cautioned to avoid comparing different approaches solely on the basis of differences in the data structures they support. An adequate appreciation of the differences must entail consideration of the operator types also."

We list some aspects that will help to make the data easy to manipulate. No additional comment is necessary in the first case.

- The number of operator types should be small.
- Very high-level (i.e., powerful) operators should be available.

It goes without saying that the operators must be precisely defined. However, it is also desirable that operators should exist at a level close to the imprecise, but very high-level, "operators" used in natural language (consider, for example, the transaction "Increase all programmers' salaries by ten percent"). Ideally each transaction would be expressible at the conceptual level in one and only one way. The burden of irrelevant decisions (concerning access strategies, for example) should be removed from the user.

- Symmetry should be preserved.

Transactions that have a naturally symmetric formulation should be expressible symmetrically in the manipulative language. For example, the queries "List all employees working for department D3" and "List all employees earning a salary of 30,000 dollars" should have similar representations.

Theoretical Base

Given the importance of the conceptual level, it is absolutely essential that it be founded on a solid base of theory [28.17]. Its behavior must be totally predictable and, to the greatest extent possible, should accord with users' intuitive expectations. Surprises, especially unpleasant ones, simply cannot be tolerated. Whatever formal system we choose as a basis for the conceptual level, we *must* be fully aware of exactly what is and is not possible in that system. Specifically, we should be familiar with all potential pitfalls and problem areas, and we should be certain that ambiguity and paradox cannot occur. In short, we should know exactly what we are doing.

28.4 THE RELATIONAL APPROACH

Let us now see how the relational approach measures up to the requirements of the previous section. First, there can be little doubt that relations are easy to understand. The number of basic data constructs is *one,* namely, the relation (or table) itself; all information in the database is represented using just this one construct, and moreover this one construct is both simple and highly familiar—people have been using tables for centuries. (We remind the user that the schema itself, and all other information in the dictionary, can also be represented in relational form, as mentioned in Chapter 7.) As for keeping distinct concepts separate, there seem to be few, if any, instances of "bundling" in the relational approach.[1] Indeed, it is significant that most of the research since 1970 into such areas as concurrency, locking, security, integrity, view definition, and so on, has taken the relational approach as a starting point precisely *because* it provides a clean conceptual base. And as for symmetry and nonredundancy, the relational approach again seems to meet the requirements. [In the latter case the normalization discipline will guarantee that the same "fact" will not appear in two places.]

   Relations are also easy to manipulate; numerous examples from this book and elsewhere can be cited in support of this statement. Moreover, the statement is true at both the tuple-at-a-time and set-at-a-time levels; in other words, very high-level operators are available, as well as the more familiar low-level operators. (The very high-level operators are those of the relational algebra and equivalent languages.) The number of distinct operators in any given language is small because there is only one type of data construct to deal with; essentially we need just one operator for each of the four basic functions retrieve, insert, delete, update. If we also consider—as we must—the operators needed for authorization and integrity purposes, we again find that a single set of operators is all that is necessary, and for the same reason. Last, relational languages generally provide what Codd [4.1] calls "symmetric exploitation": the ability to access a relation by specifying

---

1. Some writers would argue that *n*-ary relations do bundle together several distinct *facts,* and that the purposes of the conceptual level are better served by an equivalent collection of binary relations. There is some merit in this position. However, we consider the distinction between the *n*-ary and binary relational views as being far less significant than that between relational views of any kind and the DBTG-like network view.

known values for any combination of its attributes, seeking the (unknown) values for its other attributes. Symmetric exploitation is possible because all information is represented in the same uniform way.

As for the question of an underlying theory, the relational approach is not only soundly based on certain aspects of mathematical set theory, it also possesses a considerable body of theory in its own right aimed specifically at its application to database problems. The normalization theory discussed in Chapter 14 provides a rigorous set of guidelines for the design of a relational schema. The theory of relational completeness provides a valuable tool for measuring the selective power of a language and for comparing different candidate languages (indeed, now that the concept has been defined, it is incumbent on the designer of any such language either to make that language complete in this sense or else to justify each and every departure from such an objective). Under the heading of theory we may also mention *closure* (discussed in Chapter 12): The result of any operation of the relational algebra, or equivalent language, is itself a relation, which allows us to write nested expressions.[2] The closure property is particularly important in the provision of support for the nonprogramming user [28.3].

28.5 THE NETWORK APPROACH

Before discussing networks in any detail, we first introduce the important notion of *essentiality* [28.3]. The declaration D of some data construct in a schema S is *essential* if there exists an instantaneous database B conforming to S such that removal from B of the construct defined by D would cause a loss of information from B. By saying that a loss of information would occur, we mean, precisely, that some relation would no longer be derivable.

We present some examples to illustrate this idea, using a simplified form of the declarative syntax of UDL (see Chapter 27).

1. Schema S1:

    ```
    BASESET COURSE(COURSE#,TITLE)
    BASESET OFFERING(COURSE#,OFF#,DATE,LOCATION)
    ```

    Both declarations are essential in S1. (Also, both basesets are relations.)

2. Schema S2:

    ```
    BASESET COURSE(COURSE#,TITLE)
    BASESET OFFERING(OFF#,DATE,LOCATION)
    FANSET  OFFERING UNDER COURSE
    ```

---

2. Incidentally, binary relations do not possess this same closure property. For example, the join of two binary relations is not a binary relation.

All three declarations are essential in S2. (The first baseset is a relation; the second is not.)

3. Schema S3:

```
BASESET  COURSE(COURSE#,TITLE)
BASESET  OFFERING(COURSE#,OFF#,DATE,LOCATION)
FANSET   OFFERING UNDER COURSE
         WHERE OFFERING.COURSE# = COURSE.COURSE#
```

The two baseset declarations are essential in S3, the fanset declaration is not; there is no information that can be derived from this database that cannot also be derived from the two basesets alone. (Again, the two basesets are relations.)

Given this notion of essentiality, we can now state an absolutely crucial distinction between the relational and network approaches. In a relational schema the entire information content of the database is represented by means of a single data construct, namely, the n-ary relation.[3] In a network schema, by contrast, there exists at least one fanset bearing information essentially; for if there did not, the schema would degenerate into a relational schema with certain explicit access paths.[4] In other words, there are at least two essential data constructs in the network approach, the baseset and the fanset. In DBTG, in particular, there are *five* data constructs, any or all of which may be used to bear information essentially:

- record type (corresponds to baseset);
- DBTG set (corresponds to fanset);
- singular set;
- ordering;
- repeating group.

Now we consider how the network approach measures up to the criteria specified earlier for the conceptual level of the system. The first criterion

---

3. Sometimes we permit relations to be ordered, but such ordering is always inessential. For example, the supplier relation may be ordered by ascending supplier number; however, the ordering is merely a convenience—we could still find (say) the supplier with the third supplier number in this sequence, even if the relation was in totally random order.

4. The suppliers-and-parts schema of Fig. 24.16 does not contain any essential fansets, and is thus not a network schema by this definition. (The inessentiality was not made explicit in the declarations, however, and the DBMS was therefore not aware of it.) Our reasons for making the fansets inessential in that example were given in the text; basically the problem was that maintaining the proper child sequence is difficult in an essential fanset under DBTG. But this is really a criticism of DBTG—it is not a state of affairs that is intrinsic to networks per se.

COMPONENT	MAJOR.P#	MINOR.P#	QUANTITY
	P1	P2	2
	P1	P4	4
	P5	P3	1
	P3	P6	3
	P6	P1	9
	P5	P6	8
	P2	P4	3

Fig. 28.1 A parts-and-components structure: Relational view.

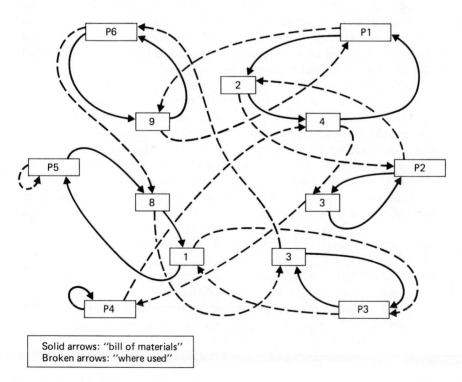

Solid arrows: "bill of materials"
Broken arrows: "where used"

Fig. 28.2 A parts-and-components structure: Network view.

was ease of understanding. A comparison of Figs. 28.1 (a repeat of Fig. 4.4) and 28.2 (a network version of the same data) suggests that, in terms of occurrences at least, networks are somewhat less easy to understand than relations. A comparison of Figs. 27.2 and 27.4 (see the previous chapter) suggests that the same is true for the schemas. A possible reason for the increase in complexity is the increase in the number of basic constructs the user has to understand and deal with.

A more severe criticism of networks is that the fanset construct bundles together at least three distinct concepts.

1. It *carries information* (either essentially or inessentially), namely, the association between the two record types involved.

2. It provides an *access path* (actually several such paths; parent to first and last child, child to next and previous child, child to parent).

3. It represents certain *integrity constraints* (primarily the constraint that each child has one parent, though the concept of membership class provides for a number of variations on this basic theme).

In addition, fansets may be used to establish a scope for authorization purposes; also the ordering of children within a given fan may be used to carry information (again, either essentially or inessentially). A result of this bundling is that, for example, programs may come to rely on an access path that is really a side effect of the way the designer chose to represent a certain integrity constraint. If that integrity constraint changes, the schema has to be restructured, with a strong likelihood of consequent impact on the corresponding program—even if that program was completely uninterested in the integrity constraint as such. As an example, the reader is invited to consider the effect on a program that lists employee numbers by department number (a) using a relation ED(EMP#,DEPT#) and (b) using a fanset DEPTEMP (parent DEPT, child EMP), if the department-to-employee correspondence changes from one-to-many to many-to-many. (In the relational case, the worst that can occur is a trivial change to the external/conceptual mapping—ED may have to be derived as a projection of a department/employee "linking" relation instead of as a projection of the employee relation. In the network case, the changes required at the conceptual level are rather more extensive, and either the program or the external/conceptual mapping will require significantly more rewriting. If the rewriting is contained within the mapping, incidentally, we will then have the situation that the program is using an access path, namely, DEPTEMP, which is no longer directly supported. See number 2 below.)

Let us examine each of the three "bundled" concepts in a little more detail.

1. Fansets represent certain associations between entities. However, not all such associations will be represented as fansets, in general; in all likelihood, not even all one-to-many associations will be so represented. As an example of one that is not, consider the association between cities and suppliers. Of course, there is no record type corresponding to cities; but if such a record type were added to the schema, would a fanset also be added with cities as parents, suppliers as children? If the answer is yes, the fanset will be inessential, unless the city field type is removed from the supplier record type. This removal is unlikely, for the following reasons: (a) Suppliers would have to be MANUAL members of the fanset (to allow for the fact that the supplier records exist *before* the city records are created); therefore (b) a new program will be needed to connect suppliers to cities; and (c) this program will need to obtain the city value for a given supplier from *somewhere*—presumably from the city field. We conclude that the addition of essential fansets with existing records as members is a nontrivial operation, which raises questions about the usefulness of the construct.

2. Fansets represent certain access paths. However, not all such paths are represented by fansets; for example, the system may provide various forms of indexing under the covers [24.6]. User programs are not dependent on the existence of such "invisible" access paths, but they very definitely are dependent on the existence of the visible paths that are represented by fansets. (This observation suggests that fansets cannot be viewed as purely logical constructs—they must be supported fairly directly at the physical level, for otherwise there is little justification for representing just these particular associations in this rather privileged manner. See number 1 above.) The question arises: Why is this particular form of access path made visible, when others are not?[5]

3. Fansets represent certain integrity constraints. However, not all such constraints are represented by fansets; indeed, most constraints are specified separately from the data structure. An example of the problems caused by bundling such constraints with the data structure has already been given. The question arises: Why are these particular constraints given this special treatment?

---

5. Fansets are actually a very general and widely applicable structure, considered purely as an access mechanism and not as a logical construct. They are thus a strong candidate for implementation at the *internal* or storage structure level (as opposed to the conceptual level). It is likely, however, that "internal" fansets would not use FIXED, MANDATORY, or AUTOMATIC membership—everything would be MANUAL and OPTIONAL. The work of Kay [25.1] supports these remarks.

A more general question arising from these three paragraphs is the following: How does the schema designer decide which associations/paths/constraints to express as fansets and which to represent in some other way?

Returning to our "ease of understanding" criteria, the last two in the list were *symmetry* and *nonredundancy*. A network schema involving essential fansets has less symmetry of representation than an equivalent relational schema, since some information is represented as records and some as links between records; it follows that such a network cannot totally support "symmetric exploitation." Second, a network schema can certainly be just as nonredundant as an equivalent relational schema (but no more so), but only if it does not involve any inessential fansets; an inessential fanset does contain some redundancy, in that the association between parent and child is represented both by field values and by links.

We turn now to *ease of manipulation*. We observe first that each information-bearing construct needs its own set of operators to manipulate it, in general. Thus, even if we restrict our attention to just record types and fansets, we see that networks necessarily require more operators than relations. The language UDL of Chapter 27 has already demonstrated the truth of this statement. For example, in DBTG we have STORE to create a record and CONNECT to create a link, ERASE to destroy a record and DISCONNECT to destroy a link, and so on. (Actually DBTG does not provide individual operators for each of the four basic functions for each information-bearing construct. However, this does not mean that such operators are not needed—it simply means that in such cases users have to program the function for themselves. For example, there is no direct way [single DML operation] to modify information that is represented by position within a repeating group. Consider, for example, what the user must do to move the fifth item in a repeating group into the third position.) The foregoing remarks are applicable regardless of operator level; thus we can certainly provide very high-level (set-at-a-time) network operators, but there will necessarily be more of them than there will be for relations.

We also need more authorization and integrity operators. Moreover, authorization and integrity controls can be quite complicated to apply. Suppose, for example, that within the department-employee fanset, employees are ordered by ascending values of the salary field, and suppose we have a user who needs to see employees by department—perhaps as an access path—but who is not allowed any access to salary information. It is not sufficient simply to omit the salary field from the user's view; the user can still discover that Smith earns more than Jones, for example, by observing that Smith follows Jones in the sequence. (Inessential information-carriers do still carry information, and corresponding controls are still necessary.)

Last, we consider the question of a supporting theory. This writer knows of no theory to assist with the design of a network schema that is as complete as the normalization theory is for relations. It is true that normalization theory can be applied to the *records* of the network, but only *after* the decision has been made as to which information is to be represented by records and which by other means—and of course this first decision is critical. The consequences of a wrong choice are likely to be instability in the schema. As an example, consider a network schema representing a subway network in which each subway line is represented by a singular set, and the order of the stations on the line is represented by the order of the records in the set (a realistic example of essential ordering). Suppose that at a later time it is required to incorporate the distance between adjacent stations into this schema. This distance is a property, not of a station per se, but rather of a pair of adjacent stations; however, adjacency is represented by ordering, not by records, which makes it difficult to introduce a distance field. If we introduce a new "pair-of-adjacent-stations" record type we can obviously use it to hold the distance field; however, the existing schema then becomes totally redundant. (The new record type would have to include a field identifying the relevant subway line.) If we place the distance field in the existing station record type (more precisely, if we incorporate a "distance to next station" field into the station record type, thus relying once again on the ordering), we introduce an unpleasant asymmetry into the schema. For example, the algorithm for computing the distance between two stations X and Y on a given line will vary significantly according to whether X precedes or follows Y on the line. The problems are entirely due to the use of ordering as an essential construct.

Another important theoretical question is the following: Is it possible to support a relational external schema on a conceptual schema that involves essential fansets? It is generally accepted that nonprogramming users, at least, will require a relational view of the database. Again, this writer knows of no completely general method of supporting such a view if the conceptual schema involves essential fansets.[6] It is not hard to produce examples that suggest that such a general mapping would be rather complex. (The information represented by the essential fanset will be represented by a foreign key in the child record in the relational view. Difficulties arise if the relational user updates this foreign key and sets it to a value not matching any existing parent record. In some situations this operation must be allowed; in others it must not.)

---

6. We note in passing that the closure properties of relations do not apply to essential fansets. For example, a "union" of two fans of a given fanset that retains all linkage information is not itself another fan.

Some Questions

We can conclude our discussion of the suitability of networks for the conceptual level by turning the problem around and asking, but not answering, a number of questions (see [28.3]). Suppose that we start with relations as the sole data construct available at the conceptual level. What is the effect of introducing new constructs (e.g., fansets) that bear information essentially?

- So far as the *system* is concerned, do not more operators become necessary? Do not concurrency, authorization, and similar controls become more complex? Hence, does not the implementation become more complex and less reliable?

- So far as the *user* is concerned, is there not an increased burden in choosing which operators to use? Is there not an increased variety of possible errors to cope with, and a correspondingly increased variety of remedial actions to consider?

- So far as the *database administrator* is concerned, are there not too many structural choices available? *Are there dependable guidelines for making these choices?* (This is one of the most critical questions of all.) Are not the mappings to the internal level significantly more complicated to define and maintain? Are not authorization and integrity constraints more complicated to specify?

If it turns out that fansets have to be *inessential* (for example, to support a relational external view), then their role at the conceptual level must again be questioned. It is interesting to note, incidentally, that Bachman himself in his Turing Award lecture [26.1] suggests that fansets are fundamentally inessential and are intended primarily for improving performance: " . . . The field named 'department code' appears in both the employee record and the department record . . . The use of the same data value as a primary key for one record and as a secondary key for a set of records is the basic concept upon which data structure sets are declared and maintained . . . With database sets, all redundant data can be eliminated, reducing the storage space required . . . Performance is enhanced . . . where the owner and some or most of the members of a set are physically stored and accessed together on the same block or page." And later: "The joint usage of the department code by both [employee and department] records and the declaration of a set based upon this data key provide the basis for the creation and maintenance of the set relationship between a department record and all the records representing the employees of that department. [A benefit of this construct is] the significant improvement in performance that accrues from using the database sets in lieu of both primary and secondary indices to gain access to all the records with a particular data key value."

28.6   CONCLUSION

Many papers have appeared over the last few years on the relative merits of different data structures and different ways of manipulating them [28.2–28.17]. In this chapter we have attempted to extract and present some of the most significant themes from these papers. In particular, we have tried to show the advantages of *n*-ary relations over DBTG-like networks; however, for an opposing point of view the reader is referred to certain of the original papers (particularly [28.8] and [28.12]).

It seems appropriate to conclude with Codd's statement of objectives for the relational approach [9.2]. They are as follows:

1. To provide a high degree of data independence.

2. To provide a community view of the data of spartan simplicity, so that a wide variety of users in an enterprise (ranging from the most computer-naive to the most computer-sophisticated) can interact with a *common* view (while not prohibiting superimposed user views for specialized purposes).

3. To simplify the potentially formidable job of the database administrator.

4. To introduce a theoretical foundation (albeit modest) into database management (a field sadly lacking in solid principles and guidelines).

5. To merge the fact retrieval and file management fields in preparation for the addition at a later time of inferential services in the commercial world.

6. To lift database application programming to a new level—a level in which sets (and more specifically relations) are treated as operands instead of being processed element by element.

No one would claim that all these objectives have now been attained; much more work remains to be done. However, a strong foundation has been established, and there seems good reason to be optimistic about the eventual outcome.

REFERENCES AND BIBLIOGRAPHY

28.1 R. Rustin (ed.). "Data Models: Data Structure Set versus Relational." *Proc. 1974 ACM SIGMOD Workshop on Data Description, Access and Control, Vol. II* (May 1974).

> The proceedings of a debate held at the 1974 SIGMOD conference. Includes references [28.2–28.5], additional comments by D. C. Tsichritzis and J. R. Lucking, and the transcript of a panel-and-audience discussion.

28.2 C. W. Bachman. "The Data Structure Set Model." In [28.1].

Presents Bachman's arguments that the two approaches are fundamentally compatible.

28.3 E. F. Codd and C. J. Date. "Interactive Support for Non-Programmers: The Relational and Network Approaches." In [28.1].

Section 28.5 of the present chapter draws heavily from this paper.

28.4 E. H. Sibley. "On the Equivalence of Data Based Systems." In [28.1].

28.5 C. J. Date and E. F. Codd. "The Relational and Network Approaches: Comparison of the Application Programming Interfaces." In [28.1].

A companion paper to [28.3]. Somewhat unfair, in that it contrasts a relational set-at-a-time language (DSL ALPHA) with a network record-at-a-time language (the DML of DBTG).

28.6 A. E. Bandurski and D. K. Jefferson. "Data Description for Computer-Aided Design." *Proc. 1975 ACM SIGMOD International Conference on Management of Data* (May 1975).

Includes some interesting criticisms of both relations and networks.

28.7 A. P. G. Brown. "Modelling a Real World System and Designing a Schema to Represent It." In [24.3].

Suggests an informal set of guidelines for designing a DBTG schema.

28.8 C. P. Earnest. "A Comparison of the Network and Relational Data Structure Models." Available from Computer Sciences Corporation, 650 N. Sepulveda Blvd., El Segundo, California 90245.

Earnest's major conclusions are: "(1) The two models are in practice not very different; (2) the relational structures are somewhat simpler than networks; but (3) the price for this is that the network model has more structural power and *more,* not less, data independence than the relational, and is therefore likely to be a better basis for a standard."

28.9 M. Stonebraker and G. Held. "Networks, Hierarchies, and Relations in Data Base Management Systems." *Proc. 1975 ACM PACIFIC Conference, San Francisco* (April 1975). Available from ACM Golden Gate Chapter, P.O. Box 24055, Oakland, California 94623.

Suggests that language level (set-at-a-time or record-at-a-time) is a more important factor than the underlying view of data.

28.10 W. C. McGee. "A Contribution to the Study of Data Equivalence." *Proc. IFIP TC-2 Working Conference on Data Base Management Systems* (eds., Klimbie and Koffeman), April 1974. North-Holland (1974).

28.11 W. C. McGee. "On the Evaluation of Data Models." *ACM Transactions on Database Systems* **1,** No. 4 (December 1976).

Defines a set of criteria for choosing a particular view of data. The criteria are as follows: simplicity, elegance, logicalness, picturability, modeling directness, modeling uniqueness, provision of structure "schemas," overlap with coresident models, partitionability, consistent terminology, proximity to implementation base, and applicability of safe implementation techniques. Of course, some of these criteria clash with others.

28.12 A. Metaxides. "Information-Bearing and Non-Information-Bearing Sets." In [24.3].

The terms "information-bearing" and "non-information-bearing" in the title of this paper are unfortunately sometimes used in place of "essential" and "inessential." As Metaxides quite rightly observes, the terms are misleading since essential and inessential constructs both bear information. The paper claims that eliminating essential sets (a) provides no data independence benefits, (b) provides no integrity benefits, (c) does not really increase simplicity (simplification in the schema is achieved only at the expense of complication in programs), (d) reduces flexibility, and (e) leads to design and update problems.

Metaxides was the DBTG chairman at the time the final report [23.1] was produced.

28.13 A. S. Michaels, B. Mittman, and C. R. Carlson. "A Comparison of the Relational and CODASYL Approaches to Data Base Management." *ACM Computing Surveys* **8,** No. 1 (March 1976).

Discusses the two approaches under the headings of data definition, data manipulation (language level, complexity), data protection, data independence, and performance. The major conclusion is that no single approach to database management is desirable (sic) and no single approach is likely to emerge as dominant in the near future.

28.14 G. M. Nijssen. "Data Structuring in DDL and the Relational Data Model." *Proc. IFIP TC-2 Working Conference on Data Base Management Systems* (eds., Klimbie and Koffeman), April 1974. North-Holland (1974).

Compares and contrasts the network and relational data structures, and proposes a discipline for network users. The "DDL" of the title is the CODASYL Data Description Language. It is interesting to compare the discipline suggested with another such discipline proposed in [28.3].

28.15 G. M. Nijssen. "Set and CODASYL Set or Coset." In [24.3].

Considers the CODASYL DDL as a language for defining conceptual schemas, and suggests a number of improvements to the language with this aim in mind. The changes proposed include the following.

- All record types should include a primary key.
- All set types should be inessential.
- All ordering should be inessential.
- A set type should be allowed to have the same record type as both owner and member.
- A set type should not be allowed to have more than one type of member.
- The concept of membership class should be replaced by a statement of whether the functional dependence of owners on members is total or partial, together with certain additional integrity constraints.

The paper includes some good illustrations of why sets should not be essential. However, the author does not discuss the question (see Section 28.5) "If sets must be inessential, what purpose are they really serving in the conceptual schema?"

28.16 K. A. Robinson. "An Analysis of the Uses of the CODASYL Set Concept." In [24.3].

Supports the contention of Section 28.5 that DBTG sets should not appear at the conceptual level but may be very useful at the internal level.

28.17 T. B. Steel, Jr. "Data Base Standardization: A Status Report." In [24.3].

An outline description of the ANSI/SPARC architecture, with emphasis on the conceptual schema. The author argues strongly for his own conviction that the only acceptable formalism for the conceptual level is that of modern symbolic logic.

28.18 E. F. Codd. "Understanding Relations, Instalment No. 4." *SIGMOD bulletin FDT* **6**, No. 4 (1974).

Includes a very clear description of the differences among the following concepts: (1) the domain concept; (2) comparability of attributes: (3) the association between a foreign key and a primary key; and (4) the DBTG set or fanset. (The differences are important; the claim is frequently made that fansets are the DBTG equivalent of one or other of the first three, and this is not the case.)

28.19 G. Polya. "How To Solve It." Princeton University Press: Princeton Paperback (second ed., 1971).

28.20 P. P. S. Chen. "The Entity-Relationship Model—Toward a Unified View of Data." *ACM Transactions on Database Systems* **1**, No. 1 (March 1976).

Answers
to Selected
Exercises

CHAPTER 1: DATABASE SYSTEM ARCHITECTURE

1.4 Security may be compromised
 (without good controls)
Integrity may be compromised
 (without good controls)
Extra hardware may be required
Performance overhead may be significant
Successful operation is crucial
 (enterprise highly vulnerable to failure)
System is likely to be complex
 (though complexity should be concealed)

CHAPTER 2: STORAGE STRUCTURES

2.4 *Values recorded in index*   *Expanded form*

Values recorded in index	Expanded form
0-2-AB	AB
1-3-CKE	ACKE
3-1-R	ACKR
1-7-DAMS,Tb	ADAMS,Tb
7-1-R	ADAMS,TR
5-1-0	ADAMSO
1-1-L	AL
1-1-Y	AY
0-7-BAILEY,	BAILEY,
6-1-M	BAILEYM

Notes
 1. The two figures preceding each recorded value represent, respectively, the number of leading characters that are the same as those in the preceding value, and the number of characters actually recorded.

2. The expanded form of each value shows what can be deduced from (a sequential scan of) the index alone, i.e., without looking at the data.

3. It is assumed that the next value of the indexed field does not have BAILEYM as its first seven characters.

If we take the 8-bit byte as the unit of storage space and assume (a) that the two counts are accommodated in a single byte, and (b) that each recorded character also requires a single byte, the percentage saving in storage space is

$$\frac{150 - 35}{150} \cdot 100 = 76.67\%.$$

The index search algorithm is as follows.

Let V be the specified value (padded with blanks if necessary to make it 15 characters long).

1. Form next expanded index entry; let N = corresponding length ($1 \le N \le 15$).

2. Compare expanded index entry with leftmost N characters of V.

3. If equal, go to step 6.

4. If index entry is high, no stored record occurrence for V exists; go to exit.

5. Go to step 1.

6. Retrieve corresponding stored record occurrence, and check V against value stored therein.

If no "next" entry exists (step 1), no stored record occurrence for V exists.

For ACKROYD,S we get a match on the third iteration; we retrieve the stored record occurrence and find that it is indeed the one we want.

For ADAMS,V we get "index entry high" on the sixth iteration, so no appropriate stored record occurrence exists.

For ALLINGHAM,M we get a match on the seventh iteration; however, the stored record occurrence retrieved is for ALLEN,S, so it is permissible to insert a new one for ALLINGHAM,M. (We are assuming here that the indexed field is the primary key, so that values should be unique.) This involves the following steps.

1. Finding space and storing the new occurrence

2. Adjusting the index entry for ALLEN,S to read

$$1-3-LLE$$

3. Inserting an index entry between those for ALLEN,S and AYRES,ST to read

$$3-1-I$$

Note that the preceding entry in the index has to be changed. In general, making a new entry in the index may affect the preceding entry or the following entry, or possibly neither—but never both.

2.5 The number of *levels* in the index is the unique positive integer k such that $n^{k-1} < N \le n^k$. Taking logs to base n, we have $k - 1 < \log_n N \le k$; hence

$$k = \text{ceil}(\log_n N),$$

where $\text{ceil}(x)$ denotes the smallest integer greater than or equal to x.

Now let the number of *blocks* in the ith level of the index be B_i (where $i = 1$ corresponds to the lowest level). We show that

$$B_i = \text{ceil}\left(\frac{N}{n^i}\right),$$

and hence that the total number of blocks is

$$\sum_{i=1}^{i=k} \text{ceil}\left(\frac{N}{n^i}\right).$$

Consider the expression

$$\text{ceil}\ \frac{\text{ceil}\left(\dfrac{N}{n^i}\right)}{n} = x,\ \text{say}.$$

Suppose $N = qn^i + r$ ($0 \le r \le n^i - 1$). Then

a) If $r = 0$,

$$x = \text{ceil}\left(\frac{q}{n}\right)$$

$$= \text{ceil}\left(\frac{qn^i}{n^{i+1}}\right)$$

$$= \text{ceil}\left(\frac{N}{n^{i+1}}\right).$$

b) If $r > 0$,

$$x = \text{ceil}\left(\frac{q+1}{n}\right).$$

Suppose $q = q'n + r'$ ($0 \le r' \le n - 1$). Then $N = (q'n + r')n^i + r = q'n^{i+1} + (r'n^i + r)$; since $0 < r \le n - 1$ and $0 \le r' \le n - 1$,

$$0 < (r'n^i + r) \le n^{i+1} - (n^i - n + 1) < n^{i+1};$$

hence $\text{ceil}\left(\dfrac{N}{n^{i+1}}\right) = q' + 1$.

But

$$x = \text{ceil}\left(\frac{q'n + r' + 1}{n}\right)$$

$$= q' + 1$$

since $1 \leq r' + 1 \leq n$. Thus in both cases (a) and (b) we have that

$$\text{ceil}\left(\frac{\text{ceil}\left(\frac{N}{n^i}\right)}{n}\right) = \text{ceil}\left(\frac{N}{n^{i+1}}\right).$$

Now, it is immediate that $B_1 = \text{ceil}(N/n)$. It is also immediate that $B_{i+1} = \text{ceil}(B_i/n)$, $1 \leq i < k$. Thus, if $B_i = \text{ceil}(N/n^i)$, then

$$B_{i+1} = \text{ceil}\left(\frac{\text{ceil}\left(\frac{N}{n^i}\right)}{n}\right) = \text{ceil}\left(\frac{N}{n^{i+1}}\right).$$

The rest follows by induction.

2.6 (a) 3. (b) 6. For example, if the four field names are A,B,C,D, and if we denote an index by the appropriate ordered combination of field names, the following indexes will suffice: ABCD, BCDA, CDAB, DABC, ACBD, BDAC. (c) In general the number of indexes required is

$$^NC_n$$

(the number of ways of selecting n elements from a set of N elements), where n is the smallest integer $\geq N/2$. For proof see Lum[2.13].

CHAPTER 3: DATA STRUCTURES AND ASSOCIATED OPERATORS

3.1 *Relational view:*

PERSON

PNAME	ADDR	---
Arthur	--	---
Bill	--	---
Charlie	--	---
Dave	--	---

SKILL

SNAME	COURSE	JOBCODE	----
Programming	--	--	----
Operating	--	--	----
Engineering	--	--	----

PERSKIL

PNAME	SNAME	DATE
Arthur	Programming	--
Bill	Operating	--
Bill	Programming	--
Charlie	Engineering	--
Charlie	Programming	--
Charlie	Operating	--
Dave	Operating	--
Dave	Engineering	--

3.2 The two possible hierarchical views consist of (a) four hierarchical occurrences, one for each person, with skills subordinate to persons; and (b) three hierarchical occurrences, one for each skill, with persons subordinate to skills.

3.3 The network view consists of four person record occurrences, three skill record occurrences, and eight "connector" record occurrences. Each connector record occurrence represents the connection between one person and one skill, and contains the date the person attended the corresponding course. Each connector is on one "person" chain and one "skill" chain.

3.4 (a) Find names of all persons having a specified skill (S, say). This is very similar to the queries Q1 and Q2 of Fig. 3.2. For the relational view of Answer 3.1, the required record-at-a-time procedure resembles the two relational procedures of Fig. 3.2; an algebraic procedure is:

```
SELECT PERSKIL WHERE SNAME=S GIVING TEMP
PROJECT TEMP OVER PNAME GIVING RESULT
```

For hierarchy (a) of Answer 3.2—persons superior to skills—the required procedure follows that shown for Q2 in Fig. 3.4; for hierarchy (b)—skills superior to persons—it follows that shown for Q1 in Fig. 3.4. For the network of Answer 3.3 the required procedure follows that for Q1 (or Q2) in Fig. 3.6.

(b) Find names of all persons having at least one skill in common with a specified person (P, say). This is much more difficult.

Relational structure of Answer 3.1

Record-at-a-time solution
do until no more PERSKIL records;
   get next PERSKIL where PNAME = P;
   add SNAME to working list;
end;
position to start of PERSKIL table;
do until no more PERSKIL records;
   get next PERSKIL;
   if SNAME exists in working list
   then merge PNAME into result list
      (eliminating duplicates);
end;
print result list;

Note that we need a "set initial position" operator (used prior to the second loop). The procedure above could be made more efficient, and the "eliminate duplicates" step would be unnecessary, if we could rely on PERSKIL being ordered in ascending (PNAME,SNAME) sequence. See Chapter 4.

Algebraic solution

```
SELECT PERSKIL WHERE PNAME=P GIVING TEMP1
PROJECT TEMP1 OVER SNAME GIVING TEMP2
JOIN TEMP2 AND PERSKIL OVER SNAME GIVING TEMP3
PROJECT TEMP3 OVER PNAME GIVING RESULT
```

Hierarchy (a) of Answer 3.2
get [next] person where PNAME = P;
do until no more skills
        under this person;
    get next skill
        under this person;
    add SNAME to working list;
end;
position to start of database;
do until no more persons;
    get next person;
    do until no more skills
            under this person;
        get next skill
            under this person;
        if SNAME exists in working list
        then
            do;
                add PNAME to result list;
                leave inner ("skills") loop;
            end;
    end;
end;
print result list;

Hierarchy (b) of Answer 3.2
do until no more skills;
    get next skill;
    get [next] person
        under this skill
        where PNAME = P;
    if found
    then add SNAME to working list;
end;
do until no more in working list;
    set S = next SNAME in working list;
    position to start of database;
    get [next] skill where SNAME = S;
    do until no more persons
            under this skill;
        get next person
            under this skill;
        merge PNAME into result list
            (eliminating duplicates);
    end;
end;
print result list;

An alternative strategy is:

```
do until no more skills;
    get next skill;
    get [next] person
        under this skill
        where PNAME = P;
    if found
    then
        do;
            position to start of persons
                    under this skill;
            do until no more persons
                    under this skill;
                get next person
                    under this skill;
                merge PNAME into result list
                    (eliminating duplicates);
            end;
        end;
end;
print result list;
```

Network of Answer 3.3

```
get [next] person where PNAME = P;
do until no more connectors
        under this person;
    get next connector
        under this person;
    get skill
        over this connector;
    add SNAME to working list;
end;
do until no more in working list;
    set S = next SNAME in working list;
    position to start of database;
    get [next] skill where SNAME = S;
    do until no more connectors
            under this skill;
        get next connector
            under this skill;
        get person
            over this connector;
        merge PNAME into result list
            (eliminating duplicates);
    end;
end;
print result list;
```

CHAPTER 4: RELATIONAL DATA STRUCTURE

```
4.2 DOMAIN   PNAME      CHARACTER (15) PRIMARY
    DOMAIN   ADDR       CHARACTER (40)
    DOMAIN   SNAME      CHARACTER (15) PRIMARY
    DOMAIN   COURSE     CHARACTER (30)
    DOMAIN   JOBCODE    CHARACTER (2)
    DOMAIN   DATE       CHARACTER (6)

    RELATION   PERSON     (PNAME,ADDR,...)
                          PRIMARY KEY  (PNAME)
    RELATION   SKILL      (SNAME,COURSE,JOBCODE,...)
                          PRIMARY KEY  (SNAME)
    RELATION   PERSKIL  (PNAME,SNAME,DATE)
                          PRIMARY KEY  (PNAME,SNAME)
```

Each attribute is assumed by default to be defined on the domain having the same name.

CHAPTER 6: SYSTEM R DATA STRUCTURE

```
6.1 CREATE TABLE   PERSON  ( PNAME    ( CHAR(15), NONULL ),
                             ADDR     ( CHAR(40) ), ... )
    CREATE TABLE   SKILL   ( SNAME    ( CHAR(15), NONULL ),
                             COURSE   ( CHAR(30) ),
                             JOBCODE  ( CHAR(2) ), ... )
    CREATE TABLE   PERSKIL ( PNAME    ( CHAR(15), NONULL ),
                             SNAME    ( CHAR(15), NONULL ),
                             DATE     ( CHAR(6) )           )
    CREATE UNIQUE INDEX   XP   ON   PERSON  ( PNAME )
    CREATE UNIQUE INDEX   XS   ON   SKILL   ( SNAME )
    CREATE UNIQUE INDEX   XPS  ON   PERSKIL ( PNAME, SNAME )
```

CHAPTER 7: SYSTEM R DATA MANIPULATION

Most of the following answers are not unique.

```
7.1 SELECT *
    FROM   J
7.2 SELECT *
    FROM   J
    WHERE  CITY='LONDON'
7.3 SELECT P#
    FROM   P
    WHERE  WEIGHT=
           (SELECT MIN(WEIGHT)
            FROM   P)
7.4 SELECT UNIQUE S#
    FROM   SPJ
    WHERE  J#='J1'
7.5 SELECT S#
    FROM   SPJ
    WHERE  P#='P1' AND J#='J1'
```

7.6
```
SELECT  JNAME
FROM    J
WHERE   J# IN
        (SELECT J#
         FROM   SPJ
         WHERE  S#='S1')
```

7.7
```
SELECT  UNIQUE COLOR
FROM    P
WHERE   P# IN
        (SELECT P#
         FROM   SPJ
         WHERE  S#='S1')
```

7.8
```
SELECT  S#
FROM    SPJ
WHERE   J#='J1'
AND     S# IN
        (SELECT S#
         FROM   SPJ
         WHERE  J#='J2')
```

7.9
```
SELECT  UNIQUE S#
FROM    SPJ
WHERE   J#='J1'
AND     P# IN
        (SELECT P#
         FROM   P
         WHERE  COLOR='RED')
```

7.10
```
SELECT  UNIQUE P#
FROM    SPJ
WHERE   J# IN
        (SELECT J#
         FROM   J
         WHERE  CITY='LONDON')
```

7.11
```
SELECT  UNIQUE S#
FROM    SPJ
WHERE   J# IN
        (SELECT J#
         FROM   J
         WHERE  CITY='LONDON'
         OR     CITY='PARIS')
AND     P# IN
        (SELECT P#
         FROM   P
         WHERE  COLOR='RED')
```

7.12
```
SELECT  UNIQUE P#
FROM    S,SPJ,J
WHERE   S.S#=SPJ.S#
AND     SPJ.J#=J.J#
AND     S.CITY=J.CITY
```

7.13 SELECT   UNIQUE P#
     FROM   SPJ
     WHERE   J# IN
            (SELECT   J#
            FROM   J
            WHERE   CITY='LONDON')
     AND   S# IN
            (SELECT   S#
            FROM   S
            WHERE   CITY='LONDON')

7.14 SELECT   J.J#
     FROM   S,SPJ,J
     WHERE   S.S#=SPJ.S#
     AND   SPJ.J#=J.J#
     AND   S.CITY¬=J.CITY

7.15 SELECT   J#
     FROM   J
     WHERE   NOT EXISTS
            (SELECT *
            FROM   S,SPJ,P
            WHERE   S.S#=SPJ.S#
            AND   P.P#=SPJ.P#
            AND   J.J#=SPJ.J#
            AND   S.CITY='LONDON'
            AND   P.COLOR='RED')

7.16 SELECT   UNIQUE S#
     FROM   SPJ
     WHERE   P# IN
            (SELECT P#
            FROM   SPJ
            WHERE   S# IN
                 (SELECT S#
                 FROM   SPJ
                 WHERE   P# IN
                     (SELECT P#
                     FROM   P
                     WHERE   COLOR='RED')))

7.17 SELECT   UNIQUE J#
     FROM   SPJ
     WHERE   P# IN
            (SELECT P#
            FROM   SPJ
            WHERE   S#='S1')

7.18 SELECT   UNIQUE S.CITY,J.CITY
     FROM   S,SPJ,J
     WHERE   S.S#=SPJ.S#
     AND   J.J#=SPJ.J#

7.19 SELECT   S.CITY,P#,J.CITY
     FROM   S,SPJ,J
     WHERE   S.S#=SPJ.S#
     AND   J.J#=SPJ.J#

```
7.20  SELECT    S.CITY,P#,J.CITY
      FROM      S,SPJ,J
      WHERE     S.S#=SPJ.S#
      AND       J.J#=SPJ.J#
      AND       S.CITY¬=J.CITY


7.21  SELECT    UNIQUE S#
      FROM      SPJ SPJX
      WHERE     EXISTS
                (SELECT *
                 FROM    SPJ SPJY
                 WHERE   NOT EXISTS
                         (SELECT *
                          FROM    SPJ SPJZ
                          WHERE   NOT EXISTS
                                  (SELECT *
                                   FROM    SPJ
                                   WHERE   S#=SPJX.S#
                                   AND     P#=SPJY.P#
                                   AND     J#=SPJZ.J#)))


7.22  SELECT    UNIQUE J#
      FROM      SPJ SPJX
      WHERE     NOT EXISTS
                (SELECT *
                 FROM    SPJ
                 WHERE   J#=SPJX.J#
                 AND     S#¬='S1')


7.23  SELECT    UNIQUE P#
      FROM      SPJ SPJX
      WHERE     NOT EXISTS
                (SELECT *
                 FROM    J
                 WHERE   CITY='LONDON'
                 AND     NOT EXISTS
                         (SELECT *
                          FROM    SPJ
                          WHERE   J#=J.J#
                          AND     P#=SPJX.P#))


7.24  SELECT    UNIQUE J#
      FROM      SPJ SPJX
      WHERE     NOT EXISTS
                (SELECT *
                 FROM    SPJ SPJY
                 WHERE   S#='S1'
                 AND     NOT EXISTS
                         (SELECT *
                          FROM    SPJ
                          WHERE   P#=SPJY.P#
                          AND     J#=SPJX.J#))
```

```
7.25  SELECT   UNIQUE  J#
      FROM     SPJ  SPJX
      WHERE    NOT  EXISTS
               (SELECT  *
               FROM     SPJ  SPJY
               WHERE    J#=SPJX.J#
               AND      NOT  EXISTS
                        (SELECT  *
                        FROM     SPJ
                        WHERE    P#=SPJY.P#
                        AND      S#='S1'))
7.26  SELECT   UNIQUE  J#
      FROM     SPJ  SPJX
      WHERE    NOT  EXISTS
               (SELECT  *
               FROM     SPJ  SPJY
               WHERE    EXISTS
                        (SELECT  *
                        FROM     SPJ
                        WHERE    S#='S1'
                        AND      P#=SPJY.P#)
               AND      NOT  EXISTS
                        (SELECT  *
                        FROM     SPJ
                        WHERE    S#='S1'
                        AND      P#=SPJY.P#
                        AND      J#=SPJX.J#))
7.27  SELECT   UNIQUE  J#
      FROM     SPJ  SPJX
      WHERE    NOT  EXISTS
               (SELECT  *
               FROM     SPJ  SPJY
               WHERE    EXISTS
                        (SELECT  *
                        FROM     SPJ
                        WHERE    P#=SPJY.P#
                        AND      J#=SPJX.J#)
               AND      NOT  EXISTS
                        (SELECT  *
                        FROM     SPJ
                        WHERE    S#='S1'
                        AND      P#=SPJY.P#
                        AND      J#=SPJX.J#))
7.28  SELECT   UNIQUE  J#
      FROM     SPJ  SPJX
      WHERE    NOT  EXISTS
               (SELECT  *
               FROM     SPJ  SPJY
               WHERE    P#  IN
                        (SELECT  P#
                        FROM     P
                        WHERE    COLOR='RED')
               AND      NOT  EXISTS
                        (SELECT  *
                        FROM     SPJ
                        WHERE    S#=SPJY.S#
                        AND      J#=SPJX.J#))
```

```
7.29  UPDATE    J
      SET       JNAME='VIDEO'
      WHERE     J#='J6'

7.30  UPDATE    P
      SET       COLOR='ORANGE'
      WHERE     COLOR='RED'

7.31  DELETE    SPJ
      WHERE     P# IN
                (SELECT P#
                 FROM    P
                 WHERE   COLOR='RED')
      DELETE    P
      WHERE     COLOR='RED'

7.32  SELECT    COUNT(UNIQUE J#)
      FROM      SPJ
      WHERE     S#='S3'

7.33  SELECT    SUM(QTY)
      FROM      SPJ
      WHERE     S#='S1'
      AND       P#='P1'

7.34  SELECT    P#,J#,SUM(QTY)
      FROM      SPJ
      GROUP     BY P#,J#
```

CHAPTER 8: EMBEDDED SQL

8.1 There are basically two ways to write such a program. The first involves two cursors, CS and CP say, defined along the following lines:

```
$LET CS BE SELECT * INTO $S#, ...
                     FROM S
                     ORDER BY S#;
$LET CP BE SELECT * INTO $P#, ...
                     FROM P
                     WHERE P# IN
                          (SELECT P# FROM SPJ
                               WHERE S# = $S#)
                     ORDER BY P#;
```

The logic in this case is essentially as follows:

```
$OPEN CS;
  DO for all suppliers;
    $FETCH CS;
     print S;
    $OPEN CP;
      DO for all parts for this supplier;
        $FETCH CP;
          print P;
      END;
  END;
```

The second approach uses a single cursor:

```
$LET  C  BE  SELECT  *  INTO  ...
                     FROM  S,P,SPJ
                     WHERE  S.S#  =  SPJ.S#
                     AND  SPJ.P#  =  P.P#
                     ORDER  BY  S.S#,P.P#;
```

Logic:

```
$OPEN  C;
 DO  for  all  joined  records;
   $FETCH  C;
    IF  S.S#  different  from  previous  iteration
    THEN  print  S  information;
    print  P  information;
 END;
```

8.2 Suppose the program includes a LET statement of the form

```
$LET  C  BE  SELECT  ...  FROM  T  ...;
```

The RDS optimizer is responsible for choosing an access path corresponding to the cursor C. Suppose it chooses an index based on field F of table T. The set of records accessible via C when C is active will then be ordered according to values of F. If the programmer were allowed to UPDATE a value of F via the cursor C—i.e., via an UPDATE statement of the form

```
$UPDATE  T  SET  F  =  ...  WHERE  CURRENT  OF  C;
```

—then the updated record would probably have to be "moved" (logically speaking), because it would now belong in a different place with respect to the ordering of the set. In other words, cursor C would effectively jump to a new position, with unpredictable results. To avoid such a situation, the user must warn the optimizer of any fields to be updated, so that access paths based on those fields will *not* be chosen.

8.3 We give a sketch of one possible solution here. (We do not claim this solution to be very efficient. How can it be improved?)

```
        GET  LIST  (GIVENP#);
        print  GIVENP#;
       $BEGIN  TRANSACTION;
        CALL  RECURSION  (GIVENP#);
       $END  TRANSACTION;
        RETURN;

RECURSION:
  PROC  (UPPER_PART)  RECURSIVE;
 $DCL  UPPER_PART;
 $DCL  LOWER_PART  INITIAL  ('  ');
 $LET  C  BE  SELECT  MINORP#
             INTO    $LOWER_PART
             FROM    COMPONENT
             WHERE   MAJORP#  =  $UPPER_PART
             AND     MINORP#  >  $LOWER_PART
             ORDER   BY  MINORP#;
```

```
DO forever;
   $OPEN C;
   $FETCH C;
   IF not found THEN RETURN;
   IF found THEN DO;
                      print LOWER_PART;
                   $CLOSE C;
                   CALL RECURSION (LOWER_PART);
                END;
END;
END; /* of RECURSION */
```

Note that the same cursor, C, is used on every invocation of RECURSION. There is no way in SQL to create new "instances" of a cursor dynamically. (By contrast, new instances of UPPER_PART and LOWER_PART are created dynamically each time RECURSION is invoked; those instances are destroyed at completion of that invocation.) Because of this fact, we have to use a trick (". . . AND MINORP# > $LOWER_PART ORDER BY MINORP#") so that, on each invocation of RE-CURSION, we ignore all immediate components (LOWER_PARTs) of the current UPPER_PART that have already been processed.

For some alternative approaches and a discussion of this problem, see reference [5.10].

8.4 In System R each target variable in the INTO clause can have an associated *indicator variable,* specified as follows:

```
INTO target [: indicator ] [, target [: indicator ]] ...
```

If a particular field to be retrieved happens to be null, the corresponding indicator is set to a negative value. If no indicator is specified, SYR_CODE is set to a negative value.

CHAPTER 9: THE EXTERNAL LEVEL OF SYSTEM R

9.1 The problem here is, how should the field SP.QTY be defined? The sensible answer seems to be that, for a given (S#, P#) pair, SP.QTY should be the *sum* of all SPJ.QTY values, taken over all J#'s for that (S#, P#) pair.

```
DEFINE VIEW  SP (S#, P#, QTY)
         AS  SELECT S#, P#, SUM(QTY)
             FROM   SPJ
             GROUP  BY J#
```

Table SP cannot be updated.

9.2 We give a simple example to show how DEFINE VIEW might be extended to define hierarchical views. The example defines a hierarchical version of view V2 (see Section 9.3), consisting of a record-type PART as root and another record-type

LOC as a dependent of that root. PART contains a single field (P#), and so does LOC (CITY).

```
DEFINE VIEW   HV2
              ( PART (P#) OVER (
                             LOC (CITY) ) )
          AS  SELECT P#, CITY
              FROM   SP, S
              WHERE  SP.S# = S.S.#
```

9.3 For retrieval operations any derivable hierarchy is valid. For update operations there are many restrictions. We do not give a complete solution to the problem, but content ourselves with an illustrative example. Consider the following hierarchy (suppliers over parts over projects):

```
DEFINE  VIEW  HSPJ
              ( HS (S#,CITY)
                OVER ( HP (P#)
                       OVER ( HJ (J#,QTY) ) )
          AS  . . .
```

which we suppose to be derived in an obvious way from the suppliers-parts-projects relational schema. We observe that the root record-type (HS) in this hierarchy is essentially identical to the underlying relation S, except that certain attributes (not the primary key) have been omitted. It would also have been possible to omit individual tuples (those not satisfying some defining predicate). We observe further that each record-type below the root (i.e., HP and HJ) consists of a primary key from another of the underlying relations together with zero or more additional attributes that are "fully functionally dependent" (see Chapter 14) on the "fully concatenated key" (see Chapter 16) of that record-type. Given this structure, updates may be performed against each of the three record-types HS, HP, HJ; any such update can be mapped into an equivalent update on the underlying relations, *except* for the following: (a) An HJ can be deleted *only* as a side effect of deleting an HP or an HS; (b) an HP can be inserted *only* if at least one subordinate HJ is inserted simultaneously.

We remark in passing that this example illustrates some guidelines that could be useful in designing a hierarchical schema. As in the case of the relational guidelines (see Chapter 14), a guiding principle is "one fact in one place"—that is, avoid redundancy. However, these guidelines are by no means as complete as those for relations. For example, they do not indicate whether the hierarchy should be suppliers over parts over projects, as above, or suppliers over projects over parts, or suppliers over both parts and projects (in that order), or one of the other nine possibilities. Nor do they indicate whether the hierarchy should contain only "SPJ" information, or whether the root, at least, should contain additional attributes for the entity-type concerned. And finally, whichever hierarchy is selected, it will still have to be supplemented by two *relations* for the nonroot entity-type.

CHAPTER 11: QUERY BY EXAMPLE

In the following we have numbered the questions as 11.*n*, where *n* is the number of
the original exercise in Chapter 7.

11.1

J	J#	JNAME	CITY
P.			

11.2

J	J#	JNAME	CITY
P.			LONDON

11.3

P	P#	PNAME	COLOR	WEIGHT	CITY
	P.PX			W	
¬				< W	

11.4

SPJ	S#	P#	J#	QTY
	P.SX		J1	

11.5

SPJ	S#	P#	J#	QTY
	P.SX	P1	J1	

11.6

J	J#	JNAME	CITY
	JX	P.JN	

SPJ	S#	P#	J#	QTY
	S1		JX	

11.7

P	P#	PNAME	COLOR	WEIGHT	CITY
	PX		P.COL		

SPJ	S#	P#	J#	QTY
	S1	PX		

11.8

SPJ	S#	P#	J#	QTY
	P.<u>SX</u>		J1	
	<u>SX</u>		J2	

11.9

SPJ	S#	P#	J#	QTY
	P.<u>SX</u>	<u>PX</u>	J1	

P	P#	PNAME	COLOR	WEIGHT	CITY
	<u>PX</u>		RED		

11.10

SPJ	S#	P#	J#	QTY
		P.<u>PX</u>	<u>JX</u>	

J	J#	JNAME	CITY
	<u>JX</u>		LONDON

11.11

P	P#	PNAME	COLOR	WEIGHT	CITY
	<u>PX</u>		RED		
	<u>PY</u>		RED		

J	J#	JNAME	CITY
	<u>JX</u>		LONDON
	<u>JY</u>		PARIS

SPJ	S#	P#	J#	QTY
	P.<u>SX</u>	<u>PX</u>	<u>JX</u>	
	P.<u>SY</u>	<u>PY</u>	<u>JY</u>	

Note that two distinct example part numbers are needed.

11.12

S	S#	SNAME	STATUS	CITY
	<u>SX</u>			<u>CX</u>

J	J#	JNAME	CITY
	<u>JX</u>		<u>CX</u>

SPJ	S#	P#	J#	QTY
	<u>SX</u>	P.<u>PX</u>	<u>JX</u>	

11.13

S	S#	SNAME	STATUS	CITY
	SX			LONDON

J	J#	JNAME	CITY
	JX		LONDON

SPJ	S#	P#	J#	QTY
	SX	P.PX	JX	

11.14

S	S#	SNAME	STATUS	CITY
	SX			C

J	J#	JNAME	CITY
	JX		¬C

SPJ	S#	P#	J#	QTY
	SX		P.JX	

11.15

S	S#	SNAME	STATUS	CITY
	SX			LONDON

P	P#	PNAME	COLOR	WEIGHT	CITY
	PX		RED		

SPJ	S#	P#	J#	QTY
¬	SX	PX	JX	
			P.JX	

11.16

SPJ	S#	P#	J#	QTY
	P.SX	PX		
	SY	PX		
	SY	PY		

P	P#	PNAME	COLOR	WEIGHT	CITY
	PY		RED		

11.17

SPJ	S#	P#	J#	QTY
	S1	PX		
		PX	P.JX	

11.18

S	S#	SNAME	STATUS	CITY
	SX			SC

J	J#	JNAME	CITY
	JX		JC

SPJ	S#	P#	J#	QTY
	SX		JX	

RESULT	SCITY	JCITY
	P.SC	P.JC

11.19

S	S#	SNAME	STATUS	CITY
	SX			SC

J	J#	JNAME	CITY
	JX		JC

SPJ	S#	P#	J#	QTY
	SX	PX	JX	

RESULT	SCITY	P#	JCITY
P.	SC	PX	JC

11.20 Add to solution 11.19:

CONDITIONS
SC ¬= JC

11.29

J	J#	JNAME	CITY
	J6	U. VIDEO	

11.30

P	P#	PNAME	COLOR	WEIGHT	CITY
	PX		RED		
U.	PX		ORANGE		

11.31

P	P#	PNAME	COLOR	WEIGHT	CITY
D.			RED		
	PX		RED		

SPJ	S#	P#	J#	QTY
D.		PX		

11.32

SPJ	S#	P#	J#	QTY
	S3		P.CNT.UNQ.ALL.JX	

11.33

SPJ	S#	P#	J#	QTY
	S1	P1		P.SUM.ALL.QX

11.34

SPJ	S#	P#	J#	QTY
		P.G.PX	P.G.JX	P.SUM.ALL.QX

Incidentally, if we wanted the result displayed in J# order within P# order here, then we could have specified "AO(1)." between the "P." and the "G." for P#, and "AO(2)." between the "P." and the "G." for J#.

CHAPTER 12: RELATIONAL ALGEBRA

12.1 (a) A INTERSECT B ≡ A MINUS (A MINUS B)
            ≡ B MINUS (B MINUS A)

(b) A DIVIDEBY B

(where A has attributes X, Y and B has attribute Z—X, Y, and Z possibly composite)

    ≡ (A MINUS ((A[X] TIMES B) MINUS A))[X]

12.2 Let A and B be any two members of the given set of named relations. Further (unnamed) relations may be derived by means of unnested algebraic expressions involving exactly one of the algebraic operators and one or both, as appropriate, of A and B. For each such unnested expression it is fairly straightforward to find a semantically equivalent SQL expression, as indicated below. (Notation is intended to be self-explanatory.)

Algebra	*SQL*
A UNION B	SELECT all-columns-of-A FROM A UNION SELECT all-columns-of-B FROM B

A MINUS B	SELECT all-columns-of-A FROM A
	WHERE NOT EXISTS
	    (SELECT * FROM B
	    WHERE all-columns-of-A
	        = all-columns-of-B)

A TIMES B	SELECT all-columns-of-A,all-columns-of-B FROM A,B
A WHERE p	SELECT all-columns-of-A FROM A WHERE p
A[x]	SELECT x FROM A (We ignore UNIQUE.)

Given that SQL allows us to store away (and give a name to) the result of any query, a procedure along the lines of the foregoing is sufficient to demonstrate the completeness of the language in Codd's original sense [12.1]. However, we indicate below how one might show completeness in the more demanding sense that any relation derivable via a single algebraic expression be derivable via a single SQL expression.

In outline the proof runs as follows.

Step 1. (Already done.) We show that, if A and B are any two members of the given set of named relations, any relation derivable via a single unnested algebraic expression involving exactly one of the algebraic operators and A and/or B may be derived via a single SQL expression.

Step 2. Now let A and B be any two relations derivable from the given set of named relations via possibly nested algebraic expressions. Further (unnamed) relations may be derived from A and B by means of expressions involving exactly one of the algebraic operators applied to one or both, as appropriate, of A and B. We show that *if* there exist SQL expressions representing A and B, *then* there exists a SQL expression representing each such derived relation.

Step 3. From Steps 1 and 2 taken together it follows that any relation derivable by means of an arbitrarily complex single algebraic expression is also derivable by means of a suitable single SQL expression.

Now for the details.

Step 1
(Already done.)

Step 2
Suppose that SQL expressions giving rise to A and B are, respectively,

```
SELECT  column-list-A  and  SELECT  column-list-B
FROM    table-list-A        FROM    table-list-B
WHERE   predicate-A         WHERE   predicate-B
```

We refer to these two expressions as QA and QB. We shall consider later whether it is reasonable to suppose that QA and QB exist.

Algebra	*SQL*
A UNION B	QA UNION QB
A MINUS B	QA AND NOT EXISTS (QB AND column-list-A = column-list-B)
A TIMES B	SELECT column-list-A,column-list-B FROM table-list-A,table-list-B WHERE predicate-A AND predicate-B
A WHERE *p*	SELECT column-list-A FROM table-list-A WHERE predicate-A AND *p*
A[*x*]	SELECT *x* FROM table-list-A WHERE predicate-A

Step 3
From Steps 1 and 2 it follows that *if* there exists a SQL expression of the assumed form corresponding to the application of a single algebraic operator, *then* there exists a SQL expression corresponding to the application of two algebraic operators in sequence and *therefore* there exists a SQL expression for a sequence of 3, 4, . . . , any number of operators.

The flaw is that there does *not* exist a SQL expression of the assumed form (SELECT-FROM-WHERE) corresponding to the algebraic UNION operator. Thus in Step 2 our assumption should have been that QA and QB were SQL expressions of the form

```
Q UNION Q UNION Q . . . . .
```

where each Q was a SELECT-FROM-WHERE block. It is left as an exercise to the reader to reexamine the "equivalences" of Step 2 under this revised assumption and to show that SQL is indeed relationally complete in the more demanding sense of the term.

12.3 The trap is that the join involves the CITY attributes as well as the S# and P# attributes.

Result:

S.S#	S.SNAME	S.STATUS	S.CITY	SP.P#	SP.QTY	P.PNAME	P.COLOR	P.WEIGHT
S1	Smith	20	London	P1	300	Nut	Red	12
S1	Smith	20	London	P4	200	Screw	Red	14
S1	Smith	20	London	P6	100	Cog	Red	19
S2	Jones	10	Paris	P2	400	Bolt	Green	17
S3	Blake	30	Paris	P2	200	Bolt	Green	17
S4	Clark	20	London	P4	200	Screw	Red	14

12.4.1 J

12.4.2 J WHERE CITY='LONDON'

12.4.3 PX ALIASES P;
PY ALIASES P;
P[P#] MINUS
    ((PX[P#,WEIGHT] TIMES PY[WEIGHT])
        WHERE PX.WEIGHT>PY.WEIGHT)[P#]

12.4.4 (SPJ WHERE J#='J1')[S#]

12.4.5 (SPJ WHERE J#='J1' AND P#='P1')[S#]

12.4.6 (J JOIN (SPJ WHERE S#='S1')[J#])[JNAME]

12.4.7 (P JOIN (SPJ WHERE S#='S1')[P#])[COLOR]

12.4.8 (SPJ WHERE J#='J1')[P#]
    INTERSECT
(SPJ WHERE J#='J2')[P#]

12.4.9 ((SPJ WHERE J#='J1') JOIN (P WHERE COLOR='RED'))[S#]

12.4.10 (SPJ JOIN (J WHERE CITY='LONDON'))[P#]

12.4.11 ((J WHERE CITY='LONDON' OR CITY='PARIS')[J#]
    JOIN SPJ
        JOIN (P WHERE COLOR='RED')[P#])[S#]

12.4.12 (J[J#,CITY] JOIN SPJ JOIN S[S#,CITY])[P#]

12.4.13 ((J WHERE CITY='LONDON')[J#]
    JOIN SPJ
        JOIN (S WHERE CITY='LONDON')[S#])[P#]

12.4.14 ((J[J#,CITY] TIMES SPJ TIMES S[S#,CITY])
    WHERE J.J#=SPJ.J# AND SPJ.S#=S.S#
        AND J.CITY¬=S.CITY)[J#]

Note that JOIN as we have defined it is of no use here.

12.4.15 J[J#] MINUS
    (((S WHERE CITY='LONDON')[S#]
        JOIN SPJ
            JOIN (P WHERE COLOR='RED')[P#])[J#])

12.4.16 (((((SPJ JOIN (P WHERE COLOR='RED')[P#])[S#])
            JOIN SPJ)[P#] JOIN SPJ)[S#]

12.4.17 ((SPJ WHERE S#='S1')[P#] JOIN SPJ)[J#]

12.4.18 `((S[S#,CITY] TIMES SPJ TIMES J[J#,CITY])`
`WHERE S.S#=SPJ.S# AND SPJ.J#=J.J#)`
`[S.CITY,J.CITY]`

12.4.19 `((S[S#,CITY] TIMES SPJ TIMES J[J#,CITY])`
`WHERE S.S#=SPJ.S# AND SPJ.J#=J.J#)`
`[S.CITY,P#,J.CITY]`

12.4.20 `((S[S#,CITY] TIMES SPJ TIMES J[J#,CITY])`
`WHERE S.S#=SPJ.S# AND SPJ.J#=J.J#`
`AND S.CITY¬=J.CITY)`
`[S.CITY,P#,J.CITY]`

12.4.21 `(SPJ[S#,P#,J#] DIVIDEBY J[J#])[S#]`

12.4.22 `(SPJ WHERE S#='S1')[J#]`
`MINUS`
`(SPJ WHERE S#¬='S1')[J#]`

12.4.23 `SPJ[P#,J#] DIVIDEBY (J WHERE CITY='LONDON')[J#]`

12.4.24 `SPJ[J#,P#] DIVIDEBY (SPJ WHERE S#='S1')[P#]`

12.4.25 `J[J#] MINUS`
`((SPJ JOIN (P[P#] MINUS`
`(SPJ WHERE S#='S1')[P#]))[J#])`

12.4.26 `SPJ[J#,S#,P#] DIVIDEBY (SPJ WHERE S#='S1')[S#,P#]`

12.4.27 `J[J#] MINUS`
`((SPJ[J#,P#] MINUS`
`(SPJ WHERE S#='S1')[J#,P#])[J#])`

12.4.28 `SPJ[J#,S#] DIVIDEBY (SPJ JOIN`
`(P WHERE COLOR='RED')[P#])[S#]`

CHAPTER 13: RELATIONAL CALCULUS

13.1 (a) True. (b) True. (c) False. (d) True. Note that *like* quantifiers can be written in any order, whereas for *unlike* quantifiers the sequence is significant. As an illustration, suppose that *x* and *y* are integers and *f* is the formula "$y > x$." It should be clear that $\forall x(\exists y(y > x))$ is true, whereas $\exists y(\forall x(y > x))$ is false. Thus interchanging unlike quantifiers changes the meaning of the formula.

13.2 For each of the following questions we give first a tuple calculus solution, then a domain calculus solution. Tuple variables and domain variables are given names as in the body of the chapter; we do not show their declarations.

13.2.1 `JX.J#,JX.JNAME,JX.CITY`

`JX,JNAMEX,CITYX WHERE J(J#:JX,`
`JNAME:JNAMEX,`
`CITY:CITYX)`

An obvious shorthand in the tuple calculus solution would be to allow simply "JX" in the target list (as an abbreviation for "JX.J#,JX.JNAME,JX.CITY").

13.2.2 `JX.J#,JX.JNAME,JX.CITY WHERE JX.CITY='LONDON'`

`JX,JNAMEX,CITYX  WHERE  J(J#:JX,`
`JNAME:JNAMEX,`
`CITY:CITYX) AND`
`CITYX='LONDON'`

13.2.3 PX.P# WHERE ∀PY(PY.WEIGHT>=PX.WEIGHT)

PX WHERE ∀WEIGHTZ(IF ∃WEIGHTX(P(P#:PX,WEIGHT:WEIGHTX) AND
                                P(WEIGHT:WEIGHTZ))
                   THEN WEIGHTZ>=WEIGHTX)

13.2.4 SPJX.S# WHERE SPJX.J#='J1'

SX WHERE SPJ(S#:SX,J#:'J1')

13.2.5 SPJX.S# WHERE SPJX.P#='P1' AND SPJX.J#='J1'

SX WHERE SPJ(S#:SX,P#:'P1',J#:'J1')

13.2.6 JX.JNAME WHERE ∃SPJX(SPJX.J#=JX.J# AND
                             SPJX.S#='S1')

JNAMEX WHERE ∃JX(J(J#:JX,JNAME:JNAMEX) AND
                 SPJ(J#:JX,S#:'S1'))

13.2.7 PX.COLOR WHERE ∃SPJX(SPJX.P#=PX.P# AND
                            SPJX.S#='S1')

COLORX WHERE ∃PX(P(P#:PX,COLOR:COLORX) AND
                 SPJ(P#:PX,S#:'S1'))

13.2.8 SPJX.S# WHERE SPJX.J#='J1' AND
                    ∃SPJY(SPJY.S#=SPJX.S# AND
                          SPJY.J#='J2')

SX WHERE SPJ(S#:SX,J#:'J1') AND
         SPJ(S#:SX,J#:'J2')

13.2.9 SPJX.S# WHERE ∃PX(PX.COLOR='RED' AND
                        SPJX.P#=PX.P# AND
                        SPJX.J#='J1')

SX WHERE ∃PX(P(P#:PX,COLOR:'RED') AND
             SPJ(S#:SX,P#:PX,J#:'J1'))

13.2.10 SPJX.P# WHERE ∃JX(JX.CITY='LONDON' AND
                         SPJX.J#=JX.J#)

PX WHERE ∃JX(SPJ(P#:PX,J#:JX) AND
             J(J#:JX,CITY:'LONDON'))

13.2.11 SPJX.S# WHERE ∃PX(∃JX(PX.COLOR='RED' AND
                              (JX.CITY='LONDON' OR
                               JX.CITY='PARIS') AND
                              SPJX.P#=PX.P# AND
                              SPJX.J#=JX.J#))

SX WHERE ∃PX(∃JX(SPJ(S#:SX,P#:PX,J#:JX) AND
                 P(P#:PX,COLOR:'RED') AND
                 (J(J#:JX,CITY:'LONDON') OR
                  J(J#:JX,CITY:'PARIS'))))

13.2.12 SPJX.P# WHERE ∃SX(∃JX(SX.CITY=JX.CITY AND
                             SPJX.S#=SX.S# AND
                             SPJX.J#=JX.J#))

```
        PX WHERE ∃SX(∃JX(∃CITYX(SPJ(S#:SX,P#:PX,J#:JX) AND
                              S(S#:SX,CITY:CITYX) AND
                              J(J#:JX,CITY:CITYX)))
```

13.2.13
```
        SPJX.P# WHERE ∃SX(∃JX(SX.CITY='LONDON' AND
                              JX.CITY='LONDON' AND
                              SX.S#=SPJX.S# AND
                              JX.J#=SPJX.J#))

        PX WHERE ∃SX(∃JX(SPJ(S#:SX,P#:PX,J#:JX) AND
                         S(S#:SX,CITY:'LONDON') AND
                         J(J#:JX,CITY:'LONDON')))
```

13.2.14
```
        SPJX.P# WHERE ∃SX(∃JX(SX.CITY¬=JX.CITY AND
                              SPJX.S#=SX.S# AND
                              SPJX.J#=JX.J#))

        PX WHERE ∃SX(∃JX(∃CITYX(∃CITYZ(SPJ(S#:SX,P#:PX,J#:JX) AND
                                       S(S#:SX,CITY:CITYX) AND
                                       J(J#:JX,CITY:CITYZ) AND
                                       CITYX¬=CITYZ))))
```

13.2.15
```
        JX.J# WHERE NOT ∃SPJX(∃SX(∃PX(SX.CITY='LONDON' AND
                                      PX.COLOR='RED' AND
                                      SPJX.S#=SX.S# AND
                                      SPJX.P#=PX.P# AND
                                      SPJX.J#=JX.J#)))

        JX WHERE J(J#:JX) AND
                 NOT ∃SX(∃PX(SPJ(S#:SX,P#:PX,J#:JX) AND
                             S(S#:SX,CITY:'LONDON') AND
                             P(P#:PX,COLOR:'RED')))
```

13.2.16
```
        SPJX.S# WHERE ∃SPJY(SPJY.P#=SPJX.P#  AND
                            ∃SPJZ(SPJZ.S#=SPJY.S# AND
                                  ∃PX(PX.P#=SPJZ.P# AND
                                      PX.COLOR='RED')))

        SX WHERE ∃PX(∃SY(∃PY(SPJ(S#:SX,P#:PX) AND
                             SPJ(P#:PX,S#:SY) AND
                             SPJ(S#:SY,P#:PY) AND
                             P(P#:PY,COLOR:'RED'))))
```

13.2.17
```
        SPJX.J# WHERE ∃SPJY(SPJX.P#=SPJY.P# AND
                            SPJY.S#='S1')

        JX WHERE ∃PX(SPJ(J#:JX,P#:PX) AND
                     SPJ(P#:PX,S#:'S1'))
```

13.2.18
```
        SX.CITY,JX.CITY WHERE ∃SPJX(SPJX.S#=SX.S# AND
                                    SPJX.J#=JX.J#)

        CITYX,CITYZ WHERE ∃SX(∃JZ(S(S#:SX,CITY:CITYX) AND
                                  J(J#:JZ,CITY:CITYZ) AND
                                  SPJ(S#:SX,J#:JZ)))
```

13.2.19
```
        SX.CITY,SPJX.P#,JX.CITY WHERE ∃SPJY(SPJY.S#=SX.S# AND
                                            SPJY.P#=SPJX.P# AND
                                            SPJY.J#=JX.J#)
```

```
          CITYX,PY,CITYZ WHERE ∃SX(∃JZ(S(S#:SX,CITY:CITYX) AND
                                     J(J#:JZ,CITY:CITYZ) AND
                                     SPJ(S#:SX,P#:PY,J#:JZ)))
13.2.20 SX.CITY,SPJX.P#,JX.CITY WHERE ∃SPJY(SPJY.S#=SX.S# AND
                                            SPJY.P#=SPJX.P# AND
                                            SPJY.J#=JX.J# AND
                                            SX.CITY⌐=JX.CITY)

          CITYX,PY,CITYZ WHERE ∃SX(∃JZ(S(S#:SX,CITY:CITYX) AND
                                     J(J#:JZ,CITY:CITYZ) AND
                                     SPJ(S#:SX,P#:PY,J#:JZ) AND
                                     CITYX⌐=CITYZ))
13.2.21 SPJX.S# WHERE ∀JX(∃SPJY(SPJY.S#=SPJX.S# AND
                               SPJY.P#=SPJX.P#  AND
                               SPJY.J#=JX.J#))

          SX WHERE ∃PX(∀JX(SPJ(S#:SX,P#:PX,J#:JX)))
13.2.22 SPJX.J# WHERE ∀SPJY(IF SPJY.J#=SPJX.J#
                           THEN SPJY.S#='S1')

          JX WHERE ∀SX(IF SPJ(S#:SX,J#:JX)
                      THEN SX='S1')
13.2.23 SPJX.P# WHERE ∀JX(IF JX.CITY='LONDON'
                         THEN ∃SPJY(SPJY.P#=SPJX.P# AND
                                    SPJY.J#=JX.J#))

          PX WHERE ∀JX(IF J(J#:JX,CITY:'LONDON')
                      THEN SPJ(P#:PX,J#:JX))
13.2.24 SPJX.J# WHERE ∀SPJY(IF SPJY.S#='S1'
                           THEN ∃SPJZ(SPJZ.J#=SPJX.J# AND
                                      SPJZ.P#=SPJY.P#))

          JX WHERE ∀PX(IF SPJ(S#:'S1',P#:PX)
                      THEN SPJ(P#:PX,J#:JX))
13.2.25 SPJX.J# WHERE ∀SPJY(IF SPJY.J#=SPJX.J#
                           THEN ∃SPJZ(SPJZ.P#=SPJY.P# AND
                                      SPJZ.S#='S1'))

          JX WHERE ∀PX(IF SPJ(J#:JX,P#:PX)
                      THEN SPJ(P#:PX,S#:'S1'))
13.2.26 SPJX.J# WHERE ∀SPJY(IF SPJY.S#='S1'
                           THEN ∃SPJZ(SPJZ.S#='S1' AND
                                      SPJZ.P#=SPJY.P# AND
                                      SPJZ.J#=SPJX.J#))

          JX WHERE ∀PX(IF SPJ(S#:'S1',P#:PX)
                      THEN SPJ(S#:'S1',P#:PX,J#:JX))
13.2.27 SPJX.J# WHERE ∀SPJY(IF SPJY.J#=SPJX.J#
                           THEN ∃SPJZ(SPJZ.P#=SPJY.P# AND
                                      SPJZ.J#=SPJX.J# AND
                                      SPJZ.S#='S1'))

          JX WHERE ∀PX(IF SPJ(P#:PX,J#:JX)
                      THEN SPJ(P#:PX,J#:JX,S#:'S1'))
```

13.2.28 `SPJX.J# WHERE ∀SPJY(IF ∃PX(PX.COLOR='RED' AND`
`                                 PX.P#=SPJY.P#)`
`                          THEN ∃SPJZ(SPJZ.S#=SPJY.S# AND`
`                                     SPJZ.J#=SPJZ.J#))`

`        JX WHERE ∀SX(IF ∃PX(SPJ(S#:SX,P#:PX) AND`
`                            P(P#:PX,COLOR:'RED'))`
`                    THEN SPJ(S#:SX,J#:JX))`

13.3 Again we give tuple calculus solutions first. Solutions are omitted if they do not differ from the corresponding solution under 13.2.

13.3.6 `JX.JNAME WHERE JX.J#=SPJX.J# AND`
`                SPJX.S#='S1'`

`        JNAMEX WHERE J(J#:JX,JNAME:JNAMEX) AND`
`                     SPJ(J#:JX,S#:'S1')`

13.3.7 `PX.COLOR WHERE PX.P#=SPJX.P# AND`
`                SPJX.S#='S1'`

`        COLORX WHERE P(P#:PX,COLOR:COLORX) AND`
`                     SPJ(P#:PX,S#:'S1')`

13.3.8 `SPJX.S# WHERE SPJX.J#='J1' AND`
`                SPJX.S#=SPJY.S# AND`
`                SPJY.J#='J2'`

`        SX WHERE SPJ(S#:SX,J#:'J1') AND`
`                 SPJ(S#:SX,J#:'J2')`

13.3.9 `SPJX.S# WHERE SPJX.J#='J1' AND`
`                SPJX.P#=PX.P# AND`
`                PX.COLOR='RED'`

`        SX WHERE P(P#:PX,COLOR:'RED') AND`
`                 SPJ(S#:SX,P#:PX,J#:'J1')`

13.3.10 `SPJX.P# WHERE SPJX.J#=JX.J# AND`
`                 JX.CITY='LONDON'`

`        PX WHERE SPJ(P#:PX,J#:JX) AND`
`                 J(J#:JX,CITY:'LONDON')`

13.3.11 `SPJX.S# WHERE SPJX.P#=PX.P# AND`
`                 SPJX.J#=JX.J# AND`
`                 PX.COLOR='RED' AND`
`                 (JX.CITY='LONDON' OR`
`                  JX.CITY='PARIS')`

`        SX WHERE SPJ(S#:SX,P#:PX,J#:JX) AND`
`                 P(P#:PX,COLOR:'RED') AND`
`                 (J(J#:JX,CITY:'LONDON') OR`
`                  J(J#:JX,CITY:'PARIS'))`

13.3.12 `SPJX.P# WHERE SPJX.S#=SX.S# AND`
`                 SPJX.J#=JX.J# AND`
`                 SX.CITY=JX.CITY`

`        PX WHERE SPJ(S#:SX,P#:PX,J#:JX) AND`
`                 S(S#:SX,CITY:CITYX) AND`
`                 J(J#:JX,CITY:CITYX)`

13.3.13 SPJX.P# WHERE SPJX.S#=SX.S# AND
                      SPJX.J#=JX.J# AND
                      SX.CITY='LONDON' AND
                      JX.CITY='LONDON'

   PX WHERE SPJ(S#:SX,P#:PX,J#:JX) AND
              S(S#:SX,CITY:'LONDON') AND
              J(J#:JX,CITY:'LONDON')

13.3.14 SPJX.P# WHERE SPJX.S#=SX.S# AND
                      SPJX.J#=JX.J# AND
                      SX.CITY⌐=JX.CITY

    PX WHERE SPJ(S#:SX,P#:PX,J#:JX) AND
               S(S#:SX,CITY:CITYX) AND
               J(J#:JX,CITY:CITYZ) AND
               CITYX⌐=CITYZ

13.3.16 SPJX.S# WHERE SPJX.P#=SPJY.P# AND
                      SPJY.S#=SPJZ.S# AND
                      SPJZ.P#=PX.P# AND
                      PX.COLOR='RED'

    SX WHERE SPJ(S#:SX,P#:PX) AND
               SPJ(P#:PX,S#:SY) AND
               SPJ(S#:SY,P#:PY) AND
               P(P#:PY,COLOR:'RED')

13.3.17 SPJX.J# WHERE SPJX.P#=SPJY.P# AND
                      SPJY.S#='S1'

    JX WHERE SPJ(J#:JX,P#:PX) AND
               SPJ(P#:PX,S#:'S1')

13.3.18 SX.CITY,JX.CITY WHERE SX.S#=SPJX.S# AND
                              SPJX.J#=JX.J#

    CITYX,CITYZ WHERE S(S#:SX,CITY:CITYX) AND
                        J(J#:JZ,CITY:CITYZ) AND
                        SPJ(S#:SX,J#:JZ)

13.3.19 SX.CITY,SPJX.P#,JX.CITY WHERE SX.S#=SPJY.S# AND
                                     SPJX.P#=SPJY.P# AND
                                     JX.J#=SPJY.J#

    CITYX,PY,CITYZ WHERE S(S#:SX,CITY:CITYX) AND
                           J(J#:JZ,CITY:CITYZ) AND
                           SPJ(S#:SX,P#:PY,J#:JZ)

13.3.20 SX.CITY,SPJX.P#,JX.CITY WHERE SX.S#=SPJY.S# AND
                                     SPJX.P#=SPJY.P# AND
                                     JX.J#=SPJY.J# AND
                                     SX.CITY⌐=JX.CITY

    CITYX,PY,CITYZ WHERE S(S#:SX,CITY:CITYX) AND
                           J(J#:JZ,CITY:CITYZ) AND
                           SPJ(S#:SX,P#:PY,J#:JZ) AND
                           CITYX⌐=CITYZ

13.3.21 `SPJX.S# WHERE ∀JX(∃SPJY(SPJY.S#=SPJX.S# AND`
`SPJY.P#=SPJX.P# AND`
`SPJY.J#=JX.J#))`

`SX WHERE ∀JX(SPJ(S#:SX,P#:PX,J#:JX))`

CHAPTER 14: FURTHER NORMALIZATION

14.1 The diagram shows all direct functional dependencies involved, both those implied by the wording of the exercise and those corresponding to "reasonable assumptions" about the semantics (stated explicitly below). The attribute names are intended to be self-explanatory.

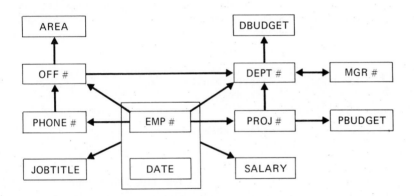

For *multivalued* dependencies, see Step 1 below. We assume that there are no additional join dependencies (i.e., JDs that are not FDs or MVDs).

Semantic assumptions
- No employee is the manager of more than one department at a time.
- No employee works in more than one department at a time.
- No employee works on more than one project at a time.
- No employee has more than one office at a time.
- No employee has more than one phone at a time.
- No employee has more than one job at a time.
- No project is assigned to more than one department at a time.
- No office is assigned to more than one department at a time.

Step 0
First observe that the hierarchical structure may be considered as an unnormalized relation DEPT0 defined on domains DEPT# (the primary key), DBUDGET,

MGR#, and three further domains whose elements are nonatomic: XEMP0, XPROJ0, and XOFFICE0, say. We may represent this unnormalized relation as

DEPT0(<u>DEPT#</u>,DBUDGET,MGR#,XEMP0,XPROJ0,XOFFICE0)

(the primary key is indicated by underlining). Now let us ignore employees and offices for a moment and concentrate on projects. Define the relation

PROJ0(<u>PROJ#</u>,PBUDGET)

to be the set of *all* PROJ#-PBUDGET pairs. Then the XPROJ0 value associated with any particular department is some subset of this set. Hence the domain XPROJ0 actually consists of the set of all subsets of PROJ0 (the so-called power set of PROJ0).

Similar remarks apply to XEMP0, XOFFICE0, and indeed to all domains in the example whose elements are nonatomic: In each case the domain is the power set of a relation defined as the set of all tuples of a particular type. We shall indicate each such power set by a prefix X. Then the complete collection of relations, normalized and unnormalized, is as follows.

```
DEPT0(DEPT#,DBUDGET,MGR#,XEMP0,XPROJ0,XOFFICE0)
EMP0(EMP#,PROJ#,OFF#,PHONE#,XJOB0)
JOB0(JOBTITLE,XSALHIST0)
SALHIST0(DATE,SALARY)
PROJ0(PROJ#,PBUDGET)
OFFICE0(OFF#,AREA,XPHONE0)
PHONE0(PHONE#)
```

Step 1

We now reduce this set to a collection of 1NF relations. This preliminary reduction process is explained by Codd [4.1] as follows. Starting with the relation at the top of the hierarchy, we take its primary key and expand each of the immediately subordinate relations by inserting this primary key. The primary key of each expanded relation is the combination of the primary key before expansion, together with the primary key copied down from the parent relation. Now we strike out from the parent relation all nonsimple attributes (i.e., those whose elements are nonatomic), remove the top node of the hierarchy, and repeat the same sequence of operations on each remaining subhierarchy. We obtain the following collection of 1NF relations. Note that we have lost the power sets. In fact, by considering each subhierarchy separately, we have immediately eliminated all multivalued dependencies that are not also functional dependencies.

```
DEPT1(DEPT#,DBUDGET,MGR#)
EMP1(DEPT#,EMP#,PROJ#,OFF#,PHONE#)
JOB1(DEPT#,EMP#,JOBTITLE)
SALHIST1(DEPT#,EMP#,JOBTITLE,DATE,SALARY)
PROJ1(DEPT#,PROJ#,PBUDGET)
OFFICE1(DEPT#,OFF#,AREA)
PHONE1(DEPT#,OFF#,PHONE#)
```

Step 2

We may now reduce the 1NF relations to an equivalent 2NF collection by eliminating nonfull dependencies. We shall consider the 1NF relations one by one.

DEPT1:   This relation is already in 2NF.

EMP1:   First observe that DEPT# is actually redundant as a component of the primary key for this relation. We may take EMP# alone as the primary key, in which case the relation is in 2NF as it stands.

JOB1:   Again, observe that DEPT# is not required as a key component. Since DEPT# is functionally dependent on EMP#, we have a non-key attribute (DEPT#) that is not fully functionally dependent on the primary key (the combination EMP#-JOBTITLE), and hence JOB1 is not 2NF. We can replace it by

JOB2(<u>EMP#,JOBTITLE</u>)

and

JOB2'(<u>EMP#</u>,DEPT#)

However, JOB2 is a projection of SALHIST2 (see below), and JOB2' is a projection of EMP1 (renamed as EMP2 below); hence both these relations may be discarded.

SALHIST1: As with JOB1, we can project out DEPT# entirely. Moreover, JOBTITLE is not required as a key component; we may take the combination EMP#-DATE as the primary key, to obtain the 2NF relation

SALHIST2(<u>EMP#,DATE</u>,JOBTITLE,SALARY)

PROJ1:   As with EMP1, we may consider DEPT# as a nonkey attribute; the relation is then 2NF.

OFFICE1:   Similar remarks apply.

PHONE1:   We can project out DEPT# entirely, since the relation (DEPT#, OFF#) is a projection of OFFICE1 (renamed as OFFICE2 below). Also, OFF# is functionally dependent on PHONE#, so we may take PHONE# alone as the primary key, to obtain the 2NF relation

PHONE2(<u>PHONE#</u>,OFF#)

Note that this is not necessarily a projection of EMP2 (phones or offices may exist without being assigned to employees), so that we cannot discard this relation.

Hence our collection of 2NF relations is

```
DEPT2(DEPT#,DBUDGET,MGR#)
EMP2(EMP#,DEPT#,PROJ#,OFF#,PHONE#)
SALHIST2(EMP#,DATE,JOBTITLE,SALARY)
PROJ2(PROJ#,DEPT#,PBUDGET)
OFFICE2(OFF#,DEPT#,AREA)
PHONE2(PHONE#,OFF#)
```

Step 3

Now we may reduce the 2NF relations to an equivalent 3NF set by eliminating transitive dependencies. The only 2NF relation that is not already 3NF is the relation

EMP2, in which OFF# and DEPT# are both transitively dependent on the primary key EMP#: OFF# via PHONE#, and DEPT# via PROJ# *and* via OFF# (and hence PHONE#). The 3NF relations (projections) corresponding to EMP2 are

```
EMP3(EMP#,PROJ#,PHONE#)
X(PHONE#,OFF#)
Y(PROJ#,DEPT#)
Z(OFF#,DEPT#)
```

However, X is PHONE2, Y is a projection of PROJ2, and Z is a projection of OFFICE2. Hence our collection of 3NF relations is

```
DEPT3(DEPT#,DBUDGET,MGR#)
EMP3(EMP#,PROJ#,PHONE#)
SALHIST3(EMP#,DATE,JOBTITLE,SALARY)
PROJ3(PROJ#,DEPT#,PBUDGET)
OFFICE3(OFF#,DEPT#,AREA)
PHONE3(PHONE#,OFF#)
```

Each of these 3NF relations is in fact BCNF, and indeed 4NF (because of the way we performed the reduction to 1NF in Step 1). By our assumption concerning JDs they are also 5NF, so the decomposition is complete. Note that in DEPT3 we have two candidate keys, DEPT# and MGR#.

We observe also that, given certain (reasonable) additional semantic constraints, this collection of relations is *strongly redundant* [4.1], in that the projection of relation PROJ3 over (PROJ#,DEPT#) is a projection of the join of EMP3 and PHONE3 and OFFICE3.

Note finally that it is possible to "spot" the 3NF relations from the functional dependence diagram. (How?)

14.2 The diagram shows all direct functional dependencies involved.

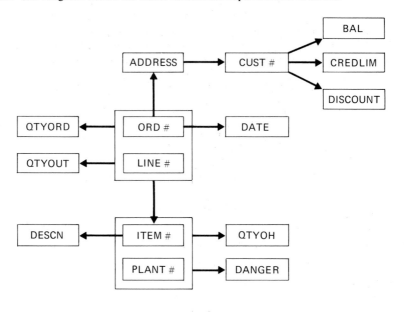

Semantic assumptions

- No two customers have the same ship-to address.

- Each order is identified by a unique order number.

- Each detail line within an order is identified by a line number, unique within the order.

4NF (5NF) relations

```
CUST(CUST#,BAL,CREDLIM,DISCOUNT)
SHIPTO(ADDRESS,CUST#)
ORDHEAD(ORD#,ADDRESS,DATE)
ORDLINE(ORD#,LINE#,ITEM#,QTYORD,QTYOUT)
ITEM(ITEM#,DESCN)
IP(ITEM#,PLANT#,QTYOH,DANGER)
```

14.3 Consider the processing that must be performed by a program handling orders. We assume that the input order specifies customer number, ship-to address, and details of the items ordered (item numbers and quantities).

```
SELECT * FROM CUST WHERE CUST.CUST#=input.CUST#
check balance, credit limit etc
SELECT * FROM SHIPTO WHERE SHIPTO.ADDR=input.ADDR AND
                          SHIPTO.CUST#=input.CUST#
(this checks ship-to address)
if everything is OK go ahead and process the order
```

If 99 percent of customers actually have only one ship-to address, it would be rather inefficient to put that address in a relation other than CUST (considering only the 99 percent, ADDR is in fact functionally dependent on CUST#). We can improve matters as follows. For each customer we designate one valid ship-to address as that customer's *primary* address. For the 99 percent, of course, the primary address is the only address. Any remaining addresses we refer to as *secondary*. Relation CUST can then be redefined as

```
CUST(CUST#,ADDR,BAL,CREDLIM,DISCOUNT)
```

and relation SHIPTO can be replaced by

```
SECOND(ADDR,CUST#)
```

Here CUST.ADDR refers to the primary address, and SECOND contains all secondary addresses (and corresponding customer numbers). These relations are 4NF. The order-processing program now looks like this:

```
SELECT * FROM CUST WHERE CUST.CUST#=input.CUST#
check balance, credit limit etc
IF CUST.ADDR¬=input.ADDR THEN
SELECT * FROM SECOND WHERE SECOND.ADDR=input.ADDR AND
                          SECOND.CUST#=input.CUST#
    (this checks ship-to address)
if everything is OK go ahead and process the order
```

The advantages of this approach are as follows:

■ Processing is simpler and marginally more efficient for 99 percent of customers.

■ If the ship-to address is omitted from the input order, the primary address could be used by default.

■ Suppose that the customer may have a different discount for each ship-to address. With the original approach (shown in the answer to Exercise 14.2), the DISCOUNT attribute would have to be moved to the SHIPTO relation, making processing still more complicated. With the revised approach, however, the primary discount (corresponding to the primary address) can be represented by an appearance of DISCOUNT in CUST, and secondary discounts by a corresponding appearance of DISCOUNT in SECOND. Both relations are still in 4NF, and the processing is again simpler for 99 percent of customers.

To sum up: Isolating exceptional cases is probably a valuable technique for obtaining the best of both worlds—i.e., combining the advantages of 4NF with the simplification in retrieval operations that may occur if the restrictions of 4NF are violated.

14.4 The diagrams illustrate the (most important) functional dependencies.

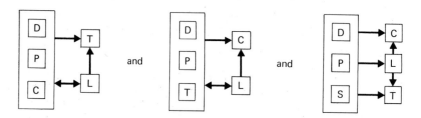

A possible collection of 4NF relations is

```
RELATION SCHED (L,T,C,D,P)
         PRIMARY KEY (L)
         ALTERNATE KEY (T,D,P)
         ALTERNATE KEY (C,D,P)
RELATION STUDY (S,L)
         PRIMARY KEY (S,L)
```

This reduction is not unique.

14.5 (a) True.

(b) True.

(c) False (but "almost true"). A binary relation R(X, Y) can be nonloss-decomposed into its two unary projections R1(X), R2(Y) if and only if R is equal to the Cartesian product of R1 and R2 (remember that join and Cartesian product are identical if the relations being joined have no common attribute). See Fig. 4.2 for an example. Such a relation satisfies the special, nontrivial MVD $\emptyset \rightarrow \rightarrow X|Y$ (where $\emptyset$ is the empty set), and is thus not 4NF.

(d) False; see (c).

(e) False (true if "A→B" is changed to "A→→B"). The "if part" is true. Counter-example for the "only if" part:

R	A	B	C
	a1	b1	c1
	a1	b2	c1
	a1	b1	c2
	a1	b2	c2

R1	A	B
	a1	b1
	a1	b2

R2	A	C
	a1	c1
	a1	c2

R is the join of R1 and R2, yet A→B does not hold in R. (Neither does A→C hold.)

(f) True.

(g) True.

(h) True.

14.6 First we introduce three relations

```
REPS       (REP#,  . . . )
AREAS      (AREA#, . . . )
PRODUCTS   (PROD#, . . . )
```

with the obvious interpretation. Second, we can represent the association between sales representatives and sales areas by a relation

```
RA  (REP#,AREA#)
```

and the association between sales representatives and products by a relation

```
RP  (REP#,PROD#)
```

(both of these are many-to-many associations).

Next, we are told that every product is sold in every area. So if we introduce the relation

```
AP  (AREA#,PROD#)
```

to represent the association between areas and products, then we have the constraint (C)

```
∀AX ∀PX ∃APX (APX.AREA# = AX.AREA# AND
              APX.PROD# = PX.PROD#)
```

(where AX, PX, APX are tuple variables for relations AREAS, PRODUCTS, AP, respectively). Note that constraint C implies that relation AP is not 4NF (see Exercise 14.5).

No two representatives sell the same product in the same area. In other words, given an (AREA#,PROD#) combination, there is exactly one responsible sales representative (REP#), so we can introduce a relation

```
APR (AREA#,PROD#,REP#)
```

in which (to make the functional dependency explicit)

```
APR.(AREA#,PROD#) → APR.REP#
```

(of course, specification of the combination AREA#–PROD# as primary key is sufficient to express this FD). Now, however, relations RA, RP, and AP are all redundant, since they are all projections of APR; they can therefore be dropped. In place of constraint C, we now need the constraint C1

```
∀AX ∀PX ∃APRX (APRX.AREA# = AX.AREA# AND
               APRX.PROD# = PX.PROD#)
```

(where APRX is a tuple variable for relation APR). This constraint certainly needs to be explicit if it is to be enforced by the DBMS, but should be stated explicitly in any case since it represents part of the semantics of the situation and must be understood by the user. Also, since every representative sells all that representative's products in all that representative's areas, we have the constraint C2

```
APR.REP# →→ APR.AREA#|APR.PROD#
```

(a multivalued dependency; relation APR is not 4NF). Again the constraint should be stated explicitly.

Thus the final design consists of relations REPS, AREAS, PRODUCTS, and APR, together with the explicit constraints C1 and C2. This exercise illustrates very clearly the point that, in general, the normalization discipline is adequate to represent *some* semantic aspects of a given problem (FDs and MVDs that are a consequence of keys), but that explicit statement of additional FDs and MVDs may also be needed for other aspects, and some aspects cannot be represented in terms of FDs and MVDs at all. It also illustrates the point that it is not always desirable to normalize "all the way" (relation APR is BCNF but not 4NF).

Note too that additional explicit constraints are also needed, over and above those discussed. For example, we need the constraint

```
∀APRX ∃AX (AX.AREA# = APRX.AREA#)
```

to express the fact that every area mentioned in APR must exist in AREAS; and similarly for products and representatives. Similar constraints are also needed in the earlier exercises in this chapter. A comprehensive discussion of constraints is beyond the scope of this text.

CHAPTER 16: IMS DATA STRUCTURE

```
16.1 COURSE    M23
     PREREQ    M16
     PREREQ    M19
     OFFERING  730813
     TEACHER   421633
     STUDENT   102141
     STUDENT   183009
        . . .   . .   . . .
     STUDENT   761620
     OFFERING  741104
     OFFERING  750106
```

```
16.2 DBD    NAME=PUBDBD
     SEGM   NAME=SUB,BYTES=45
     FIELD  NAME=(SUB#,SEQ),BYTES=7,START=1
     FIELD  NAME=SUBNAME,BYTES=38,START=8
     SEGM   NAME=PUB,PARENT=SUB,BYTES=45
     FIELD  NAME=(PUBNAME,SEQ,M),BYTES=44,START=1
     FIELD  NAME=AMFLAG,BYTES=1,START=45
     SEGM   NAME=DETAILS,PARENT=PUB,BYTES=25
     FIELD  NAME=(DATE,SEQ,M),BYTES=6,START=1
     FIELD  NAME=PUBHOUSE,BYTES=19,START=7
     FIELD  NAME=JNVOLISS,BYTES=19,START=7
     SEGM   NAME=AUTHOR,PARENT=PUB,BYTES=50
     FIELD  NAME=(AUTHNAME,SEQ),BYTES=16,START=1
     FIELD  NAME=AUTHADDR,BYTES=34,START=17
```

Note the M specifications for PUBNAME and DATE.

CHAPTER 17: THE EXTERNAL LEVEL OF IMS

```
17.1 PCB    TYPE=DB,DBDNAME=PUBDBD,KEYLEN=67
     SENSEG NAME=SUB,PROCOPT=G
     SENSEG NAME=PUB,PARENT=SUB,PROCOPT=G
     SENSEG NAME=DETAILS,PARENT=PUB,PROCOPT=G
     SENSEG NAME=AUTHOR,PARENT=PUB,PROCOPT=G
```

CHAPTER 18: IMS DATA MANIPULATION

```
18.1     GU  SUB(SUBNAME='INFORMATION RETRIEVAL')
     GNP GNP AUTHOR
         add author name to result list (eliminating duplicates)
         go to GNP
```

```
18.2     GU SUB
     GN  GN PUB*D
            AUTHOR(AUTHNAME='GRACE'|AUTHNAME='HOBBS')
            add publication name to result list
            go to GN
```

Notice that "or" is represented by | (vertical bar). "And" is represented by an ampersand. With this code a publication will appear twice in the list if Grace and Hobbs are both authors of that publication.

```
18.3     GU SUB
     GN  GN SUB*D
            PUB(AMFLAG='M')
            AUTHOR(AUTHNAME='BRADBURY')
            add subject name to result list (eliminating duplicates)
            go to GN
```

Note that it might be more efficient to issue another 'GN SUB' before branching back. Note, too, that if we did not care whether the publication concerned was an article or a monograph, we could omit the second SSA; IMS would assume that an unconditional SSA on PUB was intended.

18.4
```
       GU   SUB
  GN   GN   PUB(AMFLAG='A')
       GNP AUTHOR(AUTHNAME='OWEN')
       if not found go to GN
       GNP DETAILS*F
       add publication name and date to result list
       go to GN
```

18.5
```
       GU   SUB
  GN   GN   PUB(AMFLAG='M')
       GNP DETAILS(PUBHOUSE='CIDER PRESS'&DATE>'700101')
       if not found go to GN
  GNP  GNP AUTHOR
       if not found go to GN
       add author name to result list (eliminating duplicates)
       go to GNP
```

18.6
```
       build PUB and DETAILS segments concatenated in I/O area
       ISRT SUB(SUBNAME='SCIENCE FICTION')
             PUB*D
             DETAILS
       build AUTHOR segment in I/O area
       ISRT AUTHOR
```

18.7
```
       GU   SUB
  GN   GN   PUB
       set counter=0
  GNP  GNP DETAILS
       if not found go to TST
       set counter=counter+1
       go to GNP
  TST  if counter=1 go to GN
       GHNP DETAILS*F
       DLET
       set counter=counter-1
       go to TST
```

18.8 The use of *V instead of GNP has the effect of reducing the number of sub-routine calls to IMS, and hence improving performance, in Questions 18.4 and 18.5. In the foregoing solution to 18.4 we can replace the GN and first GNP (and the "if not found go to GN") by a single GN

```
       GN PUB(AMFLAG='A')
          AUTHOR(AUTHNAME='OWEN')
```

and the second GNP by

```
       GN PUB*DV
          DETAILS*F
```

(Note the use of two command codes within a single SSA.) The replacements in 18.5 are similar, except that the D and F command codes are not required.

CHAPTER 19: THE INTERNAL LEVEL OF IMS

19.1

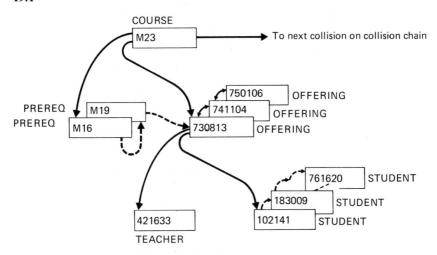

Broken arrows represent hierarchical pointers, solid arrows child/twin pointers.

19.2

Segment	Data	Pointers (number)	Prefix size	Occurrences per PDBR occurrence (average number)	Data bytes per PDBR occurrence (number)	Prefix bytes per PDBR occurrence (number)
COURSE	256	3	18	1	256	18
PREREQ	36	1	10	2	72	20
OFFERING	20	4	22	8	160	176
TEACHER	24	1	10	12	288	120
STUDENT	26	1	10	128	3328	1280
					4104	1614

(A pad byte has been added to the STUDENT segment.)
Ratio prefix bytes to data bytes = 1614/4104 = 39% approximately.
Ratio prefix bytes to total bytes = 1614/5718 = 28% approximately.

19.3 Cases (a) and (b) are impossible because hierarchical pointers are not allowed to cross the boundary between two DSGs. Case (c) may be specified as follows:

```
        DBD      . . .
P DATASET . . .
        SEGM     NAME=COURSE, . . .
Q DATASET . . .
        SEGM     NAME=PREREQ, . . .
        SEGM     NAME=OFFERING, . . .
P DATASET
        SEGM     NAME=TEACHER, . . .
R DATASET . . .
        SEGM     NAME=STUDENT, . . .
```

Case (a) is the only one possible if the storage structure is HISAM (and then only if the supporting access method is ISAM/OSAM).

CHAPTER 20: IMS LOGICAL DATABASES

20.1 The diagram shows a possible pair of PDBs. Observe that PALINK and APLINK are paired segments and that virtual pairing is being used. APLINK has been (arbitrarily) chosen to be the virtual member of the pair (in practice such a choice is made on the basis of performance criteria).

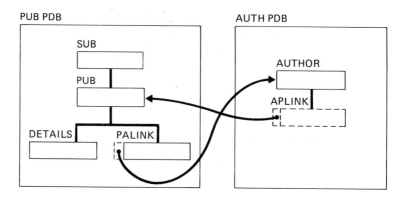

The following LDBs may be defined. (Intersection data and logical-parent fully concatenated keys are not shown.)

SPDA LDB

APD LDB

APS LDB

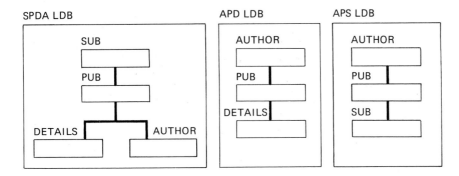

The PUB and AUTH physical DBDs are essentially similar to the AREA and BIRD physical DBDs of Figs. 20.16 and 20.17. The most significant difference is in the specification of the SEQ field for APLINK (the virtual member of the pair):

```
SEGM   NAME=APLINK,POINTER=PAIRED,
       PARENT=AUTHOR,SOURCE=((PALINK,,PUBPDBD))
FIELD  NAME=(FCKEY,SEQ),START=1,BYTES=51
FIELD  NAME=SUB#,START=1,BYTES=7
FIELD  NAME=PUBNAME,START=8,BYTES=44
```

The sequence field is the *fully concatenated* logical parent key, i.e., the combination of SUB# and PUBNAME.

The three logical DBDs are essentially similar to the logical DBD of Fig. 20.9.

20.5 For the EDUC PDB (Fig. 20.21):

```
DBD      NAME=EDUCPDBD, . . .
SEGM     NAME=COURSE,POINTER=TWIN, . . .
LCHILD   NAME=(CP,EDUCPDBD),PAIR=PC,POINTER=SNGL
FIELD    NAME=(COURSE#,SEQ),BYTES=3,START=1
FIELD    NAME=TITLE, . . .
FIELD    NAME=DESCRIPN, . . .
SEGM     NAME=CP,POINTER=(LPARNT,TWIN,LTWIN),
         PARENT=((COURSE),(COURSE,PHYSICAL,EDUCPDBD))
FIELD    NAME=(COURSE#,SEQ), . . .
SEGM     NAME=PC,POINTER=PAIRED,PARENT=COURSE,
         SOURCE=((CP,,EDUCPDBD))
FIELD    NAME=(COURSE#,SEQ), . . .
```

For the EDCP LDB (Fig. 20.22):

```
DBD      NAME=EDCPLDBD,ACCESS=LOGICAL
DATASET  LOGICAL
SEGM     NAME=COURSE,SOURCE=((COURSE,,EDUCPDBD))
SEGM     NAME=PREREQ,PARENT=COURSE,
         SOURCE=((CP,,EDUCPDBD),(COURSE,,EDUCPDBD))
```

For the EDPC LDB (Fig. 20.22):

```
DBD        NAME=EDPCLDBD,ACCESS=LOGICAL
DATASET    LOGICAL
SEGM       NAME=PREREQ,SOURCE=((COURSE,,EDUCPDBD))
SEGM       NAME=COURSE,PARENT=PREREQ,
           SOURCE=((PC,,EDUCPDBD),(COURSE,,EDUCPDBD))
```

20.6 If we assume that segments are presented for loading in physical hierarchical sequence, it will not in general be true that the logical parent will already exist when a logical child is submitted for insertion (although it *is* always so with the sample data of Exercise 20.3). Thus, after the data has been loaded into the database, it will be necessary to run a utility program against it to resolve all logical relationships. Alternatively, the "loading" process could involve COURSE segments only, and a subsequent updating program could then be run to insert all the dependent segments as a separate operation.

20.7 We give a sketch of a possible approach (with acknowledgments to Don Chamberlin).

PDBs:

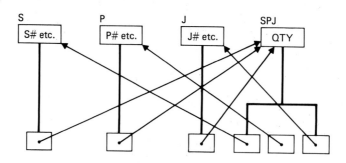

LDBs:

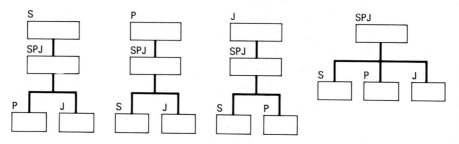

20.8 For retrieval-only applications there is no problem. The effect on applications that perform update operations on any of the databases (PDBs or LDBs) will depend on the insert/delete/replace rules specified for the segments involved. See [19.1].

CHAPTER 21: IMS SECONDARY INDEXING

21.1 The user sees

(a)

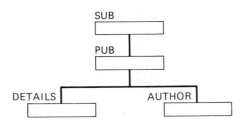

In this case the hierarchical structure is unchanged.

(b)

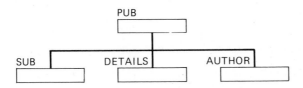

(c)

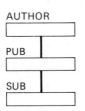

In all three cases (a), (b), and (c), the structure is seen in AUTHNAME sequence, with as many occurrences of the root as there are AUTHOR occurrences in the original database and, for each root occurrence, the corresponding number of occurrences of each of the dependents. See the answer to Exercise 21.6.

21.2 Index DBD:

```
DBD     NAME=AUTHXDBD,ACCESS=INDEX
SEGM    NAME=XSEG,BYTES=16
FIELD   NAME=(AUTHNAME,SEQ,M),BYTES=16,START=1
LCHILD  NAME=(PUB,PUBDBD),INDEX=XAUTH
```

For PUBDBD the following two additional statements are needed for the PUB segment:

```
LCHILD  NAME=(XSEG,AUTHXDBD),POINTER=INDX
XDFLD   NAME=XAUTH,SRCH=AUTHNAME,SEGMENT=AUTHOR
```

Corresponding PCB:

```
PCB     TYPE=DB,...,KEYLEN=32,PROCSEQ=AUTHXDBD
SENSEG NAME=PUB
SENSEG NAME=SUB,PARENT=PUB
SENSEG NAME=DETAILS,PARENT=PUB
SENSEG NAME=AUTHOR,PARENT=PUB
```

21.3
```
        GU    PUB(XAUTH='ADAMS')
    TST if not found, exit
        print PUBNAME
        GN    PUB(XAUTH='ADAMS')
        go to TST
```

21.4
```
        PUB    : AUTHNAME (i.e., XAUTH)
        SUB    : AUTHNAME followed by SUB#
        DETAILS: AUTHNAME followed by DATE
        AUTHOR : AUTHNAME followed by AUTHNAME
                 (the two names are not necessarily the same)
```

21.5
```
        Get    : no restrictions
        Insert : not allowed for PUB or SUB
        Delete : not allowed for PUB or SUB
        Replace: not allowed for PUBNAME, SUB#, DATE, AUTHNAME
```

21.6
```
        PUB    : 12000
        SUB    : 12000
        DETAILS: 18000
        AUTHOR : 14400
```

21.7 A possible method of supporting key-sequential access to root segments in HDAM.

CHAPTER 24: DBTG DATA STRUCTURE

24.1 (To be compared with the answer to Exercise 16.2.)

```
SCHEMA NAME IS PUB-SCHEMA.

RECORD NAME IS SUB;
    DUPLICATES ARE NOT ALLOWED FOR SUBNO IN SUB.
    02 SUBNO        ; TYPE IS CHARACTER 7.
    02 SUBNAME      ; TYPE IS CHARACTER 38.
RECORD NAME IS PUB;
    02 PUBNAME      ; TYPE IS CHARACTER 44.
    02 AMFLAG       ; TYPE IS BIT       1.

RECORD NAME IS DETAILS;
    02 DATE         ; TYPE IS CHARACTER 6.
    02 PHJV         ; TYPE IS CHARACTER 19.

RECORD NAME IS AUTHOR;
    02 AUTHNAME     ; TYPE IS CHARACTER 16.
    02 AUTHADDR     ; TYPE IS CHARACTER 34.
```

```
SET NAME IS SUBJECTS;
    OWNER IS SYSTEM;
    ORDER IS SORTED BY DEFINED KEYS
    DUPLICATES ARE NOT ALLOWED.
    MEMBER IS SUB;
        INSERTION IS AUTOMATIC
        RETENTION IS FIXED;
        KEY IS ASCENDING SUBNO IN SUB.

SET NAME IS SUBPUB;
    OWNER IS SUB;
    ORDER IS SORTED BY DEFINED KEYS
    DUPLICATES ARE ALLOWED.
    MEMBER IS PUB;
        INSERTION IS AUTOMATIC
        RETENTION IS FIXED;
        KEY IS ASCENDING PUBNAME IN PUB;
        SET SELECTION IS BY APPLICATION. (default, not specified
                                                    explicitly)

SET NAME IS PUBDET;
    OWNER IS PUB;
    ORDER IS SORTED BY DEFINED KEYS
    DUPLICATES ARE ALLOWED.
    MEMBER IS DETAILS;
        INSERTION IS AUTOMATIC
        RETENTION IS FIXED;
        KEY IS DESCENDING DATE IN DETAILS;
        SET SELECTION IS BY APPLICATION. (default, not specified
                                                    explicitly)

SET NAME IS PUBAUTH;
    OWNER IS PUB;
    ORDER IS SORTED BY DEFINED KEYS
    DUPLICATES ARE NOT ALLOWED.
    MEMBER IS AUTHOR;
        INSERTION IS AUTOMATIC
        RETENTION IS FIXED;
        KEY IS ASCENDING AUTHNAME IN AUTHOR;
        SET SELECTION IS BY APPLICATION. (default, not specified
                                                    explicitly)
```

Notes

1. AMFLAG has been declared as BIT 1 simply to show that BIT is a permissible data-type.

2. The ordering in set PUBDET has been specified as descending date sequence simply to show that this can be done. A like feature in IMS would have considerably simplified Exercise 18.7.

3. The singular set SUBJECTS has been introduced in order that SUB occurrences may be sequenced on SUBNO (as in the corresponding IMS database).

4. Membership class has been specified in all cases as AUTOMATIC FIXED. This is to make the DBTG structure reflect as closely as possible the corresponding IMS structure (in which no child segment can exist independently of its parent).

5. DUPLICATES ARE ALLOWED means that, for example, two publications on the same subject may have the same title, and that the relative position of two member records with the same sort control key will be determined by the DBMS, not by the user. For information on other DUPLICATES options, see [23.4].

6. SET SELECTION for the three nonsingular sets is shown as BY APPLICATION, to match most closely the situation in IMS. (BY APPLICATION is actually specified by *omitting* the SET SELECTION clause, but for clarity we show it explicitly.)

24.2 `SCHEMA NAME IS MANAGERIAL-STRUCTURE.`

```
RECORD NAME IS EMP;
      DUPLICATES ARE NOT ALLOWED FOR ENO IN EMP.
      02 ENO . . .

      RECORD NAME IS LINK.

      SET NAME IS EL;
            . . .
            OWNER IS EMP;
            MEMBER IS LINK;
            . . .

      SET NAME IS LE;
            . . .
            OWNER IS LINK;
            MEMBER IS EMP;
            . . .
```

Note that membership must be MANUAL in at least one of these two sets (why?).

24.3 `SCHEMA NAME IS S-P-J-SCHEMA.`

```
RECORD NAME IS S;
      DUPLICATES ARE NOT ALLOWED FOR SNO IN S.
      02 SNO    ; TYPE IS CHARACTER 5.
      02 SNAME  ; TYPE IS CHARACTER 20.
      02 STATUS ; TYPE IS FIXED DECIMAL 3.
      02 CITY   ; TYPE IS CHARACTER 15.

RECORD NAME IS P;
      DUPLICATES ARE NOT ALLOWED FOR PNO IN P.
      02 PNO    ; TYPE IS CHARACTER 6.
      02 PNAME  ; TYPE IS CHARACTER 20.
      02 COLOR  ; TYPE IS CHARACTER 6.
      02 WEIGHT ; TYPE IS FIXED DECIMAL 4.

RECORD NAME IS J;
      DUPLICATES ARE NOT ALLOWED FOR JNO IN J.
      02 JNO    ; TYPE IS CHARACTER 4.
      02 JNAME  ; TYPE IS CHARACTER 20.
      02 CITY   ; TYPE IS CHARACTER 15.
```

```
RECORD NAME IS SPJ;
     DUPLICATES ARE NOT ALLOWED FOR SNO IN SPJ,
                                     PNO IN SPJ,
                                     JNO IN SPJ.
     02 SNO    ; TYPE IS CHARACTER 5.
     02 PNO    ; TYPE IS CHARACTER 6.
     02 JNO    ; TYPE IS CHARACTER 4.
     02 QTY    ; TYPE IS FIXED DECIMAL 5.

SET NAME IS S-SPJ;
     OWNER IS S;
     ORDER IS SORTED BY DEFINED KEYS
     DUPLICATES ARE NOT ALLOWED.
     MEMBER IS SPJ;
         INSERTION IS AUTOMATIC
         RETENTION IS FIXED;
         KEY IS ASCENDING PNO IN SPJ, JNO IN SPJ;
         SET SELECTION IS BY VALUE OF SNO IN S.

SET NAME IS S-SET;
     OWNER IS SYSTEM;
     ORDER IS SORTED BY DEFINED KEYS
     DUPLICATES ARE NOT ALLOWED.
     MEMBER IS S;
         INSERTION IS AUTOMATIC
         RETENTION IS FIXED;
         KEY IS ASCENDING SNO IN S.

SET NAME IS P-SPJ;
     OWNER IS P;
     ORDER IS SORTED BY DEFINED KEYS
     DUPLICATES ARE NOT ALLOWED.
     MEMBER IS SPJ;
         INSERTION IS AUTOMATIC
         RETENTION IS FIXED;
         KEY IS ASCENDING JNO IN SPJ, SNO IN SPJ;
         SET SELECTION IS BY VALUE OF PNO IN P.

SET NAME IS P-SET;
     OWNER IS SYSTEM;
     ORDER IS SORTED BY DEFINED KEYS
     DUPLICATES ARE NOT ALLOWED.
     MEMBER IS P;
         INSERTION IS AUTOMATIC
         RETENTION IS FIXED;
         KEY IS ASCENDING PNO IN P.

SET NAME IS J-SPJ;
     OWNER IS J;
     ORDER IS SORTED BY DEFINED KEYS
     DUPLICATES ARE NOT ALLOWED.
     MEMBER IS SPJ;
         INSERTION IS AUTOMATIC
         RETENTION IS FIXED;
         KEY IS ASCENDING SNO IN SPJ, PNO IN SPJ;
         SET SELECTION IS BY VALUE OF JNO IN J.
```

```
SET NAME IS J-SET;
    OWNER IS SYSTEM;
    ORDER IS SORTED BY DEFINED KEYS
    DUPLICATES ARE NOT ALLOWED.
    MEMBER IS J;
        INSERTION IS AUTOMATIC
        RETENTION IS FIXED;
        KEY IS ASCENDING JNO IN J.
```

24.4 `SCHEMA NAME IS PARTS-AND-COMPONENTS.`

```
    RECORD NAME IS PART;
        DUPLICATES ARE NOT ALLOWED FOR PNO IN PART.
        02 PNO . . .

    RECORD NAME IS LINK.
        02 QTY. . .

    SET NAME IS BM;
        . . .
        OWNER IS PART;
        MEMBER IS LINK;
        . . .

    SET NAME IS WU;
        . . .
        OWNER IS PART;
        MEMBER IS LINK;
        . . .
```

24.5 (a) `SCHEMA NAME IS AREA-BIRD-SURVEY.`

```
    RECORD NAME IS AREA-REC;
        DUPLICATES ARE NOT ALLOWED FOR ANO IN AREA-REC.
        02 ANO    ; TYPE IS CHARACTER 3.
        02 ANAME  ; TYPE IS CHARACTER 24.
        02 ADESCN ; TYPE IS CHARACTER 473.

    RECORD NAME IS BIRD-REC;
        DUPLICATES ARE NOT ALLOWED FOR BNAME IN BIRD-REC;
        DUPLICATES ARE NOT ALLOWED FOR SNAME IN BIRD-REC.
        02 BNAME  ; TYPE IS CHARACTER 44.
        02 SNAME  ; TYPE IS CHARACTER 44.
        02 BDESCN ; TYPE IS CHARACTER 412.

    RECORD NAME IS SIGHTING.
        02 DATE    ; TYPE IS CHARACTER 6.
        02 REMARKS ; TYPE IS CHARACTER 494.

    SET NAME IS AREA-SET;
        OWNER IS SYSTEM;
        ORDER IS SORTED BY DEFINED KEYS
        DUPLICATES ARE NOT ALLOWED.
        MEMBER IS AREA-REC;
            INSERTION IS AUTOMATIC
            RETENTION IS FIXED;
            KEY IS ASCENDING ANO IN AREA-REC.
```

```
SET NAME IS BIRD-SET;
    OWNER IS SYSTEM;
    ORDER IS SORTED BY DEFINED KEYS
    DUPLICATES ARE NOT ALLOWED.
    MEMBER IS BIRD-REC;
        INSERTION IS AUTOMATIC
        RETENTION IS FIXED;
        KEY IS ASCENDING SNAME IN BIRD-REC.

SET NAME IS AREA-SIGHTINGS;
    OWNER IS AREA-REC;
    ORDER IS NEXT.
    MEMBER IS SIGHTING;
        INSERTION IS AUTOMATIC
        RETENTION IS MANDATORY;
        SET SELECTION IS BY APPLICATION.

SET NAME IS BIRD-SIGHTINGS;
    OWNER IS BIRD-REC;
    ORDER IS NEXT.
    MEMBER IS SIGHTING;
        INSERTION IS AUTOMATIC
        RETENTION IS MANDATORY;
        SET SELECTION IS BY APPLICATION.
```

Since the SIGHTING record does not contain a data-item corresponding to ANO IN AREA-REC or a data-item corresponding to SNAME (or BNAME) in BIRD-REC, it is not possible to define a sort control key for SIGHTINGs with respect to the sets BIRD-SIGHTINGS and AREA-SIGHTINGS. It therefore becomes the responsibility of the programmer to maintain SIGHTING records in bird name sequence within area and area number sequence within bird, if these sequences are required. ORDER IS NEXT means that the programmer must procedurally select the predecessor of the new record in the set before creating that new record.

(b) The following alterations should be made to schema (a).

- Eliminate DATE from the SIGHTING record.

- Introduce a new type of record:

```
RECORD NAME IS DATE-REC;
    DUPLICATES ARE NOT ALLOWED FOR DATE IN DATE-REC.
    02 DATE  ; TYPE IS CHARACTER 6.
```

- Introduce a new type of set:

```
SET NAME IS DATE-SIGHTINGS;
    OWNER IS DATE-REC;
    ORDER IS NEXT.
    MEMBER IS SIGHTING;
        INSERTION IS AUTOMATIC
        RETENTION IS MANDATORY;
        SET SELECTION IS BY APPLICATION.
```

CHAPTER 25: THE EXTERNAL LEVEL OF DBTG

25.1 A couple of observations may be helpful. If O is old, any program currently executing ERASE operations against O will *probably* have to be changed (together with the corresponding subschema). If M is old and membership class is AUTOMATIC, any program currently executing STORE operations against M will have to be changed (together with the corresponding subschema).

CHAPTER 26: DBTG DATA MANIPULATION

The currency table in Section 26.2 should be completed as follows.

Current of run-unit	P 'P2'
Current S occurrence	S 'S4'
Current P occurrence	P 'P2'
Current SP occurrence	SP 'S4/P2/200'
Current record of set S-SP	SP 'S4/P2/200' (member)
Current record of set P-SP	P 'P2' (owner)
Current S-SP occurrence	owned by S 'S4'
Current P-SP occurrence	owned by P 'P2'
Current record of realm S-SP-P	P 'P2'

Throughout the remaining answers we assume that declarative procedures for exception handling have been established as in the example in Section 26.3.

26.1.1
```
MOVE 'NO' TO NOTFOUND
MOVE 'J1' TO JNO IN J
FIND ANY J USING JNO IN J
IF NOTFOUND = 'NO'
   MOVE 'NO' TO EOF
   FIND FIRST SPJ WITHIN J-SPJ
   PERFORM UNTIL EOF = 'YES'
      GET SPJ
      (add SNO IN SPJ to result list
      unless already present)
      FIND NEXT SPJ WITHIN J-SPJ
   END-PERFORM
END-IF
```

26.1.2
```
MOVE 'NO' TO EOF
MOVE 'J1' TO JNO IN J
MOVE 'P1' TO PNO IN SPJ
FIND SPJ WITHIN J-SPJ USING PNO IN SPJ
PERFORM UNTIL EOF = 'YES'
   GET SPJ
   (add SNO IN SPJ to result list)
   FIND DUPLICATE WITHIN J-SPJ USING PNO IN SPJ
END-PERFORM
```

26.1.3
```
      MOVE 'NO' TO NOTFOUND
      MOVE 'J1' TO JNO IN J
      FIND ANY J USING JNO IN J
      IF NOTFOUND = 'NO'
         MOVE 'NO' TO EOF
         FIND FIRST SPJ WITHIN J-SPJ
         PERFORM UNTIL EOF = 'YES'
            GET SPJ
            FIND OWNER IN P-SPJ
            GET P
            IF COLOR IN P = 'RED'
               (add SNO IN SPJ to result list
                unless already present)
            END-IF
         END-PERFORM
      END-IF
```

26.1.4 First we construct a table LONJNO containing JNO values for projects in London.

```
      MOVE 'NO' TO EOF
      MOVE 'LONDON' TO CITY IN J
      FIND J WITHIN J-SET USING CITY IN J
      PERFORM VARYING I FROM 1 BY 1 UNTIL EOF = 'YES'
         GET J
         MOVE JNO IN J TO LONJNO (I)
         FIND DUPLICATE WITHIN J-SET USING CITY IN J
      END-PERFORM
```

Now we scan P occurrences, looking for parts for which there exist SPJ occurrences linking the part to every one of the N London projects just found.

```
      IF I > 1
         SUBTRACT 1 FROM I GIVING N
         MOVE 'NO' TO EOF
         FIND FIRST P WITHIN P-SET
         PERFORM UNTIL EOF = 'YES'
            GET P
            PERFORM VARYING I FROM 1 BY 1 UNTIL I > N
                                           OR EOF = 'YES'
               MOVE LONJNO (I) TO JNO IN SPJ
               FIND SPJ WITHIN P-SPJ CURRENT USING JNO IN SPJ
            END-PERFORM
            IF EOF = 'YES'
               MOVE 'NO' TO EOF
               (add PNO IN P to result list)
            END-IF
            FIND NEXT P WITHIN P-SET
         END-PERFORM
      END-IF
```

26.1.5
```
         MOVE 'NO' TO EOF
         FIND FIRST J WITHIN J-SET
         PERFORM UNTIL EOF = 'YES'
            GET J
            MOVE 'NO' TO EOF
            MOVE 'NO' TO BADJ
            FIND FIRST SPJ WITHIN J-SPJ
            PERFORM UNTIL EOF = 'YES' OR BADJ = 'YES'
               FIND OWNER WITHIN P-SPJ
               GET P
               IF COLOR IN P = 'RED'
                  MOVE 'YES' TO BADJ
               ELSE
                  FIND OWNER WITHIN S-SPJ
                  GET S
                  IF CITY IN S = 'LONDON'
                     MOVE 'YES' TO BADJ
                  ELSE
                     FIND NEXT SPJ WITHIN J-SPJ
                  END-IF
               END-IF
            END-PERFORM
            IF EOF = 'YES'
               MOVE 'NO' TO EOF
               (add JNO IN J to result list)
            END-IF
            FIND NEXT J WITHIN J-SET
         END-PERFORM
```

26.1.6 We make use of a keep list, KX, of length 2. Our solution could be made more efficient if duplicates were eliminated as early as possible instead of only at the final stage.

```
         LD KX LIMIT IS 2.

         MOVE 'NO' TO NOTFOUND
         MOVE 'S1' TO SNO IN S
         FIND ANY S USING SNO IN S
         IF NOTFOUND = 'NO'
            MOVE 'NO' TO EOF
            FIND FIRST SPJ WITHIN S-SPJ
            PERFORM UNTIL EOF = 'YES'
               KEEP USING KX
               FIND OWNER WITHIN P-SPJ
               FIND FIRST SPJ WITHIN P-SPJ
               PERFORM UNTIL EOF = 'YES'
                  KEEP USING KX
                  FIND OWNER WITHIN S-SPJ
                  FIND FIRST SPJ WITHIN S-SPJ
                  PERFORM UNTIL EOF = 'YES'
                     GET SPJ
                     (add PNO IN SPJ to result list
                     unless already present)
                     FIND NEXT SPJ WITHIN S-SPJ
```

```
              END-PERFORM
              MOVE 'NO' TO EOF
              FIND LAST WITHIN KX
              FREE LAST WITHIN KX
              FIND NEXT SPJ WITHIN P-SPJ
          END-PERFORM
          MOVE 'NO' TO EOF
          FIND LAST WITHIN KX
          FREE LAST WITHIN KX
          FIND NEXT SPJ WITHIN S-SPJ
      END-PERFORM
   END-IF
```

26.1.7
```
      MOVE 'NO' TO EOF
      FIND FIRST S WITHIN S-SET
      PERFORM UNTIL EOF = 'YES'
         GET S
         FIND FIRST SPJ WITHIN S-SPJ
         PERFORM UNTIL EOF = 'YES'
            FIND OWNER IN J-SPJ
            GET J
            (add <CITY IN S,CITY IN J> to result list
             unless already present)
            FIND NEXT SPJ WITHIN S-SPJ
         END-PERFORM
         MOVE 'NO' TO EOF
         FIND NEXT S WITHIN S-SET
      END-PERFORM
```

26.1.8 This problem is surprisingly difficult to handle efficiently. Our solution retrieves the entire set of P occurrences one at a time, on the face of it not a very desirable procedure. But the Format 2 FIND cannot be used (why not?), and the Format 6 FIND would actually be even less efficient (why?). (*Hint:* To see why the Format 2 FIND cannot be used, consider what would happen if red parts were to be deleted, not just modified.)

```
      MOVE 'NO' TO EOF
      FIND FIRST P WITHIN P-SET
      PERFORM UNTIL EOF = 'YES'
         GET COLOR IN P
         IF COLOR IN P = 'RED'
            MOVE 'ORANGE' TO COLOR IN P
            MODIFY COLOR IN P
         END-IF
         FIND NEXT P WITHIN P-SET
      END-PERFORM
      COMMIT
```

26.1.9 We assume that an SPJ occurrence for S1/P1/J1 exists; however, we do not assume that an SPJ occurrence for S2/P1/J1 does not already exist. The first step, therefore, is to FIND and GET the SPJ occurrence for S2/P1/J1 if it exists, so that the appropriate QTY value can be added to the QTY value for S1/P1/J1 to form the new QTY value for S2/P1/J1. If it does not exist, of course, nothing need be added to the QTY value for S1/P1/J1. We also delete the SPJ occurrence for S2/P1/J1 if it exists.

```
MOVE 'NO' TO EOF
MOVE 'S2' TO SNO IN S
MOVE 'P1' TO PNO IN SPJ
MOVE 'J1' TO JNO IN SPJ
FIND SPJ WITHIN S-SPJ USING PNO IN SPJ, JNO IN SPJ
IF EOF = 'NO'
   GET QTY IN SPJ
   MOVE QTY IN SPJ TO TEMPQTY
   ERASE SPJ
ELSE
   MOVE 'NO' TO EOF
   MOVE ZERO TO TEMPQTY
END-IF
```

We now proceed to FIND, MODIFY, and RECONNECT the SPJ occurrence for S1/P1/J1.

```
MOVE 'S1' TO SNO IN S
FIND SPJ WITHIN S-SPJ USING PNO IN SPJ, JNO IN SPJ
GET QTY IN SPJ
ADD TEMPQTY TO QTY IN SPJ
MOVE 'S2' TO SNO IN SPJ
MODIFY SNO IN SPJ, QTY IN SPJ
MOVE 'S2' TO SNO IN S
RECONNECT SPJ WITHIN S-SPJ
COMMIT
```

26.3 The membership class of LINK in EL would probably be AUTOMATIC, since it would be unreasonable for a LINK occurrence not to be connected to a superior (manager) EMP occurrence. Assuming that LINK's membership is AUTOMATIC, then, the membership class of EMP in LE must be MANUAL, to allow at least one EMP occurrence (at the top of the tree) not to be subordinate to any others.

We assume that SET SELECTION for EL is BY VALUE OF ENO IN EMP and that SET SELECTION for LE is BY APPLICATION.

```
MOVE 'E8' TO ENO IN EMP
STORE LINK (no UWA data for this record)
MOVE 'E15' TO ENO IN EMP
MOVE . . .   (create E15 EMP occurrence in UWA)
STORE EMP
CONNECT EMP TO LE
COMMIT
```

26.4.1
```
MOVE 'NO' TO EOF
FIND FIRST PART WITHIN PART-SET
PERFORM UNTIL EOF = 'YES'
   GET PART
   (print PNO IN PART)
   FIND FIRST LINK WITHIN BM
   PERFORM UNTIL EOF = 'YES'
      FIND OWNER WITHIN WU
            RETAINING PART-SET, BM CURRENCY
      GET PART
      (print PNO IN PART, i.e., component no.)
      FIND NEXT LINK WITHIN BM
   END-PERFORM
   MOVE 'NO' TO EOF
   FIND CURRENT PART WITHIN PART-SET
   FIND FIRST LINK WITHIN WU
   PERFORM UNTIL EOF = 'YES'
      FIND OWNER WITHIN BM
            RETAINING PART-SET, WU CURRENCY
      GET PART
      (print PNO IN PART, i.e., assembly no.)
      FIND NEXT LINK WITHIN WU
   END-PERFORM
   MOVE 'NO' TO EOF
   FIND NEXT PART WITHIN PART-SET
END-PERFORM
```

26.4.2 LD STACK LIMIT IS 10. (limit of 10 is arbitrary)

```
MOVE 'NO' TO NOTFOUND
MOVE GIVEN-PNO TO PNO IN PART
FIND ANY PART USING PNO IN PART
IF NOTFOUND = 'NO'
   GET PART
   (print PNO IN PART)
   MOVE ZERO TO STACK-DEPTH
   MOVE 'NO' TO EOF
   PERFORM UNTIL STACK-DEPTH < ZERO
      FIND NEXT LINK WITHIN BM
      IF EOF = 'NO'
         GET LINK
         KEEP USING STACK
         ADD 1 TO STACK-DEPTH
         FIND OWNER WITHIN WU
         GET PART
         (print PNO IN PART)
      ELSE
         IF STACK-DEPTH > ZERO
               FIND LAST WITHIN STACK
               FREE LAST WITHIN STACK
               MOVE 'NO' TO EOF
         END-IF
         SUBTRACT 1 FROM STACK-DEPTH
      END-IF
   END-PERFORM
END-IF
```

CHAPTER 27: THE UNIFIED DATABASE LANGUAGE

We present COBOL versions of the enrollment procedure (cf. Figs. 27.5, 27.6, and 27.7; see also the comparative counts in Fig. 27.9).

Relational:

```
MOVE 'YES' TO APPLICATION-OK
PERFORM PREREQ MATCHING GIVEN
                UNTIL APPLICATION-OK = 'NO'
   IF EXISTS (STUDENT MATCHING GIVEN ON EMPNO
                        WHERE COURSENO OF STUDENT = PRENO OF PREREQ)
      CONTINUE
      ELSE MOVE 'NO' TO APPLICATION-OK
   END-IF
END-PERFORM
IF APPLICATION-OK = 'YES'
   CREATE STUDENT FROM GIVEN, SPACES
END-IF
```

Hierarchical:

```
MOVE 'YES' TO APPLICATION-OK
FIND UNIQUE (COURSE MATCHING GIVEN)
PERFORM PREREQ UNDER COURSE
                UNTIL APPLICATION-OK = 'NO'
   IF EXISTS (STUDENT MATCHING GIVEN
              WHERE UNIQUE (COURSENO OF COURSE OVER STUDENT)
                                        = PRENO OF PREREQ)
      CONTINUE
      ELSE MOVE 'NO' TO APPLICATION-OK
   END-IF
END-PERFORM
IF APPLICATION-OK = 'YES'
   FIND UNIQUE (OFFERING MATCHING GIVEN UNDER COURSE)
   CREATE STUDENT FROM EMPNO OF GIVEN, SPACES
                CONNECTING UNDER OFFERING
END-IF
```

Network:

```
MOVE 'YES' TO APPLICATION-OK
FIND UNIQUE (COURSE MATCHING GIVEN)
PERFORM PREREQ UNDER COURSE VIA HASPRE
                UNTIL APPLICATION-OK = 'NO'
   IF EXISTS (STUDENT WHERE
                  UNIQUE (EMPNO OF EMPLOYEE OVER STUDENT)
                                        = EMPNO OF GIVEN
              AND UNIQUE (COURSENO OF COURSE OVER STUDENT)
                                        =
                  UNIQUE (COURSENO OF COURSE OVER PREREQ
                                        VIA PREOF))
```

```
      CONTINUE
      ELSE MOVE 'NO' TO APPLICATION-OK
   END-IF
END-PERFORM
IF APPLICATION-OK = 'YES'
   FIND UNIQUE (OFFERING MATCHING GIVEN UNDER COURSE)
   FIND UNIQUE (EMPLOYEE MATCHING GIVEN)
   CREATE STUDENT FROM EMPNO OF GIVEN, SPACES
                  CONNECTING UNDER OFFERING,
                             UNDER EMPLOYEE
END-IF
```

Throughout the following solutions we use "print" as a convenient generic short-hand for PUT SKIP LIST and other PL/I output operators.

27.1.1 We show a variety of solutions to this exercise, in order to illustrate a number of UDL features.

Relational, record-level, 1st solution:

```
DO SPJ WHERE SPJ.J# = 'J1';
   print SPJ.S#;
END;
```

If we wish to guarantee that the results are printed in, say, ascending supplier number sequence, we can include the specification ORDER (UP SPJ.S#) in the DO statement. In the absence of an ORDER specification, the iteration is performed according to the declared ordering for the underlying baseset (SPJSET)—i.e., system-defined (default) ordering, in this particular case. We ignore ORDER in most of our solutions.

Relational, record-level, 2nd solution:

```
DO SPJ.S# WHERE SPJ.J# = 'J1'
          NOSET ASSIGNTO(TEMP#);
   print TEMP#;
END;
```

Here the iteration is performed over a "sliced set"—i.e., over a set of S# fields, rather than over a set of SPJ records. "SPJ.S# WHERE . . ." is a set expression (actually a "sliced-set reference") that does not designate a set of existing records in the database but rather a set of records that are derived in some way from such records. It is not permitted to set a cursor to point to a derived record; hence the NOSET specification, and hence also the ASSIGNTO specification, which is required and which causes a copy of the current record to be assigned to the indicated variable.

Relational, record-level, 3rd solution:
This solution eliminates duplicate supplier numbers.

```
DO DISTINCT(SPJ.S# WHERE SPJ.J# = 'J1')
       NOSET ASSIGNTO(TEMP#);
   print TEMP#;
END;
```

NOSET and ASSIGNTO are required whenever the DO-loop scope is specified as a DISTINCT reference.

Relational, set-level:

```
print DISTINCT(SPJ.S# WHERE SPJ.J# = 'J1');
```

Network, record-level, 1st solution:

```
FIND UNIQUE(J WHERE J.J# = 'J1');
DO SPJ UNDER J;
   print SPJ.S#;
END;
```

Network, record-level, 2nd solution:

```
DO SPJ WHERE UNIQUE(J.J# OVER SPJ) = 'J1';
   print UNIQUE(S.S# OVER SPJ);
END;
```

This solution is likely to be less efficient than the previous one, unless the implementation recognizes that it need only look at SPJ records that are "under project J1."

Network, record-level, 3rd solution:

```
DO S WHERE EXISTS(SPJ UNDER S
                      WHERE UNIQUE(J.J# OVER SPJ) = 'J1');
   print S.S#;
END;
```

Network, set-level:

```
print S.S# WHERE EXISTS(SPJ UNDER S
                      WHERE UNIQUE(J.J# OVER SPJ) = 'J1');
```

For the remaining questions we give record-level solutions only.

27.1.2

Relational:

```
DO SPJ WHERE SPJ.J# = 'J1' & SPJ.P# = 'P1';
   print SPJ.S#;
END;
```

Network:

```
DO SPJ WHERE UNIQUE(J.J# OVER SPJ) = 'J1'
         & UNIQUE(P.P# OVER SPJ) = 'P1';
   print UNIQUE(S.S# OVER SPJ);
END;
```

27.1.3

Relational:

```
DO S.S# WHERE EXISTS(SPJ MATCHING S
                      WHERE SPJ.J# = 'J1' &
                             UNIQUE(P.COLOR MATCHING SPJ) = 'RED')
            NOSET ASSIGNTO(TEMP#);
  print TEMP#;
END;
```

Network:

```
DO S.S# WHERE EXISTS(SPJ UNDER S
                     WHERE UNIQUE(J.J# OVER SPJ) = 'J1' &
                           UNIQUE(P.COLOR OVER SPJ) = 'RED')
               NOSET ASSIGNTO(TEMP#);
   print TEMP#;
END;
```

27.1.4

Relational:

```
DO P WHERE ¬EXISTS(J WHERE J.CITY = 'LONDON' &
                   ¬EXISTS(SPJ WHERE SPJ.P# = P.P# &
                           SPJ.J# = J.J#));
   print P.P#;
END;
```

Network:

A network solution can be obtained from the relational solution by replacing
SPJ.P# and SPJ.J# by UNIQUE (P.P# OVER SPJ) and UNIQUE (J.J# OVER
SPJ), respectively.

27.1.5

Relational:

```
DO J WHERE ¬EXISTS(SPJ MATCHING J
                   WHERE UNIQUE(P.COLOR MATCHING SPJ) = 'RED'
                         & UNIQUE(S.CITY MATCHING SPJ) = 'LONDON');
   print J.J#;
END;
```

Network:

A network solution can be obtained from the relational solution by replacing the
first MATCHING by UNDER and the other two MATCHINGs by OVER.

27.1.6

Let X, Y, Z be cursors for record type SPJ.

Relational:

```
DO P WHERE EXISTS(X→SPJ MATCHING P WHERE
                  EXISTS(Y→SPJ MATCHING X→SPJ ON S# WHERE
                         EXISTS(Z→SPJ MATCHING Y→SPJ ON P#
                                WHERE Z→SPJ.S# = 'S1')));
   print P.P#;
END;
```

Network:

```
DO P WHERE EXISTS(X→SPJ UNDER P WHERE
                  EXISTS(Y→SPJ UNDER UNIQUE(S OVER X→SPJ) WHERE
                         EXISTS(Z→SPJ UNDER UNIQUE(P OVER Y→SPJ)
                                WHERE UNIQUE(S.S# OVER Z→SPJ)
                                      = 'S1')))
   print P.P#;
END;
```

27.1.7

Let PAIR be declared as follows:

```
DCL 1 PAIR,
       2 SC . . . ,
       2 JC . . . ;
```

Relational:

```
DO DISTINCT((S.CITY,J.CITY)
               WHERE EXISTS(SPJ WHERE SPJ.S# = S.S# &
                                      SPJ.J# = J.J#))
               NOSET ASSIGNTO(PAIR);
    print PAIR;
END;
```

Network:

A network solution can be obtained from the relational solution by replacing SPJ.S# and SPJ.J# by UNIQUE (S.S# OVER SPJ) and UNIQUE (J.J# OVER SPJ), respectively.

27.1.8

Relational/network, record-level:

```
DO P WHERE P.COLOR = 'RED';
   ASSIGN 'ORANGE' TO P.COLOR;
END;
COMMIT;
```

Relational/network, set-level:

```
ASSIGN ('ORANGE' TO P.COLOR
          DO P WHERE P.COLOR = 'RED');
COMMIT;
```

The embedded DO specification within the ASSIGN here is analogous to an embedded DO specification within a data list in current PL/I GET and PUT statements.

27.1.9

Relational:

```
FIND UNIQUE(SPJ WHERE SPJ.S# = 'S1' &
                      SPJ.P# = 'P1' &
                      SPJ.J# = 'J1')
                                    SET (X);
FIND UNIQUE(SPJ WHERE SPJ.S# = 'S2' &
                      SPJ.P# = 'P1' &
                      SPJ.J# = 'J1')
                                    SET (Y)
FOUND
   DO;
       ASSIGN (X→SPJ.QTY+Y→SPJ.QTY) TO Y→SPJ.QTY;
       FREE X→SPJ;
   END;
NOTFOUND
   ASSIGN 'S2' TO X→SPJ.S#;
COMMIT;
```

Network:

```
FIND UNIQUE(SPJ WHERE UNIQUE(S.S# OVER SPJ) = 'S1' &
                      UNIQUE(P.P# OVER SPJ) = 'P1' &
                      UNIQUE(J.J# OVER SPJ) = 'J1')
                                    SET (X);
FIND UNIQUE(SPJ WHERE UNIQUE(S.S# OVER SPJ) = 'S2' &
                      UNIQUE(P.P# OVER SPJ) = 'P1' &
                      UNIQUE(J.J# OVER SPJ) = 'J1')
                                    SET (Y)
FOUND
   DO;
       ASSIGN (X→SPJ.QTY+Y→SPJ.QTY) TO Y→SPJ.QTY;
       FREE X→SPJ;
   END;
NOTFOUND
   RECONNECT X→SPJ UNDER UNIQUE(S WHERE S.S# = 'S2');
COMMIT;
```

27.2.1
Relational:

```
DO PART IN PART_SET;    /* iterate over all parts */
   print PART.P#;
   DO COMPONENT WHERE MAJORP# = PART.P#;
      print MINORP#;
   END;
   DO COMPONENT WHERE MINORP# = PART.P#;
      print MAJORP#;
   END;
END;
```

Network:

```
DO PART IN PART_SET;
   print PART.P#;
   DO COMPONENT UNDER PART VIA BM;
      print UNIQUE(PART.P# OVER COMPONENT VIA WU);
   END;
   DO COMPONENT UNDER PART VIA WU;
      print UNIQUE(PART.P# OVER COMPONENT VIA BM);
   END;
END;
```

27.2.2
Relational:

```
      CALL EXPLODE(GIVENP#);

EXPLODE:
   PROC(UPPERP#) RECURSIVE;
   DCL UPPERP# . . . ;
   DCL X CURSOR RECTYPE(COMPONENT);
   print UPPERP#;
   DO COMPONENT WHERE MAJORP# = UPPERP# SET(X);
      CALL EXPLODE(X→MINORP#);
   END;
END /* EXPLODE */;
```

Network:

The following procedure uses cursor values to communicate between levels of the explosion (unlike the relational solution, which uses part numbers).

```
FIND UNIQUE(PART WHERE PART.P# = GIVENP#) SET(P);
CALL EXPLODE(P);

EXPLODE:
    PROC(PU) RECURSIVE;
    DCL (PU,PL) CURSOR RECTYPE(PART),
        X CURSOR RECTYPE(COMPONENT);
    print PU→PART.P#;
    DO COMPONENT UNDER PU→PART VIA BM SET(X);
        FIND UNIQUE(PART OVER X→COMPONENT VIA WU) SET(PL);
        CALL EXPLODE(PL);
    END;
END /* EXPLODE */;
```

27.3

Hierarchical:

```
FIND UNIQUE(COURSE WHERE COURSE.COURSE# = GIVEN.COURSE#) SET(C1);
DO PREREQ UNDER C1→COURSE;
    FIND UNIQUE(COURSE WHERE COURSE.COURSE# = PREREQ.PRE#) SET(C2);
    DO OFFERING UNDER C2→COURSE;
        print OFFERING;
    END;
END;
```

27.4

(a) *Relational:* The obvious approach is to map each record directly into an isomorphic stored record, and to add an index on the primary key for each record type. In fact, since PREREQs and TEACHERs are "all key," the index alone would be sufficient in these two cases—no data records are needed at all; however, we assume here that data records do exist in all cases.

Hierarchical: Map each fanset into a stored fanset. Each parent record has a pointer to the first child. Each child record has a pointer to the next child and a pointer to the parent. Also, index COURSEs and EMPLOYEEs on their primary key.

Network: Same approach as for the hierarchical case.

(b) Let:

c = the number of COURSEs,

e = the number of EMPLOYEEs,

p = the average number of PREREQs per COURSE,

x = the average number of OFFERINGs per COURSE,

y = the average number of STUDENTs per OFFERING, and

z = the average number of TEACHERs per OFFERING.

(Note that the average number of STUDENTs per EMPLOYEE will then be cxy/e.)

Assume 4-byte pointers; assume also for simplicity that an index consists solely of a set of entries, one for each indexed record, and that each entry consists of just a key value and a pointer (i.e., ignore index levels above the "index set" [see Chapter 2], also the fact that indexes are typically compressed). Then storage space requirements are as follows.

Relational:

COURSEs	$c(36 + (3 + 4))$	$= 43c$
PREREQs	$cp(6 + (6 + 4))$	$= 16cp$
OFFERINGs	$cx(24 + (6 + 4))$	$= 34cx$
STUDENTs	$cxy(13 + (9 + 4))$	$= 26cxy$
TEACHERs	$cxz(12 + (12 + 4))$	$= 28cxz$
EMPLOYEEs	$e(24 + (6 + 4))$	$= 34e$

Total $= c(2x(13y + 14z + 17) + 16p + 43) + 34e$ bytes.

(If we assume that PREREQs and TEACHERs are subsumed by the corresponding indexes, this total reduces by $6c(p + 2xz)$ bytes.)

Hierarchical:

COURSEs	$c(36 + 4 + 4 + (3 + 4))$	$= 51c$
PREREQs	$cp(3 + 4 + 4)$	$= 11cp$
OFFERINGs	$cx(21 + 4 + 4 + 4 + 4)$	$= 37cx$
STUDENTs	$cxy(7 + 4 + 4)$	$= 15cxy$
TEACHERs	$cxz(6 + 4 + 4)$	$= 14cxz$
EMPLOYEEs	$e(24 + (6 + 4))$	$= 34e$

Total $= c(x(15y + 14z + 37) + 11p + 51) + 34e$ bytes.

Network:

COURSEs	$c(36 + 4 + 4 + 4 + (3 + 4))$	$= 55c$
PREREQs	$cp(4 + 4 + 4 + 4)$	$= 16cp$
OFFERINGs	$cx(21 + 4 + 4 + 4 + 4)$	$= 37cx$
STUDENTs	$cxy(1 + 4 + 4 + 4 + 4)$	$= 17cxy$
TEACHERs	$cxz(4 + 4 + 4 + 4)$	$= 16cxz$
EMPLOYEEs	$e(24 + 4 + 4 + (6 + 4))$	$= 42e$

Total $= c(x(17y + 16z + 37) + 16p + 55) + 42e$ bytes.

As an illustration, suppose $c = 100$, $e = 1000$, $p = 3$, $x = 8$, $y = 16$, and $z = 1.5$. Then the three expressions evaluate as follows.

Relational:	436,700 bytes
Hierarchical:	280,800 bytes
Network:	318,700 bytes

(c) We concentrate on the loop portion of the procedure, which is executed p times on the average (assuming that the given employee has attended all relevant prerequisite courses). In all three cases each iteration of the loop involves two calls to the DBMS; one to move to the next PREREQ, and one to check for existence of a STUDENT. Thus the total number of calls is $2p$ in every case. However, the calls themselves get progressively more complex, and the DBMS has to do correspondingly more work, as we step from relations to hierarchies to networks. The expressions derived below give some indication of this increase in complexity. The reader is cautioned, however, not to take these figures as any absolute measure of performance.

Relational: We make the (reasonable) assumption that all index entries for PREREQs of the given COURSE are in the same physical index block. Then each PREREQ after the first will involve exactly one direct access to the database. (A smart implementation might realize that the data record access is unnecessary, since the data values are already available from the index entry, but we do not assume such an implementation.) Turning now to the EXISTS test, we note that the test is for a STUDENT having a given primary key value, and that therefore the result of the test can be determined from the index alone—no access is needed to the data itself. Moreover, it is again likely that all STUDENT index entries for the given COURSE are in the same physical block, but we do not make this assumption. Thus our final expression for the number of database records (data records and index records) accessed in the loop is simply $2p$ (p for the PREREQs and p for the STUDENT index records).

Hierarchical: Since each PREREQ under the given COURSE points directly to the next, we can again assume that each PREREQ involves only one access. The EXISTS test is more complicated, however. If we assume that the implementation will search down from the top of the hierarchy, we have:

> one access to the COURSE index on the basis of PREREQ.PRE#
> one access to the corresponding COURSE
> scan half the x corresponding OFFERINGs (on average)
> for each—
> > one access to OFFERING
> > scan all y corresponding STUDENTs
> > for each—
> > > one access to STUDENT

So the final expression is

$$p(1 \; + \; 1 \; + \; 1 \; + \; (x/2) \, (1 \; + \; y)) = ((xy/2) \; + \; (x/2) \; + \; 3)p.$$

Network: Again we assume one access per PREREQ. However, there are now two strategies for the EXISTS test, one searching down from the prerequisite COURSE and one searching down from the given EMPLOYEE. For the first of these, we have:

> one access to COURSE via PREOF parent pointer
> scan half the x corresponding OFFERINGs (on average)
> for each—
> > one access to OFFERING
> > scan all y corresponding STUDENTs
> > for each—
> > > one access to STUDENT
> > > one access to EMPLOYEE via ATTENDS parent pointer

So the first possibility is

$$p(1 \; + \; 1 \; + \; (x/2) \, (1 \; + \; y \, (1 \; + \; 1))) = (xy \; + \; (x/2) \; + \; 2)p.$$

For the second strategy, we have:

> scan half the cxy/e STUDENTs for the given EMPLOYEE
> for each—
>> one access to STUDENT
>> one access to OFFERING via HASSTU parent pointer
>> one access to COURSE via HASOFFER parent pointer

So the second possibility is

$$p(1 + (cxy/2e)(1 + 1 + 1)) = ((3cxy/2e) + 1)p.$$

Note that both the network expressions would be much worse in the absence of parent pointers.

Taking the same values for c, e, p, x, and y as in part (b) of the answer, these expressions evaluate as follows:

Relational:		6
Hierarchical:		213
Network:	(1)	402
	(2)	61 to the nearest integer.

List of
Acronyms

We list below some of the more important acronyms introduced in the text, together with their meanings.

ANSI/SPARC	literally, American National Standards Institute/Systems Planning and Requirements Committee; used to refer to the three-level database architecture described in Chapter 1
BCNF	Boyce/Codd normal form
DBA	database administrator
DBD	database description (IMS)
DBMS	database management system
DBTG	Data Base Task Group
DDL	data description language; data definition language
DEDB	data entry database (IMS)
DK/NF	domain/key normal form
DML	data manipulation language
DSDL	data storage description language (DBTG)
DSG	data set group (IMS)
DSL	data sublanguage
FD	functional dependency
FSA	field search argument (IMS)
GN	get next (IMS)
GNP	get next within parent (IMS)
GSAM	generalized sequential access method (IMS)
GU	get unique (IMS)
HDAM	hierarchical direct access method (IMS)

HIDAM	hierarchical indexed direct access method (IMS)
HISAM	hierarchical indexed sequential access method (IMS)
HSAM	hierarchical sequential access method (IMS)
IMS	Information Management System
ISAM	indexed sequential access method
JD	join dependency
LDB	logical database (IMS)
LDBR	logical database record (IMS)
MSDB	main storage database (IMS)
MVD	multivalued dependency
OSAM	overflow sequential access method (IMS)
PCB	program communication block (IMS)
PDB	physical database (IMS)
PDBR	physical database record (IMS)
PJ/NF	projection-join normal form
PSB	program specification block (IMS)
QBE	Query By Example
QUEL	query language (INGRES)
RDS	relational data system (System R)
r-s-e	record selection expression (DBTG)
RSI	research storage interface (System R)
RSS	research storage system (System R)
SHISAM	simple HISAM (IMS)
SHSAM	simple HSAM (IMS)
SQL	structured query language (System R)
SRA	stored record address
SSA	segment search argument (IMS)
TID	tuple ID (System R, INGRES)
UDL	unified database language
UFI	user-friendly interface (System R)
UWA	user work area (DBTG)
VSAM	virtual storage access method
WFF	well-formed formula
XD	indexed (IMS)
1NF	first normal form
2NF	second normal form
3NF	third normal form
4NF	fourth normal form
5NF	fifth normal form (same as PJ/NF)

Index

Entries marked with an asterisk (for example, *ADABAS) are database management systems or software systems in some closely related field.